ESSENTIALS OF CONTEMPORARY MANAGEMENT

FIRST CANADIAN EDITION

Gareth R. Jones
Texas A&M University

Jennifer M. George
Texas A&M University

Nancy Langton
University of British Columbia

McGraw-Hill Ryerson

Toronto   Montréal   Boston   Burr Ridge, IL   Dubuque, IA   Madison, WI
New York   San Francisco   St. Louis   Bangkok   Bogotá   Caracas
Kuala Lumpur   Lisbon   London   Madrid   Mexico City   Milan
New Delhi   Santiago   Seoul   Singapore   Sydney   Taipei

Essentials of Contemporary Management
First Canadian Edition

ISBN: 0-07-091816-3

1 2 3 4 5 6 7 8 9 10 TCP 0 9 8 7 6 5

Care has been taken to trace ownership of copyright material contained in this text; however, the publisher will welcome any information that enables them to rectify any reference or credit for subsequent editions.

Vice President, Editorial and Media Technology: Pat Ferrier
Executive Sponsoring Editor: Nicole Lukach
Developmental Editors: Tracey Haggert/Su Mei Ku
Director of Marketing: Jeff MacLean
Marketing Manager: Kelly Smyth
Manager, Editorial Services: Kelly Dickson
Copy Editor: Cheryl Cohen
Permissions Research: Alison Derry/Permissions Plus
Additional Research: Lesley Mann
Senior Production Coordinator: Madeleine Harrington
Composition: Bookman Typesetting Co.
Cover Design: Greg Devitt
Cover Photos: Stock Illustration Source/Bob Commander
Printer: Transcontinental Printing Group

National Library of Canada Cataloguing in Publication Data

Jones, Gareth R.

  Essentials of contemporary management / Gareth R. Jones, Jennifer M. George, Nancy Langton. – 1st Canadian ed.

Includes bibliographical references and index.

ISBN 0-07-091816-3

  1. Management.   I. George, Jennifer M.   II. Langton, Nancy   III. Title.

HD31.J63 2004   658   C2003-907055-7

Brief Contents

Contents

Preface

Welcome to the first Canadian edition of *Essentials of Contemporary Management.* This is a developed-in-Canada product, specially derived from the first Canadian edition of *Contemporary Management* to meet the needs of instructors and institutions that want a briefer, focused approach to a management text. Based on reviews and other market research we found that potential users want chapters that are short, have the right balance of theory and application material, and are relevant for student learning. In order to accomplish this, we took the first Canadian edition of *Contemporary Management* and have done the following:

- written fewer and briefer chapters that present more focused theoretical discussions
- added more headers to the material to guide student reading
- added more figures and tables to help clarify material
- introduced *Roles in Contrast: Questions* at the beginning of the chapter to highlight how the material might be viewed differently by managers and employees
- introduced each major section of the chapter with a short management scenario, called *Think About It,* followed by questions
- introduced *Roles in Contrast: Considerations* at the end of the chapter to highlight tips that managers and employees can take from the material, again to emphasize how learning about management is not just for managers, but for everyone
- added *Management for You, Managing Ethically,* and *You're the Management Consultant* to the experiential learning features at the end of the chapter.

In emphasizing that management is for everyone, and not just for managers and would-be managers, *Essentials of Contemporary Management* takes a contemporary approach to the study of management and can help anyone who works in an organization understand how and why priorities get set.

Emphasis on Applied Management

Our contemporary approach means that we have gone to great lengths to bring the manager back into the subject matter of management. That is, we have written the text from the perspective of current or future managers to illustrate, in a hands-on way, the problems and opportunities they face and how they can effectively meet these challenges. Throughout the chapters we emphasize important issues managers face and how management theory, research, and practice can help them and their organizations be effective.

Rich and Relevant Examples

An important feature of our book is the way we use real-world examples and stories about managers and companies to drive home the applied lessons to students. Our reviewers were unanimous in their praise of the sheer range and depth of the rich, interesting examples we use to illustrate the chapter material and make it come alive. We've included coverage of large and small firms, from a variety of industries in both the public sector and the private sector, from across the provinces and territories.

Each chapter opens with *A Case in Contrast*, a feature that contrasts the behaviours and actions of two managers and organizations to help demonstrate the uncertainty and challenges surrounding the management process. We cover such organizations as Calgary-based WestJet and Petro-Canada; Montreal-based Gildan Activewear; Toronto-based Altamira Investment Services and Willow Manufacturing; Mississauga, Ontario-based Moore Wallace Inc.; and Vancouver-based QLT and the City of Vancouver.

NEW! The substantive part of each chapter is bracketed by two new features: *Roles in Contrast: Questions* and *Roles in Contrast: Considerations*. These features, developed by Nancy Langton for the Canadian market, highlight for students the different experiences managers and nonmanagers might have when encountering the material. They are intended to specifically illustrate the point that "management is not just for managers".

NEW! Most major headings in each chapter start with a new *Think About It* feature developed by Nancy Langton. Each *Think About It* provides a short vignette, relevant to the section, and is followed by one or more questions. The vignette is then explored further in the unfolding of that section.

Each chapter contains the feature *Tips for Managers,* which distills the lessons that students can take from the chapter and use to develop their management skills.

Each chapter also contains two *Management Cases*. Some of the cases were written specifically for this textbook, while others are taken directly from the pages of Canadian print media, including the *National Post, The Globe and Mail,* the *Ottawa Citizen* and *The Vancouver Sun.* The cases taken from the media show students, in full detail, real-world examples of relevant managerial action. Through both kinds of end-of-chapter cases, students will be introduced to organizations such as the CBC; Guelph, Ontario-based Sleeman Breweries Ltd.; Moncton, New Brunswick-based Amcor PET Packaging; Toronto-based The Brothers Markle Inc.; Aurora, Ontario-based Magna Corporation; and such Canadian managers as Belinda Stronach (of Magna), Cynthia Trudell (now with Brunswick Corporation), Vic De Zen (Royal Group Technologies Ltd.), and Mac Voisin (M and M Meat Shops).

Finally, the book also contains two *Integrative Cases* to help instructors and students alike apply a broad range of theory to the organizational and managerial problems of Canadian Tire and Kooshies Baby Products.

Experiential Learning Features

We have devoted considerable time and attention to developing state-of-the-art experiential end-of-chapter learning exercises that we hope will also drive home the meaning of management to students. Grouped together at the end of each chapter in the section called *Management in Action,* they include:

TOPICS FOR DISCUSSION AND ACTION A set of chapter-related questions and points for reflection, some of which ask students to research actual management issues and learn first-hand from practising managers.

BUILDING MANAGEMENT SKILLS A self-development exercise that asks students to apply what they have learned to their own experience of organizations and managers or to the experiences of others.

NEW! **MANAGEMENT FOR YOU** A feature developed by Nancy Langton to help students apply material to their daily lives. Each chapter gives several suggestions for how students can use insights from the chapter to plan, lead, organize, or control their lives.

NEW! **MANAGING ETHICALLY** A new feature included for the Canadian market to give students the opportunity to consider ethical issues that relate to chapter material.

NEW! **YOU'RE THE MANAGEMENT CONSULTANT** An exercise that presents a realistic scenario in which a manager/organization faces some kind of challenge, problem, or opportunity, and the student plays the role of a management consultant offering advice and recommending a course of action based on the chapter content.

SMALL GROUP BREAKOUT EXERCISE A unique exercise designed to allow instructors to use interactive experiential exercises in groups of three to four students. The instructor calls on students to break up into small groups, simply by turning to people around them; all students take part in the exercise in class, and a mechanism is provided for the different groups to share what they have learned with each other.

EXPLORING THE WORLD WIDE WEB Two internet exercises designed to draw students into the web and give them experience of the new information systems while applying what they have learned.

MANAGEMENT CASE A case for discussion, drawing on contemporary, real-world managers and organizations, which we have written to highlight chapter themes and issues.

MANAGEMENT CASE IN THE NEWS An actual article, from the business pages of a publication such as *The Globe and Mail* or the *National Post,* that shows students how practising managers are facing the issues they have just studied.

Our idea is that instructors can select from these exercises and vary them over the semester so that students can learn the meaning of management through many different avenues. These exercises complement the chapter material and have been class-tested to add to the overall learning experience, and students report that they both learn from and enjoy them.

Integrated Learning System

Great care was used in the creation of the supplemental materials to accompany *Essentials of Contemporary Management.* Whether you are a seasoned faculty member or a newly minted instructor, we hope you will find our support materials to be among the most thorough and thoughtful available.

i-Learning Sales Specialist

Your integrated learning *(i*-learning) sales specialist is a McGraw-Hill Ryerson representative who has the experience, product knowledge, training, and support to help you assess and integrate any of the products, technology, and services that are noted below into your course for optimum teaching and learning performance. Whether you want tips on using our test bank software, on helping your students improve their grades, or on putting your entire course online, your *i*-learning sales specialist is there to help. Contact your local *i*-learning sales specialist to learn how to maximize all McGraw-Hill Ryerson resources.

i-Learning Services Program

McGraw-Hill Ryerson offers a unique *i*-Services package designed for Canadian faculty. Our mission is to equip providers of higher education with superior tools and resources required for excellence in teaching. For additional information visit **www.mcgrawhill.ca/highereducation/eservices/**.

Instructors' Supplements

Instructor's CD ROM

(Includes an electronic version of the Instructor's Manual, the Brownstone Computerized Test Bank and Microsoft® PowerPoint® Presentations.)

Instructors can use this electronic resource to access the supplements listed below that are associated with the text and create custom presentations, exam questions, and Microsoft® PowerPoint® lecture slides. All of these instructor's supplements are also available for download in the Instructor's Resource Centre of the Online Learning Centre (OLC) at **www.mcgrawhill.ca/college/jones**.

Instructor's Manual The *Instructor's Manual,* prepared by Laurel Donaldson, Douglas College, includes a wealth of information to assist instructors in presenting this text and their course to its best advantage. It includes lecture notes, answers to end-of-chapter questions, and other valuable aids.

Brownstone Computerized Test Bank The computerized test bank has been prepared by Michael Hockenstein, Vanier College, to provide a variety of testing methods for instructors. The Brownstone software allows instructors to design their own examinations from a series of multiple-choice, true/false, and essay questions for each chapter. Each question is ranked in terms of difficulty and page-referenced to the textbook.

Microsoft® PowerPoint® Presentations A complete set of PowerPoint slides is provided for each chapter.

Essentials of Contemporary Management Video Package

The video package contains carefully selected segments from various CBC programs chosen by Michael Hockenstein, Vanier College, as well as segments from the McGraw-Hill Management Video Library. It is an excellent supplement to lectures and useful for generating in-class discussions.

PageOut

McGraw-Hill's unique point-and-click course website tool enables users to create a full-featured, professional quality course website without knowing HTML coding. PageOut is free for instructors, and lets you post your syllabus online, assign McGraw-Hill OLC content, add web links, and maintain an online grade book. (If you are short on time, we even have a team ready to help you create your site.)

Primis Online

You can customize this text and save your students money off bookstore prices by using McGraw-Hill's Primis Online digital database, the largest online collection of texts, readings, and cases. Contact your McGraw-Hill *i*-learning sales specialist for more information.

WebCT/BlackBoard

This text is available in two of the most popular course-delivery platforms—WebCT and BlackBoard—for more user-friendly and enhanced features. Contact your McGraw-Hill *i*-learning sales specialist for more information.

Instructor Online Learning Centre—www.mcgrawhill.ca/college/jones

Essentials of Contemporary Management includes a password-protected website for instructors. The site offers downloadable supplements including those found on the instructors' CD-ROM, and a series of other resources.

Student Supplements

Student Online Learning Centre–www.mcgrawhill.ca/college/jones

The *Essentials of Contemporary Management* Online Learning Centre (OLC) prepared by Laurel Donaldson, Douglas College, is a website that follows the text chapter by chapter, with additional materials and quizzes to enhance the text and the classroom experience. Students can review concepts or prepare for exams by taking the self-grading quizzes that accompany each chapter or work through interactive exercises. The site also contains web links to relevant management sites and resources and other supplemental information that complements the text material.

Student CD ROM

Every copy of *Essentials of Contemporary Management* comes packaged with a free Student CD ROM, created by Jennifer E. Cliff, University of Alberta, which is loaded with interactive exercises, quizzes, video cases, links to management sites and more. The Student CD features a multimedia case study on Yahoo! complete with video clips, video notes and case study quizzes. You will also find valuable study aids including chapter quizzes, links to management sites and interactive application exercises designed to help you assess your personal management style and test your project management skills.

Student Study Guide

This valuable student resource, prepared by Laurel Donaldson, Douglas College, includes learning objectives, a detailed outline of each of the chapters, as well as multiple-choice and true/false application questions. This comprehensive learning aid will assist students in their understanding of key concepts, and help them prep for exams.

Acknowledgments

I would like to thank several people for the help they provided as I worked on this text. First and foremost, I would like to express particular appreciation to Su Mei Ku, my very talented "day-to-day" developmental editor, who put in long and exhausting hours helping me to get the manuscript in order. She knew and understood how to make things easier for me so that I could concentrate fully on the writing and research process. And she was always available, cheerleading all the way. Lesley Mann provided valuable research assistance for this project. Lesley has an uncanny sense for knowing the kinds of background material I need for my book projects and she outdid herself in making sure that examples are both current and relevant. Cheryl Cohen did an outstanding job of copyediting, dedicating herself to the task of eliminating the numerous inconsistencies and misspellings that can crop up in a book of this length. I really enjoyed her careful attention to detail, her goodwill in working with me, and her sense of humour and honesty as we tried to make this the most student-friendly read possible. Alison Derry did a great job in getting the photos that you see, as well as acquiring myriad permissions. Finally, Kelly Dickson (Manager, Editorial Services & Design) managed the production of this book efficiently and good-naturedly, and was always ready to help out in whatever way needed. There is always the danger in singling out people that others get forgotten. The McGraw team as a whole should be acknowledged for any help they provided that was not specifically mentioned.

Irene Khoo, my divisional assistant at UBC, deserves special mention for helping to keep the project on track, doing some of the word processing, managing the courier packages and faxes, and always being attentive to detail. I could not ask for a better, more dedicated, or more cheerful assistant. She really helps keep everything together.

Finally, I want to acknowledge the many reviewers of this Canadian edition for their detailed, helpful, and timely comments. They made a number of great suggestions that helped improve this textbook:

John Brownlee-Baker (Capilano College)
Lewis Callahan (Lethbridge Community College)
Laurel Donaldson (Douglas College)
Frances Ford (New Brunswick Community College)
Robert Fournier (Red Deer College)
Jai Goolsarran (Centennial College)
Alec Lee (Camosun College)
Murray Kernaghan (Assiniboine College)
Louis Masson (Southern Alberta Institute of Technology)
David O'Leary (Capilano College)
Brian Paul (Yukon College)
Penny Perrier (Sault College/Algoma University College)
Barbara Smith (Niagara College)
Don Smith (Georgian College)
Heather Stevens (George Brown College)

Christine Tomchak (Humber College)
Rae Verity (Southern Alberta Institute of Technology)
Vic De Witt (Red River College)

I dedicate this book to my father, Peter X. Langton. He was a man of many talents, and he would have been amused beyond words to watch me write a text on management. To my family I give silent acknowledgment for everything else.

Nancy Langton
November 2003

About the Authors

Gareth Jones is a Professor of Management in the Lowry Mays College and Graduate School of Business at Texas A&M University. He received both his BA and PhD from the University of Lancaster, UK. He previously held teaching and research appointments at the University of Warwick, Michigan State University, and the University of Illinois at Urbana–Champaign.

He specializes in both strategic management and organizational theory and is well known for his research that applies transaction cost analysis to explain many forms of strategic behaviour. He is currently interested in strategy process and issues concerning the development of trust and the role of affect in the strategic decision-making process. He has published many articles in leading journals of the field and his recent work has appeared in the *Academy of Management Review, Journal of International Business Studies, Human Relations,* and the *Journal of Management.* One of his articles won the *Academy of Management Journal* Best Paper Award, and he is one of the most prolific authors in the *Academy of Management Review.* He is serving or has served on the editorial boards of the *Academy of Management Review,* the *Journal of Management,* and *Management Inquiry.* In addition to his academic achievements, Gareth is co-author of three other major textbooks in the management discipline, including organizational behaviour, organizational theory, and strategic management.

Jennifer George is also a Professor of Management in the Lowry Mays College and Graduate School of Business at Texas A&M University. She received her BA in Psychology/Sociology from Wesleyan University, her MBA in Finance from New York University, and her PhD in Management and Organizational Behavior from New York University.

She specializes in organizational behaviour and is well known for her research on affect and mood, their determinants, and their effects on various individual and group-level work outcomes. She is the author of many articles in leading peer-reviewed journals, and her recent work has appeared in the *Academy of Management Review,* the *Journal of Management,* and *Human Relations.* One of her papers won the Academy of Management's Organizational Behavior Division Outstanding Competitive Paper Award. She is, or has been, on the editorial review boards of the *Journal of Applied Psychology, Academy of Management Journal, Journal of Management,* and *Journal of Managerial Issues,* and was a consulting editor for the *Journal of Organizational Behavior.* She is a Fellow in the American Psychological Association, the American Psychological Society, and the Society for Industrial and Organizational Psychology.

With her husband, Gareth Jones, she has written a leading textbook in organizational behaviour. They have also collaborated on two children, Nicholas, who is nine, and Julia, who is eight.

Nancy Langton received her PhD from Stanford University. Since completing her graduate studies, Professor Langton has taught at the University of Oklahoma and the University of British Columbia. Currently a member of the Organizational Behaviour and Human Resources division in the Sauder School of Business, University of British Columbia, and academic director of the Business Families Centre at UBC, she teaches at the undergraduate, MBA and PhD level and conducts executive programs on family business issues, time management, attracting and retaining employees, as well as women and management issues.

Professor Langton has received several major three-year research grants from the Social Sciences and Humanities Research Council of Canada (SSHRC), and her research interests have focused on human resource issues in the workplace, including pay equity, gender equity, and leadership and communication styles. She is currently conducting longitudinal research with entrepreneurs in the Greater Vancouver Region, looking specifically at their human resource practices. Her research has appeared in such journals as *Administrative Science Quarterly, American Sociological Review, Organizational Studies, Sociological Quarterly, Journal of Management Education*, and *Gender, Work and Organizations*. She has won Best Paper commendations from both the Academy of Management and the Administrative Sciences Association of Canada, and in 2003 won the Best Women's Entrepreneurship Paper Award given by the Washington, DC-based Center for Women's Business Research for work with Jennifer Cliff (University of Alberta) and Howard Aldrich (University of North Carolina). She has also published two textbooks on organizational behaviour.

Professor Langton routinely wins high marks from her students for teaching. She has been nominated many times for the Commerce Undergraduate Society Awards, and has won several honourable mention plaques. In 1998 she won the University of British Columbia Faculty of Commerce's most prestigious award for teaching innovation, The Talking Stick. The award was given for Professor Langton's redesign of the undergraduate organizational behaviour course as well as the many activities that were a spinoff of these efforts. In 2001 she was part of the UBC MBA Core design team that won the national Alan Blizzard Award, which recognizes innovation in teaching. At heart, Professor Langton enjoys being a teacher. But she also is a quilter and an accomplished pizza maker. She wishes she had more time for these latter two activities.

Online
LearningCenter
with POWERWEB

www.mcgrawhill.ca/college/jones

FOR THE STUDENT

- Want to get higher grades?

- Want instant feedback on your comprehension *and* retention of the course material?

- Want to know how ready you *really* are to take your next exam?

- Want the extra help at *your* convenience?

Of course you do!

Then check out your
Online Learning Centre!

- Online Quizzes
- Web Resources
- Web Exercises
- Journal Entries

ESSENTIALS OF CONTEMPORARY MANAGEMENT

FIRST CANADIAN EDITION

FOR THE INSTRUCTOR

- Want an easy way to test your students prior to an exam that *doesn't* create more work for you?

- Want to access your supplements *without* having to bring them all to class?

- Want to integrate current happenings into your lectures *without* all the searching and extra work?

- Want an *easy* way to get your course on-line?

- Want to *free up more time* in your day to get more done?

Of course you do!

Then check out your
Online Learning Centre!

- Downloadable Supplements
- PageOut
- Online Resources

McGraw-Hill Ryerson

Higher Learning. Forward Thinking.™

Part 1

CHAPTER 1

MANAGERS AND MANAGING

Learning Objectives

1. Describe what management is, what managers do, what organizations are for, and how managers use the resources of their organization efficiently and effectively to achieve organizational goals.

2. Explain how planning, organizing, leading, and controlling (the four principal managerial functions) differ, and how managers' ability to handle each one can affect an organization's performance.

3. Differentiate among the three levels of management, and understand the responsibilities of managers at different levels in the organizational hierarchy.

4. Identify the roles managers perform and the skills they need to carry out those roles effectively.

5. Explain the key challenges managers face in the Canadian environment.

6. Discuss the principal challenges managers face in today's increasingly competitive global environment.

Roles in Contrast: Questions

MANAGERS	EMPLOYEES
What is management?	Are managers really important?
What do I need to know about management roles?	What do managers do?
What skills do managers need?	If I wanted to be a manager, what kinds of skills might I need?

A Case in Contrast

WestJet Brings Back Its First CEO

When Clive Beddoe was honoured at the end of 2000 as Entrepreneur of the Year, he was in his second stint as CEO and president of Calgary-based WestJet Airlines Ltd. (www.westjet.com).[1] Beddoe founded the airline in 1996 with Don Bell, Mark Hill, and Tim Morgan, but he stepped aside to be executive chairman when Steve Smith, formerly of Air Canada, was appointed CEO in early 1999. The two men could not have been more different in their management styles.

Beddoe started WestJet having no experience running an airline. However, he and his co-founders had a solid business plan. Their intention was to copy the successful Dallas, Texas-based discount carrier Southwest Airlines. They would do this by running a low-cost operation with short flights on selected routes, very low fares, and high quality customer service.

WestJet is the fastest-growing airline ever launched in Canada and one of the most profitable in North America. Beddoe insists, however, that it's not the business plan but WestJet's corporate culture that accounts for the airline's extraordinary performance. "The entire environ-ment is conducive to bringing out the best in people," he says. "It's the culture that creates the passion to succeed."

Beddoe's leadership strength is that he understands how to manage people. Or more precisely, he understands how to get his employees to manage themselves. WestJet sets performance goals for employees, but workers have the freedom to do their jobs without interference from supervisors.

Many of WestJet's job applicants come from outside the airline industry. "We prefer it that way," says Beddoe. "This is a new culture, a new vision. It's better to start with a clean slate."

WestJet employees are expected to have enthusiasm and a sense of humour. One thing Beddoe doesn't want is employees who want to be part of a union. So he created the Pro-Active Communication Team (PACT, for short), an employee association for all employees that helps management address employee concerns before they become a problem.

Clive Beddoe, CEO of WestJet (second from right), won the 2000 Canadian Entrepreneur of the Year award along with company co-founders (from left to right) Donald Bell, Tim Morgan, and Mark Hill.

Steve Smith did not work out as CEO of WestJet, and was forced to resign. However, he was given a second chance to run a discount airline: Air Canada chose him in August 2001 to lead one of its spinoffs, Calgary-based Zip.

In early 1999, Beddoe decided he no longer wanted to run the day-to-day business of the carrier, preferring to take on the role of executive chair. WestJet hired Steve Smith to become WestJet's second CEO. Smith, a well-respected executive in the aviation community with more than 20 years' experience, was running Air Canada's regional airline, Air Ontario, at the time. The WestJet co-founders thought he was well suited to take their airline from a private concern into a public company. WestJet's board also liked Smith's amiable, energetic personality.

However, his experience at Air Ontario, where he frequently dealt with hostile unions, had left Smith with more of a top-down management style than WestJet was used to. Beddoe says that Smith "treated PACT like a union, and they resented that immediately. He came from a background where you just weren't open and straightforward, [where] you don't play all your cards at once. Well, we don't do that."

About 18 months after Smith was hired, WestJet's board asked for his resignation because of "a difference in philosophy as to management style." Under his leadership, employees had become "agitated, morale suffered and the culture that built the airline was at risk."

Statistics underscore that it really was his managerial philosophy that cost Smith his job. During his tenure there was a sharp increase in earnings, with a 120-percent rise in share price during his last year, including a three-for-two stock split. Thus, from a bottom-line perspective, Smith was successful, although by the time of his dismissal, some of the core senior executives were threatening to quit. Smith rarely comments on his departure from WestJet, but has acknowledged that his management style didn't mesh with WestJet's collaborative approach.

OVERVIEW

The story of WestJet's two CEOs illustrates many of the challenges facing people who become managers: Managing a company is a complex activity, and managers must learn the skills and acquire the knowledge necessary to become effective managers. Management is clearly more an art form than a science. Even effective managers make mistakes, and success at one company does not necessarily guarantee success at another.

In this chapter, we look at what managers do and what skills and abilities they must develop if they are to manage their organizations successfully over time. We also identify the different kinds of managers that organizations need, and the skills and abilities they must develop if they are to be successful. Finally, we identify some of the challenges that Canadian managers must address if their organizations are to grow and prosper.

WHAT IS MANAGEMENT?

When you think of a manager, what kind of person comes to mind? Do you see someone who, like Clive Beddoe, can determine the future prosperity of a large for-profit company? Or do you see the administrator of a not-for-profit organization such as a school, library, health care organization or charity? Or do you think of the person in charge of your local McDonald's restaurant or Wal-Mart store? Do you realize that even employees are being asked to assume some managerial functions, and that management occurs even in informal groups? In other words, these days almost everyone is called upon to manage, although the scope of that responsibility will vary. What, then, does management mean?

Management takes place in **organizations,** which are collections of people who work together and coordinate their actions to achieve a wide variety of goals.[2] **Management** is the planning, organizing, leading, and controlling of resources to achieve goals effectively and efficiently. **Resources** are assets such as people, machinery, raw materials, information, skills, and financial capital. A **manager** is a person responsible for supervising the use of a group or organization's resources to achieve its goals.

Achieving High Performance: A Manager's Goal

Organizational performance is a measure of how efficiently and effectively managers use resources to satisfy customers and achieve organizational goals. For instance, the principal goal of Steve Jobs is to manage Apple Computer so that it produces personal computers that customers are willing to buy; the principal goal of doctors, nurses, and hospital administrators is to increase their hospital's ability to make sick people well; the principal goal of each McDonald's restaurant manager is to produce burgers, fries, and shakes that people want to eat and pay for. Organizational performance increases in direct proportion to increases in efficiency and effectiveness (see Figure 1.1).

Efficiency is a measure of how well or how productively resources are used to achieve a goal.[3] Organizations are efficient when managers minimize the amount of input resources (such as labour, raw materials, and component parts) or the amount of time needed to produce a given output of goods or services. For example, McDonald's recently developed a more efficient fat fryer that not only reduces (by 30 percent) the amount of oil used in cooking but also speeds up the cooking of french fries. A manager's responsibility is to ensure that an organization and its

organizations
Collections of people who work together and coordinate their actions to achieve goals.

management
The planning, organizing, leading, and controlling of resources to achieve organizational goals effectively and efficiently.

resources
Assets such as people, machinery, raw materials, information, skills, and financial capital.

manager
A person who is responsible for supervising the use of an organization's resources to achieve its goals.

organizational performance
A measure of how efficiently and effectively a manager uses resources to satisfy customers and achieve organizational goals.

Figure 1.1 | Efficiency, Effectiveness, and Performance in an Organization

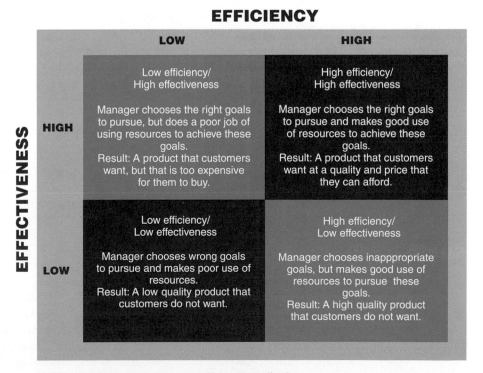

High-performing organizations are efficient *and* effective.

efficiency
A measure of how well or productively resources are used to achieve a goal.

effectiveness
A measure of the appropriateness of the goals an organization is pursuing and of the degree to which the organization achieves those goals.

Boliden AB's Myra Falls
www.boliden.ca/
operations/myrafalls.htm

members perform, as efficiently as possible, all the activities that are needed to provide goods and services to customers.

Effectiveness is a measure of the appropriateness of the goals that managers have selected for the organization to pursue, and of the degree to which the organization achieves those goals. Management expert Peter Drucker compared the two this way: Efficiency is doing things right; effectiveness is doing the right thing.[4] Organizations are effective when managers choose appropriate goals and then achieve them. Some years ago, for example, managers at McDonald's decided on the goal of providing breakfast service to attract more customers. This goal was a smart choice, because sales of breakfast food now account for more than 30 percent of McDonald's revenues. High-performing organizations such as Campbell Soup, McDonald's, Wal-Mart, Intel, Home Depot, IKEA, and the March of Dimes are simultaneously efficient and effective, as shown in Figure 1.1.

Managers who are effective are those who choose the right organizational goals to pursue and have the skills to use resources efficiently. Consider, for example, the way in which Kjell Larsson, the mine manager at Myra Falls copper and zinc mine, turned a hostile situation around in a unionized workplace.

MANAGERIAL FUNCTIONS

Think About It

How to Be an Effective Mine Manager

When Swedish-controlled Boliden AB bought Vancouver Island's Myra Falls copper and zinc mine in 1998, it faced a considerable challenge. The mine had a history of rough management-union relations, even for the mining industry.[5] Work stoppages had preceded the last two union contracts. The existing agreement had come after just a one-day strike, but the previous contract was an arbitrated decision after a bitter 16-month strike-lockout. Employees still felt a lot of anger about the negotiations.

Once the purchase was completed, the company sent Kjell Larsson over from Sweden to be the mine manager. Larsson asked every one of the miners how the mine's operation could be improved. Together, the miners and the managers identified five key problem areas and then formed teams to figure out how to solve the problems. Larsson and Boliden represent a new form of management, particularly in a unionized environment.

Question
1. What do managers do?

Henri Fayol
www.lib.uwo.ca/
business/fayol.html

The job of management is to help an organization make the best use of its resources to achieve its goals. How do managers accomplish this objective? They do so by performing four essential managerial functions: planning, organizing, leading, and controlling (see Figure 1.2). French manager Henri Fayol first outlined the nature of these managerial activities around the start of the 20th century in *General and Industrial Management,* a book that remains the classic statement of what managers must do to create a high-performing organization.[6]

Managers at all levels and in all departments—whether in small or large organizations, for-profit or not-for-profit organizations, or organizations that operate in one country or throughout the world—are responsible for performing these four functions, and we will look at each in turn. How well managers perform them determines how efficient and effective their organization is. Individuals who are not managers can also be involved in planning, organizing, leading, and controlling, so understanding these processes is important for everyone.

Figure 1.2 | Four Functions of Management

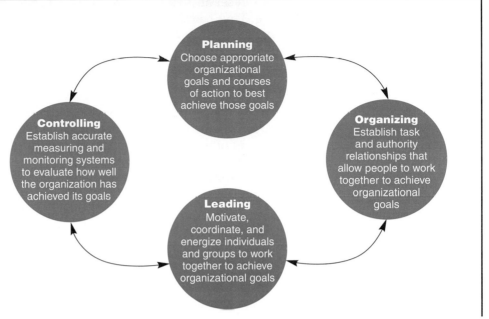

Planning

planning

Identifying and selecting appropriate goals and courses of action; one of the four principal functions of management.

Planning is a process used to identify and select appropriate goals and courses of action. There are three steps in the planning process: (1) deciding which goals the organization will pursue, (2) deciding what courses of action to adopt to attain those goals, and (3) deciding how to allocate organizational resources to attain the goals. How well managers plan determines how effective and efficient their organization is—its performance level.[7] For the managers at Myra Falls, part of the planning process was determining how the new management would work with unionized employees who felt hostile after a series of lengthy strikes under the previous management.

strategy

A cluster of decisions about what goals to pursue, what actions to take, and how to use resources to achieve goals.

The outcome of planning is a **strategy,** a cluster of decisions concerning what organizational goals to pursue, what actions to take, and how to use resources to achieve goals. For instance, WestJet's strategy is to be a low-cost provider in the Canadian discount airline market. Planning is a difficult activity because, normally, it's not immediately clear which goals an organization should pursue or how best to pursue them. Choosing the right strategy is risky because managers commit organizational resources for activities that could either succeed or fail. The failure of many of the dot-coms is attributable to managers trying to make money quickly, without business plans or long-term vision. In Chapter 5, we focus on the planning process and on the strategies organizations can select to respond to opportunities or threats.

Organizing

organizing

Structuring workplace relationships in a way that allows members of an organization to work together to achieve organizational goals; one of the four principal functions of management.

Organizing is a process used to structure workplace relationships in a way that allows members of an organization to work together to achieve organizational goals. Organizing involves grouping people into departments according to the kinds of job-specific tasks they perform. In organizing, managers also lay out the lines of authority and responsibility between different individuals and groups, and they decide how best to coordinate organizational resources, and in particular, human resources. When Boliden took over the Myra Falls mine, managers decided to share some responsibility with the employees. "The leadership we recognize here are management and union," says Dave Bazowsky, who has worked in human resources at Myra Falls. The union is involved in everything from training to strategic planning. Thus coordination is more of a shared responsibility at the mine.

The outcome of organizing is the creation of an **organizational structure,** a formal system of task and reporting relationships that coordinates and motivates organizational members so that they work together to achieve organizational goals. Organizational structure determines how an organization's resources can best be used to create goods and services.

We examine the organizing process in Chapters 6 and 7. In Chapter 6, we consider the organizational structures that managers can use to coordinate and motivate people and other resources. In Chapter 7, we look at the important roles that an organization's culture, values, and norms play in binding people and departments together so that they work toward organizational goals.

Leading

In **leading,** managers articulate a clear vision, and make sure that organizational members understand their individual roles in achieving organizational goals. Leadership depends on the use of power, influence, vision, persuasion, and communication skills for two important tasks: to coordinate the behaviours of individuals and groups so that their activities and efforts are in harmony, and to encourage employees to perform at a high level. The outcome of good leadership is a high level of motivation and commitment among organizational members. The leadership at the Myra Falls mine encouraged union members to be involved and participate in decisions, and this led employees to have greater motivation and commitment to their jobs.

We discuss the issues involved in managing and leading individuals and groups in Chapters 8 through 12. In Chapters 8 and 9, we examine the best ways to encourage high motivation and commitment among employees. In Chapter 10, we look at the way groups and teams achieve organizational goals, and the coordination problems that can arise when people work together in groups and teams. In Chapter 11, we consider how to manage employees through human resource practices. In Chapter 12 , we consider how communication and coordination problems can arise between people and functions, and how managers can try to manage these problems through bargaining and negotiation. Understanding how to manage and lead effectively is an important skill. You might be interested to know that CEOs have just a few short months to prove to investors that they are able to communicate a vision and carry it out. Recent studies suggest that investors and analysts give CEOs only 14 to 18 months to show results.[8]

Controlling

In **controlling,** managers evaluate how well an organization is achieving its goals and take action to maintain or improve performance. For example, managers monitor the performance of individuals, departments, and the organization as a whole to see whether they are all meeting desired performance standards. If standards are not being met, managers take action to improve performance. Individuals working in groups also have the responsibility of controlling, because they have to make sure the group achieves its goals and completes its actions. At the Myra Falls mine, goals are achieved by making everyone aware of them. Everyone is involved in budget discussions, and employees can easily find out information about the company—such as tonnes mined each day, percentage of ore, extract shipped, progress against budget, and safety measures.

The outcome of the control process is the ability to measure performance accurately and regulate organizational efficiency and effectiveness. In order to exercise

---

organizational structure
A formal system of task and reporting relationships that coordinates and motivates organizational members so that they work together to achieve organizational goals.

leading
Articulating a clear vision and energizing and empowering organizational members so that everyone understands their individual roles in achieving organizational goals; one of the four principal functions of management.

controlling
Evaluating how well an organization is achieving its goals and taking action to maintain or improve performance; one of the four principal functions of management.

control, managers must decide which goals to measure—perhaps goals pertaining to productivity, quality, or responsiveness to customers—and then they must design information and control systems that will provide the data they need to assess performance. These mechanisms provide feedback to the manager, and the manager provides feedback to employees. The controlling function also allows managers to evaluate how well they themselves are performing the other three functions of management—planning, organizing, and leading—and to take corrective action.

We cover the most important aspects of the control function in Chapter 13, where we outline the basic process of control and examine some control systems that managers can use to monitor and measure organizational performance.

The four managerial functions—planning, organizing, leading, and controlling—are essential to a manager's job. At all levels in a managerial hierarchy, and across all departments in an organization, effective management means making decisions and managing these four activities successfully.

TYPES OF MANAGERS

Think About It

CEO and President Shares Power With Her Managers

Lee McDonald, president and CEO of Barrie, Ontario-based Southmedic Inc., started her company in a home office with two employees in 1983.[9] The company manufactures and distributes surgical instruments for hospital operating rooms. By 1998 it had a staff of 55, and in 2001 its building facilities covered 5400 square metres. McDonald won the 1997 Canadian Woman Entrepreneur of the Year Award for International Competitiveness and in 1999, 2000, and 2001 she was one of *Chatelaine's* Top 100 Woman Entrepreneurs and *Profit's* Top 100 Woman Entrepreneurs.

McDonald says her success was sparked by her custom manufacturing division. "We are one of the few companies in North America able to take a prototype from design to packaging in the short time of six weeks. The big companies can do it but not at my speed."

Southmedic's management structure is different than the big companies as well. While she holds the positions of CEO and president, McDonald shares power with her managers. "I believe in a horizontal management team. There are no pyramids here. I couldn't structure the company as if the world depended on me. My managers have a lot of autonomy," she explains. McDonald chose this flattened, more participative structure for Southmedic to accommodate her own needs. Because of the business, she has a heavy travel schedule. More important, she has three young children at home. "I have to be able to come and go without this place falling apart," she says.

Question
1. What are the different types of managers?

To perform efficiently and effectively, larger organizations traditionally employ three types of managers—first-line managers, middle managers, and top managers—arranged in a hierarchy (see Figure 1.3). Typically, first-line managers report to middle managers, and middle managers report to top managers. Managers at each level have different but related types of responsibilities for using organizational resources to increase efficiency and effectiveness. The managers working at Southmedic help Lee McDonald manage the company, and fill in for her when she is travelling on business.

Figure 1.3 | Management Hierarchy

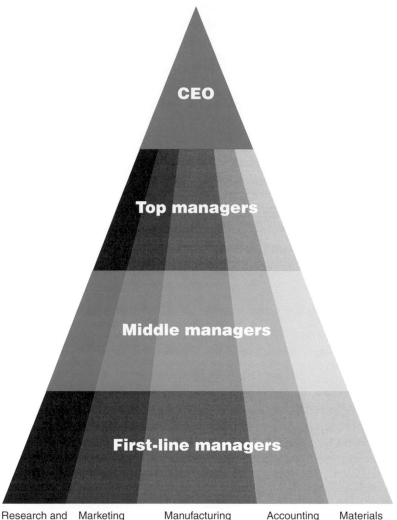

An entrepreneur founds an organization, takes the role of chief executive officer (CEO) and begins the management task of organizing.

As more and more employees are hired, the CEO realizes the need to create a hierarchy of managers.

Top managers are hired and together with the CEO become responsible for planning, identifying, and selecting appropriate goals and courses of action.

Middle managers are hired and become responsible for the effective management of organizational resources, including supporting first-line managers.

First-line managers are hired and take on the day-to-day task of leading and controlling human and other resources.

At the same time that the organization is dividing vertically into hierarchical levels, it also divides horizontally into departments: groups of people who work together and possess similar skills or use the same knowledge, tools, or techniques to perform their jobs. Managers and employees become members of a particular department, such as manufacturing, marketing, or research and development.

The final result of this division vertically and horizontally is an organizational structure.

department
A group of people who work together and possess similar skills or use the same knowledge, tools, or techniques to perform their jobs.

These three types of managers are grouped into departments according to their specific job responsibilities. A **department**—such as manufacturing, accounting, or engineering—is a group of people who work together and possess similar skills or use the same kind of knowledge, tools, or techniques to perform their jobs. As Figure 1.3 indicates, first-line, middle, and top managers, who differ from one another by virtue of their job-specific responsibilities, are found in each of an organization's major departments. Below, we examine the reasons why organizations use a hierarchy of managers and group them into departments. We then examine some recent changes that have been taking place in managerial hierarchies.

Levels of Management

First-Line Managers

first-line managers
Managers who are responsible for the daily supervision and coordination of nonmanagerial employees.

At the base of the managerial hierarchy are **first-line managers** (often called supervisors). They are responsible for the daily supervision and coordination of the nonmanagerial employees who perform many of the specific activities necessary to produce goods and services. First-line managers may be found in all departments of an organization.

Examples of first-line managers include the supervisor of a work team in the manufacturing department of a car plant, the head nurse in the obstetrics department of a hospital, and the chief mechanic overseeing a crew of mechanics in the service department of a new-car dealership.

Middle Managers

middle managers
Managers who supervise first-line managers and are responsible for finding the best way to use resources to achieve organizational goals.

Middle managers supervise the first-line managers, and have the responsibility of finding the best way to organize human and other resources to achieve organizational goals. To increase efficiency, middle managers try to find ways to help first-line managers and nonmanagerial employees make better use of resources in order to reduce manufacturing costs or improve the way services are provided to customers. To increase effectiveness, middle managers are responsible for evaluating whether the goals that the organization is pursuing are appropriate and for suggesting to top managers ways in which goals should be changed. A major part of the middle manager's job is to develop and fine-tune skills and know-how—manufacturing or marketing expertise, for example—that allow the organization to be efficient and effective. Middle managers also coordinate resources across departments and divisions. Middle managers make the thousands of specific decisions that go into the production of goods and services: Which first-line supervisors should be chosen for this particular project? Where can we find the highest quality resources? How should employees be organized to allow them to make the best use of resources?

Middle managers perform an important role in organizations. For instance, behind a first-class sales force, look for the sales manager responsible for training, motivating, and rewarding salespeople. Behind a committed staff of secondary school teachers, look for the principal who energizes them to look for ways to obtain the resources they need to do an outstanding and innovative job in the classroom.

Top Managers

top managers
Managers who establish organizational goals, decide how departments should interact, and monitor the performance of middle managers.

In contrast to middle managers, **top managers** are responsible for the performance of all departments.[10] They have cross-departmental responsibility and they're responsible for connecting the parts of the organization together. Top managers help carry out the organizational vision; they establish organizational goals, such as which goods and services the company should produce; they decide how the different departments should interact; and they monitor how well middle managers

Andrea Jung—CEO of Avon, the famous cosmetic producer—advanced to that rank after first serving as the company's president and chief operating officer.

top-management team
A group composed of the CEO, the president, and the heads of the most important departments.

in each department use resources to achieve goals.[11] Top managers are ultimately responsible for the success or failure of an organization, and their performance is continually scrutinized by people inside and outside the organization, such as employees and investors.[12]

Top managers report to a company's chief executive officer—such as WestJet CEO Clive Beddoe, Shaw Communications CEO Jim Shaw, and Quebecor CEO Pierre Karl Péladeau—or to the president of the organization, who is second-in-command. In some organizations one person holds the title of both CEO and president, such as Lee McDonald at Southmedic and Paul Godfrey, president and CEO of the Toronto Blue Jays. The CEO and president are responsible for developing good working relationships among the top managers who head the various departments (manufacturing and marketing, e.g.), and who usually have the title *vice-president*. A central concern of the CEO is the creation of a smoothly functioning **top-management team,** a group composed of the CEO, the president, and the department heads most responsible for helping to achieve organizational goals.[13] The CEO also has the responsibility of setting the vision for the organization.

The relative importance of each of the four managerial functions—planning, organizing, leading, and controlling—to any particular manager depends on the manager's position in the managerial hierarchy.[14] As managers move up the hierarchy, they spend more time planning and organizing resources to maintain and improve organizational performance (see Figure 1.4). Top managers devote most of their time to planning and organizing, the functions that are so crucial to determining an organization's long-term performance. The

Figure 1.4 | **Relative Amount of Time That Managers Spend on the Four Managerial Functions**

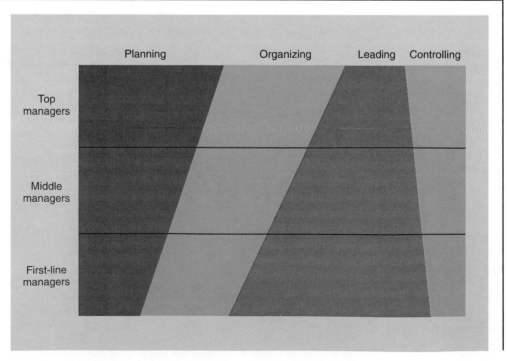

lower a manager's position in the hierarchy, the more time he or she spends leading and controlling first-line managers or nonmanagerial employees.

RECENT CHANGES IN MANAGERIAL HIERARCHIES

Think About It

Managing From the Bottom at WestJet

Clive Beddoe, president and CEO of Calgary-based WestJet Airlines Ltd., believes that letting employees manage themselves is the key to WestJet's success.[15] Because WestJet's employees are spread throughout the country, Beddoe organized his company to be managed from the bottom. Employees are encouraged to perform their jobs without interference from supervisors. "I don't direct things," says Beddoe. "We set some standards and expectations, but [I] don't interfere in how our people do their jobs." For instance, flight attendants are asked to serve customers in a caring, positive, and cheerful manner. How they do that is left up to them.

Questions
1. Do employees always need managers?
2. How can employees be encouraged to take on more responsibility?

The tasks and responsibilities of managers at different levels have been changing dramatically in recent years. Increasingly, top managers are encouraging lower-level managers to look beyond the goals of their own departments and take a cross-departmental view to find new opportunities to improve organizational performance. Stiff competition for resources—both at home and abroad—has put increased pressure on all managers to improve efficiency, effectiveness, and organizational performance. To respond to these pressures, many organizations have been changing the managerial hierarchy.[16]

Restructuring

restructuring

Downsizing an organization by eliminating the jobs of large numbers of top, middle, and first-line managers and nonmanagerial employees.

To decrease costs, CEOs and their top-management teams have been **restructuring** organizations to reduce the number of employees on the payroll. Restructuring can involve flattening the organization by cutting out some hierarchical layers, reducing the number of departments or the number or types of product lines, selling off parts of the business, closing plants, or even deciding to outsource some of the functions within the organization. Often, restructuring involves downsizing, or eliminating the jobs of large numbers of top, middle, or first-line managers and nonmanagerial employees. Downsizing has been a frequent event in Canada recently. Restructuring promotes efficiency by reducing costs and allowing the organization to make better use of its remaining resources. Large for-profit organizations today typically employ 10-percent fewer managers than they did 10 years ago. Canadian National Railway, Nortel Networks Corporation, General Motors, and many other organizations have eliminated several layers of middle management. The middle managers who still have jobs at these companies have had to assume additional responsibilities and are under increasing pressure to perform. For instance, when Indigo Books & Music Inc. removed a layer of management from all its stores in May 2000, each store's general manager had to handle responsibilities of the marketing, purchasing, and operations managers who had previously reported to the general manager.

Not everyone agrees that restructuring has a positive impact on society at large. For instance, when he was industry minister, federal politician John Manley said,

"It's part of my job to push the corporate sector and urge them to take into account the enormous damage it does when you cast people aside instead of retraining them."[17] Moreover, when polled, 58 percent of Canadians did not find it acceptable for profitable corporations to lay off employees.[18] Len Brooks, executive director of the Clarkson Centre for Business Ethics & Board Effectiveness at the University of Toronto, says laying off employees to maximize profit and improve cash flow "is really a dumb idea. Only a third of its practitioners achieve their financial objectives while paying a huge price as employee morale craters."[19] Many studies show that "surviving employees become narrow-minded, self-absorbed, and risk averse [after downsizing]. Morale sinks, productivity drops, and survivors distrust management."[20] For instance, Professor Terry Wagar, of the Department of Management at Saint Mary's University in Halifax, surveyed almost 2000 firms across Canada and found that companies that downsized during the 1990s suffered a variety of negative consequences. These included less favourable employer-employee relations, and decreases in efficiency and employee satisfaction.[21]

Empowerment and Self-Managed Teams

empowerment
Expanding employees' tasks and responsibilities.

self-managed teams
Groups of employees who supervise their own activities and monitor the quality of the goods and services they provide.

Another major change in management has taken place at the level of first-line managers, who typically supervise the employees engaged in producing goods and services. Many organizations have taken two steps to reduce costs and improve quality. One is the **empowerment** of the workforce, expanding employees' tasks and responsibilities so that they have more authority and accountability. The other is the creation of **self-managed teams**—groups of employees who are given responsibility for supervising their own activities and for monitoring the quality of the goods and services they provide. At WestJet, CEO Clive Beddoe has created an empowered workforce. He believes that his management from the bottom gives employees pride in what they do. "They are the ones making the decisions about what they're doing and how they're doing it," says Beddoe.

Under both empowerment and self-managed teams, employees assume many of the responsibilities and duties previously performed by first-line managers.[22] What is the role of the first-line manager in this new work context? First-line managers act as coaches or mentors whose job is not to tell employees what to do, but to provide advice and guidance and help teams find new ways to perform their tasks more efficiently.[23] The unionized workers at the Myra Falls copper mine are an example of empowered employees who are asked to share in the decision making of the company. Similarly, WestJet's employees are encouraged to perform their jobs in ways that meet the company's overall objectives without interference from supervisors.

Tips for Managers

Managing Resources

1. Talk to customers to assess whether the goods or services that an organization provides adequately meet all needs and how they might be improved.

2. Analyze how an organization can better obtain or use resources to increase efficiency and effectiveness.

3. Critically assess how the skills and know-how of departments are helping an organization to achieve a competitive advantage. Take steps to improve skills whenever possible.

4. Count the number of managers at each level in the organization and analyze how to increase efficiency and effectiveness of the workforce.

MANAGERIAL ROLES AND SKILLS

Think About It

The Many Roles of Management

Terri Patsos Stanley is the president of Boston Short-Term Rentals, a small company that provides high quality apartments for business travellers who don't want to stay in hotels.[24] She enjoys the variety of her work and relishes the pleasure of meeting the senior managers, actors, and overseas visitors who stay in the apartments. To keep costs down and customers happy, Patsos Stanley has had to learn a variety of managerial roles. Apparently, she performs her roles effectively; since its start in 1995, her company has grown rapidly in size and revenues.

Question
1. What are the roles that managers need to learn?

Though we might like to think that a manager's job is highly structured and that management is a logical, orderly process in which managers try hard to make rational decisions, being a manager often involves acting emotionally and relying on gut feelings. Quick, immediate reactions to situations rather than deliberate thought and reflection are an important aspect of managerial action.[25] Often, managers are overloaded with responsibilities, do not have time to analyze every nuance of a situation, and therefore make decisions in uncertain conditions without being sure which outcomes will be best.[26] Moreover, for top managers in particular, the current situation is constantly changing, and a decision that seems right today may prove to be wrong tomorrow.

Henry Mintzberg
www.henrymintzberg.com

role
The specific tasks that a person is expected to perform because of the position he or she holds in an organization.

Despite all this flux, however, it is important to note that the roles managers need to play and the skills they need to use have changed little since the early 1970s, when McGill University Professor Henry Mintzberg detailed 10 specific roles that effective managers undertake. A **role** is a set of specific tasks that a person is expected to perform because of the position he or she holds in an organization. Although the roles that Mintzberg described overlap with Fayol's model, they are useful because they focus on what managers do in a typical hour, day, or week.[27] Below, we discuss these roles and then examine the skills effective managers need to develop.

Managerial Roles Identified by Mintzberg

Mintzberg examined all the specific tasks that managers need to perform as they plan, organize, lead, and control organizational resources, and he reduced them to 10 roles.[28] Managers assume each of these roles in order to influence the behaviour of individuals and groups inside and outside the organization. People inside the organization include other managers and employees. People outside the organization include shareholders, customers, suppliers, the local community in which an organization is located, and any local or government agency that has an interest in the organization and what it does.[29] Mintzberg grouped the 10 roles into three broad categories: *interpersonal, informational,* and *decisional* (see Table 1.1). Managers often perform several of these roles simultaneously.

Interpersonal Roles

Managers assume interpersonal roles in order to coordinate and interact with organizational members and provide direction and supervision for employees and for

Table 1.1 | Managerial Roles Identified by Mintzberg

Type of Role	Specific Role	Examples of Role Activities
INTERPERSONAL	Figurehead	Outline future organizational goals to employees at company meetings; open a new corporate headquarters building; state the organization's ethical guidelines and the principles of behaviour employees are to follow in their dealings with customers and suppliers.
	Leader	Provide an example for employees to follow; give direct commands and orders to subordinates; make decisions concerning the use of human and technical resources; mobilize employee support for specific organizational goals.
	Liaison	Coordinate the work of managers in different departments; establish alliances between different organizations to share resources to produce new goods and services.
INFORMATIONAL	Monitor	Evaluate the performance of managers in different functions and take corrective action to improve their performance; watch for changes occurring in the external and internal environment that may affect the organization in the future.
	Disseminator	Inform employees about changes taking place in the external and internal environment that will affect them and the organization; communicate to employees the organization's vision and purpose.
	Spokesperson	Launch a national advertising campaign to promote new goods and services; give a speech to inform the local community about the organization's future intentions.
DECISIONAL	Entrepreneur	Commit organizational resources to develop innovative goods and services; decide to expand internationally to obtain new customers for the organization's products.
	Disturbance handler	Move quickly to take corrective action to deal with unexpected problems facing the organization from the external environment, such as a crisis like an oil spill, or from the internal environment, such as producing faulty goods or services.
	Resource allocator	Allocate organizational resources among different functions and departments of the organization; set budgets and salaries of middle and first-level managers.
	Negotiator	Work with suppliers, distributors, and labour unions to reach agreements about the quality and price of input, technical, and human resources; work with other organizations to establish agreements to pool resources to work on joint projects.

the organization as a whole. A manager's first interpersonal role is to act as a *figurehead*–the person who symbolizes an organization or a department. Assuming the figurehead role, the chief executive officer determines the direction or mission of the organization and informs employees and other interested parties about what the organization is seeking to achieve. Managers at all levels act as figureheads and role models who establish the appropriate and inappropriate ways to behave in the organization. Terri Patsos Stanley is the figurehead who provides the personal touch her guests expect; she is the person they can contact if problems arise.

In fact, Patsos Stanley has learned the importance of a hands-on approach to managing her company. She and her employees personally greet the new arrivals and perform the activities that porters, the concierge, and front desk staff do in the typical hotel.

A manager's role as a *leader* is to encourage subordinates to perform at a high level and to take steps to train, counsel, and mentor subordinates to help them reach their full potential. A manager's power to lead comes both from formal authority, due to his or her position in the organization's hierarchy, and from his or her personal qualities, including reputation, skills, and personality. The personal behaviour of a leader affects employee attitudes and behaviour; indeed, subordinates' desire to perform at a high level–and even whether they desire to arrive at work on time and not to be absent often–depends on how satisfied they are with working for the organization. With her small staff of carpenters, electricians, interior decorators, and maintenance workers, Patsos Stanley acts like a leader, energizing them to provide the quick service that guests expect.

In performing as a *liaison,* managers link and coordinate the activities of people and groups both inside and outside the organization. Inside the organization, managers are responsible for coordinating the activities of people in different departments to improve their ability to cooperate. Outside the organization, managers are responsible for forming linkages with suppliers, customers, or the organization's local community in order to obtain scarce resources. People outside an organization often come to equate the organization with the manager they are dealing with, or with the person they see on television or read about in the newspaper. Patsos Stanley takes on the liaison role when she links her guests to organizations that provide services they may need such as dry cleaning, catering, or hairdressing.

Informational Roles

Informational roles are closely associated with the tasks necessary to obtain and transmit information. First, a manager acts as a *monitor* and analyzes information from inside and outside the organization. With this information, a manager can effectively organize and control people and other resources. For instance, Patsos Stanley uses a sophisticated computer system to evaluate the performance of Boston Short-Term Rentals by occupancy rates, customer complaints, and other indicators of the quality of her service. The system helps her to respond quickly to problems as they arise.

Acting as a *disseminator,* the manager transmits information to other members of the organization to influence their work attitudes and behaviour. For instance, Patsos Stanley uses information technology (IT) to update her staff about changes in visitor arrivals and departures. In the role of spokesperson, a manager uses information to promote the organization so that people both inside and outside the organization respond positively. For instance, Patsos Stanely is always on the phone telling visitors the benefits of staying in an apartment that they know nothing about rather than in a hotel room.

Decisional Roles

Decisional roles are closely associated with the methods that managers use to plan strategy and utilize resources. In the role of *entrepreneur,* a manager must decide which projects or programs to initiate and how to invest resources to increase organizational performance. As a *disturbance handler,* a manager assumes responsibility for handling an unexpected event or crisis that threatens the organization's access to resources. In this situation, a manager must also assume the roles of figurehead and leader to rally employees so they can help secure the resources needed to avert the problem. Patsos Stanley engages in the disturbance handler role when she deals with unexpected problems such as plumbing breakdowns in the middle of the night.

Under typical conditions, *resource allocator* is one of the important roles a manager plays—deciding how best to use people and other resources to increase organizational performance. For instance, Patsos Stanley decides how much money to spend to refurbish and upgrade the apartments to maintain their luxury appeal. While engaged as a resource allocator, the manager must also be a *negotiator,* reaching agreements with other managers or groups claiming the first right to resources, or with the organization and outside groups such as shareholders or customers. For instance, Patsos Stanely contracts with other organizations, such as cleaning or painting companies, to obtain the most economical services her business requires.

Managerial Skills

To successfully perform their roles, managers must have certain skills. Research has shown that formal education, training, and experience help managers to acquire three principal types of skills: *conceptual, human,* and *technical.*[30] As you might expect, the level of these skills that a manager needs depends on his or her level in the managerial hierarchy (see Figure 1.5).

Conceptual Skills

conceptual skills
The ability to analyze and diagnose a situation and to distinguish between cause and effect.

Conceptual skills are demonstrated by the ability to analyze and diagnose a situation and to distinguish between cause and effect. Planning and organizing require a high level of conceptual skill, as does performing the managerial roles discussed above. Top managers require the best conceptual skills, because their primary responsibilities are planning and organizing.[31] Conceptual skills allow managers to understand the big picture confronting an organization. The ability to focus on the big picture lets the manager see beyond the situation immediately at hand and consider choices while keeping the organization's long-term goals in mind.

Human Skills

human skills
The ability to understand, alter, lead, and control the behaviour of other individuals and groups.

Human skills include the ability to understand, alter, lead, and control the behaviour of other individuals and groups. The ability to communicate and give feedback, to coordinate and motivate people, to give recognition, to mould individuals into a cohesive team, and to play politics effectively distinguishes effective from ineffective managers. By all accounts, Clive Beddoe of WestJet and Kjell Larsson of the Myra Falls mine possess human skills.

To manage interpersonal interactions effectively, each person in an organization needs to learn how to empathize with other people–to understand their viewpoints and the problems they face. One way to help managers understand their personal

Figure 1.5 | **Conceptual, Human, and Technical Skills Needed by Three Levels of Management**

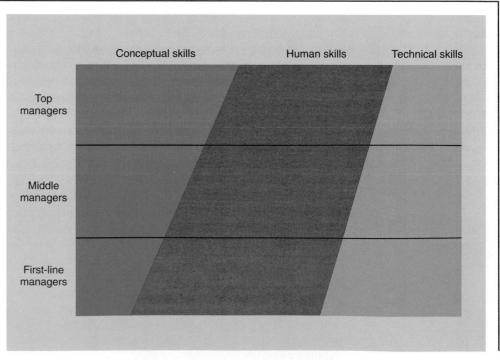

strengths and weaknesses is to have their superiors, peers, and subordinates provide feedback about their performance in the roles that Mintzberg identified. Managers also need to be able to manage politics effectively so that they can deal with resistance from those who disagree with their goals. Effective managers use political strategies to influence others and gain support for their goals, while overcoming resistance or opposition.

Technical Skills

Technical skills are the job-specific knowledge and techniques that are required to perform an organizational role. Examples include a manager's specific manufacturing, accounting, or marketing skills. Managers need a range of technical skills to be effective. The array of technical skills a person needs depends on his or her position in the organization. The manager of a restaurant, for example, may need cooking skills to fill in for an absent cook, accounting and bookkeeping skills to keep track of receipts and costs and to administer the payroll, and aesthetic skills to keep the restaurant looking attractive for customers.

Effective managers need all three kinds of skills—conceptual, human, and technical. The absence of even one type can lead to failure. Michael Kavanagh, human resources director for Vancouver-based Crystal Decisions, highlights this point. He says that at Crystal, a large computer software company, "We place a lot of emphasis on behavioural [human] skills. It's the difference between who gets hired and who doesn't. Your technical skills get you in the door, but your behavioural skills are increasingly criteria in enhancing your employment opportunities." Management skills, roles, and functions are closely related, and wise managers or prospective managers are constantly in search of the latest educational contributions to help them develop the conceptual, human, and technical skills they need to function in today's changing and increasingly competitive environment.

technical skills
Job-specific knowledge and techniques that are required to perform an organizational role.

Crystal Decisions
www.crystaldecisions.
com

Tips for Managers

Tasks and Roles

1. Estimate how much time managers spend performing each of the four tasks of planning, organizing, leading, and controlling. Decide if managers are spending the right amount of time on each task.

2. Decide which of Mintzberg's 10 managerial roles managers are performing well or poorly.

3. Based on this analysis, take steps to ensure that managers possess the right levels of conceptual, technical, and human skills to perform their jobs effectively.

CHALLENGES FOR MANAGEMENT IN THE CANADIAN ENVIRONMENT

Think About It

Canadian Armed Forces Face Diversity

A recent report by a special advisory board set up by former defence minister Art Eggleton found that women, visible minorities, and Aboriginal peoples remain underrepresented in the Canadian Armed Forces, with the army lagging behind both the navy and the air force.[32] The report said that the army tended to have a poor attitude toward women: Participants and instructors in combat training centres and battle schools claimed that "women are too weak to be in the combat arms." In addition, many soldiers believe that physical standards have been lowered so women can qualify. Perhaps the biggest problem, however, is that "soldiers tended to dismiss diversity training as a waste of time."

The board recommended that army leadership lead by example on integration questions. It also suggested that the military improve recruiting materials, do a better job of attracting women and minorities, and make fitness tests "less a measure of mere strength and more a gauge of ability to perform tasks." The latter might help to fight the view that there was a double standard in fitness tests.

Questions
1. Can the Canadian Forces be examined just like any other organization?
2. How does the legal environment affect organizations?
3. Why does managing diversity matter?

Managing in Canada presents a number of unique challenges and opportunities. Though these will be addressed throughout the textbook, we will identify them briefly here.

Organizational Size

It is important to recognize that managers don't manage only in large organizations. There are management responsibilities in organizations of every size. You may think managers primarily manage large manufacturing operations, but you may not realize that only 14.5 percent of Canadians work in manufacturing organizations. This is fewer than the 19 percent of Canadians who work in public sector jobs (those in the local, provincial, or federal government). Most Canadians (around 75 percent) work in the service sector of the economy.[33] You may also think that most people work in large **publicly held organizations** such as Ford Motor Company of Canada, or Nortel Networks. However, large organizations represent only 3 percent of the organizations in Canada. Of the almost 438 000 organizations in Canada in 2000 that had 5 or more employees, nearly 87 percent employed fewer than 50 people.[34] Big business hires just over 40 percent of all employees in Canada, while small businesses hire about 34 percent of all employees.[35] In 2003, about 15 percent of the labour force was self-employed, meaning that these people were managing themselves.[36]

publicly held organizations
Companies whose shares are available on the stock exchange for public trading by brokers or dealers.

The Types of Organizations

Large organizations are often publicly held, so that the managers report to boards of directors that are responsible to shareholders. This represents one form of organization in Canada. There are also numerous **privately held organizations,** both large and small. Privately held organizations, whose shares are not available on the stock exchange, can be individually owned, family owned, or owned by some other group of individuals. Other organizational forms, such as partnerships and cooperatives, also require managers.

Many managers work in the *public sector* as civil servants, for municipal, provincial, or federal governments. The challenges of managing within government departments can be quite different from the challenges of managing in publicly held organizations. Critics argue that governments have no measurable performance objectives, and therefore employees feel less accountable for their actions. Public sector organizations also come under greater scrutiny for how they deal with diversity issues.

In addition to working directly for the government, some managers and employees work for Crown corporations. These are structured like private sector corporations,

privately held organizations
Companies whose shares are not available on the stock exchange but are privately held.

with boards of directors, CEOs, and so on. Rather than being owned by shareholders, however, they are owned by governments. The employees of a Crown corporation are not civil servants. Managers in Crown corporations are more independent than the senior bureaucrats who manage government departments.

Many of Canada's larger organizations are actually subsidiaries of American parent organizations—including Sears, Safeway, General Motors and Ford Motor Company. This means that managers in these companies often report to American top managers, and are not always free to set their own goals and targets. Conflicts can arise between Canadian managers and the American managers to whom they report about how things should be done.

The Political and Legal Climate

About 30 percent of Canadian employees are unionized, and this presents an additional challenge to management. In unionized organizations, managers must learn to work with unions and union leaders to create a positive work climate. Organizations with unionized employees are governed by the collective agreements negotiated between management and the union(s).

Canadian organizations are affected by Canadian law at a number of levels. The Competition Bureau determines whether there is too little competition in an industry, and rules on what companies must do to increase competition. For instance, the Competition Bureau ruled that Chapters Inc. and Indigo Books & Music Inc. would have to sell 13 superstores and refrain from opening new stores for two years if they were to merge, which they did on June 13, 2001 under the Chapters Inc. name. This ruling affected the plans that the managers of Chapters Inc. could make until mid-2003.

Canadian companies are also affected by interprovincial trade rules, marketing boards, and whether they are in the regulated sector (which includes agriculture, telecommunications, utilities, and transportation, e.g.). Canada has greater regulation of firms than does either the United States or the United Kingdom.[37] These rules and regulations can affect the products that firms are able to provide, or the prices at which goods must be sold. Thus regulations impact managers' abilities to make decisions freely.

Canadian organizations are also affected by trade barriers from other countries. These are discussed more fully in Chapter 2. Many organizations are also affected by the Human Rights Act and the Employment Equity Act, which have an impact on how they manage diversity in the workplace, a topic we cover in Chapter 3. We briefly illustrate all of these challenges below.

Managing a Diverse Workforce

The face of Canada has changed considerably in the past 20 years, and thus another challenge for managers is to recognize the need to treat human resources in a fair and equitable manner. In the past, white male employees dominated the ranks of management, but today the workplace also includes, for example, women, First Nations peoples, Asian Canadians, African Canadians, and Indo-Canadians. Moreover, today's workplace is much more likely to include gays and lesbians, the elderly, and people with disabilities. Managers must recognize the value of a diverse workforce, such as the ability to take advantage of the skills and experiences of different kinds of people.[38] When managers fail to understand how diversity might affect the workplace, they can encounter difficulties such as those experienced by the Canadian Armed Forces.

Even though some managers resist diversity initiatives, managers who value their diverse employees are the managers who best succeed in promoting performance over the long run.[39] Today, more and more organizations are realizing that people are their most important resource and that developing and protecting human resources is an important challenge for management in a competitive global environment. Introducing cultural sensitivity into the workplace is one of the many tasks managers have to face. We discuss many of the issues surrounding the management of a diverse Canadian workforce in Chapter 3.

CHALLENGES FOR MANAGEMENT IN A GLOBAL ENVIRONMENT

Think About It

How Mountain Equipment Co-op Faces the Globalization Challenge

At Vancouver-based Mountain Equipment Co-op (MEC), determining the appropriate strategy for running a business in a global economy raises more questions than solutions.[40] MEC prides itself on being about values while it sells fleece, Gore-Tex, and crampons, and keeps its eye on the bottom line.

The co-op uses workers in Asian factories to produce about 20 percent of its goods. With company growth and concern about prices, some of the production had to be moved to lower-wage countries such as China and Vietnam. At the annual general meeting in April 2001, co-op members voted on whether MEC should stop contracting work to China. CEO Peter Robinson, a human rights activist, was sympathetic to the resolution proposed. "It gives us an opportunity to talk about where we came from and where we are going. We have to talk about what we can do beyond the factory."

Though MEC does evaluate labour practices at manufacturing plants that produce its goods, idealistic co-op members are concerned about China's human rights progress. Globalization forces companies to wrestle with the challenge of being politically correct while providing affordable merchandise to their customers.

Questions
1. Should organizations manufacture in countries that have poor human rights practices?
2. Should companies make sure that they are doing enough for employment in their own countries before contracting out to lower-wage plants in poorer countries?

global organizations
Organizations that operate and compete in more than one country.

Mountain Equipment Co-op
www.mec.ca

Canadian firms are less likely to operate only within their own borders these days. Not only do firms face competition domestically, but they also face global competition. The rise of **global organizations**—organizations that operate and compete in more than one country—has put severe pressure on many organizations to improve their performance and to identify better ways to use their resources. The successes of German chemical companies Schering and Hoescht, Italian furniture manufacturer Natuzzi, Korean electronics companies Samsung and Lucky Goldstar, and Brazilian plane maker Empresa Brasileira de Aeronautica SA (Embraer)—all global companies—are putting pressure on organizations in other countries to raise their level of performance in order to compete successfully.

Canada has been slow historically to face the global challenge. The list of the Top 100 Global Companies of 1998 does not include any Canadian firms. The majority are American, but there are several entries from Switzerland, as well as the United Kingdom, France, and Sweden. Today, managers who make no attempt to learn and adapt to changes in the global environment find themselves reacting rather than innovating, and their organizations often become uncompetitive and fail.[41] Three major challenges stand out for Canadian managers in today's global economy: building a competitive advantage, maintaining ethical standards, and utilizing new kinds of information systems and technologies.

Building a Competitive Advantage

competitive advantage
The ability of one organization to outperform other organizations because it produces desired goods or services more efficiently and effectively than competitors do.

If Canadian managers and organizations are to reach and remain at the top of the competitive environment, they must build a **competitive advantage.** Competitive advantage is the ability of one organization to outperform other organizations because it produces desired goods or services more efficiently and effectively than its competitors. The four building blocks of competitive advantage are superior *efficiency, quality, innovation,* and *responsiveness to customers* (see Figure 1.6).

Increasing Efficiency

Organizations increase their efficiency when they reduce the quantity of resources (such as people and raw materials) they use to produce goods or services. In today's competitive environment, organizations are constantly seeking new ways to use their resources to improve efficiency. Many organizations are training their workers in new skills and techniques to increase their ability to perform many new and different tasks. Canada could do more on the training front, however. Japanese and German companies invest far more in training employees than do Canadian companies.

In addition to training employees, organizations sometimes work together to increase efficiency. For instance, Montreal-based Radio-Canada and *La Presse* signed a partnership agreement in early 2001 to combine their efforts in such areas as the internet, special events, and marketing. Guy Crevier, president and publisher of *La Presse,* noted that the agreement would "increase the efficiency of the partners." They also planned to share the infrastructure costs for foreign bureaus and the cost and results of public opinion polls.[42]

Managers must improve efficiency if their organizations are to compete successfully with companies operating in Mexico, Malaysia, and other countries where employees are paid comparatively low wages. New methods must be devised either to increase efficiency or to gain some other competitive advantage—

Figure 1.6 | Building Blocks of Competitive Advantage

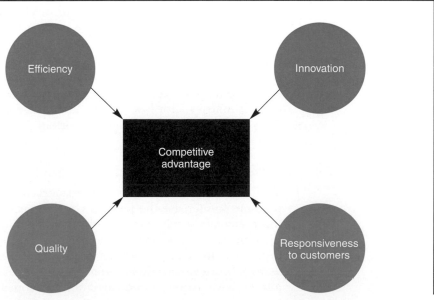

Today's steel rolling mills are almost all under the control of highly skilled employees who use state-of-the-art, computer-controlled production systems to increase operating efficiency.

innovation
The process of creating new goods and services or developing better ways to produce or provide goods and services.

higher quality goods, for example—if the loss of jobs to low-cost countries is to be prevented.

Globalization does not necessarily mean that companies are abandoning superior conditions at home in order to save money in low-cost countries. MEC ended contracts with three Vancouver factories because of labour or technological conditions. Nevertheless, globalization does force companies to wrestle with the challenge of being politically correct while providing affordable merchandise to their customers.

Increasing Quality

The challenge from global organizations such as Korean electronics manufacturers, Mexican agricultural producers, and European marketing and financial firms has also increased pressure on companies to improve the quality of goods and services delivered. One major thrust to improve quality has been to introduce the quality-enhancing techniques known as *total quality management* (TQM). Employees involved in TQM are often organized into quality control teams and are given the responsibility of continually finding new and better ways to perform their jobs; they also are given the responsibility for monitoring and evaluating the quality of the goods they produce.

Increasing Innovation

Innovation—the process of creating new goods and services that customers want, or developing better ways to produce or provide goods and services—poses a special challenge. Managers must create an organizational setting in which people are encouraged to be innovative. Typically, innovation takes place in small groups or teams; management passes on control of work activities to team members and creates an organizational culture that rewards risk-taking. Understanding and managing innovation and creating a work setting that encourages risk-taking are among the most difficult managerial tasks. As we saw earlier in the chapter, WestJet has accomplished innovation by its management-from-the-bottom policy.

Increasing Responsiveness to Customers

Organizations use their products and services to compete for customers, so training employees to be responsive to customers' needs is vital for all organizations, but particularly for service organizations. Retail stores, banks, and restaurants, for example, depend entirely on their employees to give high quality service at a reasonable cost.[43] As Canada and other countries move toward a more service-based economy (in part because of the loss of manufacturing jobs to China, Malaysia, and other countries with low labour costs), managing behaviour in service organizations is becoming increasingly important.

Maintaining Ethical Standards

While mobilizing organizational resources, all managers are under considerable pressure to increase the level at which their organizations perform. For example, top managers receive pressure from shareholders to increase the performance of the entire organization in order to boost the stock price, improve profits, or raise dividends. In turn, top managers may then pressure middle managers to find new ways to use organizational resources to increase efficiency or quality in order to attract new customers and earn more revenues.

Pressure to increase performance can be healthy for an organization because it causes managers to question the organization's operations and encourages them to find new and better ways to plan, organize, lead, and control. However, too much pressure to perform can be harmful.[44] It may induce managers to behave unethically in dealings with individuals and groups both inside and outside the organization.[45] For example, a purchasing manager for a large retail chain might buy inferior clothing as a cost-cutting measure, or, to secure a large foreign contract, a sales manager in a large defence company might offer bribes to foreign officials. As another example, in early 2001, supervisory procedures at BMO Nesbitt Burns were investigated by the Manitoba Securities Commission and the Investment Dealers Association after a number of client complaints against brokers in the Winnipeg office. Among other charges, brokers were alleged to have churned client accounts to increase their own personal commissions.[46] The resulting settlement called for the biggest penalty of its kind to the commission.

When managers act unethically, some individuals or groups may obtain short-term gains, but in the long run the organization and people inside and outside the organization will pay. In Chapter 3, we discuss the nature of ethics and the importance of managers and all members of an organization behaving ethically as they pursue organizational goals.

Utilizing New Information Systems and Technologies

Another important challenge facing Canadian managers is the pressure to increase performance through new information systems and technologies.[47] Canadian companies have been slower to adopt new technologies than their American counterparts, lagging behind the United States by two decades when it comes to corporate and government spending on information technology, a recent Conference Board of Canada report found. As a result, the United States enjoys higher productivity and economic growth rates.[48] The importance of information systems and technologies is discussed in greater detail in Chapter 4.

SUMMARY AND REVIEW

WHAT IS MANAGEMENT? A manager is a person responsible for supervising the use of an organization's resources to meet its goals. An organization is a collection of people who work together and coordinate their actions to achieve a wide variety of goals. Management is the process of using organizational resources to achieve organizational goals effectively and efficiently through planning, organizing, leading, and controlling. An efficient organization makes the most productive use of its resources. An effective organization pursues appropriate goals and achieves these goals by using its resources to create the goods or services that customers want.

MANAGERIAL FUNCTIONS According to Fayol, the four principal managerial functions are planning, organizing, leading, and controlling. Managers at all levels of the organization and in all departments perform these functions. Effective management means managing these activities successfully.

TYPES OF MANAGERS Organizations typically have three levels of management. First-line managers are responsible for the day-to-day supervision of nonmanagerial employees. Middle managers are responsible for developing and utilizing organizational resources efficiently and effectively. Top managers have cross-departmental responsibility. The top managers' job is to establish appropriate goals for the entire organization and to verify that department managers are using

Chapter Summary

WHAT IS MANAGEMENT?
• Achieving High Performance: A Manager's Goal

MANAGERIAL FUNCTIONS
• Planning
• Organizing
• Leading
• Controlling

TYPES OF MANAGERS
• Levels of Management

resources to achieve those goals. To increase efficiency and effectiveness, some organizations have altered their managerial hierarchies by restructuring, by empowering their workforces, and by using self-managed teams.

RECENT CHANGES IN MANAGERIAL HIERARCHIES Managers' tasks and responsibilities have been changing dramatically in recent years. Organizations have become flatter, and large numbers of top, middle, and first-line managers have been cut, increasing the managerial responsibilities of those remaining. Some organizations are empowering more employees at all levels, giving them more authority and accountability. Organizations have also introduced self-managed teams, which are responsible for supervising their own activities.

MANAGERIAL ROLES AND SKILLS According to Mintzberg, managers play 10 different roles: figurehead, leader, liaison, monitor, disseminator, spokesperson, entrepreneur, disturbance handler, resource allocator, and negotiator. Three types of skills help managers perform these roles effectively: conceptual, human, and technical skills.

CHALLENGES FOR MANAGEMENT IN THE CANADIAN ENVIRONMENT Canada's environment presents many interesting challenges to managers: different types and sizes of organizations; a number of national and international laws; labour unions; and a diverse workforce.

CHALLENGES FOR MANAGEMENT IN A GLOBAL ENVIRONMENT Today's competitive global environment presents three main challenges to managers: building a competitive advantage by increasing efficiency, quality, innovation, and responsiveness to customers; behaving ethically toward people inside and outside the organization; and utilizing new information systems and technologies.

Roles in Contrast: Considerations

MANAGERS	EMPLOYEES
In order to be an effective manager, I need to learn about planning, organizing, leading, and controlling	Managers perform a variety of functions to help organizations achieve goals. As an employee, talking with my manager about the overall goals may help me understand the specific job I'm assigned.
It's important to achieve some level of expertise in interpersonal, informational, *and* decisional roles. Focusing on some roles to the exclusion of others will make me a less effective manager.	Managers often have bigger-picture concerns than their immediate employees, and thus it's important to understand those concerns to work effectively with my manager.
Managers need not only technical skills, but conceptual and human skills as well. Human skills are critically important to all managers, so it is worthwhile for me to develop those skills.	If I want to be a manager, I'll need not only technical skills, but conceptual and human skills as well. Human skills are critically important to all managers, so it is worthwhile to develop those skills.

MANAGEMENT in Action

Topics for Discussion and Action

1. Describe the difference between efficiency and effectiveness, and identify real organizations that you think are, or are not, efficient and effective.
2. In what ways can managers at each of the three levels of management contribute to organizational efficiency and effectiveness?
3. Identify an organization that you believe is high performing and one that you believe is low performing, using the criteria of effectiveness and efficiency. Give 10 reasons why you think the performance levels of the two organizations differ so much.
4. Choose an organization such as a school or a bank, visit it, and then list the different kinds of organizational resources it uses.
5. Visit an organization, and talk to first-line, middle, and top managers about their respective management roles in the organization. What do they do to help the organization be efficient and effective?
6. Ask a middle or top manager, perhaps someone you already know, to give examples of how he or she performs the managerial functions of planning, organizing, leading, and controlling. How much time does he or she spend in performing each function?
7. Mintzberg followed managers for his research on what they do. Try to find a cooperative manager who will allow you to follow him or her around for a day. List the types of roles the manager plays, and indicate how much time he or she spends performing them.
8. What are the building blocks of competitive advantage? Why is obtaining a competitive advantage important to managers?
9. What are some of the challenges that Canadian managers face? To what extent are these challenges specific to Canada?
10. In what ways do you think managers' jobs have changed the most over the past 15 years? Why have these changes occurred?

Building Management Skills

THINKING ABOUT MANAGERS AND MANAGEMENT

Think of an organization that has provided you with work experience, and the manager to whom you reported (or talk to someone who has had extensive work experience); then answer these questions.

1. Think of your direct supervisor. If he or she belongs to a department, what department is it? At what level of management is this person?
2. How do you characterize your supervisor's approach to management? For example, which particular management functions and roles does this person perform most often? What kinds of management skills does this manager have?
3. Do you think the functions, roles, and skills of your supervisor are appropriate for the particular job he or she performs? How could this manager improve his or her task performance?
4. How did your supervisor's approach to management affect your attitudes and behaviour? For example, how well did you perform as a subordinate, and how motivated were you?
5. Think of the organization and its resources. Do its managers use organizational resources effectively? Which resources contribute most to the organization's performance?
6. Describe how the organization treats its human resources. How does this treatment affect the attitudes and behaviours of the workforce?

7. If you could give your manager one piece of advice or change one management practice in the organization, what would it be?
8. How aware are the managers in the organization of the need to increase efficiency, quality, innovation, or responsiveness to customers? How well do you think the organization performs its prime goals of providing the goods or services that customers want or need the most?

Management for You

In each chapter you will find the Management for You *feature, which gives you ideas on how to apply this material to your personal life. We do this to help reinforce the idea that management isn't just for managers—all of us manage our lives and can apply many of the concepts in this book.*

Think about where you hope to be in you life five years from now (i.e., your major goal). What is your competitive advantage for achieving your goal? What do you need to plan, organize, lead and control to make sure that you reach your goal? Looking over Mintzberg's managerial roles (Table 1.1), which roles seem comfortable for you? What areas need improvement?

Small Group Breakout Exercise

OPENING A NEW RESTAURANT

Form groups of 3 or 4 people, and appoint 1 group member as the spokesperson who will communicate your findings to the entire class when called on by the instructor. Then discuss the following scenario.

You and 2 partners have decided to open a large restaurant in your local community that will serve breakfast, lunch, and dinner between 7 a.m. and 10 p.m. Each of you is investing $75 000 in the venture, and together you have secured a bank loan for $450 000 more to begin operations. You and your partners have little experience in the food industry beyond serving meals or eating in restaurants, and you now face the task of deciding how you will manage the restaurant and what your respective roles will be.

1. Decide what your respective managerial roles in the restaurant will be. For example, who will be responsible for the necessary departments and specific activities? Describe your managerial hierarchy.
2. Which building blocks of competitive advantage do you need to establish to help your restaurant succeed? What criteria will you use to evaluate how successfully you are managing the restaurant?
3. Discuss the most important decisions that must be made about (a) planning, (b) organizing, (c) leading, and (d) controlling, to allow you and your partners to use organizational resources effectively and build a competitive advantage.
4. For each managerial function, list the issue that will contribute the most to your restaurant's success.

Managing Ethically

Recently, six global pharmaceutical companies admitted that they conspired to artificially raise the price of vitamins on a global basis. This involved a Swiss firm, a German firm, and four others. The decision to inflate the prices came from senior managers in each company through a joint decision. This unethical action resulted in passing on unfair expenses to the customers. In several meetings around the world they worked out the details that went undiscovered for many years. Once they were caught, there was jail for some and continuing prosecution for others; all were fired.

The result of this situation was that each company agreed to create a special position of ethics officer to oversee behaviour in the organization. Why are some people unethical while others would not even consider doing what is described above? Is ethics an internal force in each individual, or can you educate people in ethics, or can people be made to be ethical? How do you define "unethical" in this case? Do you think it is possible for businesses to be ethical? What was the gain for the managers?

Exploring the World Wide Web

SPECIFIC ASSIGNMENT

Enter Magna International's website (www.magnaint.com), and click on "Company Info." From there, click on both "Corporate Constitution" and "Employee's Charter." You should print out both documents. Also click on "Our Founder."

1. What expectations does Magna International have for its employees and managers?
2. What is Frank Stronach's "Fair Enterprise" system?

GENERAL ASSIGNMENT

Search for the website of a company in which a manager discusses his or her approach to planning, organizing, leading, or controlling. What is that manager's approach to managing? What effects has this approach had on the company's performance?

You're the Management Consultant

PROBLEMS AT ACHIEVA

You have just been called in to help managers at Achieva, a fast-growing internet software company that specializes in business-to-business (B2B) network software. Your job is to help Achieva solve some management problems that have arisen because of its rapid growth.

Customer demand to license Achieva's software has boomed so much in just two years that more than 50 new software programmers have been added to help develop a new range of software products. Achieva's growth has been so swift that it still operates informally, its organizational structure is loose and flexible, and programmers are encouraged to find solutions to problems as they go along. Although this structure worked well in the past, you have been told that problems are arising.

There have been increasing complaints from employees that good performance is not being recognized in the organization and that they do not feel equitably treated. Moreover, there have been complaints about getting managers to listen to new ideas and to act on them. A bad atmosphere is developing in the company, and recently several talented employees have left. Your job is to help Achieva's managers solve these problems quickly and keep the company on the fast track.

Questions

1. What kinds of organizing and controlling problems is Achieva suffering from?
2. What kinds of management changes need to be made to solve them?

MANAGEMENT CASE

The Challenges of Heading the CBC

When Robert Rabinovitch was appointed president at the Canadian Broadcasting Corporation in November 1999, the announcement was greeted with enthusiasm by friends and CBC employees alike.[49] Ted Johnson, a senior executive with Power Corp., remarked: "This is a man with remarkable people skills, strategic vision, and understanding of technology. But no one should be fooled by the charm—he is as tough as he has to be."

In his early months, he was a popular president with the employees because of his clear, passionate vision for the corporation. CBC staff were excited when he opposed new licence conditions imposed by the Canadian Radio-television and Telecommunications Commission (CRTC) shortly after he took over. The CRTC wanted the CBC to stop broadcasting foreign blockbuster films, produce more regional programming, and reduce professional sports coverage. Rabinovitch refused, saying, "There's no way the CBC can implement these decisions." He projected that these changes would cost the CBC $50 million in revenue.

By spring 2001, Rabinovitch's honeymoon with his employees was clearly over. A study completed then shows that morale among CBC staff had dropped significantly during the previous two years, and much of their unhappiness was directed at senior management. Employees felt that management was untrustworthy, and lacked competence and a clear direction.

Managing an organization such as the CBC is not easy. The CBC has had sharp drops in its viewing and listening audiences, deep budget cuts, huge layoffs, and an often-hostile relationship with the Prime Minister's Office. Rabinovitch's predecessor, Perrin Beatty, faced numerous battles with CBC chair Guylaine Saucier, who is well connected to the Liberal Party. She wanted Prime Minister Jean Chrétien to fire Beatty, and when he didn't, she undermined Beatty's authority, making it difficult for him to run the company.

Almost three-quarters of the corporation's annual budget of $1.2 billion comes from the federal government. The rest comes from commercial revenue, and not everyone believes that the CBC should be running commercials. Between 1990 and 2000, $414 million was cut from the CBC's budget.

Management at CBC struggles to balance the books because, by law, the corporation has to break even every year. To cope, the CBC has engaged in numerous rounds of layoffs. Between 1990 and early 2000, the CBC cut 1740 employees. "The corporation has been through so many of these layoffs that they have become routine," says Mike Sullivan, national representative of the Communications Energy and Paperworkers Union of Canada, which represents 2100 CBC technicians. "To CBC management, it's like eating candy. They think, 'It's so easy, why would we look at other ways of saving money?'"

The broadcaster has made numerous programming changes in the past few years, most of which employees didn't understand. The changes seemed to be made for no obvious reason. "Senior managers seem to be addicted to this sort of organizational change," one source said. "It doesn't help that they seem to score points for it."

Rabinovitch is trying to figure out how to reduce costs and create a more viable CBC. He faces a lot of challenges. The government dictates many of the policies that the CBC must make with regard to programming. Meanwhile the corporation faces competition from cable companies and television networks—in both the United States and Canada—that produce their own programming. Another challenge facing Rabinovitch is labour unions. More than 90 percent of the CBC's costs come from union contracts. This takes away some of Rabinovitch's flexibility to replace underperforming staff with creative younger talent.

Questions

1. How might Robert Rabinovitch's approach to management be affected by conditions at the CBC?
2. What can Rabinovitch do to build a competitive advantage at the CBC?

MANAGEMENT CASE

From the Pages of *The Globe and Mail* Managers Crucial to Curbing Turnover

Ernst and Young is putting its managers under the microscope with a confidential employee poll.

The professional services firm is hoping to cull candid information from its workers to help its managers become more effective and help curb turnover.

"People leave managers. They don't leave organizations," says Keith Bowman, the company's director of human resources.

"For the last five years, people have had an incredible number of work opportunities. They are more likely to look for other jobs and leave. The role of the manager is absolutely fundamental to keeping people from leaving."

Starting next month, Ernst and Young employees will be asked about their managers: "How well does the individual foster a positive work environment and help our people grow?"

Staff can respond electronically to one of several preselected ratings, from not well to extremely well. All responses are anonymous.

This approach comes at a time when the working world is under siege by an employee retention crisis—one that observers say will only get more severe in the years to come as an impending labour shortage of almost one million workers is expected across all industries in Canada.

As a result, organizations are desperate to understand how to keep top talent from job-hopping.

Their desperation is well founded, given that one in three workers will resign from his job in the next two years, according to a new survey by The Hay Group.

Ineffective managers are a major factor in the increasing rates of departure, says the research company, which interviewed over one million employees in 330 organizations around the world.

"Poor managers have a huge impact on employee turnover. Management's inability to adapt to the times will continue to contribute dramatically to sustaining high levels of turnover," says Ron Grey, managing director of The Hay Group Canada.

"We have seen significant problems with senior managers who have not recognized the changing relationship with workers and continue to operate using historical methods," he says.

As the workplace becomes more team-based and virtual, the role of managers must also change, Mr. Bowman says.

"If you have the right people, you do not need to manage them. More work is team-based. More work is done from home. Managers should look for results and output, not whether their people are in the office at 9 a.m."

The Hay Group survey found the main reason workers left was that they felt their skills weren't being used. The second-most cited reason was the inability of top managers to be effective leaders.

For instance, only 30 to 40 percent of workers surveyed said they felt their bosses were eager to help advance their careers.

Managers were also criticized for tolerating workers who underperform—creating a key source of dissatisfaction among their peers, Mr. Grey says. Over half of the employees surveyed said their employers routinely accept poor performers who shirk responsibility. Many top workers respond by leaving.

To add insult to injury, Mr. Grey says, managers often don't understand why so many people are eager to leave and change jobs.

"Managers have a degree of blind loyalty that makes it difficult for them to understand the views of other employees," Mr. Grey says.

Workplace consultants urge managers to become better communicators, to treat employees as individuals and help foster career development.

KMPG's chief human resources officer, Lorne Burns, says many of the firm's employees leave because they are "cherry-picked" by their clients, not because of bad management. The company has started rerecruiting former employees who may want to return.

Still, Mr. Burns says, old-style management techniques that rely on close supervision, hierarchy and paternalistic methods are the most common reasons organizations are given for high turnover.

"People feel trapped. They are unhappy with the working relationship they have with their managers and want to get out."

Source: Natalie Southworth, freelance journalist, "Managers Crucial to Curbing Turnover," *The Globe and Mail*, May 30, 2001, p. M1.

Questions

1. How does management style affect turnover?
2. What can managers do to make sure that employees are less likely to quit their jobs?

THE EVOLUTION OF MANAGEMENT THEORY

Management theory concerning appropriate management practices has evolved in modern times. The so-called classical management theories emerged around the start of the 20th century. These include scientific management, which focuses on matching people and tasks to maximize efficiency, and administrative management, which focuses on identifying the principles that will lead to the creation of the most efficient system of organization and management. Behavioural management theories, developed both before and after the Second World War, focus on how managers should lead and control their workforces to increase performance. Management science theory, developed during the Second World War, has become more important as researchers have developed rigorous analytical and quantitative techniques to help managers measure and control organizational performance. Finally, theories were developed during the 1960s and 1970s to help explain how the external environment affects the way organizations and managers operate.

SCIENTIFIC MANAGEMENT THEORY

The evolution of modern management began in the closing decades of the 19th century, after the Industrial Revolution had swept through Europe, Canada, and the United States. Small workshops run by skilled workers who produced hand-manufactured products (a system called crafts production) were replaced by large factories. In these factories, hundreds or even thousands of unskilled or semi-skilled employees controlled the sophisticated machines that made products.

Many of the managers and supervisors had only technical knowledge, and were unprepared for the social problems that occur when people work together in large groups (as in a factory or shop system). Managers began to search for new ways to manage their organizations' resources, and soon they began to focus on how to increase the efficiency of the employee-task mix.

Job Specialization and the Division of Labour

The Adam Smith
Institute
www.adamsmith.org

The famous Scottish economist Adam Smith was one of the first to look at the effects of different manufacturing systems.[1] He compared the relative performance of two different manufacturing methods. The first was similar to crafts-style production, in which each employee was responsible for all of the 18 tasks involved in producing a pin. The other had each employee performing only 1 or a few of the 18 tasks that go into making a completed pin.

Smith found that factories in which employees specialized in only 1 or a few tasks had greater performance than factories in which each employee performed

Figure A1.1 | The Evolution of Management Theory

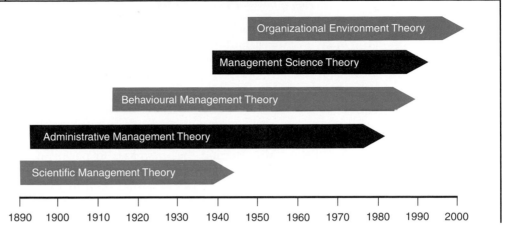

all 18 pin-making tasks. In fact, Smith found that 10 employees specializing in a particular task could, between them, make 48 000 pins a day, whereas those employees who performed all the tasks could make only a few thousand at most.[2] Smith reasoned that this difference in performance was due to the fact that the employees who specialized became much more skilled at their specific tasks, and, as a group, were thus able to produce a product faster than the group of employees in which everyone had to perform many tasks. Smith concluded that increasing the level of **job specialization**—the process by which a division of labour occurs as different employees specialize in different tasks over time—increases efficiency and leads to higher organizational performance.[3]

Based on Adam Smith's observations, early management practitioners and theorists focused on how managers should organize and control the work process to maximize the advantages of job specialization and the division of labour.

job specialization

The process by which a division of labour occurs as different employees specialize in different tasks over time.

F.W. Taylor and Scientific Management

Frederick W. Taylor (1856–1915) is best known for defining the techniques of **scientific management**, the systematic study of relationships between people and tasks for the purpose of redesigning the work process to increase efficiency. Taylor believed that the production process would become more efficient if the amount of time and effort that each employee spent to produce a unit of output (a finished good or service) could be reduced. He noted that increased specialization and the division of labour could increase efficiency. Taylor believed that the way to create the most efficient division of labour could best be determined by means of scientific management techniques, rather than intuitive or informal rule-of-thumb knowledge. Based on his experiments and observations as a manufacturing manager in a variety of settings, he developed four principles to increase efficiency in the workplace:[4]

scientific management

The systematic study of relationships between people and tasks for the purpose of redesigning the work process to increase efficiency.

The F. W. Taylor Project
attila.stevens-
tech.edu/~rdowns/

- Principle 1. *Study the way workers perform their tasks, gather all the informal job knowledge that workers possess, and experiment with ways of improving the way tasks are performed.*

- Principle 2. *Codify the new methods of performing tasks into written rules and standard operating procedures.*

- Principle 3. *Carefully select workers so that they possess skills and abilities that match the needs of the task, and train them to perform the task according to the established rules and procedures.*

- Principle 4. *Establish a fair or acceptable level of performance for a task, and then develop a pay system that provides a reward for performance above the acceptable level.*

By 1910, Taylor's system of scientific management had become known and, in many instances, faithfully and fully practised.[5] However, managers in many organizations chose to use the new principles of scientific management selectively. This decision ultimately resulted in problems. For example, some managers using scientific management saw increases in performance, but rather than sharing performance gains with employees through bonuses as Taylor had advocated, they simply increased the amount of work that each employee was expected to do. Thus, employees found they were required to do more work for the same pay. Employees also learned that increases in performance often resulted in layoffs, because fewer employees were needed. In addition, the specialized, simplified jobs were often monotonous and repetitive, and many employees became dissatisfied with their jobs.

Scientific management brought many employees more hardship than gain, and left them with a distrust of managers who did not seem to care about their well-being.[6] These dissatisfied employees resisted attempts to use the new scientific management techniques and at times even withheld their job knowledge from managers to protect their jobs and pay.

Taylor's work has had an enduring effect on the management of production systems. Managers in every organization, whether it produces goods or services, now carefully analyze the basic tasks that must be performed and try to create work systems that will allow their organizations to operate most efficiently.

The Gilbreths

The Gilbreth Network
gilbrethnetwork.
tripod.com

Two prominent followers of Taylor were Frank Gilbreth (1868–1924) and Lillian Gilbreth (1878–1972), who refined Taylor's analysis of work movements and made many contributions to time-and-motion study.[7] Their aims were to (1) break up a particular task into individual actions, and analyze each step needed to perform the task, (2) find better ways to perform each step, and (3) reorganize each of the steps so that the action as a whole could be performed more efficiently—at less cost in time and effort.

The Gilbreths often filmed an employee performing a particular task and then separated the task actions, frame by frame, into their component movements. Their goal was to maximize the efficiency with which each individual task was performed so that gains across tasks would add up to enormous savings of time and effort.

In workshops and factories, the work of the Gilbreths, Taylor, and many others had a major effect on the practice of management. In comparison with the old crafts system, jobs in the new system were more repetitive, boring, and monotonous as a result of the application of scientific management principles. Employees became more dissatisfied. Frequently, the management of work settings became a game between employees and managers: Managers tried to introduce work practices to increase performance, and employees tried to hide the true potential efficiency of the work setting in order to protect their own well-being.[8]

ADMINISTRATIVE MANAGEMENT THEORY

administrative management
The study of how to create an organizational structure that leads to high efficiency and effectiveness.

Side by side with scientific managers studying the person-task mix to increase efficiency, other researchers were focusing on **administrative management**—the study of how to create an organizational structure that leads to high efficiency and effectiveness. Organizational structure is the system of task and authority relationships that control how employees use resources to achieve the organization's goals. Two of the most influential views regarding the creation of efficient systems of organizational administration were developed in Europe. Max Weber, a German professor of sociology, developed one theory. Henri Fayol, the French manager, developed the other.

The Theory of Bureaucracy

Max Weber (1864–1920) wrote at the start of the 20th century, when Germany was undergoing its Industrial Revolution.[9] To help Germany manage its growing industrial enterprises at a time when it was striving to become a world power, Weber developed the principles of **bureaucracy**—a formal system of organization and administration designed to ensure efficiency and effectiveness.

bureaucracy
A formal system of organization and administration designed to ensure efficiency and effectiveness.

* Principle 1. *In a bureaucracy, a manager's formal authority derives from the position he or she holds in the organization.*

  In a bureaucratic system of administration, obedience is owed to a manager, not because of any personal qualities that he or she might possess—such as personality, wealth, or social status—but because the manager occupies a position that is associated with a certain level of authority and responsibility.[10]

* Principle 2. *In a bureaucracy, people should occupy positions because of their performance, not because of their social standing or personal contacts.*

  This principle was not always followed in Weber's time and is often ignored today. Some organizations and industries are still affected by social networks in which personal contacts and relations, not job-related skills, influence hiring and promotional decisions.

* Principle 3. *The extent of each position's formal authority and task responsibilities, and its relationship to other positions in an organization, should be clearly specified.*

authority
The power to hold people accountable for their actions and to make decisions concerning the use of organizational resources.

  When the tasks and **authority** associated with various positions in the organization are clearly specified, managers and employees know what is expected of them and what to expect from each other. Moreover, an organization can hold all its employees strictly accountable for their actions when each person is completely familiar with his or her responsibilities.

* Principle 4. *For authority to be exercised effectively in an organization, positions should be arranged hierarchically. This helps employees know whom to report to and who reports to them.*[11]

  Managers must create an organizational hierarchy of authority that makes it clear (a) who reports to whom and (b) to whom managers and employees should go if conflicts or problems arise. This principle is especially important in the Armed Forces, Canadian Security Intelligence Service (CSIS), Royal Canadian Mounted Police (RCMP), and other organizations that deal with sensitive issues where there could be major repercussions.

rules
Formal written instructions that specify actions to be taken under different circumstances to achieve specific goals.

standard operating procedures (SOPs)
Specific sets of written instructions about how to perform a certain aspect of a task.

norms
Unwritten rules and informal codes of conduct that prescribe how people should act in particular situations.

* Principle 5. *Managers must create a well-defined system of rules, standard operating procedures (SOPs), and norms so that they can effectively control behaviour within an organization.*

  Rules, SOPs, and norms provide behavioural guidelines that improve the performance of a bureaucratic system because they specify the best ways to accomplish organizational tasks. **Rules** are formal written instructions that specify actions to be taken under different situations to achieve specific goals. **SOPs** are specific sets of written instructions on how to perform a certain aspect of a task. **Norms** are unwritten rules and informal codes of conduct on how to act in particular situations. Companies such as McDonald's and Wal-Mart have developed extensive rules and procedures to specify the types of behaviours that are required of their employees, such as, "Always greet the customer with a smile."

Weber believed that organizations that implement all five principles will establish a bureaucratic system that will improve organizational performance. The specification of positions and the use of rules and SOPs to regulate how tasks are performed make it easier for managers to organize and control the work of subordinates. Similarly, fair and equitable selection and promotion systems improve managers' feelings of security, reduce stress, and encourage organizational members to act ethically and further promote the interests of the organization.[12]

If bureaucracies are not managed well, however, many problems can result. Sometimes, managers allow rules and SOPs—"bureaucratic red tape"—to become so cumbersome that decision making becomes slow and inefficient and organizations are unable to change. When managers rely too much on rules to solve problems and not enough on their own skills and judgment, their behaviour becomes inflexible. A key challenge for managers is to use bureaucratic principles to benefit, rather than harm, an organization.

Fayol's Principles of Management

Working at the same time as Weber but independently of him, Frenchman Henri Fayol (1841–1925), the CEO of Comambault Mining, identified 14 principles (summarized in Table A1.1) that he believed to be essential to increasing the efficiency of the management process.[13] Some of the principles that Fayol outlined have faded from contemporary management practices, but most have endured.

The principles that Fayol and Weber set forth still provide a clear and appropriate set of guidelines that managers can use to create a work setting that makes efficient and effective use of organizational resources. These principles remain the foundation of modern management theory; recent researchers have refined or developed them to suit modern conditions. For example, Weber's and Fayol's concerns for equity and for establishing appropriate links between performance and reward are central themes in contemporary theories of motivation and leadership.

Table A1.1 | Fayol's 14 Principles of Management

Division of Labour   Job specialization and the division of labour should increase efficiency, especially if managers take steps to lessen employees' boredom.

Authority and Responsibility   Managers have the right to give orders and the power to exhort subordinates for obedience.

Unity of Command   An employee should receive orders from only one superior.

Line of Authority   The length of the chain of command that extends from the top to the bottom of an organization should be limited.

Centralization   Authority should not be concentrated at the top of the chain of command.

Unity of Direction   The organization should have a single plan of action to guide managers and employees.

Equity   All organizational members are entitled to be treated with justice and respect.

Order   The arrangement of organizational positions should maximize organizational efficiency and provide employees with satisfying career opportunities.

Initiative   Managers should allow employees to be innovative and creative.

Discipline Managers need to create a workforce that strives to achieve organizational goals.

Remuneration of Personnel   The system that managers use to reward employees should be equitable for both employees and the organization.

Stability of Tenure of Personnel   Long-term employees develop skills that can improve organizational efficiency.

Subordination of Individual Interests to the Common Interest   Employees should understand how their performance affects the performance of the whole organization.

Esprit de Corps   Managers should encourage the development of shared feelings of comradeship, enthusiasm, or devotion to a common cause.

BEHAVIOURAL MANAGEMENT THEORY

behavioural management
The study of how managers should behave in order to motivate employees and encourage them to perform at high levels and be committed to achieving organizational goals.

Mary Parker Follett Foundation
www.follettfoundation.org

The **behavioural management** theorists writing in the first half of the 20th century all chose a theme that focused on how managers should personally behave in order to motivate employees and encourage them to perform at high levels and be committed to the achievement of organizational goals.

The Work of Mary Parker Follett

If F.W. Taylor is considered to be the father of management thought, Mary Parker Follett (1868–1933) serves as its mother.[14] Much of her writing about management and about the way managers should behave toward employees was a response to her concern that Taylor was ignoring the human side of organization. Follett also proposed that knowledge and expertise, and not managers' formal authority deriving from their position in the hierarchy, should decide who would lead at any particular moment. She believed, as do many management theorists today, that power is fluid and should flow to the person who can best help the organization achieve its goals. Follett took a horizontal view of power and authority, in contrast to Fayol, who saw the formal line of authority and vertical chain of command as being most essential to effective management. Follett's behavioural approach to management was radical for its time.

The Hawthorne Studies and Human Relations

Probably because of its radical nature, Follett's work was unappreciated by managers and researchers until quite recently. Instead, researchers continued to follow in the footsteps of Taylor and the Gilbreths. One focus was on how efficiency might be increased through improving various characteristics of the work setting, such as job specialization or the kinds of tools employees used. One series of studies was conducted from 1924 to 1932 at the Hawthorne Works of the Western Electric Company.[15] This research, now known as the Hawthorne studies, began as an attempt to investigate how characteristics of the work setting–specifically the level of lighting or illumination–affect employee fatigue and performance. The researchers conducted an experiment in which they systematically measured employee productivity at various levels of illumination.

Hawthorne Studies
www.wikipedia.org/wiki/
Hawthorne_studies

informal organization
The system of behavioural rules and norms that emerge in a group.

One of the main implications of the Hawthorne studies was that the behaviour of managers and employees in the work setting is as important in explaining the level of performance as the technical aspects of the task. Managers must understand the workings of the **informal organization**, the system of behavioural rules and norms that emerge in a group, when they try to manage or change behaviour in organizations. Many studies have found that, as time passes, groups often develop elaborate procedures and norms that bond members together, allowing unified action either to cooperate with management in order to raise performance or to restrict output and undermine organizational goals.[16] The Hawthorne studies demonstrated the importance of understanding how the feelings, thoughts, and behaviour of work-group members and managers affect performance. It was becoming increasingly clear to researchers that understanding behaviour in organizations is a complex process that is critical to increasing performance.[17] Indeed, the increasing interest in the area of management known as **organizational behaviour**–the study of the factors that have an impact on how individuals and groups respond to and act in organizations–dates from these early studies.

organizational behaviour
The study of the factors that have an impact on how individuals and groups respond to and act in organizations.

Theory X and Theory Y

Several studies after the Second World War revealed how assumptions about employees' attitudes and behaviour affect managers' behaviour. Perhaps the most

Douglas McGregor
www.lib.uwo.ca/busines/
dougmcgregor.html

Theory X

Negative assumptions about employees that lead to the conclusion that a manager's task is to supervise them closely and control their behaviour.

Theory Y

Positive assumptions about employees that lead to the conclusion that a manager's task is to create a work setting that encourages commitment to organizational goals and provides opportunities for imagination, initiative, and self-direction.

influential approach was developed by Douglas McGregor. He proposed that two different sets of assumptions about work attitudes and behaviours dominate the way managers think and affect how they behave in organizations. McGregor named these two contrasting sets of assumptions *Theory X* and *Theory Y*.[18]

According to the assumptions of **Theory X**, the average employee is lazy, dislikes work, and will try to do as little as possible. Moreover, employees have little ambition and wish to avoid responsibility. Thus, the manager's task is to counteract employees' natural tendencies to avoid work. To keep employees' performance at a high level, the manager must supervise them closely and control their behaviour by means of rewards and punishments.

Theory Y assumes that employees are not inherently lazy, do not naturally dislike work, and, if given the opportunity, will do what is good for the organization. According to Theory Y, the characteristics of the work setting determine whether employees consider work to be a source of satisfaction or punishment; and managers do not need to control employees' behaviour closely in order to make them perform at a high level, because employees will exercise self-control when they are committed to organizational goals. It is the manager's task to create a work setting that encourages commitment to organizational goals and provides opportunities for employees to be imaginative and to exercise initiative and self-direction.

MANAGEMENT SCIENCE THEORY

management science theory

An approach to management that uses rigorous quantitative techniques to help managers make full use of organizational resources.

Management science theory is a contemporary approach to management that focuses on the use of rigorous quantitative techniques to help managers make maximum use of organizational resources to produce goods and services. In essence, management science theory is a contemporary extension of scientific management. There are many branches of management science, each of which deals with a specific set of concerns:

- *Quantitative management* uses mathematical techniques—such as linear and non-linear programming, modelling, simulation, queuing theory, and chaos theory—to help managers decide, for example, how much inventory to hold at different times of the year, where to build a new factory, and how best to invest an organization's financial capital.

- *Operations management (or operations research)* provides managers with a set of techniques that they can use to analyze any aspect of an organization's production system to increase efficiency.

- *Total quality management (TQM)* focuses on analyzing an organization's input, conversion, and output activities to increase product quality.[19]

- *Management information systems (MIS)* help managers design information systems that provide information about events occurring inside the organization as well as in its external environment—information that is vital for effective decision making.

All these subfields of management science provide tools and techniques that managers can use to help improve the quality of their decision making and increase efficiency and effectiveness.

ORGANIZATIONAL ENVIRONMENT THEORY

An important milestone in the history of management thought occurred when researchers went beyond the study of how managers can influence behaviour within organizations to consider how managers control the organization's relationship with

organizational environment
The set of forces and conditions that operate beyond an organization's boundaries but affect a manager's ability to acquire and use resources.

open system
A system that takes in resources from its external environment and converts them into goods and services that are then sent back to that environment for purchase by customers.

closed system
A system that is self-contained and thus not affected by changes that occur in its external environment.

entropy
The tendency of a system to dissolve and disintegrate because it loses the ability to control itself.

synergy
Performance gains that result when individuals and departments coordinate their actions.

contingency theory
The idea that managers' choice of organizational structures and control systems depends on—is contingent on—characteristics of the external environment in which the organization operates.

its external environment, or **organizational environment**—the set of forces and conditions that operate beyond an organization's boundaries but affect a manager's ability to acquire and use resources. Resources in the organizational environment include the raw materials and skilled people that an organization needs to produce goods and services, as well as the support of groups—such as customers who buy these goods and services—that provide the organization with financial resources. The importance of studying the environment became clear after the development of open-systems theory and contingency theory during the 1960s.

The Open-Systems View

One of the most influential views of how an organization is affected by its external environment was developed by Daniel Katz, Robert Kahn, and James Thompson in the 1960s.[20] These theorists viewed the organization as an **open system**—a system that takes in resources from its external environment and converts or transforms them into goods and services that are then sent back to that environment, where they are bought by customers.

The system is said to be "open" because the organization draws from and interacts with the external environment in order to survive; in other words, the organization is open to its environment. A **closed system**, in contrast, is a self-contained system that is not affected by changes that occur in its external environment. Organizations that operate as closed systems, that ignore the external environment and that fail to acquire inputs, are likely to experience **entropy**, the tendency of a system to dissolve and disintegrate because it loses the ability to control itself.

Researchers using the open-systems view are interested in how the various parts of a system work together to promote efficiency and effectiveness. Systems theorists like to argue that "the parts are more than the sum of the whole"; they mean that an organization performs at a higher level when its departments work together rather than separately. **Synergy**, the performance gains that result when individuals and departments coordinate their actions, is possible only in an organized system. The recent interest in using teams comprising people from different departments reflects systems theorists' interest in designing organizational systems to create synergy and thus increase efficiency and effectiveness.

Contingency Theory

Another milestone in management theory was the development of **contingency theory** in the 1960s by Tom Burns and G.M. Stalker in the United Kingdom and Paul Lawrence and Jay Lorsch in the United States.[21] Recognizing that organizations need to acquire valuable resources, the crucial message of contingency theory is that there is no one best way to organize: The organizational structures and the control systems that managers choose depend on—are contingent on—characteristics of the external environment in which the organization operates.

An important characteristic of the external environment that affects an organization's ability to obtain resources is the degree to which the environment is changing. Changes in the organizational environment include: changes in technology, which can lead to the creation of new products (such as compact discs) and result in the disappearance of existing products (eight-track tapes); the entry of new competitors (such as foreign organizations that compete for available resources); and unstable economic conditions. In general, the more quickly the organizational environment is changing, the greater are the problems associated with gaining access to resources and the greater is the manager's need to find ways to coordinate the activities of people in different departments in order to respond to the environment quickly and effectively.

The basic idea behind contingency theory that there is no one best way to design or lead an organization—has been incorporated into other areas of management theory, including leadership theories.

CHAPTER **2**

MANAGING THE ORGANIZATIONAL ENVIRONMENT

Learning Objectives

1. Explain why being able to perceive, interpret, and respond appropriately to the organizational environment is crucial for managers' success.

2. Identify the main forces in an organization's general and task environments, and describe the challenges that each force presents to managers.

3. Discuss the main ways in which managers can manage the external environment.

Roles in Contrast: Questions

MANAGERS	EMPLOYEES
What is happening in the environment that might affect this business?	What do I notice about the environment that may have an impact on my job, or on the way it's done?
How might I respond to changes in the business environment to protect or increase sales?	Do I need to think about acquiring new skills to respond to changes in the environment?
Are there new opportunities to which this business should respond?	Are there new opportunities for me to consider for my career?

A CASE IN CONTRAST

FROM CROWN CORPORATION TO PRIVATIZATION

Calgary-based Petro-Canada (Petrocan; www.petro-canada.ca) was established in 1975 by the Liberal government under Pierre Trudeau to provide Canadians with "a window on the energy industry." Petrocan was to bring some Canadian ownership to the energy sector, which was dominated at the time by foreign companies. It has been called "a money pit for Canadian tax-payers in its early years."[1] It was also viewed with suspicion by others in the energy industry, "as both a spy agency and unfair competition."[2]

Ian Doig, who writes an energy newsletter, says of that time: "There was never any love lost between the industry in those days and Petro-Canada . . . a company owned by the state inside a red building."[3]

As a Crown corporation, Petrocan did not face the same financial realities as other oil firms. It was allowed to explore far and wide, including the East Coast, the Arctic, and the untested oil-sands. It also made a series of corporate acquisitions to increase cash flow, resulting very shortly in huge debt, something most private corporations would not have been able to bear.

Wilbert (Bill) Hopper was the chairman and CEO of Petro-Canada from its start until 1993. He had a "divide-and-conquer management strategy, flat-tering people to their faces and then denigrating them behind their backs."[4] Moreover, he "used to boast that he was nearly impossible to fire."[5]

Unlike the way things usually work in public cor-porations, Hopper did not face challenges from his board of directors over his management of the company. The sole shareholder of the com-pany from 1976 to 1991 was the government.

Wilbert (Bill) Hopper was the first CEO of Petro-Canada. Hopper's management style did not survive Petrocan's privatization.

Jim Stanford, chairman and CEO of Petro-Canada from 1993 to 1999, successfully oversaw much of the privatization of Petrocan.

Hopper's first real challenge to his management practices came in 1991, when privatization brought a change in Petrocan's governance structure. Between 1991 and 1993, the government sold a 30-percent interest in the company. The first shares were offered for $13; a year later, the second issue, at $8.25, did not sell out. Nearly a year later, the price was down to $7.25. The move toward privatization was not as successful as had been hoped.

To understand why Petrocan might have had difficulties with privatization, we should note that for many years the company benefited from large subsidies and favouritism from the government. Also, just when most oil and gas companies were aggressively reducing debt, nonperforming assets, and employees, Petrocan's debt increased.

As a manager, Hopper did not easily adapt to the new environment facing Petrocan, but tended to resist the changes that were necessary to make the company profitable. While he engaged in some corporate downsizing, he found it easier to get rid of employees than corporate assets.

Finally, in January 1993, a group of disgruntled directors voted to remove him. They were concerned that Hopper was depressing the long-term value of Petrocan, because of his "refusal to cut waste and reduce the company's payroll."[6]

Jim Stanford, a long-time Petrocan employee, replaced Hopper. He immediately began to cut costs. Eight months after he took over, Petrocan's publicly traded shares were trading at $12.50.

Stanford faced a very different organizational environment than Hopper. Stanford says, "The major turning point [making it possible for his success] was when the company ceased to be a Crown corporation and the federal government started selling its stock."[7] Stanford also oversaw further privatization of the company. In the fall of 1995, the government sold an additional 52 percent of its shares at $14.65 a share.

Stanford is credited with turning Petro-Canada "from a staid Crown corporation into a profitable, dynamic energy giant."[8] At the end of 1999, Stanford stepped down, and Ron Brenneman, former head of corporate planning at Exxon Corp., took over as chief executive officer. Stanford's final year was one of the most profitable in Petro-Canada's history, because of high oil prices.

At the time that Stanford stepped down, Duncan Mathieson, an analyst at Scotia Capital Markets in Toronto, noted, "Compared to what it was five years ago, it's a massively different company."[9] The company is also viewed with a lot less suspicion. Alan MacFadyen, a professor of economics at the University of Calgary, says that Calgarians now view Petrocan "as being independent, and of functioning with much the same objectives as other companies. And that's what people in the industry here feel comfortable with."[10]

 **OVERVIEW**

Bill Hopper and Jim Stanford faced very different environments during the time that each was CEO at Petro-Canada. They also took different actions that had different outcomes. All managers face a rich array of forces that they must recognize and respond to quickly and appropriately if their organizations are to survive and prosper. The external environment is uncertain and unpredictable because it is complex and constantly changing. Managers must position their organizations to deal efficiently and effectively with new developments. Hopper saw no need to make his company profitable, because it was a Crown corporation. When the environment changed, and the company started to privatize, he was not prepared to make the necessary changes. As a result, he lost his job. Stanford rose to the challenge of privatization by taking proper action and turning Petrocan into a successful, profitable operation. Petrocan's growth continues; it is one of the largest energy companies in Canada.[11]

In this chapter, we examine the organization's external environment in detail. We describe it and identify the principal forces—both task and general—that create pressure and influence managers and thus affect the way organizations operate. We conclude with a study of several methods that managers can use to help organizations adjust and respond to forces in the organization's environment. By the end of the chapter, you will understand the steps managers must take to ensure that organizations adequately address and appropriately respond to their external environment.

WHAT IS THE ORGANIZATIONAL ENVIRONMENT?

organizational environment
The set of forces and conditions that can affect the way an organization operates.

internal environment
The forces operating within an organization and stemming from the organization's structure and culture.

external environment
The forces operating outside an organization that affect how the organization functions.

task environment
The set of forces and conditions that start with suppliers, distributors, customers, and competitors and affect an organization's ability to obtain inputs and dispose of its outputs, because they influence managers on a daily basis.

general environment
The economic, technological, socio-cultural, demographic, political and legal, and global forces that affect an organization and its task environment.

The **organizational environment** is a set of forces and conditions, such as technology and competition, that can affect the way the organization operates, and the way managers engage in planning and organizing.[12] These forces change over time and thus present managers with *opportunities* and *threats*. The organizational environment can be divided into the internal environment and the external environment. The **internal environment** consists of forces operating within an organization and stemming from the organization's structure and culture. The **external environment** consists of forces operating outside an organization that affect how an organization functions. We generally divide the organization's external environment into two major categories: the task environment and the general environment. All three of these environments are shown in Figure 2.1.

The **task environment** is a set of external forces and conditions that start with suppliers, distributors, customers, and competitors, and affect an organization's ability to obtain inputs, or raw materials, and dispose of its outputs, or finished products. When managers turn on the radio or television, arrive at their offices, open their mail, or look at their computer screens, they are likely to learn about problems facing them because of changing conditions in their organization's task environment.

The **general environment** is a wide-ranging set of external factors—including economic, technological, socio-cultural, demographic, political and legal, and global forces—that affect the organization and its task environment directly or indirectly. For the individual manager, opportunities and threats resulting from changes in the general environment are often more difficult to identify and respond to than are events in the task environment. In Chapter 5, we examine how managers analyze their environment, using SWOT (strengths, weaknesses, opportunities, and threats) analysis.

Some changes in the external environment, such as the introduction of new technology or the opening of foreign markets, create opportunities for managers to obtain resources or enter new markets and thereby strengthen their organizations. In contrast, the rise of new competitors, an economic recession, or an oil shortage poses a threat that can devastate an organization if managers are unable to obtain resources or sell the organization's goods and services. The ability of managers to perceive, interpret, and respond to forces in the organizational environment is critical to an organization's performance.

Figure 2.1 | Forces in the Organizational Environment

Although the task, general, and internal environments influence each other, we leave detailed discussion of how to manage the internal environment until Parts 3 and 4. In this chapter, we explore the nature of the external forces and consider how managers can respond to them.

THE TASK ENVIRONMENT

Think About It

It's Hard to Get into the Lottery Ticket Printing Business

Only three companies in the world print all of the lottery and gaming tickets that are produced: Two are in the United States and the third is Winnipeg-based Pollard Banknote.[13] Pollard Banknote employs more than 900 people at production facilities in Canada, the United States, and France. It can produce six billion lottery tickets annually, and it serves customers in 40 jurisdictions.

Laurie Pollard, the company's owner, attributes his success to deciding to specialize in the printing business, and then taking first-mover advantage. "We were the first in Canada to develop break-open or pull-tab tickets," he says. "We had markets very quickly in Saskatchewan, Alberta and Ontario." Shortly afterward, the federal and provincial governments became vitally interested in developing lotteries themselves, and so Pollard met with government people to get the contract to supply all of the instant lottery products. Pollard's first challenge was to produce a "very highly sophisticated and very secure document." He then had to guarantee security of the tickets, so vendors would have no way of knowing whether or not they had winning tickets. A sample of every batch of tickets goes through rigorous testing twice: once at Pollard's and then at the independent lab of the client's choice, at Pollard Banknote's expense.

These days, Pollard Banknote can count on brand loyalty for its continuing success. There is strict plant security, and staff members are trained to uphold the high security standards.

Questions
1. What factors affect a manager's ability to obtain inputs and dispose of outputs?
2. How do suppliers, distributors, customers, and competitors present opportunities and threats to managers?

Pollard Banknote Limited
www.pollardbanknote.
com

Forces in the task environment result from the actions of suppliers, distributors, customers, and competitors (see Figure 2.1). These four groups affect a manager's ability to obtain resources and distribute outputs on a daily, weekly, and monthly basis and thus have a significant impact on short-term decision making. Referring to Pollard Banknote, we discuss each of these factors in turn.

Suppliers

suppliers

Individuals and organizations that provide an organization with the input resources that it needs to produce goods and services.

Suppliers are the individuals and organizations that provide an organization with the input resources (such as raw materials, component parts, or employees) that it needs to produce goods and services. In return, the supplier receives compensation for those goods and services. An important aspect of a manager's job is to ensure a reliable supply of input resources. When the federal and provincial governments in Canada became interested in developing lotteries, they needed a secure supplier with high quality control standards. Pollard Banknote met that challenge.

Changes in the nature, number, or types of suppliers lead to opportunities and threats that managers must respond to if their organizations are to prosper. Often, when managers do not respond to a threat, they put their organization at a competitive disadvantage. If Pollard Banknote had not developed a secure printing system, the government lotteries would have been at jeopardy.

One major supplier-related threat that confronts managers arises when suppliers have a strong bargaining position with an organization. They can then raise the prices of the inputs they supply to the organization. A supplier's bargaining position is especially strong if (1) the supplier is the sole source of an input and (2) the input is vital to the organization.[14] Pollard Banknote has only two other competitors, which puts it in a strong bargaining position with the federal and provincial governments.

Distributors

distributors

Organizations that help other organizations sell their goods or services to customers.

Distributors are organizations that help other organizations sell their goods or services to customers. The decisions that managers make about how to distribute products to customers can have important effects on organizational performance. For many years, Apple Computer refused to let others sell its computers, which meant that customers had to buy directly from Apple. Thus, potential customers who shopped at large computer stores with a variety of products were less likely to buy an Apple computer, since it would not be sold there.

The changing nature of distributors and distribution methods can also bring opportunities and threats for managers. If distributors are so large and powerful that they can control customers' access to a particular organization's goods and services, they can threaten the organization by demanding that it reduce the prices of its goods and services.[15] For example, before Chapters was taken over by Indigo Books & Music, publishers complained that Chapters had used its market share to force them into dropping their wholesale prices to the book retailer. Because Chapters was the largest distributor of books to customers in Canada, publishers felt compelled to comply with Chapters' demands.

In contrast, the power of a distributor may be weakened if there are many options. Demand for service from regional phone companies has declined greatly with the advent of cellphones and the larger number of service providers.

Customers

customers

Individuals and groups that buy the goods and services that an organization produces.

Customers are the individuals and groups that buy the goods and services that an organization produces. Dell Canada's customers can be divided into several distinct groups: (1) individuals who purchase personal computers, or PCs, for home use, (2) small companies, (3) large companies, (4) government agencies, and (5) educational institutions. Changes in the numbers and types of customers or changes in customers' tastes and needs result in opportunities and threats. An organization's success depends on its response to customers. When Eaton's failed in the late 1990s, much of the reason for its failure was its lack of responsiveness to changing customer needs. Managers' abilities to identify an organization's main customers and produce the goods and services they want are a crucial factor affecting organizational and managerial success.

Competitors

competitors

Organizations that produce goods and services that are similar to a particular organization's goods and services.

One of the most important forces that an organization confronts in its task environment is competitors. **Competitors** are organizations that produce goods and services that are similar to a particular organization's goods and services. In other words, competitors are organizations that are vying for the same customers. Pollard Banknote has only two competitors, both in the United States.

Rivalry between competitors can be the most threatening force that managers must deal with. A high level of rivalry often results in price competition, and falling prices reduce access to resources and cause profits to decrease. Today, competition in the personal computer industry is intense as all the major players battle to increase their market share by offering customers better-equipped machines at lower prices.

Barriers to Entry

barriers to entry

Factors that make it difficult and costly for an organization to enter a particular task environment or industry.

Although the rivalry between existing competitors is a major threat, so is the possibility that new competitors will enter the task environment. In general, the potential for new competitors to enter a task environment (and thus boost the level of competition) depends on barriers to entry.[16] **Barriers to entry** are factors that make it difficult and costly for an organization to enter a particular task environment or industry.[17] The higher the barriers to entry, the smaller the number of competitors in an organization's task environment and thus the lower the threat of competition. With fewer competitors, it is easier to obtain customers and keep prices high. Airlines are the classic example of barriers to entry. Montreal-based Air Canada operates as a near monopoly because of the high cost of establishing an airline. In 2001 alone, Royal Airlines and CanJet were swallowed up by Canada 3000, and Roots Air was bought out by Air Canada after only one month of operation. Canada 3000 then went out of operation at the end of 2001. Competitors such as Jetsgo, Tango, Zip, and a revitalized CanJet Airlines have since appeared, and have also struggled to gain market share. Air Canada's near monopoly has not resulted in the airline being successful in recent years, however.

Air Canada
www.aircanada.ca

Barriers to entry result from two main sources: economies of scale and brand loyalty (see Figure 2.2). **Economies of scale** are the cost advantages associated with large operations. Economies of scale result from factors such as being able to manufacture products in large quantities, buy inputs in bulk, or be more effective than competitors at making use of organizational resources by fully utilizing employees' skills and knowledge. If organizations already in the task environment are large and enjoy significant economies of scale, then their costs are lower than the costs of potential entrants will be, and newcomers will find it very expensive to enter the industry. In the *Management Case* at the end of this chapter, we discuss Sleeman Breweries, where the production of premium beers does not allow for the economies of scale faced by Molson and Labatt.

Brand loyalty is customers' preference for the products of organizations that currently exist in the task environment. If established organizations enjoy significant brand loyalty, then a new entrant will find it extremely difficult and costly to obtain a share of the market. Newcomers must bear the huge advertising costs of building customer awareness of the good or service they intend to provide.[18] Pollard Banknote is in an industry that has high barriers to entry. Its success is due to brand loyalty. At Pollard Banknote, a sample of every batch of tickets goes through rigorous testing twice: once at Pollard's in-house laboratory, and then at the independent lab of the client's choice, at Pollard Banknote's expense. It would be very expensive for new competitors to meet these standards, and they would have difficulty building up trust to the level that Pollard has done already.

In some cases, government regulations function as a barrier to entry. For example, until the late 1980s, government regulations prohibited third parties from reselling long-distance service in Canada. This prevented competition with the established long-distance companies —Bell Canada, SaskTel, and NBTel. When the regulations were amended to allow other companies to compete, the opportunities and threats facing companies in the telephone industry changed. Even more competition opened up when the Canadian Radio-television and Telecommunications Commission (CRTC) allowed for competition in long-distance calls to areas outside of Canada. The government has also established regulations that make it difficult to establish private hospitals.

In summary, high barriers to entry create a task environment that is highly threatening and causes difficulty for managers trying to gain access to the customers

Frank Stronach, chair of Aurora, Ontario-based Magna Entertainment Corp., thinks that the Canadian government should not be limiting competition as it did by granting the Ontario Jockey Club a monopoly over slot machines at racetracks in Toronto. Stronach would like to open a racetrack in Ontario, but not without lucrative slot machines on site.

economies of scale
Cost advantages associated with large operations.
brand loyalty
Customers' preference for the products of organizations that currently exist in the task environment.

Figure 2.2 | Barriers to Entry and Competition

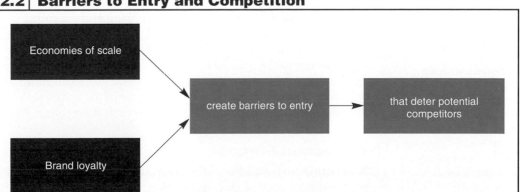

and other resources an organization needs. Conversely, low barriers to entry result in a task environment where competitive pressures are more moderate and managers have greater opportunities to acquire the customers and other resources they need for their organizations to be effective.

THE GENERAL ENVIRONMENT

Think About It

NB Power Faces Deregulation

In January 2001, New Brunswick Premier Bernard Lord and Energy Minister Jeannot Volpé outlined a 10-year plan for the future of electricity and natural gas production in the province.[19] Volpé explained that the policy is "a change in regulation to allow the province to participate in a competitive energy market." Effectively it encourages market-based rates for electricity. Large industries would have the opportunity to "generate their own power or shop for cheap power on the North American grid."

Managers at NB Power had to figure out how to operate in this new environment, after having a monopoly on power generation and transmission since the 1920s. NB Power's large industrial customers—including McCain Foods Ltd., the Irving group of companies, and other pulp and paper producers—can explore alternatives for cheaper sources of energy under the new policy. Thus managers face a number of critical decisions on how to manage in a less regulated environment.

Question

1. To what extent do managers face constraints from the external environment while trying to keep their organizations successful?

Managers must concern themselves not only with finding suppliers and customers. They must also pay attention to the larger environment around them. Economic, technological, demographic, political, and legal forces in an organization's general environment can have profound effects on the organization's task environment, effects that may be ignored by some managers. For example, technology in the telecommunications industry has made it possible for companies to offer their customers a variety of products. In the past, consumers simply chose the cheapest long-distance package or the best telephone system, but now they're looking at enhanced communication products—such as local calling, cellphone options, long distance, internet access, and videoconferencing—that are offered as part of the package. Telephone providers who failed to expand their range of offerings quickly have had difficulty keeping customers.

Managers must constantly analyze forces in the general environment because these forces affect long-term decision making and planning. With the changes in regulations, managers at NB Power faced a competitive environment, after operating in a monopoly environment for more than 80 years. Below we examine each of the major forces in the general environment in turn, exploring their impact on managers and on the organization's task environment, and examining how managers can deal with them. In Chapter 5, we examine one of the major tasks involved in planning—the careful and thorough analysis of forces in the general environment.

Economic Forces

Economic forces affect the general health and well-being of a nation or the regional economy of an organization. They include interest rates, inflation, unem-

NB Power
www.nbpower.com

economic forces
Interest rates, inflation, unemployment, economic growth, and other factors that affect the general health and well-being of a nation or the regional economy of an organization.

ployment, and economic growth. Economic forces produce many opportunities and threats for managers. Low levels of unemployment and falling interest rates mean a change in the customer base: More people have more money to spend, and as a result organizations have an opportunity to sell more goods and services. Good economic times affect supplies: Resources become easier to acquire, and organizations have an opportunity to flourish.

In contrast, worsening macroeconomic conditions pose a threat because they limit managers' ability to gain access to the resources their organization needs. Profit-oriented organizations such as retail stores and hotels have fewer customers for their goods and services during economic downturns. Not-for-profit organizations such as charities and colleges receive fewer donations during economic downturns. Even a moderate deterioration in national or regional economic conditions can seriously affect performance.

Poor economic conditions make the environment more complex and managers' jobs more difficult and demanding. Managers may need to reduce the number of individuals in their departments and increase the motivation of remaining employees, and managers and workers alike may need to identify ways to gain and use resources more efficiently. Successful managers realize the important effects that economic forces have on their organizations and they pay close attention to changes in the national and regional economy in order to respond appropriately.

Technological Forces

technology
The combination of skills and equipment that managers use in the design, production, and distribution of goods and services.

technological forces
Outcomes of changes in the technology that managers use to design, produce, or distribute goods and services.

Technology is the combination of skills and equipment that managers use in the design, production, and distribution of goods and services. **Technological forces** are outcomes of changes in the technology that managers use to design, produce, or distribute goods and services. Technological forces have increased greatly since the Second World War because the overall pace of technological change has sped up so much.[20] Computers have become increasingly faster and smaller. Transportation speed has increased. Distribution centres are able to track goods in ways that were unthinkable even 10 years ago.

Technological forces can have profound implications for managers and organizations. Technological change can make established products obsolete overnight—for example, eight-track tapes and black and white televisions—forcing managers to find new products to make. Although technological change can threaten an organization, it also can create a host of new opportunities for designing, making, or distributing new and better kinds of goods and services. Managers must move quickly to respond to such changes if their organizations are to survive and prosper.

Changes in information technology also are changing the very nature of work itself within organizations, and the manager's job. Telecommuting and teleconferencing are now everyday activities that provide opportunities for managers to supervise and coordinate employees working from home or other locations. Even students engage in telecommuting, communicating with classmates and instructors via email or discussion forums, and completing assignments at home. This has changed the way instructors do their jobs.

Demographic Forces

demographic forces
Outcomes of changes in, or changing attitudes toward, the characteristics of a population, such as age, gender, ethnic origin, race, sexual orientation, and social class.

Demographic forces are outcomes of changes in, or changing attitudes toward, the characteristics of a population, such as age, gender, ethnic origin, race, sexual orientation, and social class. Like the other forces in the general environment, demographic forces present managers with opportunities and threats and can have major implications for organizations. Over the past 30 years, for example, women have entered the workforce in increasing numbers. Between 1973 and 1999, the percentage of working-age women in the workforce grew from 48 to 78 percent in

Canada and from 50 to 77 percent in the United States.[21] The dramatic increase in the number of working women has focused public concern on issues such as equal pay for equal work and sexual harassment at work. Managers must address these issues if they are to attract and make full use of the talents of female employees. We discuss the important issue of workforce diversity at length in Chapter 3.

Changes in the age distribution of a population are another example of a demographic force that affects managers and organizations. Currently, most industrialized nations are experiencing the aging of their populations as a consequence of falling birth and death rates and the aging of the baby boom generation. The aging of the population is increasing opportunities for organizations that cater to older people; the recreation and home health care industries, for example, are seeing an upswing in demand for their services.

The aging of the population also has several implications for the workplace. Most significant are a relative decline in the number of young people joining the workforce and an increase in active employees willing to postpone retirement past the traditional retirement age of 65. These changes suggest that organizations will need to find ways to motivate older employees and use their skills and knowledge, an issue that many Western societies have yet to tackle.

political and legal forces

Outcomes of changes in laws and regulations, such as the deregulation of industries, the privatization of organizations, and increased emphasis on environmental protection.

The Competition Act
http://laws.justice.gc.ca
/en/C-34

Political and Legal Forces

Political and legal forces result from political and legal developments within society and significantly affect managers and organizations. Political processes shape a society's laws; for instance, public pressure for corporations to be more environmentally conscious has strengthened pollution laws in Canada. Laws constrain the operations of organizations and managers and thus create both opportunities and threats.[22] For example, in much of the industrialized world there has been a strong trend toward deregulation of industries previously controlled by the state and privatization of organizations once owned by the state. The *Case in Contrast* discussed the effects of privatization on Petro-Canada and at the beginning of this section we discussed the effects of deregulation on NB Power.

Deregulation and privatization are just two examples of political and legal forces that can create challenges for organizations and managers. Others include increased emphasis on safety in the workplace and on environmental protection and the preservation of endangered species. Successful managers carefully monitor changes in laws and regulations in order to take advantage of the opportunities they create and counter the threats they pose in an organization's task environment.

The Competition Act of 1986 provides more legislation that affects how companies may operate. Under this act, the Bureau of Competition Policy acts to maintain and encourage competition in Canada. For example, if two major competing companies consider merging, they face intense scrutiny from the bureau. When Heather Reisman and Gerry Schwartz bought Chapters in 2001, they had to receive approval before they could merge Chapters with their Indigo bookstores. The bureau imposed a number of conditions before approving the merger, including the sale or closure of 20 stores and a code of conduct for dealing with publishers. Chapters was forced to accept this code because of complaints about the way the company had treated publishers in the past. These rules restrict the way that the new company, Indigo Books & Music Inc., can do business until 2006.

Government policy regarding whether publications such as the *National Post* are owned by Canadians affects whether advertisers can deduct the cost of an ad from their taxes. So when Conrad Black renounced his Canadian citizenship, Hollinger International Inc. had to restructure its ownership to be sure that at least three-quarters of the paper was still owned by Canadians.

Global Forces

Global forces are outcomes of changes in international relationships, changes in nations' economic, political, and legal systems, and changes in technology. Perhaps the most important global force affecting managers and organizations is the increasing economic integration of countries around the world.[23] Developments such as the North American Free Trade Agreement (NAFTA), the free-trade agreements enforced by the World Treaty Organization (WTO), and the growth of the European Union (EU) have led to a lowering of barriers to the free flow of goods and services between nations.[24]

Falling trade barriers have created enormous opportunities for organizations in one country to sell goods and services in other countries. But by allowing foreign companies to compete for an organization's domestic customers, falling trade barriers also pose a serious threat, because they increase competition in the task environment. After NAFTA was signed, one of the major challenges facing Canadian managers was how to compete successfully against American companies moving into this country. Zellers and the Bay, for instance, faced strong challenges from Wal-Mart as well as smaller boutique operations.

Despite evidence that countries are becoming more similar to one another and that the world is on the verge of becoming a "global village," countries still differ across a range of political, legal, economic, and cultural dimensions. When an organization operates in the global environment, it confronts a series of forces that differ from country to country and world region to world region.

The Impact of Political and Economic Forces

In recent years, two large and related shifts in political and economic forces have taken place globally (see Figure 2.3).[25] One is the shift away from **totalitarian regimes**, where those in charge allow no opposition, toward more democratic regimes. This change has been most dramatic in Eastern Europe and the former Soviet Union, where totalitarian communist regimes collapsed during the late 1980s and early 1990s. The other shift—toward **representative democracy**, where voters elect a government that makes decisions on their behalf—has occurred from Latin America to Africa.

Accompanying this change in political forces has been a worldwide shift away from **command economies** (where the government owns all businesses) and **mixed economies** (where only some sectors are government-owned) and toward **free-market economies** (where competition determines prices).[26] This economic shift began with the realization that government involvement in economic activity often blocks economic growth. Thus, a wave of privatization and deregulation has swept over the world, from the former communist countries to Latin America, Asia, and Western Europe.

These trends are good news for managers of global organizations because they result in the expansion of opportunities for exporting and investment abroad. The managers of many Western companies have had a lot of trouble establishing business operations in Eastern Europe and China, however. For example, when the Chiquita banana company entered the Czech Republic in 1990, it found that Czech citizens apparently had difficulty understanding why something of better quality should cost more. Chiquita was forced to switch to lower quality bananas after discovering that consumers were unwilling to pay higher prices for superior bananas.[27]

The Impact of National Culture

Differences among national cultures have important implications for managers. First, management practices that are effective in Canada might not work in Japan,

Figure 2.3 | Changes in Political and Economic Forces

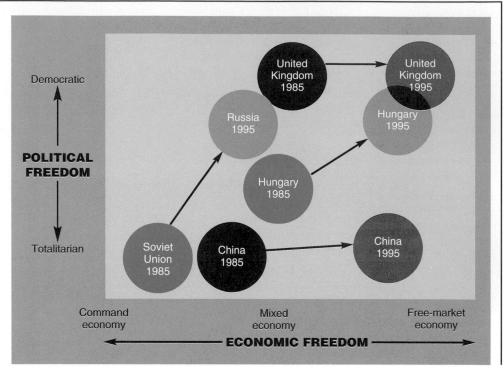

Hungary, or Mexico, because of differences in national culture. For example, pay-for-performance systems used in Canada, which emphasize the performance of individuals alone, are less suitable in Japan, where individual performance in pursuit of group goals is the value that receives emphasis.

A culturally diverse management team can be a source of strength in the global marketplace. Organizations that employ managers from a variety of cultures appreciate better how national cultures differ than do organizations with culturally similar management teams, and they tailor their management systems and behaviours to the differences.

Tips for Managers

Forces in the Environment

1. List the forces in an organization's task environment that affect it the most. Analyze changes taking place that may result in opportunities or threats for the organization.

2. List the forces in the general environment that affect an organization the most. Analyze changes taking place that may result in opportunities or threats for the organization.

3. Devise a plan indicating how your managers propose to take advantage of opportunities or counterthreats that arise from environmental forces and what kinds of resources they will need to do so.

Managing the External Environment

Think About It

Starbucks Goes to Vienna and Bans Smoking in a City of Smokers

When Starbucks went to Vienna in December 2001, it rose to some new challenges.[28] Vienna is filled with cafés and the people think of themselves as snobbish about coffee. Starbucks decided to ban smoking at its stores, even though 40 percent of Europeans smoke. Skeptics were sure the plan would fail, but Starbucks has been a "resounding success," with three additional stores opened within the first six months.

Starbucks went against the culture not only with its smoking ban, but also with its business model. Viennese typically linger with their coffee, meeting friends, smoking, enjoying pastries with cream and marzipan, and reading free newspapers. In Viennese coffee shops, customers drink their beverages from china cups delivered by waiters in black dinner jackets.

Starbucks couldn't match the Viennese pastries, and didn't even try. They sell the Viennese staple, apple strudel, and a few cakes with poppy seeds, but otherwise the customers enjoy Starbucks' blueberry muffins and chocolate-chip cookies. They're not the same as in Canada, though, where "the muffins are nearly the size of human heads and the cookies rival hubcaps." The pastries in Austria are smaller, and have half the sugar.

Questions
1. What considerations do managers face when expanding their businesses?
2. How can managers reduce the threats that come from the environment?

As previously discussed, an important task for managers is to understand how forces in the task and general environments create opportunities for, and threats to, their organizations. To analyze the importance of opportunities and threats in the external environment, managers must measure (1) the level of complexity in the environment and (2) the rate at which the environment is changing. With this information, they can plan better and choose the best goals and courses of action.

The complexity of the external environment depends on the number and potential impact of the forces that managers must respond to in the task and general environments. A force that seems likely to have a significant negative impact is a potential threat to which managers must devote a high level of organizational resources. A force likely to have a marginal impact poses little threat to an organization and requires only a minor commitment of managerial time and attention. A force likely to make a significant positive impact warrants a considerable commitment of managerial time and effort to take advantage of the opportunity. When Starbucks went to Vienna, the company had to think carefully about its no-smoking policy, since it would be the only coffee shop in the city to ban smoking.

In general, the larger an organization is, the greater the number of environmental forces that managers must respond to. Compare, for example, the external environment facing the manager of a small country diner with that facing top managers at Starbucks' headquarters. At the local level, the main concern of a diner manager is to ensure there are enough inputs, such as food supplies and restaurant employees, to provide customers with fast and efficient service. In contrast, top managers at Starbucks must determine how to distribute food supplies to restaurants in the most efficient ways; how to ensure that the organization's practices do not discriminate against any ethnic groups or older workers; how to respond to customers' preferences for different types of pastries in different countries; and how to deal with competition from other coffee shops that have tried to create a more personalized environment for customers than Starbucks does. Clearly, the more forces managers must deal with, the more complicated is the management process.

environmental change
The degree to which forces in the task and general environments change and evolve over time.

Environmental change is the degree to which forces in the task and general environments change and evolve over time. Change is problematic for an organization and its managers because the consequences of change can be difficult to predict.[29] Managers can try to forecast or simply guess about future conditions in the task environment, such as where and how strong the new competition may be. But, confronted with a complex and changing task environment, managers cannot be sure that decisions and actions taken today will be suitable in the future. This uncertainty makes their jobs especially challenging. It also makes it vitally important for managers to understand the forces that shape the external environment.

To manage the external environment, managers need to:
1. List the types and relative strengths of the forces that affect their organizations' task and general environments the most.
2. Analyze the way changes in these forces may result in opportunities or threats for their organizations.
3. Draw up a plan indicating how they propose to take advantage of those opportunities or counter those threats, and what kinds of resources they will need to do so.

An understanding of the external environment is necessary so that managers can anticipate how the task environment might look in the future and decide on the actions to pursue if the organization is to prosper. Starbucks' decision to avoid selling Viennese pastries acknowledged the company's likelihood to do this poorly, and instead, they chose the muffins and cookies they already sold, but with less sugar.

Reducing the Impact of Environmental Forces

Finding ways to reduce the number and potential impact of forces in the external environment is the job of all managers in an organization.

- The principal task of the CEO and top-management team is to devise strategies that will allow an organization to take advantage of opportunities and counter threats in its general and task environments (see Chapter 5 for a discussion of this vital topic).

- Middle managers in an organization's departments collect relevant information about the task environment, such as (1) the future intentions of the organization's competitors, (2) the identity of new customers for the organization's products, and (3) the identity of new suppliers of crucial or low-cost inputs.

- First-line managers find ways to use resources more efficiently to hold costs down or to get close to customers and learn what they want.

Managers are organized in different departments that allow the external environment to be monitored and addressed. Figure 2.4 illustrates different departments and their relationship to the environment.

Managers as Agents of Change

It is important to note that, although much of the change that takes place in the external environment is independent of a particular organization (e.g., basic advances in biotechnology or plastics), a significant amount of environmental change is the direct consequence of actions taken by managers within organizations.[30] As explained in the appendix to Chapter 1, an organization is an open system: It takes in inputs from the environment and converts them into goods and services that are sent back to the environment. Thus, change in the environment is

Figure 2.4 | How Managers Use Functions to Manage Forces in the Task and General Environments

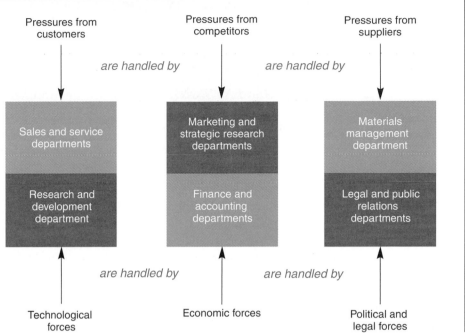

a two-way process (see Figure 2.5). Often, however, the choices that managers make about which products to produce, and even about how to compete with other organizations, affect the environment in many ways. Starbucks' quick success in Vienna may well end up changing the face of all coffee houses in the city.

Tips for Managers

Managing the External Environment

1. To assess the level of uncertainty in the environment, analyze its level of complexity and rate of change.

2. Once the number and importance of the forces in the environment have been determined, decide how to build and develop departments to respond to them.

3. After analyzing your customers, competitors, and suppliers, decide which managers should be responsible for identifying and responding to their needs.

Figure 2.5 | Change in the Environment as a Two-Way Process

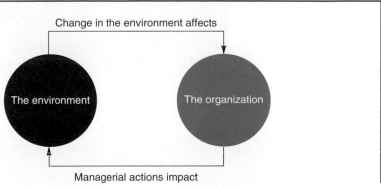

Chapter Summary

SUMMARY AND REVIEW

WHAT IS THE ORGANIZATIONAL ENVIRONMENT? The organizational environment is the set of forces and conditions that affect a manager's ability to acquire and use resources. The organizational environment has two components: the internal environment and the external environment. The external environment can be divided into the task environment and the general environment.

THE TASK ENVIRONMENT The task environment is the set of forces and conditions that originate with suppliers, distributors, customers, and competitors and that influence managers on a daily basis.

THE GENERAL ENVIRONMENT The general environment includes wider-ranging economic, technological, demographic, political and legal, and global forces that affect an organization and its task environment.

MANAGING THE EXTERNAL ENVIRONMENT Two factors affect the nature of the opportunities and threats that organizations face: (1) the level of complexity in the environment and (2) the rate of change in the environment. Managers must learn how to analyze the forces in the environment in order to respond effectively to opportunities and threats.

Roles in Contrast: Considerations

MANAGERS	EMPLOYEES
I need to be aware of the environment, to position the business, and to be aware of threats and opportunities that may come along.	Scanning the environment is a manager's responsibility to help position the organization. As an employee, I can learn to scan the environment to better understand my own position in the organization.
When I truly understand all the different aspects of the environment, I can use this information to adjust to changes that might be occurring, thus increasing my chances for increased sales.	Scanning the environment might open up opportunities for me to learn more skills which might make me more effective in my current job, or give me the credentials to move to another job.
An understanding of the environment makes it possible to know whether there are new customers, suppliers, or other opportunities that should be pursued.	Understanding the organizational environment may give me ideas of other careers that are available, or business opportunities that I might want to pursue.

MANAGEMENT in Action

Topics for Discussion and Action

1. Why is it important for managers to understand the nature of the environmental forces that are acting on them and their organization?

2. Choose an organization, and ask a manager in that organization to list the types and strengths of forces in the organization's task environment. Ask the manager to pay particular attention to identifying opportunities and threats that result from pressures and changes in customers, competitors, and suppliers.

3. Read the business section of your local newspaper, to get an idea of task and general forces that affect the organizations in your community. What local conditions have a major impact on organizations in your area?

4. Which organization is likely to face the most complex task environment: a biotechnology company trying to develop a cure for cancer, or a large retailer such as Zellers or the Bay? Why?

5. The population is aging because of declining birth rates, declining death rates, and the aging of the baby boom generation. What might some of the implications of this demographic trend be for (a) a pharmaceutical company, (b) the home construction industry, and (c) the agenda of political parties?

6. Currently, most households and businesses in Canada, the United Kingdom, the United States, and a number of other countries do not have a choice of electricity supplier. But as a result of deregulation, within a decade the average business and household will be able to choose from among several competing suppliers. How might this development alter the task environment facing a manager in an electric utility?

7. The textile industry has a labour-intensive manufacturing process that uses unskilled and semiskilled workers. What are the implications of the shift to a more open global environment for textile companies whose manufacturing operations are based in high-wage countries such as Australia, Canada, and the United States?

8. After the passage of the North American Free Trade Agreement, some Canadian companies shifted production operations to Mexico to take advantage of lower labour costs and lower standards for environmental and worker protection. As a result, they cut their costs and were better able to survive in an increasingly competitive global environment. Was their behaviour ethical—that is, did the ends justify the means?

9. Go to the library and gather information that allows you to compare and contrast the political, economic, and cultural systems of the United States, Mexico, and Canada. In what ways are the countries similar? How do they differ? How might the similarities and differences influence the activities of managers at an enterprise such as Wal-Mart, which does business in all three countries?

Building Management Skills

ANALYZING AN ORGANIZATION'S TASK AND GENERAL ENVIRONMENTS

Pick an organization that you know. It can be an organization where you have worked or currently work, or it can be an organization that you interact with regularly as a customer (such as the college or university that you are currently attending). Then do the following:

1. Describe the main forces in the task environment that are affecting the organization.
2. Describe the main forces in the general environment that are affecting the organization.
3. Try to determine whether the organization's task and general environments are relatively stable or changing rapidly.
4. Explain how environmental forces affect the job of an individual manager within this organization. How do they determine the opportunities and threats that its managers must confront?

Management for You

You are considering organizing an event to raise funds for a special cause (e.g., children living in poverty, breast cancer research, literacy, or something of your choice). Think about who you might invite to this event (i.e., your "customers"—those who will buy tickets to the event). What type of event might appeal to them? What suppliers might you approach for help in organizing the event? What legal issues might you face in setting up this event? After considering all these issues, how difficult is the environment you face in holding this event?

Small Group Breakout Exercise

HOW TO ENTER THE COPYING BUSINESS

Form groups of 3 to 5 people, and appoint 1 group member as the spokesperson who will communicate your findings to the whole class when called on by the instructor. Then discuss the following scenario.

You and your partners have decided to open a small printing and copying business in a college town of 100 000 people. Your business will compete with companies such as Kinko's. You know that more than 50 percent of small businesses fail in their first year, so to increase your chances of success, you have decided to do a detailed analysis of the task environment of the copying business in order to analyze the opportunities and threats you will encounter. As a group:

1. Decide what you must know about (a) your future customers, (b) your future competitors, and (c) other critical forces in the task environment, if you are to be successful.
2. Evaluate the main barriers to entry into the copying business.
3. Based on this analysis, list some of the steps you will take to help your new copying business succeed.

Managing Ethically

You are a manager for a drug company that has developed a pill to cure river blindness, a common disease in Africa. It was a quick and easy solution, but there were no buyers because the people afflicted or who could be are too poor to buy the pills. Should you shelve the pills and wait until the market can pay the price? What other alternatives might you have?

Exploring the World Wide Web

SPECIFIC ASSIGNMENT

Examine the environment that the communications company Nortel Networks Corporation faces as it pursues its activities around the globe. Explore Nortel's website (www.nortel networks.com), and click on "Corporate Information" and "Corporate Citizenship." Explore these locations and other relevant ones for information about Nortel's environment.

1. What major forces in the task and general environments present opportunities and threats for Nortel?
2. How are Nortel's managers managing these forces?

GENERAL ASSIGNMENT

Search for the website of a company that has a complex, rapidly changing environment. What forces in its environment are creating the strongest opportunities and threats? How are managers trying to respond to these opportunities and threats?

You're the Management Consultant

THE CHANGING ENVIRONMENT OF RETAILING

You have been called in to advise the top managers of a major clothing store who are facing a crisis. This clothing store has been the leader in its market for the past 15 years. In the past 3 years, however, two other major clothing store chains have opened up and they have steadily been attracting your customers—your sales are down 30 percent. To find out why, the managers surveyed former customers and learned that customers perceive the store is just not keeping up with changing fashion trends and new forms of customer service. In examining the way the store operates, managers realize that over time the 10 buyers who purchase the clothing and accessories for your store have been buying increasingly from the same clothing suppliers and have become reluctant to try new ones. Moreover, salespeople rarely, if ever, make suggestions for changing the way the store operates, and the culture of the store has become conservative and opposed to risk.

Questions

1. Analyze the major forces in the task environment of a retail clothing store.
2. Devise a program that will help managers and employees to better understand and respond to their store's task environment.

MANAGEMENT CASE

The Brewing Industry

For many years now, the Canadian brewing industry has effectively been a duopoly, dominated by Labatt Brewing Co. and Molson Inc., which together control some 90 percent of the market.[31] The only other national player in the industry is Guelph, Ontario-based Sleeman Breweries Ltd., which has gained 5 percent of the national market since its 1988 revival, with niche brands such as Stroh, Okanagan Spring, and Upper Canada.

As a new competitor, Sleeman has worked cautiously to build up its market share, working in partnership with more experienced breweries. It started in 1988 with the help of former Detroit-based Stroh Brewery Co., which bought 20 percent of the shares and offered its expertise as one of the biggest US breweries. From that beginning, Sleeman has steadily expanded as a regional maker of premium craft beers.

Sleeman's strategy for growth has been to buy up "craft beer makers that had a reputation for making high-quality natural brews in small quantities."[32] Purchases include Okanagan Spring Brewery in Vernon, BC; Upper Canada Brewing in Toronto; Montreal's La Brasserie Seigneuriale; and the bankrupt Maritime Beer Co. in Dartmouth, Nova Scotia. With these and other purchases, Sleeman has become a national beer maker.

In 2000, Sleeman started its entrance into the US market, by teaming up with Boston Beer Co. to market its Samuel Adams brand in Canada, in exchange for which Boston would market Sleeman's products in the United States. Sleeman also acquired the Canadian rights to Stroh's low-priced American beers, including Old Milwaukee, Rainier, and Stroh's. Of this move, John Sleeman, chair and CEO, said, "This will counterbalance the premium-priced beers [Sleeman] has specialized in, providing extra volume for the plants and insulating the company from the vagaries of the domestic beer market."[33] Sleeman tries to avoid competing directly with Molson and Labatt: "We compete with them in the value-priced segment, but they don't have strong entries in the premium categories."[34]

With the concentration of sales in the hands of just three major Canadian players, Canada's small brewers looked for help from the federal government. In September 2000, about 70 of them from across the country asked Ottawa for a reduction in the excise tax charged by Ottawa. "This industry is threatened," said Pierre Paquin, general manager of the newly formed Canadian Council of Regional Brewers. "We're not saying give us handouts. We're saying, give us a field where we can play too."[35] The craft-brewing industry employs about 3300 people directly and indirectly in Canada. Industry members see themselves as small business owners who should not have to pay the same rate of excise tax as Canadian beer giants Molson and Labatt. "Canadian brewers, regardless of size, pay about $2.30 in excise tax on a case of beer," said Donald Ross of Granville Island Brewing, chair of the Craft Brewers Association of British Columbia. "But it costs a small brewer as much as $260 to make a hectolitre, about 12 cases of beer, compared with $128 for the big breweries."[36] Craft breweries rely on employees rather than machines to produce their beer, and thus their labour costs are considerably higher. Other countries extract less tax from small brewers. "In the United States, for instance, the big brewers pay about Cdn$1.88 a case in excise taxes while the small brewers pay about 74 cents," said Ross.

John Wiggins, of Creemore Springs Brewery Ltd. and chair of the Ontario Small Brewers Association, said the current excise tax situation "creates an uneven playing field. By dumping us into the same pot as the large brewers and charging us the same amount, it's actually making us non-competitive. It's punitive to our section of the industry."[37] The success of the large brewers resulted from two factors. First, economies of scale allowed them to keep the costs of making beer low and to make higher profits as their market increased. At the same time, their national presence permitted them to engage in large-scale advertising campaigns and develop national brand names for their beers. The smaller brewers have higher costs and mainly regional customers.

A number of forces affect even the Canadian giants in the industry, however. First, sales of beer are flat in Canada because many customers have switched to wine or wine coolers. Second, social attitudes toward drinking, and in particular toward drinking and driving, have changed. Concern over the health effects of drinking alcohol has increased, and organizations such as MADD (Mothers Against Drunk Driving) and SADD (Students Against Destructive Decisions) have lobbied for tighter control over sales of alcohol to minors and for strengthening legal penalties for drunk driving.

One of the most interesting forces affecting the large brewers has been an increase in competition from small regional beer makers and import beer makers who are capitalizing on Canadian customers' demands for new tastes and higher beer quality.

Questions

1. What are the principal forces in the external environment facing the major brewers?
2. How has the level of uncertainty changed over time in the brewing industry? What is the source of these changes?

MANAGEMENT CASE — IN THE NEWS

From the Pages of *Business Week* Levi's Is Hiking up Its Pants

Back in September, Levi Strauss & Co. was all set to ship to retailers its newest invention: a line of blue jeans called Special Reserve. Samples had been made. Stores had placed orders. Levi's had even handed out T-shirts with the Special Reserve logo at an August sales meeting in Palm Springs, Calif.

But weeks before the debut, an unprecedented thing occurred. Thomas A. Fanoe—two months into his reign as president of Levi's USA—pulled the plug on the launch and sent nearly a year's worth of work into the circular file. Why? Because Special Reserve, which was likely to appeal to consumers 25 years and up, didn't solve Levi's core problem: teenage indifference.

That's quite a turnabout for a brand once synonymous with rebellious youth. While Levi retains its hold over the baby boomers who built the brand into mythic proportions, the company has neglected the whims of the latest crop of teens. "They missed all the kids, and those are your future buyers," says Bob Levy, owner of Dave's Army & Navy Store in New York, which devotes 50 percent of its shelves to Levi products.

The oversight has cost it dearly. With shrinking teen sales one of the key factors in the erosion of its once dominant market share, Levi Strauss was forced to announce on Nov. 3 that it would shutter 11 of its US plants and lay off one-third of its North American workforce. The news followed a similar announcement in February in which Levi's said it would lay off 1000 salaried US employees.

Of course, increased competition added to Levi's tight fit. But the San Francisco clothing giant's biggest problem is plummeting market share: In 1990, Levi Strauss had 30.9 percent of the US blue jeans market, but it has just 18.7 percent today, according to estimates by Tactical Retail Solutions Inc., a researcher in New York. Most troubling has been the drop among consumers aged 15 to 19. Levi says it enjoyed a 33 percent share of their jeans dollars in 1993, vs. about 26 percent now.

Missing those buyers can be a long-term mistake. "It's very important that you attract this age group," says Gordon Harton, vice-president for the Lee brand at rival VF Corp. "By the time they're 24, they've adopted brands that they will use for the rest of their lives. Worse, since teens set fashion trends that influence even older shoppers, the defection to other brands affects sales all down the product line."

Caught with its pants down, the US$7 billion company is scrambling to get back on track. Top management is giving virtually every aspect of the Levi's brand the once-over. Some products are being repositioned, while others are being scrapped altogether. Hiring policies are being reviewed to cultivate new talent and bring in fresh ideas. And marketing initiatives, including the company's 67-year-old relationship with ad agency Foote, Cone & Belding, are being completely revamped. "We are examining every element of the marketing, big M, of the Levi's brand," says Fanoe. "That means product, distribution, advertising, public relations, customer service. Everything."

How did the undisputed king of denim get into this hole? Levi Chairman and CEO Robert D. Haas says it was, in part, the classic corporate goof: taking your eyes off the ball. Projects during the last decade, such as expanding the casual clothing line Dockers and launching its upscale cousin Slates distracted executives from the threat to Levi's core jeans brand. "When you try to take on too many things, you are not as attentive to the warning signs," he concedes.

The warning signs became sirens at a July 31 meeting, when top US managers learned the results of a yearlong research project into what the kids of baby boomers—called the Echo Boom generation—think of the world's largest branded-apparel maker. The news wasn't good.

For half a day, executive product managers, and marketers of the Levi's brand in the US watched teen after teen on video talking about the blue-jeans king as if it were a has-been. Levi's, they said, was uncool, more suitable for their parents or older siblings than for fashion-conscious kids. "That was scary," recalls Stephen Goldstein, vice-president for marketing and research for Levi's USA. "Kids say they love the Levi's brand. But if you ask them whether it's 'with it,' they'll say no."

Meanwhile, the competition had made inroads. Top-end designers such as Tommy Hilfiger and Ralph Lauren have squeezed Levi on one end, while private labels sold by low-priced retailers such as J.C. Penney Co. and Sears, Roebuck & Co. have come on strong from the other direction. Trends such as wide-legged and baggy jeans took hold without response from Levi. "Levi Strauss was zagging when the world was zigging," says retail consultant Alan Millstein. "The company totally missed the significance of the inner city and the huge impact it

has on trends. It tells me they're sleepy in their marketing."

But Levi execs seem to be waking up. The decision to scrap Special Reserve came in tandem with a move to pump up Levi's Silver Tab brand, the eight-year-old jeans line that is considered more stylish among young consumers. Indeed, the median age of those who buy Silver Tab apparel is 18, compared with about 25 for other Levi's products. With its baggier fits and use of more than just denim fabrics, kids tag Silver Tab as Levi's hippest clothes. So the company plans to expand the line to include more tops, more trendy styles, and new khaki pants.

To catch teens' attention, Levi plans to spend five times as much in 1998 as it did this year on promoting Silver Tab. And for all its brands, it's also increasing marketing aimed specifically at teens. For instance, Levi is sponsoring concerts in New York and San Francisco for up-and-coming bands playing music known as Electronica. It's also outfitting characters on hot TV shows, such as *Friends* and *Beverly Hills 90210*. "As the Echo Boom generation goes, so goes Levi Strauss & Co.," says Goldstein. "We have to be relevant to this population."

The quest to jazz up Levi's image has also left the company searching for a new ad agency: A review, which includes longtime agency Foote, Cone & Belding, is under way. Although Levi has attempted to target teens in its latest ads, so far that hasn't translated into improved sales. Levi says its most recent TV campaign—featuring images such as a young man driving through a car wash with the windows down—has logged positive response from young consumers on the company's Web site. But when kids hit the stores and found them stocked mostly with traditional styles, Goldstein concedes, they didn't buy.

Another way Levi hopes to overcome that problem is by working over its retail presentation and the packaging and labelling of all its goods. In 1998, the company says it will come out with jazzier, more colourful packaging aimed at giving its products a more exciting, youthful look. And Levi has ditched plans to open more than 100 new stores in malls around the country. Instead, it will follow Nike Inc.'s retail approach and open a handful of grand flagship stores in big cities. The first one is set to open in San Francisco in 1999.

But marketing and products aren't all that's getting a makeover. The company is also shaking up management. Now, Levi is considering a plan calling for 30 percent of all new management jobs to be filled by outsiders. Critics argue that one reason Levi appears to be losing touch with what's happening in the marketplace is that it doesn't recruit enough outside executives or solicit enough independent opinions. "It has always been insular, paternalistic, and, quite frankly, a little smug," says Isaac Lagnado, president of Tactical Retail Solutions.

Will this work? Most industry experts believe that the 140-year-old apparel giant can right itself—given its vast resources and still formidable market presence. But it's likely to be a difficult, multiyear process. Retailer Levy says the wake-up call comes none too soon. "They are facing the problem," he says. "That's important because they weren't doing it before." No one is more confident than Haas. "From time to time, any brand is likely to have periods of great strength and relevancy and periods of regrouping and refocusing," he says. "We're going to restore the Levi's brand with consumers." The trick will be to keep the generation that grew up on Bob Dylan, while understanding the new age of Electronica.

Source: L. Himelstein, "Levi's Is Hiking up Its Pants," *Business Week,* December 1, 1997, pp. 71, 75.

Questions

1. What factors in its environment are giving rise to opportunities and threats for Levi Strauss?
2. How are Levi's managers trying to manage these opportunities and threats?

3

MANAGING ETHICS, SOCIAL RESPONSIBILITY, AND DIVERSITY

Learning Objectives

1. Describe the concept of ethics, and the different models of ethics.

2. Describe the concept of social responsibility, and detail the ways in which organizations can encourage both ethical and socially responsible behaviour among their employees.

3. Define diversity, and explain why the effective management of diverse employees is both an ethical issue and a means for an organization to improve its performance.

4. Identify instances of sexual harassment, and discuss how to prevent its occurrence.

Roles in Contrast: Questions

MANAGERS	EMPLOYEES
How do I make ethical decisions?	How do I make ethical decisions?
To what extent should I be concerned with my company being socially responsible?	Do I want to work for a socially responsible organization?
What can I do to manage diversity effectively?	What can I do to improve the situation when working with a diverse group of co-workers?

A CASE IN CONTRAST

ETHICAL STANCES AT PEMBINA AND BRIDGESTONE

When an oil pipeline running between Taylor and Prince George, BC ruptured in the early hours of August 1, 2000, Calgary-based Pembina Pipeline Corporation (www.pembina.com) had a nightmare in the making on its hands. Pembina was the owner of the pipeline, which spilled about one million litres of light crude oil into the Pine River. It was the largest-ever spill on a river in Western Canada, and there were threats to the drinking water supply of the local area.

Pembina immediately issued a bare-bones news release, and then hired Calgary-based Communication Incorporated (CI) to handle its media relations. CI told Pembina's CEO, Bob Michaleski, to "Talk about as much as you can, give as much information as you can and never lie."[1]

Michaleski had bought the pipeline that burst just 12 hours before the spill occurred. So he certainly could have tried to place the blame elsewhere. Instead, he remained steadfast in accepting responsibility by continuing to say: "It's

our pipeline, our spill, and our responsibility." That earned Pembina big credibility points with media and public alike.

Even though the oil spill caused widespread environmental damage to the river, Mayor Charlie Lasser of Chetwynd, BC, the small town whose drinking water was affected, proclaimed five months later, "We turned a liability into an asset." The town brought in a dowser, who helped to find sources for two new wells. Pembina Pipeline paid to find and develop the new wells.

Pembina also paid millions of dollars for cleanup and repairs, while facing a production curtailment at the Husky Oil Refinery in Prince George until the pipeline could be repaired.

At almost the same time that Pembina was facing its oil spill crisis, Japanese tire maker Bridgestone (www.bridgestone.co.jp) was facing a public relations disaster of its own making. Its Firestone Tires subsidiary faced a voluntary

After one of its pipelines burst in Chetwynd, BC, Pembina Pipeline quickly got to work on cleaning up the spill, and making things right for the small community.

Masatoshi Ono, CEO of Bridgestone, was slow to admit fault after his company's Firestone tires were linked to an unusually high number of accidents.

recall of 6.5 million tires in August 2000 and a mandated recall of another 1.4 million by the US National Highway Traffic Safety Administration. The tires were linked to 46 deaths in Venezuela and 88 deaths in the United States as a result of shredding, peeling, or blowouts in accidents mainly involving Ford Motor Company's Explorer sport-utility vehicle.

As the Bridgestone crisis unfolded in September 2000, Bridgestone engaged in progressive acts of damage control, rather than admitting responsibility for the tire failures. For instance, Yoichiro Kaizaki, Bridgestone's president at the time, told a news conference that he had learned as early as May that the tires were linked to an unusually high number of accidents. He also admitted that the company's headquarters in Tokyo was slow to take action after learning about the accidents.[2]

Masatoshi Ono, then CEO of Bridgestone Corp., testified before the US Congress that he did not know the reason for the Firestone tire failures. Meanwhile, John Lampe, then executive vice-president of Bridgestone's US operations, suggested that it was not its tires, but the tendency of Ford Motor Company's Explorer to roll over that was responsible for many of the fatal crashes being reviewed by regulators.[3]

Still, most investors saw the major problem as a tire issue. Richard Hilgert, an analyst with Fahnestock and Co., noted: "The consumer seems to have voted with its pocketbook and they're buying Ford vehicles. They are comfortable with the Explorer product as long as it's equipped with tires other than Firestone."

The effect on Bridgestone was enormous. Profits plunged 80 percent in 2000.[4] The recall cost the company $510 million (US) at its Firestone subsidiary in the United States in 2000 alone. Kaizaki stepped down in March 2001, acknowledging that his company's image was badly hurt and that there was no telling when the damage would end. However, he denied that his resignation was related to the crisis. "I am not resigning to take responsibility for the recall. I decided on this move to strengthen our management in a rapidly changing global environment and to win back the trust of our customers and shareholders," he said.[5]

Ford's US operations also took a hit as a result of the tire scandal, with decreased sales and profits, although Oakville, Ontario-based Ford Canada's "operational highlights included 283 000 new car and truck sales in 2000, making it the second-best sales year since 1989," noted Bob Girard, Ford Canada's vice-president, general sales.[6] "We're pleased to see that Canadians continue to have confidence in our vehicles," said Ford spokesperson Lauren More.[7] Consumers may have been more sympathetic to Ford, which immediately tried to help its customers get tire replacements while providing clearer information about the cause of the crisis.

Bridgestone managers seem to have put what they incorrectly thought were the interests of their company ahead of their customers' interests. Managers at Pembina Pipeline put the local community's interests first. Bridgestone's stance harmed the company's reputation in the short run. By 2003, it was starting to regain its sales in the American market, but it had taken several years to recover. Meanwhile, among the residents of Chetwynd and those of British Columbia more broadly, Pembina gained a reputation for being socially responsible and has been quite successful in recent years.

OVERVIEW

As the behaviour of Pembina and Bridgestone executives suggests, managers may interpret their responsibilities to their customers and to their organizations in very different ways. Pembina accepted responsibility immediately, and then helped to restore the water supply. Bridgestone's managers postponed action and, to safeguard the profits of their company, did not confront the fact that their product was defective and dangerous. As a result, car companies such as Ford continued to buy Bridgestone's tires, and the potential for accidents increased.

The ways in which managers view their responsibilities to the individuals and groups that are affected by their actions are central to the discussion of ethics and social responsibility, and to the discussion of organizational performance as well. In this chapter, we explore what it means to behave ethically. We describe how managers and organizations can behave in a socially responsible way toward the individuals and groups in their organizational environment.

We then focus on one particular aspect of ethical behaviour that is receiving increasing attention today: how to manage diversity to ensure that everyone an organization employs is fairly and equitably treated. Managers' ability and desire to behave ethically and to manage diversity effectively are central concerns in today's complex business environment. Increasingly, if managers ignore these issues or fail to act appropriately, their organizations are unlikely to prosper in the future.

We also discuss sexual harassment, which is both unethical and illegal, and a behaviour that managers and organizations—military as well as civilian—must confront and respond to in a serious manner. By the end of the chapter, you will appreciate why ethics, diversity, and sexual harassment are issues that make a manager's job both more challenging and more complex.

WHAT ARE ETHICS?

Think About It

Should Canadians Be Doing Business in Sudan?

During 1999 and 2000, Calgary-based Talisman Energy Inc. came under increasing fire from church and human rights organizations and the United States for its stake in an oil project in Sudan.[8] Critics said Sudan uses oil revenues to fund its civil war. Though the Canadian government backed off from its threat to impose sanctions in February 2000, at the same time the United States slapped sanctions on the consortium operating the Sudan project, of which Talisman owned 25 percent.

The United States justified its sanctions by noting that Talisman "provided a new source of hard currency for a regime that has been responsible for massive human-rights abuses—including slavery—and sponsoring terrorism outside Sudan."[9] Jim Buckee, president and chief executive officer, in responding to sanctions by the United States defended Talisman's actions. He said that his company was not in the business of peacemaking "and shouldn't be expected to take on the dirty work of governments."[10] The foreign affairs minister at that time, Lloyd Axworthy, responding to the US sanctions, said that, "Other countries have no business making laws for Canadian companies." He also suggested that Talisman needs to make its own decisions, but did not support Canadian intervention in the company's policies. "They could look seriously at some monitoring agency on human rights abuses. These are company decisions," Axworthy said.[11] Talisman stayed firm in Sudan until March 2003, watching its share prices continue to fall. Though the company felt it was actually doing some good in Sudan, investors did not, and it was time to pull out.

Questions
1. How do you decide whether an action is ethical?
2. If companies are not breaking laws of the countries where they are doing business, do they need to be held to the ethical standards of their home country?

---

ethics

Moral principles or beliefs about what is right or wrong.

Talisman Energy Inc. www.talisman-energy.com

The questions raised about Talisman's actions in Sudan highlight ethical concerns. **Ethics** are moral principles or beliefs about what is right or wrong. These beliefs guide individuals in their dealings with other individuals and groups who have a concern in a particular situation (stakeholders), and they provide a basis for deciding if behaviour is right and proper.[12] Ethics help people determine moral responses to situations in which the best course of action is unclear.

Managers often experience an ethical dilemma when they confront a situation that requires them to choose between two courses of action, especially if each decision is likely to serve the interests of one particular stakeholder group to the detriment of the other.[13] To make an appropriate decision, managers must weigh the competing claims or rights of the various stakeholder groups. Sometimes, making a decision is easy because some obvious standard, value, or norm of behaviour applies. In other cases, managers have trouble deciding what to do.

Making Ethical Decisions

Philosophers have debated for centuries about the specific criteria that should be used to determine whether decisions are ethical or unethical. Three models of what determines whether a decision is ethical—the *utilitarian, moral rights,* and *justice* models—are summarized in Table 3.1.[14] In theory, each model offers a different and complementary way of determining whether a decision or behaviour is ethical, and all three models should be used to sort out the ethics of a particular course of action. Ethical issues are seldom clear-cut, however, and the interests of different stakeholders often conflict, so it is often extremely difficult for a decision maker to use these models to identify the most ethical course of action. That is why many experts on ethics propose the following practical guide to determine whether a decision or behaviour is ethical.[15] A decision is probably acceptable on ethical grounds if a person can answer "yes" to each of these questions:
1. Does my decision fall within the accepted values or standards that typically apply in the organizational environment?
2. Am I willing to see the decision communicated to all stakeholders affected by it—for example, by having it reported in newspapers or on television?
3. Would the people with whom I have a significant personal relationship, such as family members, friends, or even managers in other organizations, approve of the decision?

---

ethical decision

A decision that reasonable or typical stakeholders would find acceptable because it aids stakeholders, the organization, or society.

unethical decision

A decision that a manager would prefer to disguise or hide from other people because it enables a company or a particular individual to gain at the expense of society or other stakeholders.

From an organizational perspective, an **ethical decision** is a decision that reasonable or typical stakeholders would find acceptable because it aids stakeholders, the organization, or society. By contrast, an **unethical decision** is a decision that a person would prefer to disguise or hide from other people because it enables a company or a particular individual to gain at the expense of society or other stakeholders. The actions of Talisman, noted above, and the comments of former foreign affairs minister Lloyd Axworthy suggest that these two parties felt the company was engaging in ethical behaviour. Though Talisman eventually sold its shares in the Sudan in 2003, the company did not rush to change its situation, even in the face of negative press.

Table 3.1 | Utilitarian, Moral Rights, and Justice Models of Ethics

Model	Managerial Implications	Problems for Managers
Utilitarian Model An ethical decision is a decision that produces the greatest good for the greatest number of people.	Managers should compare and contrast alternative courses of action based on the benefits and costs of those alternatives for different organizational stakeholder groups. They should choose the course of action that provides the most benefits to stakeholders. For example, managers should locate a new manufacturing plant at the place that will most benefit its stakeholders.	How do managers decide on the relative importance of each stakeholder group? How are managers to measure precisely the benefits and harms to each stakeholder group? For example, how do managers choose among the interests of stockholders, employees, and customers?
Moral Rights Model An ethical decision is a decision that best maintains and protects the fundamental rights and privileges of the people affected by it. For example, ethical decisions protect people's rights to freedom, life and safety, privacy, free speech, and freedom of conscience.	Managers should compare and contrast alternative courses of action based on the effect of those alternatives on stakeholders' rights. They should choose the course of action that best protects stakeholders' rights. For example, decisions that would involve significant harm to the safety or health of employees or customers are unethical.	If a decision will protect the rights of some stakeholders and hurt the rights of others, how do managers choose which stakeholder rights to protect? For example, in deciding whether it is ethical to snoop on an employee, does an employee's right to privacy outweigh an organization's right to protect its property or the safety of other employees?
Justice Model An ethical decision is a decision that distributes benefits and harms among stakeholders in a fair, equitable, or impartial way.	Managers should compare and contrast alternative courses of action based on the degree to which the action will promote a fair distribution of outcomes. For example, employees who are similar in their level of skill, performance, or responsibility should receive the same kind of pay. The allocation of outcomes should not be based on arbitrary differences such as gender, race, or religion.	Managers must learn not to discriminate between people because of observable differences in their appearance or behaviour. Managers must also learn how to use fair procedures to determine how to distribute outcomes to organizational members. For example, managers must not give people they like bigger raises than they give to people they do not like or bend the rules to help their favourites.

codes of ethics
Formal standards and rules, based on beliefs about right or wrong, that managers can use to help themselves make appropriate decisions with regard to the interests of their stakeholders.

societal ethics
Standards that govern how members of a society are to deal with each other on issues such as fairness, justice, poverty, and the rights of the individual.

professional ethics
Standards that govern how members of a profession are to make decisions when the way they should behave is not clear-cut.

individual ethics
Personal standards that govern how individuals interact with other people.

Codes of Ethics

Codes of ethics are formal standards and rules, based on beliefs about right or wrong, that managers can use to help themselves make appropriate decisions with regard to the interests of their stakeholders.[16] Ethical standards embody views about abstractions such as justice, freedom, equity, and equality (see Table 3.1). An organization's code of ethics derives from three main sources in the organizational environment: (1) **societal ethics,** governing how everyone deals with each other on issues such as fairness, justice, poverty, and the rights of the individual; (2) **professional ethics**, governing how members of the profession make decisions when the way they should behave is not clear-cut; and (3) the **individual ethics,** or personal standards for interacting with others, of the organization's top managers (see Figure 3.1).

Shell Canada's code of ethics states the following:

Shell Canada's reputation and credibility are based upon its total commitment to ethical business practices. To safeguard the Shell reputation, employees must conduct themselves in accordance with the highest ethical standards and also be perceived to be acting ethically at all times.[17]

The company's ethics web page (http://66.46.47.14/code/values/commitments/ethics.html) describes in some detail how different stakeholders are to interpret the code of ethics.

Figure 3.1 | Sources of an Organization's Code of Ethics

Societal ethics
The values and standards embodied in a society's laws, customs, practices, and norms and values

Organization's code of ethics derives from

Professional ethics
The values and standards that groups of managers and workers use to decide how to behave appropriately

Individual ethics
Personal values and standards that result from the influence of family, peers, upbringing, and involvement in significant social institutions

Ethics and Stakeholders

organizational stakeholders

Shareholders, employees, customers, suppliers, and others who have an interest, claim, or stake in an organization and in what it does.

The individuals and groups that have an interest, claim, or stake in an organization and in what it does are known as *organizational stakeholders*.[18] **Organizational stakeholders** include shareholders, managers, nonmanagerial employees, customers, suppliers, the local community in which an organization operates, and even citizens of the country in which an organization operates. To survive and prosper, an organization must effectively satisfy its stakeholders.[19] Stockholders want dividends, managers and employees want salaries and stable employment, and customers want high quality products at reasonable prices. If stakeholders do not receive these benefits, they may withdraw their support for the organization: Stockholders will sell their stock, managers and workers will seek jobs in other organizations, and customers will take their business elsewhere.

Managers are the stakeholder group that determines which goals an organization should pursue to benefit stakeholders most, and how to make the most efficient use of resources to achieve those goals. In making such decisions, managers often have to juggle the interests of different stakeholders, including themselves.[20] Managerial decisions that may benefit some stakeholder groups and harm others involve questions of ethics. The Talisman decision to do business in Sudan may have been profitable for shareholders for a time, but many people questioned the impact on Sudanese because of the civil war that was allegedly funded by oil revenues. This did eventually lead Talisman to leave Sudan.

Ethics and National Culture

Views about what is ethical vary among societies. For example, ethical standards accepted in Canada and the United States are not accepted in all other countries. In many economically poor countries, bribery is standard practice to get things done—such as getting a telephone installed or a contract awarded. In Canada and many other Western countries, bribery as part of doing business in one's home country is considered unethical and often illegal. Bribing foreign public officials is widespread, however. The US government reported that between 1994 and 2001, bribery was uncovered in more than 400 competitions for international contracts.[21] A recent study found that some Asian governments were far more tolerant of corruption than others. Singapore, Japan and Hong Kong scored relatively low on corruption (0.83, 2.5, and 3.77 out of 10, respectively), and Vietnam, Indonesia, India, the Philippines, and Thailand scored as the most corrupt of the 12 Asian countries surveyed.[22]

While Canada has no national laws regarding codes of ethics, in 1997 a coalition of Canadian companies developed a new international code of ethics. The code is voluntary and deals with issues such as the environment, human rights, business conduct, treatment of employees, and health and safety standards. Supporters of the Canadian code include the Alliance of Manufacturers & Exporters Canada, the Conference Board of Canada, and the Business Council on National Issues. Alcan Inc., Komex International Ltd., Shell Canada Ltd., and Talisman Energy Inc. are among the companies that have signed the code. Former foreign affairs minister Lloyd Axworthy hailed the code as a way of putting Canadian values into the international arena.[23] Interpretation of what Canadian companies should be doing is not always clear, however, as the situation with Talisman suggests.

What Behaviours Are Ethical?

A key ethical decision for managers is how to divide harms and benefits among stakeholder groups.[24] Suppose a company has a few very good years and makes high profits. Who should receive these profits—managers, employees, stockholders, or customers? For example, as oil prices soared throughout the world in 2000 and 2001, Canadian oil industry profits reached record highs. Customers, whose heating bills rose greatly, thought they should get some of their money back in rebates.

The decision about how to divide profits among managers, employees, stockholders, and even customers might not seem to be an ethical issue, but it is—and in the same manner as how to apportion harms or costs among stakeholders when things go wrong.[25] For instance, it is not unusual for companies to engage in restructurings—resulting in massive layoffs—to improve their bottom line, and perhaps increase returns to stockholders, who are the legal owners of a corporation. Are layoffs of managers and employees ethical? Managers at some companies try to make the layoffs less painful by introducing generous early retirement programs that give employees full pension rights if they retire early. Employees are sometimes paid a month's or several months' salary for each year of service to the company.

Publishers hoped that Heather Reisman would be friendlier to the publishing industry than Chapters' former CEO, Larry Stephenson.

Managers also face ethical dilemmas when choosing how to deal with certain stakeholders. For example, suppliers provide an organization with its inputs and expect to be paid within a reasonable amount of time. Some managers, however, consistently delay payment to make the most use of their organization's money. This practice can hurt a supplier's cash flow and threaten its very survival.

An organization that is a powerful customer and buys large amounts of particular suppliers' products is in a position to demand that suppliers reduce their prices. If an organization does this, suppliers earn lower profits and the organization earns more. Is this behaviour just "business as usual," or is it unethical?

Before it was bought out by Heather Reisman of Indigo Books & Music Inc. and Gerry Schwartz of Onex Corporation, Toronto-based Chapters controlled between 40 and 70 percent of the Canadian retail book market.[26] It owned its own wholesale distribution company, and because of its large orders, Chapters demanded the lowest unit costs from publishers, usually a 50-percent discount, "or else."[27] Some publishers were relieved when Reisman took over from Chapters CEO Larry Stephenson, viewing her as friendlier to the publishing industry and less likely to demand such steep discounts from already struggling publishers.

Sometimes it is suppliers who can take advantage of situations in the market to gain higher profits. After California's energy crisis in 2000 and 2001, a report was filed with the US Federal Energy Regulatory Commission claiming that BC Hydro "reaped US$176 million in 'excessive' profits by price gouging California utilities."[28] BC Hydro was accused of offering "power at a range of high prices and sometimes in large amounts when the state was most desperate."[29] BC Hydro officials "acknowledge they did anticipate periods of severe power shortages and planned for them by letting their reservoirs rise overnight and then opening them to create hydro electricity, which could be produced inexpensively but sold for a premium." But BC Hydro officials say they played by the rules of the electricity trade marketplace. "It was the marketplace that determined what the price of electricity would be at any given time," said BC Hydro spokesman Ian Cousins. We can readily raise the question: Was this good business, or was this unethical behaviour?

BC Hydro
www.bchydro.com

In addition to suppliers and distributors, customers are a critical stakeholder group because, as noted in Chapter 1, organizations depend on them for their very survival. Customers have the right to expect an organization to provide goods and services that will not harm them. As well, local communities and the general public have an interest or stake in whether the decisions that managers make are ethical. The quality of a city's school system or police department, the economic health of its downtown area, and its general level of prosperity all depend on choices made by managers of organizations.

In sum, managers face many ethical choices as they deal with the different and sometimes conflicting interests of organizational stakeholders. Deciding what behaviour is ethical is often a difficult task that requires managers to make tough choices that will benefit some stakeholders and harm others.

Promoting Ethics

A 2000 ethics survey by KPMG found that nearly two-thirds of Canadian firms promote values and ethical practices. However, more than half of the companies surveyed had not designated a senior manager responsible for ethical issues. Only 14 percent evaluated their employees in terms of ethical performance.[30] Despite a seeming lack of commitment to concrete actions by Canada's companies, there are many ways in which managers can communicate their desire for employees at all levels to behave ethically toward organizational stakeholders.

Establishing Ethical Control Systems

Perhaps the most important step to encourage ethical behaviour is to develop a code of ethics that is given to every employee and published regularly in company newsletters and annual reports. The "Integrity Program" at Calgary-based Nexen Inc. (formerly Canadian Occidental Petroleum Ltd.) covers such issues as business conduct, employee and human rights, and the environment. Each division at Nexen has an integrity leader who is supposed to make sure that the message about the company's commitment to ethics spreads throughout the organization.[31] At UPS Canada, employees must develop an action plan around their codes of conduct. Managers are assessed on matters such as integrity and fair treatment.[32]

The next step is to provide a visible means of support for ethical behaviour. Increasingly, organizations are creating the role of ethics officer, or

Nexen Inc. Integrity
Program
www.nexeninc.com/Our_
Commitment/Business_
Practices/

ethics ombudsman
An ethics officer who monitors an organization's practices and procedures to be sure they are ethical.

ethics ombudsman, to monitor their ethical practices and procedures. The ethics ombudsman is responsible for communicating ethical standards to all employees, for designing systems to monitor employees' conformity to those standards, and for teaching managers and nonmanagerial employees at all levels of the organization how to respond to ethical dilemmas appropriately.[33] Because the ethics ombudsman has organization-wide authority, organizational members in any department can discuss instances of unethical behaviour by their managers or co-workers without fear of retribution. This arrangement makes it easier for everyone to behave ethically. In addition, ethics ombudsmen can provide guidance when organizational members are uncertain about whether an action is ethical. Some organizations have an organization-wide ethics committee to provide guidance on ethical issues and help write and update the company code of ethics.

Developing an Ethical Culture

An organization can also communicate its position on ethics and social responsibility to employees by making ethical values and norms a central part of its organizational culture. A number of companies try to encourage ethical behaviour through their corporate culture, emphasizing such values as honesty, trust, respect, and fairness. (We discuss organizational culture in depth in Chapter 7.) It is important to note that when organizational members abide by the organization's values and norms, those values and norms become part of each individual's personal code of ethics. Thus, an employee who faces an ethical dilemma automatically responds to the situation in a manner that reflects the ethical standards of the organization. High standards and strong values and norms help individuals resist self-interested action and recognize that they are part of something bigger than themselves.[34]

The manager's role in developing ethical values and standards in other employees is very important. Employees naturally look to those in authority to provide leadership, and managers become ethical role models whose behaviour is scrutinized. If top managers are not ethical, their subordinates are not likely to behave in an ethical manner. They may think that, if it's all right for a top manager to engage in ethically dubious behaviour, it's all right for them too.

Ethical control systems such as codes of ethics and regular training programs help employees learn an organization's ethical values. However, KPMG reported in 2000 that 61 percent of Canadian companies surveyed gave no ethics training at all, and a third of Canadian businesses provide managers with less than one hour of training a year.[35]

Tips for Managers

Championing Ethical Behaviour

1. Analyze the way stakeholders will be affected by managerial decisions and ensure that managers make decisions in such a way that they can defend them to all of those who will be affected by their actions.

2. Develop a written code of ethics for an organization and encourage members of different areas to develop specific guidelines that will help them know how to behave when confronted by an ethical dilemma.

3. Ensure that all managers are responsible for helping their subordinates learn how to determine whether an action is unethical or not and to discover instances of unethical behaviour.

4. Ensure that managers serve as role models and always act ethically and with integrity.

SOCIAL RESPONSIBILITY

Think About It

Communicopia.Net's Socially Responsible Advantage

Jason Mogus, twenty-something president of Vancouver-based Communicopia.Net, uses his leadership to practise what he believes. Employees do not work overtime at Communicopia, and they are encouraged to use public transportation and bikes to get to work. The company also carefully considers the supplies purchased: Paper cannot be made from old-growth trees, and coffee must be the organic fair-trade variety. Discounts are given to nonprofit groups when they need web design services.[36]

Question

1. Why would being socially responsible make a difference?

social responsibility

A manager's duty or obligation to make decisions that promote the well-being of stakeholders and society as a whole.

There are many reasons why it is important for managers and organizations to act ethically and to do everything possible to avoid harming stakeholders. However, what about the other side of the coin? What responsibility do managers have to provide benefits to their stakeholders and to adopt courses of action that enhance the well-being of society at large? The term **social responsibility** refers to a manager's duty or obligation to make decisions that nurture, protect, enhance, and promote the welfare and well-being of stakeholders and society as a whole. Many kinds of decisions signal an organization's interest in being socially responsible (see Table 3.2).

Approaches to Social Responsibility

obstructionist approach

Disregard for social responsibility; willingness to engage in and cover up unethical and illegal behaviour.

The strength of organizations' commitment to social responsibility ranges from low to high (see Figure 3.2).[37] At the low end of the range is an **obstructionist approach**. Obstructionist managers choose not to behave in a socially responsible way. Instead, they behave unethically and illegally and do all they can to prevent knowledge of their behaviour from reaching other organizational stakeholders and society at large.

Table 3.2 | Forms of Socially Responsible Behaviour

Managers are being socially responsible and showing their support for their stakeholders when they:

- Provide severance payments to help laid-off workers make ends meet until they can find another job;
- Provide workers with opportunities to enhance their skills and acquire additional education so they can remain productive and do not become obsolete because of changes in technology;
- Allow employees to take time off when they need to and provide extended health care and pension benefits for employees;
- Contribute to charities or support various civic-minded activities in the cities or towns in which they are located;
- Decide to keep open a factory whose closure would devastate the local community;
- Decide to keep a company's operations in Canada to protect the jobs of Canadian workers rather than move abroad;
- Decide to spend money to improve a new factory so that it will not pollute the environment;
- Decline to invest in countries that have poor human rights records;
- Choose to help poor countries develop an economic base to improve living standards.

Figure 3.2 | Approaches to Social Responsibility

defensive approach

Minimal commitment to social responsibility; willingness to do what the law requires and no more.

Λ **defensive approach** indicates at least a commitment to ethical behaviour. Managers adopting this approach do all they can to ensure that their employees behave legally and do not harm others. But when making ethical choices, these managers put the claims and interests of their shareholders first, at the expense of other stakeholders.

Some economists believe that managers in a capitalist society should always put stockholders' claims first. They suggest that if such choices are unacceptable or are considered unethical to other members of society, then society must pass laws and create rules and regulations to govern the choices managers make.[38] From a defensive point of view, it is not managers' responsibility to make socially responsible choices; their job is to abide by the rules that have been legally established.

accommodative approach

Moderate commitment to social responsibility; willingness to do more than the law requires if asked.

An **accommodative approach** is an acknowledgment of the need to support social responsibility. Accommodative managers agree that organizational members ought to behave legally and ethically, and they try to balance the interests of different stakeholders against one another so that the claims of stockholders are seen in relation to the claims of other stakeholders. Managers adopting this approach want to make choices that are reasonable in the eyes of society and want to do the right thing when called on to do so. Wal-Mart Canada has been criticized for its policy of doing business with third-party suppliers—such as Hampton Industries, Sutton Creations, Global Gold, Stretch-O-Rama, Cherry Stix, and By Design—that import goods from Myanmar (Burma), which engages in forced labour, including that of children. In defence of the company's actions, Wal-Mart Canada spokesman Andrew Pelletier noted, "We have a policy we are looking at, of monitoring vendors sourcing from other countries."[39] The company started with a defensive approach, focusing on not doing anything illegal, but has moved to a more accommodative style.

proactive approach

Strong commitment to social responsibility; eagerness to do more than the law requires and to use organizational resources to promote the interests of all organizational stakeholders.

Managers taking a **proactive approach** actively embrace the need to behave in socially responsible ways, go out of their way to learn about the needs of different stakeholder groups, and are willing to use organizational resources to promote the interests of stockholders as well as other stakeholders. Jason Mogus and Communicopia.Net take a proactive approach to social responsibility.

Why Be Socially Responsible?

There are several advantages to social responsibility by managers and organizations. First, employees and society benefit directly because organizations (rather than the government) bear some of the costs of helping employees. Second, it has been said that if all organizations in a society were socially responsible, the quality of life as a whole would be higher.[40] Indeed, several management experts have argued that the way organizations behave toward their employees determines many of a society's values and norms and the ethics of its citizens. Experts point to Japan, Sweden, Germany, the Netherlands, and Switzerland as countries where

McDonald's is one of the many global organizations that have declared a commitment to be socially responsible—it supports a proactive stance on the issues and wants its customers to support this stance too.

Communicopia.Net
www.communicopia.net

social audit

A tool that allows managers to analyze the profitability and social returns of socially responsible actions.

organizations are very socially responsible and where, as a result, crime and unemployment rates are relatively low, the literacy rate is relatively high, and socio-cultural values promote harmony between different groups of people. Other reasons for being socially responsible are that it is the right thing to do and that companies that act responsibly toward their stakeholders benefit from increasing business and see their profits rise.[41]

Jason Mogus, president of Communicopia.Net, finds that being socially responsible is a competitive advantage: "The times that we are in right now are tough times for a lot of high-tech firms, and the ones that are thriving are the ones that really did build community connections and have strong customer and employee loyalty," says Mogus. "If everyone's just there for the stock price and it goes underwater, then what you have is a staff of not very motivated workers."[42]

Given these advantages, why would anyone quarrel over organizations and their managers pursuing social responsibility? One response is that a commitment to social responsibility could benefit some stakeholders and not others. For instance, some shareholders might think they are being harmed financially when organizational resources are used for socially responsible courses of action. Some people argue that business has only one kind of responsibility: to use its resources for activities that increase its profits and thus reward its stockholders.[43]

How should managers decide which social issues they will respond to, and to what extent their organizations should trade profits for social gain? Obviously, illegal behaviour should not be tolerated, and all managers and workers should be alert to its occurrence and report it promptly. The need to behave legally is only one of the criteria managers can use to decide which social actions to undertake. A **social audit** allows managers to consider both the organizational and the social effects of particular decisions. The audit ranks various courses of action according to both their profitability and their social benefits.

Evidence suggests that, in the long run, managers who behave in a socially responsible way will most benefit all organizational stakeholders (including stockholders). It appears that socially responsible companies, in comparison with less responsible competitors, are less risky investments, tend to be somewhat more profitable, have a more loyal and committed workforce, and have better **reputations**; these qualities encourage stakeholders (including customers and suppliers) to establish long-term business relationships with the companies.[44] Socially responsible companies are also sought out by communities, which encourage such organizations to locate in their cities and offer them incentives such as property-tax reductions and the construction of new roads and free utilities for their plants. Thus, there are many reasons to believe that, over time, strong support of social responsibility brings the most benefits to organizational stakeholders (including stockholders) and society at large.

reputation
The esteem or high repute that individuals or organizations gain when they behave ethically.

MANAGING AN INCREASINGLY DIVERSE WORKFORCE

Think About It

Sweetgrass Comes to the RCMP

To help Aboriginal cadets take part in spiritual practices while in training, the RCMP training academy in Regina created an Aboriginal Heritage Room, with cedar walls, Plains Indian artifacts, and reproductions of old photographs of Aboriginal Canadians.[45]

At the opening ceremony in December 2000, Piapot First Nation elder Art Kaiswatum used the sweet-smelling smoke of burning buffalo sage to cleanse the room. The Heritage Room makes it possible for Aboriginal cadets to practise ceremonies, meet with elders, and discuss their culture. Cadet Dustin Ward, from the Mi'kmaq reserve in New Brunswick, finds the Heritage Room "one more sign that the RCMP welcomes First Nations Mounties. It shows the children hope that they can come here some day and be an RCMP cadet."

Question
1. What types of accommodations should companies make for employees from different cultures, or with different needs?

One of the most important issues in management to emerge over the past 30 years has been the increasing diversity of the workforce. In Chapter 2, we addressed issues of diversity that result from organizations' expansion into the global environment. Here, we address diversity as it occurs closer to home—in an organization's workforce. **Diversity** is dissimilarity—differences—among people due to age, gender, race, ethnicity, religion, sexual orientation, socio-economic background, and capabilities/disabilities (see Figure 3.3). Diversity raises important ethical issues and social responsibility issues as well. It is also a critical issue for organizations, one that if not handled well can bring an organization to its knees, especially in our increasingly global environment.

diversity
Differences among people in age, gender, race, ethnicity, religion, sexual orientation, socio-economic background, and capabilities or disabilities.

Canada has become a truly diverse country, although this might not be apparent to everyone. Based on the 2001 census, on average 13 percent of Canada's population are visible minorities.[46] However, this varies widely across the country. In British Columbia, 22 percent of the residents are visible minorities, the highest proportion of any province. Ontario is second, with 19 percent of its population being visible minorities. These concentrations are much higher in Vancouver and

Figure 3.3 | Sources of Diversity in the Workforce

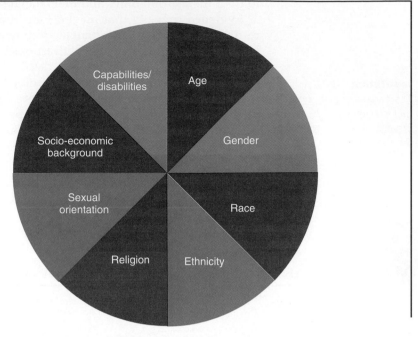

Toronto, however—in both of these cities, visible minorities make up about 37 percent of the population. By contrast, only 0.8 percent of the population are visible minorities in Newfoundland and Labrador and Nunavut, 7.9 percent in Manitoba, and 11 percent in Alberta. There are many more women and minorities—including people with disabilities and gays and lesbians—in the workforce than ever before, and most experts agree that diversity is steadily increasing.

Why is diversity such a pressing issue both in the popular press and for managers and organizations? There are several reasons:

• There is a strong ethical imperative in many societies to see that all people receive equal opportunities and are treated fairly and justly. Unfair treatment is also illegal.

• Effectively managing diversity can improve organizational effectiveness. When managers manage diversity well, they not only encourage other managers to treat diverse members of an organization fairly and justly, but also realize that diversity is an important resource that can help an organization gain a competitive advantage.

• Embracing diversity encourages employee participation, and thus encourages differences of opinions/ideas that are beneficial to the organization.

Saskatchewan-born Aboriginal Pauline Busch provides an example of how an organization that is visibly open to minority employees can make those individuals more willing to join the organization. Busch worked alongside the commanding officer's Aboriginal advisory committee for two years to get the Heritage Room in Regina established. She remembered the decision in the late 1980s to allow Aboriginal Mounties to wear their hair in braids, if they wanted. "There's nothing that warms a child's heart and pride as seeing another Aboriginal person in the red serge, fully outlined with the braids."[47]

In the rest of this section, we examine why effectively managing diversity makes sense. Then we look at the steps that managers can take to manage diversity effectively in their organizations.

The Ethical Need to Manage Diversity Effectively

Effectively managing diversity not only makes good business sense, but is an ethical obligation in Canadian society. Two moral principles provide managers with guidance when they try to meet this obligation: distributive justice and procedural justice.

distributive justice
A moral principle calling for the distribution of pay raises, promotions, and other organizational resources to be based on meaningful contributions that individuals have made and not on personal characteristics over which they have no control.

Distributive Justice

The principle of **distributive justice** dictates that the distribution of pay raises, promotions, job titles, interesting job assignments, office space, and other organizational resources among members of an organization be fair. The distribution of these outcomes should be based on the meaningful contributions that individuals have made to the organization (such as time, effort, education, skills, abilities, and performance levels) and not on irrelevant personal characteristics over which individuals have no control (such as gender, race, or age).[48] Managers have an obligation to ensure that distributive justice exists in their organizations. This does not mean that all members of an organization receive identical or similar outcomes; rather, it means that members who receive more outcomes than others have made much greater or more significant contributions to the organization.

Is distributive justice common in organizations in corporate Canada? Probably the best way to answer this question is to say that things are getting better. Fifty years ago, **overt discrimination** (knowingly and willingly denying diverse individuals access to opportunities and outcomes in an organization) against women and minorities was not uncommon; today, organizations are inching closer toward the ideal of distributive justice. Statistics comparing the treatment of women and minorities with the treatment of white men suggest that most managers would need to take a proactive approach in order to achieve distributive justice in their organizations. For instance, Toronto-based Bank of Montreal has worked diligently to advance women through the ranks since 1991, after discovering that, even though 75 percent of its employees were women, only 9 percent of them were in management positions.[49] After bank managers introduced some changes, women held 23 percent of the executive positions at the Bank of Montreal in 1997. The Bank of Montreal continues to monitor its hiring and promotion of women and other diverse groups. Since 2001, senior managers have been given annual hiring and retention goals for members of the four designated groups. A portion of their bonus is tied to success on this front.[50]

overt discrimination
Knowingly and willingly denying diverse individuals access to opportunities and outcomes in an organization.

In many countries, managers have not only an ethical obligation to strive to achieve distributive justice in their organizations, but also a legal obligation to treat all employees fairly. Managers risk being sued by employees who feel that they are not being fairly treated.

Procedural Justice

procedural justice
A moral principle calling for the use of fair procedures to determine how to distribute outcomes to organizational members.

The principle of **procedural justice** requires managers to use fair procedures to determine how to distribute outcomes to organizational members.[51] This principle applies to typical procedures such as appraising subordinates' performance, deciding who should receive a raise or a promotion, and deciding whom to lay off when an organization is forced to downsize.

Procedural justice exists, for example, when managers (1) carefully appraise a subordinate's performance, (2) take into account any environmental obstacles to high performance beyond the subordinate's control, such as lack of supplies, machine breakdowns, or dwindling customer demand for a product, and (3) ignore irrelevant personal characteristics such as the subordinate's age or ethnicity. Like distributive justice, procedural justice is necessary not only to ensure ethical conduct but also to avoid costly lawsuits.

Human Rights Act
http://laws.justice.gc.ca/e
n/H-6

Employment Equity Act
http://laws.justice.gc.ca/
en/E-5.401

Effectively Managing Diversity Makes Good Legal Sense

A variety of legislative acts affect diversity management in Canada. Under the Canadian Human Rights Act, it is against the law for any employer or provider of service that falls within federal jurisdiction to make unlawful distinctions based on the following prohibited grounds: race, national or ethnic origin, colour, religion, age, sex (including pregnancy and childbirth), marital status, family status, mental or physical disability (including previous or present drug or alcohol dependence), pardoned conviction, or sexual orientation. Employment with the following employers and service providers is covered by the Human Rights Act: federal departments, agencies, and Crown corporations; Canada Post; chartered banks; national airlines; interprovincial communications and telephone companies; interprovincial transportation companies; and other federally regulated industries, including certain mining operations.

In addition to the Human Rights Act, Canada's Employment Equity Act of 1995 lists four protected categories of employees: Aboriginal peoples (whether Indian, Inuit, or Metis); persons with disabilities; members of visible minorities (non-Caucasian in race or nonwhite in colour); and women. The reasoning behind the Employment Equity Act is that individuals should not face employment barriers due to being a woman, a person with a disability, an Aboriginal person, or a member of a visible minority. Thus the federal legislation aims at ensuring that members of these four groups are treated equitably. Employers affected by the Canadian Human Rights Act are also covered by the Employment Equity Act.

A number of provinces have their own legislation, including employment equity acts, governing employers in their provinces. Many companies have difficulty complying with equity acts, as recent audits conducted by the Canadian Human Rights Commission show. In an audit of 180 companies, only Status of Women Canada; Elliot Lake, Ontario-based AJ Bus Lines; the National Parole Board; Canadian Transportation Agency; Les Méchins, Quebec-based Verreault Navigation; and Nortel Networks were compliant on their first try.[52]

Effectively Managing Diversity Makes Good Business Sense

Though organizations are forced to follow the law, the diversity of organizational members can be a source of competitive advantage in more than a legal sense, as it helps an organization to provide customers with better goods and services.[53] The variety of points of view and approaches to problems and opportunities that diverse employees provide can improve managerial decision making. Just as the workforce is becoming increasingly diverse, so too are the customers who buy an organization's goods or services.

Diverse members of an organization are likely to be attuned to what goods and services diverse segments of the market want and do not want. Major car companies, for example, are increasingly assigning women to their design teams to ensure that the needs and desires of female customers (a growing segment of the market) are taken into account in new car design.

Effectively managing diversity makes good business sense for another reason. More and more, consumer and civil rights organizations are demanding that companies think about diversity issues from a variety of angles. For instance, Toronto-based Royal Bank of Canada found its efforts to acquire North Carolina-based Centura Banks Inc. under attack by Inner City Press/Community on the Move (ICP), a US civil rights group. In April 2001, the group asked

Women wearing the hajib, the traditional head cover of Muslim women, face discrimination when they look for jobs in Canada. A recent study found that when visibly Muslim women asked whether jobs were available, they were told there were no jobs available or were not given a chance to apply for a job almost 40 percent of the time.

American and Canadian regulators to delay approval of the acquisition to allow further investigation of alleged abusive lending practices carried out by Centura. "Centura's normal interest rate lending disproportionately denies and excludes credit applications from people of colour," said Matthew Lee, ICP executive director.[54] ICP alleged that, in two American cities, Centura denied applications for home purchase from Black people three times more frequently than applications from White people. The group wanted Royal Bank to guarantee that it would end the alleged unfair lending practices.

Being aware of diversity issues extends beyond employees to include the issues of suppliers, clients, and customers. Nestlé Canada recently announced that it was planning to do away with its nut-free products because trying to keep the production area free of nut products seemed more costly than it was beneficial. Nestlé Canada was soon deluged with protests from Canadian families who had relied upon such products as Kit Kat, Mirage, Coffee Crisp, and Aero chocolate bars; and Smarties. Between 1 and 2 percent of all Canadians, and perhaps as many as 8 percent of children, are allergic to peanuts and/or other nuts, which is why the protest was so vocal. Within a month, Nestlé Canada announced that it would go back to producing these candies in a nut-free facility to appease its consumers with this particular disability. Nestlé's initial decision factored in "a growing public demand for chocolate with nuts, as well as the need to protect jobs at its Toronto plant."[55] Nestlé senior vice-president Graham Lute still wants to expand Nestlé's manufacturing in Canada, but says, "We'll just execute it in a different way, but not as attractive a way as it would have been before, from a sheer business point of view."[56] In other words, the attention to this particular diversity issue has caused the company to rethink part of its business strategy.

Increasing Diversity Awareness

It is natural to see other people from your own point of view, because your feelings, thoughts, attitudes, and experiences guide how you perceive and interact with others. The ability to appreciate diversity, however, requires people to become aware of other perspectives and the various attitudes and experiences of others. Many diversity awareness programs in organizations strive to increase managers' and employees' awareness of (1) their own attitudes, biases, and stereotypes, and (2) the differing perspectives of diverse managers, subordinates, co-workers, and customers. Diversity awareness programs often have these goals:[57]

- Providing organizational members with accurate information about diversity;

- Uncovering personal biases and stereotypes;

- Assessing personal beliefs, attitudes, and values, and learning about other points of view;

- Overturning inaccurate stereotypes and beliefs about different groups;

- Developing an atmosphere in which people feel free to share their differing perspectives;

- Improving understanding of others who are different from oneself.

The creation of the Aboriginal Heritage Room in Regina helped Aboriginal cadets feel more comfortable in the workplace, and also helped others understand more about Aboriginal culture.

Techniques for Increasing Diversity Awareness and Skills

Many managers use a varied approach to increase diversity awareness and skills in their organizations: films and printed materials are supplemented by experiential

RCMP Commander Giuliano Zaccardelli (right) wafts buffalo sage smoke during a smudging ceremony while Timothy Kaiswatum, of the Piapot First Nation, holds the sage. The smudging was part of the opening ceremonies of the Aboriginal Heritage Room at the RCMP training academy in Regina.

bias

The systematic tendency to use information about others in ways that result in inaccurate perceptions.

stereotype

Simplistic and often inaccurate beliefs about the typical characteristics of particular groups of people.

exercises to uncover any hidden **bias** (the systematic tendency to use information about others in ways that result in inaccurate perceptions) or **stereotype** (simplistic and often inaccurate belief about the typical characteristics of particular groups of people). Sometimes simply providing a forum for people to learn about and discuss their differing attitudes, values, and experiences can be a powerful means for increasing awareness. Also useful are role-playing exercises in which people act out problems that result from lack of awareness, and then indicate the increased understanding that comes from appreciating others' viewpoints. Accurate information and training experiences can debunk stereotypes. Group exercises, role plays, and diversity-related experiences can help organizational members develop the skills they need to work effectively with a variety of people.

Managers sometimes hire outside consultants to provide diversity training. For instance, Trevor Wilson, president of Toronto-based Omnibus Consulting, has presented employment equity programs to such clients as IBM Canada Ltd., Molson Inc., and National Grocers Co. Ltd.[58] Some organizations have their own in-house diversity experts, such as Maureen Geddes at Chatham, Ontario-based Union Gas.

The Importance of Top-Management Commitment to Diversity

When top management is truly committed to diversity, top managers embrace diversity through their actions and example, spread the message that diversity can be a source of competitive advantage, deal effectively with diverse employees, and are willing to commit organizational resources to managing diversity. That last step alone is not enough. If top managers commit resources to diversity (such as providing money for training programs) but as individuals do not value diversity, any steps they take are likely to fail.

Some organizations recruit and hire women for first-level and middle-management positions, but after being promoted into middle management, some of these female managers quit to start their own businesses. A major reason for their departure is their belief that they will not be promoted into top-management positions because of a lack of commitment to diversity among members of the top-management team. As Professor David Sharp of the Richard Ivey School of Business notes, "It seems that some Canadian women entrepreneurs are neither born, nor made. They are pushed."[59] The Bank of Montreal is an example of an organization that has been very proactive in making sure women will not leave, through its efforts to aggressively promote women to upper-management positions.

By now, it should be clear that managers can take a variety of steps to manage diversity effectively. Many companies and their managers continue to develop and experiment with new diversity initiatives to meet this ethical and business challenge. Although some steps prove unsuccessful, it is clear that managers must make a long-term commitment to diversity. Training sessions oriented toward the short term are doomed to failure: Participants quickly slip back into their old ways of doing things. The effective management of diversity, like the management of the organization as a whole, is an ongoing process: It never stops and never ends.

Tips for Managers

Managing an Increasingly Diverse Workforce

1. Make sure that managerial decision making conforms to the values of distributive and procedural justice.

2. Be careful that managers do not treat subordinates who are similar to them more favourably than those who are different.

3. Help managers to understand their stereotypes and why they are likely to be inaccurate.

4. Clearly communicate to subordinates your managerial commitment to effective diversity management.

5. Provide ongoing diversity training for subordinates.

SEXUAL HARASSMENT

Think About It

Zero Tolerancee Leads to Firing

Murdoch Carriere, former head of forest-firefighting operations in Saskatchewan, was fired in spring 2003 after an investigation concluded he had sexually harassed and intimidated his female staff.[60] Carriere had worked for the Saskatchewan government for 32 years. A variety of complaints were brought against him. One employee said he had humiliated her when he introduced her to Premier Lorne Calvert as "pet" during a meeting with other ministers.

The six women who complained also claimed that Carriere had kissed and hugged them, and touched them inappropriately. Carriere did not deny that he hugged or touched the women, but said it was not sexual. He was initially reprimanded, and then demoted and transferred to another office. However, the government later decided that its zero-tolerance policy for sexual harassment required that he be fired.

Questions
1. What is sexual harassment?
2. What can be done to eliminate sexual harassment?

There have been several notable cases of sexual harassment in recent years. For instance, the Canadian Armed Forces were subject to intense media scrutiny during 1998 for alleged cover-ups of sexual harassment. University campuses across Canada have seen a dramatic increase in the number of sexual harassment complaints, according to Paddy Stamp, sexual harassment officer at the University of Toronto.[61] Sexual harassment is apparently common in the workplace: A survey conducted by York University in 1999 found that 48 percent of working Canadian women reported that they had experienced some form of sexual harassment in the previous year.

The Supreme Court of Canada defines **sexual harassment** as unwelcome behaviour of a sexual nature in the workplace that negatively affects the work environment or leads to adverse job-related consequences for the employee. In 1987, the court ruled that employers will be held responsible for harassment by their employees. The court also said that the employers should promote a workplace free of harassment. The court recommended that employers have clear guidelines to prevent harassment, including procedures to investigate complaints.

Although women are the most frequent victims of sexual harassment—particularly those in male-dominated occupations, or those who occupy positions stereotypically associated with certain gender relationships (such as a female secretary reporting to a male boss)—men can be victims too. Several male employees at Jenny Craig in the United States said that they were subject to lewd and inappropriate comments from female co-workers and managers.[62] To date, there have been no media reports of women sexually harassing either men or women in Canada.

Sexual harassment seriously damages the victims as well as the reputation of the organization. It is not only unethical, but also illegal. Beyond the negative publicity, sexual harassment can cost organizations large amounts of money. Managers have an ethical obligation to ensure that they, their co-workers, and their subordinates never engage in sexual harassment, even unintentionally.

Forms of Sexual Harassment

There are two basic forms of sexual harassment: *quid pro quo sexual harassment* and *hostile work environment sexual harassment*. **Quid pro quo sexual harassment** occurs when a harasser asks or forces an employee to perform sexual favours to keep a job, receive a promotion or raise, obtain some other work-related opportunity, or avoid receiving negative consequences such as demotion or dismissal.[63] This "Sleep with me, honey, or you're fired" form of harassment is the more extreme form and leaves no doubt in anyone's mind that sexual harassment has taken place.[64] A study conducted by York University in 1999 found that only 3 percent of working Canadian women reported having experienced quid pro quo sexual harassment.[65]

Hostile work environment sexual harassment is more subtle. It occurs when organizational members are faced with an intimidating, hostile, or offensive work environment because of their gender.[66] Lewd jokes, sexually oriented comments, displays of pornography, displays or distribution of sexually oriented objects, and sexually oriented remarks about someone's physical appearance are examples of hostile work environment sexual harassment. About 45 percent of working Canadian women reported this form of harassment in the recent study at York University. Barbara Orser, a researcher with the Conference Board of Canada, noted that "sexual harassment is more likely to occur in workplace environments that tolerate bullying, intimidation, yelling, innuendo and other forms of discourteous behaviour."[67]

A hostile work environment interferes with organizational members' ability to perform their jobs effectively and has been deemed illegal by the courts. Managers who engage in hostile work environment harassment or allow others to do so risk

---

sexual harassment
Unwelcome behaviour of a sexual nature in the workplace that negatively affects the work environment or leads to adverse job-related consequences for the employee.

quid pro quo sexual harassment
Asking or forcing an employee to perform sexual favours in exchange for some reward or to avoid negative consequences.

hostile work environment sexual harassment
Telling lewd jokes, displaying pornography, making sexually oriented remarks about someone's personal appearance, and other sex-related actions that make the work environment unpleasant.

costly lawsuits for their organizations, as was the experience of Aurora, Ontario-based Magna International Inc. A former saleswoman in the parts maker's Detroit sales office brought a sexual harassment case against the company, alleging that she faced harassment in the office.[68] She also alleged that her male co-workers regularly entertained customers at area strip clubs. That case is still under investigation, though auto industry executives and observers acknowledge that some purchasing executives for the auto makers are entertained at strip clubs.[69]

Steps Managers Can Take to Eradicate Sexual Harassment

Managers have an ethical obligation to eradicate sexual harassment in their organizations. There are many ways to accomplish this objective. Here are four initial steps that managers can take to deal with the problem.[70]

- *Develop and clearly communicate a sexual harassment policy endorsed by top management.* This policy should include prohibitions against both quid pro quo and hostile work environment sexual harassment. It should contain: (1) examples of types of behaviour that are unacceptable, (2) a procedure for employees to use to report instances of harassment, (3) a discussion of the disciplinary actions that will be taken when harassment has taken place, and (4) a commitment to educate and train organizational members about sexual harassment.

- *Use a fair complaint procedure to investigate charges of sexual harassment.* Such a procedure should: (1) be managed by a neutral third party, (2) ensure that complaints are dealt with promptly and thoroughly, (3) protect and fairly treat victims, and (4) ensure that alleged harassers are fairly treated.

- *When it has been determined that sexual harassment has taken place, take corrective actions as soon as possible.* These actions can vary depending on the severity of the harassment. When harassment is extensive, prolonged over a period of time, of a quid pro quo nature, or severely objectionable in some other manner, corrective action may include firing the harasser.

- *Provide sexual harassment education and training to organizational members, including managers.* Managers at DuPont, for example, developed DuPont's "A Matter of Respect" program to help educate employees about sexual harassment and stop it from happening.

Barbara Orser, a researcher with the Conference Board of Canada, noted that most large Canadian organizations have harassment policies on paper. However, many lack a clear resolution process.

Chapter Summary

SUMMARY AND REVIEW

WHAT ARE ETHICS? Ethics are moral principles or beliefs about what is right or wrong. These beliefs guide people in their dealings with other individuals and groups that have an interest in the situation at hand (stakeholders) and provide a basis for deciding whether behaviour is right and proper. Many organizations have a formal code of ethics derived mainly from societal ethics, professional ethics, and the individual ethics of the organization's top managers. Managers can apply ethical standards to help themselves decide on the proper way to behave toward organizational stakeholders.

SOCIAL RESPONSIBILITY Social responsibility refers to a manager's duty to make decisions that nurture, protect, enhance, and promote the well-being of stakeholders and society as a whole. Managers generally take one of four approaches to the issue of socially responsible behaviour: obstructionist, defensive, accommodative, or proactive. Promoting ethical and socially responsible behaviour is a major managerial challenge.

MANAGING AN INCREASINGLY DIVERSE WORKFORCE Diversity refers to differences among people due to age, gender, race, ethnicity, religion, sexual orientation, socio-economic background, and capabilities or disabilities. Effectively managing diversity is an ethical obligation that makes good business sense. Diversity can be managed effectively if top management is committed to principles of distributive and procedural justice, values diversity as a source of competitive advantage, and is willing to devote organizational resources to increasing employees' diversity awareness and diversity skills. Managers need to ensure that they and their subordinates appreciate the value that diversity brings to an organization, understand why diversity should be celebrated rather than ignored, and have the ability to interact and work effectively with men and women who are physically challenged or are of a diverse race, age, gender, ethnicity, nationality, or sexual orientation.

SEXUAL HARASSMENT Two forms of sexual harassment are quid pro quo sexual harassment and hostile work environment sexual harassment. Steps that managers can take to halt sexual harassment include developing and communicating a sexual harassment policy endorsed by top management, using fair complaint procedures; ensuring prompt corrective action when harassment occurs; and training and educating organizational members on sexual harassment.

Roles in Contrast: Considerations

MANAGERS	EMPLOYEES
I should determine whether the decisions I make are consistent with my organization's values, whether I would be comfortable if my decisions were reported in the newspaper, and whether those whom I respect and trust would approve of my decisions.	I should determine whether the decisions I make are consistent with my organization's values, whether I would be comfortable if my decisions were reported in the newspaper, and whether those whom I respect and trust would approve of my decisions.
Many people believe that organizations should be socially responsible and that the benefits outweigh the costs. I would need to consider what issues might be of particular importance for my organization.	Socially responsible organizations often ask their employees to do volunteer work, and engage in community activities. This is something I might investigate.
I should develop an environment where people feel comfortable exchanging different perspectives and points of view.	I should be aware of biases and stereotypes on my part that might make people uncomfortable.

MANAGEMENT in Action

Management in Action
Topics for Discussion and Action

1. Why is it important for people and organizations to behave ethically?

2. Ask a manager to describe an instance of ethical behaviour that she or he observed and an instance of unethical behaviour. What caused these behaviours, and what were the outcomes?

3. Search business magazines such as *Report on Business* or *Canadian Business* for an example of ethical or unethical behaviour, and use the material in this chapter to analyze it.

4. Which stakeholder group should managers be most concerned about when they decide on their approach to social responsibility? Why?

5. Discuss why violations of the principles of distributive and procedural justice continue to occur in modern organizations. What can managers do to support these principles in their organizations?

6. Discuss an occasion when you may have been treated unfairly because of stereotypical thinking. What stereotypes were applied to you? How did they result in your being unfairly treated?

7. Choose a *National Post* Business 500 company not mentioned in the chapter. Conduct library research to determine what steps this organization has taken to effectively manage diversity and eliminate sexual harassment.

Building Management Skills

SOLVING DIVERSITY-RELATED PROBLEMS

Think about the last time that you (1) were treated unfairly because you differed from a decision maker on a particular dimension of diversity, or (2) observed someone else being treated unfairly because that person differed from a decision maker on a particular dimension of diversity. Then answer these questions.

1. Why do you think the decision maker acted unfairly in this situation?

2. In what ways, if any, were biases, stereotypes, or overt discrimination involved in this situation?

3. Was the decision maker aware that he or she was acting unfairly?

4. What could you or the person who was treated unfairly have done to improve matters and rectify the injustice on the spot?

5. Was any sexual harassment involved in this situation? If so, what kind was it?

6. If you had authority over the decision maker (e.g., if you were his or her manager or supervisor), what steps would you take to ensure that the decision maker no longer treated diverse individuals unfairly?

Management for You

Identify an issue that presented an ethical dilemma for you. Analyze the situation and the stakeholders involved using the three models of ethics. How did the decision you made compare to the decisions you might arrive at using these models? The next time you faced an ethical dilemma, would you consider using just one of these models? Why or why not?

Small Group Breakout Exercise

WHAT IS ETHICAL BEHAVIOUR?

Form groups of 3 to 5 people, and appoint 1 group member as the spokesperson who will communicate your findings to the class when called on by the instructor. Then discuss the following scenario.

You are the managers of the functions of a large hospital, and you have been charged with the responsibility to develop a code of ethics to guide the members of your organization in their dealings with stakeholders. To guide you in creating the ethical code, do the following.

1. Discuss the various kinds of ethical dilemmas that hospital employees—doctors, nurses, pharmacists—may encounter in their dealings with stakeholders such as patients or suppliers.
2. Identify a specific behaviour that the 3 kinds of hospital employees mentioned in Item 1 might exhibit, and characterize the behaviour as ethical or unethical.
3. Based on this discussion, identify 3 standards or values that you will incorporate into your personal ethical code to help yourself determine whether a behaviour is ethical or unethical.

Managing Ethically

The state of California is having an energy crisis. You are a manager at BC Hydro. You have discovered that it is possible to anticipate periods of severe power shortages and plan for them by letting your reservoirs rise overnight and then opening them to create hydroelectricity. Electricity can thus be produced inexpensively but sold for a premium. Your research of the law suggests that this behaviour would be consistent with what is allowed under the rules of the electricity trade marketplace. Is this good business, or is this unethical behaviour?

Exploring the World Wide Web

SPECIFIC ASSIGNMENT

This exercise looks at how Procter & Gamble Canada describes its stance on workplace diversity. Explore Procter & Gamble's website (www.pg.com/canada) and, in particular, look under the section "Working at P&G Canada" to find the company's statement on diversity, and some words of wisdom. Also look under the section "Introduction to Procter & Gamble" located on the home page and follow the links to find out about the company's purpose, values, and principles.

1. In what ways does Procter & Gamble show its support for a diverse workforce?
2. To what extent do you think the company's policies on diversity contribute to supporting Procter & Gamble's purpose, values, and principles?

GENERAL ASSIGNMENT

Search for a company website that has an explicit statement of the company's approach to workplace diversity. What is its approach, and how does this approach support the company's main goals?

You're the Management Consultant

STRIVING FOR ETHICS IN AN ADVERTISING AGENCY

Sam Bernstein was recently hired as the vice-president for human resources in an advertising agency. The agency has been plagued by accusations that certain employees engage in unethical conduct ranging from conflicts of interest with clients to using expense accounts for family vacations. While a task force composed of high-ranking managers in the agency has been formed to investigate these allegations and propose a course of action to deal with any lapses in ethical conduct on the part of the agency's employees, Bernstein has been asked to proactively address the issue of organizational ethics as part of his objectives for the year. He has found out that the agency does not have an actual code of ethics. Whenever legal questions arise, the agency employs freelance attorneys for advice, and if necessary, action. The organization does have policies forbidding conflicts of interest with clients and use of expense accounts for personal travel. However, top management is concerned that these policies are too vague and not taken seriously.

As an expert in ethics, Bernstein has come to you for help. He doesn't know where to start to address this seemingly huge task, or even what he should be striving to accomplish. Advise Bernstein.

MANAGEMENT CASE

Is It Right to Use Child Labour?

In recent years, the number of Canadian and US companies that buy their inputs from low-cost foreign suppliers has been growing, and concern about the ethics associated with employing young children in factories has been increasing. In Pakistan, children as young as six work long hours in deplorable conditions to make rugs and carpets for export to Western countries. There are children in poor countries throughout Africa, Asia, and South America who work in similar conditions.

Opinions about the ethics of child labour vary widely. Some believe that the practice is totally reprehensible and should be outlawed on a global level. Another view, championed by *The Economist* magazine (www.economist.com), is that, while nobody wants to see children working in factories, citizens of rich countries need to recognize that in poor countries a child is often the family's only breadwinner. Thus, denying children employment would cause whole families to suffer, and correcting one wrong (child labour) might produce a greater wrong (poverty). Instead, *The Economist* favours regulating the conditions under which children are employed and hopes that over time, as poor countries become richer, the need for child employment will disappear.

Many Canadian and US retailers buy their clothing from low-cost foreign suppliers, and managers in these companies have had to take their own ethical stance on child labour. In Chapter 1, we discussed how Mountain Equipment Co-op (www.mec.ca) was facing demands from some of its members to discontinue manufacturing clothing in China. Wal-Mart

Canada (www.walmart.com) has been criticized for its policy of doing business with third-party suppliers—such as Hampton Industries, Sutton Creations, Global Gold, Stretch-O-Rama, Cherry Stix and By Design—that import goods from Myanmar (Burma), which engages in forced labour, including that of children. In defence of the company's actions, Wal-Mart Canada spokesman Andrew Pelletier noted, "We have a policy we are looking at, of monitoring vendors sourcing from other countries. . . . For other corporations, our expectation is that they would take their direction from the Canadian government, that's what we would recommend they would do."

At present, the Canadian government, unlike the US government, does not have regulations governing the use of child labour in foreign countries by Canadian companies.

Questions

1. Should Canada develop regulations governing the use of child labour in foreign countries by Canadian companies?
2. You are the manager of a company considering setting up a factory in a foreign country that allows child labour. What would be the benefits to your company for deciding not to use child labour?
3. You are the manager of a company considering setting up a factory in a foreign country that allows child labour. Should you simply rely on the laws of that country when deciding what to do about child labour? Why or why not?

MANAGEMENT CASE ——————————————— IN THE NEWS

From the Pages of *Canadian Business* Stuff Your Gold Watch

In many cultures, the elderly are respected, even revered, by younger generations. Senior citizens are trusted advisers, admired for their wisdom. Sir Winston Churchill was 66 when he first became prime minister of Britain in 1940 and 81 when he retired. South Africans elected 76-year-old Nelson Mandela as president in 1994.

Our very own prime minister is old enough to have been collecting old age pension cheques at 24 Sussex for a couple of years now, and senior citizen CEOs run some of the country's most powerful corporations: Ken Thomson is 76; Jimmy Pattison is 71; Izzy Asper is 67. I guess owning the joint helps, because what do the rest of us schmoes get for our 65th birthdays? Not reverence, that's for sure—more like a swift kick in the ass as we carry the vestiges of our working lives out the door.

It's really quite shocking that, in a time when human rights laws protect child pornography buffs, it hasn't occurred to lawmakers that mandatory retirement is a blatant display of discrimination. Of course some professions, such as law enforcement and the military, necessarily retire their employees at a younger age. But time

and time again, the Supreme Court of Canada has ruled in favor of forced retirement. (An interesting side note: the mandatory retirement age for Supreme Court justices is 75, not 65.)

Not all the top judges have agreed, however, that mental competence, adaptability and energy magically disappear once you hit the arbitrary age of 65. Madame Justice Claire L'Heureux-Dubé, herself 73, wrote about the case of a Vancouver doctor who was forced to resign his hospital post: "One is no less competent the day after one's 65th birthday, than the day before. Fundamentally it is a question of personal dignity and fairness."

Not all the provinces are guilty. In Quebec and Manitoba, employers have to come up with rationale other than age for giving employees their pink slips. In the US, it's illegal to force anyone into retirement as long as they are willing and able to work. But the Ontario Human Rights Commission (OHRC), perhaps prompted by the United Nations' declaration of 1999 as the International Year of Older Persons, only recently decided to launch a public policy review into age discrimination. "Aging," notes an OHRC discussion paper released this past July, "is something that all individuals who do not die prematurely will eventually experience."

And with premature deaths at an all-time low—senior citizens now account for 12% of Canada's population and by 2030 will make up 23%—mandatory retirement is bound to be a big-ticket issue. Ontario's provincewide public consultations will be held in November, and you can bet a fair number of its 1.5 million seniors will descend on the hearings, along with more than a few aging boomers indignant—and terri- fied—at the thought of being unceremoniously given the boot in a few years.

And rightly so. While more and more people are retiring to lives of leisure in their 50s, many don't have enough savings or large enough pen- sions to allow them to quit at 65. Others simply don't relish the thought of 15 or 20 years of arts and crafts or helping kiddies cross the street at lunchtime.

There are, of course, a couple of valid argu- ments in favor of mandatory retirement. A

favorite of youngsters everywhere is that forced retirement makes way for a whole new genera- tion to move up the ranks. Don't pull out the knit- ting needles just yet, though: according to a study conducted by the Canada Pension Plan, people are far more likely to die in their first year of retirement than in subsequent years. But with a full 41 working years stretching ahead of me, I'm willing to take my chances. Any seniors out there willing to swap their CPP cheques for an exciting new career in journalism, give me a call.

Source: D. Calleja, "Stuff Your Gold Watch: Why Hasn't It Occurred to Canadian Lawmakers That Forced Retirement is Blatant Discrimination?" *Canadian Business*, October 16, 2000, p. 131.

Questions

1. How are different stakeholder groups affected by mandatory retirement policies?
2. What kinds of ethical issues does mandatory retirement raise?

CHAPTER 4

THE MANAGER AS A DECISION MAKER

Learning Objectives

1. Differentiate between programmed and nonprogrammed decisions, and explain why nonprogrammed decision making is a complex, uncertain process.

2. Describe the six steps that managers should take to make the best decisions.

3. Explain how cognitive biases can affect decision making and lead managers to make poor decisions.

4. Identify the advantages and disadvantages of group decision making, and describe techniques that can improve it.

5. Explain the role that organizational learning and creativity play in helping managers to improve their decisions.

6. Differentiate between data and information, and list the characteristics of useful information.

Roles in Contrast: Questions

MANAGERS	EMPLOYEES
How do I make good decisions?	How do I make good decisions?
What biases might affect the decisions I make?	What biases might affect the decisions I make?
What can I do to make sure that the teams I lead do not make faulty decisions?	If I'm working on a team, what must I do to make sure the team doesn't make poor decisions?

A Case in Contrast

A Tale of Two Decisions at Calling Systems International

August 14, 2003, 9:30 a.m.: Sharon Eastman glances one last time at her presentation slides. "This new product proposal looks unbeatable," she thinks. "I've covered every base and looked at the issue from every angle. I know the technology; I can handle any question that Redland throws at me. He has to approve this."

Sharon Eastman is the marketing manager at Calling Systems International (CSI), a 350-employee, Halifax-based company that makes computer-controlled telephone calling and answering equipment. CSI was the creation of Alan Redland, an energetic man with a domineering personality and seemingly unlimited faith in his own vision. In its first five years, CSI has already made the *Profit* magazine list of the 100 fastest-growing small companies in Canada. Eastman was hired 12 months ago as a newly minted MBA. Before getting her MBA, she worked as a computer systems engineer for IBM.

Eastman's responsibilities at CSI include looking for new product opportunities. She has found what she thinks is a gem. Three months ago, she was visiting the credit collection department of a large bank to which CSI was trying to sell its equipment. The staff of this department try to collect bad debts from delinquent loan customers over the phone. Eastman noticed that many of the employees spent an enormous amount of time dialing numbers, getting busy signals, or getting no answer at all. Little of their time was spent actually talking to delinquent customers.

Finding the right way to frame your arguments is an important part of the process of convincing others to take your ideas seriously and support your position. Managing the perceptions of individuals and groups is an important part of the decision-making process.

"Wow," thought Eastman. "It should be possible to predict how often a telephone operator gets no answer, or a busy signal. We could also find out how long, on average, an operator talks to someone over the phone. We could write a computer program that takes this into account. This program could be used to control an automated dialing system. We could use a mathematical algorithm to predict when an operator will come free and how much time will be needed to get a 'live' person on the other end of the phone line. The dialing system—let's call it a predictive dialing system—would then know when to dial in order to match up a free telephone operator with a 'live' person. The result? Telephone operators would waste no time dialing, listening to busy signals, or getting no answer. Brilliant!"

Over the past three months, Eastman had worked on the idea with two engineers at CSI. She concluded that the idea not only was technically feasible, but could be a commercial gold mine. Now she has to present her new product proposal to CSI's executive committee, which includes Redland and three other senior managers. They could OK the idea or kill it.

August 14, 2003, 11:00 a.m.: An angry and dejected Eastman bursts through her office door and flings her presentation slides against the opposite wall. Her office mate, Ron, looks up and raises an eyebrow. "I gather things didn't go too well, then?"

"It was awful, a complete disaster. Redland has just come back from some seminar at the University of Alberta on the information superhighway. He has decided that the company has to become involved in that area. He thinks he has seen the future, and we should be part of it. He wouldn't even let me explain my idea. He just kept asking me, 'How does this fit with our information superhighway strategy?'" What information superhighway strategy? I didn't know we had one!

"Didn't any of the other executive committee members speak up on your behalf?" asks Ron. "I know that Mike Kidder and John Matsuka were excited by the idea. They told me so."

"They just hung on every word Redland said and nodded in agreement," replies Eastman.

March 12, 2004, 9:30 a.m.: Eastman sits waiting for the summons from the executive team. "Here we go again, Predictive Dialing Systems Proposal Mark II," thinks Eastman. "It should be different this time."

Eastman's faith is not ill-placed. Two months earlier, CSI was taken over by a large telecommunications company. Redland and the rest of the executive team left and have been replaced by a team of managers from the acquiring company.

March 12, 2003, 3:30 p.m.: An exhausted-looking Eastman stumbles into her office and slumps into her chair.

"Where on earth have you been?" asks Ron.

"With the new executive team," replies Eastman. "They have been quizzing me for hours about the project. We didn't stop for lunch. They wanted to know absolutely everything. How big was the potential market? How much would the predictive dialing system sell for? What were my data sources? What were my assumptions? They challenged every single assumption I made! How did I know that this was technically feasible? How long would it take to get a predictive dialing system to market? And on and on and on!"

"And?" asks Ron.

Eastman takes a deep breath, "And they liked the idea, but not enough to give me the go-ahead yet. They want some specific information on various topics. But they said that if things do check out, they will invest in the project. And if they do, I get to head it!"[1]

OVERVIEW

The *Case in Contrast* describes how two different management teams approached the same decision—namely, whether to pursue Sharon Eastman's new product idea. The first team dismissed Eastman's proposal without exploring it because it was not the brainchild of Alan Redland, the company's domineering CEO. The second management team not only listened to Eastman but bombarded her with questions, vigorously challenging the assumptions behind her proposal to see if it could work.

The purpose of this chapter is to examine how managers make decisions, and to explore how individual, group, and organizational factors affect the quality of the decisions they make and thus determine organizational performance. We discuss the nature of managerial decision making and examine some models of the decision-making process that help reveal the complexities of successful decision making. Then we outline the main steps of the decision-making process; in addition, we explore the biases that may cause capable managers to make poor decisions both as individuals and as members of a group. Finally, we examine how managers can promote organizational learning and creativity and improve the quality of their decision making. By the end of this chapter, you will understand the crucial role that decision making plays in creating a high-performing organization.

THE NATURE OF MANAGERIAL DECISION MAKING

Think About It

Mountain Equipment Co-op Struggles to "Build Green" in Montreal

When Vancouver-based Mountain Equipment Co-op (MEC) decided to built a new store in Montreal, using ecologically friendly practices, managers did not consider all the obstacles. Consequently, when it tried to carry out the decision, the company ran into unexpected problems.[2]

Recycled building materials are not easily available in Montreal, and contractors do not favour their use. "We had contractors quoting us cheaper prices for new material, which is really counterintuitive," said architect Andrew Todd of Montreal-based Duschenes & Fish/DFS Inc., one of the firms that won the building contract for the Montreal store. Another architect on the project noted that if MEC wants to use salvaged material, it should not be thinking about a new building.

Question
1. How do decisions affect a person's ability to act?
2. What kinds of decisions do people make?

When Belinda Stronach took over as CEO of Magna International in February 2001, one of her first major decisions was to realign the company along five product lines: Magna Steyr, Tesma, Intier, Decoma, and Cosma. This structure gave each management team greater flexibility and autonomy in making decisions. Stronach's father, Frank Stronach (shown with her here), founded the company.

Every time a manager acts to plan, organize, direct, or control organizational activities, he or she makes a stream of decisions. In opening a new restaurant, for example, managers have to decide where to locate it, what kinds of food to provide to customers, what kinds of people to employ, and so on. In Chapter 1, where we considered Mintzberg's managerial roles, we described four decision-making roles managers have. We also noted in Chapter 1 the importance of managers having conceptual skills. Decision making is a basic part of every task in which a manager is involved, and in this chapter we study how decisions are made.

Decision making is the process by which managers analyze the options facing them and make determinations, or decisions, about specific organizational goals and courses of action. Good decisions result in the selection of suitable goals and courses of action that increase organizational performance; bad decisions result in lower performance.

decision making
The process by which managers analyze the options facing them and make decisions about specific organizational goals and courses of action.

Programmed and Nonprogrammed Decision Making

Regardless of the specific decision that a manager is responsible for, the decision-making process is either programmed or nonprogrammed.[3]

Programmed Decision Making

programmed decision making
Routine, virtually automatic decision making that follows established rules or guidelines.

Programmed decision making is a routine, virtually automatic process. Programmed decisions are decisions that have been made so many times in the past that managers have been able to develop rules or guidelines to be applied when certain situations inevitably occur. Programmed decision making takes place for much of the day-to-day running of an organization, for example when the office manager needs to order supplies. He or she can rely on long-established decision rules such as these:

- *Rule 1.* When the storage shelves are three-quarters empty, order more copy paper.

- *Rule 2.* When ordering paper, order enough to fill the shelves.

This decision making is called "programmed" because the office manager does not need to make judgments constantly about what should be done. Managers can develop rules and guidelines to regulate all kinds of routine organizational activities.

Nonprogrammed Decision Making

nonprogrammed decision making
Nonroutine decision making that occurs in response to unusual, unpredictable opportunities and threats.

Nonprogrammed decision making occurs when there are no ready-made decision rules that managers can apply to a situation. Why are there no rules? The situation is unexpected, and managers lack the information they would need to develop rules to cover it. Examples of nonprogrammed decision making include decisions to invest in a new kind of technology, to develop a new kind of product, to launch a new promotional campaign, to enter a new market, or to expand internationally. In the remainder of this chapter, when we talk about decision making, we are referring to nonprogrammed decision making because it is the kind that causes the most problems for managers.

COMPARING DECISION-MAKING MODELS

Think About It

Head or Heart Decision?

The Warm Company, with headquarters in Seattle, Washington, manufactures products for quilters, crafters, and stitchers throughout the world.[4] In early 2003, owners Jim and Evelyn Chumbley of Seattle decided to close their East Coast warehouse and distribution facility in Fletcher, North Carolina. The Chumbleys had already bought a building 140 kilometres south of Seattle for the new facility. All that was left to do was notify North Carolina employees that they were welcome to relocate to Seattle if they wanted to keep their jobs, and the Chumbleys planned to do this in person. At the plant, they met Peggy Watkins, a 38-year-old woman who has Down's syndrome and had worked at the plant for three years. Watkins was devastated by the news. She would not be able to move to Seattle on her own, and feared losing her job and her friends at the plant. After speaking with both Watkins and her manager, Barry Brown, the Chumbleys "made a decision of the heart instead of the profit margin."

Questions

1. What does the Chumbleys' decision tell us about engaging in decision making?
2. How should managers make nonprogrammed decisions and how do they make the decisions?

The rational and the administrative decision-making models reveal many of the assumptions, complexities, and pitfalls that affect decision making. We compare and contrast them below.

The Rational Model

rational decision-making model

A prescriptive approach to decision making based on the idea that the decision maker can identify and evaluate all possible alternatives and their consequences and rationally choose the most suitable course of action.

optimum decision

The best decision in light of what managers believe to be the most desirable future consequences for their organization.

One of the earliest models of decision making, the **rational model** (also referred to as the *classical model*), is prescriptive, which means that it specifies how decisions *should* be made. Managers using the rational model make a series of simplifying assumptions about the nature of the decision-making process (see Figure 4.1). The idea behind the rational model is that once managers recognize the need to make a decision, they should be able to make a complete list of *all* alternatives. For each alternative they should be able to list all consequences, and they can then make the best choice. In other words, the rational model assumes that managers have access to *all* the information they need to make the **optimum decision**, which is the best decision possible in light of what they believe to be the most desirable future consequences for their organization. Furthermore, the rational model assumes that managers can easily list their own preferences for each alternative and rank them from least to most preferred in order to make the optimum decision. When we look back at the Chumbleys' decision, however, it's clear that until they actually travelled to North Carolina, they did not have the information about the employee with Down's syndrome and did not realize that their preference for an ethical decision was higher than their preference for an economic decision.

The Administrative Model

James March and Herbert Simon were aware that many managers are similar to the Chumbleys, and do not have access to all the information they need to make a decision. Moreover, they pointed out that even if all information were readily available, many managers would lack the mental or psychological ability to absorb and evaluate it correctly. As a result, March and Simon developed the

Figure 4.1 | The Rational Model of Decision Making

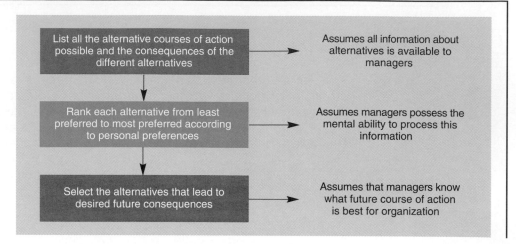

List all the alternative courses of action possible and the consequences of the different alternatives	→	Assumes all information about alternatives is available to managers
Rank each alternative from least preferred to most preferred according to personal preferences	→	Assumes managers possess the mental ability to process this information
Select the alternatives that lead to desired future consequences	→	Assumes that managers know what future course of action is best for organization

administrative model

An approach to decision making that explains why decision making is basically uncertain and risky and why managers usually make satisficing rather than optimum decisions.

administrative model of decision making to explain why decision making is always basically an uncertain and risky process—and why managers can rarely make decisions in the manner prescribed by the rational model. The administrative model is based on three important concepts: *bounded rationality, incomplete information,* and *satisficing.*

Bounded Rationality

bounded rationality

Cognitive limitations that constrain one's ability to interpret, process, and act on information.

March and Simon pointed out that human decision-making capabilities are bounded by people's limitations in their ability to interpret, process, and act on information.[5] **Bounded rationality** thus describes the situation in which the number of alternatives and the amount of information are so great that it is difficult for the manager to evaluate everything before making a decision.[6] This may explain the Chumbleys' need to reconsider their decision once they received more information.

Incomplete Information

uncertainty

Unpredictability.

Even if managers did have an unlimited ability to evaluate information, they still would have incomplete information. Information is incomplete because the full range of decision-making alternatives is unknowable in most situations, and the consequences are uncertain.[7] Because of **uncertainty**, the probabilities of alternative outcomes cannot be determined, and future outcomes are *unknown.* Another reason why information may be incomplete is that much of the information that managers have at their disposal is **ambiguous information**. Its meaning is not clear—it can be interpreted in multiple and often conflicting ways.[8]

ambiguous information

Information that can be interpreted in multiple and often conflicting ways.

Satisficing

satisficing

Searching for and choosing acceptable, or satisfactory, ways to respond to problems and opportunities, rather than trying to make the best decision.

Faced with bounded rationality and incomplete information, March and Simon argue, managers do not try to discover every alternative. Rather, they use a strategy known as **satisficing**, exploring a limited sample of possible alternatives.[9] When managers satisfice, they search for and choose acceptable, or satisfactory, ways to respond to problems and opportunities, rather than trying to make the best decision.[10] For instance, the purchasing manager for Ford Canada would likely engage in a limited search to identify supplies. This might involve asking a limited number of suppliers for their terms, trusting that they are representative of suppliers in general, and making a choice from that set. Although this course of action is

intuition

Ability to make sound decisions based on past experience and immediate feelings about the information at hand.

judgment

Ability to develop a sound opinion based on one's evaluation of the importance of the information at hand.

reasonable from the point of view of the purchasing manager, it may mean that a potentially superior supplier is overlooked.

March and Simon pointed out that managerial decision making is often more art than science. In the real world, managers must rely on their intuition and judgment to make what seems to them to be the best decision in the face of uncertainty and ambiguity.[11] **Intuition** is a person's ability to make sound decisions based on past experience and immediate feelings about the information at hand. **Judgment** is a person's ability to develop a sound opinion because of the way he or she evaluates the importance of the information available in a particular context. For reasons that we examine later in this chapter, both intuition and judgment are often flawed and can result in poor decision making.

STEPS IN THE DECISION-MAKING PROCESS

The conditions for an optimum decision rarely exist. To help managers make the best decision possible, researchers have developed a step-by-step model of the decision-making process and the issues and problems that managers confront at each step. There are six steps that managers should consciously follow to make a good decision (see Figure 4.2).[12] We review them in the remainder of this section.

Recognize the Need for a Decision

The first step in the decision-making process is to recognize the need for a decision. Managers face decisions that arise both internally and as a consequence of changes

Figure 4.2 | Six Steps in Decision Making

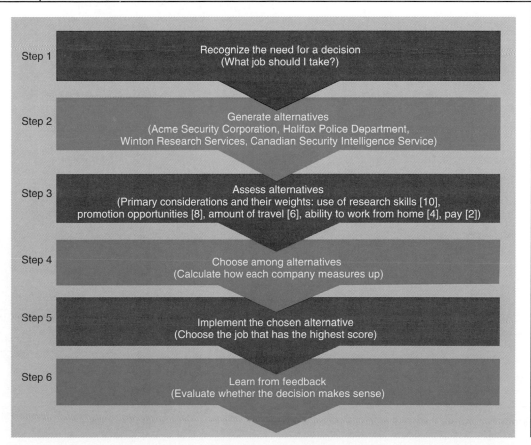

Step 1 — Recognize the need for a decision (What job should I take?)

Step 2 — Generate alternatives (Acme Security Corporation, Halifax Police Department, Winton Research Services, Canadian Security Intelligence Service)

Step 3 — Assess alternatives (Primary considerations and their weights: use of research skills [10], promotion opportunities [8], amount of travel [6], ability to work from home [4], pay [2])

Step 4 — Choose among alternatives (Calculate how each company measures up)

Step 5 — Implement the chosen alternative (Choose the job that has the highest score)

Step 6 — Learn from feedback (Evaluate whether the decision makes sense)

in the external environment.[13] Once a decision maker recognizes the need to make a decision, the person will need to diagnose the issue or problem, in order to determine all the factors underlying the problem. In the Chumbleys' case, the downturn in the economy prompted the need to evaluate whether they should continue operating both an East Coast and a West Coast facility.

Generate Alternatives

Having recognized the need to make a decision, a manager must generate a set of feasible alternative courses of action to take in response to the opportunity or threat. The failure to properly generate and consider different alternatives is one reason why managers sometimes make bad decisions.[14] The Chumbleys likely generated a number of alternatives, including downsizing the North Carolina plant; investing even more money in it; and doing everything at their current West Coast facility.

Assess Alternatives

Once managers have listed a set of alternatives, they must evaluate the advantages and disadvantages of each one.[15] The key to a good assessment of the alternatives is being able to define the opportunity or threat exactly, and then specifying the criteria that *should* influence the selection of alternative ways of responding to the problem or opportunity.

One reason for bad decisions is that managers often fail to specify the criteria that are important in reaching a decision.[16] In general, successful managers use four criteria to evaluate the pros and cons of alternative courses of action (see Figure 4.3):

1. *Practicality.* Managers must decide whether they have the capabilities and resources to implement the alternative, and they must be sure that the alternative will not threaten the ability to reach other organizational goals.
2. *Economic feasibility.* Managers must decide whether the alternatives make sense economically and fit the organization's performance goals. Typically, man-

Figure 4.3 | General Criteria for Evaluating Possible Courses of Action

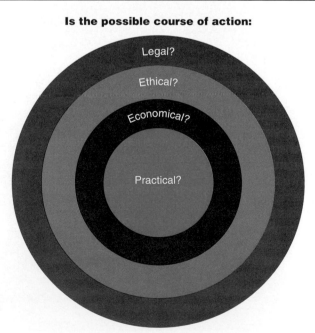

Is the possible course of action:

Legal?

Ethical?

Economical?

Practical?

agers perform a cost-benefit analysis of the various alternatives to determine which one is likely to have the best financial payoff.

3. *Ethicality.* Managers must ensure that a possible course of action is ethical and that it will not unnecessarily harm any stakeholder group. Many of the decisions that managers make may help some organizational stakeholders and harm others (see Chapter 3).

4. *Legality.* Managers must ensure that a possible course of action is legal and will not violate any domestic and international laws or government regulations.

For each of the possible alternatives that the Chumbleys considered, they might have applied the four criteria above. Some alternatives would have seemed more practical or economical, and they might not have been aware of any ethical problems with their decision.

Choose Among Alternatives

Once the set of alternative solutions has been carefully evaluated, the next task is to rank the various alternatives (using the criteria discussed in the previous section) and make a decision. When ranking alternatives, managers must be sure that all of the available information is brought to bear on the problem or issue at hand. Identifying all relevant information for a decision does not mean that the manager has complete information, however; in most instances, information is incomplete.

It is likely the Chumbleys determined that it would be more practical and economical to move all of the work to the Seattle area, and that is why they bought the new building. There was also nothing illegal about their decision. However, once they went to North Carolina to announce the decision to their employees, they were confronted with the ethical consequences of their decision. They had recently lost their own son, who was also disabled. At that point, the Chumbleys decided that ethical considerations should be given greater weight than economic considerations in their final decision.

The disastrous breakup of the Columbia space shuttle illustrates the importance of bringing all available information to bear on the decision-making process and making sure the alternative courses of action are evaluated using all relevant criteria.

Implement the Chosen Alternative

Once a decision has been made and an alternative has been selected, the alternative must be implemented and many subsequent and related decisions must be made. Although the need to make further decisions may seem obvious, many managers make the initial decision and then fail to act on it.[17] This is the same as not making a decision at all.

Managers often fail to get buy-in from those around them before making a decision. However, successful implementation requires participation. One study found that participation was used in only 20 percent of decisions, even though broad participation in decisions led to success 80 percent of the time. By contrast, the most common form of decision-making tactics, power or persuasion, used in 60 percent of decisions, are successful in only one of three decisions.[18]

To ensure that a decision is implemented, top managers must let middle managers participate in decisions, and then give them the responsibility to make the follow-up decisions necessary to achieve the goal. They must give middle managers enough resources to achieve the goal, and they must hold the middle managers accountable for their performance. If the middle managers succeed in implementing the decision, they should be rewarded; if they fail, they should be subject to sanctions.

Learn from Feedback

The final step in the decision-making process is learning from feedback. Managers who do not evaluate the results of their decisions do not learn from experience; instead, they stagnate and are likely to make the same mistakes again and again.[19] To avoid this problem, managers must establish a formal procedure for learning from the results of past decisions. The procedure should include these steps:

1. Compare what actually happened to what was expected to happen as a result of the decision.
2. Explore why any expectations for the decision were not met.
3. Develop guidelines that will help in future decision making.

Individuals who always strive to learn from past mistakes and successes are likely to continuously improve the decisions they make. The Chumbleys will still need to evaluate their decision, even though they have changed their original decision to close the North Carolina facility.

Tips for Managers

Managing the Decision-Making Process

1. Recognize that it is impossible for managers to make the optimum decision, and direct their actions toward making the best decision possible.

2. To make the best decision possible, learn to use intuition and judgment to uncover acceptable alternatives and to choose between them.

3. Constantly monitor changes in organizational performance and in the environmental forces to discover if there are any opportunities or threats that should be addressed.

4. Create a set of clearly defined criteria to frame opportunities and threats, and apply these criteria consistently.

5. Encourage managers at all levels to make problem solving a major part of their jobs and to generate as many feasible alternatives as possible.

6. Be aware of the role people's preferences and interests play in generating alternative courses of action, and learn how to manage coalitions to promote effective decision making.

7. Once an alternative course of action has been chosen, take steps to implement the decision. Request periodic updates on the situation from the managers responsible for implementing the chosen alternative.

8. Learn from your successes and mistakes and use this information to improve your next decision.

BIASES IN DECISION MAKING

Think About It

Turning Pestilence into Profit

When the mountain pine beetle struck millions of hectares of prime northern BC forests recently, the forestry industry viewed it as a disaster.[20] The beetle carries a fungus that stains the trees blue. "Nobody wants blue stain in their wood and just having a tree with something called a fungus is not to most people's liking," says Larry Pedersen, British Columbia's chief forester. The industry watched in alarm as Japan, its largest market, rejected the lumber. However, log-home builders Dean and Lori Gunderson, owners of Quesnel, BC-based Eagleye Precision Log Homes, did not let assumptions about customer biases get in their way. Instead, they discovered that when the blue-stained logs dry, they turn gold, creating a tiger-stripe motif to their log homes. They started marketing the logs to US clients. It turns out that Americans much prefer these logs over the noninfected logs. "It definitely gives us a market edge," says Lori Gunderson.

Questions
1. What kinds of biases do individuals have when making decisions?
2. How do these affect decision-making ability?

In the 1970s, two psychologists, Daniel Kahneman and Amos Tversky, suggested that because all decision makers are subject to bounded rationality, they tend to use **heuristics**, rules of thumb that simplify the process of making decisions.[21] Kahneman and Tversky argued that rules of thumb are often useful because they help decision makers make sense of complex, uncertain, and ambiguous information. Sometimes, however, the use of heuristics can lead to systematic errors in the way decision makers process information about alternatives and make decisions. **Systematic errors** are errors that people make over and over and that result in poor decision making. Because of cognitive biases, which are caused by systematic errors, otherwise capable managers may end up making bad decisions.[22] Four sources of bias that can negatively affect the way managers make decisions are prior hypotheses, representativeness, the illusion of control, and escalating commitment (see Figure 4.4).

heuristics
Rules of thumb that simplify decision making.

systematic errors
Errors that people make over and over again and that result in poor decision making.

Prior Hypothesis Bias

Decision makers who have strong prior beliefs about the relationship between two variables tend to make decisions based on those beliefs *even when presented with evidence that their beliefs are wrong*. In doing so, they are falling victim to **prior hypothesis bias**. Moreover, decision makers tend to seek and use information that is consistent with their prior beliefs and to ignore information that contradicts those beliefs. At Calling Systems International (CSI), profiled in the *Case in Contrast,* we saw CEO Alan Redland reject Sharon Eastman's new product proposal because it was not consistent with his prior beliefs about what CSI should be doing. Eagleye Precision Log Homes went against the prior hypothesis bias of the BC forest industry, however, and gained a market edge when it was able to sell the pine-beetle-infested lumber.

prior hypothesis bias
A cognitive bias resulting from the tendency to base decisions on strong prior beliefs even if evidence shows that those beliefs are wrong.

representativeness bias
A cognitive bias resulting from the tendency to generalize inappropriately from a small sample or from a single vivid case or episode.

Representativeness Bias

Many decision makers inappropriately generalize from a small sample or even from a single vivid case or episode. An interesting example of the **representativeness bias** occurred as more and more investors perceived that Amazon.com was going to be the next great business model and invested in dot-com companies

Figure 4.4 | **Sources of Cognitive Bias at the Individual and Group Levels**

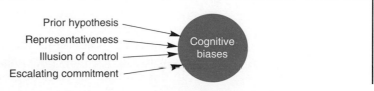

Eagleye Precision
Log Homes
www.eagleyeloghomes.
com

illusion of control
A source of cognitive bias resulting from the tendency to overestimate one's own ability to control activities and events.

that had no serious business plan. The investors made the mistake of thinking that marketing on the internet would be good for any new company. BC lumber producers had encountered Japanese buyers who rejected the pine-beetle-infested lumber, and assumed that this response was representative of all lumber buyers. Eagleye Precision Log Homes wisely challenged that bias.

Illusion of Control

Other errors in decision making result from the **illusion of control**, the tendency of decision makers to overestimate their ability to control activities and events. Top-level managers seem to be particularly prone to this bias. Having worked their way to the top of an organization, they tend to have an exaggerated sense of their own worth and are overconfident about their ability to succeed and to control events.[23] The illusion of control causes managers to overestimate the odds of a favourable outcome and, consequently, to make inappropriate decisions. For example, in the 1980s, Nissan was run by Katsuji Kawamata, an autocratic manager who thought he had the skills to run the car company alone. He made all the decisions—decisions that resulted in a series of spectacular mistakes, including changing the company's name from Datsun to Nissan—and Nissan's share of the North American market fell dramatically.

Escalating Commitment

escalating commitment
A source of cognitive bias resulting from the tendency to commit additional resources to a project even if evidence shows that the project is failing.

Having already committed significant resources to a course of action, some managers commit more resources to the project *even if they receive feedback that the project is failing.*[24] Feelings of personal responsibility for a project apparently bias the analysis of decision makers and lead to **escalating commitment**. They decide to increase their investment of time and money in a course of action and ignore evidence that it is illegal, unethical, uneconomical, or impractical (see Figure 4.3). Often, the more appropriate decision would be to "cut and run."

A tragic example of where escalating commitment can lead is the Columbia shuttle disaster. Apparently, managers were so anxious to keep the shuttle program on schedule that they ignored or discounted any evidence that falling debris might seriously compromise the shell of the shuttle. Thus, information about potential disaster was downplayed, even during the flight of the doomed shuttle.

Be Aware of Your Biases

How can managers avoid the negative effects of cognitive biases and improve their decision-making and problem-solving abilities? Managers must become aware of biases and their effects, and they must identify their own personal style of making decisions.[25] One useful way for managers to analyze their decision-making style is to review two decisions that they made recently—one that turned out well and one that turned out poorly. Problem-solving experts recommend that a manager start by determining how much time he or she spent on each of the decision-making steps, such as gathering information to identify the pros and cons of alternatives or ranking the alternatives, to make sure that sufficient time is being spent on each step.[26]

Another recommended technique for examining decision-making style is for managers to list the criteria they typically use to assess and evaluate alternatives—the heuristics (rules of thumb) they typically employ, their personal biases, and so on—and then critically evaluate the appropriateness of these different factors.

Many individual managers are likely to have difficulty identifying their own biases, so it is often advisable for managers to study their own assumptions by working with other managers to help expose weaknesses in their decision-making style. In this context, the issue of group decision making becomes important.

GROUP DECISION MAKING

Think About It

Kids Help Improve Decision Making at The BrainStore

When senior managers at Credit Suisse Group, one of Switzerland's top banks, wanted to phase out a passbook-savings plan that Swiss families had cherished for years, they could have made the decision themselves.[27] Instead, hoping that a group decision would yield a better outcome, the bank hired nine children to help five executives explore alternatives.

The executives were actually getting help from The BrainStore, an "idea factory" in Biel, Switzerland, which recognizes the importance of diversity in putting together creative ideas. It uses an international network of kids to help the company brainstorm for its most challenging projects. The cross-generational teams developed a set of raw ideas for Credit Suisse. The ideas then went through the remaining steps in The BrainStore assembly line: "compression (in which a team of in-house employees and outside experts sorts through ideas and picks out the best ones); testing (research and prototype); and finishing (marketing campaigns and positioning strategies)." Markus Mettler, one of the company's founders, suggests that it is this assembly-line process that keeps innovation flowing, by making sure that all parts of the decision-making process get carried out.

Question

1. Do groups make decisions differently than individuals?

The BrainStore
www.brainstore.com

Many, perhaps most, important organizational decisions are made by groups of managers rather than by individuals. Group decision making is superior to individual decision making in several respects. When managers work as a team to make decisions and solve problems, their choices of alternatives are less likely to fall victim to the biases and errors discussed previously. They are able to draw on the combined skills, competencies, and accumulated knowledge of group members, and thereby improve their ability to generate feasible alternatives and make good decisions. Group decision making also allows managers to process more information and to correct each other's errors. In the implementation phase, all managers affected by the decisions agree to cooperate. When a group of managers makes a decision, as opposed to one top manager making a decision and imposing it on subordinate managers, it's more probable that the decision will be implemented successfully.

Nevertheless, some disadvantages are associated with group decision making. Groups often take much longer than individuals to make decisions. Getting two or more managers to agree to the same solution can be difficult because managers' interests and preferences are often different. In addition, just like decision making by individual managers, group decision making can be undermined by biases. A major source of group bias is groupthink.

groupthink

A pattern of faulty and biased decision making that occurs in groups whose members strive for agreement among themselves at the expense of accurately assessing information relevant to a decision.

The Perils of Groupthink

Groupthink is a pattern of faulty and biased decision making that occurs in groups whose members strive for agreement among themselves at the expense of accurately assessing information relevant to a decision.[28] When individuals are subject to groupthink, they collectively embark on a course of action without developing appropriate criteria to evaluate alternatives. Typically, a group rallies around a strong individual and the course of action that the individual supports. Group members become blindly committed to that course of action without evaluating its merits. Commitment is often based on an emotional—rather than objective—assessment of the best course of action.

We have all seen the symptoms of the groupthink phenomenon:[29]

- *Illusion of invulnerability.* Group members become overconfident, and this enables them to take extraordinary risks.

- *Assumption of morality.* Group members believe that the group's objectives are morally right, and so they don't debate the ethics of their actions.

- *Rationalized resistance.* No matter how strongly the evidence may contradict their basic assumptions, group members rationalize that their assumptions are correct and the negative evidence is faulty.

- *Peer pressure.* Members who express doubts about any of the group's shared views are pressured to ignore their concerns and to support the group.

- *Minimized doubts.* Members who have doubts or hold differing points of view may keep silent about their misgivings and even minimize to themselves the importance of their doubts.

- *Illusion of unanimity.* If someone doesn't speak, it's assumed that he or she agrees with the group. In other words, silence becomes viewed as a "Yes" vote.

In the *Case in Contrast,* groupthink was probably at work when the first executive team at Calling Systems International, headed by Alan Redland, dismissed Sharon Eastman's new product proposal. Despite previously expressing support for Eastman's idea, two members of the executive team merely nodded their agreement with Redland when he criticized the proposal—a sure sign that pressures toward agreement were at work in this group. Pressures for agreement and harmony within a group have the unintended effect of discouraging individuals from raising issues that run counter to majority opinion.

There is considerable anecdotal evidence to suggest the negative implications of groupthink in organizational settings, but very little empirical work has been conducted in organizations on the subject of groupthink.[30] In fact, more recently, groupthink has been criticized for overestimating the link between the decision-making process and its outcome[31] and for suggesting that its effect is uniformly negative.[32] A study of groupthink in five large corporations reported that elements of groupthink may affect decision making differently. For instance, the illusion of vulnerability, the belief in inherent group morality, and the illusion of unanimity often led to greater team performance, counter to what the original groupthink proposals suggest.[33]

Improving Group Decision Making

A variety of steps can be taken to improve group decision making.[34] Managers should encourage group leaders to be impartial in their leadership, and actively seek input from all group members. Leaders should avoid expressing their own opinions in the early stages of discussion.

devil's advocacy
Critical analysis of a preferred alternative, made by a group member who plays the role of devil's advocate to defend unpopular or opposing alternatives for the sake of argument.

Another strategy to improve group decision making is to encourage one group member to play the role of devil's advocate. **Devil's advocacy** is a critical analysis of a preferred alternative to pinpoint its strengths and weaknesses before it is implemented (see Figure 4.5).[35] Typically, one member of the decision-making group plays the role of devil's advocate. The devil's advocate critiques and challenges the way the group evaluated alternatives and chose one over the others. The purpose of devil's advocacy is to identify all the reasons that might make the preferred alternative unacceptable after all. In this way, decision makers can be made aware of the possible perils of recommended courses of action.

Another way to improve group decision making is to promote diversity in decision-making groups.[36] Bringing together male *and* female managers, from various

Figure 4.5 | Devil's Advocacy

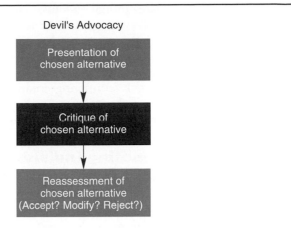

ethnic, national, and functional backgrounds, broadens the range of life experiences and opinions that group members can draw from as they generate, assess, and choose among alternatives. Moreover, diverse groups are sometimes less prone to groupthink because group members already differ from each other and thus are less subject to pressures for uniformity. The Swiss firm The BrainStore takes advantage of diversity to improve decision making by mixing children and managers together, as we saw earlier.

ORGANIZATIONAL LEARNING AND CREATIVITY

Think About It

BMW Employees Celebrate Their Creativity

In March 2003, some of the employees at BMW's Mini factory in Oxford, England had to decide between go-karting for an evening or making a trip to a comedy club.[37] The employees, who worked in the Mini body shop, had come up with the month's best money-saving idea for the factory: The company could save more than $250,000 by halving the number of soundproofing foam blocks put in roofs. The evening out was to be the reward for their suggestion.

BMW's German managers and the plant's union leaders are united in a common goal: improving employee creativity to cut costs. The annual employee bonus of $570 is tied not only to meeting standard quality and productivity targets, but also to each employee generating an average of three ideas and saving $1,750 a year. In 2002, the voluntary suggestion scheme generated 10 339 ideas (more than 2 per employee) and saved the plant more than $13 billion.

Question
1. How can managers improve the decision-making environment, so that more creative alternatives are brought forward?

organizational learning
The process through which managers seek to improve employees' desire and ability to understand and manage the organization and its task environment.

The quality of managerial decision making ultimately depends on innovative responses to opportunities and threats. How can managers increase their ability to make nonprogrammed decisions—decisions that will allow them to adapt to, modify, and even drastically alter their task environments so that they can continually increase organizational performance? The answer: by encouraging organizational learning.[38]

Organizational learning is the process through which managers seek to improve employees' desire and ability to understand and manage the organization

learning organization
An organization in which managers try to maximize the ability of individuals and groups to think and behave creatively and thus maximize the potential for organizational learning to take place.

creativity
A decision maker's ability to discover original and novel ideas that lead to feasible alternative courses of action.

and its task environment so that employees can make decisions that constantly raise organizational effectiveness.[39] A **learning organization** is one in which managers do everything possible to maximize the ability of individuals and groups to think and behave creatively and thus maximize the potential for organizational learning to take place. At the heart of organizational learning is **creativity**, the ability of a decision maker to discover original ideas that lead to feasible alternative courses of action. Encouraging creativity among managers is such a pressing organizational concern that many organizations hire outside experts to help them develop programs to train their managers in the art of creative thinking and problem solving.

Promoting Individual Creativity

Research suggests that individuals are most likely to be creative when certain conditions are met. First, people must be given the opportunity and freedom to generate new ideas. Creativity declines when managers look over the shoulders of talented employees and try to "hurry up" a creative solution. How would you feel if your boss said you had one week to come up with a new product idea to beat the competition? Creativity results when individuals have an opportunity to experiment, to take risks, and to make mistakes and learn from them. Companies that have a lot of innovation foster that through their formal structure and expectations. For instance, in one recent year, 3M launched more than 200 new products. To encourage this level of development, managers are told that 30 percent of sales are expected to come from products less than four years old.[40]

Once managers have generated alternatives, creativity can be encouraged by providing employees with constructive feedback so that they know how well they are doing. Ideas that seem to be going nowhere can be eliminated and creative energies refocused in other directions. Ideas that seem promising can be promoted, and help from other managers can be obtained as well.[41]

It is also important for top managers to stress the importance of looking for alternative solutions and to visibly reward employees who come up with creative ideas. Being creative can be demanding and stressful. Employees who believe that they are working on important, vital issues will be motivated to put forth the high levels of effort that creativity demands.

Despite the importance of fostering creativity in organizations, in a recent survey of 500 CEOs, only 6 percent felt that they were doing a great job at managing their creative people. John MacDonald, co-founder of Richmond, BC-based MacDonald Dettwiler & Associates Ltd. (MDA), suggests that "managing creative people is a bit like riding herd on a thousand prima donnas. They are all highly individual people who don't follow the herd, so managing them is a challenge."[42]

Promoting Group Creativity

To encourage creativity at the group level, organizations can make use of group problem-solving techniques that promote creative ideas and innovative solutions. These techniques can also be used to prevent groupthink and to help managers and employees uncover biases. Here, we look at three group decision-making techniques: *brainstorming*, the *nominal group technique*, and the *Delphi technique*.

Brainstorming

brainstorming
A group problem-solving technique in which individuals meet face to face to generate and debate a wide variety of alternatives from which to make a decision.

Brainstorming is a group problem-solving technique in which individuals meet face to face to generate and debate a wide variety of alternatives from which to make a decision.[43] Generally, from 5 to 15 individuals meet in a closed-door session and proceed like this:

- One person describes in broad outline the problem the group is to address.

- Group members then share their ideas and generate alternative courses of action.

- As each alternative is described, group members are not allowed to criticize it, and everyone withholds judgment until all alternatives have been heard. One member of the group records the alternatives on a flip chart.

- Group members are encouraged to be as innovative and radical as possible. Anything goes; and the greater the number of ideas put forth, the better. Moreover, group members are encouraged to "piggyback"—that is, to build on each other's suggestions.

- When all alternatives have been generated, group members debate the pros and cons of each and develop a short list of the best alternatives.

Brainstorming is very useful in some problem-solving situations—for example, when trying to find a new name for a perfume or for a model of car. But sometimes individuals working alone can generate more alternatives. The main reason, it seems, is the **production blocking** that occurs in groups because members cannot always simultaneously make sense of all the alternatives being generated, think up additional alternatives, and remember what they were thinking.[44]

Nominal Group Technique

To avoid production blocking, the **nominal group technique** is often used. It provides a more structured way of generating alternatives in writing and gives each individual more time and opportunity to generate alternative solutions. The nominal group technique is especially useful when an issue is controversial and when different people might be expected to champion different courses of action. Generally, a small group of people meets in a closed-door session and adopts the following procedures:

- One person outlines the problem to be addressed, and 30 or 40 minutes are allocated for each group member to write down ideas and solutions. Group members are encouraged to be innovative.

- Individuals take turns reading their suggestions to the group. One person writes the alternatives on a flip chart. No criticism or evaluation of alternatives is allowed until all alternatives have been read.

- The alternatives are then discussed, one by one, in the sequence in which they were first proposed. Group members can ask for clarifying information and critique each alternative to identify its pros and cons.

- When all alternatives have been discussed, each group member ranks all the alternatives from most preferred to least preferred, and the alternative that receives the highest ranking is chosen.[45]

Delphi Technique

Both nominal group technique and brainstorming require people to meet together to generate creative ideas and engage in joint problem solving. What happens if people are in different cities or in different parts of the world and cannot meet face to face? Videoconferencing is one way to bring distant people together to brainstorm. Another way is to use the **Delphi technique**, a written approach to creative problem solving.[46] The Delphi technique works like this:

- The group leader writes a statement of the problem and a series of questions to which participating individuals are to respond.

- The questions are sent to the managers and departmental experts who are most knowledgeable about the problem; they are asked to generate solutions and mail the questionnaire back to the group leader.

Delphi technique
www.learn-usa.com/
acf001.htm

production blocking
A loss of productivity in brainstorming sessions due to the unstructured nature of brainstorming.

nominal group technique
A decision-making technique in which group members write down ideas and solutions, read their suggestions to the whole group, and discuss and then rank the alternatives.

Delphi technique
A decision-making technique in which group members do not meet face to face but respond in writing to questions posed by the group leader.

- The group leader records and summarizes the responses. The results are then sent back to the participants, with additional questions to be answered before a decision can be made.

- The process is repeated until a consensus is reached and the most suitable course of action is clear.

Tips for Managers

Improving Decision Making

1. Be aware of the operation of cognitive biases and test the assumptions managers use to frame problems, select alternatives, and make decisions.
2. Recognize the advantages of using diverse decision-making groups.
3. Use devil's advocacy to guard against groupthink.
4. Take all possible steps to promote creativity at the individual and group level and make a technique such as brainstorming a routine part of the problem-solving process.

INFORMATION AND THE MANAGER'S JOB

Think About It

How Much Should an Airline Ticket Cost?

When Calgary-based WestJet Airlines Ltd. tries to determine how many tickets from each fare class should be assigned to future flight schedules, it analyzes historical booking patterns on every flight. "We have seasonality models, event models, time-of-day models, and all of those run through our forecast every night and are optimized nightly based on that day's sales," said Brenda Crockstad, WestJet's director of revenue and scheduling.[47] These models help the airline know how many seats it must sell at the lowest and the highest prices to make a profit.

Question
1. What tools do managers have to help them make decisions?

In order for managers to generate and assess their alternatives in making a decision, they need access to data and information both from inside the organization and from external stakeholders. When deciding how to price a seat sale, for example, the WestJet marketing manager needs information about how consumers will react to different prices. She needs information about unit costs because she does not want to set the price below the costs of flying. She also needs data about how many people (and what class of flyer–business or vacation) are likely to fly on any given day. WestJet also needs information about competitors' prices, since its pricing strategy should be consistent with its competitive strategy. Some of this information can come from outside the organization (e.g., from consumer surveys) and some from inside the organization (information about flight costs comes from operations). As this example suggests, managers' ability to make effective decisions rests on their ability to acquire and process information.

Information is not the same as data.[48] **Data** are raw, unsummarized, and unanalyzed facts such as volume of sales, level of costs, or number of customers. **Information** is data that are organized in a meaningful fashion, such as in a graph showing the change in sales volume or costs over time. The distinction between

data
Raw, unsummarized, and unanalyzed facts.

information
Data that are organized in a meaningful fashion.

data and information is important because one of the uses of information technology is to help managers transform data into information in order to make better managerial decisions. **Information technology** is the means by which information is acquired, organized, stored, manipulated, and transmitted. Rapid advances in the power of information technology—specifically, through the use of computers—are having a fundamental impact on information systems and on managers and their organizations.[49]

information technology
The means by which information is acquired, organized, stored, manipulated, and transmitted.

Attributes of Useful Information

When we evaluated the rational decision-making process earlier in this chapter, we noted that it is often difficult for individuals to have access to all possible information needed to make a decision. While information is still collected from individuals, much information is now accessed through information technology (websites, databases, and the like). Regardless of how it is acquired, individuals need to decide whether the information is useful. Four factors determine the usefulness of information: quality, timeliness, completeness, and relevance (see Figure 4.6).

Quality

Accuracy and reliability determine the quality of information.[50] The greater the accuracy and reliability are, the higher is the quality of information. For an information system to work well, the information that it provides must be of high quality. If managers conclude that the quality of information provided by their information system is low, they are likely to lose confidence in the system and stop using it. Alternatively, if managers base decisions on low quality information, poor and even disastrous decision making can result. For example, the partial meltdown of the nuclear reactor at Three Mile Island in Pennsylvania during the 1970s was the result of poor information caused by an information system malfunction. The information system indicated to engineers controlling the reactor that there was enough water in the reactor core to cool the nuclear pile, although this was in fact not the case. The consequences included the partial meltdown of the reactor and the release of radioactive gas into the atmosphere.

Timeliness

Information that is timely is available when it is needed for managerial action, not after the decision has been made. In today's rapidly changing world, the need for

Figure 4.6 | Factors Affecting the Usefulness of Information

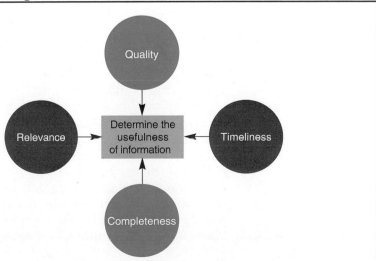

real-time information
Frequently updated
information that reflects
current conditions.

timely information often means that information must be available on a real-time basis.[51] **Real-time information** is information that reflects current conditions. In an industry that experiences rapid changes, real-time information may need to be updated frequently. Airlines use real-time information on the number of flight bookings and competitors' prices to adjust their prices on an hour-to-hour basis to maximize their revenues.

Completeness

Information that is complete gives managers all the information they need to exercise control, achieve coordination, or make an effective decision. We have already noted that because of uncertainty, ambiguity, and bounded rationality, managers have to make do with incomplete information.[52] One of the functions of information systems is to increase the completeness of the information that managers have at their disposal.

Relevance

Information that is relevant is useful and suits a manager's particular needs and circumstances. Irrelevant information is useless and may actually hurt the performance of a busy manager who has to spend valuable time determining whether information is relevant. Given the massive amounts of information that managers are now exposed to and humans' limited information-processing capabilities, the people who design information systems need to make sure that managers receive only relevant information.

Chapter Summary

SUMMARY AND REVIEW

THE NATURE OF MANAGERIAL DECISION MAKING Programmed decisions are routine decisions that are made so often that managers have developed decision rules to be followed automatically. Nonprogrammed decisions are made in response to situations that are unusual or unique; they are nonroutine decisions.

COMPARING DECISION-MAKING MODELS The rational model of decision making assumes that decision makers have complete information, are able to process that information in an objective, rational manner, and make optimum decisions. The administrative model suggests that managers are boundedly rational, rarely have access to all the information they need to make optimum decisions, and consequently satisfice and rely on their intuition and judgment when making decisions.

STEPS IN THE DECISION-MAKING PROCESS When making decisions, managers should take these six steps: recognize the need for a decision, generate alternatives, assess alternatives, choose among alternatives, implement the chosen alternative, and learn from feedback.

BIASES IN DECISION MAKING Most of the time, managers are fairly good decision makers. On occasion, however, problems result because human judgment is adversely affected by the operation of cognitive biases that result in poor decisions. Cognitive biases are caused by systematic errors in the way decision makers process information and make decisions. Sources of these errors include prior hypotheses, representativeness, the illusion of control, and escalating commitment. Managers should undertake a personal decision audit to become aware of their biases in order to improve their decision making.

GROUP DECISION MAKING Many advantages are associated with group decision making, but there are also several disadvantages. One major source of poor decision making is groupthink. Afflicted decision makers collectively embark on a dubious course of action without questioning the assumptions that underlie their decision. Managers can improve the quality of group decision making by using techniques such as devil's advocacy and by increasing diversity in the decision-making group.

ORGANIZATIONAL LEARNING AND CREATIVITY Organizational learning is the process through which managers seek to improve employees' desire and ability to understand and manage the organization and its task environment so that employees can make decisions that constantly raise organizational effectiveness. Managers must take steps to promote organizational learning and creativity at the individual and group levels to improve the quality of decision making.

INFORMATION AND THE MANAGER'S JOB Computer-based information systems are central to the operation of most organizations. By providing managers with high quality, timely, relevant, and relatively complete information, properly implemented information systems can improve managers' ability to coordinate and control the operations of an organization and to make effective decisions. Moreover, information systems can help the organization to achieve a competitive advantage through their beneficial impact on productivity, quality, innovation, and responsiveness to customers.

Roles in Contrast: Considerations

MANAGERS	EMPLOYEES
Following the six steps in decision making can help me to make sure that I try to collect several alternatives, rather than relying on the first alternative that I think of.	Following the six steps in decision making can help me to make sure that I try to collect several alternatives, rather than relying on the first alternative that I think of.
When making decisions, I need to be aware that biases enter into them, and that I may not be perceiving all information correctly.	When making decisions, I need to be aware that biases enter into them, and that I may not be perceiving all information correctly.
Try to make sure that someone on the team will take the devil's advocate role, or take that role on personally, to make sure that all alternatives are carefully explored.	I need to be aware that groups can become so wrapped up in team spirit that members may fail to question each other as they engage in decision making.

MANAGEMENT in Action

Topics for Discussion and Action

1. What are the main differences between programmed decision making and nonprogrammed decision making?
2. In what ways do the rational and administrative models of decision making help managers appreciate the complexities of real-world decision making?
3. Ask a manager to recall the best and the worst decisions he or she ever made. Try to determine why these decisions were so good or so bad.
4. Why do capable managers sometimes make bad decisions? What can individual managers do to improve their decision-making skills?

5. In what kinds of groups is groupthink most likely to be a problem? When is it least likely to be a problem? What steps can group members take to ward off groupthink?
6. What is organizational learning, and how can managers promote it?
7. To be useful, information must be timely, relevant, of high quality, and as complete as possible. Describe the negative impact that a tall management hierarchy, when used as an information system, can have on these desirable attributes.
8. Ask a manager to describe the main kinds of information systems that he or she uses on a routine basis at work.

Building Management Skills

HOW DO YOU MAKE DECISIONS?

Pick a decision you made recently that has had important consequences for you. This decision could be about which college or university to attend, which major to select, whether to take a part-time job, or which part-time job to take. Using the material in this chapter, analyze the way in which you made the decision.

1. Identify the criteria you used, either consciously or unconsciously, to guide your decision making.
2. List the alternatives you considered. Were these all possible alternatives? Did you unconsciously (or consciously) ignore some important alternatives?
3. How much information did you have about each alternative? Did you base the decision on complete or incomplete information?
4. Try to remember how you reached the decision. Did you sit down and consciously think

through the implications of each alternative, or did you make the decision on the basis of intuition? Did you use any rules of thumb to help you make the decision?
5. In retrospect, do you think that your choice of alternative was shaped by any of the cognitive biases discussed in this chapter?
6. Having answered those five questions, do you think in retrospect that you made a reasonable decision? What, if anything, might you do to improve your ability to make good decisions in the future?

Management for You

Suppose your uncle said that he would help you purchase an existing business. How would you go about making a decision on which business you might purchase, and whether you should take him up on his offer?

Small Group Breakout Exercise

BRAINSTORMING

Form groups of 3 or 4 people, and appoint 1 member as the spokesperson who will communicate your findings to the whole class when called on by the instructor. Then discuss the following scenario.

You and your partners are trying to decide which kind of restaurant to open in a centrally located shopping centre that has just been built in your city. The problem confronting you is that the city already has many restaurants that provide different kinds of food in all price ranges. You have the resources to open any type of restaurant. Your challenge is to decide which type is most likely to succeed.

Use the brainstorming technique to decide which type of restaurant to open. Follow these steps.

1. As a group, spend 5 or 10 minutes generating ideas about the alternative kinds of restaurants that you think will be most likely to succeed. Each group member should be as innovative and creative as possible, and no suggestion should be criticized.
2. Appoint one group member to write down the alternatives as they are identified.
3. Spend the next 10 or 15 minutes debating the pros and cons of the alternatives. As a group, try to reach a consensus on which alternative is most likely to succeed.
4. After making your decision, discuss the pros and cons of the brainstorming method, and decide whether any production blocking occurred.
5. When called on by the instructor, the spokesperson should be prepared to share your group's decision with the class, as well as the reasons why you made your decision.

Managing Ethically

In the late 1990s, IBM announced that it had fired the three top managers of its Argentine division because of their involvement in a scheme to secure a $340-million contract for IBM to provide and service the computers of one of Argentina's largest state-owned banks. The three executives paid $19 million of the contract money to a third company, CCR, which paid about $8 million to fake companies. This $8 million was then used to bribe the bank executives who agreed to give IBM the contract.

The bribes were not necessarily illegal under Argentine law. Moreover, the three managers argued that all companies have to pay bribes to get new business contracts in Argentina and that they were doing nothing that managers in other companies were not also doing. Is paying bribes ethical or unethical under these circumstances? If bribery is common in a particular country, what effect would this likely have on the country's economy and culture?

Exploring the World Wide Web

SPECIFIC ASSIGNMENT

This exercise examines the decisions facing Brampton, Ontario-based Nortel Networks Limited with the plummet in stock prices that happened throughout 2001 and 2002.

Scan Nortel's website (www.nortelnetworks.com) to get a feel for this innovative company. In particular, from the home page click on "Corporate Information," and "News and Events," and read the stories about current decisions being made at Nortel.

1. What opportunities and threats do Nortel and Frank Dunn, the CEO and president, currently face?
2. What kinds of decisions does Dunn need to make at the present time?

GENERAL ASSIGNMENT

Search for a website that describes a company whose managers have just made a major decision. What was the decision? Why did they make it? How successful has it been?

You're the Management Consultant

DECISION MAKING IN THE OIL FIELD

Michael Silverstein is a top manager who was recently hired by an oil field services company in Alberta to help them respond more quickly and proactively to potential opportunities in their market. He has been on the job eight months and reports to the chief operating officer (COO), who reports to the CEO. Thus far, he has come up with three initiatives he carefully studied, thought were noteworthy, and proposed and justified to the COO. The COO seemed cautiously interested when Silverstein presented the proposals and each time indicated he would think about them and discuss them with the CEO because considerable resources were involved. Each time, Silverstein never heard back from the COO and when a few weeks passed, he casually asked the COO if there was any news on the proposal in question. For the first proposal, the COO said, "We think it's a good idea but the timing is off. Let's shelve it for the time being and reconsider it next year." For the second proposal, the COO said, "Mike [the CEO] reminded me that we tried that two years ago and it wasn't well received in the market. I am surprised I didn't remember it myself when you first described the proposal but it came right back to me once Mike mentioned it." For the third proposal, the COO simply said, "We're not convinced it will work."

Silverstein has come to you for advice. He believes that his three proposed initiatives are viable ways to seize opportunities in the marketplace, yet he cannot proceed with any of them. Moreover, with each proposal he has invested a considerable amount of time, and he has even worked to bring others on board to support the proposals just to have them shot down by the CEO. When he interviewed for the position, both the COO and the CEO claimed they wanted an outsider to help them "step out of the box and innovate," yet his experience to date has just been the opposite. As an expert in decision making, you are the person he has come to for advice.

Questions

1. Use the steps of the decision-making model to develop a set of recommendations for Silverstein.
2. What should Silverstein do?

MANAGEMENT CASE ━━━━━━━━━━━━━━ IN THE NEWS

From the Pages of the *National Post* CP Wants to Be Leaner, Meaner: To Sell off Core Business

Canadian Pacific Ltd. is looking to divest at least one of its five core businesses this year, says David O'Brien, the company's chairman, president and chief executive.

During a conference call with analysts to discuss year-end results yesterday, Mr. O'Brien said the conglomerate is determined to reduce the range of its businesses, but he did not elaborate on how this would be done.

"I would have to say that our highest priority within the next 12 months is to further narrow the focus of Canadian Pacific, so that would be strategic priority number one," he said.

Investors have long complained CP suffers from a holding company discount in which the market value of the conglomerate is lower than the value of the parts individually.

For example, analysts say that CP's 91% stake in PanCanadian Petroleum has a market value of $8 billion, while CP itself has a market capitalization of $13.4 billion. The rail unit, Canadian Pacific Railway Co., is valued at $4 billion to $5 billion by some analysts, leaving its extensive coal, hotel and shipping arm with negligible stock market value.

Mr. O'Brien disputed analyst methods of reckoning the value of the individual units in a November interview. He said the discount is exaggerated and is really only 12%. However, he did concede at the time that something has to go.

"We're obviously not going to build five global businesses, we don't have the financial capacity to do that nor the intention. But we do think we can build a couple of global businesses," he said.

Figuring out what CP might keep or sell has become a parlour game for analysts and other industry observers.

Most agree the railway is a likely candidate for divestiture because Mr. O'Brien himself has said it is too small to be a buyer in the expected coming consolidation of the railway industry in North America.

Yesterday, he quashed rumours that CP was contemplating a sale of the unit to Canadian National Railway Co. "We have not had any discussions with CN, are not having any discussions with respect to a merger or sale to CN, nor are we contemplating a sale to any other party," he said.

Seizing on comments made by Mr. O'Brien in the past that CP has a bias toward energy and hotels, many analysts expect shipping and the railway units will be put on the block.

Mr. O'Brien cautioned against such speculation in November. However, he also conceded at the time that energy and hotels offer the best growth opportunities for the company.

Source: P. Fitzpatrick, "CP Wants to Be Leaner, Meaner: To Sell off Core Business," *Financial Post (National Post)*, January 23, 2001, pp. C1, C8.

Questions

1. Evaluate O'Brien's actions in terms of the six-step decision-making process described in this chapter (see Figure 4.2).
2. Do you think O'Brien might be suffering from any of the cognitive biases described in the chapter? Which ones?
3. Do you think O'Brien has charted the right course for Canadian Pacific? What new opportunities and threats might be on the horizon?

MANAGEMENT CASE

IN THE NEWS

From the Pages of *Fortune* How Disney Keeps Ideas Coming

Starting with *The Little Mermaid*, a string of animated blockbusters has earned the Walt Disney Co. some US$5 billion since 1989. By any count, that's a tribute to how Disney not only sates its own notorious appetite for ever fatter profits but also gets the best out of that often-prickly-but-you-can't-live-without-'em bunch of folks, "the creatives." Most important, Disney sees to it that good ideas keep coming from all directions and that movies meet their deadlines. Peter Schneider, 45, president of feature animation, tells how a Gong Show for all his staffers—not to mention Ping-Pong with CEO Michael Eisner, who knows how to lose a game—helps the process.

How does a Gong Show get you the best ideas? We have people thinking about what we should do next all the time. But lots of other people in the building, including secretaries, want to present their ideas too. So three times a year they get to do just that, pitching what they think would make a good animated film, to me, Michael Eisner, Roy Disney, and my executive VP, Tom Schumacher.

Isn't that a pretty scary audience? Well, people with ideas get some help from their co-workers. Development helps them shape their pitch, for instance, so that it can be presented in three to five minutes, and coaches them on things such as the sort of visuals they could use. And if you're scared to death, someone else will hold your hand when you're up there. On the day of the Gong Show, it's very formal. The four of us all sit at a table and the room is full of people with ideas they want to submit. That way everybody gets to hear all of the ideas. It's not as though you're pitching alone. There's a group supporting you. We usually have about 40 presenters. That morning we pick names at random, so there's no advance order, but each person knows when it's his or her turn.

Still, it must be tough for people to get up and say what they think to Michael Eisner. That's key, though. You have to create an environment where people feel safe about their ideas. And you do that by setting the example. Senior management has to take on the responsibility of saying, "Michael, you're wrong." When people see us saying that, it gives them permission to say it too.

Once all the ideas are presented, the four of us talk about which ones we liked and what aspects we liked about some of the others. Somebody may have a great concept, but the story may not be very good. Or somebody may have a great title. What we can't do is say, "Oh, that's fabulous. Great pitch, guys!" and when they leave, mumble, "What an idea! That was awful!" You must have immediate communication and not worry about people's egos and feelings and how to do it gently enough. You have to tell people why an idea didn't work. We don't pull our punches. If you do that enough, and people don't get fired or demoted, they begin to understand that no matter how good, bad, or indifferent the idea, it can be expressed, accepted, and thought about.

What films came out of the Gong Show? Most of Disney's animated features, in fact. In the case of *Hercules*, an animator came up with the central idea that a man is judged by his inner strength and not his outer strength. The title was also his idea, but we didn't go for his story line. In the end that came from the two guys who became the directors of the film.

Did the guy with the original idea get paid for it? If we buy the pitch, the presenter usually gets what we'd pay for a first treatment. [Schneider would not give specifics, but a US$20 000 payment, spread over the period between an accepted pitch and a movie's release, is not unusual.]

How does a good idea become a business? First we come up with a core value for each story. I hate calling anything a mission statement, but I suppose it could be called that. The core value puts process in creativity. It's written down, and we all talk about it. It's not mysterious or ethereal. It's a value that we hang on to in terms of judging whether we're doing a good job. Are we telling the story we agreed to tell? You can't manage anything that doesn't have agreed-upon goals and direction.

How do you reach an agreement? It's a very collective approach to our work. We spend a lot of time in meetings arguing, discussing, and trying to come to a consensus. For instance, there was a lot of initial debate about what story we were telling with *The Hunchback of Notre Dame*. People thought we could never make it work. So we went back to the book and asked questions. What was the fundamental value of the book? What could the story be? What should it be? We discussed what changes we were going to make to have it tell our tale. As everybody gave their input, the debate moved along a little bit and changed. We eventually decided that our story would be about discovering self-value.

But there's a time to talk and a time to start making the film. Yes, and that's the dilemma. As soon as you make the process concrete, it's wrong—but you have to lock things up or you can't go forward. You want to keep things in flux, in change, in chaos, until everybody says, "Gosh, that's exactly right." At the same time, there has to be a system and a certain amount of expectation. You have to say, "Within these boundaries, you will create. This is the budget. This is as big as it gets. These are your limitations. Make it work within this framework." And then be open to the judgment of, "My God, the framework's not right. Let's change it."

Do deadlines help you draw boundaries and do they play a role in managing creativity? They're a key ingredient to creativity. If you let people work on blank canvases with no rules, they tend to think too much. A deadline says, "By five o'clock tomorrow, you will have this up on storyboard, good, bad, or indifferent"—because we'll all come in and talk about it. We'll have something to react to. It'll spark the next idea.

Who sets the deadlines? Who's in charge? It's unclear who really is in charge of our process. Certainly the directors and the producers are the day-to-day point people. But there's a lot of give and take with Michael, Roy, Tom, and myself. The four of us are always asking if we're telling the story, if it's correct, if it's good. It's the dialogue that makes it work. At the end of the day, I think the idea of Disney animation is in charge. There's never really a possessiveness in terms of a particular person. I think you can assign it to a group of people.

But there must be some sort of hierarchy? I'm a very big believer in hierarchy, one that is not too structured. I don't think you can create things without it. When I first came here ten years ago, it was very flat. There was no real acknowledgment in the animation ranks of who was good and who was not so good. Now it's very clear who the top five people in our business are. It gives people a sense of what they're progressing toward creatively.

The other kind of hierarchy is clearly that you have directors, an art director, a head of background. Each of these people is charged with leadership in terms of their troops. By and large we try to choose someone who is a great manager and a great artist. Those are very hard skills to find together. There has to be a certain sense of judgment, of quality, of speed, and the ability to say, "This is not good enough, not fast enough. You can do more. I expect more." Or to say, "Take your time. This is really important. Go slow." A real sense of judgment and an ability to communicate it.

How much autonomy do you give those who lead a Disney project? It's about putting the pieces together to allow people to do their job. It's about people clicking. So you want leadership to pick leadership. You want directors to pick their own art directors, the art directors to pick their head of background, heads of background to pick their own crew. You want people to have a sense of being chosen and wanted on a picture, not assigned, transferred, or exiled to it. You want people to say, "God, they want me."

How often can you do that? Seventy-five percent of the time. The other times we arrogantly say, even to directors, "Just do it." On one of our most successful projects, we told the director to shut up and do it. He was a very talented man but a bit indecisive in terms of where he wanted to go with his career. He didn't know if it was the right project. I said to him, "You've

been offered to direct a major animated movie. Do it." He said, "But I don't think I like this and that." "Then change it," I said, "Get in there and start working." He did, and he became ecstatic about the work. But it was the process of it, not that he came in saying, "I know what to do with this movie." It was the process: Going to work, drawing the drawing, talking about it, arguing about it, fighting about it, redoing it, being there.

But aren't you always going to have tension between the production side of the business and the creative side? Always is right. But it's very healthy. Production's job is to ask whether every decision is worth it. We recently discussed making a small change at the end of *Hunchback*. We were in our last weeks, and the final four shots didn't quite fire off. We were talking about 30 feet of film, which is a significant change. Production said, "Guys, it's 30 feet." And we said, "Yeah, but it doesn't work." They finally agreed, but we didn't go with our first choice, which was time-consuming and expensive, and figured out a way to make the change faster and for less money.

People are getting more comfortable with the idea that this is not about us and them. One of our managers organized a Ping-Pong tournament during lunch hours last year, and the winners played a final game with Michael Eisner and [president] Mike Ovitz. They said, "Oh, my God, Michael Eisner's playing Ping-Pong in our building. Wow, I'm important." I'm not sure they say that directly. But where else would the CEO be playing Ping-Pong with an hourly artist? The big guys lost the game, which goes to show people didn't feel they had to let Eisner win. The lines of hierarchy are so blurred that it makes no difference who you are to get access.

Source: J. McGowan, "How Disney Keeps Ideas Coming," *Fortune*, April 1, 1996, pp. 131–33.

Questions

1. How does the Walt Disney Company try to encourage its employees to be creative and innovative?
2. How would you describe Disney's approach to decision making?

CHAPTER 5

THE MANAGER AS A PLANNER AND STRATEGIST

Learning Objectives

1. Describe the three steps of the planning process.

2. Explain the relationship between planning and strategy.

3. Explain the role of planning in predicting the future and in mobilizing organizational resources to meet future contingencies.

4. Outline the main steps in SWOT analysis.

5. Differentiate among corporate-, business-, and functional-level strategies.

6. Describe the vital role that strategy implementation plays in determining managers' ability to achieve an organization's mission and goals.

Roles in Contrast: Questions

MANAGERS	EMPLOYEES
Do I need to plan?	Is planning really necessary?
Why are vision and mission statements important?	How might strategic planning help me?
What do I need to think about in creating a strategy for my department?	Why is knowing my company's strategy important to me?

A Case in Contrast

Gerald Pencer Starts a Cola War

Coca-Cola (www.coca-cola.com) and Pepsi-Cola (www.pepsi.com) are household names worldwide. In 1995, together they controlled more than 70 percent of the global soft-drink market and more than 75 percent of the US soft-drink market. Their success can be attributed in part to the overall strategy that Coca-Cola and PepsiCo developed to produce and promote their products. Both companies decided to build global brands by manufacturing the soft-drink concentrate that gives cola its flavour and then selling the concentrate in syrup form to bottlers throughout the world. Coca-Cola and PepsiCo charge the bottlers a premium price for the syrup; they then invest part of the proceeds in advertising to build and maintain brand awareness. The bottlers are responsible for producing and distributing the actual cola. They add carbonated water to the syrup, package the resulting drink, and distribute it to vending machines, supermarkets, restaurants, and other retail outlets.

The bottlers leave all the advertising to Coca-Cola and PepsiCo. In addition, the bottlers must sign an exclusive agreement that prohibits them from distributing competing cola brands. A Coke or Pepsi bottler cannot bottle any other cola drink. This strategy has two major advantages for Coca-Cola and PepsiCo. First, it forces bottlers to enter into exclusive agreements, which create a high barrier to entry into the industry; any potential competitors that might want to produce and distribute a new cola product must create their own distribution network rather than use the existing network. Second, the large amount of money spent on advertising (in 2000, Coca-Cola spent $2.55 billion, and PepsiCo $1.95 billion) to develop a global brand name has helped Coca-Cola and PepsiCo differentiate their products so that consumers are more likely to buy a Coke or Pepsi than a lesser-known cola. Moreover, brand loyalty allows both companies to charge a premium or comparatively high

Which of these colas tastes the best? That depends on your personal preferences. However, there is no doubt which cola costs the least—that produced by the Cott Corporation, which makes cola for organizations such as Safeway Canada and Loblaw's, including its President's Choice brand pictured here.

price for what is, after all, merely coloured water and flavouring. This differentiation strategy has made Coca-Cola and PepsiCo two of the most profitable companies in the world.

Cott Corporation
www.cott.com

With Coca-Cola and Pepsi the dominant players in the soft-drink market, new entrants had to devise a different strategy to compete. Toronto-based Cott Corporation came up with a new plan for competing in the cola market in the early 1990s and created a new strategy to attract customers. Cott's strategy was to produce a low-priced cola that it would manufacture and bottle. Cott would then sell the cola directly to major retail establishments (such as supermarket chains) as a private-label "house brand," thus bypassing the bottlers. Cott introduced this plan first in Canada and then quickly expanded into the United States because of interest in this product. Retailers are attracted to Cott's cola because its low cost allows them to make 15-percent more profit than they receive from selling Coke or Pepsi.[1]

To put this strategy into practice, Cott planned to do no advertising (so that it could charge a low price for its cola) and to take advantage of efficient national distribution systems that retailers such as Toronto-based Loblaw Companies Limited had created in recent years. This low-cost strategy enabled Cott to circumvent the barrier to entry created by the exclusive distribution agreements that Coca-Cola and PepsiCo have signed with their bottlers. Cott delivers its products to the regional distribution centres of stores such as Loblaw's, and then Loblaw's and others handle distribution and advertising from that point on.

Cott went on to supply an international network of bottlers by offering to sell cola concentrate for as little as one-sixth of the price that Coca-Cola and PepsiCo charge. In April 1994, for example, Cott launched a cola product in the United Kingdom for Sainsbury's, the biggest UK food retailer. Sold as "Sainsbury's Classic Cola," the product was priced 30-percent below Coke and Pepsi. Within four weeks of the launch, Cott had won a 60-percent share of all cola sales at Sainsbury's, equal to a quarter of the entire UK take-home cola market. Cott also scored big in its home province of Ontario, where Cott's private-label brands now account for 31 percent of the entire cola market. Building on this success, by mid-1994 Cott had signed supply agreements with 90 retail chains around the world, including major retailers in the United Kingdom, France, Spain, Japan, and the United States.

By 1999, Pepsi had virtually conceded the "cola war," relying instead on its Frito-Lay snack division. Even though Coke faced serious global problems in 1999, it lost no market share to Pepsi—it commands 54 percent internationally to Pepsi's 15 percent. Pepsi is stronger in the United States, but its market share was generally static at about 31 percent through the 1990s and continuing into 2002, while Coke's increased to 44 percent from 40 percent during the 1990s and has remained there since.[2] Although Cott went through two years of painful restructuring in 1998–2000, following the death of founder Gerald Pencer, the company remains the world's largest retailer-brand beverage supplier, with three core markets: Canada, the United States, and the United Kingdom.[3]

OVERVIEW

As the *Case in Contrast* suggests, there is more than one way to compete in an industry. To find a workable way to enter and compete in an industry, managers must study the way other organizations behave and identify their strategies. By studying the strategies of Coca-Cola and PepsiCo, Gerald Pencer was able to devise a strategy that allowed him to enter the cola industry and take on these global giants. So far, Cott has had considerable success.

In an uncertain competitive environment, managers must engage in thorough planning to find a strategy that will allow them to compete effectively. This chapter explores the manager's role both as planner and as strategist. We discuss the different elements involved in the planning process, including its three major steps: (1) determining an organization's mission and major goals, (2) choosing strategies to realize the mission and goals, and (3) selecting the appropriate way of organizing resources to put the strategies into practice. We also discuss scenario planning and SWOT analysis, important techniques that managers use to analyze their current situation. By the end of this chapter, you will understand the role managers play in the planning and strategy-making process to create high-performing organizations.

AN OVERVIEW OF THE PLANNING PROCESS

Think About It

Grocery Founder Lacks Planning

The mission of Saskatoon-based The Grocery Go-pher is very simple: "Our mission is to provide each customer with dependable, exceptional service. Purchasing quality grocery items and delivering them to your door (with a smile) is very important to us."

Though the mission was clear, Grocery Go-pher founder Tracy Jeffrey discovered the hard way that you need more than a mission to run a business. You also need a plan. Though her business did well, she regrets not having created a business plan when she started. "I really didn't understand what a business plan was for," she says.[4] "When you don't do a business plan, you end up in a situation where you're five years down the road and you don't know what your main objective as a business is." Tracy ended up selling the business she had run for six years to Kurt Kreuger when she finished her BComm in marketing at the University of Saskatchewan.

Questions
1. What is planning?
2. Why is it important?

planning

Identifying and selecting suitable goals and courses of action; one of the four principal functions of management.

strategy

A cluster of decisions about what goals to pursue, what actions to take, and how to use resources to achieve goals.

Planning, as we noted in Chapter 1, is a process that managers use to identify and select suitable goals and courses of action for an organization.[5] It is also one of the four managerial functions identified by French manager Henri Fayol. The organizational plan that results from the planning process details the goals of the organization and specifies how managers intend to attain those goals. The cluster of decisions and actions that managers take to help an organization attain its goals is its **strategy**. Thus, planning is both a goal-making and a strategy-making process.

In most organizations, planning is a three-step activity (see Figure 5.1). The first step is *determining the organization's vision, mission, and goals*.

Figure 5.1 | Three Steps in Planning

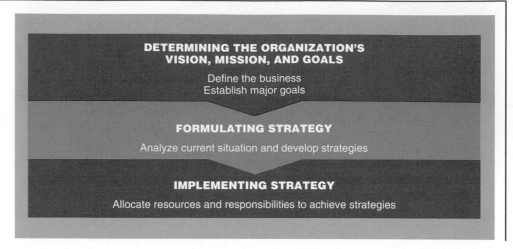

**DETERMINING THE ORGANIZATION'S
VISION, MISSION, AND GOALS**

Define the business
Establish major goals

FORMULATING STRATEGY

Analyze current situation and develop strategies

IMPLEMENTING STRATEGY

Allocate resources and responsibilities to achieve strategies

---

vision statement

A broad declaration of the big picture of the organization and/or a statement of its dreams for the future.

mission statement

A broad declaration of an organization's purpose that identifies the organization's products and customers, and distinguishes the organization from its competitors.

goal

A desired future outcome that an organization strives to achieve.

- A **vision statement** reveals the big picture of the organization, its dream for the future. When Bill Gates founded Microsoft, his vision was "a computer on every desk, in every home and in every office." Steve Ballmer, Microsoft's current CEO, sees this vision as insufficient in today's high-tech world, and has developed a new vision: "Empower people anytime, anywhere, on any device."[6]

- A **mission statement** is a broad declaration of an organization's overriding purpose; this statement is intended to identify an organization's products and customers, as well as to distinguish the organization in some way from its competitors.

- A **goal** is a desired future outcome that an organization strives to achieve. Generally the goals are set based on the vision and mission of the organization.

Even non-profit organizations have vision and mission statements. For instance, the vision statement of the Girl Guides of Canada is "Every girl in Canada wants to be and can be a member of Girl Guides of Canada–Guides du Canada: a vibrant, dynamic movement for girls, shaping a finer world." Their mission statement is "Girl Guides of Canada–Guides du Canada is a movement for girls, led by women. It challenges girls to reach their potential and empowers them to give leadership and service as responsible citizens of the world."

The second step is *formulating strategy*. Managers analyze the organization's current situation and then conceive and develop the strategies necessary to attain the organization's mission and goals.

The third step is *implementing strategy*. Managers decide how to allocate the resources and responsibilities required to implement the chosen strategies among individuals and groups within the organization.[7] In subsequent sections of this chapter, we look in detail at the specifics of each of these steps.

Before going on to learn more about planning, you might want to consider the words of Ron Zambonini, CEO of Ottawa based Cognos, who noted that planning went out of fashion during the dot-com years. Speaking of dot-com founders, he said: "You see them in California, and, to a certain extent, here too. They work . . . 90 hours a week, but the whole goal they have is not to build a business or a company. [All they really want is] someone to buy them out."[8] Unfortunately, many of those companies folded, and were not bought out. Planning may have helped them be more successful.

Who Plans?

General Electric
Company (GE)
www.ge.com

division
A business unit that has its
own set of managers and
functions or departments
and competes in a distinct
industry.

In large organizations, planning usually takes place at three levels of management: corporate, business or division, and department or functional. Figure 5.2 shows the link between the three steps in the planning process and these three levels. To understand this model, consider how General Electric (GE), a large organization that competes in many different businesses, operates.[9] GE has three main levels of management: corporate level, business level, and functional level (see Figure 5.2). At the corporate level are CEO and Chairman Jeffrey Immelt, three other top managers, and their corporate support staff. Below the corporate level is the business level. At the business level are the different divisions of the company. A **division** is a business unit that competes in a distinct industry; GE has more than 150 divisions, including GE Capital, GE Aircraft Engines, GE Lighting, GE

Figure 5.2 | **Levels of Planning at General Electric**

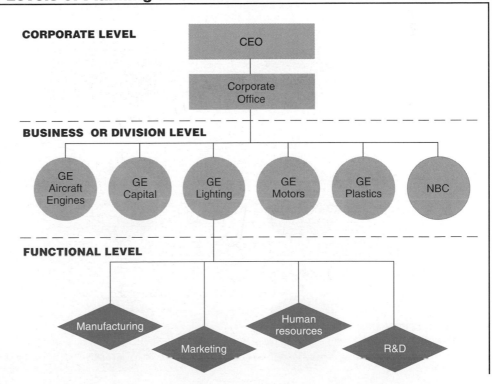

divisional managers
Managers who control the various divisions of an organization.

corporate-level plan
Top management's decisions relating to the organization's mission, overall strategy, and structure.

corporate-level strategy
A plan that indicates the industries and national markets in which an organization intends to compete.

Motors and Industrial Systems, GE Plastics, and NBC. Each division has its own set of **divisional managers**. In turn, each division has its own set of functions or departments—manufacturing, marketing, human resources, R&D, and so on. Thus, GE Aircraft Engines has its own marketing function, as do GE Lighting, GE Motors, and NBC.

Corporate-Level Planning

At GE, as at other large organizations, planning takes place at each level. In general, corporate-level planning is the primary responsibility of top managers.[10] The **corporate-level plan** contains decisions relating to the organization's mission and goals, overall (corporate-level) strategy, and structure (see Figure 5.3). **Corporate-level strategy** indicates the industries and national markets in which an organization intends to compete. One of the goals stated in GE's corporate-level plan is that GE should be first or second in market share in every industry in which it competes. A division that cannot attain this goal may be sold to another company. Another GE goal is the acquisition of other companies to help build market share. Over the past decade, GE has acquired several financial services companies and has transformed the GE Capital into one of the largest financial service operations in the world.

At General Electric, the corporate-level goal that GE be first or second in every industry in which it competes was first articulated by former CEO Jack Welch, who stepped down in September 2001. Now, Welch's hand-selected successor, Jeffrey Immelt, and his top-management team decide in which industries GE should compete.

Even though corporate-level planning is the responsibility of top managers, lower-level managers can be and usually are given the opportunity to become

Figure 5.3 | Levels and Types of Planning

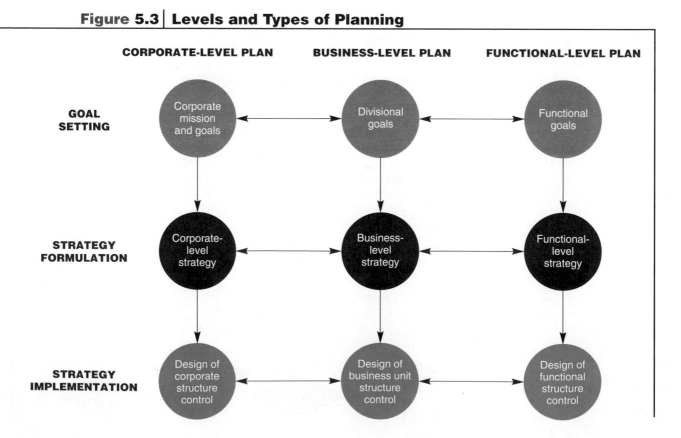

involved in the process. At General Electric and many other companies, divisional and functional managers are encouraged to submit proposals for new business ventures to the CEO and top managers, who evaluate the proposals and decide whether to fund them.[11] Corporate-level managers are also responsible for approving business- and functional-level plans to ensure that they are consistent with the corporate plan.

Business-Level Planning

business-level plan
Divisional managers' decisions relating to divisions' long-term goals, overall strategy, and structure.

business-level strategy
A plan that indicates how a division intends to compete against its rivals in an industry.

The corporate-level plan provides the framework within which divisional managers create their business-level plans. At the business level, the managers of each division create a **business-level plan** that details (1) long-term goals that will allow the division to meet corporate goals, and (2) the division's business-level strategy and structure. **Business-level strategy** states the methods a division or business intends to use to compete against its rivals in an industry. Managers at GE Lighting (currently number two in the global lighting industry behind the Dutch company Philips Electronics N.V.) develop strategies designed to help the division take over the number-one spot and better contribute to GE's corporate goals. The lighting division's competitive strategy might emphasize, for example, trying to reduce costs in all departments in order to lower prices and gain market share from Philips. GE is currently planning to expand its European lighting operations, which are based in Hungary.[12]

Functional-Level Planning

function
A unit or department in which people have the same skills or use the same resources to perform their jobs.

functional managers
Managers who supervise the various functions—such as manufacturing, accounting, and sales— within a division.

functional-level plan
Functional managers' decisions relating to the goals that functional managers propose to pursue to help the division reach its business-level goals.

functional-level strategy
A plan that indicates how a function intends to achieve its goals.

time horizon
The intended duration of a plan.

A **function** is a unit or department in which people have the same skills or use the same resources to perform their jobs. Examples include manufacturing, accounting, and sales. The business-level plan provides the framework within which **functional managers** devise their plans. A **functional-level plan** states the goals that functional managers propose to pursue to help the division attain its business-level goals, which, in turn, will allow the organization to achieve its corporate goals. A **functional-level strategy** sets forth the actions that managers intend to take at the level of departments such as manufacturing, marketing, and R&D to allow the organization to reach its goals. Thus, for example, consistent with GE Lighting's strategy of driving down costs, the manufacturing function might adopt the goal "To reduce production costs by 20 percent over three years," and its functional strategy to achieve this goal might include (1) investing in state-of-the-art European production facilities, and (2) developing an electronic global business-to-business network to reduce the cost of inputs and inventory-holding costs.

An important issue in planning is ensuring *consistency* in planning across the three different levels. Functional goals and strategies should be consistent with divisional goals and strategies, which in turn should be consistent with corporate goals and strategies, and vice versa. Once complete, each function's plan is normally linked to its division's business-level plan, which, in turn, is linked to the corporate plan. Although many organizations are smaller and less complex than GE, most do their planning as GE does and have written plans to guide managerial decision making.

Time Horizons of Plans

Plans differ in their **time horizon**, or intended duration. Managers usually distinguish among long-term plans with a horizon of five years or more, intermediate-term plans with a horizon between one and five years, and short-term plans with a horizon of one year or less.[13] Typically, corporate- and business-level goals and strategies require long- and intermediate-term plans, and functional-level goals and strategies require intermediate- and short-term plans.

Although most organizations operate with planning horizons of five years or more, it would be inaccurate to infer from this that they undertake major planning exercises only once every five years and then "lock in" a specific set of goals and strategies for that time period. Most organizations have an annual planning cycle, which is usually linked to their annual financial budget (even though a major planning effort may be undertaken only every few years).

Although a corporate- or business-level plan may extend over five years (or more), it is typically treated as a *rolling plan*, a plan that is updated and amended every year to take into account changing conditions in the external environment. Thus, the time horizon for an organization's 2004 corporate-level plan might be 2009; for the 2005 plan it might be 2010; and so on. The use of rolling plans is essential because of the high rate of change in the environment and the difficulty of predicting competitive conditions five years in the future. Rolling plans allow managers to make any mid-course corrections that environmental changes warrant, or to change the thrust of the plan altogether if it no longer seems appropriate. The use of rolling plans allows managers to plan flexibly, without losing sight of the need to plan for the long term.

Standing Plans and Single-Use Plans

policy

A general guide to action.

Another distinction often made between plans is whether they are standing or single-use plans. Managers create standing and single-use plans to help achieve an organization's specific goals. *Standing plans* are used in situations where programmed decision making is appropriate. When the same situations occur repeatedly, managers develop policies, rules, and standard operating procedures (SOPs) to control the way employees perform their tasks. A **policy** is a general guide to action; as outlined in the Appendix to Chapter 1, a *rule* is a formal, written guide to action, and an *SOP* is a written instruction describing the exact series of actions that should be followed in a specific situation. For example, an organization may have a standing plan about ethical behaviour by employees. This plan includes a policy that all employees are expected to behave ethically in their dealings with suppliers and customers; a rule that requires employees to report any gift worth more than $10 that is received from a supplier or customer; and an SOP that obliges the recipient of the gift to make the disclosure in writing within 30 days.

In contrast, *single-use plans* are developed to handle nonprogrammed decision making in unusual or one-of-a-kind situations. Examples of single-use plans include *programs* (integrated sets of plans for achieving certain goals), and *projects* (specific action plans created to complete various aspects of a program). One of NASA's major programs was to reach the moon, and one project in this program was to develop a lunar module capable of landing on the moon and returning to Earth.

Why Planning Is Important

Essentially, planning is determining where an organization is at the present time and deciding where it should be in the future and how to move it forward. When managers plan, they must consider the future and forecast what may happen in order to take action in the present, and gather organizational resources to deal with future opportunities and threats. As we have discussed in previous chapters, however, the external environment is uncertain and complex, and managers typically must deal with incomplete information and bounded rationality. This is one reason why planning is so complex.

Almost all managers engage in planning, and all *should* do so because planning helps to predict future opportunities and threats. The absence of a plan often results in hesitation, false steps, and mistaken changes of direction that can hurt an organization or even lead to disaster. Planning is important for four main reasons:

1. It's a useful way of getting managers to take part in decision making about the appropriate goals and strategies for an organization.
2. It's necessary to give the organization a sense of direction and purpose.[14] By stating which organizational goals and strategies are important, a plan keeps managers on track so that they use the resources under their control effectively.
3. A plan helps coordinate managers of the different functions and divisions of an organization to ensure that they all pull in the same direction. Without a good plan, it is possible that the members of the manufacturing function will produce more products than the members of the sales function can sell, resulting in a mass of unsold inventory.
4. A plan can be used as a device for controlling managers within an organization. A good plan specifies not only which goals and strategies the organization is committed to, but also who is responsible for putting the strategies into action to attain the goals. When managers know that they will be held accountable for attaining a goal, they are motivated to do their best to make sure the goal is achieved.

Effective Plans

Effective plans have four qualities:[15]

- *Unity.* At any one time only one central guiding plan should be put into operation.

- *Continuity.* Planning does not just happen once. Rather, plans are built, refined, and modified so that at all levels—corporate, business, and functional—fit together into one broad framework.

- *Accuracy.* Managers need to make every attempt to collect and use all available information at their disposal in the planning process.

- *Flexibility.* Plans should be altered if the situation changes.

By making sure that plans have these characteristics, planners ensure that multiple goals and plans do not cause confusion and disorder. Managers must recognize that it's important not to be bound to a static plan, because situations change. They must also recognize that uncertainty exists and that information is almost always incomplete, so that one does the best planning possible, and then reviews the plans as situations change or more information becomes available.

Scenario Planning

One of the most difficult aspects of making plans is predicting the future, which can be very uncertain. In the face of uncertainty, one of the most widely used planning techniques is scenario planning. **Scenario planning** (also known as *contingency planning*) is the generation of multiple forecasts of future conditions followed by an analysis of how to respond effectively to each of those conditions.

Scenario planning generates "multiple futures"—or scenarios of the future—based on different assumptions about conditions that *might prevail* in the future, and then develops different plans that detail what a company *should do* in the event that any of these scenarios actually occur. Managers use scenario planning to generate different future scenarios of conditions in the environment. They then develop responses to the opportunities and threats facing the different scenarios, and then develop a set of plans based on these responses. The great strength of scenario planning is its ability not only to anticipate the challenges of an uncertain future but also to educate managers to think about the future—to think strategically.[16]

Many businesses in Ontario learned the hard way that not having contingency plans in case of a public health crisis can lead to disaster. After severe acute

scenario planning

The generation of multiple forecasts of future conditions followed by an analysis of how to respond effectively to each of those conditions; also called *contingency planning.*

respiratory syndrome (SARS) hit Toronto, businesses struggled to figure out what they would do when public health officials ordered employees into quarantine. When 739 companies were surveyed by the Ontario Chamber of Commerce in April 2003, 78 percent said that they did not have a contingency plan in place for public health crises.[17]

Tips for Managers

Planning

1. Think ahead by using exercises such as scenario planning on a regular basis.
2. See plans as a guide to action. Don't feel boxed in by plans that may no longer be appropriate in a changing environment.
3. Make sure that the plans created at each of the three organizational levels are compatible with one another and that managers at all levels recognize how their actions fit into the overall corporate plan. Give managers at all levels the opportunity to take part in the planning process to best analyze an organization's present situation and the future scenarios that may affect it.

DETERMINING THE ORGANIZATION'S VISION, MISSION, AND GOALS

Think About It

Native Healing Centre Comes to General Hospital

The Regina General Hospital opened its Native Healing Centre in December 1999 after staff did needs assessment planning to further refine the organization's vision, mission, and goals.[18] The hospital recognized that the services it provided did not necessarily meet the needs of patients from the Aboriginal community who felt challenged by being from a minority culture, did not speak English, and had different beliefs about how to deal with personal well-being. Therefore, it developed a strategy to expand its services by working with those in the Aboriginal community to create a healing centre for Aboriginal patients.

Jim Saunders, interim chief executive officer of the Regina Health District, says, "The healing centre enables us to understand their culture and their health needs and it allows us to meet those needs much more effectively than in any other setting." The role of the centre is to build trust and respect with patients. Staff members work as intermediaries between the hospital and its clients, helping the patients to understand hospital policies and procedures, while being knowledgeable and respectful of the Aboriginal culture's traditional healing approach.

Questions
1. How are vision and mission statements related to the planning process?
2. How can vision and mission statements be used to better serve client and customer interests?

Determining the organization's vision, mission, and goals is the first step of the planning process. Once these are agreed upon and formally stated in the corporate plan, they guide the next steps by defining which strategies are appropriate and which are inappropriate.[19]

Defining the Vision

Vision differs from other forms of organizational direction setting in several ways:

A vision has clear and compelling imagery that offers an innovative way to improve, which recognizes and draws on traditions, and connects to actions that people can take to realize change. Vision taps people's emotions and energy. Properly articulated, a vision creates the enthusiasm that people have for sporting events and other leisure time activities, bringing that energy and commitment to the workplace.[20]

The organization's vision is generally set by the CEO.

Setting the Mission

The organization's mission is supposed to flow from the vision for the organization. To determine an organization's mission, managers must first define its business so that they can identify what kind of value they will provide to customers. To define the business, managers must ask three questions:[21] (1) Who are our customers? (2) What customer needs are being satisfied? (3) How are we satisfying customer needs? These questions identify the customer needs that the organization satisfies and the way the organization satisfies those needs. Answering these questions helps managers to identify not only what customer needs they are satisfying now but what needs they should try to satisfy in the future and who their true competitors are. All of this information helps managers determine the mission and then establish appropriate goals. The mission statements of Montreal-based Gildan Activewear Inc.; Brampton, Ontario-based Nortel Networks; and Montreal-based Bombardier Inc. are presented in Figure 5.4.

Workers' Compensation Board of British Columbia www.worksafebc.com

Establishing Major Goals

Once the business is defined, managers must establish a set of primary goals to which the organization is committed. Developing these goals gives the organization a sense of direction or purpose. For example, the mission of the Workers' Compensation Board (WCB) of British Columbia is the safety, protection, and health of workers. Based on this mission, the WCB has established the following goals:[22]

- Creation of workplaces that are safe and secure from injury and disease;

- Successful rehabilitation and return to work of injured workers;

Figure 5.4 | Three Mission Statements

COMPANY	MISSION STATEMENT
Bombardier	Bombardier's mission is to be the leader in all the markets in which it operates. This objective will be achieved through excellence in the fields of aerospace, rail transportation equipment, recreational products, financial services and services related to its products and core businesses.
Nortel Networks	Delivering greater value for customers worldwide through integrated network solutions spanning data and telephony.
Gildan Activewear	Gildan Activewear is dedicated to being the lowest-cost manufacturer and leading marketer of branded basic activewear to wholesale channels of distribution both in North America and internationally. To attain this goal, we will deliver the best in quality, service and price to our customers and, ultimately, to the end-users of our activewear products.

- Fair compensation for workers suffering injury or illness on the job;

- Sound financial management to ensure a viable WCB system;

- Protection of the public interest.

Effective goals have three characteristics: They are ambitious, they are realistic, and they are stated in terms of time period for accomplishment. The best statements of organizational goals are ambitious—that is, they stretch the organization and require managers to improve organizational performance capabilities.[23] Although goals should be challenging, they should be realistic. Challenging goals give managers an incentive to look for ways to improve an organization's operation, but a goal that is unrealistic and impossible to attain may prompt managers to give up.[24] The time period in which a goal is expected to be achieved should be stated. Time constraints are important because they emphasize that a goal must be reached within a reasonable period; they inject a sense of urgency into goal attainment and act as a motivator.

Communicating Goals: Management by Objectives

management by objectives

A system of evaluating subordinates for their ability to achieve specific organizational goals or performance standards.

To allow managers to monitor progress toward achieving goals, many organizations use some version of management by objectives (MBO). **Management by objectives** is a system of evaluating subordinates for their ability to achieve specific organizational goals or performance standards.[25] Most organizations make some use of management by objectives because it is pointless to establish goals and then fail to communicate the goals and their measurement to employees. Management by objectives involves three specific steps:

- Step 1. *Specific goals and objectives are established at each level of the organization.*

Management by objectives starts when top managers establish overall organizational objectives, such as specific financial performance targets. Objective setting then cascades down throughout the organization as managers at the divisional and functional levels set their own objectives to achieve the corporate objectives.[26] Finally, first-line managers and workers jointly set objectives that will contribute to achieving functional goals.

- Step 2. *Managers and their subordinates together determine the subordinates' goals.*

An important characteristic of management by objectives is its participatory nature. Managers at every level sit down with the subordinate managers who report directly to them, and together they determine appropriate and feasible goals for the subordinate and bargain over the budget that the subordinate will need so as to achieve his or her goals. The participation of subordinates in the objective-setting process is a way of strengthening their commitment to achieve their goals.[27] Another reason why it is so important for subordinates (both individuals and teams) to participate in goal setting is so they can tell managers what they think they can realistically achieve.[28]

- Step 3. *Managers and their subordinates periodically review the subordinates' progress toward meeting goals.*

Once specific objectives have been agreed upon for managers at each level, managers are accountable for meeting those objectives. Periodically, they sit down with their subordinates to evaluate their progress. Normally, salary raises and promotions are linked to the goal-setting process. (The issue of how to design reward systems to motivate managers and other organizational employees is discussed in Chapter 8.) The evaluation of whether goals were achieved is part of the control process, which we discuss in Chapter 13.

FORMULATING STRATEGY

Think About It

Campbell Soup Refocuses Itself

The Campbell Soup Company is one of the oldest and best-known companies in the world. However, in recent years it has seen demand plummet for its major products, including condensed soup, as customers have switched from high-salt, processed soups to healthier low-fat, low-salt varieties. Indeed, the company's condensed-soup business fell by 20 percent between 1998 and 2000. By 2001, Campbell's market share and profits were falling, and its new CEO, Douglas Conant, had to decide what to do to turn the company around and maintain its market position.

One of Conant's first actions was to introduce a thorough SWOT planning exercise. An analysis of the environment identified the growth of the organic and health food segment of the food market and the increasing number of other kinds of convenience foods as threats to Campbell's core soup business. The analysis of the environment also revealed three growth opportunities. One opportunity was in a growing market for health and sports drinks, in which the company already was a competitor with its V8 juice; the second was the growing market for salsas, in which the company competed with its Pace salsa; and the third was in chocolate products, where Campbell's Godiva brand had enjoyed increasing sales throughout the 1990s.

Questions
1. Why is formulating corporate strategy important?
2. How does a company do a SWOT analysis?

strategy formulation
Analysis of an organization's current situation followed by the development of strategies to accomplish the organization's mission and achieve its goals.

Strategy formulation includes analyzing an organization's current situation and then developing strategies to accomplish the organization's mission and achieve its goals.[29] Strategy formulation begins with managers analyzing the factors within an organization and outside—in the task and general environments—that affect or may affect the organization's ability to meet its current and future goals. *SWOT analysis* and the *Five Forces Model* are two techniques managers use to analyze these factors.

SWOT Analysis

SWOT analysis
A planning exercise in which managers identify organizational strengths (S) and weaknesses (W), and environmental opportunities (O) and threats (T).

SWOT analysis is the first step in strategy formulation at any level. It is a planning exercise in which managers identify organizational strengths (S) and weaknesses (W), and environmental opportunities (O) and threats (T). Based on a SWOT analysis, managers at the different levels of the organization select corporate-, business-, and functional-level strategies to best position the organization to achieve its mission and goals (see Figure 5.5).

The first step in SWOT analysis is to identify an organization's strengths and weaknesses that characterize the present state of their organization, and then consider how the strengths will be maintained and the weaknesses overcome.

At Campbell Soup, SWOT analysis identified a number of major weaknesses. These included staffing levels that were too high relative to its competitors, and high costs associated with manufacturing its soups because of the use of old, outdated machinery. Also, CEO Douglas Conant noted that Campbell Soup had a very conservative culture; people seemed afraid of taking risks, something that was a real problem in the fast-changing food industry where customer tastes are always changing and new products must be developed constantly. At the same time, the SWOT analysis identified an enormous strength. Campbell Soup enjoyed huge

Figure 5.5 | Planning and Strategy Formulation

economies of scale because of the large quantity of food products that it makes, and it also had a first-rate research and development division that had the capability to develop exciting new food products.

The second step in SWOT analysis begins when managers embark on a full-scale SWOT planning exercise to identify potential opportunities and threats in the environment that affect the organization at the present or may affect it in the future. Managers then consider how to take advantage of opportunities and overcome threats to the organization. As we noted earlier, Campbell's threats were coming from the health food market, but there were a number of opportunities in other directions.

With the SWOT analysis completed, and strengths, weaknesses, opportunities, and threats identified, managers can begin the planning process and determine strategies for achieving the organization's mission and goals. The resulting strategies should enable the organization to attain its goals by taking advantage of opportunities, countering threats, building strengths, and correcting organizational weaknesses. Using the information gained from the SWOT analysis, Conant and his managers decided that Campbell's needed to better meet the needs of a more health-oriented society. The company called on its product development skills to revitalize its core products and modify or reinvent them to appeal to health-conscious and busy consumers who did not want to take the time to prepare old-fashioned condensed soup. This meant developing products that would sell in the health, sports, snack, and luxury food segments of the market.

Another major need that managers saw was to find new ways to deliver products to customers. To increase sales, Campbell's needed to tap into new food outlets–such as corporate cafeterias, college dining halls, and other mass eateries–to expand consumers' access to its foods. Finally, Campbell's had to decentralize authority to managers at lower levels in the organization and give them the responsibility to bring new kinds of soups, salsas, and chocolate products to the market. In this way Conant hoped to revitalize Campbell's slow-moving culture and speed the flow of improved and new products to the market.

Tim Penner, CEO of Toronto-based Procter & Gamble Canada, used SWOT analysis to save the jobs of employees at P&G's Brockville, Ontario plant.[30] Penner knew that the Cincinnati, Ohio-based parent company was planning to consolidate the production of laundry detergent in the United States. This threatened the jobs of the Brockville employees. Penner searched for new opportunities, suggesting to head office that P&G centralize the manufacturing of fabric softener sheets and electrostatic cleaning sheets for the Swiffer sweeper in Brockville. Penner convinced his American bosses that the strengths of the Ontario plant included a

P&G Canada
www.pg.com

highly educated workforce that was also known for its commitment and productivity. As a result, Brockville's loss of laundry detergent production turned into a victory for Canadian jobs. Penner defines his mandate to include "aggressively selling Canada as a possible site for new products and reorganized operations." Penner's strategy has paid off. When he became CEO in 1999, P&G Canada was the seventh-largest revenue generator in the world for the US multinational. Three years later, he had taken his company to third place.

The Five Forces Model

Michael Porter's Five Forces Model is a well-known model that helps managers isolate particular forces in the external environment that are potential threats. Porter identified five factors (the first four are also discussed in Chapter 2) that are major threats because they affect how much profit organizations that compete within the same industry can expect to make:

- *The level of rivalry among organizations in an industry.* The more that companies compete against one another for customers—for example, by lowering the prices of their products or by increasing advertising—the lower is the level of industry profits (low prices mean less profit).

- *The potential for entry into an industry.* The easier it is for companies to enter an industry—because, for example, barriers to entry are low (see Chapter 2)—the more likely it is for industry prices and therefore industry profits to be low.

- *The power of suppliers.* If there are only a few suppliers of an important input, then (as discussed in Chapter 2) suppliers can drive up the price of that input, and expensive inputs result in lower profits for the producer.

- *The power of customers.* If only a few large customers are available to buy an industry's output, they can bargain to drive down the price of that output. As a result, producers make lower profits.

- *The threat of substitute products.* Often, the output of one industry is a substitute for the output of another industry (plastic may be a substitute for steel in some applications, e.g.). Companies that produce a product with a known substitute cannot demand high prices for their products, and this constraint keeps their profits low.

Porter argued that when managers analyze opportunities and threats, they should pay particular attention to these five forces because they are the major threats that an organization will encounter. It is the job of managers at the corporate, business, and functional levels to formulate strategies to counter these threats so that an organization can respond to both its task and general environments, perform at a high level, and generate high profits.

FORMULATING CORPORATE-LEVEL STRATEGIES

Think About It

E.D. Smith Explores Its Options

E.D. Smith & Sons Ltd., famous for its jams and pie fillings, spent several years in the early 2000s trying to find a strategy that made sense for the Winona, Ontario-based company.[31] Llewellyn Smith, the chair and CEO, was the third-generation Smith to run the business, which had annual sales of about $140 million. As Smith noted, the company was "too big to be a regional player and too small to be taken seriously by the big multinational buyers."

Smith's strategic planning was affected by two realities: Though E.D. Smith & Sons Ltd. was started by his great-grandfather in 1882, and passed down through four generations, Smith's three children did not plan to work in the business. More importantly, the company had lost considerable money when it purchased a food-packing plant in Byhalia, Mississippi, with the idea of supplying jam to Wal-Mart. Unfortunately, business with Wal-Mart never materialized. Smith considered two options: sell out to a big multinational, or buy another company to grow in size and compete with the multinationals. His preference was to form an alliance that would help him meet his goal of being a significant player in the US market.

Smith's corporate-level strategy did not work out and he ended up selling the company in January 2002, to a Canadian-controlled investment firm. Stephen Lister, managing partner of Imperial Capital Corp. of Toronto, said that his company is "excited about partnering with an experienced and dedicated team of [E.D. Smith] employees to build on the company's wonderful legacy. Working closely with the team, we will realize our vision of becoming a significant player in the North American food industry."

Questions
1. What factors affect corporate-level strategies?
2. Is selling a business a failure in corporate-level strategy?

Corporate-level strategy is a plan of action concerning which industries and countries an organization should invest its resources in to achieve its mission and goals. In developing a corporate-level strategy, managers ask: How should the growth and development of the company be managed in order to increase its ability to create value for its customers (and thus increase performance) over the long run? Managers of most organizations have the goal to grow their companies and actively seek out new opportunities to use the organization's resources to create more goods and services for customers. That is what Llewellyn Smith was trying to do with E.D. Smith.

In addition, some managers must help their organizations respond to threats due to changing forces in the task or general environment. For example, customers may no longer be buying the kinds of goods and services a company is producing (manual typewriters, eight-track tapes, black and white televisions), or other organizations may have entered the market and attracted customers away (this happened to Xerox when its patents expired and many companies rushed into the market to sell photocopiers). Or the markets may become saturated, as happened in the telecommunications industry recently, when more high-speed fibre optic networks were built than the market demanded. Top managers aim to find the best strategies to help the organization respond to these changes and improve performance.

The principal corporate-level strategies that managers use to help a company grow, to keep it on top of its industry, and to help it retrench and reorganize in order to stop its decline are: concentration on a single business; diversification; international expansion; and vertical integration.

These four strategies are all based on one idea: An organization benefits from pursuing a strategy only when it helps *further increase the value of the organization's goods and services for customers.* To increase the value of goods and services, a corporate-level strategy must help an organization, or one of its divisions, differentiate and add value to its products either by making them unique or special or by lowering the costs of value creation. Sometimes formulation of a corporate-level strategy presents difficult challenges, as was the case with E.D. Smith & Sons.

Concentration on a Single Business

Most organizations begin their growth and development with a corporate-level strategy aimed at concentrating resources in one business or industry in order to develop a strong competitive position within that industry. For example, Winnipeg-based Peak of the Market bought Winnipeg-based Stella Produce because it would allow the cooperative to increase its packaging capacity while adding another recognized brand name.[32] This decision by Peak of the Market's president and CEO, Larry McIntosh, continued the company's concentration on a single business while bringing it new growth opportunities. Similarly, E.D. Smith & Sons focused on fruit growing and jam production as its core business to become Canada's largest jam producer.

Sometimes, concentration on a single business becomes an appropriate corporate-level strategy when managers see the need to reduce the size of their organizations in order to increase performance. Managers may decide to get out of certain industries, for example, when particular divisions lose their competitive advantage. Managers may sell off those divisions, lay off workers, and concentrate remaining organizational resources in another market or business to try to improve performance. In contrast, when organizations are performing effectively, they often decide to enter new industries in which they can use their resources to create more value.

Diversification

diversification

Expanding operations into a new business or industry and producing new goods or services.

Diversification is the strategy of expanding operations into a new business or industry and producing new goods or services.[33] Examples of diversification include PepsiCo's diversification into the snack-food business with the purchase of Frito-Lay, Time-Warner's diversification into internet services with the acquisition of AOL, and Quebecor Media Inc.'s move into broadcasting with its acquisition of Vidéotron ltée. There are two main kinds of diversification: related and unrelated.

Related Diversification

related diversification

Entering a new business or industry to create a competitive advantage in one or more of an organization's existing divisions or businesses.

synergy

Performance gains that result when individuals and departments coordinate their actions.

Related diversification is the strategy of entering a new business or industry to create a competitive advantage in one or more of an organization's existing divisions or businesses. Related diversification can add value to an organization's products if managers can find ways for its various divisions or business units to share their valuable skills or resources so that synergy is created.[34] **Synergy** is obtained when the value created by two divisions cooperating is greater than the value that would be created if the two divisions operated separately.

In pursuing related diversification, managers often seek to find new businesses where they can use the existing skills and resources in their departments to create synergies, add value to the new business, and hence improve the competitive position of the company. Alternatively, managers may acquire a company in a new industry because they believe that some of the skills and resources of the *acquired* company might improve the efficiency of one or more of their existing divisions. If successful, such skill transfers can help an organization to lower its costs or better differentiate its products, because they create synergies between divisions.

One way to achieve diversification is by forming partnerships, something *The Toronto Star* recently announced it would do with the CBC. The two companies intend to maintain editorial independence while pooling some editorial, promotions, and internet activity.

Unrelated Diversification

unrelated diversification

Entering a new industry or buying a company in a new industry that is not related in any way to an organization's current businesses or industries.

Managers pursue **unrelated diversification** when they enter new industries or buy companies in new industries that are not related in any way to their current businesses or industries. One of the main reasons for pursuing unrelated diversification is that, sometimes, managers can buy a poorly performing company, transfer their management skills to that company, turn its business around, and increase its performance, all of which creates value.

Another reason for pursuing unrelated diversification is that buying businesses in different industries lets managers use a *portfolio strategy*, which is dividing financial resources among divisions to increase financial returns or spread risks among different businesses, much as individual investors do with their own portfolios. For instance, managers may transfer funds from a rich division (a "cash cow") to a new and promising division (a "star") and, by allocating money appropriately between divisions, create value. In one specific example, when Imperial Capital bought E.D. Smith & Sons Ltd., it was following what it describes as "an acquisition strategy that identifies recession-resistant niche businesses in profitable, low-risk industries poised for consolidation."[35] Toronto-based Brascan Corp. is one of the last large Canadian conglomerates that continues to pursue this diversified strategy. Under CEO Bruce Flatt it has focused its development on three of its multiple lines: real estate (Toronto-based Brookfield Properties), financial services (Toronto-based Brascan Financial), and power generation (Masson-Angers, Quebec-based Brascan Power).[36] Nevertheless, the company also owns Toronto-based Noranda Inc., a mining subsidiary, and Toronto-based Nexfor Inc., a paperboard company. Though used as a popular explanation in the 1980s for unrelated diversification, portfolio strategy started running into increasing criticism in the 1990s.[37] Today, many companies and their managers are abandoning the strategy of unrelated diversification because there is evidence that too much diversification can cause managers to lose control of their organizations' core business so that they end up reducing value rather than creating it.[38] Since the 1990s, there has been a trend among many diversified companies to sell off unrelated divisions and concentrate organizational resources on their core business and related diversification.[39] For instance, Toronto-based George Weston Ltd., the food processing and supermarket giant, announced in February 2001 that it would sell Blacks Harbour, New Brunswick-based Connors Bros., a fish processing operation, so that it could acquire Bestfoods Baking Co. Chairman Galen Weston explained that the move would allow the company "to go forward in the baking and the supermarket business."[40] The company did not feel that it held a competitive advantage in the fish processing industry.

International Expansion

As if planning the appropriate level of diversification were not a difficult enough decision, corporate-level managers also must decide on the appropriate way to compete internationally. When E.D. Smith & Sons decided to move into the American market, it was partnered with Toronto-based Loblaw Cos. Ltd., which was intending to sell E.D. Smith jams to Wal-Mart. Unfortunately Loblaw's was not successful in getting a contract from Wal-Mart, and E.D. Smith's expansion to the United States did not pay off.

A basic question confronts the managers of any organization that competes in more than one national market: To what extent should the organization customize features of its products and marketing campaign to different national conditions?[41] If managers decide that their organization should sell the same standardized product in each national market in which it competes, and use the same basic marketing approach, they adopt a **global strategy**.[42] Such companies undertake very little, if any, customization to suit the specific needs of customers in different countries. But if managers decide to customize products and marketing strategies to specific national conditions, they adopt a **multidomestic strategy**. Japan's Matsushita Electric has traditionally pursued a global strategy, selling the same basic TVs and VCRs in every market in which it does business and often using the same basic marketing approach. However, even McDonald's has had to customize its food products for the global market. When McDonald's went to India, it had to sell chicken burgers and mutton burgers rather than beef burgers.

global strategy
Selling the same standardized product and using the same basic marketing approach in each national market.

multidomestic strategy
Customizing products and marketing strategies to specific national conditions.

Mars, Incorporated, the candy maker, previously used a multidomestic strategy and sold its candy under different brand names in the different countries in which it operated. Now it has changed to a global strategy to reduce costs and sells the candy under the same name throughout the world, as this billboard in Russia suggests.

Both global and multidomestic strategies have advantages and disadvantages. The major advantage of a global strategy is the significant cost savings associated with not having to customize products and marketing approaches to different national conditions. The major disadvantage of pursuing a global strategy is that, by ignoring national differences, managers may leave themselves vulnerable to local competitors that do differentiate their products to suit local tastes.

The advantages and disadvantages of a multidomestic strategy are the opposite of those of a global strategy. The major advantage of a multidomestic strategy is that, by customizing product offerings and marketing approaches to local conditions, managers may be able to gain market share or charge higher prices for their products. The major disadvantage is that customization raises production costs and puts the multidomestic company at a price disadvantage because the company often has to charge prices higher than the prices charged by competitors pursuing a global strategy. Obviously, the choice between these two strategies calls for trade-offs.

Vertical Integration

When an organization is doing well in its business, managers often see new opportunities to create value by either producing their own inputs or distributing their own outputs. Managers at E.&J. Gallo Winery, for example, realized that they could lower Gallo's costs if they produced their own wine bottles rather than buying them from a glass company. As a result, Gallo established a new division to produce glass bottles.

vertical integration
A strategy that allows an organization to create value by producing its own inputs or distributing and selling its own outputs.

Vertical integration is the corporate-level strategy through which an organization becomes involved in producing its own inputs (backward vertical integration) or distributing and selling its own outputs (forward vertical integration).[43] A steel company that supplies its iron ore needs from company-owned iron ore mines is using backward vertical integration. When Steve Jobs announced in 2001 that Apple Computer would open 25 retail stores to sell Macintosh machines directly to consumers, he showed that Apple was engaging in forward vertical integration.

Figure 5.6 illustrates the four main stages in a typical raw-materials-to-consumer value chain; value is added at each stage. Typically, the primary operations of an organization take place in one of these stages. For a company based in the assembly stage, backward integration would involve establishing a new division in intermediate manufacturing or raw-material production, and forward integration would involve establishing a new division to distribute its products to wholesalers or to sell directly to customers. A division at one stage receives the product made by the division in the previous stage, transforms it in some way—adding value—and then transfers the output at a higher price to the division at the next stage in the chain.

As an example of how the value chain works, consider the cola segment of the soft-drink industry, discussed in the *Case in Contrast*. Raw-materials suppliers include sugar companies and G.D. Searle & Co., manufacturer of the artificial sweetener NutraSweet, which is used in diet colas. These companies sell their products to companies—such as Coca-Cola, PepsiCo, and Cott Corporation—that mix these inputs with others to produce the cola concentrate that they market. In the process, they add value to these inputs. The concentrate producers then sell the concentrate to bottlers, who add carbonated water to the concentrate and package the resulting drink—again adding value to the concentrate. Next, the bottlers sell the packaged product to various distributors, including retail stores such as Costco and Safeway, and fast-food chains such as McDonald's. These distributors add value by making the product accessible to customers. Thus, value is added by companies at each stage in the raw-materials-to-consumer chain.

A major reason why managers pursue vertical integration is that it allows them either to add value to their products, by making them special or unique, or to lower the costs of value creation. For example, Coca-Cola and PepsiCo, in a case of forward vertical integration to build brand loyalty and enhance the differentiated appeal of their colas, decided to buy up their major bottlers to increase control over marketing and promotion efforts—which the bottlers had been handling.[44] An example of using forward vertical integration to lower costs is Matsushita Electric's decision to open company-owned stores to sell its own products and thus keep the profit that independent retailers otherwise would earn.[45]

Even though vertical integration can help an organization to grow rapidly, it can be a problem when forces in the organizational environment conflict with the strategies of the organization and make it necessary for managers to reorganize or retrench. Vertical integration can make an organization less flexible in responding

Figure 5.6 | Stages in a Vertical Value Chain

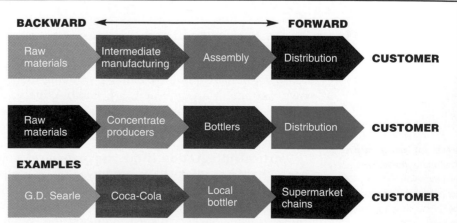

to changing environmental conditions. For example, IBM used to produce most of its own components for mainframe computers. Doing this made sense in the 1960s, but it became a major handicap for the company in the fast-changing computer industry of the 1990s. The rise of organization-wide networks of personal computers has meant slumping demand for mainframes. As demand fell, IBM found itself with an excess-capacity problem, not only in its mainframe assembly operations but also in component operations. Closing down this capacity cost IBM more than $7.75 billion in 1993 and clearly limited the company's ability to pursue other opportunities.[46] When considering vertical integration as a strategy to add value, managers must be careful because sometimes vertical integration will actually reduce an organization's ability to create value when the environment changes.

Something managers need to consider when deciding on possible expansion strategies is the human costs of consolidating operations. While Air Canada initially projected $880 million in "synergies" from merging with Canadian Airlines, that figure was at least $150 million less because of the difficulty of bringing the two employee groups together. CEO Robert Milton noted that it was "an emotionally charged process . . . perceived to create winners and losers."[47] Management from the two merged companies can also clash, creating political struggles, as was seen in the public battling between the management of Montreal-based Abitibi-Consolidated Inc., a pulp and paper giant, and Montreal-based Quebecor.

FORMULATING BUSINESS-LEVEL STRATEGIES

Think About It

Canada's Brewers Use Different Strategies to Define Their Markets

Guelph-based Sleeman Breweries Ltd. prides itself on its premium beer, which has allowed the company to become a leading brewer and distributor of premium beer in Canada and the third-largest brewing company in the country. The company also sells low-priced beer, however, through Canadian distribution rights for Stroh and Old Milwaukee, among others. Meanwhile, Canada's two largest breweries are more focused on competing with each other: Molson's Canadian against Labatt's Blue. Canadian and Blue are mid-priced beers, and Molson and Labatt have remained largely out of the premium and discount markets.

Question
1.   How do companies choose their business strategies?

Sleeman Breweries Ltd.
www.sleeman.ca

Michael Porter, the researcher who developed the Five Forces Model discussed earlier, also formulated a theory of how managers can select a business-level strategy, a plan to gain a competitive advantage in a particular market or industry.[48] According to Porter, managers must choose between the two basic ways of increasing the value of an organization's products: higher quality or lower costs. Porter also argues that managers must choose between serving the whole market or serving just one segment or part of a market. Given those choices, managers choose to pursue one of four business-level strategies: cost-leadership, differentiation, focused low-cost, or focused differentiation (see Table 5.1).

cost-leadership strategy

Driving the organization's costs down below the costs of its rivals.

Cost-Leadership Strategy

With a **cost-leadership strategy**, managers try to gain a competitive advantage by focusing the energy of all the organization's departments or functions on driving

Table 5.1 | Porter's Business-Level Strategies

Strategy	Number of Market Segments Served	
	Many	Few
Cost-leadership	✓	
Focused low-cost		✓
Differentiation	✓	
Focused differentiation		✓

the organization's costs down below the costs of its rivals. This strategy means manufacturing managers must search for new ways to reduce production costs, R&D managers must focus on developing new products that can be manufactured more cheaply, and marketing managers must find ways to lower the costs of attracting customers. According to Porter, organizations following a low-cost strategy can sell a product for less than their rivals sell it and yet still make a profit because of their lower costs. Thus, organizations that pursue a low-cost strategy hope to enjoy a competitive advantage based on their low prices.

differentiation strategy
Distinguishing an organization's products from the products of competitors in dimensions such as product design, quality, or after-sales service.

Differentiation Strategy

With a **differentiation strategy**, managers try to gain a competitive advantage by focusing all the energies of the organization's departments or functions on distinguishing the organization's products from those of competitors in one or more important dimensions, such as product design, quality, or after-sales service and support. For instance, St. Stephen, New Brunswick-based Ganong Bros. Ltd. is a small player in the chocolate market in Canada. It differentiates itself from bigger boxed-chocolate makers by focusing on the assorted chocolates market, where it ranks second in Canada. It's Fruitfull brand, made with real fruit purée and packaged like chocolates, has a 43-percent share of fruit jelly sales.[49]

Often, the process of making products unique and different is expensive. This strategy, for example, often requires managers to increase spending on product design or R&D to make the product stand out, and costs rise as a result. However, organizations that successfully pursue a differentiation strategy may be able to charge a *premium price* for their products, a price usually much higher than the price charged by a low-cost organization. The premium price allows organizations pursuing a differentiation strategy to recoup their higher costs.

Coca-Cola and PepsiCo, profiled in the *Case in Contrast,* are clearly pursuing a strategy of differentiation. Both companies spend enormous amounts of money on advertising to differentiate, and create a unique image for, their products. Molson and Labatt also use a differentiation strategy, with beer that is neither the most expensive on the market (a strategy closer to Sleeman) or the lowest-priced (a strategy that Sleeman also uses for some of the products it distributes). Canadian and Blue are presented to consumers as having distinct taste and quality.

John Sleeman, CEO of Sleeman Breweries Ltd., produces premium-priced beer, to distinguish his company from the mid-price beer strategies of Molson and Labatt.

"Stuck in the Middle"

According to Porter's theory, managers cannot simultaneously pursue both a cost-leadership strategy and a differentiation strategy.

Porter identified a simple correlation: Differentiation raises costs and thus necessitates premium pricing to recoup those high costs. For example, if Cott Corporation suddenly began to advertise heavily to try to build a strong brand image for its products, Cott's costs would rise. Cott could then no longer make a profit simply by pricing its cola lower than Coca-Cola or Pepsi. According to Porter, managers must choose between a cost-leadership strategy and a differentiation strategy. He says that managers and organizations that have not made this choice are "stuck in the middle." According to Porter, organizations stuck in the middle tend to have lower levels of performance than do those that pursue a low-cost or a differentiation strategy. To avoid being stuck in the middle, top managers must instruct departmental managers to take actions that will result in either low cost or differentiation.

However, exceptions to this rule can be found. In many organizations, managers have been able to drive costs down below those of rivals and simultaneously differentiate their products from those offered by rivals.[50] For example, Toyota's production system is reportedly the most efficient in the world. This efficiency gives Toyota a low-cost strategy vis-à-vis its rivals in the global car industry. At the same time, Toyota has differentiated its cars from those of rivals on the basis of superior design and quality. This superiority allows the company to charge a premium price for many of its popular models.[51] Thus, Toyota seems to be simultaneously pursuing both a low-cost and a differentiated business-level strategy. This example suggests that although Porter's ideas may be valid in most cases, very well-managed companies such as Toyota, McDonald's, and Compaq may have both low costs and differentiated products.

Focused Low-Cost and Focused Differentiation Strategies

focused low-cost strategy
Serving only one segment of the overall market and being the lowest-cost organization serving that segment.

Both the differentiation strategy and the cost-leadership strategy are aimed at serving most or all segments of the market. Porter identified two other business-level strategies that aim to serve the needs of customers in only one or a few market segments.[52] A company pursuing a **focused low-cost strategy** serves one or a few segments of the overall market and aims to be the lowest-cost company serving that segment. This is the strategy that Cott Corporation adopted. Cott focuses on large retail chains and strives to be the lowest-cost company serving that segment of the market. A major reason for Cott's low costs is the fact that the company does not advertise, which allows Cott to underprice both Coke and Pepsi.

focused differentiation strategy
Serving only one segment of the overall market and trying to be the most differentiated organization serving that segment.

By contrast, a company pursuing a **focused differentiation strategy** serves just one or a few segments of the market and aims to be the most differentiated company serving that segment. BMW pursues a focused strategy, producing cars exclusively for higher-income customers. Sleeman has followed this strategy in producing its premium beers.

As these examples suggest, companies pursuing either of these focused strategies have chosen to specialize in some way—by directing their efforts at a particular kind of customer (such as serving the needs of babies or affluent customers) or even the needs of customers in a specific geographical region (customers on the East or West Coast).

FORMULATING FUNCTIONAL-LEVEL STRATEGIES

As discussed earlier in the chapter, a *functional-level strategy* is a plan of action to improve the ability of an organization's departments to create value. It is concerned with the actions that managers of individual departments (such as manufacturing or marketing) can take to add value to an organization's goods and services and thereby increase the value customers receive.

There are two ways in which departments can add value to an organization's products:

1. Departmental managers can lower the costs of creating value so that an organization can attract customers by keeping its prices lower than its competitors' prices.
2. Departmental managers can add value to a product by finding ways to differentiate it from the products of other companies.

For instance, the marketing and sales departments at Molson and Labatt add value by building brand loyalty and finding more effective ways to attract customers. Each organizational function has an important role to play in lowering costs or adding value to a product (see Table 5.2).

In trying to add value or lower the costs of creating value, all functional managers should pay attention to these four goals:[53]

1. *To attain superior efficiency.* Efficiency is a measure of the amount of inputs required to produce a given amount of outputs. The fewer the inputs required to produce a given output, the higher is the efficiency and the lower the cost of outputs.
2. *To attain superior quality.* Here, quality means producing goods and services that are reliable—they do the job they were designed for and do it well.[54] Providing high quality products creates a brand-name reputation for an organization's products. In turn, this enhanced reputation allows the organization to charge a higher price.
3. *To attain superior innovation.* Anything new or unusual about the way in which an organization operates or the goods and services it produces is the result of innovation. Innovation leads to advances in the kinds of products, production processes, management systems, organizational structures, and strategies that an organization develops. Successful innovation gives an organization something unique that its rivals lack. This uniqueness may enhance the value added

Table 5.2 | **How Functions Can Lower Costs and Create Value or Add Value to Create a Competitive Advantage**

Value-creating Function	Ways to Lower the Cost of Creating Value (Low-cost Advantage)	Ways to Add Value (Differentiation Advantage)
Sales and marketing	• Find new customers • Find low-cost advertising methods	• Promote brand-name awareness and loyalty • Tailor products to suit customers' needs
Materials management	• Use just-in-time inventory system/computerized warehousing • Develop long-term relationships with suppliers and customers	• Develop long-term relationships with suppliers to provide high quality inputs • Reduce shipping time to customers
Research and development	• Improve efficiency of machinery and equipment • Design products that can be made more cheaply	• Create new products • Improve existing products
Manufacturing	• Develop skills in low-cost manufacturing	• Increase product quality and reliability
Human resource management	• Reduce turnover and absenteeism • Raise employee skills	• Hire highly skilled employees • Develop innovative training programs

and thereby allow the organization to differentiate itself from its rivals and attract customers who will pay a premium price for its product.

4. *To attain superior responsiveness to customers.* An organization that is responsive to customers tries to satisfy their needs and give them exactly what they want. An organization that treats customers better than its rivals treats them provides a valuable service for which customers may be willing to pay a higher price.

The important issue to remember here is that all of these techniques can help an organization achieve a competitive advantage by lowering the costs of creating value or by adding value above and beyond that offered by rivals.

PLANNING AND IMPLEMENTING STRATEGY

Think About It

Finning Goes From SWOT to Implementing Strategy

While analyzing its strengths and weaknesses (during a SWOT analysis), Edmonton-based Finning International Inc.'s managers discovered a crucial weakness: Safety management results were not very good. To address this, the managers created a health, safety, and environment committee at the board of directors' level. The company then appointed a safety manager to monitor progress quarterly on all safety statistics. All operations (Canadian, European, and Chilean) report directly to the committee on their progress on safety and environmental issues.

Question
1. What is the relationship between strategic planning and implementation?

After conducting a SWOT analysis and identifying appropriate strategies to attain an organization's mission and goals, managers confront the challenge of putting those strategies into action. Strategy implementation is a five step process:

1. Allocating responsibility for implementation to the appropriate individuals or groups;
2. Drafting detailed action plans that specify how a strategy is to be implemented;
3. Establishing a timetable for implementation that includes precise, measurable goals linked to the attainment of the action plan;
4. Allocating appropriate resources to the responsible individuals or groups;
5. Holding specific individuals or groups responsible for reaching corporate, divisional, and functional goals.

As the case of Finning illustrates, the planning process goes beyond the mere identification of strategies; it also includes actions taken to ensure that the organization actually implements its strategies. One of the difficulties Air Canada has faced in recent years is that it has not articulated a clear strategy, particularly in creating Tango and Jetsgo to operate alongside the parent airline. Customers face stressed airline employees who are not clear on the real priorities of the airline. By contrast, Southwest Airlines has communicated a very clear strategy to its employees: Flights are to be an enjoyable, affordable experience for travellers, and employees are to make sure that happens while keeping costs down and improving turnaround time. Armed with this strategy, all Southwest Airlines employees know what is expected of them in a crisis, and pilots and fight attendants pitch in to help in whatever ways are necessary to meet this strategy.

It should be noted that the plan for implementing a strategy may require radical redesign of the structure of the organization, the adoption of a program for changing the culture of the organization and the development of new control systems. We address the first two issues in the next two chapters. The issues of control we discuss in Chapter 13.

Tips for Managers

1. Periodically define an organization's business to determine how well it is achieving its mission. Use this planning exercise to determine its future goals.

2. Make SWOT analysis an integral part of the planning process.

3. Always be alert for opportunities to increase the value of an organization's goods and services so it can better serve its customers' needs.

4. Ensure that functional managers focus on finding new ways to lower the costs of value creation or to add value to products so that an organization can pursue both a low-cost and a differentiation strategy.

5. Carefully assess the costs and benefits associated with using a corporate-level strategy and enter a new business only when it can be clearly demonstrated that the business will increase the value of your products.

Chapter Summary

SUMMARY AND REVIEW

AN OVERVIEW OF THE PLANNING PROCESS Planning is a three-step process: (1) determining an organization's mission and goals, (2) formulating strategy, and (3) implementing strategy. Managers use planning to identify and select appropriate goals and courses of action for an organization and to decide how to allocate the resources they need to attain those goals and carry out those actions. A good plan builds commitment for the organization's goals, gives the organization a sense of direction and purpose, coordinates the different functions and divisions of the organization, and controls managers by making them accountable for specific goals. In large organizations, planning takes place at three levels: corporate, business or division, and department or functional. While planning is typically the responsibility of a well-defined group of managers, the subordinates of those managers should be given every opportunity to have input into the process and to shape the outcome. Long-term plans have a time horizon of five years or more; intermediate-term plans, between one and five years; and short-term plans, one year or less.

DETERMINING THE ORGANIZATION'S VISION, MISSION, AND GOALS Determining the organization's vision and mission requires managers to define the business of the organization and establish major goals. Strategy formulation requires managers to perform a SWOT analysis and then choose appropriate strategies at the corporate, business, and functional levels.

FORMULATING STRATEGY At the corporate level, organizations use strategies such as concentration on a single business; diversification; international expansion; and vertical integration to help increase the value of the goods and services provided to customers. At the business level, managers are responsible for developing a successful low-cost or differentiation strategy, either for the whole market or for a particular segment of it. At the functional level, departmental managers strive to develop and use their skills to help the organization either add value to its products by differentiating them or lower the costs of value creation.

PLANNING AND IMPLEMENTING STRATEGY Strategy implementation requires managers to allocate responsibilities to suitable individuals or groups; draft detailed action plans that specify how a strategy is to be implemented; establish a timetable for implementation that includes precise, measurable goals linked to the attainment of the action plan; allocate appropriate resources to the responsible individuals or groups; and hold individuals or groups accountable for reaching goals.

Roles in Contrast: Considerations

MANAGERS	EMPLOYEES
Planning gives a sense of direction and purpose, and helps determine the steps needed to get something done.	Planning can help me ensure that projects get completed in a timely fashion, and in a way that I had hoped.
Vision and mission statements help organizational members know what the company stands for, and how it intends to interact with customers or clients.	Making long-term plans for myself, by looking toward the future and understanding opportunities and threats, can help me achieve my important goals.
Within my department I need to consider how I can help create value by keeping costs down, or creating better products.	If I understand whether my manager's objectives are to keep costs low or to develop more innovative products, then when I'm making decisions about my own work, I can make decisions that are consistent with my manager's strategy.

MANAGEMENT in Action

Topics for Discussion and Action

1. Describe the three steps of planning. Explain how they are related.
2. How can scenario planning help managers predict the future?
3. Ask a manager about the kinds of planning exercises he or she regularly uses. What are the purposes of these exercises, and what are their advantages or disadvantages?
4. What is the role of divisional and functional managers in the formulation of strategy?
5. Why is it important for functional managers to have a clear grasp of the organization's mission when developing strategies within their departments?
6. What is the relationship among corporate-, business-, and functional-level strategies, and how do they create value for an organization?
7. Ask a manager to identify the corporate-, business-, and functional-level strategies used by his or her organization.

Building Management Skills

HOW TO ANALYZE A COMPANY'S STRATEGY

Pick a well-known business organization that has received recent media coverage and for which you can get a number of years' annual reports from your school library or on the internet. For this organization, do the following.

1. From the annual reports, identify the main strategies pursued by the company over a 10-year period.
2. Try to identify why the company pursued these strategies. What reason was given in the annual reports, press reports, and elsewhere? What goals and objectives did the company say it had?
3. Document whether and when any major changes in the strategy of the organization occurred. If changes did occur, try to identify the reason for them.
4. If changes in strategy occurred, try to determine the extent to which they were the result of long-term plans and the extent to which they were responses to unforeseen changes in the company's task environment.
5. What is the main industry that the company competes in?
6. What business-level strategy does the company seem to be pursuing in this industry?
7. What is the company's reputation with regard to productivity, quality, innovation, and responsiveness to customers in this industry? If the company has attained an advantage in any of these areas, how has it done so?
8. What is the current corporate-level strategy of the company? What is the company's stated reason for pursuing this strategy?
9. Has the company expanded internationally? If it has, identify its largest international market. How did the company enter this market? Did its mode of entry change over time?

Management for You

Think ahead to five years from now, to consider what it is that you might like to be doing with your life. Develop your own vision and mission statements. Establish a set of goals that will help you achieve your vision and mission.

Develop a SWOT analysis for considering what you want to be doing in five years. What are your strengths and weaknesses? What are the opportunities and threats in carrying out this plan?

Develop a five-year plan that maps out the steps you need to take in order to get to where you want to be with your life at that time.

Small Group Breakout Exercise

PLANNING FOR NEW DEVELOPMENT

Form groups of 3 or 4 people, and appoint 1 member as the spokesperson who will communicate your findings to the class when called on by the instructor. Then discuss the following scenario.

You are a team of city planners for the City of Vancouver. Vancouver's east side is known as the poorest postal code in the country. Recently the city bought the old Woodward's building, and is trying to decide what to do with it. It is considering a mix of social housing, artists' lofts, and retail areas. Can the city create a heart in this poverty-stricken area? You have been asked to come up with a plan of action to determine what to do.

1. Describe the new building project's purpose.
2. Identify the short-term and long-term objectives for the project and how these will be evaluated.
3. Using scenario planning, analyze the pros and cons of each alternative.

Managing Ethically

A major department store has received repeated criticism for selling clothes that are produced in low-cost developing world countries. The CEO of the department store knows that suppliers are paying 5-percent better than the going rate of wages in these countries, and feels that this is fair enough. Working conditions at suppliers' factories are no worse than at other factories in those countries. The CEO has come to you to check her assumptions that as long as the suppliers are buying from manufacturing plants that have better-than-average working conditions for the country where the company is located, nothing further needs to be done. What would you advise her? How would you justify your advice?

Exploring the World Wide Web

SPECIFIC ASSIGNMENT

This exercise follows up on the activities of McDonald's Corporation (www.mcdonalds.com), which is vertically integrating on a global level. Research McDonald's website to get a feel for this global giant. In particular, focus on McDonald's most recent annual report and its descriptions of the company's goals and objectives.

1. What are the main elements of McDonald's strategy at the corporate, business, and functional levels?
2. How successful has the company been recently?
3. Has the strategy of McDonald's Canada been any different than its parent operation's?

GENERAL ASSIGNMENT

Search for a website that contains a good description of a company's strategy. What is the company's mission? Use the concepts and terminology of this chapter to describe the company's strategy to achieve its mission.

You're the Management Consultant

PLANNING A NEW SUPERMARKET

A group of investors in your city is considering opening a new upscale supermarket to compete with the major supermarket chains that are currently dominating the city's marketplace. They have called you in to help them determine what kind of upscale supermarket they should open. In other words, how can they use planning to develop a competitive advantage against existing supermarket chains?

Questions

1. List the supermarket chains in your city and identify their strengths and weaknesses.
2. What business-level strategies are these supermarkets currently pursuing?
3. What kind of supermarket would do best against the competition? What kind of business-level strategy should it pursue?

MANAGEMENT CASE ———————————— IN THE NEWS

From the Pages of *The Financial Post Daily* De Zen and the Art of Home Maintenance

He's the plastic version of Magna Inc.'s Frank Stronach, but that's not to say Vic De Zen is a cheap imitation. Like Stronach, De Zen, the chairman, president and chief executive of Royal Group Technologies Ltd., arrived in Canada as a poor immigrant tool and die maker and went on to establish an empire. But where Stronach made his fortune as an auto parts magnate, De Zen, 56, has built an $850-million-a-year company in the plastics business.

And today, he's embarking on an ambitious plan to extend Royal's domain further by housing the world in its revolutionary plastic homes.

"If you have an operation on your heart, it's plastic. And in your knee, it's plastic. Without plastic, we're going to die," says De Zen during a kinetic interview at his company's Woodbridge, Ont. head office.

Twice during the rapid-fire conversation he springs from his chair—once to fetch a bottle of Crown Royal as a gift for a visitor and another time to drag him by the sleeve to a window looking out on a 75-hectare field that will soon be home to a giant warehouse.

Like its boss, Royal is a company on the move, with plans to add 180 000 square metres of manufacturing space to its existing 495 000 square metres around the world.

Much of this expansion is being driven by demand for plastic window frames, blinds and siding, which have yielded compound annual revenue growth averaging 21.8% over the past five years.

Earnings hit $97.5 million ($1.21 a share) in 1997, for 33% compounded annual growth over five years.

"The guy is driven. He sets the tone for his company and all those ideas that flow come from him. He's a great ideas man," says Farras Shammas of the Canadian Plastics Industry Association. "I guess it's one man's vision. Put simply, Vic is a visionary, there's no doubt about it."

Analysts are keen on the stock, valuing it like a growth stock rather than a building materials company. Even if, as expected, the building materials division slows down with a cooling economy and rising interest rates, the burgeoning housing division is expected to continue strong.

Investors have been equally positive, bidding Royal stock up from a low of $30 last year to a

52-week high of $48 this spring. Yesterday, the shares (RYG/TSE) closed at $44, up 5 cents.

Royal's results are evident even in the company's parking lot, which looks like a Mercedes dealership.

It's made De Zen, who owns 20% of the shares and 80% of the votes, a rich man. He gets around on a Canadair regional jet and hanging in the boardroom is a picture of him linking arms with Prime Minister Jean Chretien.

But it hasn't always been so cushy. De Zen was born near Venice and apprenticed in Switzerland before coming to Canada in 1962 with $20. Legend has it he was at work an hour later putting up TV antennas with his brother.

After repeated disappointments with bad bosses, in 1970 he and two partners pooled $58 000 in savings to set up a line of plastic extrusion machines that was Royal Plastics. His take-home pay was $35 a week.

Among the many lessons learned was self-reliance. De Zen still remembers the frustration of looking for someone to repair equipment whenever there were problems. "I had no spare parts and I didn't know what to do. I had very little money and every time I called somebody in they overcharged me," he says. "If nobody is feeding you, you have to grow your own food."

Today, Royal is totally vertically integrated. Its various units are involved in every stage of the business, from providing chemicals and compounding to designing and making machinery, building its own plants and transporting its products with a 250-truck fleet that picks up scrap for recycling.

In April, it went a step further, agreeing to pay $82 million for a polyvinyl chloride resin plant in Sarnia, Ont., from Imperial Oil Ltd.

In an age when many companies are outsourcing work to concentrate on core businesses, De Zen has no qualms about Royal's strategy. For him, outsourcing is like leasing a car when you can afford to buy it.

Moreover, he says, integration allows the company to control quality, respond more quickly to customer needs and develop new ideas in months rather than years.

"How can you compete in world markets today? The Americans are big and they are super businessmen. If you cannot make it faster than them and better, customers won't deal with you," he says.

All this sets up Royal for its newest and biggest venture yet, the construction of plastic houses through the Royal Building System.

In some ways, plastic houses are an old idea. When Disneyland opened its Tomorrowland theme park in 1955, among the exhibits were plastic houses set not too far from the Moonliner. Since then, multinationals such as General Electric Co. have tried to build plastic houses and failed. Royal's houses, developed after $50 million in spending and seven prototypes since 1990, may change that.

The building system works somewhat like a giant Lego set. Instead of blocks, though, it uses hollow panels that slot together and are then filled with cement. Once finished with brick or siding, the resulting house looks like a regular home, only it feels more solid inside. It's also cheaper and faster to build, with three semi-skilled workers able to put up a 550-square-foot home in three days for about US$16 000.

"With the building system they don't cut down any more trees, it's maintenance-free, very competitive and it lasts over 200 years," says De Zen.

Home sales could grow to 40% of Royal's total revenue by 2002 from less than 10% in 1997, he expects.

Royal sees the potential market as vast, having received building code approval in about 25 countries. It has made sales throughout the world, including in South America, Russia, Eastern Europe, Taiwan and the southern U.S., where termites and damp weather feast on traditional wooden structures.

Among the big sales last year were a $40-million, 800-home project in Russia, a $10-million, 2160-home complex in the Philippines, a $14-million, 460-unit resort and casino in St. Kitts, and a $5-million, 400-home deal in Argentina.

In Canada, the homes are also beginning to gain acceptance, with sales to such diverse customers as remote First Nations groups and the luxury condo market.

The system has commercial applications too, with Shell Oil Co. using it to erect at least 70 car washes and a 2000-square-metre office in Houston. Royal has formed a 50-50 joint venture with Shell Chemical Holdings Inc. to develop the market for Royal structures for such things as convenience stores, service centres, research facilities and office buildings.

De Zen himself doesn't live in a plastic house—his wife refuses to move from their home in the country—but his son is building an 1800-square-metre plastic monster home for himself.

Despite the growing financial returns—the backlog for homes is about $150 million—De Zen says the greatest satisfaction comes from helping shelter the poor.

This was brought home when he toured Antigua after a hurricane in 1995 destroyed most houses but left standing homes and a school built with the Royal System.

"People were kissing me, they thought I was like the Pope," he recalls. "They called me in. 'Come on, eat and drink with us,' they said. '"My friend is dead, but I'm alive.'"

Source: P. Fitzpatrick, "De Zen and the Art of Home Maintenance," *The Financial Post Daily*, May 13, 1998, p. 10.

Questions

1. Use Porter's Five Forces Model to analyze the nature of competition in Royal Group Technologies' industry.
2. What business- and functional-level strategies is Vic De Zen pursuing to compete in this industry?

MANAGEMENT CASE ─────────────────── IN THE NEWS

From the Pages of *Canadian Plastics* Holding Its Own

This New Brunswick-based operation, one of Amcor PET Packaging's five bottle manufacturing plants in Canada, has seen a number of changes in the Atlantic Canada bottling market in recent years. One of the company's long-time customers, Coca Cola, pulled out of the Maritimes when it decided to consolidate its operations in Quebec. While soft drink beverage bottles still form the bulk of the Moncton plant's business, bottled water now accounts for 15 to 20 percent of sales and has seen significant growth during the last few years.

"We've been very encouraged by the growth of the water market," says plant manager David Kinnear. The plant is currently supplying a number of companies with water bottles in 355 mL, 500 mL, 1 L and 1.5 L sizes. It is also looking to secure more bottled water business in the near future. As the bottled water market has grown, large beverage companies have also entered the market, Kinnear says, noting that Pepsi sponsors the Aquafina label and Coca Cola has the Desani brand.

The company's main customers in the beverage business are Pepsi, Cott, Big 8 and Cassidy beverages, for which it supplies bottles in sizes ranging from 250 mL to 2 L. It makes bottles in clear and green, which are made from pre-colored PET. It also has the capability to make a blue-tinted bottle for water using color concentrate.

The facility has three Husky injection molding machines for making pre-forms, and three Krupp Coroplast machines, as well as one Milacron machine, for stretch-blowing the pre-forms into bottles. Blow machines run at a rate of between 2700 and 10 100 bottles per hour. Palletized bottles are usually aged 72 hours before shipping and stored in a high-ceilinged warehouse capable of accommodating three-high pallet stacking.

The Moncton operation has its own budget, and, as well, is empowered to meet its production targets and develop new business. As a member of the Amcor PET Packaging family, however, the facility receives considerable R&D and marketing support at the corporate level, Kinnear stresses. All resin pricing is negotiated through Amcor's central corporate offices.

There is a high priority placed on reducing costs at the company, as there is in the bottling industry as a whole, notes Kinnear. Designing bottles that are lighter in weight is one strategy used to cut raw material costs. For instance, in 1981 a 2 L bottle weighed about 68 g, compared with 47 g today. As bottles become lighter, the goal to take out still more weight and meet all the performance criteria required for bottles becomes more of a challenge. Amcor, and as it was once known, Twinpak, have been at the forefront in the use of advanced technology to build lighter, stronger bottles through investment in corporate research and development.

At the plant level, employees are encouraged to suggest and implement ways to cut costs and improve efficiencies. The plant's maintenance staff often manufactures parts that frequently need to be replaced in production equipment, thus saving the premium on parts bought from dealers. Kinnear says the stable, mature workforce of 53 employees contributes to the facility's ability to control costs and maintain an edge on competitors.

While allowing with typical Maritime modesty that the plant's goal is to maintain the business it has, Kinnear says it is always on patrol for new business and growth. "We are always looking for new opportunities. Every day we ask ourselves what steps we can take to find new business and customers."

Source: M. LeGault, "Holding Its Own: Growth in the Bottled Water Business Has Enabled Amcor PET Packaging's Moncton Plant to Maintain Its Position as the Leading Bottle Manufacturer in Atlantic Canada," *Canadian Plastics*, December 2000, p. 16.

Questions

1. What strategies did David Kinnear use to increase the profitability of the Moncton plant?
2. What kinds of control systems does Kinnear use with his employees? How does the control system support productivity?
3. What kinds of corporate- and business-level strategies is Kinnear working on to help increase Amcor's performance?

Part 4

CHAPTER 6

MANAGING ORGANIZATIONAL STRUCTURE

Learning Objectives

1. Identify the factors that influence managers' choice of an organizational structure.

2. Explain how managers group tasks into jobs that are motivating and satisfying for employees.

3. Describe the organizational structures managers can design, and explain why they choose one structure over another.

4. Explain why there is a need to both centralize and decentralize authority.

5. Explain why managers who seek new ways to increase efficiency and effectiveness are using strategic alliances and network structures.

Roles in Contrast: Questions

MANAGERS	EMPLOYEES
How should I organize the tasks within individual jobs?	How might organizational structure affect me?
What is the best way to organize divisions?	Why does my company organize us into geographic divisions?
What is the best organizational structure to use?	What happens when managers are laid off?

A CASE IN  CONTRAST

ALTAMIRA MOVES FROM ITS ENTREPRENEURIAL ROOTS TO A TEAM STRUCTURE

Altamira Investment Services Ltd. (www.altamira.com) was the poster child for the Canadian mutual fund industry from 1987 to the mid-1990s. Founded in the late 1960s in Toronto, the company had developed an entrepreneurial style that served it well in its early years. By the early 1990s, Altamira was seen as the little no-load company that could, because it was one of the hottest firms in the no-load sector and was attracting lots of money from investors.

By the mid-1990s, however, the company's entrepreneurial style was not working as well. Altamira had grown too large, too fast, and little consideration had been given to adjusting the organizational structure to suit the new times. The environment for mutual fund companies had changed considerably over the company's 30-year history: Regulations were being rewritten, new market entrants were using e-business, established companies were making new alliances to increase their global capacities,

and consumers were demanding a more integrated approach to their wealth management needs.[1]

The company was also facing internal problems: There had been a bitter battle for ownership of Altamira; the company's flagship mutual fund was not doing well; one of its star performers had resigned under a cloud of suspicion; and clients had become impatient and taken millions of dollars elsewhere.

In early 1998, Altamira named Gordon Cheesbrough as CEO to turn the company around. Cheesbrough had been chief executive at ScotiaMcLeod Inc., the investment dealer arm of the Bank of Nova Scotia. Though Altamira was struggling when Cheesbrough arrived, he immediately recognized that there were a number of things that the company did well. These included having a smart group of people who were "loyal to the company and committed to

Gordon Cheesbrough, CEO of Altamira Investment Services Ltd., instituted more of a team structure at the company when he arrived in 1998.

When Frank Mersch, formerly the "star" fund manager at Altamira, departed the company, the need for structural changes in the organization became obvious.

putting it back on top."[2] The company also had a good reputation for direct-to-client services and a history of innovation.

He also saw a number of things that had to change. One serious problem was that the lagging performance of the Altamira Equity Fund was affecting the entire company. Because it represented 35 percent of the company's mutual fund assets, the fund's performance had a large impact on everyone's morale. Frank Mersch had been the fund manager for Altamira Equity for a number of years, and was considered a star. In fact, Mersch was the face of Altamira during the 1980s and early 1990s.

However, with the departure of Mersch as the result of being disciplined by the Ontario Securities Commission for trading in a penny stock, it became obvious that Altamira's largest organizational structure problem was its star system of portfolio management. "If Altamira hadn't invented it, we certainly had put our name on it," said Cheesbrough. While that system had greatly benefited Altamira for a number of years, Cheesbrough did not see it as the way to move the company forward. "One person cannot carry a company on his or her shoulders. The star system inhibits team-building. It hampers succession planning and expansion into new areas that require new skills. And it affects the morale of employees who live in the star's shadow."[3]

Cheesbrough's goal was to create a team-based corporate structure for Altamira, while keeping the unique qualities and spirit that had made the company successful in the past. Creating a team was not an easy task, however. When Cheesbrough arrived, there were 14 highly talented, highly competitive portfolio managers. Their competitive drive was directed at each other, however, rather than toward the competition. "So I quickly called the managers together and told them that, from now on, we would be fighting the competition and not each other," said Cheesbrough.[4]

Building the team was not always easy. As Cheesbrough noted, communication wasn't open or frequent at the company when he started there. Often, employees found out important company news by reading it in the newspaper. So he insisted that people had to be treated as team members, not as competitors. The company began weekly meetings so that portfolio managers could share market information and develop ideas for new products. "In short, we started thinking about maximizing our performance and service capabilities as a fund family, not just as individual funds," says Cheesbrough.[5]

TA Associates Inc. of Boston, which bought 35 percent of Altamira in 1997, feels that Cheesbrough did the right thing by moving to a team structure. Mersch's departure "made room to do what needed to be done anyway, which was to move more to a team management approach. . . . You've got a lot more cooperation than ever before and the investment results are, I think, starting to show that," said Andrews McLane, a managing director at TA.[6] Altamira's structure also helped it build a strong reputation for customer service. The company was named the top mutual fund company for client service for three years in a row, starting in 1999.[7] Altamira considered an initial public offering (IPO) in late 2000. However, National Bank of Canada purchased it in June 2002. In the end, the team structure was not enough to overcome the struggling equity markets of the early 2000s.

OVERVIEW

As the *Case in Contrast* suggests, the challenge facing Altamira Investment Services was to identify the best way to operate in the new, more competitive industry environment. Under Gordon Cheesbrough, Altamira radically changed the way it organized its employees and other resources to meet that challenge, and the company improved.

In Part 4, we examine how managers can organize human and other resources to create high-performing organizations. To organize, managers must design an organization that makes the best use of resources to produce the goods and services customers want.

By the end of this chapter, you will be familiar not only with various organizational structures but also with various factors that determine the organizational design choices that managers make. Then in Chapter 7, we examine issues surrounding the organization's culture and what it takes for an organization to achieve change.

DESIGNING ORGANIZATIONAL STRUCTURE

Think About It

Cascades Inc.'s Product Structure

Kingsey Falls, Quebec-based Cascades Inc., Canada's second-largest pulp and paper company, has more than 80 mills and plants in Canada, the United States, France, Germany, and Sweden.[8] The company's strength has been absorbing and turning around money-losing acquisitions. While Alain Lemaire is president and CEO, his two brothers Bernard and Laurent are also a part of the business.

Cascades has several publicly traded subsidiaries, including Cascades Boxboard Group Inc., Cascades Tissue Group Inc., and Cascades Fine Papers Group Inc., and owns a 41-percent share in Boralex Inc. The first three are in the pulp and paper business, producing tissues, container-board packaging, boxboard packaging, and fine papers. Boralex is an energy producer headed by brother Bernard. Each of the companies is treated as a separate entity, based on product.

The Lemaires emphasize decentralized, entrepreneurial management, a style once viewed as unwieldy and complicated. However, other Canadian forest products companies, such as Montreal-based Avenor Inc. and Domtar, are now following Cascades' lead and decentralizing their operations. Under Cascades' novel corporate structure, each subsidiary company operates like a federation of small and medium-sized businesses. In fact, each mill within a subsidiary operates as a separate business unit, accountable for its own bottom line. The company uses profit sharing to motivate its employees, but employees get to share only in the profits generated by the mill they work for. The managers at each individual operation have to be both more responsible and more accountable for operations, while encouraging employees to take more ownership of their job performance.

Question

1. What factors affect how managers group the different parts of their business?

Organizing is the process by which managers establish the structure of working relationships among employees to allow them to achieve organizational goals

organizational structure

A formal system of both task and reporting relationships that coordinates and motivates organizational members so that they work together to reach organizational goals.

organizational design

The process by which managers make specific organizing choices that result in a particular kind of organizational structure.

efficiently and effectively. **Organizational structure** is the formal system of task and reporting relationships that determines how employees use resources to reach organizational goals.[9] **Organizational design** is the process by which managers make specific organizing choices that result in the construction of a particular organizational structure.[10]

How do managers design a structure? The way an organization's structure works depends on the organizing choices managers make about four issues:

- how to group tasks into individual jobs;

- how to group jobs into functions and divisions;

- how to coordinate and allocate authority in the organization among jobs, functions, and divisions;

- whether to pursue a more formal or flexible structure.

GROUPING TASKS INTO JOBS: JOB DESIGN

Think About It

Sadie Hawkins Lives at Windsor Auto Plants

At DaimlerChrysler AG's Windsor plants, unionized employees can switch jobs once a year in a practice known as "Sadie Hawkins day."[11] The automaker posts all unionized jobs, and employees bid on them by seniority. This gives employees the opportunity to bid for more interesting work, or less physically demanding work, as they see fit.

During its contract negotiations with the Canadian Autoworkers union in late 2002, the company tried to eliminate this practice. So many employees ask to switch jobs that it results in a 40-percent job turnover each year, and involves expensive retraining for employees who change jobs. The company asked employees to accept a job rotation system instead, where they would learn several key jobs, and rotate through them. This would allow more flexibility for the company.

Questions
1. How do tasks get grouped into jobs?
2. Is there a best way to group jobs?

job design

The process by which managers decide how to divide tasks into specific jobs.

The first step in organizational design is **job design**, the process by which managers decide how to divide tasks into specific jobs. Managers at McDonald's, for example, have decided how best to divide the tasks required to provide customers with fast, cheap food in each McDonald's restaurant. After experimenting with different job arrangements, McDonald's managers decided on a basic division of labour among chefs and food servers. Managers allocated all the tasks involved in actually cooking the food (putting oil in the fat fryers, opening packages of frozen french fries, putting beef patties on the grill, making salads, and so on) to the job of chef. They allocated all the tasks involved in giving the food to customers (such as greeting customers; taking orders; putting fries and burgers into bags; adding salt, pepper, and serviettes; and taking money) to food servers. They also created other jobs—the job of dealing with drive-through customers, the job of keeping the restaurant clean, and the job of shift manager responsible for overseeing employees and responding to unexpected events. The result of the job design process is a *division of labour* among employees, one that McDonald's and other managers have discovered through experience is most efficient.

Establishing an appropriate division of labour among employees is a critical part of the organizing process, one that is vital to increasing efficiency and effectiveness. At McDonald's, the tasks associated with chef and food server were split into different jobs because managers found that, for the kind of food McDonald's serves, this approach was most efficient. When employees are given fewer tasks to perform (so that their jobs become more specialized), they become more productive at performing the tasks that constitute their job.

A strict division of labour is not the only way to organize jobs in a fast food restaurant, however. At Subway sandwich shops, there is no division of labour among the people who make the sandwiches, wrap the sandwiches, give them to customers, and take the money. The roles of chef and food server are combined into one role. This different division of tasks and jobs is efficient for Subway and not for McDonald's because Subway serves a limited menu of mostly submarine-style sandwiches that are prepared to order. Subway's production system is far simpler than McDonald's, because McDonald's menu is much more varied and its chefs must cook many different kinds of foods.

job simplification

Reducing the number of tasks that each worker performs.

Managers of every organization must analyze the range of tasks to be performed and then create jobs that best allow the organization to give customers the goods and services they want. In deciding how to assign tasks to individual jobs, however, managers must be careful not to go too far with **job simplification**–the process of reducing the number of tasks that each employee performs.[12] Too much job simplification may reduce efficiency rather than increase it if workers find their simplified jobs boring and monotonous, become demotivated and unhappy, and as a result perform at a low level.

Job Enlargement and Job Enrichment

Researchers have looked at ways to create a division of labour and design individual jobs to encourage employees to perform at a higher level and be more satisfied with their work. Based on this research, they have proposed job enlargement and job enrichment as better ways than job simplification to group tasks into jobs.

Employees at Subway follow the carefully designed work procedures that allow the company to provide a large variety of sandwiches to customers quickly at peak times.

job enlargement
Increasing the number of different tasks in a given job by changing the division of labour.

Job enlargement increases the *number of different tasks* in a given job by changing the division of labour.[13] For example, because Subway food servers make the food as well as serve it, their jobs are "larger" than the jobs of McDonald's food servers. The idea behind job enlargement is that increasing the range of tasks performed by an employee will reduce boredom and fatigue and may increase motivation to perform at a high level—increasing both the quantity and the quality of goods and services provided.

job enrichment
Increasing the degree of responsibility a worker has over his or her job.

Job enrichment increases the *degree of responsibility* a worker has over his or her job by, for example, (1) empowering employees to experiment to find new or better ways of doing the job, (2) encouraging employees to develop new skills, (3) allowing employees to decide how to do the work and giving them the responsibility for deciding how to respond to unexpected situations, and (4) allowing employees to monitor and measure their own performance.[14] The idea behind job enrichment is that increasing employees' responsibility increases their involvement in their jobs and thus increases their interest in the quality of the goods they make or the services they provide.

In general, managers who make design choices that increase job enrichment and job involvement are likely to increase the degree to which workers behave flexibly rather than rigidly or mechanically. Narrow, specialized jobs are likely to lead people to behave in predictable ways; employees who perform a variety of tasks and who are allowed and encouraged to discover new and better ways to perform their jobs are likely to act flexibly and creatively. Thus, managers who enlarge and enrich jobs create a flexible organizational structure, and those who simplify jobs create a more formal structure. If employees are also grouped into self-managed work teams, the organization is likely to be flexible because team members provide support for each other and can learn from one another.

One of the tensions at the Windsor DaimlerChrysler plant when management tried to get rid of Sadie Hawkins Day was the extent to which managers wanted employees to behave flexibly, rather than perform well-defined jobs. Some union members feared that jobs would be lost if there was too much flexibility. They were also concerned that employees who have difficulty doing some jobs, but are well suited for others, might lose their jobs completely if Sadie Hawkins Day was eliminated.

GROUPING JOBS INTO FUNCTIONS AND DIVISIONS

Think About It

From Geographic to Market Structure at Royal Bank

How do you create a structure for providing bank services for corporate clients, and ensure they get the attention they need? Toronto-based RBC Dominion Securities Inc. (part of the Royal Bank group) did so by creating a global banking division responsible for handling the major tasks of global banking in a more integrative fashion.[15] Previously, clients were contacted by both a corporate banker and an investment banker who would try to get new business. Under the restructuring, each relationship officer takes responsibility for all aspects of a client's needs: debt, equity, or advisory services. The 200 relationship officers are divided into eight industry groups: communications and technology, diversified industries, energy, financial institutions, mining, forest products, real estate, and the public sector.

Due to the restructuring, corporate clients now have industry specialists serving their needs, whereas previously the divisions were made according to geographic regions. Under the previous structure, customers were not getting the level of personalized service they required. Meanwhile, the bankers' talents were stretched thin because clients from different industries had different needs. RBC's change from a geographic to a market structure makes it easier for the salesforce to serve its customers.

Question

1. What is the best way to organize divisions: by function, product, market, or geography?

Once managers have decided which tasks to allocate to which jobs, they face the next organizing decision: how to group jobs together to best match the needs of the organization's environment, strategy, technology, and human resources. Most top-management teams decide to group jobs into departments and develop a functional structure to use organizational resources. As the organization grows, managers design a divisional structure or a more complex matrix or product team structure.

Choosing a structure and then designing it so that it works as intended is a significant challenge. As noted in Chapter 5, managers reap the rewards of a well-thought-out strategy only if they choose a suitable type of structure initially and then execute the strategy. The ability to make the right kinds of organizing choices is often what sets effective and ineffective managers apart.

Functional Structure

functional structure

An organizational structure composed of all the departments that an organization requires to produce its goods or services.

A function is a group of people, working together, who possess similar skills or use the same kind of knowledge, tools, or techniques to perform their jobs. Manufacturing, sales, and research and development are often organized into functional departments. A **functional structure** is an organizational structure composed of all the departments that an organization requires to produce its goods or services. Pier 1 Imports, a home furnishings company, uses a functional structure to supply its customers with a range of goods from around the world to satisfy their desires for new and innovative products.

Pier 1's main functions are finance and administration, merchandising (purchasing the goods), stores (managing the retail outlets), logistics (managing product distribution), marketing, human resources, and real estate. Each job inside a function exists because it helps the function perform the activities necessary for high organizational performance. Thus, within the logistics department are all the jobs necessary to distribute and transport products efficiently to stores. Inside the marketing department are all the jobs (such as promotion, photography, and visual communication) that are necessary to increase the appeal of Pier 1's products to customers.

There are several advantages to grouping jobs according to function. First, when people who perform similar jobs are grouped together, they can learn from watching one another. Thus they become more specialized and can perform at a higher level. The tasks associated with one job often are related to the tasks associated with another job, which encourages cooperation within a function. Second, when people who perform similar jobs are grouped together, managers can monitor and evaluate their performance more easily.[16] Finally, as we saw in Chapter 2, managers like functional structure because it allows them to create the set of functions they need for scanning and monitoring the task and general environments.[17]

As an organization grows, and its strategy changes to produce a wider range of goods and services for different kinds of customers, several problems can make a functional structure less efficient and effective.[18] First, managers in different functions may find it more difficult to communicate and coordinate with one another when they are responsible for several different kinds of products, especially as the organization grows both domestically and internationally. Second, functional managers may become so preoccupied with supervising their own specific departments and achieving their departmental goals that they lose sight of organizational goals. If that happens, organizational effectiveness will suffer because managers will be viewing issues and problems facing the organization only from their own, relatively narrow, departmental perspectives.[19] Both of these problems can reduce efficiency and effectiveness.

Divisional Structures: Product, Geographic, and Market

divisional structure

An organizational structure composed of separate business units within which are the functions that work together to produce a specific product for a specific customer.

As the problems associated with growth and diversification increase over time, managers must search for new ways to organize their activities to overcome the problems linked with a functional structure. Most managers of large organizations choose a **divisional structure** and create a series of business units to produce a specific kind of product for a specific kind of customer. Each division is a collection of functions or departments that work together to produce the product. The goal behind the change to a divisional structure is to create smaller, more manageable units within the organization. There are three forms of divisional structure (see Figure 6.1).[20] When managers organize divisions according to the type of good or

Figure 6.1 | Product, Market, and Geographic Structures

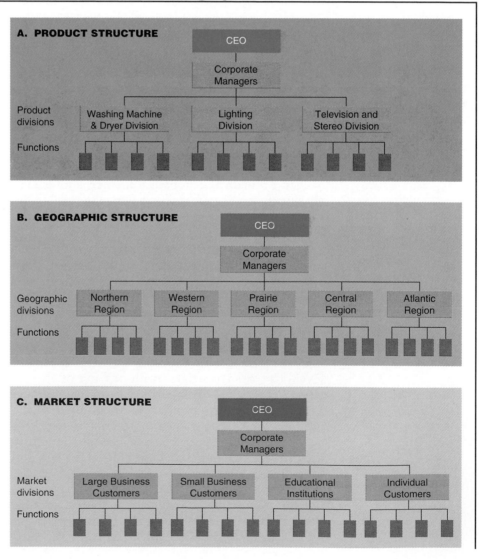

A. PRODUCT STRUCTURE

CEO

Corporate Managers

Product divisions: Washing Machine & Dryer Division | Lighting Division | Television and Stereo Division

Functions

B. GEOGRAPHIC STRUCTURE

CEO

Corporate Managers

Geographic divisions: Northern Region | Western Region | Prairie Region | Central Region | Atlantic Region

Functions

C. MARKET STRUCTURE

CEO

Corporate Managers

Market divisions: Large Business Customers | Small Business Customers | Educational Institutions | Individual Customers

Functions

service they provide, they adopt a *product* structure. When managers organize divisions according to the area of the country or world they operate in, they adopt a *geographic* structure. When managers organize divisions according to the types of customers they focus on, they adopt a *market* structure.

Product Structure

product structure
An organizational structure in which each product line or business is handled by a self-contained division.

Using a **product structure** (see Figure 6.1A), managers place each distinct product line or business in its own self-contained division and give divisional managers the responsibility for devising an appropriate business-level strategy to allow the division to compete effectively in its industry or market.[21] Each division is self-contained because it has a complete set of all the functions—marketing, R&D, finance, and so on—that it needs to produce or provide goods or services efficiently and effectively. Functional managers report to divisional managers, and divisional managers report to top or corporate managers.

Grouping functions into divisions focused on particular products has several advantages for managers at all levels in the organization. First, a product structure allows functional managers to specialize in only one product area, so they are able to build expertise and fine-tune their skills in this particular area. Second, each division's managers can become experts in their industry; this expertise helps them choose and develop a business-level strategy to differentiate their products or lower their costs while meeting the needs of customers. Third, a product structure frees corporate managers from the need to supervise each division's day-to-day operations directly; this latitude allows corporate managers to create the best corporate-level strategy to maximize the organization's future growth and ability to create value. Corporate managers are likely to make fewer mistakes about which businesses to diversify into or how best to expand internationally, for example, because they are able to take an organization-wide view.[22] Corporate managers also are likely to better evaluate how well divisional managers are doing, and they can intervene and take corrective action as needed.

The extra layer of management, the divisional management layer, can improve the use of organizational resources. Moreover, a product structure puts divisional managers close to their customers and lets them respond quickly and appropriately to the changing task environment. Organizations sometimes change their divisional strategy because of market changes. When RBC moved from geographic to product organization, Gordon Nixon, the president and CEO at RBC Financial Group Inc., explained that the change was to help clients who wanted services and products delivered as efficiently as possible. The restructuring means that there will be a single accountability for all of the products that RBC Dominion Securities delivers to clients.

RBC Dominion
Securities
www.rbcinvestments.com

Geographic Structure

geographic structure
An organizational structure in which each region of a country or area of the world is served by a self-contained division.

When organizations expand rapidly both at home and abroad, functional structures can create special problems, because managers in one central location may find it increasingly difficult to deal with the different problems and issues that may arise in each region of a country or area of the world. In these cases, a **geographic structure**, in which divisions are broken down by geographical location, is often chosen (see Figure 6.1B). To achieve the corporate mission of providing next-day mail service, Fred Smith, chair, president, and CEO of Federal Express, chose a geographic structure and divided up operations by creating a division in each region. Large retailers often use a geographic structure. Since the needs of retail customers differ by region—for example, umbrellas in Vancouver and down-filled parkas in the Prairies and the East—a geographic structure gives regional retail managers the flexibility they need to choose products that best meet the needs of regional customers.

Telus Communications
Inc.
www.telus.com

market structure
An organizational structure
in which each kind of
customer is served by a
self-contained division; also
called *customer structure*.

Market Structure

Sometimes, the pressing issue managers face is how to group functions according to the type of customer buying the product, in order to tailor the organization's products to each customer's unique demands. Burnaby, BC-based Telus is structured around six customer-focused business units: Consumer Solutions, focused on households and individuals; Business Solutions, focused on small- to medium-sized businesses and entrepreneurs; Client Solutions, focused on large organizations in Canada; Partner Solutions, focused on Canadian and global carriers into and within Canada; Wireless Solutions, focused on people and businesses on the go; and Telus Québec, a Telus company for the Quebec marketplace.

To satisfy the needs of diverse customers, Telus adopts a **market structure** (also called a *customer structure*), which groups divisions according to the particular kinds of customers they serve (see Figure 6.1C). A market structure allows managers to be both responsive to the needs of their customers and able to act flexibly to make decisions in response to customers' changing needs.

Matrix and Product Team Designs

Moving to a product, market, or geographic divisional structure means managers can respond more quickly and flexibly to the particular set of circumstances they confront. However, when the environment is dynamic and rapidly changing, and uncertainty is high, even a divisional structure may not provide managers with enough flexibility to respond to the environment quickly enough. When technology or customer needs are changing rapidly and the environment is very uncertain, managers must design the most flexible organizational structure available: a *matrix structure* or a *product team structure* (see Figure 6.2).

Matrix Structure

matrix structure
An organizational structure
that simultaneously groups
people and resources by
function and by product.

In a **matrix structure**, managers group people and resources in two ways simultaneously: by function and by product.[23] Employees are grouped into *functions* to allow them to learn from one another and become more skilled and productive. Employees are also grouped into *product teams*, in which members of different functions work together to develop a specific product. The result is a complex network of reporting relationships among product teams and functions that makes the matrix structure very flexible (see Figure 6.2A). Each person in a product team reports to two managers: (1) a functional manager, who assigns individuals to a team and evaluates their performance from a functional point of view, and (2) the manager of the product team, who evaluates their performance on the team.

The functional employees assigned to product teams change over time as the specific skills that the team needs change. At the beginning of the product development process, for example, engineers and R&D specialists are assigned to a product team because their skills are needed to develop new products. When a provisional design has been established, marketing experts are assigned to the team to gauge how customers will respond to the new product. Manufacturing personnel join when it is time to find the most efficient way to produce the product. As their specific jobs are completed, team members leave and are reassigned to new teams. In this way, the matrix structure makes the most use of human resources.

To keep the matrix structure flexible, product teams are empowered and team members are responsible for making most of the important decisions involved in product development.[24] The product team manager acts as a facilitator, controlling the financial resources and trying to keep the project on time and within budget. The functional managers try to ensure that the product is the best that it can be in order to make the most of its differentiated appeal.

Figure 6.2 | Matrix and Product Team Structures

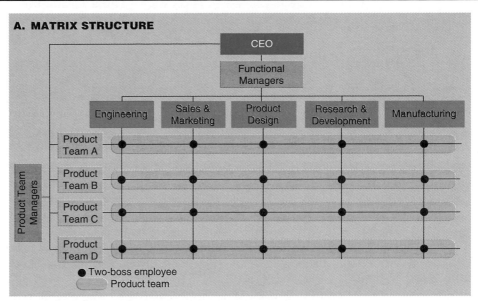

A. MATRIX STRUCTURE

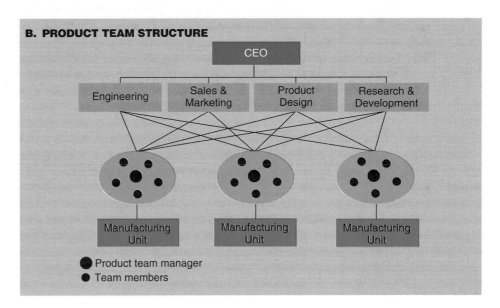

B. PRODUCT TEAM STRUCTURE

High-tech companies have been using matrix structures successfully for many years. These companies operate in environments where new product developments happen monthly or yearly and the need to innovate quickly is vital to the organization's survival. The matrix structure provides enough flexibility for managers to keep pace with a changing and increasingly complex environment. For this reason, matrixes also have been designed by managers who want to control international operations as they move abroad and face problems of coordinating their domestic and foreign divisions.[25] Motorola, for example, operates a global matrix structure because it hopes to obtain synergies from cooperation among its worldwide divisions.

A global matrix structure allows an organization's domestic divisions to supply its foreign divisions quickly with knowledge about new R&D advances in order to help the foreign divisions gain a competitive advantage in their local markets. Likewise, the foreign divisions can transmit new product marketing ideas to domestic divisions that may give the domestic divisions an advantage in the domestic market. The expression "Think locally but act globally" describes the way managers in global matrix structures should behave.[26]

Product Team Structure

The dual reporting relationships that are at the heart of a matrix structure have always been difficult for managers and employees to deal with. Often, the functional manager and the product manager make conflicting demands on team members, who do not know which manager to satisfy first. Also, functional and product team managers may come into conflict over precisely who is in charge of which team members and for how long. To avoid these problems, managers have devised a way of organizing people and resources that still allows an organization to be flexible but makes its structure easier to operate: a product team structure.

product team structure

An organizational structure in which employees are permanently assigned to a cross-functional team and report only to the product team manager or to one of his or her direct subordinates.

cross-functional team

A group of individuals from different departments brought together to perform organizational tasks.

The **product team structure** differs from a matrix structure in two ways: (1) It does away with dual reporting relationships for employees, and (2) functional employees are permanently assigned to a cross-functional team that is empowered to bring a new or redesigned product to market. A **cross-functional team** is a group of individuals brought together from different departments to perform organizational tasks. When individuals are grouped into cross-departmental teams, the artificial boundaries between departments disappear, and a narrow focus on departmental goals is replaced with a general interest in working together to achieve organizational goals. The results of such changes have been dramatic: For example, Chrysler Canada's use of cross-functional teams has reduced the time it takes to retool for a new product from months to just weeks.

Members of a cross-functional team report only to the product team manager or to one of his or her direct subordinates. The functional managers have only an informal, advisory relationship with members of the product teams. These managers counsel and help cross-functional team members, share knowledge among teams, and provide new technological developments that can help improve each team's performance (see Figure 6.2B).[27]

COORDINATING FUNCTIONS AND DIVISIONS

Think About It

Procter & Gamble's New World Hierarchy

Until 1995, managers in each P&G division, in every country in which the company operated, were more or less free to make their own decisions.[28] Thus, managers in charge of the soap and detergent division in the United Kingdom operated independently from managers in the soap and detergent divisions in France and Germany. Moreover, even within the United Kingdom, the soap and detergent division operated independently from other UK Procter & Gamble divisions such as the health care and beauty products divisions. Top managers saw that this highly decentralized global decision making was reducing opportunities for synergies that could come from cooperation not only among managers of the same kind of division in the different countries (soap and detergent divisions throughout Europe) but also in different divisions operating in the same country or world region. So Procter & Gamble UK's top managers pioneered a new organizational structure.

Questions
1. Why do organizations group authority relationships the way they do?
2. Is there one best way to coordinate authority?

In organizing, managers' first task is to group functions and divisions and create the organizational structure best suited to the contingencies they face. Managers' next task is to ensure that there is sufficient coordination among functions and divisions so that organizational resources are used efficiently and effectively. Having discussed how managers divide organizational activities into jobs, functions, and divisions to increase efficiency and effectiveness, we now look at how they put the parts back together.

Allocating Authority

authority
The power to hold people accountable for their actions and to make decisions concerning the use of organizational resources.

hierarchy of authority
An organization's chain of command, specifying the relative authority of each manager.

span of control
The number of subordinates who report directly to a manager.

As organizations grow and produce a wider range of goods and services, the size and number of their functions and divisions increase. To coordinate the activities of people, functions, and divisions, and to allow them to work together effectively, managers must develop a clear hierarchy of authority.[29] **Authority** is the power vested in a manager to make decisions and use resources to achieve organizational goals by virtue of his or her position in an organization. The **hierarchy of authority** is an organization's chain of command—the relative authority that each manager has—extending from the CEO at the top, down through the middle managers and first-line managers, to the nonmanagerial employees who actually make goods or provide services. Every manager, at every level of the hierarchy, supervises one or more subordinates. The term **span of control** refers to the number of subordinates who report directly to a manager.

Tall and Flat Organizations

As an organization grows in size (normally measured by the number of its managers and employees), its hierarchy of authority normally lengthens, making the organizational structure taller. A *tall* organization has many levels of authority relative to company size; a *flat* organization has fewer levels relative to company size (see Figure 6.3).[30] As a hierarchy becomes taller, problems may result that make the organization's structure less flexible and that slow managers' response to changes in the organizational environment.

For instance, communication problems may arise. When an organization has many levels in the hierarchy, it can take a long time for the decisions and orders of upper-level managers to reach managers further down in the hierarchy, and it can take a long time for top managers to learn how well their decisions worked out. Feeling out of touch, top managers may want to verify that lower-level managers are following orders and may require written confirmation from them. Middle managers, who know they will be held strictly accountable for their actions, start devoting more time to the process of making decisions in order to improve their chances of being right. They might even try to avoid responsibility by making top managers decide what actions to take.

Another communication problem that can result is the distortion of commands and orders being transmitted up and down the hierarchy, which causes managers at different levels to interpret differently what is happening. Distortion of orders and messages can be accidental, occurring because different managers interpret messages from their own narrow functional perspectives. Or it can be intentional, occurring because managers low in the hierarchy decide to interpret information to increase their own personal advantage.

Another problem with tall hierarchies is that usually they indicate an organization is employing many managers, and managers are expensive. Managerial salaries, benefits, offices, and secretaries are a huge expense for organizations. Large companies such as IBM and General Motors pay their managers billions of dollars a year. Throughout the 1990s, hundreds of thousands of middle managers were laid off as companies tried to reduce costs by restructuring and downsizing their workforces.

Figure 6.3 | Tall and Flat Organizations

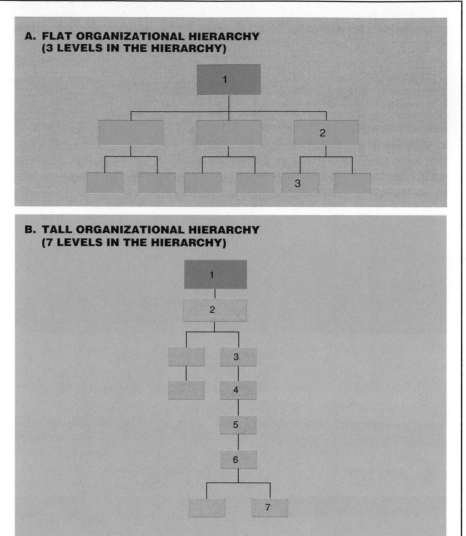

The Minimum Chain of Command

To ward off the problems that result when an organization becomes too tall and employs too many managers, top managers need to work out whether they are employing the right number of middle and first-line managers, and to see whether they can redesign their organizational structure to reduce the number of managers. Top managers might well follow a basic organizing principle—the principle of the minimum chain of command—which states that top managers should always construct a hierarchy with the fewest levels of authority necessary to use organizational resources efficiently and effectively.

Effective managers constantly scrutinize their hierarchies to see whether the number of levels can be reduced—for example, by eliminating one level and giving the responsibilities of managers at that level to managers above and empowering employees below. This practice has become more common in Canada and the United States as companies that are battling low-cost foreign competitors search for new ways to reduce costs.

One organization that is trying to empower staff is Ducks Unlimited Canada of Stonewall, Manitoba, a private nonprofit charitable organization, founded by

sportsmen, that is devoted to preserving wetlands and associated waterfowl habitats.[31] The company recently went through a reorganization, flattening its management structure. The 330 staff members have been divided into groups to focus on different areas critical to the future of the organization. They are examining such issues as performance, development, and job classification.

Gary Goodwin, director of human resources, explains that "the reorganization was essentially to help empower employees, making it easier for people working in the field to make decisions quickly without having to go up and down the proverbial power ladder."

Centralization and Decentralization of Authority

Another way in which managers can keep the organizational hierarchy flat is to decentralize authority to lower-level managers and nonmanagerial employees.[32] If managers at higher levels give lower-level employees the responsibility to make important decisions and only manage by exception, then the problems of slow and distorted communication noted previously are kept to a minimum. Moreover, fewer managers are needed because their role is not to make decisions but to act as coach and facilitator and to help other employees make the best decisions. In addition, when decision making is low in the organization and near the customer, employees are better able to recognize and respond to customer needs.

Decentralizing authority allows an organization and its employees to behave flexibly even as the organization grows and becomes taller. This is why managers are so interested in empowering employees, creating self-managed work teams, establishing cross-functional teams, and even moving to a product team structure. These design innovations help keep the organizational structure flexible and responsive to complex task and general environments, complex technologies, and complex strategies.

While more organizations are taking steps to decentralize authority, too much decentralization has certain disadvantages. If divisions, functions, or teams are given too much decision-making authority, they may begin to pursue their own goals at the expense of organizational goals. Managers in engineering design or R&D, for example, may become so focused on making the best possible product that they fail to realize that the best product may be so expensive that few people will be willing or able to buy it. Also, with too much decentralization, lack of communication among functions or among divisions may prevent possible synergies among them from ever materializing, and organizational performance suffers. As the *Case in Contrast* shows, Altamira's lack of communication among the portfolio managers under the star system resulted in a great deal of competition that was not

Sam Markle, left, and brother Jack, owners of Toronto-based The Brothers Markle Inc., keep their company lean, even in good times. With 10 employees, and heavy reliance on subcontracting, their organizational structure is flat.

helpful to the company as a whole when the internal and external environment of the company started to change.

Top managers have to look for the balance between centralization and decentralization of authority that best meets the organization's needs. If managers are in a stable environment, using well-understood technology, and producing staple kinds of products (such as cereal, canned soup, books, or televisions), there is no pressing need to decentralize authority, and managers at the top can maintain control of much of the organizational decision making.[33] However, in uncertain, changing environments where high-tech companies are producing state-of-the-art products, top managers must empower employees and allow teams to make important strategic decisions so that the organization can keep up with the changes taking place.

Procter & Gamble chose to centralize rather than decentralize its management structure. Global operations were divided into four main areas—North America, Europe, the Middle East and Africa, and Asia. In each area, P&G created a new position—global executive vice-president—and made the person in that position responsible for overseeing the operation of all the divisions within his or her world region. Each global executive vice-president is responsible for getting the various divisions within his or her area to cooperate and to share information and knowledge that will lead to synergies; thus, authority is centralized at the world area level. All of these new executive vice-presidents report directly to the president of Procter & Gamble, further centralizing authority.

Tips for Managers

Choosing a Divisional Structure

1. If an organization begins to produce a wider range of products, and especially if it enters new businesses or industries, evaluate whether a move to a product structure will keep the organization more competitive.

2. If your organization grows and expands regionally or nationally, evaluate whether a move to a geographic structure will keep the organization more competitive.

3. If an organization begins to serve different kinds of customers, evaluate whether or not a move to a market structure will keep the organization more competitive.

4. No matter what kind of structure an organization uses, periodically analyze its hierarchy of authority and keep the number of levels in the hierarchy to a minimum.

OVERALL STRUCTURE: FORMAL OR FLEXIBLE?

Think About It

Two Restaurants, Two Styles

When you walk into McDonalds, there is a limited selection of menu items, and you can count on most of them being available every day. Supervisors make all important decisions; employees are closely supervised and follow well-defined rules and standard operating procedures. At Vancouver's Blue Water Café, by contrast, you can take a seat at the sushi bar and ask the chef on duty to create a meal of his choice. Your meal will be prepared from a selection of fish that are fresh that day, and you may not be able to get the same meal the next day. The owner doesn't direct the choices of the sushi chef. Several different servers will take your drink and dessert orders, and check on you during dinner, because the focus is on making sure the diner is enjoying the experience, not rigidly defining areas in the restaurant for each person to serve. Waitstaff help each other serve all customers.

Questions
1. Why are some organizations more mechanistic than others?
2. What are the consequences of having a rigid organizational structure, or a more flexible one?

Earlier in this chapter, we discussed the choices managers make in deciding how tasks should be organized into jobs and jobs should be grouped into departments.

Managers also need to determine how formal or flexible they want the organization to be.

Burns and Stalker proposed two basic ways in which managers can organize and control an organization's activities to respond to characteristics of its external environment: They can use a formal *mechanistic structure* or a flexible *organic structure*.[34] Figure 6.4 illustrates the differences between these two types of structures. After describing these two structures, we discuss what factors managers consider when choosing between them.

Mechanistic Structures

mechanistic structure
An organizational structure in which authority is centralized at the top of the hierarchy, tasks and roles are clearly specified, and employees are closely supervised.

When the environment around an organization is stable, managers tend to choose a mechanistic structure to organize and control activities and make employee behaviour predictable. In a **mechanistic structure**, authority is centralized at the top of the managerial hierarchy, and the vertical hierarchy of authority is the main means used to control subordinates' behaviour. Tasks and roles are clearly specified, subordinates are closely supervised, and the emphasis is on strict discipline and order. Everyone knows his or her place, and there is a place for everyone. A mechanistic structure provides the most efficient way to operate in a stable environment because it allows managers to obtain inputs at the lowest cost, giving an organization the most control over its conversion processes and enabling the most efficient production of goods and services with the smallest expenditure of resources. This explains McDonald's mechanistic structure.

Organic Structures

organic structure
An organizational structure in which authority is decentralized to middle and first-line managers and tasks and roles are left ambiguous to encourage employees to cooperate and respond quickly to the unexpected.

In contrast, when the environment is changing rapidly, it is difficult to obtain access to resources. Managers need to organize their activities in a way that allows them to cooperate, to act quickly to obtain resources (such as new types of wood to produce new kinds of furniture), and to respond effectively to the unexpected. In an **organic structure**, authority is decentralized to middle and first-line managers to encourage them to take responsibility and act quickly to pursue scarce resources. Departments are encouraged to take a cross-departmental or functional perspective, and authority rests with the individuals and departments best positioned to control the current problems the organization is facing. Control in an organic structure is much looser than it is in a mechanistic structure, and reliance on shared norms to guide organizational activities is greater. This is somewhat rep-

Figure 6.4 | Mechanistic vs. Organic Organizations

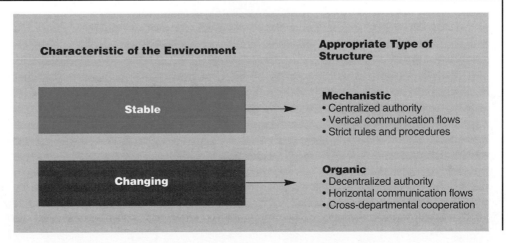

Characteristic of the Environment	Appropriate Type of Structure
Stable	**Mechanistic** • Centralized authority • Vertical communication flows • Strict rules and procedures
Changing	**Organic** • Decentralized authority • Horizontal communication flows • Cross-departmental cooperation

resentative of Blue Water Café, where restaurant staff are dependent on what is fresh and available each day to create their menus.

Managers in an organic structure can react more quickly to a changing environment than can managers in a mechanistic structure. However, an organic structure is generally more expensive to operate, so it is used only when needed—when the organizational environment is unstable and rapidly changing. Organic structures may also work more effectively if managers establish semistructures that govern "the pace, timing, and rhythm of organizational activities and processes." In other words, introducing a bit of structure while preserving most of the flexibility of the organic structure may reduce operating costs.[35]

Factors Affecting Choice of Organizational Structure

Organizational structures need to fit the factors or circumstances that affect the company the most and cause them the most uncertainty.[36] Thus, there is no "best" way to design an organization: Design reflects each organization's specific situation. Four factors are important determinants of organizational structure: the nature of the organizational environment, the type of strategy the organization pursues, the technology the organization uses, and the characteristics of the organization's human resources (see Figure 6.5).[37]

The Organizational Environment

In general, the more quickly the external environment is changing and the greater the uncertainty within it, the greater are the problems a manager faces in trying to gain access to scarce resources. In this situation, to speed decision making and communication and make it easier to obtain resources, managers typically make organizing choices that bring flexibility to the organizational structure.[38] They are likely to decentralize authority and empower lower-level employees to make important operating decisions. In contrast, if the external environment is stable, if resources are readily available, and if uncertainty is low, then less coordination and communication among people and functions is needed to obtain resources, and managers can make organizing choices that bring more formality to the organizational structure. Managers in this situation prefer to make decisions within a clearly defined hierarchy of authority and use extensive rules and standard operating procedures to govern activities.

Figure 6.5 | **Factors Affecting Organizational Structure**

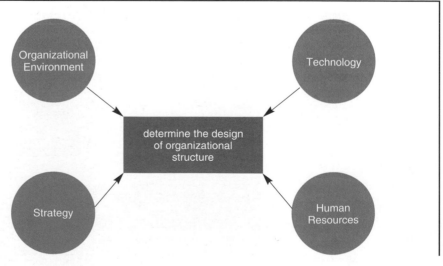

As we discussed in Chapter 2, change is rapid in today's marketplace, and increasing competition both at home and abroad is putting greater pressure on managers to attract customers and increase efficiency and effectiveness. Thus, there has been growing interest in finding ways to structure organizations—such as through empowerment and self-managed teams—to allow people and departments to behave flexibly. The *Case in Contrast* shows how Altamira moved toward a more flexible structure through its use of teams.

Strategy

As discussed in Chapter 5, once managers decide on a strategy, they must choose the right means to implement it. Different strategies often call for the use of different organizational structures. For example, a differentiation strategy aimed at increasing the value customers perceive in an organization's goods and services usually succeeds best in a flexible structure. Flexibility assists a differentiation strategy because managers can develop new or innovative products quickly—an activity that requires extensive cooperation among functions or departments. In contrast, a low-cost strategy that is aimed at driving down costs in all functions usually fares best in a more formal structure, which gives managers greater control over the expenditures and actions of the organization's various departments.[39]

In addition, at the corporate level, when managers decide to expand the scope of organizational activities by, for example, vertical integration or diversification, they need to design a flexible structure to provide sufficient coordination among the different business divisions.[40] As discussed in Chapter 5, many companies have been divesting businesses because managers have been unable to create a competitive advantage to keep them up to speed in fast-changing industries. By moving to a more flexible structure, such as a product division structure, divisional managers gain more control over their different businesses.

Finally, expanding internationally and operating in many different countries challenges managers to create organizational structures that allow organizations to be flexible on a global level.[41] As we discuss later, managers can group their departments or functions and divisions in several ways to allow them to pursue an international strategy effectively.

Technology

Technology is the combination of skills, knowledge, tools, machines, computers, and equipment that are used in the design, production, and distribution of goods and services. As a rule, the more complicated the technology that an organization uses, the more difficult it is for managers and employees to impose strict control on technology or to regulate it efficiently.[42] Thus, the more complicated the technology, the greater is the need for a flexible structure to enhance managers' and employees' ability to respond to unexpected situations and give them the freedom to work out new solutions to the problems they encounter. In contrast, the more routine the technology, the more appropriate a formal structure is, because tasks are simple and the steps needed to produce goods and services have been worked out in advance.

The nature of an organization's technology is an important determinant of its structure. Today, there is a growing use of computer-controlled production, and a movement toward using self-managed teams (groups of employees who are given the responsibility for supervising their own activities and for monitoring the quality of the goods and service they provide) to promote innovation, increase quality, and reduce costs. As a result, many companies are trying to make their structures more flexible to take advantage of the value-creating benefits of complex technology.

Human Resources

A final important factor affecting an organization's choice of structure is the characteristics of the human resources it employs. In general, the more highly skilled an organization's workforce and the more people are required to work together in groups or teams to perform their tasks, the more likely is the organization to use a flexible, decentralized structure. Highly skilled employees or employees who have internalized strong professional values and norms of behaviour as part of their training usually desire freedom and autonomy and dislike close supervision. Accountants, for example, have learned the need to report company accounts honestly and impartially, and doctors and nurses have absorbed the obligation to give patients the best care possible.

Flexible structures, characterized by decentralized authority and empowered employees, are well suited to the needs of highly skilled people. Similarly, when people work in teams, they must be allowed to interact freely, which also is possible in a flexible organizational structure. Thus, when designing an organizational structure, managers must pay close attention to the workforce and to the work itself.

In summary, an organization's external environment, strategy, technology, and human resources are the factors to be considered by managers seeking to design the best structure for an organization. The greater the level of uncertainty in an organization's environment, the more complex its strategy and technology, and the more highly qualified and skilled its workforce, the more likely managers will design a structure that is flexible. The more stable an organization's environment, the less complex and better understood its strategy or technology, and the less skilled its workforce, the more likely managers will design an organizational structure that is formal and controlling.

Tips for Managers

Designing Structure and Jobs

1. Carefully analyze an organization's environment, strategy, technology, and human resources to decide which type of organizational structure to use.

2. To create a more formal structure, carefully define the limits of each employee's job, create clear job descriptions, and evaluate each employee on his or her individual job performance.

3. To create a more flexible structure, enlarge and enrich jobs and allow employees to expand their jobs over time. Also, encourage employees to work together, and evaluate both individual and group performance.

4. Use the job characteristics model to guide job design and recognize that most jobs can be enriched to make them more motivating and satisfying.

STRATEGIC ALLIANCES AND NETWORK STRUCTURE

Think About It

Membertou Development Seeks Jobs for the Mi'kmaq

Starting in early 2001, leaders of the Cape Breton Mi'kmaq First Nations community signed joint venture agreements with SNC-Lavalin Group Inc., Sodexho Marriott Services Canada Ltd., Ledgers Canada, Georgia-Pacific Corporation, and Clearwater Fine Foods through the Membertou Development Corporation.[43] For the 1000-person band, with an unemployment rate of 50 percent, the agreements should mean more jobs. The companies will find it easier to bid on government contracts, since their use of Aboriginal employees will be viewed favourably.

Bernd Christmas, CEO of Halifax-based Membertou Development Corp., explained what he saw as the key benefit of the partnerships. "We have to develop our own revenue streams and get away from dependency on the federal government. That's the only way to true self-government."

The terms of the venture mean that Clearwater Fine Foods will be able to buy all the snow crab of Membertou fishers, and has agreed to hire 20 Aboriginal employees for its processing line, which represents a third of the plant's workforce. The Georgia-Pacific agreement is expected to bring jobs in the mining sector, and Ledgers Canada will work with the band to provide financial consulting services. The SNC-Lavalin agreement with Membertou says it will "explore jointly mutually beneficial collaborative efforts to develop projects in the Maritime provinces."

Questions

1. What kinds of ventures and alliances can companies engage in?
2. What are the advantages of these alliances?

Membertou Development
Corporation
www.membertou.ca

strategic alliance

An agreement in which managers pool or share their organization's resources and know-how with a foreign company, and the two organizations share the rewards and risks of starting a new venture.

joint venture

A strategic alliance among two or more companies that agree to establish jointly and share the ownership of a new business.

network structure

A series of strategic alliances that an organization creates with suppliers, manufacturers, and distributors to produce and market a product.

boundaryless organization

An organization whose members are linked by computers, faxes, computer-aided design systems, and video teleconferencing, and who rarely, if ever, see one another face to face.

Recently, innovations in organizational structure—strategic alliances, joint ventures, and network structures—have been sweeping through Canadian, American, and European businesses. These structures allow for considerably more flexibility by creating links outside the organization. We cover each of these in turn.

Strategic Alliances and Joint Ventures

Many people use the terms *strategic alliance* and *joint venture* interchangeably, but technically they are different. A **strategic alliance** is a formal agreement that commits two or more companies to exchange or share their resources in order to produce and market a product.[44] A **joint venture** is a strategic alliance among two or more companies that agree to establish jointly and share the ownership of a new business.

Japanese car companies such as Toyota and Honda have formed a series of strategic alliances with suppliers of inputs such as car axles, gearboxes, and air-conditioning systems. More and more Canadian, American, and European organizations are relying on strategic alliances to gain access to low-cost foreign sources of inputs. This approach allows managers to keep costs low.

Network Structure

A **network structure** is a series of strategic alliances that an organization creates with suppliers, manufacturers, and distributors to produce and market a product. For instance, Handspring, which is known for its PDAs (personal digital assistants), doesn't actually make them. A network of partner companies manufacture, design, ship and support Handspring's products. Handspring's role is to manage the network. Network structures allow an organization to bring resources (workers especially) together on a long-term basis in order to find new ways to reduce costs and increase the quality of products—without experiencing the high costs of operating a complex organizational structure (such as the costs of employing many managers).

The ability of managers to develop networks to produce or provide the goods and services customers want, rather than creating a complex organizational structure to do so, has led many researchers and consultants to popularize the idea of a **boundaryless organization** composed of people who are linked by computers, faxes, computer-aided design systems, and video teleconferencing, and who rarely, if ever, see one another face to face. This structure is also referred to as *network organizations, learning organizations,* or *virtual corporations*.[45] People are used when their services are needed, much as in a matrix structure, but they are not formal members of an organization. They are functional experts who form an alliance with an organization, fulfill their contractual obligations, and then move on to the next project.

Two Winnipeg-based firms—Cardinal Capital Management Inc. (whose president, Tim Burt, is shown here) and Lawton Partners Financial Planning Services Limited—formed a strategic alliance to strengthen each of their businesses. Cardinal will provide investment management for Lawton's clients, and Lawton will provide financial planning, estate planning and tax-advantaged planning strategies. Clients of both companies will thus have a broader array of services available to them.

iGen Knowledge
Solutions Inc.
www.igeninc.com

business-to-business (B2B) networks
A group of organizations that join together and use software to link themselves to potential global suppliers to increase efficiency and effectiveness.

outsourcing
Using outside suppliers and manufacturers to produce goods and services.

The Brothers Markle
www.brothersmarkle.com

New Westminster, BC-based iGEN Knowledge Solutions Inc. operates as a virtual organization to bring technical solutions to its business clients. Associates work from home offices connected by wireless technologies and the internet, and collaborate to solve client problems. The virtual model allows fast cycle times for idea implementation, service delivery, and product development. The model also makes it easy to set up operations in different regions of the country without large overhead costs.

Leadership in virtual organizations may be more important and more difficult than in conventional organizations. A study of a number of successful virtual organizations found that the most important factor was a leader organization with a strategically important core competence.[46] The leader organization manages and inspires the other organizational relationships. Because virtual organizations have similar characteristics to voluntary organizations, leaders need to be able to build trust while recognizing that they do not have authority or full control over partners.

The push to lower costs has also led to the development of electronic **business-to-business (B2B) networks** in which most or all of the companies in an industry (e.g., car makers) use the same software platform to link to each other and establish industry specifications and standards. Then, these companies jointly list the quantity and specifications of the inputs they require and invite bids from the thousands of potential suppliers around the world. Suppliers also use the same software platform so electronic bidding, auctions, and transactions are possible between buyers and sellers around the world. The idea is that high-volume standardized transactions can help drive down costs at the industry level.

Outsourcing

The use of **outsourcing** is increasing rapidly as organizations recognize the many opportunities that the approaches offer to reduce costs and increase organizational flexibility. Canadian companies spent almost $49 billion on outsourcing in 1999.[47] Toronto-based The Brothers Markle Inc., a sign-making company, outsources more than 50 percent of its work. Why the management team does this is described in this chapter's *Management Case in the News*.

Companies that specialize in outsourced work, such as EDS Corporation—which manages the information systems of large organizations like Xerox and Eastman Kodak—are major beneficiaries of this new approach. While many companies use outsourcing, not all have been successful at implementing it. Managers should be aware of the following concerns when considering its use: (1) choosing the wrong activities to outsource, (2) choosing the wrong vendor, (3) writing a poor contract, (4) failing to consider personnel issues, (5) losing control over the activity, (6) ignoring the hidden costs, and (7) failing to develop an exit strategy (for either moving to another vendor or deciding to bring the activity back in-house.)[48] A review of 91 outsourcing activities found that writing a poor contract and losing control of the activity were the most likely reasons for an outsourcing venture to fail. Designing organizational structure is becoming an increasingly complex management function. To maximize efficiency and effectiveness, managers must carefully assess the relative benefits of having their own organization perform a functional activity versus forming an alliance with another organization to perform the activity. It is still not clear how B2B networks and other forms of electronic alliances between companies will develop in the future.

Chapter Summary

DESIGNING ORGANIZATIONAL STRUCTURE

GROUPING TASKS INTO JOBS: JOB DESIGN

- Job Enlargement and Job Enrichment

GROUPING JOBS INTO FUNCTIONS AND DIVISIONS

- Functional Structure
- Divisional Structures: Product, Geographic, and Market
- Matrix and Product Team Designs

COORDINATING FUNCTIONS AND DIVISIONS

- Allocating Authority

OVERALL STRUCTURE: FORMAL OR FLEXIBLE?

- Mechanistic Structures
- Organic Structures
- Factors Affecting Choices in Organizational Structure

STRATEGIC ALLIANCES AND NETWORK STRUCTURE

- Strategic Alliances and Joint Ventures
- Network Structure
- Outsourcing

SUMMARY AND REVIEW

DESIGNING ORGANIZATIONAL STRUCTURE Organizational structure is the formal system of both task and reporting relationships that determines how employees use resources to achieve organizational goals. The way an organization's structure works depends on how tasks are grouped into individual jobs; how jobs are grouped into functions and divisions; how coordination and allocating authority are accomplished; and whether the structure is formal or flexible.

GROUPING TASKS INTO JOBS: JOB DESIGN Job design is the process by which managers group tasks into jobs. To create more interesting jobs, and to get workers to act flexibly, managers can enlarge and enrich jobs.

GROUPING JOBS INTO FUNCTIONS AND DIVISIONS Managers can choose from many kinds of organizational structures to make the best use of organizational resources. Depending on the specific organizing problems they face, managers can choose from functional, product, geographic, market, matrix, and product team structures.

COORDINATING FUNCTIONS AND DIVISIONS No matter which structure managers choose, they must decide how to distribute authority in the organization, how many levels to have in the hierarchy of authority, and what balance to strike between centralization and decentralization to keep the number of levels in the hierarchy to a minimum. As organizations grow, managers must increase integration and coordination among functions and divisions.

OVERALL STRUCTURE: FORMAL OR FLEXIBLE? Overall organizational structure is determined by conditions of the environment. When the environment is stable, a mechanistic structure is appropriate. When the environment is changing rapidly, an organic structure is more appropriate. An organic structure is more flexible. To avoid many of the communication and coordination problems that emerge as organizations grow, managers are adopting more flexible structures. The four main determinants of organizational structure are the external environment, strategy, technology, and human resources. In general, the higher the level of uncertainty associated with these factors, the more appropriate is a flexible, adaptable structure as opposed to a formal, rigid one.

STRATEGIC ALLIANCES AND NETWORK STRUCTURE In a strategic alliance, managers enter into a contract with another organization to provide inputs or to perform a functional activity. If managers enter into a series of these contracts and a substantial number of activities are performed outside their organization, they have created a network structure.

Roles in Contrast: Considerations

MANAGERS	EMPLOYEES
Task can be organized simply, so that individuals perform a few tasks repeatedly, or they can be organized in a more complex way, which gives the employee more responsibility.	Some organizations are more flexible, and others are more structured. If I prefer clear routines and expectations, a flexible structure might not be comfortable.
Divisions can be organized in a variety of ways, including products and geography. They should be organized in a way that provides the best support to customers and clients, based on their needs.	Typically companies organize divisions to match client needs. For instance, a geographic structure might make sense if the company serves a variety of countries, and it's important to understand the culture of the clients in order to better serve them.
There is no one best organizational structure. The chosen structure will depend on the environment, corporate strategy, and technology.	When managers are laid off, the chain of command becomes broader. If I work in such a situation, I could be expected to take on more responsibilities.

MANAGEMENT in Action

Topics for Discussion and Action

1. Would a flexible or a more formal structure be appropriate for these organizations: (a) a large department store, (b) one of the big accounting firms, (c) a biotechnology company? Explain your reasoning.
2. Using the job characteristics model as a guide, discuss how a manager can enrich or enlarge subordinates' jobs.
3. How might a salesperson's or secretary's job be enlarged or enriched to make it more motivating?
4. When and under what conditions might managers change from a functional structure to (a) a product, (b) a geographic, or (c) a market structure?
5. How do matrix structure and product team structure differ? Why is product team structure more widely used?
6. Find a manager and identify the kind of organizational structure that his or her organization uses to coordinate its people and resources. Why is the organization using that structure? Do you think a different structure would be more appropriate? Which one?
7. With the same or another manager, discuss the distribution of authority in the organization. Does the manager think that decentralizing authority and empowering employees is appropriate?
8. Compare the pros and cons of using a network structure to perform organizational activities, and performing all activities in-house or within one organizational hierarchy.

Building Management Skills

UNDERSTANDING ORGANIZING

Think of an organization you know—perhaps one you have worked in—such as a store, restaurant, office, church, or school. Then answer the following questions.

1. Which contingencies are most important in explaining how the organization is organized? Do you think it is organized in the best way?
2. Using the job characteristics model, how motivating do you think the job of a typical employee in this organization is? Can you think of any ways in which a typical job could be enlarged or enriched?
3. What kind of organizational structure does the organization use? If it is part of a chain, what kind of structure does the entire organization use? What other structures discussed in the chapter might allow the organization to operate more effectively? For example, would the move to a product team structure lead to greater efficiency or effectiveness? Why or why not?
4. How many levels are there in the organization's hierarchy? Is authority centralized or decentralized? Describe the span of control of the top manager and of middle or first-line managers.
5. Is the distribution of authority appropriate for the organization and its activities? Would it be possible to flatten the hierarchy by decentralizing authority and empowering employees?
6. What are the main integrating mechanisms used in the organization? Do they provide sufficient coordination among individuals and functions? How might they be improved?
7. Now that you have analyzed the way in which this organization is organized, what advice would you give its managers to help them improve the way it operates?

Management for You

Choose an organization for which you have worked. How did the structure of your job and the organization affect your job satisfaction? Did the tasks within your job make sense? In what ways could they be better organized? What structural changes would you make to this organization? Would you consider making this a taller or flatter organization? How would the changes you have proposed improve responsiveness to customers and your job satisfaction?

Small Group Breakout Exercise

BOB'S APPLIANCES

Form groups of 3 or 4 people, and appoint 1 member as the spokesperson who will communicate your findings to the whole class when called on by the instructor. Then discuss the following scenario.

Bob's Appliances sells and services household appliances such as washing machines, dishwashers, stoves, and refrigerators. Over the years, the company has developed a good reputation for the quality of its customer service, and many local builders are customers at the store. Recently, some new appliance retailers, including Circuit City and Future Shop, have opened stores that also provide numerous appliances. In addition to appliances, however, to attract more customers these stores carry a complete range of consumer electronics products, including television sets, stereos, and computers. Bob Lange, the owner of Bob's Appliances, has decided that if he is to stay in business he must widen his product range and compete directly with the chains.

In 2001, he decided to build a new 1800-square-metre store and service centre, and he is now hiring new employees to sell and service the new line of consumer electronics. Because of his company's increased size, Lange is not sure of the best way to organize the employees. Currently, he uses a functional structure; employees are divided into sales, purchasing and accounting, and repair. Bob is wondering whether selling and servicing consumer electronics is so different from selling and servicing appliances that he should move to a product structure (see figure) and create separate sets of functions for each of his two lines of business.[49]

You are a team of local consultants that Bob has called in to advise him as he makes this crucial choice. Which structure do you recommend? Why?

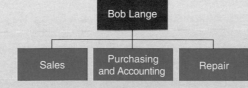

FUNCTIONAL STRUCTURE

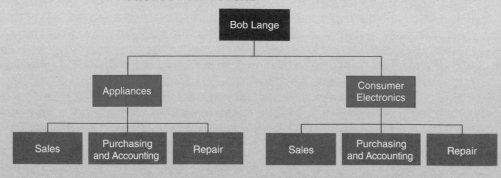

PRODUCT STRUCTURE

Managing Ethically

In many businesses—such as chicken-processing plants, small engineering companies, furniture makers, warehouses, and offices—unskilled workers perform the same repetitive task for many hours a day, day in and day out, and often for years if they stay at the same job. Boredom is common, as is the development of bodily ailments such as skin conditions, muscle fatigue, and carpal tunnel syndrome. Is it ethical for managers to allow workers to perform repetitive tasks for long periods of time? What kinds of standards would you use to decide this issue? To what degree should job redesign be used to change such a situation and enrich jobs if it also would raise costs and make a company less competitive? How could organizational structure be redesigned to make this problem less prevalent?

Exploring the World Wide Web

SPECIFIC ASSIGNMENT

Enter the website of the German publishing company Bertelsmann (www.bertelsmann.com). Click on "Bertelsmann AG," then on "Essentials."

1. What are Bertelsmann's mission and corporate goals?

2. What kind of organizational structure does Bertelsmann have?
3. What is Bertelsmann's approach to managing its structure (its approach to decentralization, delegation, and so on)?

GENERAL ASSIGNMENT

Search for a website that tells the story of how an organization changed its structure in some way to increase its efficiency and effectiveness.

You're the Management Consultant

SPEEDING UP WEBSITE DESIGN

You have been called in as a consultant by the top functional managers of a website design, production, and hosting company whose new animated website designs are attracting a lot of attention and a lot of customers. Currently, your employees are organized into different functions such as hardware, software design, graphic art, website hosting, as well as functions such as marketing and human resources. Each function takes its turn to work on a new project from initial customer request to final online website hosting.

The problem this company is experiencing is that it typically takes one year from the initial idea stage to the time that the website is up and running and the company wants to halve this time to protect and expand its market niche. The managers believe their current functional structure is the source of the problem: It is not allowing employees to develop websites fast enough to satisfy customers' demands. They want you to suggest a better one.

Questions

1. Discuss ways in which you can improve the way the current functional structure operates to speed website development.
2. Discuss the pros and cons of using (a) multidivisional, (b) matrix, or (c) product-team structures to reduce website development time.
3. Which of these structures do you think is most appropriate and why?

MANAGEMENT CASE

The Organizing Approach at Microsoft

Microsoft, the biggest and most profitable software company in the world, has been called the best 15 000-person company in the United States.[50] These 15 000 employees generated over $7.75 billion in revenues in 1996 alone. Perhaps even more impressive is the fact that since Bill Gates founded Microsoft in 1974, more than 2000 of these employees have become millionaires because of the stock options that Microsoft uses to attract and retain talented employees. Gates himself is the richest man in the United States, having a fortune estimated at more than $93 billion. What is the secret of Microsoft's success?

At the level of individual employees, Microsoft's philosophy of managing the company is evident in the sorts of people the company recruits and selects. Microsoft goes to the best software departments in colleges and universities across the country and spends a lot of time recruiting people who like to work hard, be imaginative and creative, and take risks. These are work values that Microsoft prizes. Employees are expected to work long hours, often 60- or 80-hour workweeks. They are expected to become experts in the specific software projects they work on and to possess up-to-the-minute information and state-of-the-art knowledge about what Microsoft and its competitors are doing. Gates meets frequently with employees on different projects and is constantly probing their knowledge to make sure they are up to date. If they lack current information, they lose credibility with him because they are not doing their job.

Beyond stock options, Microsoft motivates employees by providing them with the latest technology, flexible (though long) work hours, and even exercise rooms on the premises of a collegiate-type "campus." The way employees are motivated is also closely linked to the way Microsoft uses groups and teamwork as the basis of its organizing process.

At Microsoft, programmers work in teams that can be as small as five or six people, and different teams work on specific software applications. Often many small teams are working on different aspects of a larger project managed by a project manager. For example, more than 300 people worked in small teams to develop Microsoft's Windows 98 operating system, a product that tried to match the user-friendliness of Apple's operating system. The use of product teams allows people to cooperate and pool their skills and resources; it promotes among team members the intense interactions that often lead to the breakthroughs that help Microsoft pioneer new products so quickly. Moreover, team members can learn from one another and control one another's behaviour.

At the organization level, Microsoft keeps the distance between managers and the teams to a minimum by keeping the organization as flat as possible—that is, by keeping the number of levels in the organizational hierarchy to a minimum. Moreover, Microsoft's structure is organized around these teams. Decentralized authority and delegation of important decisions to each team give them maximum autonomy and freedom to be creative and to take risks. Microsoft is able to delegate so much authority because the company pays so much attention to recruiting the right kinds of employees and because each team's performance is appraised regularly to ensure that all teams are on top of their projects.

Questions

1. What are the main elements in Bill Gates' organizing approach?
2. What organizing problems do you think might emerge in Microsoft as it continues to grow?

MANAGEMENT CASE

From the Pages of *The Toronto Star* Survival of the Fittest

Caution: There may be economic rough waters ahead. The key to surviving an economic slow-down is to batten down the hatches before the major storm hits—and don't overload your boat.

No one knows this better than Sam and Jack Markle. The two brothers, owners of Toronto-based The Brothers Markle Inc., learned this lesson the hard way. They've been producing some of the most innovative signage for a veritable Who's Who of Canadian business for some four decades.

But the award-winning duo was hit hard by the last recession in the mid-'90s and was forced to downsize from a 24 000-square-foot facility and 40 employees.

Their formula for survival? They stay healthy by staying lean even in the best of times. They say they operate much more efficiently now with a 7500-square-foot plant, 10 employees, and subcontracting 50 percent of their work to specialty manufacturers.

"Before we tried to do everything inhouse, which required more equipment and more over-head, but the way we're operating now we almost don't have to tighten our belts if business drops," says Jack, 61. "We also don't go after every opportunity; rather we focus on what we do best, which is specialized custom work, so much so that we find other sign companies referring their clients to us for the difficult or unusual projects."

The brothers say they are big enough to have all the necessary equipment and staff, yet small enough to provide hands-on management and personalized service. "With so much competition and choice, you need to build good relationships with your customers—that's the key to empower-ing your business," explains Sam, 68. "Clients want to know that their needs are understood and that they're valued."

Sam adds that most companies make the same mistake: They're too fat in the good times and then they panic in the bad times and go too lean.

"You need to find a comfortable medium so that when the economy slows down you don't have to overreact just to stay afloat."

This is great advice, considering it's difficult even to find economists who agree on when, or if, we're heading for a recession.

The Markle brothers say their formula for staying lean also includes controlling their fixed overhead, motivating their staff, and offering unique products that give them a competitive advantage, like their computerized directories for building lobbies.

It's also important to remember to reinvest in the health of your company during the good times.

This might mean keeping a rainy day fund, sort of like a health insurance policy for your business.

Moreover, at no time should the success of your business be seen as a licence to waste money, because the economy can take an unexpected turn for the worse.

Source: Written by Risha Gotlieb, freelance writer and author. Article originally appeared in *The Toronto Star*, May 17, 2001.

Questions

1. What type of organizational structure does The Brothers Markle have?
2. What advantages and disadvantages does this sort of structure bring to the company?

CHAPTER 7

ORGANIZATIONAL CULTURE AND CHANGE

Learning Objectives

1. Explain what organizational culture is and its role in guiding behaviour in organizations.

2. Explain how culture is taught to employees.

3. Identify what is involved in managing organizational change.

4. Explain how managers could help to overcome resistance to change.

Roles in Contrast: Questions

MANAGERS	EMPLOYEES
What is my role in maintaining organizational culture?	How does organizational culture affect me?
How might the company's culture affect my ability to manage?	How might an organization's culture affect the rewards I receive?
How can I increase the chances of making change happen in my organization?	Why do I resist change?

A Case in Contrast

Corporate Cultures Affect Openness and Decision Making

When the space shuttle Columbia exploded on re-entry in February 2003, officials at the National Aeronautics and Space Administration (www.nasa.gov) expressed shock and horror.[1] It was the second shuttle disaster in recent years. Immediately NASA searched for possible mechanical failures that might have led to the latest tragedy.

Though foam striking the shuttle created the hole that led to the Columbia explosion, management failure is the root cause of the disaster. Both members of the board that investigated the accident and former NASA employees described "attitudes of superiority, fear of retribution by lower-level employees, communications problems and strained relationships between key divisions of NASA" as part of the organization's management problems.

The pressure on engineers to remain silent, even when they have safety questions, was illustrated in decisions made by Linda Ham, head of Columbia's mission management team. After it became clear that Columbia had been hit by foam during launch, Ham refused to seek spy satellite pictures of the shuttle, which might have

shown any damage to the vehicle while it was still in flight. She said she failed to act because she didn't know who was making the request for the images. After the accident she discovered that the requests had come from engineers who had taken part in meetings with her, but would not speak up after she insisted the photos weren't necessary.

At Burnaby-based Creo Inc. (www.creo.com), an open, sharing environment characterizes the company.[2] It is the world's largest independent supplier of pre-press systems for the graphics arts industry.

Creo has one of the lowest turnover rates in the industry, and CEO Amos Michelson says that is because Creo is an attractive place to work. The company's culture aims to make employees happy. The company has maintained that culture even as it has grown considerably. As one manager remarked, "The culture that was founded when the company was really small still exists."

Michelson, as CEO, sets the tone for the company. "The CEO is the protector of the culture," he says. In contrast to NASA's culture,

Differing organizational cultures can affect employee behaviour, including how open employees are with sharing information. Both NASA and Creo have been successful in a variety of ways, but NASA has suffered two shuttle disasters that were blamed on management failures to listen and a flawed organizational culture.

Michelson demands that Creo employees reach consensus for most decisions. He also insists that information be shared throughout the organization so that employees can more effectively meet the needs of customers. David Brown, corporate vice-president of business strategy, says, "We encourage people to do what's right, and not what they're told."

Also unlike NASA, Creo is anti-hierarchical. Thus, employees are more likely to speak up if they encounter problems. Creo's culture reinforces that all employees are valued: There are few special privileges for senior managers and all employees receive stock options.

Creo's commitment to open communication is also revealed in its 360-degree feedback system. It is not unusual for up to 30 people—who work under, beside, and above the person being evaluated—to participate in the feedback. The company wants to discourage employees who "manage up" or are just trying to impress their superiors.

Creo maintains its culture by carefully selecting new employees. Job applicants meet with up to 10 employees, who all have an equal say in the hiring decision, regardless of their rank. If applicants do not fit the company's culture, they are not hired, regardless of their technical skills. Creo is more concerned with hiring people who work well in a team-driven environment.

Both NASA and Creo have created strong organizational cultures that have led to many successes. However, NASA's culture also gets blamed for its failures. NASA says it will change its culture, though. NASA administrator Sean O'Keefe said he is committed to "creating an atmosphere in which we're all encouraged to raise our hand and speak out when there are life-threatening hazards." Nobel Prize-winner Douglas Osheroff, a Stanford University physicist, is less convinced that NASA can change its culture. "Culture is a very funny thing, of course. It is the way people intuitively behave to a situation."

OVERVIEW

As the *Case in Contrast* suggests, the culture of an organization can lead to very different employee behaviour at different companies. Creo encourages participation and involves employees in hiring and decision making. NASA has a hierarchical structure, and questions are silenced. As a result of the different ways that managers interact with their employees, Creo and NASA created very different cultures in their organizations. As we recall from Chapter 6, organizational structure provides an organization with a skeleton; organizational culture provide the muscles, sinews, nerves, and sensations that allow managers to regulate and govern the organization's activities. Organizational culture also affects the ability of the organization to engage in change when necessary. As we saw from the NASA example, organizations do not change easily, even when they have faced two shuttle disasters.

In this chapter, we look at how culture works, and how it is taught to organizational members. This continues our discussion from the previous chapter about how managers organize human and other resources to create high-performing organizations We will examine why culture can inspire employees to achieve great goals, and why it can also lead to organizational failure. We will look at how to manage change successfully, in the face of strong culture, and how to overcome resistance to change. By the end of this chapter, you will understand how culture helps convey meaning and purpose to employees. You will also understand the vital role that change plays in building competitive advantage and creating a high-performing organization.

ORGANIZATIONAL CULTURE

Think About It

Nokia's Finnish Ways

In less than 10 years, Nokia became the world's largest wireless phone maker, with more than a 30-percent share of the global market. Nokia's managers believe that the secret of its success lies in its organizational and national culture—in the stories and language of the company itself and the country in which it is headquartered, Finland.[3]

Matti Alahuhta, president of Nokia Mobile Phones, believes that Nokia's cultural values are based on the Finnish character: Finns are down-to-earth, rational, and straightforward people. They are also very friendly and democratic people who do not believe in a rigid hierarchy based on a person's authority or social class. Nokia's culture reflects these values because innovation and decision making are pushed right down to the bottom line, to teams of employees who take up the challenge of developing the ever smaller and more sophisticated phones for which the company is known. Bureaucracy is kept to a minimum at Nokia. Its culture is based on informal and personal relationships and norms of cooperation and teamwork.

Question
1. How does a company's culture help it succeed?

organizational culture
A system of shared meaning, held by organization members, that distinguishes the organization from other organizations.

Organizational culture refers to a system of shared meaning, held by organization members, that distinguishes the organization from other organizations.[4] Culture is the "glue" that keeps organizational members together, and guides their behaviour. New employees learn the organizational culture from their managers and other employees.

Culture can be viewed as something that both helps employees make sense of the organization and guides employee behaviour. In essence, culture defines the rules of the game:

> *Culture by definition is elusive, intangible, implicit, and taken for granted. But every organization develops a core set of assumptions, understandings, and implicit rules that govern day-to-day behaviour in the workplace. Until newcomers learn the rules, they are not accepted as full-fledged members of the organization. Transgressions of the rules on the part of high-level executives or front-line employees result in universal disapproval and powerful penalties. Conformity to the rules becomes the primary basis for reward and upward mobility.[5]*

values
The stable, long-lasting beliefs about what is important.

Organizational culture can control individuals and groups in an organization through shared values, norms, standards of behaviour, and expectations. **Values** are the stable, long-lasting beliefs about what is important. **Norms** are unwritten rules or guidelines that prescribe appropriate behaviour in particular situations. Norms emerge from values.[6]

norms
Unwritten rules or guidelines for appropriate behaviour in particular situations.

Organizational culture is not an externally imposed system of constraints, such as direct supervision or rules and procedures. Rather, employees internalize organizational values and norms and then let those values and norms guide their decisions and actions. Just as people in society at large generally behave in accordance with socially acceptable values and norms, such as the norm that people should line up at the checkout counters in supermarkets, so are individuals in an organizational setting mindful of the force of organizational values and norms.

Levels of Culture

artifacts
Aspects of an organization's culture that one sees, hears, and feels.

Culture exists at two levels in an organization: the visible level and the invisible level. We see culture through its **artifacts**. These are what you see, hear, and feel when you are within an organization. For instance, organizations have different dress policies, have different ways of organizing office space, and have different ideas of what should be displayed on company walls. The things you see reveal the organization's culture.

beliefs
The understandings of how objects and ideas relate to each other.

assumptions
The taken-for-granted notions of how something should be in an organization.

At the invisible level of culture are the values, beliefs, and assumptions that make up the organizational culture. **Beliefs** are the understandings of how objects and ideas relate to each other. **Assumptions** are the taken-for-granted notions of how something should be. Because of basic assumptions that are held by organizational members, it can be difficult to introduce change. Darren Entwistle, CEO of Burnaby, BC-based Telus, struggled through negotiations with employees during 2003 because of basic assumptions of employees. Those based in Alberta, who had merged into Telus, were quite happy with a variable-pay program that Entwistle proposed, and they assumed they would be rewarded for good performance. Those based in British Columbia, where management-employee relations were more antagonistic, assumed the program would end up lowering their pay by expecting them to work harder than they were currently working.[7] These differing assumptions made it difficult for Telus management to reach agreement with BC employees about having a variable-pay program.

The values and assumptions of an organization are not easily observed. Thus, we look to organizational artifacts (i.e., the things we can observe) to help us uncover the values and assumptions. For instance, managers' and employees' behaviour often reveals the organization's values and assumptions. When employees continue talking to each other in front of a waiting customer, they signal that employees are more important than customers to this organization.

Creating a Strong Organizational Culture

Culture is created and sustained in three ways:[8]

1. The founders and/or senior managers of the organization hire and keep only employees who think and feel the way they do.
2. The management indoctrinates and socializes these employees to their way of thinking and feeling.
3. Top managers serve as role models. By observing their behaviour, employees identify with them and internalize their beliefs, values, and assumptions.

In an organization, values and norms make it clear to organizational members what goals they should pursue and how they should behave to reach those goals. Thus, values and norms perform the same function as formal goals, written rules, or direct supervision. Research shows that having a strong culture usually pays off, except in times of a changing environment.[9] Those companies with stronger cultures tend to have better returns on investment, higher net income growth, and larger increases in share price than firms with weaker cultures. However, strong culture can be a liability when the environment is changing. Organizations with strong cultures have greater difficulty adapting to change.

Managers can influence the kinds of values and norms that develop in an organization. Some managers might cultivate values and norms that let subordinates know they are welcome to perform their roles in innovative and creative ways. Employees are thus encouraged to be entrepreneurial and willing to experiment and go out on a limb even if there is a significant chance of failure. At organizations such as Nortel Networks, Lucent Technologies, and 3M Canada, top managers encourage employees to adopt such values in order to support organizational commitment to innovation as a source of competitive advantage.

Other managers, however, might cultivate values and norms that let employees know that they should always be conservative and cautious in their dealings with others. Thus, these employees should always consult with their superiors before making important decisions, and should always put their actions in writing so they can be held accountable for whatever happens. In any setting where caution is needed—nuclear power stations, large oil refineries, chemical plants, financial institutions, insurance companies—a conservative, cautious approach to making decisions might be highly appropriate.[10] Caution when used inappropriately, however, may stifle employees' ability to innovate or communicate. NASA's culture, for instance, encouraged too much caution in communicating concerns. Joseph Grenny, a NASA engineer, notes that "The NASA culture does not accept being wrong." The culture doesn't accept that "there's no such thing as a stupid question"; instead "the humiliation factor always runs high," he said.[11]

Difficulties arise when two organizations with different cultures merge. For instance, when Calgary-based TransCanada PipeLines Ltd. and Nova Corporation merged in 1998, different cultures led to conflicts in bringing the two companies together. Nova and TransCanada treated their employees very differently. TransCanada had a more traditional, top-down management control structure. Nova relied on its culture of empowering employees to govern their behaviour. One Nova employee described the merger as "GI Joe meets the Care Bears."[12] Three years later the two companies had not completely resolved their cultural differences.

TransCanada PipeLines Limited
www.transcanada.com

Nova Chemicals Corporation
www.novachem.com

Teaching the Culture to Employees

Managers deliberately cultivate and develop the organizational values and norms that are best suited to their task and general environments, strategy, or technology. Organizational culture is transmitted to and shared with organizational members through the values of the founder; the process of socialization; ceremonies and rites; and stories and language (see Figure 7.1).

Values of the Founder

One manager who has a very important impact on the kind of organizational culture that emerges in an organization is the founder. An organization's founder and his or her personal values and beliefs have a substantial influence on the values, norms, and standards of behaviour that develop over time within the organization.[13] Founders set

Figure 7.1 | Factors Creating a Strong Organizational Culture

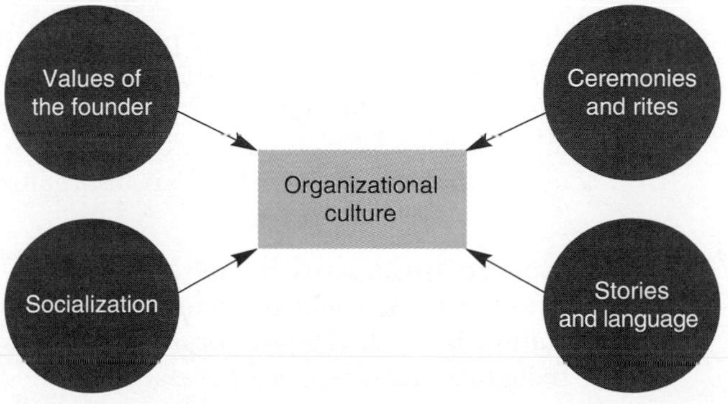

the stage for the way cultural values and norms develop because they hire other managers to help them run their organizations. It is reasonable to assume that founders select managers who share their vision of the organization's goals and what it should be doing. In any case, new managers quickly learn from the founder what values and norms are appropriate in the organization and thus what is desired of them. Subordinates imitate the style of the founder and, in turn, transmit his or her values and norms to their subordinates. Gradually over time, the founder's values and norms permeate the organization.[14]

A founder who requires a great display of respect from subordinates and insists on things such as formal job titles and formal modes of dress encourages subordinates to act in this way toward their subordinates. Often, a founder's personal values affect an organization's competitive advantage. Frank Stronach, founder of Aurora, Ontario-based Magna Corporation, believes that his employees should show a "strong sense of ownership and entrepreneurial energy." He practises this belief by diverting 10 percent of pre-tax profit to profit-sharing programs for his employees. Similarly, managers' salaries are deliberately set "below industry standards" so that managers will earn more through profit-sharing bonuses. To further emphasize managerial responsibility, Magna's managers are given considerable autonomy over buying, selling, and hiring. Through these policies of profit-sharing and empowerment, Stronach has developed a workforce that has made Magna one of the largest and most profitable companies in the country.

Similarly, Richard Branson of the Virgin Group, known for his entrepreneurial style, challenges his managers to act like him. All of his small companies are headed by managing directors who have a stake in the company they run. He wants his managers to operate the companies as if they were their own. Branson's style of management has made Virgin a success in a number of different markets it has entered.

Frank Stronach, Magna International
www.magnaint.com/
magnaweb.nsf/
webpages/

Richard Branson, Virgin Group
www.virgin.com/aboutus/
autobiography/

organizational socialization

The process by which newcomers learn an organization's values and norms and acquire the work behaviours necessary to perform jobs effectively.

Socialization

Over time, organizational members learn from each other which values are important in an organization and the norms that specify appropriate and inappropriate behaviours. Eventually, organizational members behave in accordance with the organization's values and norms—often without realizing they are doing so. **Organizational socialization** is the process by which newcomers learn an organization's values and norms and acquire the work behaviours necessary to perform jobs effectively.[15] As a result of their socialization experiences, organizational members internalize an organization's values and norms and behave to fit in with them, not only because they think they have to but because they think that these values and norms describe the right and proper way to behave.[16]

Most organizations have some kind of socialization program to help new employees "learn the ropes"—the values, norms, and culture of their organization. The military, for example, is well known for the rigorous socialization process it uses to turn raw recruits into trained soldiers. Many organizations put new recruits through a rigorous training program to provide them with the knowledge they need not only to perform well in their jobs but also to represent the company to its clients. Thus, through the organizational socialization program, the founder and top managers of an organization can transmit to employees the cultural values and norms that shape the behaviour of organizational members.

Ceremonies and Rites

Another way in which managers can try to create or influence an organizational culture is by developing organizational ceremonies and rites—formal events that recognize incidents of importance to the organization as a whole and to specific

Table 7.1 | Organizational Rites

Type of Rite	Example of Rite	Purpose of Rite
Rite of passage	Induction and basic training	Learn and internalize norms and values
Rite of integration	Office Christmas party	Build common norms and values
Rite of enhancement	Presentation of annual award	Motivate commitment to norms and values

employees.[17] The most common rites that organizations use to transmit cultural norms and values to their members are rites of passage, of integration, and of enhancement (see Table 7.1).[18]

Rites of passage determine how individuals enter, advance within, or leave the organization. The socialization programs developed by military organizations (such as the Canadian Armed Forces) or by large accountancy firms are rites of passage. Likewise, the ways in which an organization prepares people for promotion or retirement are rites of passage.

Sometimes, rites of passage can get out of hand. Fraternities, sororities, sports teams, and even the military have been known to use hazing to initiate members. Activities can include "sleep deprivation, public nudity and childish pranks or, at worst, extreme drunkenness, gross racial slurs, even beatings."[19] The videotaped hazing rituals at CFB Petawawa caused the Airborne Regiment to be disbanded in 1995. While the goal of the hazing might have been to desensitize new recruits to the brutality of war, many Canadians felt that the practice had gone too far.

Rites of integration, such as office parties, company cookouts, and shared announcements of organizational successes, both build and reinforce common bonds among organizational members. Southwest Airlines is well known for its efforts to develop ceremonies and rituals to bond employees to the organization by showing them that they are valued members. Southwest holds cookouts in the parking lot of its Dallas headquarters, and Herb Kelleher, the founder and chair, personally attends each employee Christmas party throughout the country. Because there are so many Christmas parties to attend, Kelleher often finds himself attending parties in July!

Rites of enhancement, such as awards dinners, newspaper releases, and employee promotions, let organizations publicly recognize and reward employees' contributions and thus strengthen their commitment to organizational values. By bonding members within the organization, rites of enhancement help promote group cohesiveness.

Flamboyant Southwest Airlines founder and chair Herb Kelleher, pictured here on a Harley-Davidson motorcycle given to him by his pilots, prepares to enjoy his company's annual Chili Cook-Off in Dallas. Such organizational rites and ceremonies help build his organization's culture.

Stories and Language

Stories and language also communicate organizational culture. Stories (whether fact or fiction) about organizational heroes and villains and their actions provide important clues about values and norms. Such stories can reveal the kinds of behaviours that are valued by the organization and the kinds of practices that are frowned on.[20] Stories about Ted Rogers, the person (hero) who made Rogers Communications the company it is today, shed light on many aspects of Rogers Communications' corporate culture.

Lucent Technologies
Canada & GROWS
www.innoversity.org/
lucent_technologies.asp

Language—through slogans, symbols, and jargon—is used to help employees come to know expectations while bonding with one another. Toronto-based Lucent Technologies Canada uses two acronyms to convey a set of expectations to employees. GROWS summarizes the behaviours expected for high performance: *G* is for global growth mind set; *R* is for results focus; *O* is for obsession with customers and competitors; *W* is for a workplace that is open, supportive, and diverse; and *S* is for speed to market. Similarly, employees are evaluated for paying attention to Lucent Canada's TOUCH: *T* is for teamwork; *O* is for obsession with customers; *U* is for uncompromising quality; *C* is for cost effectiveness; and *H* is for helping others excel.[21]

Material Symbols

The organization's layout is a material symbol, and so are the size of offices; whether individuals wear uniforms or have a dress code; and the kinds of cars that top executives are given.[22] Material symbols convey to employees who is important, how much distance there is between top management and employees, and what kinds of behaviour are appropriate. For example, in *A Case in Contrast* in Chapter 10, we describe Toronto-based Willow Manufacturing, where everyone from the CEO down wears a uniform to convey the message that everyone in the company is part of a team.

Similarly, Alain Batty, the president and CEO of Ford Motor Company of Canada, Ltd., has the same kind of huge desk in his office in Toronto as William Clay Ford Jr., chair and CEO of Ford Motor Company, and every other Ford divisional head. The office buildings for all of Ford's operations are also similar. Founder Henry Ford believed it was more efficient to organize office space this way.[23] At Bolton, Ontario-based Husky Injection Molding Systems, employees and management share the parking lot, dining room, and even washrooms, conveying the sense of an egalitarian workplace.

The concept of organizational language encompasses not only spoken language but how people dress, the offices they occupy, the cars they drive, and the degree of formality they use when they address one another. IBM Canada, long known for its dark-blue suits, introduced less formal clothing in 1993 so that customers would feel more comfortable when interacting with the company.[24] When employees "speak" and understand the language of their organization's culture, they know how to behave in the organization and what attitudes are expected of them.

ORGANIZATIONAL CULTURE AND CHANGE

Think About It

Sunflower Has to Fire Abusive Managers

Sunflower Electric Power Corporation, a generation and transmission cooperative, almost went bankrupt in 2000.[25] A state committee of inquiry set up to find out the source of the problem put the blame on its CEO. They decided that he had created an abusive culture based on fear and blame that encouraged managers to fight over and protect their turf. Managers were afraid to rock the boat or make suggestions, because they could not predict what would happen to them.

The CEO was fired and a new CEO, Chris Hauck, was appointed to change the cooperative's culture. He found this difficult, because his senior managers were so used to the values and norms of the previous CEO. One top manager, for example, frequently berated one supervisor until the man became physically sick. Hauck fired this and other abusive managers as a signal that such behaviour would no longer be tolerated. With the help of consultants he went about the slow process of changing values and norms to emphasize cooperation, teamwork, and respect for others.

Questions
1. Why is organizational culture so difficult to change?
2. What can be done to encourage organizational change?

To understand how widespread the need for change in Canadian organizations is, consider the findings of a 1999 study of 309 human resource executives across a variety of industries. All of them reported that they were going through at least one of the following changes: mergers, acquisitions, divestitures, global competition, management, and/or organizational structure.[26]

A variety of organizational factors can be changed, such as the structure, the technology, or the people. Often, however, it is not possible to change any of these without changing culture, because culture signals to employees what behaviour is appropriate and what is not inappropriate. Culture can even prevent an organization from making necessary changes in the workplace. For instance, employees were so afraid of some of the managers at Sunflower that even hiring new CEO Chris Hauck to turn things around was not enough to make change happen. Hauck had to fire other abusive managers to send the signal that this behaviour was inappropriate and would not be tolerated by the new CEO.

Organizations that want to move in a new direction must alter policies, structures, behaviours, and beliefs in order to get from how "we've always done it" to how things will be done in the future. Thus even the changes in the production system need to be carried out within the context of examining and changing an organization's culture. Managers play a crucial role in changing culture because employees watch their behaviour to assess what is and is not important.

Edgar Schein identifies five mechanisms that alert employees to what management finds important in the culture.[27] These mechanisms are:

- *Attention.* Those things to which the leader directs employee attention (i.e., what is criticized, praised, or asked about). These things communicate what the leader and the employee value.

- *Reactions to crises.* The reaction of the leader and managers to crisis conveys to employees the core values of the organization. For instance, when companies face financial difficulties, employees receive the message from downsizing that people do not matter in this organization.

- *Role modelling.* Leaders communicate to employees strong messages about their values through their actions. In other words, actions speak louder than words when employees are trying to determine what the culture of the organization is. Sunflower's new CEO, Chris Hauck, signalled what type of behaviour he expected by firing some of his managers.

- *Allocation of rewards.* Rewards such as pay increases or promotions signal to employees how one succeeds in the organization.

- *Criteria for selection and dismissal.* The leader's decisions about what kinds of employees to recruit or dismiss send a signal to all about what kinds of employees are valued.

In order to change the culture of the organization, managers need to consider these mechanisms and the messages they are sending to employees. Thus, they need to look at how they recruit and dismiss, how they reward, how they act, and what things they bring to employees' attention. Changes in these activities may well result in resistance, but successful change will require the consistent application of new procedures and rewards. We discuss how to deal with resistance to change below.

Managing Organizational Change

Think About It

Moore Meets the Paperless Revolution

Mississauga, Ontario-based Moore Wallace Inc. has had to reinvent itself in recent years.[28] Through the early and mid-1990s, Moore, a manufacturer of business forms and labels, was viewed as a solid company. In 1997 shares were trading at around $30, and its business was growing. However, by December 2000, shares were trading at $3.95.

The reason for the fall in share prices? The company took to heart the notion of the "paperless office" and set out to transform Moore into a "leader in electronic publishing and related services." Then-CEO Ed Tyler did so by spending a lot of cash on acquisitions and buying back shares. Observers suggested the company had lost its discipline and focus and thrown away its cash.

By 2003, and two CEOs later, Moore (www.moore.com) seemed back on track once again. In fact, it had returned to what it always did well: making various business forms, printing and mailing monthly bills for other companies, and printing annual reports.

Questions
1. How do managers know when change is necessary?
2. How can managers make sure they introduce change effectively?

Deciding how to change an organization is a complex matter, not least because change disrupts the status quo and poses a threat, prompting employees to resist attempts to alter work relationships and procedures. Several experts have proposed a model that managers can follow to introduce change successfully while effectively managing conflict and politics.[29] Figure 7.2 outlines the steps that managers must take to manage change effectively. In the rest of this section we examine each one.

Assessing the Need for Change

Assessing the need for change calls for two important activities: recognizing that there is a problem and identifying its source. As the *Case in Contrast* shows, this is not always easy. NASA generally has been reluctant to address management failures after problems arise, and more willing to look for and address mechanical failures. When the Columbia Accident Investigation Board issued its report in the summer of 2003, it listed many of the same management failures that were identified after the Challenger disaster of 1983. NASA is not unique in this approach. Sometimes the need for change is obvious, such as when an organization's performance is suffering. Often, however, managers have trouble determining that something is going wrong because problems develop gradually; organizational

Figure 7.2 | Four Steps in the Organizational Change Process

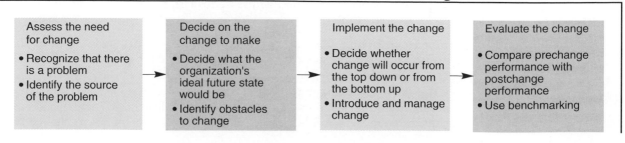

Assess the need for change	Decide on the change to make	Implement the change	Evaluate the change
• Recognize that there is a problem • Identify the source of the problem	• Decide what the organization's ideal future state would be • Identify obstacles to change	• Decide whether change will occur from the top down or from the bottom up • Introduce and manage change	• Compare prechange performance with postchange performance • Use benchmarking

When Wayne Sales took over as president and CEO of Canadian Tire, signs of the need for change were all over: The stock price had dropped $15 in the previous year, sales were dropping, and Home Hardware, Wal-Mart and Home Depot were taking away his customers.

performance may slip for a number of years before it becomes obvious. This is what happened at NASA. Thus, during the first step in the change process, managers need to recognize that there is a problem that requires change.

Often, a gap between desired and actual performance signals that there is a problem. By looking at performance measures—such as falling market share or profits, rising costs, or employees' failure to meet their established goals or stay within budgets—managers can see whether change is needed. These measures are provided by organizational control systems (discussed in Chapter 13). For Moore, the rapid drop in share price, from $30 to less than $4, indicated a serious problem with the company.

If there is a gap between desired and actual performance, managers need to discover the source of the problem. They do this by looking both inside and outside the organization. Outside the organization, they must examine how changes in environmental forces may be creating opportunities and threats that are affecting internal work relationships. Perhaps the emergence of low-cost foreign competitors has led to conflict among different departments that are trying to find new ways to gain a competitive advantage. In Moore's case, the increasing use of computers and online storage made the company wonder whether paper would become obsolete, which is why Moore started its paperless office strategy. Managers also need to look within the organization to see whether its structure and culture are causing problems between departments. Perhaps a company does not have the integrating mechanisms in place to allow different departments to respond to low-cost competition (see Chapter 6).

Deciding on the Change to Make

Once managers have identified the source of the problem, they must decide what they think the organization's ideal future state would be. In other words, they must decide where they would like their organization to be in the future—what kinds of goods and services it should be offering, what its business-level strategy should be, how the organizational structure should be changed, and so on. During this step, managers also must engage in planning how they are going to attain the organization's ideal future state. McDonald's is at a crossroads because consumers are starting to move away from a constant diet of Cokes and Big Macs, and looking for something a bit healthier. McDonald's can see this in its bottom line, but managers don't know how to meet the challenge. In part, their continued success over the past 30 years makes it difficult to determine a new strategy.

This step in the change process also includes identifying obstacles or sources of resistance to change. Managers must analyze the factors that may prevent the company from reaching its ideal future state. Obstacles to change are found at the corporate, divisional, departmental, and individual levels of the organization.

Corporate-level changes in an organization's strategy or structure—even seemingly trivial changes—may significantly affect how divisional and departmental managers behave. Suppose that to compete with low-cost foreign competitors, top managers decide to increase the resources spent on state-of-the-art machinery and reduce the resources spent on marketing or R&D. The power of manufacturing managers would increase, and the power of marketing and R&D managers would fall. This decision would alter the balance of power among departments and might lead to increased politics and conflict as departments start fighting to retain their status in the organization. An organization's present strategy and structure are powerful obstacles to change.

Organizational culture also can make change easier or harder. Organizations with entrepreneurial, flexible cultures, such as high-tech companies, are much easier to change than are organizations with more rigid cultures such as those sometimes found in large bureaucratic organizations like the military or General Motors.

The same obstacles to change exist at the divisional and departmental levels as well. Division managers may differ in their attitudes toward the changes that top managers propose and will resist those changes if their interests and power seem threatened. Managers at all levels usually fight to protect their power and control over resources. Given that departments have different goals and time horizons, they may also react differently to the changes that other managers propose. When top managers are trying to reduce costs, for example, sales managers may resist attempts to cut back on sales expenditures if they believe that problems stem from manufacturing managers' inefficiencies.

At the individual level, too, people are often resistant to change because change brings uncertainty and uncertainty brings stress. For example, individuals may resist the introduction of a new technology because they are uncertain about their abilities to learn it and effectively use it.

These obstacles make organizational change a slow process. Managers must recognize these potential obstacles to change and take them into consideration. Some obstacles can be overcome by improving communication so all organizational members are aware of both the need for change and the nature of the changes being made. Empowering employees and inviting them to take part in the planning for change also can help overcome resistance and reduce employees' fears. Emphasizing big-picture goals, such as organizational effectiveness and gaining a competitive advantage, can make organizational members who resist a change realize that the change is ultimately in everyone's best interests because it will increase organizational performance. The larger and more complex an organization is, the more complex is the change process.

Introducing the Change

top-down change
Change that is introduced quickly throughout an organization by upper-level managers.

Generally, managers can introduce and manage change from the top down or from the bottom up.[30] **Top-down change** is implemented quickly: Top managers identify the need for change, decide what to do, and then move quickly to introduce the changes throughout the organization. For example, top managers may decide to restructure and downsize the organization and then give divisional and departmental managers specific goals to achieve. With top-down change, the emphasis is on making the changes quickly and dealing with problems as they arise. This is how Ed Tyler handled the changes at Moore.

bottom-up change
Change that is introduced gradually and involves managers and employees at all levels of an organization.

Bottom-up change is typically more gradual. Top managers consult with middle and first-line managers about the need for change. Then, over time, these low-level managers work with nonmanagerial employees to develop a detailed plan for change. A major advantage of bottom-up change is that it can reduce uncertainty and resistance to change. The emphasis in bottom-up change is on participation and on keeping people informed about what is going on.

Lewin's Three-Stage Model of Change

Kurt Lewin identified a three-step process that organizations could use to manage change successfully: *unfreeze* the status quo, *move* to a new state, and *refreeze* the new change to make it permanent.[31]

driving forces
Forces that direct behaviour away from the status quo.

Organizations in their ordinary state reflect the status quo. To move toward a new state, unfreezing is necessary. Unfreezing, the process by which an organization overcomes the resistance to change, can occur in one of three ways, as shown in Figure 7.3. **Driving forces**, which direct behaviour away from the status quo,

Figure 7.3 | Unfreezing the Status Quo

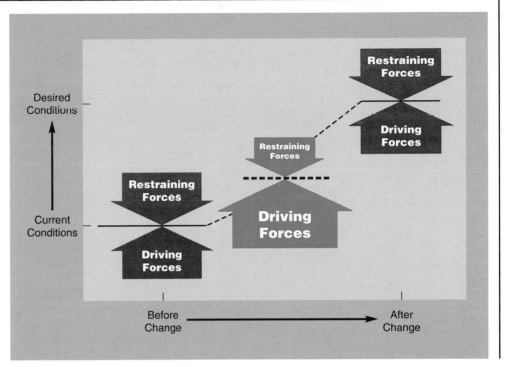

restraining forces

Forces that prevent movement away from the status quo.

can be increased. **Restraining forces**, which hinder movement from the existing equilibrium, can be decreased. One can also combine the first two approaches.

Individuals generally resist change, and therefore managers must take steps to break down that resistance. They can increase the driving forces by promising new rewards or benefits if employees work toward the change. Managers can also remove some of the restraining forces. For instance, if employees fear change because they don't know how to use the new technology, training could be given to reduce that fear. When resistance to change is extremely high, managers may have to work on both the driving and the restraining forces for unfreezing to be successful.

Moving involves getting the change process itself underway. Once change has been implemented, the behaviours have to be refrozen so that they can be sustained over time. Otherwise, change is likely to be short-lived, and employees are likely to go back to the previous state. Refreezing balances the driving and restraining forces to prevent the old state from arising again.

To refreeze the change, managers need to put permanent driving forces into place. For instance, the new bonus system could reinforce specific new changes. Over time, the norms of the employee work groups and managers will also help solidify the change if senior managers have sufficiently reinforced the new behaviour.

Evaluating the Change

The last step in the change process is to evaluate how successful the change effort has been in improving organizational performance.[32] Using measures such as changes in market share, profits, or the ability of managers to meet their goals, managers compare how well an organization is performing after the change with how well it was performing before. After Ed Tyler started making changes at Moore, share prices plunged. However, when Robert Burton replaced Tyler in

December 2002, he took the company on a path of going back to basics, and the company's share price started to rise.

Managers also can use **benchmarking**, comparing their performance on specific dimensions with the performance of high-performing organizations to decide how successful the change effort has been. For example, when Xerox was doing poorly in the 1980s, it benchmarked the efficiency of its distribution operations against those of L.L. Bean, the efficiency of its central computer operations against those of John Deere, and its marketing abilities against those of Procter & Gamble. Those companies are renowned for their skills in those different areas, and by studying how they performed, Xerox was able to dramatically increase its own performance.

benchmarking
Comparing performance on specific dimensions with the performance of high-performing organizations.

Tips for Managers

Introducing Change

1. Assess the need for change by examining your department's performance.

2. Clearly communicate what needs to be changed and why.

3. Use rewards that encourage individuals to engage in new behaviours.

MANAGING CHANGE IN A UNIONIZED ENVIRONMENT

Think About It

How to Tackle Featherbedding

When Paul Tellier (now CEO and president at Bombardier) took over at Montreal-based Canadian National Railway (CN), he had to deal with a unionized workforce that was quite resistant to change. In fact, the unions had negotiated a practice of "featherbedding," where union members whose jobs had been abolished were still being paid, even though they were not working. And even if CN had jobs for these employees in other provinces, the employees had the right to refuse jobs if they didn't want to move.[33] These practices created great difficulties for Tellier when he first tried to turn CN around.

Question
1. What can managers do to encourage change in unionized environments?

When managers work in a unionized environment, they may have some other considerations to face. Two consultants who have worked with a number of Canadian organizations in recent years note four essential elements for managing change in a unionized environment:[34]

- *An effective system for resolving day-to-day issues.* Employees should have alternatives to the formal grievance process so that they feel they can be heard easily. If the workplace is open to hearing workers' issues, this will underscore a commitment to participation and empowerment.

- *A jointly administered business education process.* Because union leaders and their members become uneasy about the effects of change on jobs, education can help employees understand the need for change. Making them more aware of company performance helps them better understand the decisions the company makes.

- *A jointly developed strategic vision for the organization.* Giving union members the opportunity to be involved in setting the vision lets them focus on how change can be made, rather than whether it should be made. The vision "should describe performance expectations, work design, organizational structure, the supply chain, governance, pay and rewards, technology, education and training, operating processes, employee involvement, employment security, and union-management roles and relations."[35]

- *A nontraditional, problem-solving method of negotiating collective agreements.* Managers need to create an atmosphere of tolerance and willingness to listen. Expanding the traditional scope of bargaining to include complex issues such as strategic plans is also helpful. Management resists bargaining over these issues, but when managers do bargain, it communicates a commitment to working jointly with unionized employees.

Chapter Summary

SUMMARY AND REVIEW

ORGANIZATIONAL CULTURE Organizational culture is the set of values, norms, standards of behaviour, and common expectations that guide how individuals and groups in an organization interact with each other and work to achieve organizational goals. Culture guides individuals and groups through shared values, norms, standards of behaviour, and expectations. Organizational culture is transmitted to employees through the values of the founder, the process of socialization, organizational ceremonies and rites, and stories and language. The way managers perform their management functions influences the kind of culture that develops in an organization.

ORGANIZATIONAL CULTURE AND CHANGE Changing the culture of an organization is difficult, and managers need to be aware of the signals they send to employees about change. If managers do not support the change themselves, it is unlikely that employees will go along with change.

MANAGING ORGANIZATIONAL CHANGE Managing organizational change is one of managers' most important and difficult tasks. Four steps in the organizational change process are assessing the need for change, deciding on the change to make, introducing the change, and evaluating how successful the change effort has been.

MANAGING CHANGE IN A UNIONIZED ENVIRONMENT To manage change in a unionized environment it is important to resolve day-to-day issues, provide education about the change, work together on developing a vision for the organization, and establish new problem-solving arrangements.

Roles in Contrast: Considerations

MANAGERS	EMPLOYEES
Managers convey the values of the organization to employees, and help socialize them. This reinforces the culture of the organization.	Organizational culture provides the context for rules and rewards in organizations. If I'm not comfortable with the culture, then it will be a less rewarding experience to work for that company.
The culture of the organization sets the tone for management, determining, for instance, how much you should involve employees in decisions. Thus it's important for you to manage in an environment where you support the culture.	Organizational culture helps determine which behaviours and activities are valuable, and which are not. So, even if I think something I'm doing should be rewarded because I think it's valuable, it might not be something that the organization's culture values.
To decrease resistance to change, provide rewards for those who take part in change behaviour, and also try to manage the fears of employees by giving them training in areas where they feel they do not have enough experience.	Individuals resist change because of fear of the unknown, and comfortableness with the way things have been done in the past. It requires some willingness to go beyond the comfortable and take part in change processes.

MANAGEMENT
in Action

Topics for Discussion and Action

1. What is organizational culture, and how does it affect the way employees behave?
2. Interview some employees of an organization, and ask them about the organization's values, norms, socialization practices, ceremonies and rites, and special language and stories. Referring to this information, describe the organization's culture.
3. What are the main obstacles to change?
4. Interview a manager about a change effort that he or she was involved in. What issues were involved? What problems were encountered? What was the outcome of the change process?
5. What difficulties do managers face when trying to introduce organizational change? How might they overcome some of these difficulties?

Building Management Skills

UNDERSTANDING CHANGE

Choose an organization you know—one that you have worked in or patronized, or one that has received extensive coverage in the popular press. The organization should be involved in only one industry or business. Answer these questions about the organization.

1. What is the output of the organization?
2. Is the organization producing its output efficiently?
3. Try to identify improvements that might be made to boost the organization's responsiveness to customers, quality, and efficiency.
4. How difficult would these changes be?

Management for You

Think of something that you would like to change in your personal life. It could be your study habits, your fitness and nutrition, the way you interact with others, or anything else that is of interest to you. What values and assumptions have encouraged the behaviour that currently exists (i.e., the one you want to change)?

What driving and restraining forces can you address in order to make the desired change?

Small Group Breakout Exercise

REDUCING RESISTANCE TO ADVANCES IN INFORMATION TECHNOLOGY

Form groups of 3 or 4 people, and appoint 1 member as the spokesperson who will communicate your findings to the whole class when called on by the instructor. Then discuss the following scenario.

You are a team of managers in charge of information and communications in a large consumer products corporation. Your company has already introduced many advances in information technology. Managers and employees have access to voice mail, email, the internet, your company's own intranet, and groupware.

Many employees use the new technology, but the resistance of some is causing communication problems. For example, all managers have email addresses and computers in their offices, but some refuse to turn their computers on, let alone send and receive email. These managers feel that they should be able to communicate as they have always done—in person, over the phone, or in writing. Thus, when managers who are unaware of their preferences send them email messages, those messages are never retrieved.

Moreover, the resistant managers never read company news sent by email. Another example of the resistance that your company is encountering concerns the use of groupware. Members of some work groups do not want to share information with others electronically.

Although you do not want to force people to use the technology, you want them at least to try it and give it a chance. You are meeting today to develop strategies for reducing resistance to the new technologies.

1. One resistant group of employees is made up of top managers. Some of them seem computer-phobic. They have never used, and do not want to start using, personal computers for any purpose, including communication. What steps will you take to get these managers to give their PCs a chance?
2. A second group of resistant employees consists of middle managers. Some middle managers resist using your company's intranet. Although these middle managers do not resist the technology per se and use their PCs for multiple purposes, including communication,

they seem to distrust the intranet as a viable way to communicate and get things done. What steps will you take to get these middle managers to take advantage of the intranet?
3. A third group of resistant employees is made up of members of groups and teams who do not want to use the groupware that has been provided to them. You think that the groupware could improve their communication and performance, but they seem to think otherwise. What steps will you take to get these members of groups and teams to start using groupware?

Managing Ethically

Some organizations, such as Arthur Andersen, the former accounting firm, and Enron, seem to have developed norms and values that caused their members to behave in unethical ways. When and why might a strong norm that

encourages high performance become one that can cause people to act unethically? How can organizations prevent their values and norms becoming "too strong"?

Exploring the World Wide Web

SPECIFIC ASSIGNMENT

Enter Hewlett-Packard's website (www.hp. com). Click on "Company Information"; then click on "About Us" and "Corporate Objectives."

1. What are the main elements of the HP Way?

2. How does the HP Way lead to an organizational culture that helps Hewlett-Packard to achieve its strategies?
3. How easy would it be to institute the HP Way and culture in other companies?

GENERAL ASSIGNMENT

Search for the website of a company that actively uses organizational culture to build competitive advantage. What kind of values and

norms is the culture based on? How does it affect employee behaviour?

You're the Management Consultant

RETAINING VALUABLE EMPLOYEES

Sam Bernstein was recently hired as the vice-president for human resources in an advertising agency. The agency has had a lot of turnover among its creative staff. The agency has no trouble attracting new talent, but turnover has become a real concern. Bernstein is determined to find out why turnover among the creative staff is so high (turnover among such employees was not high at other agencies where Bernstein worked). You are an expert in understanding organizational culture, and Bernstein has come to you for help. He wants to know what specific steps he should take to determine why so many members of the creative staff are leaving the agency, and what he can do to change this situation.

MANAGEMENT CASE ———————————————— IN THE NEWS

From the Pages of *The Boston Globe* Fostering Corporate Culture

When Brown University buddies Tom First and Tom Scott launched their juice company, Nantucket Nectars, six years ago, they deliberately made things as informal as possible.

No hierarchy. No dress code. No stodgy corporate culture.

The free-spirited attitude of the blond beach boys is flaunted throughout their Brighton-based company, from the dogs roaming the purple-toned offices to the naked man pictured jumping into the harbor on their juice labels.

But now, as juice sales approach US$20 million, Nantucket Nectars is outgrowing its fraternity house culture, and "Tom and Tom" (as they're known) are grappling with how to manage that growth without destroying the entrepreneurial spirit that has made the company special.

"It's one of my biggest fears," admits First, 29, whose baby face belies his intensity. "Once you start departmentalizing, you lose that."

Whether identified by purple walls or conservative blue suits, a company's culture has everything to do with its success—or failure.

That's especially true within start-up companies, where hard-driving employees typically put in long hours for relatively low pay.

IBM's paternalistic culture—often identified by its propensity toward blue suits and red ties—fostered deep employee loyalty with promises of good benefits, good pay and, until recently, a lifetime job.

Too often, company cultures—especially at start-up firms—are measured by what people wear to work or how much time they spend playing games in the corridors. But while blue jeans and Nerf basketball games might inspire creativity or relieve tension, they are not what make the culture.

A company's culture has more to do with its employees' behaviour, values and expectations. When employees understand and share a company's mission and values, specialists say, they are more productive, and the company is more prosperous.

So where does a company's culture come from?

Whether intentional or not, it's typically spawned by the founder early in the company's life.

First and Scott, 30, set the work ethic for Nantucket Nectars long before selling a single bottle of juice. During summers on Nantucket, they spent long hours selling supplies from a boat, shucking scallops, even walking dogs—anything to earn money and a reputation for service.

"Nantucket's a close-knit community. We needed to be respected as businesspeople, and not just seen as college kids passing through," First says.

Today, Nantucket Nectars's employees put in equally long hours. The office is lit up well past 8 p.m., and many staffers drop in on weekends to take care of business.

The founders didn't initially realize the example they were setting. About two months ago,

First called the staff together and encouraged them to leave at 6 p.m. each night.

The problem, says staffer Wink Mleczko, is that employees thought they were guilty of being inefficient.

"I'm like a tornado," First confesses. "I have tunnel vision. People look at their leaders and I have to be real careful about the tone I set."

Whether or not the founder of a company thinks much about cultural issues during its start-up phase, those issues become critical as a company matures, specialists and entrepreneurs agree.

"How you maintain a culture during explosive growth is probably the No. 1 thing that I worry about," says Frank Ingari, chief executive of Shiva Corp., a US$118 million company that makes equipment and software for telecommuters.

In his view, a company's culture has to fit not only the employee, but the employee's family, too. Not surprisingly, then, Shiva encourages employees to work from home on flexible schedules, if it fits their lifestyle.

"I don't care whether people are working here or there, as long as they are self-starters, self-motivators and hard workers," Ingari says.

Pamela Reeve, president and chief executive of Lightbridge Inc., a Waltham-based provider of software for the cellular communications industry, shares Ingari's obsession with managing culture.

"You have to pay as much attention to cultural issues as you do to your financing or marketing. To me, it's one of the assets that has to be managed and fertilized and watered."

Without a clearly defined culture, employees may try to clone themselves in the image of the company's leader—by wearing similar clothes or adopting various personality traits—rather than embrace the leader's ideas and principles, says William Bygrave, director of the Center for Entrepreneurial Studies at Babson College.

Another problem as companies grow, adds Babson colleague Julian Lange, is that "people try to divine what's happening in the company by reading titles."

At Lightbridge, Reeve tried to head off that situation by giving her company a very flat organization. "We have very little structure," she says. "Sure, someone has to have spending responsibility

and someone has to have responsibility for hiring and training. But that's all in the background. We're very team-oriented. I don't run the team. I'm just on it."

She compares the situation to her first whitewater rafting trip. The guide led the group through tumultuous waters, but he steered from the back of the boat.

To promote teamwork among the company's 300 employees, Lightbridge holds frequent brown bag lunches where goals are discussed, and ties performance incentives to companywide accomplishments, not individual ones.

When the company moved into larger office space at the end of a particularly stressful period of growth, Reeve invited art therapists in for a day to help employees design artwork that reflected the company's culture.

"We needed to put our soul in the building," she says.

In one exercise, each employee was assigned to paint a small area on a large canvas, which was their "home." The space between each area was their "neighborhood." Together, employees decided how to paint those common areas. The result is an "eclectic mix of colorful abstract paintings displayed throughout Lightbridge's offices.

The art helps tie employees together, something that becomes more difficult as companies grow beyond the start-up phase.

At Nantucket Nectars, weekly staff meetings include a guest speaker—an employee "who has to stand up and talk about their whole life, and what inspires them," First says. "We're so busy, sometimes we don't respect what other people do.

I wanted everyone to understand who the people are and how they're helping this company."

"You have to respect the fact that your employees are smart," says David Blohm, president of software company Virtual Entertainment, who has used similar teambuilding tactics.

At his last company, Mathsoft Inc., which he founded in 1985 and took public in 1993, Blohm made sure every employee was plugged in by requiring them to demonstrate the company's software products to colleagues.

"We wanted them to talk about the product benefits, like they were demonstrating them to their in-laws. We wanted them to talk about it at that level. That raises the level of understanding and empathy for the customer," Blohm says.

To produce the cultural flavour of a small company, many entrepreneurs search for ways to bring employees together, whether for Halloween parties, pizza and beer blasts, or summer barbecues.

At Molten Metal Technology Inc. in Waltham, it's breakfast. Each Friday, two of the company's most recent hires are responsible for preparing breakfast for the rest of their colleagues.

In the beginning, when there were only a dozen or so employees, it was easy. "You just stopped and got a bag of bagels," says Ian Yates, vice-president of sales and market development for the environmental technology company.

Now, however, Molten Metal has 300 employees, including 150 at its Waltham headquarters. But the tradition continues, with some newcomers going all out, preparing everything from pancakes to such ethnic favorites as breakfast burritos. The company picks up the tab.

"It's a small price to pay for the benefit, which is bringing people together," says Yates. "We don't want the first chance for people to meet to be in a meeting or on a project.

If you know someone first, you'd be surprised how much better you listen to them."

Another meeting place at Molten Metal is the fifth-floor atrium, where employees and executives talk over business issues, while shooting pool or playing table tennis or air hockey.

Having fun is actually part of the 7-year-old company's mission statement. But in the end, what makes any company's culture work is a shared sense of passion for the company's objectives.

"We're part of a team that is dedicated to changing the way the world deals with waste," Yates says. "We're pulling on the same end of the rope together. That's pretty powerful. It makes the time playing table tennis more fun."

Source: From the pages of *The Boston Globe,* J. Muller, "Fostering Corporate Culture," *The Boston Globe*, February 4, 1996, p. 73.

Questions

1. What factors influence the values and norms of Nantucket Nectars' culture?
2. What factors make it easy or difficult to create or change an organization's culture?

MANAGEMENT CASE ————————— IN THE NEWS

From the Pages of the *National Post* In the Clutches of a Slowdown

It is going to be an uneasy Christmas for Canadian employees of DaimlerChrysler AG's embattled North American unit who must wait until February to hear if they will still have jobs after Chrysler announces its restructuring plan.

In 1924, Walter P. Chrysler made auto history by introducing the Chrysler Six, the world's first affordable car that incorporated four-wheel hydraulic brakes and a high-compression engine that had more power than all other comparable engines. A year later, he established Chrysler Corp., which expanded rapidly, closing the year with about 3000 dealers across the United States and an impressive US$17-million profit.

Since then, Chrysler has had its ups and downs. It managed to maintain growth throughout the Great Depression, for example, despite the cool public reception to the 1934 Airflow—a

revolutionary vehicle with a teardrop front designed by Chrysler engineer Carl Breer and Orville Wright, the legendary aviator.

More recently, Lee Iacocca and a government bailout helped the automaker avoid bankruptcy in 1980, when a Middle East oil embargo and competition from fuel-efficient Japanese imports wreaked havoc with North American automakers. Chrysler dodged potential ruin again in the early Nineties by remaking itself as a nimble manufacturer of consumer favourites such as its LH series of sedans and Viper sports car.

Today, however, the North American icon, which merged with Daimler-Benz AG two years ago to create a global automotive powerhouse, faces what some insiders consider the biggest challenge of its rocky 76-year history.

"It's like a corporate version of *The Perfect Storm*. Too much hit us at once," says one U.S. manager who thinks even a heroic effort by the company's new German management team may not be enough to drive Chrysler out of the ditch.

Now that the U.S. auto bubble has burst, General Motors Corp., Ford Motor Co. and Chrysler are throttling back production to fight bloated inventories. This month, for example, the Big Three have trimmed overtime and idled operations that employ about 20 000 workers at assembly plants in Ontario and Quebec.

Plant shutdowns have a direct impact on the Big Three's earnings because automakers count revenues from new vehicles when they are built, not when they are sold. As a result, each of the Detroit trio has issued earnings warnings for the fourth quarter.

But Chrysler, which generated half of DaimlerChrysler's profits last year, is already deep in the red.

The unit is expected to lose about US$1.25-billion in the fourth quarter, twice its US$512-million third-quarter loss, due to the combined effect of high product launch expenditures and stiffer competition in key market segments, which has forced the company, and its rivals, to rely on costly consumer incentives to keep vehicles moving off dealer lots. Although the division is still expected to post a small profit for 2000, next year could be a different story.

"We believe the competitive market environment will continue to intensify and that our underlying financial performance, particularly in the U.S., will reflect this," Juergen Schrempp, DaimlerChrysler chairman, said in a letter to shareholders this week. "Indeed, if the automobile industry, especially in the U.S., becomes weaker in 2001, we will face a year which is even more challenging than 2000."

According to industry watchers, Chrysler's latest financial crisis was set in motion a few years ago when executives of the company that started off with affordability as its goal miscalculated what consumers would pay.

"They really missed the boat three or four years ago," says Dennis DesRosiers, an automotive industry consultant who thinks the management team that generated record profits in the mid-Nineties began to believe their own headlines and let costs escalate.

"They were operating in a 3% to 5% price increase world at a time when consumers were wanting to pay less and less."

Mr. Schrempp also blames Chrysler's former management for the unit's sad state of affairs, which has reduced the value of the once-mighty company to zero in the eyes of shareholders and generated calls to break up the 1998 merger that was once billed as a "marriage made in heaven."

Indeed, Mr. Schrempp was outraged by a series of production cuts announced by Chrysler management in October after he told analysts the division's problems were under control and it would return to profitability in the fourth quarter.

That embarrassment led Mr. Schrempp—who has since admitted he always intended the merger to be a takeover—to take a chainsaw through Chrysler's headquarters last month. In what has been dubbed the Auburn Hills Massacre, James Holden, Chrysler boss, was told to hit the road and take his top sales, administrative and public relations executives along for the ride.

Under the new leadership of Dieter Zetsche, a Mercedes-Benz veteran, and Wolfgang Bernhard, chief operating officer, the company is now firmly in the hands of German executives, who are working on a massive restructuring plan expected to be made public in February.

Mr. Schrempp has already laid the groundwork for a huge layoff, stating Chrysler is staffed for a company that owns 20% of the market, not the 14.5% it actually controls.

As a result, Mr. Zetsche is expected to slash up to 20 000 jobs and close at least one of Chrysler's 13 assembly operations in Canada and the United States.

Although he says the goal "is to have as little negative impact on people as possible," Mr. Zetsche has warned the company's 125 000 employees to expect "painful" measures next year. He has already temporarily shut down plants for one-week periods to further cut production and ordered suppliers to cough up a 5% price reduction starting on Jan. 1, and find another 10% by 2003.

Mr. Zetsche freely admits the stakes are high for all concerned.

"Every job, including mine," is on the line, he told reporters this week, in his first meeting with media since being put behind the wheel at Chrysler. "And I am up for that."

According to union officials, the best that Canada's 14 000 unionized Chrysler workers can hope for is probably getting away with a few more temporary shutdowns at operations in Windsor and Brampton, Ont., and having overtime shifts "taken out of the production picture."

Industry watchers disagree over the worst-case scenario. But some say Chrysler's commercial van assembly operation in Windsor is high on the list of targets for permanent closure. Company insiders also think the Pillette Road operation, which employs about 2000 workers, is a "likely target to anyone who knows the history of the plant."

Buzz Hargrove, president of the Canadian Auto Workers union, says he would be "shocked" if Chrysler closed any plants, especially the Pillette operation, which is undergoing a $1.5-billion expansion meant to make it "the most versatile manufacturing plant on the face of the Earth."

The union boss thinks Mr. Zetsche is smart enough to take into account that Chrysler's Canadian production has increased from 394 000 units in 1990 to 797 000 last year because Canadian autoworkers are more efficient than their U.S. cousins.

But Mr. Hargrove is nervous because Mr. Zetsche may act in the short-term interest of shareholders or succumb to U.S. union pressure to let Canada feel most of the pain, something he says the Big Three have done before.

Whatever happens, union leaders on both sides of the border say they will not reopen contracts to help cut costs.

Mr. Zetsche, who says there are positive and negative issues associated with doing business in Canada, refuses to guarantee the Pillette plant's future, which now reportedly hinges on the Dodge MAXXcab, a luxury pickup/SUV concept vehicle in need of a home for mass production.

"There is nothing to tell you because no decision has been made," Mr. Zetsche told the *Financial Post* this week, adding he intends to rethink every dollar spent.

But that is the easy stuff, according to Mike Flynn, director of the Office for the Study of Automotive Transportation at the University of Michigan, who thinks fixing cultural problems will be much harder.

"There were two real problems with the merger right from the start," he says. "The first was that it never was a merger of equals, which made it a bit of a charade. . . . The second difficulty was that you were taking one of the more hierarchical car companies in the world and trying to integrate it with one of the least hierarchical car companies in the world."

Insiders say employee morale at DaimlerChrysler's head office in Stuttgart, Germany, has improved since Mr. Zetsche replaced Mr. Holden, because the general feeling is that the "overpaid Americans" would "rather play golf" than put in overtime to make the merger work.

But Mr. Zetsche faces serious morale problems in the United States, where angry managers think Daimler took advantage of Chrysler's cash reserves to acquire stakes in Mitsubishi Motors Corp. and Hyundai Motor Co. and then used U.S. executives as scapegoats when market conditions got tough.

According to some estimates, DaimlerChrysler's cash reserves are dwindling fast. Prior to its US$36-billion acquisition by Daimler-Benz in 1998, Chrysler had socked away about US$9-billion to ensure it would not go broke in a weak car market as it nearly did in 1980.

Source: T. Watson, "In the Clutches of a Slowdown: Plant Closures Might Loom in DaimlerChrysler's Future as the Carmaker Tries to Correct Past Management Errors, a Misread of What Consumers Wanted to Drive off the Lot and a Clash of Cultures from its Recent Merger," *Financial Post (National Post)*, December 23, 2000, p. D7.

Questions

1. What are some of the forces for change that DaimlerChrysler has faced over its lifetime?
2. In what ways have employees been involved in the changes at DaimlerChrysler?
3. What does DaimlerChrysler need to do to ensure that its managers and employees remain committed to change?

CHAPTER **8**

MOTIVATION

Learning Objectives

1. Explain what motivation is and why managers need to be concerned about it.

2. Describe from the point of view of expectancy theory and equity theory what managers should do to have a highly motivated workforce.

3. Explain how goals and needs motivate people and what kinds of goals are especially likely to result in high performance.

4. Explain why and how managers can use pay as a major motivation tool.

Roles in Contrast: Questions

MANAGERS	EMPLOYEES
How can I motivate employees?	What motivates me?
Can I make things easier for employees to be motivated?	How will setting goals help to motivate me?
How is equity related to motivation?	Is it fair that some people are paid more than others?

A CASE IN CONTRAST

MOTIVATING EMPLOYEES AT EASTMAN KODAK AND MARS

George Fisher, as CEO of Eastman Kodak (www.kodak.com), the well-known photographic products company, and John and Forrest Mars Jr., the brothers who run the privately owned candy company Mars Inc., could not have chosen more different ways to motivate their employees.[1]

Fisher's approach to motivation included raising levels of responsibility, and encouraging employees to make decisions in a timely manner and to take risks in order to meet quality, customer satisfaction, and product development goals. Fisher set specific, difficult goals for his employees to attain, but gave them the responsibility to figure out how to meet the goals. In contrast, the Mars brothers like to call the shots and are reluctant to share responsibility, even with top managers. As one former manager at Mars put it, "Senior managers are scared of the Mars boys. They are like Russian czars, dictatorial in spirit and manner. There's a court around them. You don't pick a fight with John or Forrest."[2] The Mars brothers are so autocratic that not even high-level managers are motivated to take risks and come up

with creative new ideas, because they are likely to get shot down by Forrest or John.

Fisher expressed confidence in his subordinates' ability to succeed. He expected high performance, made it clear that shortfalls would not go unnoticed, and held employees accountable for reaching their difficult goals. Forrest and John Mars not only do not express confidence in their subordinates but frequently criticize them and their capabilities and are prone to angry outbursts when things displease them. Former Mars managers suggest that Forrest and John are such difficult people to work for that they make other hard-hitting CEOs look like Barney, the purple dinosaur character for young children. Some Mars employees feel that the Mars brothers have little faith in employees' competence and capabilities, given their tendencies to be so critical.

George Fisher, as CEO of Kodak, and John and Forrest Mars Jr., the brothers who run the candy company Mars Inc., could not have chosen more different ways to motivate their employees. Fisher liked to give employees the responsibility of making decisions and the opportunity to take risks. The Mars brothers like to call the shots and are reluctant to share responsibility, even with top managers.

Fisher has an informal, approachable style; he practically never raises his voice or shows anger or displeasure. He treated Kodak employees so well that they wanted to do a good job to help him turn the company around. As Carl Kohrt, former general manager of the $2.5-billion health sciences unit, says, "It's like talking to your father . . . You don't want to disappoint him." The Mars brothers are anything but approachable. Their frequent angry outbursts and tirades motivate employees to avoid them whenever possible.

Positive feedback for a job well done is an integral part of Fisher's approach to motivation. He took great pains to make sure that he was accessible to Kodak employees so that he could help spur them on and provide positive feedback and praise. For example, Fisher often visited with Kodak researchers for updates on their projects, and he praised their efforts. The only feedback the Mars brothers seem to provide is negative. They are impatient and use a variety of punishments on employees who disappoint them, including criticizing and berating them in front of their co-workers.

Consistent with his approachable style, Fisher was always available to talk to employees and had breakfast in the company cafeteria for this purpose. He encouraged all employees to send him email and some days received as many as 30 such messages. His secretary printed out the messages, and Fisher personally responded to each one with a handwritten note on the printout, typically within a day. Fisher showed that he cared about what his employees thought, gave them input on their ideas, and commended them for good suggestions. The Mars brothers do not welcome input from their employees. Managers and employees at all levels are afraid of them, are reluctant to stand up for what they believe in if it might not be what the brothers want to hear, and are reluctant to interact with them. "Fear of Forrest" causes many Mars employees to keep their opinions to themselves so as to avoid Forrest Mars' angry outbursts.

How are the Mars brothers able to attract employees despite what some former Mars executives claim is a very negative approach to motivation? They do it by paying salaries that are twice as large as the salaries paid by other companies in their industry. George Fisher also used pay to motivate; he did it, however, by linking pay to performance levels. Even researchers in Kodak's labs are held accountable for progress on their projects, including ensuring that projects are completed in a timely fashion.

How does the difference in Fisher's and the Mars brothers' styles of motivating employees affect their companies' performance? Kodak, under Fisher, performed better than it had for decades, and at the time of his retirement in 2000, Kodak remained the world's number-one film seller with 36 percent of the market. Meanwhile, Mars has been losing market share in the candy industry both in the United States and in Western Europe.

OVERVIEW

Even with the best strategy in place and an appropriate organizational architecture, an organization will be effective only if its members are motivated to perform at a high level. George Fisher clearly realizes this. One reason why leading is such an important managerial activity is that it entails ensuring that each member of an organization is motivated to perform highly and help the organization achieve its goals. When managers are effective, the outcome of the leading process is a highly motivated workforce. A key challenge for managers of organizations both large and small is to encourage employees to perform at a high level.

In this chapter, we describe what motivation is, where it comes from, and why managers need to promote high levels of it for an organization to be effective and achieve its goals. We examine important theories of motivation: *needs theories, expectancy theory, goal-setting theory, reinforcement theory,* and *equity theory.* Each provides managers with important insights about how to motivate organizational members. The theories are complementary in that each focuses on a somewhat different aspect of motivation. Considering all of the theories together will give managers a rich understanding of the many issues and problems involved in encouraging high levels of motivation throughout an organization. Last, we consider the use of pay as a motivation tool. By the end of this chapter, you will understand what it takes to have a highly motivated workforce.

The Nature of Motivation

Think About It

Motivating Retail Workers

Working in a retail store does not pay well. More than 60 percent of store employees earn less than $12 an hour, which is the national average wage, and the jobs often come with no benefits and no training. Turnover in these jobs is also quite high.[3]

To combat turnover, managers in the Bombay Co. home furnishings chain hold "Take Five" sessions with each sales staff member twice daily to discuss performance and goals. Assistant store managers also keep a "brag book." In these they record employees' achievements. At Staples, there are rally meetings each morning before the store opens to try to motivate employees and discuss performance.

Questions
1. What motivates employees?
2. Can rally meetings, brag books, and goal sessions take the place of pay in motivating?

motivation
Psychological forces that determine the direction of a person's behaviour in an organization, a person's level of effort, and a person's level of persistence.

intrinsically motivated behaviour
Behaviour that is performed for its own sake.

extrinsically motivated behaviour
Behaviour that is performed to acquire material or social rewards or to avoid punishment.

Motivation is the psychological forces that determine the *direction* of a person's behaviour in an organization, a person's level of *effort,* and a person's level of *persistence* in the face of obstacles.[4] People are motivated to obtain certain outcomes that they desire. An outcome is anything a person gets from a job or organization. Some outcomes, such as autonomy, responsibility, a feeling of accomplishment, and the pleasure of doing interesting or enjoyable work, result in intrinsically motivated behaviour. Other outcomes, such as pay, job security, benefits, and vacation time, result in extrinsically motivated behaviour. **Intrinsically motivated behaviour** is behaviour that is performed for its own sake; the source of motivation is actually to perform the behaviour, and motivation comes from doing the work itself. **Extrinsically motivated behaviour** is behaviour that is performed to acquire material or social rewards or to avoid punishment; the source of motivation is the consequences of the behaviour, not the behaviour itself.

Organizations hire people to obtain important inputs. An input is anything a person contributes to his or her job or organization, such as time, effort, education, experience, skills, knowledge, and actual work behaviours. Inputs such as these are necessary for an organization to achieve its goals. Managers strive to motivate members of an organization to contribute inputs—through their behaviour, effort, and persistence—that help the organization achieve its goals. They do this by making sure that members of an organization obtain the outcomes they desire when they make valuable contributions to the organization.

This alignment between employees and organizational goals as a whole can be described by the motivation equation shown in Figure 8.1. Managers aim to ensure that people are motivated to contribute important inputs to the organization, that these inputs are put to good use or focused in the direction of high performance, and that high performance results in employees obtaining the outcomes they desire.

The main theories of motivation that we cover in this chapter fall into one of two categories: needs theories and process theories. *Needs theories* focus on the types of needs individuals have that will lead them to be motivated, while *process theories* explore how one actually motivates someone. Each of the theories of motivation we discuss focuses on one or more aspects of the motivation equation in Figure 8.1. Together, the theories provide a comprehensive set of guidelines for managers to follow to promote high levels of employee motivation. Effective managers such as George Fisher in the *Case in Contrast* tend to follow many of these guidelines, whereas ineffective managers often fail to follow them and seem to have trouble motivating organizational members.

NEEDS THEORIES

Think About It

Treating People Right at Pazmac Enterprises

Steve Scarlett, owner of Langley, BC-based Pazmac Enterprises, recognizes the importance of addressing employees' needs in order to motivate them.[5] The employees at Scarlett's machine shop enjoy perks often associated with employees in the high-tech industry: During the work week, they have access to personal trainers, a fully equipped exercise room, and a swimming pool. On weekends, the company organizes guided hikes, snowshoeing expeditions, and other activities as desired.

These are great extrinsic rewards, but Scarlett also provides intrinsic rewards. There are no job titles at the company so that there are fewer barriers, and relationships can more easily be formed among all employees. All employees are involved in decision making. "I believe business needs to be planned diplomatically—we talk things out," says Scarlett.

"I treat people the way I'd want to be treated. At business school, you learn all about managing fixed assets and depreciation of equipment, but not a moment is spent on the value of people," Scarlett says. He tries very conscientiously to meet the needs of his employees to keep them motivated.

Question
1. How can we use needs to motivate individuals?

---

need
A requirement or necessity for survival and well-being.

needs theories
Theories of motivation that focus on what needs people are trying to satisfy at work and what outcomes will satisfy those needs.

A **need** is a requirement or necessity for survival and well-being. The basic premise of need theories is that people are motivated to obtain outcomes at work that will satisfy their needs. **Needs theories** suggest that in order to motivate a person to contribute valuable inputs to a job and perform at a high level, a manager must determine what needs the person is trying to satisfy at work and ensure that the person receives outcomes that help to satisfy those needs when the person performs at a high level and helps the organization achieve its goals.

We discuss two needs theories below: Abraham Maslow's *hierarchy of needs* and Frederick Herzberg's *motivator-hygiene theory*. These theories describe needs that people try to satisfy at work. In doing so, the theories provide managers with

Figure 8.1 | The Motivation Equation

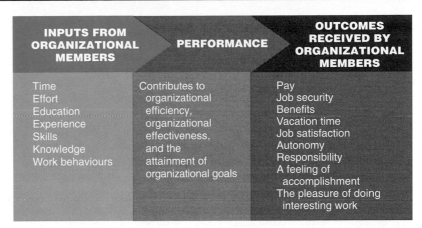

INPUTS FROM ORGANIZATIONAL MEMBERS	PERFORMANCE	OUTCOMES RECEIVED BY ORGANIZATIONAL MEMBERS
Time Effort Education Experience Skills Knowledge Work behaviours	Contributes to organizational efficiency, organizational effectiveness, and the attainment of organizational goals	Pay Job security Benefits Vacation time Job satisfaction Autonomy Responsibility A feeling of accomplishment The pleasure of doing interesting work

insights about what outcomes will motivate members of an organization to perform at a high level and contribute inputs to help the organization achieve its goals.

Abraham Maslow
www.ship.edu/~cgboeree/
maslow.html

Maslow's hierarchy of needs

An arrangement of five basic needs that, according to Maslow, motivate behaviour. Maslow proposed that the lowest level of unmet needs is the prime motivator and that only one level of needs is motivational at a time.

Maslow's Hierarchy of Needs

Psychologist Abraham Maslow proposed that everyone aims to satisfy five basic kinds of needs: physiological needs, safety needs, belongingness needs, esteem needs, and self-actualization needs (see Table 8.1).[6] He suggested that these needs constitute a **hierarchy of needs**, with the most basic or compelling needs–physiological and safety needs–at the bottom. Maslow argued that these lowest-level needs must be met before a person will strive to satisfy needs higher up in the hierarchy, such as self-esteem needs. Once a need is satisfied, he proposed, it no longer is a source of motivation, and needs at the next highest level become motivators.

Although Maslow's theory identifies needs that are likely to be important sources of motivation for many people, research does not support his contention that there is a needs hierarchy or his notion that only one level of needs is motivational at a time.[7] Nevertheless, a key conclusion can be drawn from Maslow's theory: People differ in what needs they are trying to satisfy at work. To have a motivated workforce that achieves goals, managers must determine which needs employees are trying to satisfy in organizations and then make sure that individuals receive outcomes that will satisfy their needs when they perform at a high level and contribute to organizational effectiveness.

In an increasingly global economy it is also important for managers to realize that citizens of different countries might differ in the needs they try to satisfy through work.[8] Some research suggests, for example, that people in Greece and Japan are especially motivated by safety needs and that people in Sweden, Norway, and Denmark are motivated by belongingness needs.[9] In poor countries with low standards of living, physiological and safety needs are likely to be the prime motivators of behaviour. As countries become wealthier and have higher standards of living, it is likely that needs related to personal growth and accomplishment (such as esteem and self-actualization) become important as motivators of behaviour.

Vancouver-based Pazmac Enterprises owner Steve Scarlett recognizes that his employees have needs other than money. Scarlett hires a personal trainer to help his employees meet their fitness goals.

Table 8.1 | Maslow's Hierarchy of Needs

	Needs	Description	Examples of How Managers Can Help People Satisfy These Needs at Work
Highest-level needs	**Self-actualization needs**	The needs to realize one's full potential as a human being	By giving people the opportunity to use their skills and abilities to the fullest extent possible
	Esteem needs	The needs to feel good about oneself and one's capabilities, to be respected by others, and to receive recognition and appreciation	By granting promotions and recognizing accomplishments
	Belongingness needs	Needs for social interaction, friendship, affection, and love	By promoting good interpersonal relations and organizing social functions such as company picnics and holiday parties
	Safety needs	Needs for security, stability, and a safe environment	By providing job security, adequate medical benefits, and safe working conditions
Lowest-level needs (most basic or compelling)	**Physiological needs**	Basic needs for things such as food, water, and shelter that must be met in order for a person to survive	By providing a level of pay that enables a person to buy food and clothing and have adequate housing

The lowest level of unsatisfied needs motivates behaviour; once this level of needs is satisfied, a person tries to satisfy the needs at the next level.

Herzberg's motivator-hygiene theory
A needs theory that distinguishes between motivator needs (related to the nature of the work itself) and hygiene needs (related to the physical and psychological context in which the work is performed). Herzberg proposed that motivator needs must be met in order for motivation and job satisfaction to be high.

Pazmac Enterprises
www.pazmac.com

Frederick Herzberg
www.lib.uwo.ca/business/
herzberg.html

Herzberg's Motivator-Hygiene Theory

According to **Herzberg's motivator-hygiene theory**, people have two sets of needs or requirements: motivator needs and hygiene needs.[10] *Motivator needs* are related to the nature of the work itself and how challenging it is. Outcomes such as interesting work, autonomy, responsibility, being able to grow and develop on the job, and a sense of accomplishment and achievement help to satisfy motivator needs. In order to have a highly motivated and satisfied workforce, Herzberg suggested, managers should take steps to ensure that employees' motivator needs are being met.

Hygiene needs are related to the physical and psychological context in which the work is performed. Hygiene needs are satisfied by outcomes such as pleasant and comfortable working conditions, pay, job security, good relationships with co-workers, and effective supervision. According to Herzberg, when hygiene needs are not met, workers will be dissatisfied, and when hygiene needs are met, workers will not be dissatisfied, that is, they will be neutral. For satisfaction to occur, the motivator needs must be met. This is illustrated in Figure 8.2. Pazmac's owner, Steve Scarlett, exhibits his understanding of Herzberg's theory. To satisfy motivator needs, he provides opportunities for his employees to be involved in decision making and ensures good relationships among employees. He also shows concerns about employees' hygiene needs. Usually machine shops are noisy and messy, the floors are covered with oil, and employees wear dirty overalls. Pazmac, however, is spotlessly clean. The lunchroom is tastefully designed, and the men's washroom is plush, with potpourri bowls and paintings on the walls.

Many research studies have tested Herzberg's propositions, and, by and large, the theory fails to receive support.[11] Nevertheless, Herzberg's formulations have contributed to our understanding of motivation in at least two ways. First, Herzberg helped to focus researchers' and managers' attention on the important

Figure 8.2 | Herzberg's Motivation-Hygiene Theory

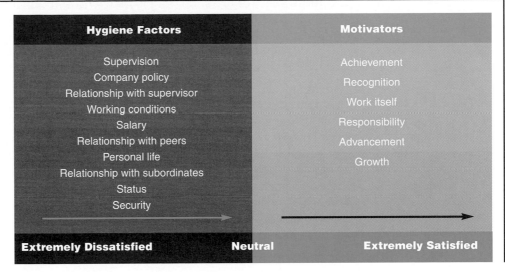

Hygiene Factors	Motivators
Supervision	Achievement
Company policy	Recognition
Relationship with supervisor	Work itself
Working conditions	Responsibility
Salary	Advancement
Relationship with peers	Growth
Personal life	
Relationship with subordinates	
Status	
Security	

Extremely Dissatisfied — **Neutral** — **Extremely Satisfied**

distinction between intrinsic motivation (related to motivator needs) and extrinsic motivation (related to hygiene needs), covered earlier in the chapter. Second, his theory helped to prompt researchers and managers to study how jobs can be designed or redesigned so that they are intrinsically motivating.

Other Needs

Clearly more needs motivate employees than the needs described by these theories. For example, more and more employees are feeling the need for work-life balance and time to take care of their loved ones while simultaneously being highly motivated at work. Interestingly enough, recent research suggests that being exposed to nature (even just by being able to see some trees from your office window) has many beneficial effects and a lack of such exposure can actually impair well-being and performance.[12] Thus, having some time during the day when one can at least see nature may be another important need.

Managers of successful companies often strive to ensure that as many of their valued employees' needs as possible are satisfied in the workplace.

Needs theories address the different needs that individuals have that could be used to motivate them. **Process theories**, which we cover below, focus on the more concrete ways of actually motivating someone. Within the process theories, we cover *expectancy theory, goal-setting theory,* and *reinforcement theory.*

process theories
Theories of motivation that explore how one actually motivates someone.

EXPECTANCY THEORY

Think About It

Motorola Promotes High Motivation in Malaysia

Motorola is a truly global organization with major operations in countries such as India and China.[13] At Motorola's plant in Penang, Malaysia, which produces walkie-talkies and cordless phones, workers have high levels of motivation. Motorola gives its Malaysian employees two days of classroom instruction in which they are taught about quality control, how to use statistical procedures, and how to work together in teams to come up with ideas to improve quality and cut costs. Employees then have, on average, 48 hours of classroom training per year to further develop their skills.

Penang managers make sure that employees are given rewards when they perform well. For instance, employees who win quality competitions are given trophies and other forms of recognition. Workers who suggest at least 100 cost-saving ideas in a year and have at least 60 percent of them implemented become members of the prestigious "100 Club." Belonging to the club does not bring many material rewards, but the employees enjoy receiving recognition.

Question
1. Is it possible to improve motivation other than by increasing rewards?

expectancy theory

The theory that motivation will be high when employees believe that high levels of effort will lead to high performance, and high performance will lead to the attainment of desired outcomes.

expectancy

In expectancy theory, a perception about the extent to which effort will result in a certain level of performance.

Mars Inc.
www.mars.com

Expectancy theory, formulated by Victor H. Vroom in the 1960s, states that motivation will be high when employees believe that high levels of effort will lead to high performance, and high performance will lead to receiving desired outcomes. Expectancy theory is one of the most popular theories of work motivation because it focuses on all three parts of the motivation equation: inputs, performance, and outcomes. Expectancy theory identifies three major factors that determine a person's motivation: *expectancy*, *instrumentality*, and *valence* (see Figure 8.3).[14]

Expectancy

Expectancy is a person's perception about the extent to which effort (an input) will result in a certain level of performance. A person's level of expectancy determines whether he or she believes that a high level of effort will result in a high level of performance. People are motivated to put forth a lot of effort on their jobs only if they think that their effort will pay off in high performance–that is, if they have a high expectancy. Think about how motivated you would be to study for a test if you thought that, no matter how hard you tried, you would get a D. In this case, expectancy is low, so overall motivation is also low.

In trying to influence motivation, managers need to make sure that their subordinates believe that if they do try hard they actually can succeed. As the *Case in Contrast* indicates, the Mars brothers' excessive criticism leads to relatively low levels of expectancy among Mars employees. They do not believe in their own ability to succeed and thus have low motivation. In addition to expressing confidence

Figure 8.3 | Expectancy, Instrumentality, and Valence

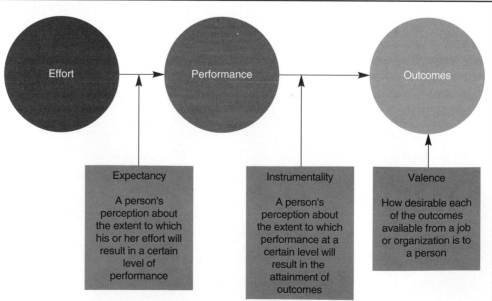

Motorola Penang
malaysia.motorola.com/
about_mot_mal/penang/

instrumentality

In expectancy theory, a perception about the extent to which performance will result in the attainment of outcomes.

in subordinates, another way for managers to boost subordinates' expectancy levels and motivation is by providing training so that people have all the expertise they need for high performance. At Motorola's plant in Penang, Malaysia, new employees are given two days of training, and then all employees are given 48 hours of training per year. The training increases their expectancy by improving their ability to perform well.

Instrumentality

Expectancy captures a person's perceptions about the relationship between effort and performance. **Instrumentality**, the second major concept in expectancy theory, is a person's perception about the extent to which performance at a certain level will result in receiving outcomes or rewards (see Figure 8.3). According to expectancy theory, employees will be motivated to perform at a high level only if they think that high performance will lead to outcomes such as pay, job security, interesting job assignments, bonuses, or a feeling of accomplishment.

Managers promote high levels of instrumentality when they clearly link performance to desired outcomes and communicate this. By making sure that rewards are given to organizational members on the basis of their performance, managers promote high instrumentality and motivation. When rewards are linked to performance in this way, high performers receive more than low performers. In the *Case in Contrast,* George Fisher raised levels of instrumentality for Kodak employees by closely linking their pay to their performance. At Motorola's Malaysian plant, managers make sure that employees see the link between performance and reward. An emphasis on quality can lead to trophies for employees, and cost-cutting ideas can lead to recognition, another form of reward. This increases the employee's instrumentality.

Valence

valence

In expectancy theory, how desirable each of the outcomes available from a job or organization is to a person.

Expectancy theory acknowledges that people differ in their preferences for outcomes or rewards. For many people, pay is the most important outcome of working. For others, a feeling of accomplishment or enjoying one's work is more important. At Motorola's Malaysian plant, the rewards to employees reflect things that they value. Salaries are relatively high ($287 a month), as are job security and promotional opportunities, which makes employees feel that they are valued members of Motorola.[15] The term **valence** refers to how desirable each of the outcomes available from a job or organization is to a person. To motivate organizational members, managers need to determine which outcomes have high valence for them—are highly desired—and make sure that those outcomes are provided when members perform at a high level. From the *Case in Contrast,* it appears that for many employees at Mars, pay that is twice the industry average has such high valence that it keeps them working for the demanding Mars brothers despite the presence of few other desirable outcomes.

Bringing It All Together

According to expectancy theory, high motivation results from high levels of expectancy, instrumentality, and valence (see Figure 8.4). If any one of these factors is low, motivation is likely to be low. No matter how tightly desired outcomes are linked to performance, if a person thinks that it is practically impossible for him or her to perform at a high level, then motivation to perform at a high level will be exceedingly low. Similarly, if a person does not think that outcomes are linked to high performance, or if a person does not desire the outcomes that are linked to high performance, then motivation to perform at a high level will be low.

Figure 8.4 | Expectancy Theory

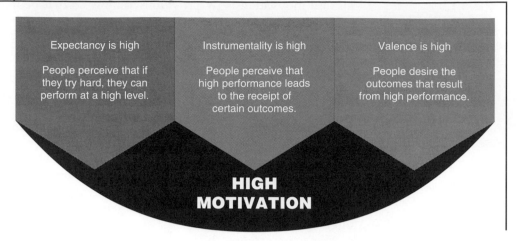

Expectancy is high	Instrumentality is high	Valence is high
People perceive that if they try hard, they can perform at a high level.	People perceive that high performance leads to the receipt of certain outcomes.	People desire the outcomes that result from high performance.

HIGH MOTIVATION

Managers of successful companies try to ensure that employees' levels of expectancy, instrumentality, and valence are high so that they will be highly motivated, as is illustrated by Motorola's efforts at managing globally.

GOAL-SETTING THEORY

goal-setting theory
A theory that focuses on identifying the types of goals that are most effective in producing high levels of motivation and performance and explaining why goals have these effects.

Goal-setting theory, developed by Ed Locke and Gary Latham, suggests that the goals that organizational members strive to achieve determine their motivation and subsequent performance. A *goal* is what a person is trying to accomplish through his or her efforts and behaviours.[16] Just as you may have a goal to get a good grade in this course, so do members of an organization have goals that they strive to meet. In the *Case in Contrast,* we mentioned that researchers in Kodak's labs have goals for finishing their projects in a timely fashion. Similarly, salespeople at the Bay strive to meet sales goals, and top managers have market share and profitability goals.

Goal-setting theory suggests that in order to result in high motivation and performance, goals must be *specific* and *difficult.*[17] Specific goals are often quantitative—a salesperson's goal to sell $200 worth of merchandise each day, a scientist's goal to finish a project in one year, a CEO's goal to reduce debt by 40 percent and increase revenues by 20 percent, a restaurant manager's goal to serve 150 customers per evening. In contrast to specific goals, vague goals such as "doing your best" or "selling as much as you can" do not have much motivational force. Difficult goals are ones that are hard but not impossible to attain.

Regardless of whether specific, difficult goals are set by managers, workers, or managers and workers together, they lead to high levels of motivation and performance. At Kodak, George Fisher set specific, difficult goals for his employees but then left decisions about how to meet the goals up to them. When managers set goals for their subordinates, it is important that their subordinates accept the goals or agree to work toward them and also that they are committed to them or really want to attain them.

As part of George Fisher's attempt to motivate his workforce, he created teams of workers who were given responsibility for developing innovative new products quickly and cost effectively. Kodak's Zebra Team, so named because of its responsibility for Kodak's black and white photographic products, achieved major gains in productivity and profitability.

Some managers find that having subordinates participate in the actual setting of goals boosts their acceptance of and commitment to the goals. It is also important for organizational members to receive *feedback* about how they are doing; feedback can often be provided by the performance appraisal and feedback component of an organization's human resource management system (see Chapter 11).

REINFORCEMENT THEORY

Think About It

Would You Want to Work in a Slaughterhouse?

Employees at a Maple Leaf Foods hog slaughterhouse in Brandon, Manitoba are known for missing a lot of work.[18] "The job sucks. That's basically it," said Scott Oldenburger. "It's cold, you stand in one spot for hours on end, you're not allowed to take a p—— unless it's on your scheduled break. It's gross." Oldenburger only worked there for about a month before he decided to quit. And he had one of the more pleasant jobs on the production line: cutting shoulders. Employees have such jobs as bung flushers, head splitters, and kidney poppers at the plant. The plant processes 45 000 hogs per week. Employees work under assembly-line conditions that are highly mechanized, with separate jobs for cutting off tongues, ears, and tails.

Question

1. How would you motivate employees who have unpleasant jobs?

reinforcement theory
A motivation theory based on the relationship between a given behaviour and its consequence.

reinforcement
Anything that causes a given behaviour to be repeated or stopped.

positive reinforcement
Giving people outcomes they desire when they perform organizationally functional behaviours well.

Reinforcement theory is a motivation theory that looks at the relationship between behaviour and its consequences. **Reinforcement** is defined as anything that causes a certain behaviour to be repeated or stopped. Four reinforcements are generally discussed in the theory: *positive reinforcement, negative reinforcement, extinction,* and *punishment.*

Positive Reinforcement

Positive reinforcement gives people outcomes they desire when they perform well. These outcomes, called positive reinforcers, include any outcomes that a person desires, such as pay, praise, or a promotion. Performing well might include producing high quality goods and services, providing high quality customer service, and meeting deadlines. By linking positive reinforcers to the positive performance, managers motivate people to perform the desired behaviours. For instance, managers at Brandon's hog slaughterhouse offer a variety of incentives to encourage workers to show up for their shifts. To be eligible for a truck raffle, held every three months, employees have to show up for every one of their shifts during that period. Employees get bonuses of 75 cents an hour for perfect attendance during shorter periods. Regular wages range from $8.25 to $13 an hour. The incentive program has paid off. Before the rewards, 12 percent of the employees skipped work each day. Since the rewards, absenteeism has dropped to about 7 to 8 percent.

Negative Reinforcement

negative reinforcement
Eliminating or removing undesired outcomes once people have performed organizationally functional behaviours.

Negative reinforcement also can be used to encourage members of an organization to perform well. Managers using negative reinforcement actually eliminate or remove undesired outcomes once the desired behaviour is performed. These undesired outcomes, called *negative reinforcers,* can include unpleasant assignments, a manager's constant nagging or criticism, or the ever-present threat of losing one's job. When negative reinforcement is used, people are motivated to perform behaviours because they want to avoid or stop receiving undesired outcomes. Managers who try to encourage salespeople to sell more by threatening them with being fired are using negative reinforcement. In this case, the negative reinforcer is the threat of job loss, which is removed once the functional behaviours are performed.

Whenever possible, managers should try to use positive reinforcement. Negative reinforcement can make for a very unpleasant work environment and even a negative culture in an organization. No one likes to be nagged, threatened, or exposed to other kinds of negative outcomes. The use of negative reinforcement sometimes causes subordinates to resent managers and try to get back at them.

Extinction

extinction

Stopping the performance of dysfunctional behaviours by eliminating whatever is reinforcing them.

Sometimes members of an organization are motivated to engage in poor performance. One way for managers to stop dysfunctional behaviours is to eliminate whatever is reinforcing the behaviours. This process is called **extinction**.

Suppose a manager has a subordinate who frequently stops by the office to chat—sometimes about work-related matters but at other times about various topics ranging from politics to last night's football game. Though the chats are fun, the manager ends up working late to catch up. To extinguish this behaviour, the manager stops acting interested in these nonwork-related conversations and keeps responses polite and friendly but brief. No longer being reinforced with a pleasurable conversation, the subordinate eventually ceases to be motivated to interrupt the manager during working hours to discuss nonwork issues.

Punishment

punishment

Administering an undesired or negative consequence when dysfunctional behaviour occurs.

When employees are performing dangerous behaviours or behaviours that are illegal or unethical, the behaviour needs to be stopped immediately. Therefore the manager will use **punishment**, administering an undesired or negative consequence to subordinates when they perform the dysfunctional behaviour. Punishments used by organizations range from verbal reprimands to pay cuts, temporary suspensions, demotions, and firings. Punishment, however, can have unintended side effects—resentment, loss of self-respect, a desire for retaliation, etc.—and should be used only when absolutely necessary. The *Case in Contrast* relates how the Mars brothers' excessive use of punishment is dysfunctional for their company.

Organizational Behaviour Modification

organizational behaviour modification (OB MOD)

The systematic application of operant conditioning techniques to promote the performance of organizationally functional behaviours and discourage the performance of dysfunctional behaviours.

When managers use reinforcement to encourage positive behaviours and discourage negative behaviours, they are engaging in **organizational behaviour modification (OB MOD)**.[19] OB MOD has been used successfully to improve productivity, efficiency, attendance, punctuality, compliance with safety procedures, and other important behaviours in a wide variety of organizations. The five basic steps in OB MOD are described in Figure 8.5.

OB MOD works best for behaviours that are specific, objective, and countable—such as attendance and punctuality, making sales, or putting telephones together—which lend themselves to careful scrutiny and control. OB MOD may be questioned because of its lack of relevance to certain kinds of work behaviours (e.g., the many work behaviours that are not specific, objective, and countable). Some people also have questioned it on ethical grounds. Critics of OB MOD suggest that it is overly controlling and robs workers of their dignity, individuality, freedom of choice, and even their creativity. Supporters counter that OB MOD is a highly effective means of promoting organizational efficiency. Both sides of this argument have some merit. What is clear, however, is that when used appropriately, OB MOD provides managers with a technique to motivate the performance of at least some positive behaviours.

Figure 8.5 | Five Steps in OB MOD

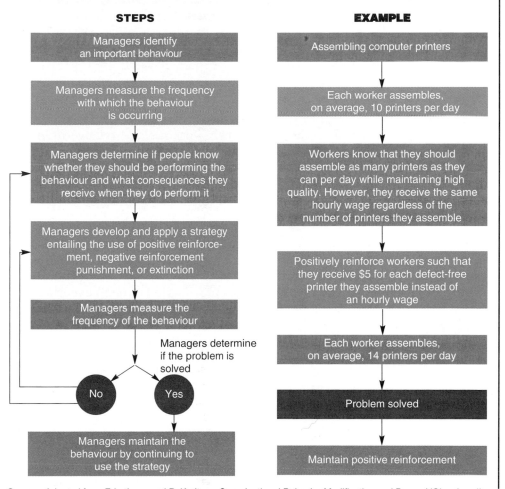

Source: Adapted from F. Luthans and R. Kreitner, *Organizational Behavior Modification and Beyond* (Glenview, IL: Scott, Foresman, 1985).

In trying to understand how all of these theories of motivation fit together, it may be helpful to remember that needs theories suggest that individuals have needs, and that they will be motivated to have these needs met. Expectancy, goal-setting and reinforcement theories show the processes by which individuals can be encouraged to behave in ways that earn rewards. Job design, which we discussed in Chapter 6, can also be a way of motivating individuals. Job rotation, job enlargement, and job enrichment can increase an employee's job satisfaction, and thus lead him or her to be more motivated in performing the job.

EQUITY THEORY

Think About It

Public Sector vs. Private Sector Pay

Greater Vancouver Regional District directors voted themselves a 60-percent pay raise in June 2003. They did this at the same time that government services were being cut across the province of British Columbia. On a percentage basis, the pay raise seems extraordinary. But what should a municipal councillor be paid? Members of Parliament earn annual salaries of $131 000, and members of the BC Legislature earn $68 500, plus expenses. Councillors earn about $40 000 a year, on average. Politicians at all three levels of government

—federal, provincial, and municipal—are expected to make complex decisions, and need the same types of skills. Many of them could make more money working in the private sector.

Questions
1. What does it mean to be paid equitably?
2. Is it fair for there to be a difference in the pay of politicians at the different governing levels?

equity theory

A theory of motivation that focuses on people's perceptions of the fairness of their work outcomes relative to their work inputs.

Equity theory is a theory of motivation that concentrates on people's perceptions of the fairness of their work *outcomes* relative to, or in proportion to, their work *inputs*. Equity theory complements need and expectancy theories by focusing on how people perceive the relationship between the outcomes they receive from their jobs and organizations and the inputs they contribute.

Equity

equity

The justice, impartiality, and fairness to which all organizational members are entitled.

Equity exists when a person perceives his or her own outcome/input ratio to be equal to a referent's outcome/input ratio. The *referent* could be another person or a group of people who are perceived to be similar to oneself; the referent also could be oneself in a previous job or one's expectations about what outcome/input ratios should be. Under conditions of equity (see Table 8.2), if a referent receives more outcomes than you receive, the referent contributes proportionally more inputs to the organization, so his or her outcome/input ratio still equals your outcome/input ratio. Similarly, under conditions of equity, if you receive more outcomes than a referent, then your inputs are perceived to be proportionally higher. Maria Lau and Claudia King, for example, both work in a shoe store in a large mall. Lau is paid more per hour than King but also contributes more inputs, including being responsible for some of the store's bookkeeping, closing the store, and periodically depositing cash in the bank. When King compares her outcome/input ratio to Lau's (her referent's), she perceives the ratios to be equitable because Lau's higher level of pay (an outcome) is proportional to her higher level of inputs (bookkeeping, closing the store, and going to the bank). In a comparison of one's own outcome/input ratio to a referent's outcome/input ratio, one's *perceptions* of outcomes and inputs (not any objective indicator of them) are key.

When equity exists, people are motivated to continue contributing their current levels of inputs to their organizations in order to receive their current levels of outcomes. Under conditions of equity, if people wish to increase their outcomes, they are motivated to increase their inputs.

Table 8.2 | Equity Theory

Condition	Person		Referent	Example
Equity	$\frac{\text{Outcomes}}{\text{Inputs}}$	=	$\frac{\text{Outcomes}}{\text{Inputs}}$	An engineer perceives that he contributes more inputs (time and effort), and receives proportionally more outcomes (a higher salary and choice job assignments), than his referent.
Underpayment inequity	$\frac{\text{Outcomes}}{\text{Inputs}}$	< (less than)	$\frac{\text{Outcomes}}{\text{Inputs}}$	An engineer perceives that he contributes more inputs but receives the same outcomes as his referent.
Overpayment inequity	$\frac{\text{Outcomes}}{\text{Inputs}}$	> (greater than)	$\frac{\text{Outcomes}}{\text{Inputs}}$	An engineer perceives that he contributes the same inputs but receives more outcomes than his referent.

Inequity

inequity
Lack of fairness.

Inequity, lack of fairness, exists when a person's outcome/input ratio is not perceived to be equal to a referent's. Inequity creates pressure or tension inside people and motivates them to restore equity by bringing the two ratios back into balance.

There are two types of inequity: underpayment inequity and overpayment inequity (see Table 8.2). **Underpayment inequity** exists when a person's own outcome/input ratio is perceived to be less than that of a referent: In comparing yourself to a referent, you think that you are not receiving the outcomes you should be, given your inputs. When the BC municipal councillors voted themselves a pay raise, they were responding to the idea that they were underpaid compared to other government decision makers. **Overpayment inequity** exists when a person perceives that his or her own outcome/input ratio is greater than that of a referent: In comparing yourself to a referent, you think that the referent is receiving fewer outcomes than he or she should be, given his or her inputs.

underpayment inequity
Inequity that exists when a person perceives that his or her own outcome/input ratio is less than the ratio of a referent.

overpayment inequity
Inequity that exists when a person perceives that his or her own outcome/input ratio is greater than the ratio of a referent.

Ways to Restore Equity

According to equity theory, both underpayment inequity and overpayment inequity create tension that motivates most people to restore equity by bringing the ratios back into balance.[20] When people experience *underpayment* inequity, they may be motivated to lower their inputs by reducing their working hours, putting forth less effort on the job, or being absent, or they may be motivated to increase their outcomes by asking for a raise or a promotion. Susan Richie, a financial analyst at a large corporation, noticed that she was working longer hours and getting more work accomplished than a co-worker who had the same position, yet they both received the exact same pay and other outcomes. To restore equity, Richie decided to stop coming in early and staying late. Alternatively, she could have tried to restore equity by trying to increase her outcomes by, for example, asking her boss for a raise.

When people experience *overpayment* inequity, they may try to restore equity by changing their perceptions of their own or their referents' inputs or outcomes. Equity can be restored when people "realize" that they are contributing more inputs than they originally thought. Equity also can be restored by perceiving the referent's inputs to be lower or the referent's outcomes to be higher than one originally thought. When equity is restored in this way, actual inputs and outcomes are unchanged. What is changed is how people think about or view their own or the referent's inputs and outcomes. Mary McMann experienced overpayment inequity when she realized that she was being paid $2 an hour more than a co-worker who had the same job as hers in a record store and who contributed the same amount of inputs. McMann restored equity by changing her perceptions of her inputs. She "realized" that she worked harder than her co-worker and solved more problems that came up in the store.

Experiencing either overpayment or underpayment inequity, you might decide that your referent is not appropriate because, for example, the referent is too different from yourself. Choosing a more appropriate referent may bring the ratios back into balance. However, when people experience *underpayment* inequity and other means of equity restoration fail, they may leave the organization.

Motivation is highest when as many people as possible in an organization perceive that they are being equitably treated—their outcomes and inputs are in balance. Top contributors and performers are motivated to continue contributing a high level of inputs because they are receiving the outcomes they deserve. Mediocre contributors and performers realize that if they want to increase their outcomes, they have to increase their inputs. Managers of effective organizations, such as George Fisher at Eastman Kodak, realize the importance of equity for motivation and performance and continually strive to ensure that employees feel they are being equitably treated.

Tips for Managers

Expectancy and Equity Theories

1. Express sincere confidence in your subordinates' capabilities and let them know that you expect them to succeed.

2. Distribute outcomes based on important inputs and performance levels and clearly communicate to your subordinates that this is the case.

3. Determine which outcomes your subordinates desire and try to gain control over as many of these as possible (i.e., have the authority to distribute or withhold outcomes).

4. Provide clear information to your subordinates about which inputs are most valuable for them to contribute to their jobs and the organization in order to receive desired outcomes.

PAY AND MOTIVATION

Think About It

What Do Employees Want?

Managers may not be giving enough consideration to what employees really want in terms of pay and benefits from the workplace.[21] According to a survey of 75 Canadian employers conducted between December 2000 and February 2001 by N. Winter Consulting Inc., employers focus on compensation for their employees. Almost 60 percent of the companies said they had changed their reward strategy in recent years, giving salary increases, incentive pay, profit sharing, and flexible benefits.

Meanwhile, surveys of employees show that they want "challenging work, continuous learning, flexible work arrangements and better communication with their employers." However, less than 10 percent of companies said they had recently introduced programs to help employees balance their work with their personal lives. Only 25 percent plan to introduce flexible hours, on-site child care or subsidized fitness to their workplace in the next two years.

Companies in the survey said they were having difficulty attracting and retaining employees. Companies may need to pay more attention to what their employees say that they want. Winter found that only 48 percent of the companies surveyed their employees to find out their needs, wants, and values.

Questions
1. How does pay motivate?
2. Is pay enough to motivate?

Once a pay level and structure are in place, managers can use pay to motivate employees to perform at a high level and attain their work goals. Pay is used to motivate entry-level workers, first-line and middle managers, and even top managers such as CEOs. Pay can be used to motivate people to perform behaviours that will help an organization achieve its goals (as at Kodak in the *Case in Contrast*), and it can be used to motivate people to join and remain with an organization (as at Mars Inc.).

Figure 8.6 | How Pay Motivates

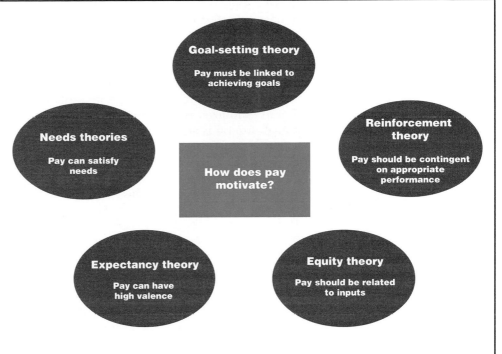

How Does Pay Motivate?

Each of the theories described in this chapter alludes to the importance of pay and suggests that pay should be based on performance (see Figure 8.6):

To motivate middle managers, many organizations are returning to pay-for-performance incentive pay systems. Here, middle managers on a team at Yoplait, the yogourt maker, celebrate the results of their high performance—bonuses that will average more than $77 000 for each person.

- *Needs theories.* People should be able to satisfy their needs by performing at a high level; pay can be used to satisfy several different kinds of needs.

- *Expectancy theory.* Instrumentality, the association between performance and outcomes such as pay, must be high for motivation to be high. Pay is also an outcome that has high valence for many people.

- *Goal-setting theory.* Outcomes such as pay should be linked to the attainment of goals.

- *Reinforcement theory.* The distribution of outcomes such as pay should be contingent on the performance of organizationally functional behaviours.

- *Equity theory.* Outcomes such as pay should be distributed in proportion to inputs (including performance levels).

As these theories suggest, to promote high motivation, managers should base the distribution of pay to organizational members on performance levels so that high performers receive more pay than low performers (other things being equal).[22]

In deciding whether to pay for performance, managers also have to determine whether to use salary increases or bonuses. Thus some pay-for-performance programs (particularly those that use bonuses) are variable-pay programs. With variable pay, earnings go up and down annually based on performance.[23] Thus, there is no guarantee that an individual will earn as much this year as last.

The number of employees affected by variable-pay plans has been rising in Canada. A 2002 survey of 191 firms by Hewitt Associates found that 76 percent of them have variable-pay plans in place, compared to 43 percent in 1994.[24] These programs are more common among nonunionized workers, although more than 30 percent of unionized companies had such plans in 2002.[25] In Canada, pay-for-performance programs are more common for nonunionized workers than unionized ones. Prem Benimadhu from the Conference Board of Canada notes, "Canadian unions have been very allergic to variable compensation."[26] In addition to wage uncertainty, employees may object to pay for performance if they feel that factors out of their control might affect the extent to which bonuses are possible.

Chapter Summary

THE NATURE OF MOTIVATION

NEEDS THEORIES

- Maslow's Hierarchy of Needs
- Herzberg's Motivator-Hygiene Theory
- Other Needs

EXPECTANCY THEORY

- Expectancy
- Instrumentality
- Valence
- Bringing It All Together

GOAL-SETTING THEORY

REINFORCEMENT THEORY

- Organizational Behaviour Modification

EQUITY THEORY

- Equity
- Inequity
- Ways to Restore Equity

PAY AND MOTIVATION

- How Does Pay Motivate?

SUMMARY AND REVIEW

THE NATURE OF MOTIVATION Motivation encompasses the psychological forces within a person that determine the direction of a person's behaviour in an organization, a person's level of effort, and a person's level of persistence in the face of obstacles. Managers strive to motivate people to contribute their inputs to an organization, to focus these inputs in the direction of high performance, and to ensure that people receive the outcomes they desire when they perform at a high level.

NEEDS THEORIES Needs theories suggest that in order to have a motivated workforce, managers should determine what needs people are trying to satisfy in organizations and then ensure that people receive outcomes that will satisfy these needs when they perform at a high level and contribute to organizational effectiveness.

EXPECTANCY THEORY According to expectancy theory, managers can promote high levels of motivation in their organizations by taking steps to ensure that *expectancy* is high (people think that if they try, they can perform at a high level), *instrumentality* is high (people think that if they perform at a high level, they will receive certain outcomes), and *valence* is high (people desire these outcomes).

GOAL-SETTING THEORY Goal-setting theory suggests that managers can promote high motivation and performance by ensuring that people are striving to achieve specific, difficult goals. It also is important for people to accept the goals, be committed to them, and receive feedback about how they are doing.

REINFORCEMENT THEORY Reinforcement theory suggests that managers can motivate people to perform highly by using *positive reinforcement* or *negative reinforcement* (positive reinforcement being the preferred strategy). Managers can motivate people to avoid performing dysfunctional behaviours by using *extinction* or *punishment*.

EQUITY THEORY According to equity theory, managers can promote high levels of motivation by ensuring that people perceive that there is equity in the organization or that outcomes are distributed in proportion to inputs. *Equity* exists when a person perceives that his or her own outcome/input ratio equals the outcome/input ratio of a referent. Inequity motivates people to try to restore equity.

PAY AND MOTIVATION Each of the motivation theories discussed in this chapter alludes to the importance of pay and suggests that pay should be based on performance.

Roles in Contrast: Considerations

MANAGERS

As a manager, it is important to be aware of the needs of individuals, because addressing their needs is one way of motivating them.

If employees do not believe they will be rewarded for hard work, or if aspects of the job make it difficult to do their work properly, they will be less motivated.

If individuals do not feel that they are rewarded fairly, they may do less work to make up for the unfairness.

EMPLOYEES

Being aware of what motivates you may make it easier to motivate yourself, or to be clearer to your manager about what motivates you.

The act of accomplishing goals is often motivational, and goal setting provides a way for you to work with your manager to set work objectives.

Many people are concerned about fairness in rewards, and will adjust their behaviour so that their work level matches the rewards they receive.

MANAGEMENT in Action

Topics for Discussion and Action

1. Interview four people who have the same kind of job (such as salesperson, waiter, or teacher), and determine what kinds of needs they are trying to satisfy at work.
2. Discuss why two people with similar abilities may have very different expectancies for performing at a high level.
3. Describe why some people have low instrumentalities even when their managers distribute outcomes based on performance.
4. Describe three techniques or procedures that managers can use to determine whether a goal is difficult.
5. Discuss why managers should always try to use positive reinforcement instead of negative reinforcement.
6. Analyze how professors try to promote equity to motivate students.

Building Management Skills

DIAGNOSING MOTIVATION

Think about the ideal job that you would like to obtain upon graduation. Describe this job, the kind of manager you would like to report to, and the kind of organization you would be working in. Then answer the following questions.

1. What would be your levels of expectancy and instrumentality on this job? Which outcomes would have high valence for you on this job? What steps would your manager take to influence your levels of expectancy, instrumentality, and valence?
2. Whom would you choose as a referent on this job? What steps would your manager take to make you feel that you were being equitably treated? What would you do if, after a year on the job, you experienced underpayment inequity?
3. What goals would you strive to achieve on this job? Why? What role would your manager play in determining your goals?
4. What needs would you strive to satisfy on this job? Why? What role would your manager play in helping you satisfy these needs?

Management for You

You are in a team with six other management students, and you have a major case analysis due in four weeks. The case project will count for 25 percent of the course mark. You are the team's leader. Several team members are having difficulty getting motivated to get started on the project. Identify ways you could motivate your team members, using needs theories, expectancy theory, goal setting, reinforcement theory, and equity theory. How will you motivate yourself?

Small Group Breakout Exercise

INCREASING MOTIVATION

Form groups of 3 or 4 people, and appoint 1 member as the spokesperson who will communicate your findings to the whole class when called on by the instructor. Then discuss the following scenario.

You are a group of partners who own a chain of 15 dry-cleaning stores in a medium-sized town. You are meeting today to discuss a problem in customer service that surfaced recently. When any one of you is spending the day or even part of the day in a particular store, clerks seem to be providing excellent customer service, spotters are making sure all stains are removed from garments, and pressers are doing a good job of pressing difficult items such as silk blouses. Yet during those same visits customers complain to you about such things as stains not being removed and items being poorly pressed in some of their previous orders; indeed, several customers have brought garments in to be redone. Customers also sometimes comment on having waited too long for service on previous visits. You are meeting today to address this problem.

1. Discuss the extent to which you believe that you have a motivation problem in your stores.
2. Given what you have learned in this chapter, design a plan to increase the motivation of clerks to provide prompt service to customers even when they are not being watched by a partner.
3. Design a plan to increase the motivation of spotters to remove as many stains as possible even when they are not being watched by a partner.
4. Design a plan to increase the motivation of pressers to do a top-notch job on all clothes they press, no matter how difficult.

Managing Ethically

You are the new CEO of a pharmaceutical company that has a reputation for compensating managers well but not employees. Top and middle managers get a 15-percent across-the-board increase, while the employees receive a 4-percent increase. The justification is that managers take the risks, make the decisions, and figure out the strategies. But in fact for years the company has been using teams to make many of the most crucial decisions for the company. And everyone has input into strategic planning. Employees also have to work extra-long hours during the busiest seasons with no overtime pay. You find morale very low. While employees seem motivated because they have a passion for the work, developing drugs to help cure major diseases, many are threatening to leave if they are not rewarded more fairly. What would you do?

Exploring the World Wide Web

SPECIFIC ASSIGNMENT

Many companies take active steps to recognize their employees for jobs well done. One such company is DuPont Canada. Scan DuPont Canada's website (ca.dupont.com) to learn more about this company. Then under "Careers in Canada" click on "Compensation & Benefits" and "Personal Development."

1. What kinds of rewards is Dupont Canada using to motivate its employees to perform at a high level?
2. How does Dupont Canada use training to motivate? How might this increase an employee's expectancy?

Find a website of a company that bases pay on performance for some or all of its employees. Describe the pay-for-performance plan in use at this company. Which employees are covered by the plan? Do you think this pay plan will foster high levels of motivation? Why or why not?

You're the Management Consultant

MOTIVATING A TEAM OF MARKETING ANALYSTS

Eva Joudoin supervises a team of marketing analysts who work on different snack products in a large food products company. The marketing analysts have recently received undergraduate degrees in business or liberal arts and have been on the job between one and three years. Their responsibilities include analyzing the market for their respective products, including looking at competitors, tracking current marketing initiatives, and planning future marketing campaigns. They also need to prepare quarterly sales and expense reports for their products and estimated budgets for the next three quarters. To prepare these reports, they need to obtain data from financial and accounting analysts assigned to their products.

When they first started on the job, Joudoin took each marketing analyst through the reporting cycle, explaining what needs to be done, how to accomplish it, and emphasizing the need for timely reports. While preparing the reports can be tedious, she thinks it is pretty straightforward and easily accomplished if the analysts plan ahead and allocate sufficient time for these tasks. When reporting time approaches, she reminds the analysts through emails and emphasizes the need for accurate and timely reports in team meetings.

According to Joudoin, this element of the analysts' jobs could not be more straightforward. However, at the end of each quarter, the majority of the analysts turn their reports in a day or two late, and worse yet, Joudoin's own supervisor (who eventually receives the reports) has indicated that information is often missing in the reports and sometimes there are errors. Once Joudoin started getting flak from her own supervisor about this problem, she realized she had better fix things, and quick. She met with the marketing analysts, explained the problem, told them to turn the reports in to her a day or two early so she could look them over, and more generally emphasized that they really needed to get their act together. Unfortunately, things have not improved much and Joudoin is spending more and more of her own time doing the reports. Joudoin has come to you for advice because you are an expert in motivation. What should she do?

MANAGEMENT CASE

Motivating With Stretch Targets

Top managers of many organizations have discovered a powerful tool to increase motivation and performance: stretch targets. Stretch targets are goals that call for dramatic improvements in key aspects of organizational performance and effectiveness, such as extraordinary increases in revenues, reductions in costs, or increases in the rate at which new products are developed and brought to market.[27] Typically, organizational goals or objectives are modest, involving changes such as a 10-percent reduction in inventory costs or a 5-percent increase in revenues. These goals seem to motivate members of an organization to achieve the specified goals in performance but often little more. Top managers who use stretch targets instead of modest goals have a vision of how much better an organization could be performing and then choose a target to motivate members of the organization to achieve this high level of performance. Much careful planning goes into the establishment of stretch targets.

At 3M, for example, Desi DeSimone was concerned about a depressed market for some of the goods the company produced, and was especially concerned about a lack of increase in revenues from new products. He decided to set a stretch target for employees to increase by 30 percent 3M's revenues from products that had been introduced within the last four years. Along with this stretch target came some changes in 3M's strategies. Rather than spending time developing products with modest potential that were similar to existing products on the market, 3M employees were encouraged to focus on developing major new products with high sales potential. Employees were also urged to bring these potential best-sellers to market quickly. As a result of the specific, difficult goal DeSimone set, the Scotch-Brite Never Rust soap pad gained 22 percent of the soap pad market from Brillo and SOS in its first 18 months on the market.

At The Boeing Company, former CEO Frank Shrontz was concerned about the slow and inefficient ways in which airplanes were produced. He decided to motivate his employees with an ambitious stretch target that would cut costs to such a great extent that Boeing would be able to lower its prices and sell more planes. After considerable planning and strategic analysis, the stretch target he decided on was a 25-percent reduction in the cost of producing a plane, while maintaining Boeing's high quality standards. At the same time, he implemented a second stretch target: reducing the amount of time it took to build a plane from 18 months to 8 months—again, while maintaining high quality. If achieved, this second stretch target would result in lower costs (due to less inventory expense) and more sales (due to decreased risk for airlines). Progress toward these stretch targets was good: New, more efficient, and less costly methods of production were implemented in practically all phases of airplane production at Boeing, and the time needed to complete a plane dropped.[28] Montreal-based Canadian National Railway's supply management department, General

Electric, and Union Pacific are other examples of companies using stretch targets.

Stretch targets seem to be powerful motivators that result in organizations and their members achieving the unthinkable in performance and effectiveness improvements. Five key aspects of stretch targets and the ways that managers implement them in organizations can account for their stunning success:

- Stretch targets are specific, difficult goals, as illustrated by the examples above.
- Managers who implement stretch targets do whatever they can to boost expectancy so employees believe they actually can reach the target. Steven Mason, who as CEO implemented stretch targets at Mead, a large paper manufacturer that has since become MeadWestvaco Corporation, suggests that one way to make sure that employees are confident that the targets are reachable is by concentrating "on things . . . [they] can control."
- Third, managers boost employees' self-confidence by demonstrating to them that other organizations have been able to reach the standards set by the stretch targets. Mason, for example, had his employees visit General Electric's successful light-bulb and appliance divisions to see what other companies have done. Like Mead, those divisions operate in mature industries with stable prices, yet they had been more profitable than many of Mead's operations because of their constant drive to increase productivity. If those divisions of GE could increase productivity in a mature industry with stable prices, why, Mason asked, couldn't Mead?
- Fourth, managers take advantage of opportunities for learning from others. At Boeing, for example, Shrontz sent teams of employees to top-performing manufacturing companies in diverse industries ranging from shipbuilding to computer manufacturing so that they could learn from and become motivated by these exemplary organizations.
- Fifth, once managers set the stretch target and employees believe they can reach it, employees are given considerable autonomy in working to achieve it, setting intermediary goals, and so forth—that is, the employees

control how they go about meeting the goal. For example, at CSX Corporation, a shipping and railroad company, former CEO John Snow indicated that once stretch targets are set, "It's people in the field who find the right path."[29] Stretch targets certainly seem to be the right path for at least some top managers to take to motivate employees to achieve dramatic improvements in organizational performance.

Questions

1. Why do stretch targets result in high levels of motivation and performance?
2. How can or should managers respond to employees who complain that a stretch target is impossible to achieve?
3. In what kinds of situations might it be particularly appropriate for managers to introduce stretch targets?
4. In what kinds of situations might stretch targets not be such a good idea?

MANAGEMENT CASE ————————————————— IN THE NEWS

From the Pages of *The Vancouver Sun* Telus Gives Stock Options to All Its Employees

While employees at some struggling telecommunications companies are bracing for pink slips, 20 000 workers at Telus Corp. got an unexpected bonus Thursday—100 stock options, with another 200 on the way.

Team Telus Options, touted as the first plan to offer options to every employee of a Canadian telecom company, will help in efforts to create "a performance culture within Telus," chief executive Darren Entwistle said.

It gives employees an incentive to work hard to ensure Telus' stock price rises—and to stick with the company since workers can only exercise the options as employees.

The plan is also open to new employees, making Burnaby-based Telus a more appealing employer as it sets out to add 500 to 1000 workers in Ontario and Quebec during three years, Entwistle said.

"The demand for talent in this industry far outstrips supply."

Only about 6.5 per cent of mid-to-large-sized businesses in Canada currently provide universal employee stock options, the Conference Board of Canada says.

Telus executives, directors and managers, who have been part of a stock-option plan for several years, are ineligible for Team Telus Options.

Often reserved for high-level executives and employees of new companies, stock options give workers the right to buy or sell stock at a specified price, by a specific date.

In the Telus plan, the first 100 options are in non-voting shares, at an exercise price of $34.88.

In two years, employees will be able to exercise them. If the stock has reached $50 by then, for example, the 100 options will be worth $1512.

Employees will be granted another 100 options in one year, and a further 100 in two years. The options must be exercised within 10 years after they are granted.

The granting of options is prominent in the computer and information-technology sector, the chemical and pharmaceutical sector and the telecommunications industry.

Pivotal Software of North Vancouver provides universal employee stock options.

"All our employees have had stock options since August of 1999, when we went public," company official Jacqueline Voci said. "It gives every employee an incentive to make the company succeed."

Crystal Decisions, formerly Seagate Software, has been giving employees stock options since the mid-1990s.

"Greg Kerfoot, the founder of the company, maintained that all employees should benefit from the growth and success of the company," Crystal official Alison MacDonald said. "We are a private company but if we go public down the road, employees can choose to exercise their options."

Consulting firm Towers Perrin says more than 90 per cent of the Fortune 1000 companies use stock options for their senior operating team.

In Canada, all but three of the top 100 companies on the TSE offer options to at least the senior management team.

However, universal employee stock option plans aren't widespread.

"It's not common for companies to offer options to every employee and it's not common enough," said Ross Birney, an associate with Rogers Group. "The companies that have done so in the past have been very successful. Why shouldn't an entry-level person benefit from the success of a company?"

The federal government relaxed tax rules on stock options last year.

The study said options not only benefit employees but help companies grow.

"Companies with a stock option plan are expected to expand up to 11 per cent faster than those without," it said.

Source: "Telus Gives Stock Options to All Its Workers," *The Vancouver Sun*, March 2, 2001, pp. C7, C8.

Questions

1. To what extent does rewarding employees with stock options support the motivation theories presented in the chapter?
2. To what extent are lower-level employees likely to find stock options as motivating as upper management?

CHAPTER 9

LEADERSHIP

Learning Objectives

1. Describe what leadership is, when leaders are effective and ineffective, and the sources of power that enables managers to be effective leaders.

2. Identify the traits that show the strongest relationship to leadership, the behaviours leaders engage in, and the limitations of the trait and behaviour models of leadership.

3. Explain how contingency models of leadership enhance our understanding of effective leadership and management in organizations.

4. Describe what transformational leadership is, and explain how managers can engage in it.

5. Characterize how gender and national culture affect leadership.

Roles in Contrast: Questions

MANAGERS	EMPLOYEES
How can I increase my power as a manager?	Is there a way that I can increase my own power in my organization?
Is there a best leadership style?	How could I use leadership theory to lead my team?
Are leaders always needed?	Is it possible to get things done without a leader?

A CASE IN CONTRAST

LEVY FOSTERS GROWTH WHILE
IRWIN FOSTERS DECLINE

Julia Levy, executive chair and former CEO of Vancouver-based QLT (www.qltinc.com), has been credited with creating a company that is a world leader in photodynamic therapy, a field of medicine that uses light-activated drugs to treat disease.[1] In contrast, George Irwin, who was CEO of Toronto-based Irwin Toy Ltd. until November 2000, has been credited with overseeing the demise of what was once the biggest toy company in Canada.

Many analysts attribute the differences in the companies' performances to their CEOs' different leadership styles.

Though Levy was named Pacific Entrepreneur of the Year by *Canadian Business* in 2000, she thought of herself as an accidental entrepreneur and CEO. She was the company's chief scientific officer, and avoided the CEO role for 13 years until QLT's board offered it to her in 1995. She accepted the job only because she felt that QLT had a team of seasoned managers on whom she could rely to overcome some of her own shortcomings.

Irwin grew up almost destined to become CEO of Irwin Toy. His grandfather had founded the company, and he was appointed president in 1990 after his father Macdonald and uncle Arnold, who had co-run the company for many years, decided that it was time for the next generation to take over. He was named CEO in 1994.

Levy was the ultimate team player when managing her company. She doesn't like to lead directly. Instead, she prefers to keep asking questions until people come up with the right answers themselves. She feels that this approach empowers employees and gives them ownership of the solutions.

Irwin's employees found him more distant, by contrast. By the time of his departure, he had "lost the confidence of many employees and family members, . . . stopped listening to the input of those around him and failed to be an effective leader."

Levy worked hard to establish trust among her QLT employees and the traditions she started

Julia Levy, executive chair and former CEO of QLT, showed consideration to her employees by listening to them and being sensitive to their needs.

George Irwin, former CEO of Irwin Toy, used a more distant leadership style, which drove a number of key employees to quit.

there have continued. Despite the pressures of being in the biotech industry, QLT is also a family-friendly employer, offering its employees a work-life balance. There is an on-site caregiver for parents who have to bring their children to work unexpectedly. There is a fitness centre, with a personal trainer, and regularly scheduled Pilates and yoga classes. On Fridays three shiatsu masseurs set up portable massage chairs in a private room at QLT and employees can sign up for appointments through the company's computer system. The company does whatever it can to help reduce employee stress, notes Linda Lupini, senior vice-president of human resources and administration. "We see people on stress-related leaves returning early to work as a result of having worked with a personal trainer," she says. "Managing stress has become a major challenge for human resource professionals everywhere. You have to take steps to deal with it." Irwin, however, was not good at dealing with people. "Part of George's problem is he didn't know how to build the morale of the people. He didn't know how to motivate them. George is a divide-and-conquer kind of person. It just was not a team effort at Irwin Toy, and that's primarily because of George. He's not a gifted leader."

Levy slowly grew her company, and knows the importance of focusing on long-term strategy. In fact, she finds that the laboratory is the perfect place to create CEOs who can lead companies in the biotech sector. "Just doing science is predicated on failure. To be a scientist and to love it means you have to be stubborn and be willing to wait a long time for pats on the head because you get far more kicks in the butt when you're doing experiments." She knows that patience and the big picture are important to keep in mind.

Irwin seems to have been more of a short-term leader. For example, in the mid-1990s, Irwin started mentoring a young employee who had been hired in the marketing department. The two became close, and instead of focusing on overall strategy for the company, Irwin started "spending more time in the marketing department working on various projects in which she was involved." His perceived favouritism toward the employee distorted reporting relationships within the marketing department, which was headed by Irwin's brother, David Irwin. Morale became so poor in the department that employees began to leave. Senior family members repeatedly asked George Irwin to get rid of the employee. Finally in the spring of 1999 she left, only to return as an account representative for an outside company hired to do promotional activities for Irwin. The remaining marketing veterans at Irwin Toy resigned.

By the time Irwin stepped down in late 2000, the internal battles at the toy company had resulted in the departure of four family members, more than a dozen middle and senior managers, most of the staff in the company's marketing and sporting goods divisions, and much of the camaraderie that once marked the company. The company was also left without a vision of how to move forward in a toy industry very different from that of the company's roots. In May 2001, the Irwin family said goodbye to the company it had owned for 75 years, selling it to Livgroup Investments Ltd. The company went out of business in December 2002.

As Levy stepped down from the position of CEO of QLT, the company was in good shape. Its sales of Visudyne have been remarkable, and the company is doing well financially. Levy's ability to work with her senior management staff and treat her employees well led QLT to its current success.

OVERVIEW

Julia Levy exemplifies how effective leadership results in a high-performing organization just as George Irwin illustrates how ineffective leadership can cripple an organization. In Chapter 1, we explained that one of the four principal tasks of managers is leading. Thus, it should come as no surprise that leadership is a key ingredient in effective management. When leaders are effective, their subordinates or followers are highly motivated, committed, and high-performing. When leaders are ineffective, chances are good that their subordinates do not perform up to their capabilities, are demotivated, and may be dissatisfied as well. As CEOs, Levy and Irwin were leaders at the very top of their organizations, but leadership is an important ingredient for managerial success at all levels of an organization: top management, middle management, and first-line management. Moreover, leadership is a key ingredient for managerial success for organizations large and small.

In this chapter, we describe what leadership is and examine the major leadership models that shed light on the factors that help make a manager an effective leader. *Trait and behaviour models* focus on what leaders are like and what they do. *Contingency models*–Fiedler's contingency model, Hersey-Blanchard's situational leadership theory, path-goal theory, and the leader substitutes model–take into account the complexity surrounding leadership and the role of the situation in leader effectiveness. We describe how managers can have dramatic effects in their organizations by means of transformational leadership. We also examine the relationship between gender and leadership. By the end of this chapter, you will have a good appreciation of the many factors and issues that managers face in their quest to be effective leaders.

Dr Julia Levy
www.qltinc.com/qltinc/
main/mainpages.cfm

THE NATURE OF LEADERSHIP

Think About It

Curtailing Coercive Power Makes Good Business Sense

Ricardo Semler was only 21 in 1979 when he took control of his family business, Semco AG, a Brazilian manufacturer of industrial products such as pumps, mixers, and propellers.[2] Use of coercive power had been the norm rather than the exception at Semco. Fear was rampant. Guards policed the factory, workers were frisked when they left for the day, their visits to the washroom were timed, and anyone who broke a piece of equipment had to pay for it. Semler found managing Semco in this manner to be so stressful that, after collapsing one day on a business trip, he vowed to make Semco "a true democracy, a place run on trust and freedom, not fear."[3] His goal was to create an ethical workplace in which all employees were treated with respect and dignity. By all reports, he has achieved his goal. Today, the company receives 1000 job applications for every open position, and managers from global organizations such as Exxon Mobil Corp. (www.mobil.com) and IBM Corp. (www.ibm.com) have travelled to Brazil to see first-hand what is happening at Semco.[4]

Questions
1. How do individual differences affect leadership style?
2. How can one use power effectively as a leader?

leadership
The process by which an individual exerts influence over other people and inspires, motivates, and directs their activities to help achieve group or organizational goals.

leader
An individual who is able to exert influence over other people to help achieve group or organizational goals.

Leadership is the process by which a person exerts influence over other people and inspires, motivates, and directs their activities to help achieve group or organizational goals.[5] The person who exerts such influence is a **leader**. When leaders are effective, the influence they exert over others helps a group or organization to achieve its performance goals. When leaders are ineffective, their influence does not contribute to, and often detracts from, goal attainment. As the *Case in Contrast* makes clear, Julia Levy was an effective leader: She influenced her senior managers by working closely with them, and the way she motivated and rewarded them has helped QLT achieve its goals. By contrast, George Irwin was an ineffective leader: He influenced a few favourite employees at Irwin Toy, but the kind of influence he exerted stood in the way of his organization reaching its goals, and his overly optimistic belief in some employees led to poor decision making.

Effective leadership increases an organization's ability to meet a variety of challenges, including the need to obtain a competitive advantage, the need to foster ethical behaviour, and the need to manage a diverse workforce fairly and equitably. Leaders who exert influence to help meet these goals increase their organization's chances of success.

In considering the nature of leadership, we first look at leadership styles and how they affect managerial tasks, and at the influence of culture on leadership styles. We then focus on the key to leadership, *power*, which can come from a variety of sources. Finally, we consider the contemporary use of empowerment and how it relates to effective leadership. Table 9.1 illustrates the comments of several Canadians about what it means to be a Canadian leader.

Personal Leadership Style and Managerial Tasks

A manager's *personal leadership style*–that is, the specific ways in which a manager chooses to influence other people–shapes the way that the manager approaches planning, organizing, and controlling (the other principal tasks of managing).

Table 9.1 | Some Thoughts About What It Means to Be a Canadian Leader

Canadian ambassador to the United States Raymond Chrétien:	I think our leadership is based upon what we are as a society. We have maintained our cohesion. We have maintained our capacity to build a tolerant, caring society that speaks to all aspects of our human development. This is why we are highly regarded.
***Maclean's* editor-in-chief Robert Lewis:**	Recently, I sat beside an American CEO at a conference and, as the discussion unfolded, he started mumbling, "You Canadians are always trying to get some kind of consensus. Why don't you stop that and make some decisions?"
ABC news anchor Peter Jennings:	I think Canadian leadership, as we've already cited in peacekeeping operations, in international conventions, in international situations, is reflected in the notion that we've had to make our way somewhat more subtly on the world stage than the United States has ever been obliged to do.
Wi-LAN Inc. founder Hatim Zaghloul:	In high-tech, we Canadians often will take longer making a decision, whereas in Silicon Valley, they would advertise their product when it's just a concept, and then they would go and build it if someone bought it. In Canada, we only advertise once it's meeting 99.99 percent of our specifications.
Olympic gold-medal rower Marnie McBean:	Canadians just don't follow the person who's shouting the loudest. . . . And I think that's where this sense of a style of Canadian leadership comes from—not from being boastful or a braggart. It comes from being able to do the job. Just sort of putting the head down, doing the job and we get our respect from our actions and from our performance.

Source: R. Lewis, "The Canadian Way: There Is a Confident Canadian Style of Leadership, and It Is Making a Global Impact," *Maclean's*, July 1, 2000, p. 26.

Consider how Julia Levy's and George Irwin's personal leadership styles affected the way they performed these other important management tasks. Julia Levy's personal style is to support and encourage other managers to assume responsibility for their performance. As a CEO, she delegated authority (an organizing task), allowed her subordinates to develop their own strategies (a planning task), and periodically reviewed their performance to evaluate their success (a control task). By contrast, Irwin's personal leadership style was to make decisions himself even when those around him urged him to consider alternatives. Irwin therefore centralized authority and decision making at Irwin Toy (an organizing task), took major responsibility for strategy development (a planning task), and forced his uncle Bryan, cousin Scott, and younger brother David to leave the company when they no longer supported his performance (a control task).

Managers at all levels and in all kinds of organizations have their own personal leadership styles, which determine not only how they lead their subordinates but also how they perform the other management tasks. Recall that Ricardo Semler found it stressful to manage Semco by creating fear in his employees, even though some other traditional Brazilian companies were and still are managed in that fashion.[6]

Power: The Key to Leadership

No matter what one's leadership style, a key component of effective leadership is found in the *power* the leader has to affect other people's behaviour and get them to act in certain ways.[7] There are several types of power: *legitimate, reward, coercive, expert,* and *referent power* (see Figure 9.1).[8] Effective leaders take steps to ensure that they have sufficient levels of each type and that they use the power they have in beneficial ways.

Legitimate Power

legitimate power

The authority that a manager has by virtue of his or her position in an organization's hierarchy.

Legitimate power is the authority a manager has by virtue of his or her position in an organization's hierarchy. This is the power, for instance, that allows managers to hire new employees, assign projects to individuals, monitor their work, and appraise their performance.

Figure 9.1 | Sources of Managerial Power

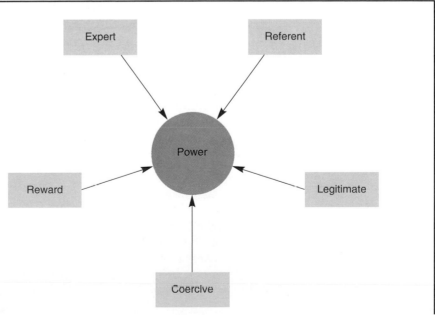

reward power

The ability of a manager to give or withhold tangible and intangible rewards.

Ricardo Semler and Semco S.A. www.t-bird.edu/ about_us/case_series/ a07980024.pdf

coercive power

The ability of a manager to punish others.

expert power

Power that is based in the special knowledge, skills, and expertise that a leader possesses.

referent power

Power that comes from subordinates' and co-workers' respect, admiration, and loyalty.

Reward Power

Reward power is the ability of a manager to give or withhold tangible rewards (pay raises, bonuses, choice job assignments) and intangible rewards (verbal praise, a pat on the back, respect). As you learned in Chapter 8, members of an organization are motivated to perform at a high level by a variety of rewards. Being able to give or withhold rewards based on performance is a major source of power that allows managers to have a highly motivated workforce.

Effective managers use their reward power in such a way that subordinates feel that they are doing a good job and their efforts are appreciated. Ineffective managers use rewards in a more controlling manner (wielding the "stick" instead of offering the "carrot"), which signals to subordinates that the manager has the upper hand. At Semco, Ricardo Semler uses reward power to get things done in a positive fashion. Employees are no longer closely monitored and can come and go when they want. Employees are allowed to choose their own managers. A record 23 percent of Semco's profits are given back to employees for a job well done. Semler even rewards top managers by sharing his title as CEO. Semler rotates the CEO position among himself and six other managers every six months.[9]

Coercive Power

Coercive power is the ability of a manager to punish others. Punishment can include verbal reprimands, reductions in pay or working hours, and actual dismissal. Punishment can have negative side effects such as resentment and retaliation and should be used only when necessary (e.g., to reduce a dangerous behaviour). Managers who rely heavily on coercive power tend to be ineffective as leaders.

Excessive use of coercive power seldom produces high performance and is questionable ethically. Sometimes it amounts to a form of mental abuse, robbing workers of their dignity and causing excessive levels of stress. Better results are obtained with reward power.

Expert Power

Expert power is based in the special knowledge, skills, and expertise that a leader possesses. The nature of expert power varies, depending on the leader's level in the hierarchy. First-line and middle managers often have technical expertise relevant to the tasks that their subordinates perform. Their expert power gives them considerable influence over subordinates.

Some top managers derive expert power from their technical expertise. Julia Levy, described in the *Case in Contrast,* is one of these. Her years of teaching science to undergraduates at the University of British Columbia gave her an edge when raising funds from investors for QLT—she was able to explain to investors what her biotech firm was doing. Many top-level managers lack technical expertise, however, and derive their expert power from their abilities as decision makers, planners, and strategists. Expert power tends to be best used in a guiding or coaching manner rather than in an arrogant, high-handed manner.

Referent Power

Referent power is more informal than the other kinds of power. **Referent power** is a function of the personal characteristics of a leader. It is the power that comes from subordinates' and co-workers' respect, admiration, and loyalty. Leaders who are likeable and whom subordinates wish to use as a role model are especially likely to possess referent power.

In addition to being a valuable asset for top managers, referent power can help first-line and middle managers be effective leaders. Sally Carruthers, for example, is the first-line manager of a group of secretaries in the finance department of a large university. Carruthers' secretaries are known to be among the best in the university. Much of their willingness to go above and beyond the call of duty has been attributed to Carruthers' warm and caring nature, which makes each of them feel important and valued. Managers can take steps to increase their referent power, such as taking time to get to know their subordinates and showing interest in and concern for them.

Empowerment: An Ingredient in Modern Management

empowerment

The process of giving employees the authority to make decisions and be responsible for their outcomes.

More and more managers today are incorporating in their personal leadership styles an aspect that at first glance seems to be the opposite of being a leader. In Chapter 1, we described how **empowerment**–the process of giving employees at all levels in the organization the authority to make decisions, be responsible for their outcomes, improve quality, and cut costs–is becoming increasingly popular in organizations. When leaders empower their subordinates, the subordinates typically take over some of the responsibilities and authority that used to reside with the leader or manager, such as the right to reject parts that do not meet quality standards, the right to check one's own work, and the right to schedule work activities. Empowered subordinates are given the power to make some of the decisions that their leaders or supervisors used to make.

At first glance, empowerment might seem to be the opposite of effective leadership because managers allow subordinates to take a more active role in leading themselves. In actuality, however, empowerment can contribute to effective leadership for several reasons:

- Empowerment increases a manager's ability to get things done because the manager has the support and help of subordinates who may have special knowledge of work tasks.

- Empowerment often increases workers' involvement, motivation, and commitment, which helps ensure that they will be working toward organizational goals.

- Empowerment gives managers more time to concentrate on their pressing concerns because they spend less time on day-to-day supervisory activities.

Effective managers such as Julia Levy realize the benefits of empowerment; ineffective managers such as George Irwin try to keep control over all decision making and force agreement from subordinates. The personal leadership style of managers who empower subordinates often includes developing subordinates, so that they can make good decisions, and being subordinates' guide, coach, and source of inspiration. Empowerment is a popular trend in Canada and the United States at companies as diverse as United Parcel Service of America Inc. (a package delivery company), Burnaby, BC-based Dominion Information Services Inc. (which publishes *Super Pages* in BC, Alberta, Ontario, and Quebec), and Langley, BC-based Redwood Plastics Corp. (a manufacturing company), and it is also taking off around the world.[10] Even companies in South Korea (such as Samsung, Hyundai, and Daewoo), in which decision making typically was centralized with the founding families, are empowering managers at lower levels to make decisions.[11]

Not every employee is a good candidate for empowerment, however. A recent study that Professor Jia Lin Xie, of the University of Toronto's Joseph L. Rotman School of Management, conducted with several others found that people who lack confidence can get ill from being put in charge of their own work. The researchers found that "workers who had high levels of control at work, but lacked confidence in their abilities or blamed themselves for workplace problems, were more likely to have lower antibody levels and experienced more colds and flus."[12]

Some of the difficulty with empowerment is that not all companies introduce it properly. Professor Dan Ondrack at the Rotman School of Management notes that for employees to be empowered, four conditions need to be met: (1) There must be a clear definition of the values and mission of the company; (2) the company must help employees acquire the relevant skills; (3) employees need to be supported in their decision making, and not criticized when they try to do something extraordinary; and (4) workers need to be recognized for their efforts.[13]

MODELS OF LEADERSHIP

Is there a difference between leadership and management? Harvard Business School Professor John Kotter suggests that "managers promote stability while leaders press for change and only organizations that embrace both sides of the contradiction can survive in turbulent times."[14] Professor Rabindra Kanungo of McGill University reports growing agreement "among management scholars that the concept of 'leadership' must be distinguished from the concept of 'supervision/management.'"[15] Leaders look to the big picture, providing vision and strategy. Managers are charged with implementing vision and strategy; they coordinate and staff the organization, and handle day-to-day problems.

Below we discuss two aspects of leadership: leading as supervision, and leading with vision.

LEADERSHIP AS SUPERVISION

Think About It

Consideration and Customer Service at Staples

Staples is a top-performing retailer with annual percentage increases in sales and profits as high as 50 percent.[16] Tom Stemberg, founder and chair of Staples, has raised customer service to an art form. He is constantly on the lookout for new ways to please customers, and salespeople at Staples go out of their way to help customers no matter how large or small their orders are. Salespeople develop close, long-term relationships with customers and strive to provide innovative solutions to their office supply problems.

One of Stemberg's guiding principles is that managers should treat subordinates in the way that they would like subordinates to treat customers. Stemberg is exceptionally considerate to the managers who report to him, and he encourages them to do likewise with their own subordinates.

Questions
1. Are there specific traits that leaders should have?
2. What kinds of behaviours should managers show?

Staples, Inc.
www.staples.com

Leadership theories developed before about 1980 focused on the supervisory nature of leadership. Thus they were concerned with managing the day-to-day functions of employees. These theories took three different approaches to how supervision could be viewed: (1) Do leaders have traits different from nonleaders? (2) Should leaders engage in particular behaviours? (3) Does the situation a leader faces matter? We briefly examine these approaches below.

The Trait Model

The trait model of leadership focused on identifying the personal characteristics that are responsible for effective leadership. Decades of research (beginning in the

1930s) and hundreds of studies indicate that certain personal characteristics do appear to be associated with effective leadership (see Table 9.2 for a list of these).[17] Traits alone, however, are not the key to understanding leader effectiveness. Some effective leaders do not possess all of these traits, and some leaders who do possess them are not effective in their leadership roles. This lack of a consistent relationship between leader traits and leader effectiveness led researchers to search for new explanations for effective leadership. Researchers began to turn their attention to what effective leaders actually do—in other words, to the behaviours that allow effective leaders to influence their subordinates to achieve group and organizational goals.

The Behavioural Models

There are a variety of behavioural models of leadership, including the Ohio Studies,[18] the Michigan Studies,[19] and Blake and Mouton's Managerial Grid.[20] These models identify two basic kinds of leader behaviours that many leaders in the United States, Germany, and other countries used to influence their subordinates: *employee-centred behaviours* (also called *consideration, concern for people,* and *supportive behaviours)* and *job-oriented behaviours* (also called *initiating structure, concern for production,* and *task-oriented behaviours).* All of the behavioural theories suggest that leaders need to consider the nature of their subordinates when trying to determine the extent to which they should perform these two types of behaviours.

employee-centred behaviour

Behaviour indicating that a manager trusts, respects, and cares about subordinates

Leaders engage in **employee-centred behaviour** when they show their subordinates that they trust, respect, and care about them. For instance, Staples' CEO Ron Sargent recalls that, when he was one of Tom Stemberg's subordinates and his newborn son was sick and in intensive care for a week, Stemberg called him every night to see how the baby was doing and provide support.[21] This helped Sargent feel more committed to Staples. Managers who truly look out for the well-being of their subordinates and do what they can to help subordinates feel good and enjoy their work are performing consideration behaviours. In the *Case in Contrast,* Julia Levy was engaging in consideration by treating her subordinates with respect, and encouraging a work/family balance for her employees; George Irwin's favouritism of an employee and disregard of other managers' concerns exemplifies a lack of consideration. With the increasing focus on the importance of high quality customer service, many managers are realizing that when they are considerate to

Table 9.2 | Traits and Personal Characteristics Related to Effective Leadership

TRAIT	DESCRIPTION
Intelligence	Helps managers understand complex issues and solve problems
Knowledge and expertise	Help managers make good decisions and discover ways to increase efficiency and effectiveness
Dominance	Helps managers influence their subordinates to achieve organizational goals
Self-confidence	Contributes to managers' effectively influencing subordinates and persisting when faced with obstacles or difficulties
High energy	Helps managers deal with the many demands they face
Tolerance for stress	Helps managers deal with uncertainty and make difficult decisions
Integrity and honesty	Help managers behave ethically and earn their subordinates' trust and confidence
Maturity	Helps managers avoid acting selfishly, control their feelings, and admit when they have made a mistake

job-oriented behaviours

Behaviours that managers engage in to ensure that work gets done, subordinates perform their jobs acceptably, and the organization is efficient and effective.

subordinates, subordinates are more likely to be considerate to customers and vice versa. Leaders engage in **job-oriented behaviours** when they take steps to make sure that work gets done, subordinates perform their jobs acceptably, and the organization is efficient and effective. Assigning tasks to individuals or work groups, letting subordinates know what is expected of them, deciding how work should be done, making schedules, encouraging adherence to rules and regulations, and motivating subordinates to do a good job are all examples of initiating structure.[22]

These two behaviours are independent of each other. Leaders can be high on both, low on both, or high on one and low on the other. You might expect that effective leaders and managers would perform both kinds of behaviours, but research has found that this is not necessarily the case. The relationship between performance of employee-oriented and job-oriented behaviours and leader effectiveness is not clear-cut. Some leaders are effective even when they do not perform either type of behaviour, and some leaders are ineffective even when they perform both kinds of behaviours. Like the trait model of leadership, the behaviour model alone cannot explain leader effectiveness. Realizing this, researchers began building more complicated models of leadership, models that focused not only on the leader and what he or she does but also on the situation or context in which leadership occurs.

Contingency Models of Leadership

Managers lead in a wide variety of situations and organizations and have various kinds of subordinates performing diverse tasks in many environmental contexts. Given the wide variety of situations in which leadership occurs, what makes a manager an effective leader in one situation (such as certain traits or certain behaviours) is not necessarily what that manager needs in order to be equally effective in a different situation. An effective army general might not be an effective university president, an effective manager of a restaurant might not be an effective manager of a clothing store, an effective coach of a football team might not be an effective manager of a fitness centre, and an effective first-line manager in a manufacturing company might not be an effective middle manager. The traits or behaviours that may contribute to a manager being an effective leader in one situation might actually result in the same manager being an ineffective leader in another situation.

Contingency models of leadership take into account the situation or context within which leadership occurs. So for instance, while behavioural theories explored whether managers should be more employee-centred or more task-centred, contingency theories answer: It depends (or is contingent) on the situation. According to contingency models, whether or not a manager is an effective leader is the result of the interplay between what the manager is like, what he or she does, and the situation in which leadership takes place. In this section, we discuss four prominent contingency models developed to shed light on what makes managers effective leaders: Fiedler's contingency model, Hersey-Blanchard's situational leadership theory, House's path-goal theory, and the leader substitutes model. As you will see, these leadership models are complementary. Each focuses on a somewhat different aspect of effective leadership in organizations.

Fiedler's Contingency Model

Fred E. Fiedler was among the first leadership researchers to acknowledge that effective leadership is contingent on, or depends on, the characteristics of the leader and of the situation. Fiedler's contingency model helps explain why a manager may be an effective leader in one situation and ineffective in another; it also suggests which kinds of managers are likely to be most effective in which situations.[23]

Fred Fiedler
www.eou.edu/~blarison/
321afied.html

Drawing from the previous behavioural studies, Fiedler identified two basic leader styles: *relationship-oriented* and *task-oriented*. All managers can be described as having one style or the other.

Relationship-oriented leaders are mainly concerned with developing good relationships with their subordinates and being liked by them. The quality of interpersonal relationships with subordinates is a prime concern for relationship-oriented leaders. Task-oriented leaders are mainly concerned with ensuring that subordinates perform at a high level. Task-oriented managers focus on task accomplishment and making sure the job gets done.

Fiedler identified three situational characteristics that are important determinants of how favourable a situation is for leading:

- *Leader-Member Relations.* The extent to which followers like, trust, and are loyal to their leader. Situations are more favourable for leading when leader-member relations are good.

- *Task Structure.* The extent to which the work to be performed is clear-cut so that a leader's subordinates know what needs to be accomplished and how to go about doing it. When task structure is high, situations are favourable for leading. When task structure is low, goals may be vague, subordinates may be unsure of what they should be doing or how they should do it, and the situation is unfavourable for leading.

- *Position Power.* The amount of legitimate, reward, and coercive power a leader has by virtue of his or her position in an organization. Leadership situations are more favourable for leading when position power is strong.

task structure

The extent to which the work to be performed is clear-cut so that a leader's subordinates know what needs to be accomplished and how to go about doing it; a determinant of how favourable a situation is for leading.

position power

The amount of legitimate, reward, and coercive power that a leader has by virtue of his or her position in an organization; a determinant of how favourable a situation is for leading.

When a situation is favourable for leading, it is relatively easy for a manager to influence subordinates so that they perform at a high level and contribute to organizational efficiency and effectiveness. Therefore it makes the most sense to be task-oriented because the relationship is already going well. In a situation unfavourable for leading, it is much more difficult for a manager to exert influence. This makes being task-oriented the most desirable behaviour for the leader. After extensive research, Fiedler determined that relationship-oriented leaders are most effective in moderately favourable situations (IV, V, VI, and VII in Figure 9.2) and task-oriented leaders are most effective in very favourable situations (I, II, and III) or very unfavourable situations (VIII).

Figure 9.2 | Fiedler's Contingency Theory of Leadership

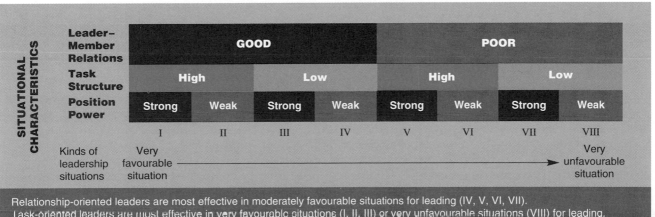

Relationship-oriented leaders are most effective in moderately favourable situations for leading (IV, V, VI, VII). Task-oriented leaders are most effective in very favourable situations (I, II, III) or very unfavourable situations (VIII) for leading.

According to Fiedler, individuals cannot change their leader style. Therefore, managers need to be placed in leadership situations that fit their style, or situations need to be changed to suit the manager. Situations can be changed, for example, by giving a manager more position power, or by taking steps to increase task structure such as by clarifying goals. Research studies tend to support Fiedler's model but also suggest that, like most theories, it needs to be adjusted.[24] Some researchers also find fault with the model's premise that leaders cannot alter their styles.

Hersey-Blanchard's Situational Leadership Theory

situational leadership theory (SLT)

A contingency model of leadership that focuses on the followers' readiness.

Paul Hersey and Ken Blanchard's **situational leadership theory (SLT)**[25] has been incorporated into leadership training programs at numerous Fortune 500 companies. More than one million managers a year are taught its basic elements.[26]

SLT compares the leader-follower relationship to that between a parent and child. Just as parents needs to give more control to a child as the child becomes more mature and responsible, so too should leaders do this with employees. Hersey and Blanchard identify four specific leader behaviours that managers can use to lead their employees: telling, selling, participating, and delegating. The styles vary in their degree of task-oriented behaviour and relationship-oriented behaviour. The appropriate style depends on the follower's ability and motivation:

- *Telling.* If a follower is *unable* and *unwilling* to do a task, the leader needs to give clear and specific directions (in other words, the leader needs to be highly directive).

- *Selling.* If a follower is *unable* but *willing*, the leader needs to display both high task orientation and high relationship orientation. The high task orientation will compensate for the follower's lack of ability. The high relationship orientation will encourage the follower to "buy into" the leader's desires (in other words, the leader needs to "sell" the task).

- *Participating.* If the follower is *able* but *unwilling*, the leader needs to use a supportive and participative style.

- *Delegating.* If the employee is both *able* and *willing*, the leader doesn't need to do much (in other words, a laissez-faire approach will work).

Figure 9.3 illustrates the relationship of leader behaviours to follower readiness.

Path-Goal Theory

path-goal theory

A contingency model of leadership proposing that leaders can motivate subordinates by identifying their desired outcomes, rewarding them for high performance and the attainment of work goals with these desired outcomes, and clarifying for them the paths leading to the attainment of work goals.

Developed by Rotman School of Management Professor Martin Evans in the late 1960s, and then expanded on by Robert House (formerly at Rotman, but now at the Wharton School of Business at the University of Pennsylvania), **path-goal theory** focuses on what leaders can do to motivate their subordinates to reach group and organizational goals.[27] The premise of path-goal theory is that effective leaders motivate subordinates to achieve goals by (1) clearly identifying the outcomes that subordinates are trying to obtain from the workplace, (2) rewarding subordinates with these outcomes for high performance and the attainment of work goals, and (3) clarifying for subordinates the paths leading to the attainment of work goals. Path-goal theory is a contingency model because it proposes that the steps that managers should take to motivate subordinates depend on both the nature of the subordinates and the type of work they do.

Based on the expectancy theory of motivation (see Chapter 8), path-goal theory provides managers with three guidelines to follow to be effective leaders:

1. *Find out what outcomes your subordinates are trying to obtain from their jobs and the organization.* These outcomes can range from satisfactory pay and job security to reasonable working hours and interesting and challenging job assignments.

Figure 9.3 | Hersey-Blanchard's Situational Leadership Styles

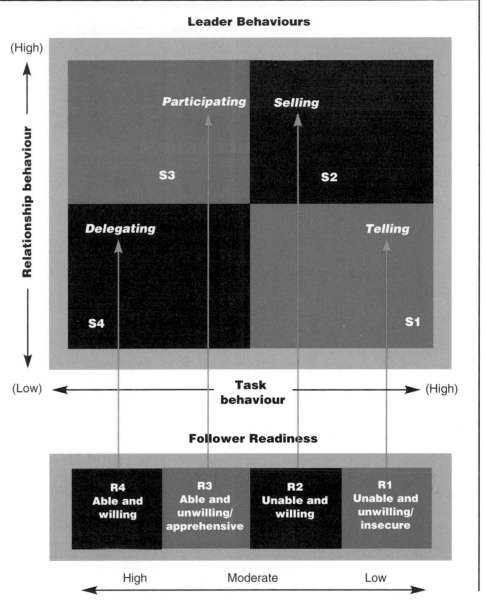

After identifying what these outcomes are, the manager should make sure that he or she has the reward power needed to distribute or withhold them.

2. *Reward subordinates for high performance and goal attainment with the outcomes they desire.*

3. *Clarify the paths to goal attainment for subordinates, remove any obstacles to high performance, and express confidence in subordinates' capabilities.* This does not mean that a manager needs to tell his or her subordinates what to do. Rather, it means that a manager needs to make sure that subordinates are clear about what they should be trying to accomplish and have the capabilities, resources, and confidence levels they need to be successful.

Path-goal theory identifies four kinds of behaviours that leaders can use to motivate subordinates:

- *Directive behaviours* include setting goals, assigning tasks, showing subordinates how to complete tasks, and taking concrete steps to improve performance.

- *Supportive behaviours* include expressing concern for subordinates and looking out for their best interests.

- *Participative behaviours* give subordinates a say in matters and decisions that affect them.

- *Achievement-oriented behaviours* motivate subordinates to perform at the highest level possible by, for example, setting very challenging goals, expecting that they be met, and believing in subordinates' capabilities.

Which of these behaviours should managers use to lead effectively? The answer to this question depends, or is contingent, on the nature of the subordinates and the kind of work they do.

Directive behaviours may be beneficial when subordinates are having difficulty completing assigned tasks, but they might be detrimental when subordinates are independent thinkers who work best when left alone. *Supportive* behaviours are often advisable when subordinates are experiencing high levels of stress. *Participative* behaviours can be particularly effective when subordinates' support of a decision is required. *Achievement-oriented* behaviours may increase motivation levels of highly capable subordinates who are bored from having too few challenges, but they might backfire if used with subordinates who are already pushed to their limit.

Effective managers seem to have a knack for determining the kinds of leader behaviours that are likely to work in different situations and result in increased efficiency and effectiveness.

To illustrate the importance of understanding that situations are different, and can require different styles, consider the fate of some of the Americans who have been recruited to run Canadian companies. Retailer Millard Barron was brought north to turn Zellers around, and American Bill Fields was supposed to save Hudson's Bay Co. Neither could replicate their US successes in Canada. Texas oilman J.P. Bryan was given the chance to restore profitability at two Canadian companies–Gulf Canada Resources Ltd. (now ConocoPhillips Company) and Canadian 88 Energy Corp. (now Esprit Exploration Limited)–and failed at both attempts.[28] These examples show the importance of understanding that one's leadership style may need to be adjusted for different companies and employees, and perhaps even for different countries.

The Leader Substitutes Model

The leader substitutes model suggests that leadership is sometimes unnecessary because substitutes for leadership are present. A **leader substitute** is something that acts in place of the influence of a leader and makes leadership unnecessary. This model suggests that under certain conditions managers do not have to play a leadership role–that members of an organization sometimes can perform highly without a manager exerting influence over them.[29] The leader substitutes model is a contingency model because it suggests that in some situations leadership is unnecessary.

leader substitute
Characteristics of subordinates or characteristics of a situation or context that act in place of the influence of a leader and make leadership unnecessary.

Both the *characteristics of subordinates*–such as their skills, abilities, experience, knowledge, and motivation–and the *characteristics of the situation or context*–such as the extent to which the work is interesting and enjoyable–can be substitutes for leadership.[30] When work is interesting and enjoyable, job holders do not need to be coaxed into performing because performing is rewarding in its own right. Similarly, when managers empower their subordinates or use *self-managed work teams* (discussed in detail in Chapter 10), the need for leadership influence from a manager is decreased because team members manage themselves.

Substitutes for leadership can increase organizational efficiency and effectiveness because they free up some of managers' valuable time and allow managers to focus their efforts on discovering new ways to improve organizational effectiveness.

Bringing It All Together

Effective leadership in organizations occurs when managers take steps to lead in a way that is appropriate for the situation or context in which leadership occurs and the subordinates who are being led. The four contingency models of leadership just discussed help managers identify the necessary ingredients for effective leadership. They are complementary in that each one looks at the leadership question from a different angle. Fiedler's contingency model explores how a manager's leadership style needs to be matched to the leadership situation that the manager is in for maximum effectiveness. Hersey-Blanchard's situational leadership theory examines the need for leaders to adjust their style to match their followers' ability and motivation. House's path-goal theory focuses on how managers should motivate subordinates and describes the specific kinds of behaviours that managers can engage in to have a highly motivated workforce. The leadership substitutes model alerts managers to the fact that sometimes they do not need to exert influence over subordinates and thus can free up their time for other important activities. Table 9.3 recaps these four contingency models of leadership.

Tips for Managers

Contingency Models of Leadership

1. If you or one of your subordinates is relationship-oriented and in a very unfavourable situation for leading, try to increase the favourability of the situation by increasing task structure or position power or improving leader-member relations.

2. Determine what outcomes your subordinates are trying to obtain from their jobs, make sure you have reward power for these outcomes, and distribute the outcomes based on performance levels.

3. Express confidence in your subordinates' capabilities and do whatever you can to help them believe in their ability to succeed. Remove any obstacles to success.

4. Explore how you can take advantage of leadership substitutes to free up some of the time you spend supervising your subordinates.

Table 9.3 | Contingency Models of Leadership

MODEL	FOCUS	KEY CONTINGENCIES
Fiedler's contingency model	Describes two leader styles, relationship-oriented and task-oriented, and the kinds of situations in which each kind of leader will be most effective	Whether or not a relationship-oriented or a task-oriented leader is effective is contingent on the situation
Hersey-Blanchard's situational leadership theory	Describes how leaders adjust their styles to match their followers' ability and motivation	The styles that managers should use are contingent on the ability and motivation of subordinates
House's path-goal theory	Describes how effective leaders motivate their followers	The behaviours that managers should engage in to be effective leaders are contingent on the nature of the subordinates and the work they do
Leader substitutes model	Describes when leadership is unnecessary	Whether or not leadership is necessary for subordinates to perform highly is contingent on characteristics of the subordinates and the situation

TRANSFORMATIONAL LEADERSHIP: LEADING WITH VISION

Think About It

Transformational Leadership in South Korea

When Hun-Jo Lee became chief executive of the once-successful Korean electrical appliance and electronics company Goldstar (since renamed LG Electronics Inc.), the company was headed for ruin.[31] Global and domestic market share was slipping, quality was declining, and even rank-and-file employees realized that bankruptcy was imminent if things did not change. Less than 10 years after Lee took over, the company recovered its spot as the top producer of washing machines, refrigerators, and colour TVs in South Korea. LG Electronics also is gaining ground globally in the areas of liquid-crystal displays and semiconductors.[32]

Question

1. How can leaders transform their employees so that companies that are performing poorly can regain market share?

transactional leadership

Leaders who guide their subordinates toward expected goals with no expectation of exceeding expected behaviour.

The trait, behavioural, and contingency theories are transactional leadership theories developed when organizations were more hierarchical, with classic lines of command. **Transactional leadership** occurs when managers guide or motivate their subordinates in the direction of established goals. Some transactional leaders use rewards and recognize appropriate behaviour. Under this kind of leadership, employees will generally meet performance expectations, though rarely will they exceed expectations.[33] Other transactional leaders emphasize correction and possibly punishment rather than rewards and recognition. This style "results in performance below expectations, and discourages innovation and initiative in the workplace."[34] While leaders should not ignore poor performance, effective leaders emphasize how to achieve expectations, rather than dwelling on mistakes.

Hierarchical organizations still dominate Canada's "Most Respected Corporations,"[35] but some organizations are trying to be more innovative, faster moving, and more responsive to employees. These organizations have turned to a different style of leadership where leaders and managers are not expected to perform only supervisory tasks but also need to focus on vision-setting activities. These theories try to explain how certain leaders can achieve extraordinary performance from their followers, and they emphasize symbolic and emotionally appealing leadership behaviours.[36]

When managers have such dramatic effects on their subordinates and on an organization as a whole, they are engaging in transformational leadership. **Transformational leadership** occurs when managers change (or transform) their subordinates in three important ways:[37]

transformational leadership

Leadership that makes subordinates aware of the importance of their jobs and performance to the organization and aware of their own needs for personal growth, and that motivates subordinates to work for the good of the organization.

1. *Transformational managers make subordinates aware of how important their jobs are for the organization and how necessary it is for them to perform those jobs as best they can so that the organization can attain its goals.* At LG Electronics, Hun-Jo Lee opened new paths of communication between nonmanagerial employees and managers, and openly shared the company's problems with employees. He made everyone feel responsible for helping to solve the problems. Decision making was decentralized, and all employees were encouraged to feel responsible for coming up with improvements, ideas for new products, and ways to increase quality.

2. *Transformational managers make their subordinates aware of the subordinates' own needs for personal growth, development, and accomplishment.* One of Lee's important steps at LG Electronics was to improve management relations with the union.

LG Electronics Inc.
www.lg.co.kr/english/

He encouraged union members to meet with him whenever they have ideas for improving things at LG Electronics.[38] He wants his employees to reach their full potential and is doing whatever he can think of to help them do that. He also empowers his employees, so they will feel free to consider new ways of doing things at the company.

3. *Transformational managers motivate their subordinates to work for the good of the organization as a whole, not just for their own personal gain or benefit.* In transforming LG Electronics, Lee explained to employees the need for change at the company, and that growth and improvement in productivity would make the company much stronger, thus benefiting everyone.

Many transformational leaders engage in transactional leadership. They reward subordinates for a job well done and notice and respond to substandard performance. But they also have their eyes on the bigger picture of how much better things could be in their organizations, how much more their subordinates are capable of achieving, and how important it is to treat their subordinates with respect and to help them reach their full potential.

Influencing Others

How do managers like Lee transform subordinates and produce dramatic effects in their organizations? There are at least three ways in which managers and other transformational leaders can influence their followers: by being a charismatic leader, by stimulating subordinates intellectually, and by engaging in developmental consideration (see table 9.4).

Being a Charismatic Leader

charismatic leader
An enthusiastic, self-confident leader able to communicate clearly his or her vision of how good things could be.

Transformational managers are **charismatic leaders**. They have a vision of how good things could be in their work groups and organizations, and it is in contrast with the status quo. Their vision usually entails dramatic improvements in group and organizational performance as a result of changes in the organization's structure, culture, strategy, decision making, and other critical processes and factors. This vision paves the way for gaining a competitive advantage.

Charismatic leaders are excited and enthusiastic about their vision and clearly communicate it to their subordinates. The excitement, enthusiasm, and self-confidence of a charismatic leader contribute to the leader's being able to inspire followers to enthusiastically support his or her vision.[39] People often think of charismatic leaders or managers as being "larger than life." The essence of charisma, however, is having a vision and enthusiastically communicating it to others. Thus, managers who appear to be quiet and earnest can also be charismatic.

Table 9.4 | Transformational Leadership

Transformational Managers

- Are charismatic
- Intellectually stimulate subordinates
- Engage in developmental consideration

Subordinates of Transformational Managers

- Have increased awareness of the importance of their jobs and high performance
- Are aware of their own needs for growth, development, and accomplishment
- Work for the good of the organization and not just their own personal benefit

Table 9.5 | Key Characteristics of a Charismatic Leader

1. *Vision and articulation.* Has a vision—expressed as an idealized goal—that proposes a future better than the status quo; is able to clarify the importance of the vision in terms that are understandable to others.

2. *Personal risk.* Willing to take on high personal risk, incur high costs, and engage in self-sacrifice to achieve the vision.

3. *Environmental sensitivity.* Able to make realistic assessments of the environmental constraints and resources needed to bring about change.

4. *Sensitivity to follower needs.* Perceptive of others' abilities and responsive to their needs and feelings.

5. *Unconventional behaviour.* Engages in behaviours that are perceived as novel and counter to norms.

Source: Based on J.A. Conger and R.N. Kanungo, *Charismatic Leadership in Organizations* (Thousand Oaks, CA: Sage, 1998), p. 94.

The most comprehensive analysis of charismatic leadership was conducted by Professor Rabindra Kanungo at McGill University, together with Jay Conger.[40] Based on studies of managers from Canada, the United States, and India, they identified five dimensions that characterize charismatic leadership. These are shown in Table 9.5.

Does charismatic leadership really make a difference? An unpublished study by Robert House and some colleagues looking at 63 American and 49 Canadian companies (including Nortel Networks, Molson, Gulf Canada [now ConocoPhillips], and Manulife Financial) found that "between 15 and 25 percent of the variation in profitability among the companies was accounted for by the leadership qualities of their CEO."[41] Charismatic leaders led more profitable companies.

An increasing body of research shows that people who work for charismatic leaders are motivated to exert extra work effort and, because they like their leaders, they express greater satisfaction.[42] One of the most cited studies of the effects of charismatic leadership was done at the University of British Columbia in the early 1980s by Jane Howell (now at the Richard Ivey School of Business, University of Western Ontario) and Peter Frost.[43] The two found that those who worked under a charismatic leader generated more ideas, produced better results, reported higher job satisfaction, and showed stronger bonds of loyalty. Howell, in summarizing these results, says, "Charismatic leaders know how to inspire people to think in new directions."[44]

The recent accounting scandals and high-profile bankruptcies of North American companies, including Enron and WorldCom, suggest some of the dangers of charismatic leadership. WorldCom Inc.'s Bernard Ebbers and Enron Corp.'s Kenneth Lay "seemed almost a breed apart, blessed with unique visionary powers" when their companies were increasing stock prices at phenomenal rates in the 1990s.[45] After the scandals, however, there was some desire for CEOs with less vision and more ethical and corporate responsibility.

Stimulating Subordinates Intellectually

Transformational managers openly share information with their subordinates so that subordinates are aware of problems and the need for change. The manager causes subordinates to view problems in their groups and throughout the organization from a different perspective, consistent with the manager's vision. Whereas in the past subordinates may not have been aware of some problems, may have viewed problems as a "management issue" beyond their concern, or may have

intellectual stimulation

Behaviour a leader engages in to make followers aware of problems and view these problems in new ways, consistent with the leader's vision.

developmental consideration

Behaviour a leader engages in to support and encourage followers and help them develop and grow on the job.

viewed problems as insurmountable, the transformational manager's **intellectual stimulation** leads subordinates to view problems as challenges that they can and will meet and conquer. The manager engages and empowers subordinates to take personal responsibility for helping to solve problems.[46]

Engaging in Developmental Consideration

When a manager engages in **developmental consideration**, he or she not only performs the consideration behaviours described earlier, such as demonstrating true concern for the well-being of subordinates, but goes one step further. The manager goes out of his or her way to support and encourage subordinates, giving them opportunities to enhance their skills and capabilities and to grow and excel on the job.[47]

Research Support

The evidence supporting the superiority of transformational leadership is overwhelmingly impressive. For example, studies of Canadian, American, and German military officers found, at every level, that transformational leaders were considered more effective than their transactional counterparts.[48] Professor Jane Howell (at the University of Western Ontario) and her colleagues studied 250 executives and managers at a major financial-services company and found that "transformational leaders had 34 percent higher business unit performance results than other types of leaders."[49] Studies also find that when leaders engage in transformational leadership, their subordinates tend to have higher levels of job satisfaction and performance.[50] Additionally, subordinates of transformational leaders may be more likely to trust their leaders and their organizations and feel that they are being fairly treated, which in turn may positively influence their work motivation (see Chapter 8).[51]

Tips for Managers

Transformational Leadership

1. Let subordinates know how their own jobs contribute to organizational effectiveness and stress the importance of high performance.
2. Help subordinates learn new skills and develop on the job.
3. Have a vision of how much better things can be in your organization and enthusiastically communicate your vision throughout the organization.
4. Share organizational problems and challenges with subordinates and engage them to help solve the problems and meet the challenges.
5. Take a personal interest in your subordinates and inspire them to accomplish as much as they can.

GENDER, CULTURE, AND LEADERSHIP

Think About It

Belinda Stronach Takes Over Magna From Her Father

Belinda Stronach became CEO of Aurora, Ontario-based Magna International in February 2001, taking over from her father, Frank Stronach, who had started the company more than 45 years before.[52] The first question many asked about Belinda was whether she got the job just because she was her father's daughter.

Observers note that Belinda is not as charismatic as Frank. She is also much more people-oriented than him. Frank Stronach was regarded as an authoritarian leader, commanding loyalty from others, but not sharing leadership. Belinda Stronach is much more team-oriented. As she notes, "It's not just about me. We have a competent team in place here and I have worked closely with that team."[53]

Question

1. Do men and women really lead differently?

There are many questions about whether men and women have different leadership styles, or whether observed differences have more to do with personality differences across people, rather than explicit gender differences. Others consider whether leadership is done the same cross-culturally, and whether our North American leadership theories apply in other countries. We consider these issues in the following sections.

Gender and Leadership

The increasing number of women entering the ranks of management as well as the problems some women face in their efforts to be hired as managers or promoted into management positions have prompted researchers to explore the relationship between gender and leadership. Although relatively more women are in management positions today than ten years ago, relatively few women are in top management in larger organizations, and, in some organizations, even in middle management. Although women make up 45 percent of the labour force in Canada, they fill only 32 percent of managerial roles, and only 12 percent of the senior management roles. Of the *National Post's* Top 150 CEOs of 2000, only 2 were women, and half of Canada's larger companies have no women in the senior ranks at all.[54] Women are represented better in smaller organizations. Industry Canada reports that in 2000, 45 percent of all small- to medium-sized enterprises reported at least one female owner.[55]

When women do advance to top-management positions, special attention is often focused on the fact that they are women, such as when Bobbi Gaunt was named to head Ford Motor Co. of Canada and Maureen Kempston Darkes was named to head General Motors of Canada.

A widespread stereotype of women is that they are nurturing, supportive, and concerned with interpersonal relations. Men are stereotypically viewed as being directive and focused on task accomplishment. Such stereotypes suggest that women tend to be more relationship-oriented as managers and engage in more consideration behaviours, whereas men are more task-oriented and engage in more initiating structure behaviours. Does the behaviour of actual male and female managers bear out these stereotypes? Do female managers lead in different ways than males? Are male or female managers more effective as leaders?

Research suggests that male managers and female managers who have leadership positions in organizations behave in similar ways.[56] Women do not engage in more consideration than men, and men do not engage in more initiating structure than women. Research does suggest, however, that leadership style may vary between women and men. Women tend to be somewhat more participative as leaders than men, involving subordinates in decision making and seeking their input.[57] Male managers tend to be less participative than female managers, making more decisions on their own and wanting to do things their own way.

Linda Hasenfratz of Guelph, Ontario-based Linamar Corporation has succeeded her father, Frank, as CEO of the company. Although she had worked in many positions including on the shop floor, some of Linamar's employees questioned her ability to lead in the male-dominated automotive parts industry when she first took over from her father.

There are at least two reasons why female managers may be more participative as leaders than male managers.[58] First, subordinates may try to resist the influence of female managers more than they do the influence of male managers. Some subordinates may never have reported to a woman before, some may inappropriately see management roles as being more appropriate for men than for women, and some may just resist being led by a woman. To overcome this resistance and encourage subordinates' trust and respect, female managers may adopt a participative approach.

A second reason why female managers may be more participative is that they sometimes have better interpersonal skills than male managers.[59] A participative approach to leadership requires high levels of interaction and involvement between a manager and his or her subordinates, sensitivity to subordinates' feelings, and the ability to make decisions that may be unpopular with subordinates but necessary for reaching goals. Good interpersonal skills may help female managers have the effective interactions with their subordinates that are crucial to a participative approach.[60] To the extent that male managers have more difficulty managing interpersonal relationships, they may shy away from the high levels of interaction with subordinates that are necessary for true participation.

Perhaps a question even more important than whether male and female managers differ in the leadership behaviours they perform is whether they differ in effectiveness. Consistent with the findings for leader behaviours, research suggests that across different kinds of organizational settings, male and female managers tend to be *equally* effective as leaders.[61] Thus, there is no logical basis for stereotypes favouring male managers and leaders or for the existence of the glass ceiling (an invisible barrier that seems to prevent women from advancing as far as they should in some organizations). Because women and men are equally effective as leaders, the increasing number of women in the workforce should result in a larger pool of highly qualified candidates for management positions in organizations, ultimately enhancing organizational effectiveness.[62]

Leadership Styles Across Cultures

Some evidence suggests that leadership styles vary not only among individuals but also among countries or cultures. Some research suggests that European managers tend to be more humanistic or people-oriented than Japanese and American managers. The collectivistic culture in Japan places prime emphasis on the group rather than the individual, so the importance of individuals' own personalities, needs, and desires is minimized. Organizations in North America tend to be very profit-oriented and thus tend to downplay the importance of individual employees' needs and desires. Many countries in Europe have a more individualistic outlook than Japan and a more humanistic outlook than the United States, which may result in some European managers being more people-oriented than their Japanese or American counterparts. European managers, for example, tend to be reluctant to lay off employees, and when a layoff is absolutely necessary, they take careful steps to make it as painless as possible.[63]

Another cross-cultural difference that has been noted is in time horizons. Managers in any two countries often differ in their time horizons, but there also may be cultural differences. Canadian and US organizations tend to have a short-run profit orientation, which results in a leadership style emphasizing short-run performance. Many of the

Samsung's managers have had to spend considerable time learning new leadership skills to influence and motivate Canadian and US employees. In these two countries, leaders need to be more direct as well as participative as compared to some Asian counterparts.

investors and creators of the dot-com companies that failed in 2000 and 2001 demonstrated very short-term objectives, along the lines of "get rich quick." Many of these companies failed to have a business plan that would guide them in a long-term strategy. By contrast, Japanese organizations tend to have a long-run growth orientation, which results in Japanese managers' personal leadership styles emphasizing long-run performance. Justus Mische, now chair at the European organization Aventis (formerly Hoechst) has suggested that "Europe, at least the big international firms in Europe, have a philosophy between the Japanese, long term, and the United States, short term."[64] Research on these and other global aspects of leadership is in its infancy, but as it continues, more cultural differences in managers' personal leadership styles may be discovered.

EMOTIONAL INTELLIGENCE AND LEADERSHIP

Do the moods and emotions leaders experience on the job influence their behaviour and effectiveness as leaders? Preliminary research suggests that this is likely to be the case. For example, one study found that when store managers experienced positive moods at work, salespeople in the stores they led provided high quality customer service and were less likely to quit.[65]

emotional intelligence
The ability to understand and manage one's own moods and emotions and the moods and emotions of other people.

Emotional intelligence is the ability to understand and manage one's own moods and emotions and the moods and emotions of other people. A leader's level of emotional intelligence may play a particularly important role in leadership effectiveness.[66] For example, emotional intelligence may help leaders develop a vision for their organizations, motivate their subordinates to commit to this vision, and energize them to enthusiastically work to achieve this vision. Moreover, emotional intelligence may enable leaders to develop a significant identity for their organization and instill high levels of trust and cooperation throughout the organization while maintaining the flexibility needed to respond to changing conditions.[67]

SUMMARY AND REVIEW

Chapter Summary

THE NATURE OF LEADERSHIP

- Personal Leadership Style and Managerial Tasks
- Power: The Key to Leadership
- Empowerment: An Ingredient in Modern Management

MODELS OF LEADERSHIP

LEADERSHIP AS SUPERVISION

- The Trait Model
- The Behavioural Models
- Contingency Models of Leadership
- Bringing It All Together

THE NATURE OF LEADERSHIP Leadership is the process by which a person exerts influence over other people and inspires, motivates, and directs their activities to help achieve group or organizational goals. Leaders are able to influence others because they possess power. The five types of power available to managers are *legitimate power, reward power, coercive power, expert power,* and *referent power.* Many managers are using empowerment as a tool to increase their effectiveness as leaders.

LEADERSHIP AS SUPERVISION The *trait model* of leadership describes personal characteristics or traits that contribute to effective leadership. However, some managers who possess these traits are not effective leaders, and some managers who do not possess all the traits are nevertheless effective leaders. The *behaviour model* of leadership describes two kinds of behaviour that most leaders engage in: consideration and initiating structure. *Contingency models* take into account the complexity surrounding leadership and the role of the situation in determining whether a manager is an effective or ineffective leader. *Fiedler's contingency model* explains why managers may be effective leaders in one situation and ineffective in another. *Hersey-Blanchard's situational leadership theory* examines the need for leaders to adjust their style to match their followers' ability and motivation. *House's path-goal theory* describes how effective managers motivate their subordinates by determining what outcomes their subordinates want, rewarding subordinates with these outcomes when they achieve their goals and perform at a high level, and clarifying the paths to goal attainment. The *leader substitutes model* suggests that sometimes managers do not have to play a leadership role because their subordinates perform highly without the manager having to exert influence over them.

TRANSFORMATIONAL LEADERSHIP: LEADING WITH VISION Transactional leaders generally only get their subordinates to meet expectations. Transformational leadership occurs when managers have dramatic effects on their subordinates and on the organization as a whole and inspire and energize subordinates to solve problems and improve performance. These effects include making subordinates aware of the importance of their own jobs and high performance; making subordinates aware of their own needs for personal growth, development, and accomplishment; and motivating subordinates to work for the good of the organization and not just their own personal gain. Managers can engage in transformational leadership by being charismatic leaders, by stimulating subordinates intellectually, and by engaging in developmental consideration. Transformational managers also often engage in transactional leadership by using their reward and coercive powers to encourage high performance.

GENDER, CULTURE, AND LEADERSHIP Female and male managers do not differ in the leadership behaviours that they perform, contrary to stereotypes suggesting that women are more relationship-oriented and men more task-oriented. Female managers sometimes are more participative than male managers, however. Research has found that women and men are equally effective as managers and leaders. Studies have found differences in leadership styles across cultures. European leaders tend to be more people-oriented than either American or Japanese leaders. Leaders also differ in their time orientations, with US and Canadian leaders being very oriented toward the short term in their approach.

EMOTIONAL INTELLIGENCE AND LEADERSHIP The moods and emotions leaders experience on the job may affect their leadership effectiveness. Moreover, emotional intelligence has the potential to contribute to leadership effectiveness in multiple ways.

Roles in Contrast: Considerations

MANAGERS	EMPLOYEES
Power comes from a variety of sources. One way to increase your power is to develop an expertise in an area that is needed for the organization, but that others don't have.	Power comes from a variety of sources. One way to increase your power is to develop an expertise in an area that is needed for the organization, but that others don't have.
There is not one best way to lead. It is important to consider the needs of the followers in determining a style that will work best for them.	When leading your team, it is important to realize that there is no best way to lead. It is important to consider the needs of the other team members in determining a style that will work best for them.
Leaders are not always needed. When employees are very motivated and have relevant technical experience, for instance, they can operate with very little leadership.	Leaders are not always needed. When employees are very motivated and have relevant technical experience, for instance, they can operate with very little leadership. This also applies to teams of which you may be a member.

MANAGEMENT
in Action

Topics for Discussion and Action

1. Describe the steps managers can take to increase their power and ability to be effective leaders.
2. Think of specific situations in which it might be especially important for a manager to engage in consideration and in initiating structure.
3. Interview an actual manager to find out how the three situational characteristics that Fiedler identified are affecting the manager's ability to provide leadership.
4. For your current job or for a future job that you expect to hold, describe what your supervisor could do to strongly motivate you to be a top performer.
5. Discuss why managers might want to change the behaviours they engage in, given their situation, their subordinates, and the nature of the work being done. Do you think managers are able to change their leadership behaviours readily? Why or why not?
6. Discuss why substitutes for leadership can contribute to organizational effectiveness.
7. Describe what transformational leadership is, and explain how managers can engage in it.
8. Find an example of a company that has dramatically turned its fortunes around and improved its performance. Determine whether a transformational leader was behind the turnaround and, if so, what this leader did.
9. Discuss why some people still think that men make better managers than women even though research indicates that men and women are equally effective as managers and leaders.

Building Management Skills

ANALYZING FAILURES OF LEADERSHIP

Think about a situation you are familiar with in which a leader was very ineffective. Then answer the following questions.

1. What sources of power did this leader have? Did the leader have enough power to influence his or her followers?
2. What kinds of behaviours did this leader engage in? Were they appropriate for the situation? Why or why not?
3. From what you know, do you think this leader was a task-oriented leader or a relationship-oriented leader? How favourable was this leader's situation for leading?
4. What steps did this leader take to motivate his or her followers? Were these steps appropriate or inappropriate? Why?
5. What signs, if any, did this leader show of being a transformational leader?

Management for You

Your school is developing a one-day orientation program for new students majoring in business. You have been asked to consider leading the group of students who will design and implement the orientation program. Develop a two- to three-page "handout" that shows whether the position is a natural fit for you. To do this, (1) identify your strengths and weaknesses in the sources of power you can bring to the project, and (2) discuss whether you would be a transactional or transformation leader and why. Provide a strong concluding statement about whether or not you would be the best leader for this task.

Small Group Breakout Exercise

IMPROVING LEADERSHIP EFFECTIVENESS

Form groups of 3 to 5 people, and appoint 1 member as the spokesperson who will communicate your findings and conclusions to the whole class when called on by the instructor. Then discuss the following scenario.

You are a team of human resource consultants who have been hired by Carla Caruso, an entrepreneur who started her own interior decorating business. At first, she worked on her own as an independent contractor. Then, because of a dramatic increase in the number of new homes being built, she decided to form her own company.

She hired a secretary/bookkeeper and 4 interior decorators. Caruso still does decorating jobs herself and has adopted a hands-off approach to leading the 4 decorators because she feels that interior design is a very personal, creative endeavour. Rather than paying the decorators on some kind of commission basis, she pays them a higher-than-average salary so that they are motivated to do what's best for their customers, not what will result in higher billings and commissions.

Caruso thought everything was going smoothly until customer complaints started coming in. These complaints were about the decorators being hard to reach, promising unrealistic delivery times, being late for or failing to keep appointments, and being impatient and rude when customers had trouble making up their minds. Caruso knows that her decorators are competent people and is concerned that she is not effectively leading and managing them. She has asked for your advice.

1. What advice can you give Caruso to either increase her power or use her existing power more effectively?
2. Does Caruso seem to be performing appropriate leader behaviours in this situation? What advice can you give her about the kinds of behaviours she should perform?
3. How can Caruso increase the decorators' motivation to deliver high quality customer service?
4. Would you advise Caruso to try to engage in transformational leadership in this situation? If not, why not? If so, what steps would you advise her to take?

Managing Ethically

One of your subordinates has noticed that your expense account reports have repeatedly overstated your expenses because you always bill for an extra day, at the "daily rate," when you go out of town on company business. Your assistant knows that you have always been in town and working at home on that extra day. He has questioned your reports, as you have now submitted 15 of these for the year. How would you use your knowledge of power to resolve this dilemma? Which use of power would be most ethical, and why?

Exploring the World Wide Web

SPECIFIC ASSIGNMENT

Many CEOs are highly visible leaders in their companies and industries. One such CEO is Mogens Smed of Calgary-based SMED International. Scan the company's website (www.smednet.com). Click on "Search" and type in "Mogens." Look at the article "Mogens Smed Looking for One Billion in Sales."

1. How would you characterize Mogens Smed's personal leadership style?
2. How might Smed's early experiences in life have affected his ability to succeed with the company he created?
3. How might Smed be considered a transformational leader?

GENERAL ASSIGNMENT

Find the website of a company that provides information on the company's missions, goals, and values, and on the company's top managers and their personal leadership styles. How might the company's missions, goals, and values impact the process of leadership in this company?

You're the Management Consultant

BRINGING BACK LUSTRE TO A BLINDS COMPANY

Jim Zhou is the CEO of a medium-sized company that makes indoor window coverings such as blinds and shades. His company has a real cost advantage in terms of being able to make custom window coverings at costs that are relatively low in the industry. However, the performance of his company has been lacklustre. In order to make needed changes and improve performance, he met with the eight other top managers in his company and made them responsible for identifying problems and missed opportunities in each of their areas and coming up with an action plan to address these problems and take advantage of opportunities.

Once their action plans received the "go ahead" from Zhou, the managers were charged with introducing their action plans in a timely fashion and monitoring the effects of their initiatives on a monthly basis for the next 8 to 12 months.

All of the managers' action plans were approved by Zhou, and a year later, most of the managers were reporting that their initiatives had been successful in addressing the problems and opportunities they had identified. However, overall company performance continued to be lacklustre and showed no signs of improvement. Zhou is confused, troubled, and starting to question both his leadership capabilities as well as his approach to change. He has come to you for help because you are an expert in leadership. He wants you to tell him why his company continues to have lacklustre performance and to advise him about what he should do next.

MANAGEMENT CASE

Cynthia Trudell: Leading in a Man's World

Cynthia Trudell, who was born in Saint John, New Brunswick, received her PhD in physical science from the University of Windsor, specializing in photochemistry—the study of gases on objects.[68] However, the slow pace and isolation of academic life convinced her to take a job in industry. Today Trudell is a member of the Automotive Hall of Fame and several US publications have referred to her as one of the top women executives in the United States.

Trudell started at Ford Motor Co. of Canada's engine plant in Windsor in 1979. Two years later, she was the senior engineering supervisor at General Motors Canada's transmission plant in Windsor, later rising to superintendent of manufacturing there. Trudell then held a variety of positions within General Motors, her last as chair and president of Saturn Corp. between 1999 and 2001. When she was appointed head of Saturn, she became the first woman ever to head a fully

integrated subsidiary of a North American automaker. In April 2001, she left General Motors to become CEO of Brunswick Corporation's Sea Ray Division, where she heads nine plants and a staff of 5000. Sea Ray is the largest manufacturer of powerboats in the world, and its products include the Sea Ray, Baja, and Boston Whaler brands.

Trudell is a study in determination. At 19, she chose her life's mantra: "When I'm dying, and they're burying me, I want to be able to shake my fist and scream back at them, 'I lived, I laughed, I learned and I loved.'" When she was appointed president of Saturn, a *New York Times* reporter commented: "Now the world's largest auto maker is about to put a true car guy in charge of its Saturn division—only the car guy is a woman."

As she started her challenge at Saturn, she recognized that she would have to turn the division into a profitable unit. And that if she didn't deliver the results, she probably shouldn't be there.

Trudell is clear about who she is as a leader. She finds bureaucracy a waste of time: "It doesn't make money for you." She gets frustrated when she thinks she knows the right way to do something and others stand in the way. Therefore, the appointment to Saturn suited her. Saturn was known for its relatively flat hierarchy and cooperative relations between union and management.

The Saturn culture values open dialogue, something that Trudell values as well. She doesn't feel that her opening position in dealing with employees is to say, "This is the way we're going to do it." Instead, she recognizes the need to explain her point of view patiently, and to win support. Still, she also recognizes that sometimes as a leader, a person has to be tough. "You can't be emotional, unless you're passionate. But if you overuse that, that loses its impact on people. Sometimes you have to show a little bit of anger because that 'stun guns' people."

She was openly supportive of Rick Wagoner, who took over as CEO and president of GM in the summer of 2000, because she thought he supported a consensus style of management. But she also knew this would be a different style of management at GM, and that some senior executives would resist. She was clear about how things should be handled to reach a more consensual style in the organization, though. "That means doing some tough stuff. It means saying, 'If you don't change your behaviour, you don't fit.'"

Trudell often relies on intuition to guide her, and believes anyone can learn to use their intuition. She suggests that decision makers should write down both what their gut and their brain are telling them, and then follow the outcome of a decision to see which gave better guidance. "People who are good at risk management are people who can get their gut helping to feed their brain. Intuition means that your senses are out there all the time. I have seen men, all of a sudden, have an intuition they didn't even know existed. If you always take the easy road, because that's what the brain says, because we'll rationalize, then people never realize their fullest potential."

One of Trudell's challenges has been to work effectively with labour unions. She has certainly earned their respect, if not their admiration. She was inspired early on in her career by a general manager she worked under who worked hard to establish better relationships with unionized employees. From that, she says, "I saw that the people who made the product were the people we all needed to support. They were the ones who made the money for us and everybody else was high-priced overhead."

Rick Chene of the Canadian Auto Workers (CAW) says that their relationship was generally positive when he worked with Trudell at Windsor. When she tried to introduce lean manufacturing in Windsor, the fights with the CAW were bitter, and there were many disagreements. But Chene noted that Trudell "would never get bent out of shape. She'd move onto other issues." When she left Windsor to move to her next position, Chene and other union executives "made sure to say good-bye—a practice that . . . is far from universal." Chene suggested that if Trudell were given the opportunity by senior management to work in her own style with union members, "I was under the impression that Cynthia could be a catalyst for improving relations with workers. But not given the opportunity, she'd be another typical GM manager."

At the time of her departure from Saturn, little explanation was given about whether she made the move herself or whether she was encouraged to move elsewhere. Her own comment at the time was, "The opportunity presented itself and I probably would have never even thought of it had it not been there." Both Saturn and Sea Ray are located in Knoxville, Tennessee.

George W. Buckley, Brunswick's chairman and chief executive officer, in announcing her appointment said, "Her technical expertise, knowledge of systems and platforms, her strong brand management skills and experience with dealer channels, plus her focus on product quality, are ideally suited to make a tremendous impact at Sea Ray."

Questions

1. In what ways does Cynthia Trudell try to exert influence over her employees? Why has she been able to exert this influence?
2. How would you describe Trudell's personal leadership style?
3. How would you apply the different leadership theories to Trudell's beliefs about management?

MANAGEMENT CASE

From the Pages of the *National Post* M&M Founder Carving Bigger Slice of Market: Specialty Meats

When Mac Voisin, who is known as the "Baron of Barbecuing," was building his M and M Meat Shops franchise network, one of the golden rules he developed was to weed out all the hard-nosed entrepreneurs, a strategy that has kept the rebels out and conformists in line.

It has allowed the self-made man to grow M and M Meat Shops into a solid operation that consists of 300 stores across Canada with sales approaching $300-million.

"[The hiring strategy] is really a personality test and what it tells us is if the person is too entrepreneurial or not entrepreneurial enough. Both extremes can cause us a whole lot of grief," said the 51-year-old Mr. Voisin, who began the business 20 years ago in Kitchener, Ont., and developed the hiring concept following a handful of unprofitable outlets.

"If they're too entrepreneurial they'll want to sell their own product and work their own hours. If they're not entrepreneurial enough, we're going to have to hold their hands, they're going to phone us all the time and keep to the store instead of being out in the community," he said. "We're looking for a happy medium."

With record sales, the company has plans to become a 500-store franchise by 2006, and an expansion into the United States has not been ruled out.

In the 1980s, Mr. Voisin left the construction business to start M and M Meat Shops with brother-in-law Mark Nowak. The big joke, he says, was that at the time anybody with a pulse and a pocketbook could buy a franchise. The lack of careful consideration resulted in poor service as squabbles between owners and franchisees resulted in lower margins.

Mr. Voisin wanted to do things differently and spent a lot of time investing in people, management and a work ethic that went beyond what a lot of other companies did.

For instance, Mr. Voisin has a fax line reserved for franchisees who want to take their concerns directly to the president. He made a commitment to respond within 24 hours and has lived up to it.

Every two years, Mr. Voisin does a friendship tour, visiting store owners from North Delta, B.C., to Pierrefonds, Que. At head office, he is known to take employees along on these tours on a moment's notice.

All sales staff are required to undergo a four-month training course in customer service. The company also fosters a strong philanthropic spirit, raising nearly $5-million for the Crohn's and Colitis Foundation of Canada over the last 12 years. It was a cause Mr. Voisin independently sought to support simply because it was a little known charity.

The company's congenial approach has earned it several national awards, including the first Canadian Franchise Association award for distinction in 1992, when M and M Meat Shops beat out iconic chains McDonald's and Burger King. "From the very beginning they looked at things very strategically," said Richard Cunningham, the trade group's president. "They did a lot of training with their management team and they were quick to go in and solve a problem before it escalated into any kind of serious level."

The idea for M and M Meat Shops was inspired out of hosting barbecues. Mr. Voisin said he was frustrated with the lack of specialty meats sold in the grocery stores. The company struggled in the first few years, but in the early 1990s it rounded a corner after introducing smaller packaged items like chicken Kiev and veal Swiss.

"We really did poorly in the first five years," Mr. Voisin said. "We never really got any outside help and we just stumbled along. Our biggest challenge was understanding the importance of the expense sheet. Entrepreneurs tend to be very sales-oriented and they don't spend a lot of time trying to figure out how to control costs."

As the company grew, he began to step back from the day-to-day operations and expanded his senior management team to include industry veterans. Sales began to jump because of a rise in microwave sales, advances in flash freezing technology and an influx of women re-entering the workforce. The company even survived the arrival of big-box competition. Loblaw Cos. Ltd., for example, generated more than $2-billion last year from its popular President's Choice specialty labels. "We really weren't greatly impacted. [Loblaws] has probably helped and hindered us. They created more awareness for us, but on the other hand they could take some customers away," he said.

Mr. Voisin said retirement is a long way away and he always sees himself playing some type of role in the company. "I'll still visit stores and run regional meetings. I'm really the custodian of the fun culture we've developed. We believe if you're having fun people will want to stick around."

Source: K. Hanson, "M&M Founder Carving Bigger Slice of Market: Specialty Meats," *Financial Post (National Post)*, October 17, 2000, p. C5.

Questions

1. How would you describe Mac Voisin's personal leadership style?
2. What leadership behaviours does Voisin engage in?
3. Is Voisin a transformational leader? Why or why not?

CHAPTER 10

MANAGING TEAMS

Learning Objectives

1. Explain why groups and teams are key contributors to organizational effectiveness.

2. Identify the different types of groups and teams that help managers and organizations achieve their goals.

3. Explain how different elements of group dynamics influence the functioning and effectiveness of groups and teams.

4. Describe how managers can motivate group members to achieve organizational goals and reduce social loafing in groups and teams.

Roles in Contrast: Questions

MANAGERS	EMPLOYEES
How do I make good decisions?	Why am I always being asked to join teams?
What can I do to help my teams be more effective?	What can I do to help my team be more effective?
What can I do to prevent groupthink in my teams?	Should I be concerned if team members seem to be fighting a lot?

A CASE IN CONTRAST

TEAMS WORK WONDERS AT WILLOW MANUFACTURING

Willow Manufacturing (www.willowcnc.com), a Toronto-based supplier of precision components, used to experience flaring tempers in its workplace often.[1] "Years ago we had all kinds of problems in our plant. Workplace violence was very much a part of our culture here, unfortunately, because of very lax hiring," says Willow's president, Dennis Wild. Managers created a "tough-boy" environment where they brow-beat staff, while employees engaged in theft and arguments. The macho attitude of the plant was also not paying off: For many years, Willow was an unorganized, money-losing business.

Willow was incorporated in 1954 at its original location on Willow Avenue in the east end of Toronto. As the company grew over the years, so did its management team, until there were seven levels of management. These layers of management led to inefficient processes that in turn led to the loss of time and money.

The plant itself was an unpleasant place to work. An inch-thick oil residue coated every surface. The factory was also noisy and smoky, which set the tone for poor employee morale and many internal disputes. The company came close to bankruptcy several times.

By the mid-1990s, Wild decided that it was time to restructure Willow to make it a better place to work, and to improve its financial situation. One of the key approaches to the turnaround was to create a team environment. Today, if you walked into Willow you would have trouble figuring out who was in charge. Everyone, from Wild on down, wears the same-style uniform because all members of the team are viewed as equally important.

To enhance team interaction, Willow's managers were given training in how to create more teamwork. Management attitudes were changed as well, with an emphasis on removing the "us-them" attitude among employees and managers. Managers were also trained to coach and facilitate rather than to boss and manage.

Willow Manufacturing went from an unorganized, money-losing business to success after Dennis Wild, the company's president, introduced effective teamwork into the workplace.

Wild notes that major housecleaning was needed to transform the company. Under his direction, the company "hauled all the old emotional skeletons out of the closet and got staff to resolve many long-term conflicts."

Once the personal issues were resolved, Willow tackled inefficient manufacturing processes. Staff members were divided into teams that redesigned procedures, then submitted their ideas to another team that would further streamline the procedures. The teams were helping each other create better manufacturing processes.

In going through changes, Willow engaged in what is known as a kaizen blitz, an attempt to create lean manufacturing systems in as short a period as possible. This put further pressure on Willow's teams. Therefore, at the end of each day, the teams met to evaluate the day's work and create a to-do list for the next day. Often, the teams were engaged in hour-by-hour planning.

Wild found that the system worked well. "It allowed us to implement improvements and make progress before we even had time to create barriers to the ideas. The key was the involvement of all employees, so that the processes we documented were sound and accepted by the people who had to use them."

Willow's vice-president, Linda Snow, says that the intensity and adrenalin rush of the kaizen blitz helped to create the successful team environment that is now part of Willow. "It was a self-imposed test in which we began to believe in our ability as a team and see how far we could stretch the improvement envelope in a short time."

The teamwork did not end once new procedures were put in place. Today, employees are consulted before a new piece of equipment is purchased. They also decide which shifts and hours they will work, giving them some control over the balance between work and family life.

Wild suggests that teamwork is essential to the company's success. "We've got a great group of people and they are the ones that are driving all of these changes, not me. It's the team that's driving the system. That is what all manufacturers need to do if they want to stay in business."

OVERVIEW

Dennis Wild and Willow Manufacturing are not alone in the shift toward using groups and teams to produce goods and services that better meet customers' needs. Companies such as Zellers, Xerox Canada, Dofasco, Toyota Canada, Westinghouse Canada, and Sears Canada are all relying on teams to help them gain a competitive advantage.[2] In this chapter, we look in detail at how groups and teams can contribute to organizational effectiveness, and at the types of groups and teams used in organizations. We discuss how different elements of group dynamics influence the functioning and effectiveness of groups, and we describe how managers can motivate group members to achieve organizational goals and reduce social loafing in groups and teams. By the end of this chapter, you will appreciate why the effective management of groups and teams is a key ingredient for organizational performance and a source of competitive advantage.

WHY THE POPULARITY OF GROUPS AND TEAMS IN THE WORKPLACE?

Think About It

Creating Workplaces That Encourage Teamwork

Markham, Ontario-based Steelcase Canada has designed its office space to support teamwork, and "transform the ways people work."[3] The company started by removing private offices, so that not even Steelcase Canada's president, Jim Mitchell, has a private office. Mitchell, those who report to him directly, and their secretaries share open offices. Some sales employees don't have offices at all, setting up their cordless phones, laptops, and portable trolleys with files in open workspace. The new space is "organized around networks of trust and social monitoring."

The company is now designed around a hub, where the operating divisions are organized, and there is space for casual interaction, as well as coffee and meals. Walls are made of glass, letting everyone see the work that the company does, including its manufacturing department. While Steelcase's layout encourages teamwork, there are areas set aside so that private meetings can be held without disruption. One of the architects in charge of the project noted that, overall, "The merging of the diverse aspects of the headquarter facilities creates an environment where the shared activities of all of these groups is productive for the organization."

Question

1. Why would a company such as Steelcase redesign its office space to support teamwork rather than individual work?

It's difficult to escape reading about teams if you pick up almost any business magazine. Teams are widely used these days. A Conference Board of Canada report found that more than 80 percent of its 109 respondents used teams in the workplace.[4] In the United States at least half of the employees at 80 percent of Fortune 500 companies work on teams, while 68 percent of small manufacturers use teams in their production areas.[5]

Teams increase an organization's competitive advantage (see Figure 10.1) by:

At Burnaby, BC-based Dominion Information Services Inc., teamwork is everything. The company publishes yellow and white telephone directories in British Columbia, Alberta, Ontario, and Quebec, as well as online at SuperPages.ca. Teamwork is a necessity for doing business and has led to a high degree of quality in the many innovative products and services the company provides.

- *Enhancing its performance.* People working in teams are able to produce more or higher quality outputs than would have been produced if each person had worked separately and all their individual efforts had been combined.

- *Increasing its responsiveness to customers.* Bringing salespeople, research and development experts, and members of other departments together in a group or cross-functional team can enhance responsiveness to customers by increasing the skills and expertise available.

- *Increasing innovation.* Managers can better encourage innovation by creating teams of diverse individuals who together have the knowledge relevant to a particular type of innovation, rather than by relying on individuals working alone.

- *Increasing employees' motivation and satisfaction.* Members of teams are likely to be more highly motivated and satisfied than they would have been while working on their own. The experience of working alongside other highly charged and motivated people can be very stimulating.

Figure 10.1 | Groups' and Teams' Contributions to Organizational Effectiveness

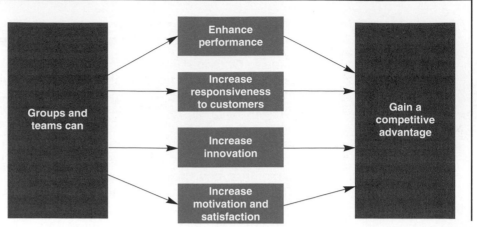

TYPES OF GROUPS AND TEAMS

Think About It

Self-Managed Teams at Langley Memorial Reduce Management Costs

Langley Memorial Hospital, in Langley, BC, has organized its materiel services department as a self-managed team.[6] The team, consisting of 3 department buyers plus 18 other full- and part-time staff for all other services, is responsible for managing inventory, adjusting the workload, and improving customer service. Staff members are encouraged to help make decisions and implement ideas. Because the team is self-managed, there is less direct supervision of staff.

Departmental performance is measured by outcome indicators such as inventory level, inventory turnover rates, in-house service levels, and lost time. Staff members compare data with previous periods "to look at trends, incremental changes, and performance indicators that compare how well [they] are doing compared with targeted benchmarks."

Questions
1. Why would an organization choose self-managed work teams?
2. What other types of teams are there in organizations?

group
Two or more people who interact with each other to reach certain goals or meet certain needs.

team
A group whose members work intensely with each other to achieve a specific common goal or objective.

top-management team
A group composed of the CEO, the president, and the heads of the most important departments.

A **group** may be defined as two or more people who interact with each other to reach certain goals or meet certain needs.[7] A **team** is a group whose members work intensely with each other to achieve a specific common goal or objective. As these definitions imply, all teams are groups but not all groups are teams. The two characteristics that distinguish teams from groups are the *intensity* with which team members work together and the presence of a *specific, overriding team goal or objective*. Organizations use a variety of groups and teams in the workplace. We describe a few of these in the next few pages (see Figure 10.2).

The Top-Management Team

A central concern of the CEO and president of a company is to form a **top-management team** to help the organization achieve its mission and goals.

Figure 10.2 | Types of Groups and Teams in Organizations

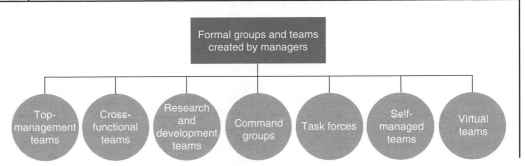

Top-management teams are responsible for developing the strategies that produce an organization's competitive advantage; most have between five and seven members. In forming their top-management teams, CEOs are well advised to stress diversity—in expertise, skills, knowledge, and experience. Thus, many top-management teams are **cross-functional teams**: They include members of different departments, such as finance, marketing, production, and engineering. Diversity helps ensure that the top-management team will have all the background and resources it needs to make good decisions.

cross-functional team
A group of individuals from different departments brought together to perform organizational tasks.

Research and Development Teams

Managers in pharmaceuticals, computers, electronics, electronic imaging, and other high-tech industries often create **research and development teams** to develop new products. Managers select R&D team members on the basis of their expertise and experience in a certain area. Sometimes R&D teams are cross-functional teams with members from departments such as engineering, marketing, and production in addition to members from the research and development department.

research and development team
A team whose members have the expertise and experience needed to develop new products.

Command Groups

Subordinates who report to the same supervisor form a **command group**. When top managers design an organization's structure and establish reporting relationships and a chain of command, they are essentially creating command groups. Command groups, often called *departments* or *units*, perform a significant amount of the work in many organizations. In order to have command groups that help an organization gain a competitive advantage, managers need to motivate group members to perform at a high level, and managers need to be effective leaders. Examples of command groups include the salespeople in the Bay who report to the same supervisor, the employees of a small swimming pool sales and maintenance company who report to a general manager, the telephone operators at the Manulife Financial insurance company who report to the same supervisor, and workers on an automobile assembly line at Ford Canada who report to the same first-line manager.

command group
A group composed of subordinates who report to the same supervisor; also called a department or unit.

Task Forces

Managers form **task forces** to accomplish specific goals or solve problems in a certain time period; task forces are sometimes called *ad hoc committees*. When Vancouver Island–based Myra Falls copper and zinc mine was purchased in 1998 by Swedish-controlled Boliden AB, the mine had been facing labour strife for years.[8] Boliden sent over a new mine manager to help get things in order. His first job was to set up five task forces geared to key problem areas. For instance, the

task force
A committee of managers or nonmanagerial employees from various departments or divisions who meet to solve a specific, mutual problem; also called an ad hoc committee.

ground support task force found that the previous owners had neglected a number of safety problems. The task forces' recommendations were followed, and $15 million worth of improvements were done. This sent a strong signal to employees that the new management team was concerned about its employees. Task forces can be a valuable tool for busy managers who do not have the time to explore an important issue in depth on their own.

Sometimes organizations need to address a long-term or enduring problem or issue facing an organization, such as how to contribute most usefully to the local community or how to make sure that the organization provides opportunities for potential employees with disabilities. Task forces that are relatively permanent are often referred to as *standing committees.* Membership in standing committees changes over time. Members may have, for example, a two- or three-year term on the committee, and memberships expire at varying times so that there are always some members with experience on the committee. Managers often form and maintain standing committees to make sure that important issues continue to be addressed.

Self-Managed Work Teams

> **self-managed (or self-directed) work teams**
> Groups of employees who supervise their own activities and monitor the quality of the goods and services they provide.

Langley Memorial Hospital
www.city.langley.bc/commun/hospital.htm

Self-managed (or self-directed) work teams, such as that found at Langley Memorial Hospital, are teams whose members are empowered and have the responsibility and autonomy to complete identifiable pieces of work. On a day-to-day basis, team members decide what the team will do, how it will do it, and which team members will perform specific tasks.[9] Managers provide self-managed work teams with their overall goals (such as assembling defect-free computer keyboards) but let team members decide how to meet those goals. Managers usually form self-managed work teams to improve quality, increase motivation and satisfaction, and lower costs. Often, by creating self-managed work teams, they combine tasks that individuals used to perform on their own, so the team is responsible for the whole set of tasks that yield an identifiable output or end product. The Conference Board of Canada found that self-directed work teams are used in a variety of manufacturing environments (e.g., the auto and chemicals industries) and service environments (e.g., hotels, banks, and airlines).[10]

Managers can take a number of steps to ensure that self-managed work teams are effective and help an organization gain a competitive advantage:[11]

- Give teams enough responsibility and autonomy to be truly self-managing. Refrain from telling team members what to do or solving problems for them even if you (as a manager) know what should be done.

- Make sure that a team's work is sufficiently complex so that it entails a number of different steps or procedures that must be performed and results in some kind of finished end product.

- Carefully select members of self-managed work teams. Team members should have the diversity of skills needed to complete the team's work, have the ability to work with others, and want to be part of a team.

- Recognize that self-managed work teams need guidance, coaching, and support, not direct supervision. Managers should be a resource for teams to turn to when needed.

- Analyze what type of training team members need, and provide it. Working in a self-managed work team often requires that employees have more extensive technical and interpersonal skills.

Managers in a wide variety of organizations have found that self-managed work teams help the organization achieve its goals.[12] However, self-managed work teams can run into trouble. Members are often reluctant to discipline one another by withholding bonuses from members who are not performing up to par or by firing members.[13]

They are also reluctant to evaluate each other's performance and determine pay levels. One reason for team members' discomfort may be the close personal relationships they sometimes develop with each other. In addition, sometimes members of self-managed work teams actually take longer to accomplish tasks, such as when team members have difficulties coordinating their efforts.

Virtual Teams

virtual team

A team whose members rarely or never meet face to face and interact by using various forms of information technology such as email, computer networks, telephones, faxes, and videoconferences.

Virtual teams are teams whose members rarely or never meet face to face and instead interact by using various forms of information technology such as email, computer networks, telephones, faxes, and videoconferences. As organizations become increasingly global and have operations in far-flung regions of the world, and as the need for specialized knowledge increases due to advances in technology, virtual teams allow managers to create teams to solve problems or explore opportunities without being limited by the need for team members to be working in the same geographic location.[14]

Take the case of an organization that has manufacturing facilities in Australia, Canada, the United States, and Mexico, and is encountering a quality problem in a complex manufacturing process. Each of its manufacturing facilities has a quality control team that is headed by a quality control manager. The vice-president for production does not try to solve the problem by forming and leading a team at one of the four manufacturing facilities; instead, she forms and leads a virtual team composed of the quality control managers of the four plants and the plants' general managers. Team members communicate via email and videoconferencing, and a wide array of knowledge and experience is brought to bear to solve the problem.

The principal advantage of virtual teams is that they enable managers to disregard geographic distances and form teams whose members have the knowledge, expertise, and experience to tackle a particular problem or take advantage of a specific opportunity.[15] Virtual teams can include members who are not employees of the organization itself. For example, a virtual team might include members of an organization that is used for outsourcing. More and more companies—including Hewlett-Packard, Pricewaterhouse Coopers, and Kodak—are either using or exploring the use of virtual teams.[16]

Beware! Teams Aren't Always the Answer

Though we have given lots of information about how teams are used in the workplace, teams are not always the best way to get work done. Because teams have increased communication demands, have more conflicts to manage, and need more meetings, the benefits of using teams have to exceed the costs.

When trying to determine if a team is appropriate to the situation, consider the following:[17]

- Can the work be performed better by an individual? If so, it is not necessary to form a team.

- Can the team provide more value than the individual? For instance, new-car dealer service departments have introduced teams that link customer service staff, mechanics, parts specialists, and sales representatives. These teams can better manage customer needs.

- Are there interdependent tasks, so that employees have to rely on each other to get work completed? Teamwork often makes interdependent work go more smoothly.

Other situations where organizations would find teams more useful include:

When work processes cut across functional lines; when speed is important (and complex relationships are involved); when the organization mirrors a complex, differentiated and rapidly changing market environment; when innovation and learning have priority; when the tasks that have to be done require online integration of highly interdependent performers.[18]

GROUP DYNAMICS

Think About It

Virtual Teams Require Planning

Doug Harrison, vice-president and managing director of Ryder System Inc. in Mississauga, Ontario, feels that his company has been transformed by using virtual teams to serve clients.[19] Ryder provides outsourced logistics for such blue-chip clients as General Motors, DaimlerChrysler, Nortel Networks, and Hewlett-Packard. It's been a challenge for managers, of course, because they are responsible for everyone on the team, not just people in their own department. The benefit, however, is that the teams allow "a much quicker response time to the market so we don't have to worry about following these departmental hierarchies," Harrison says.

Getting this to work at Ryder required new skills and new thinking for everyone. "We spent a lot of time training people and coaching our management to get out of their old thought processes of operating a hierarchical organization and start thinking about this team environment."

Question
1. What factors help groups to function more effectively?

Ryder Canada
www.ryder.com/north_
america_cae.shtml

How groups and teams function and how effective they will ultimately be depends on a number of characteristics and processes known collectively as *group dynamics*. In this section, we discuss five key elements of group dynamics: group size and roles; group leadership; group development; group norms; and group cohesiveness. As we mentioned earlier in the chapter, teams and groups are not the same thing, though some of their processes are similar. Thus, much of what we call group dynamics here also applies to teams.

Group Size and Roles

Managers need to take group size and group roles into account as they create and maintain high-performing groups and teams.

Group Size

The number of members in a group can be an important determinant of members' motivation and commitment and of group performance. There are several advantages to keeping a group relatively small—between two and nine members. Compared with members of large groups, members of small groups tend to

- interact more with each other and find it easier to coordinate their efforts;

- be more motivated, satisfied, and committed;

- find it easier to share information;

- be better able to see the importance of their personal contributions for group success.

Recognizing these advantages, Nathan Myhrvold, former chief technology officer at Microsoft Corporation, found that eight is the ideal size for the types of R&D teams he would form to develop new software.[20] A disadvantage of small rather than large groups is that members of small groups have fewer resources available to accomplish their goals.

Large groups—with 10 or more members—also offer some advantages. They have at their disposal more resources to achieve group goals than do small groups. These resources include the knowledge, experience, skills, and abilities of group members as well as their actual time and effort. Large groups also have advantages stemming from the **division of labour**—splitting the work to be performed into particular tasks and assigning tasks to individuals. Individuals who specialize in particular tasks are likely to become skilled at performing those tasks and contribute significantly to high group performance.

Large groups suffer a number of problems, including greater communication and coordination difficulties and lower levels of motivation, satisfaction, and commitment. It is clearly more difficult to share information and coordinate activities when you are dealing with 16 people rather than 8. Moreover, members of large groups might not feel that their efforts are really needed and sometimes might not even feel a part of the group.

As a general rule of thumb, groups should have no more members than necessary to achieve a division of labour and provide the resources needed to achieve group goals. Group size is too large when[21]

- members spend more time communicating what they know to others rather than applying what they know to solve problems and create new products;

- individual productivity decreases;

- group performance suffers.

Group Roles

In forming groups and teams, managers need to communicate clearly the expectations for each group role, what is required of each member, and how the different roles in the group fit together to accomplish group goals. A **group role** is a set of behaviours and tasks that a member of a group is expected to perform because of his or her position in the group. Members of cross-functional teams, for example, are expected to perform roles relevant to their special areas of expertise. Managers also need to realize that group roles change and evolve as a group's tasks and goals change and as group members gain experience and knowledge. Thus, to get the performance gains that come from experience or "learning by doing," managers should encourage group members to take the initiative to modify their assigned roles by taking on extra responsibilities as they see fit. This process, called **role making**, can enhance individual and group performance.

Beyond the simple roles that each person fulfills in order to complete the task at hand, two major kinds of roles need to be discussed: task-oriented roles and maintenance roles. **Task-oriented roles** are performed by group members to make sure that the group accomplishes its tasks. **Maintenance roles** are carried out to make sure that team members have good relationships. For teams to be effective, there needs to be some balance between task orientation and relationship maintenance. Table 10.1 identifies a number of task-oriented and maintenance roles that you might find in a team.

In self-managed work teams and some other groups, group members themselves are responsible for creating and assigning roles. Many self-managed work teams also pick their own team leaders. When group members create their own roles, managers should be available in an advisory capacity, helping group members effectively settle conflicts and disagreements. At Johnsonville Foods, for example, the position

division of labour
Splitting the work to be performed into particular tasks and assigning tasks to individual workers.

group role
A set of behaviours and tasks that a member of a group is expected to perform because of his or her position in the group.

role making
Taking the initiative to modify an assigned role by taking on extra responsibilities.

task-oriented roles
Roles performed by group members to make sure the task gets done.

maintenance roles
Roles performed by group members to make sure there are good relations among group members.

Table 10.1 | Roles Required for Effective Group Functioning

	Function	Description	Example
Roles that build task accomplish-ment	Initiating	Stating the goal or problem, making proposals about how to work on it, setting time limits.	"Let's set up an agenda for discussing each of the problems we have to consider."
	Seeking information and opinions	Asking group members for specific factual information related to the task or problem, or for their opinions about it.	"What do you think would be the best approach to this, Jack?"
	Providing information and opinions	Sharing information or opinions related to the task or problems.	"I worked on a similar problem last year and found . . ."
	Clarifying	Helping one another understand ideas and suggestions that come up in the group.	"What you mean, Sue, is that we could . . .?"
	Elaborating	Building on one another's ideas and suggestions.	"Building on Don's idea, I think we could . . ."
	Summarizing	Reviewing the points covered by the group and the different ideas stated so that decisions can be based on full information.	Appointing a recorder to take notes on a blackboard.
	Consensus testing	Periodic testing about whether the group is nearing a decision or needs to continue discussion.	"Is the group ready to decide about this?"
Roles that build and maintain a group	Harmonizing	Mediating conflict among other members, reconciling disagreements, relieving tensions.	"Don, I don't think you and Sue really see the question that differently."
	Compromising	Admitting error at times of group conflict.	"Well, I'd be willing to change if you provided some help on . . ."
	Gatekeeping	Making sure all members have a chance to express their ideas and feelings and preventing members from being interrupted.	"Sue, we haven't heard from you on this issue."
	Encouraging	Helping a group member make his or her point. Establishing a climate of acceptance in the group.	"I think what you started to say is important, Jack. Please continue."

Source: D. Ancona, T. Kochan, M. Scully, J. Van Maanen, D.E. Westney, "Team Processes," in *Managing for the Future* (Cincinnati, OH: South-Western College Publishing, 1996), p. 9.

titles of first-line managers were changed to "advisory coach" to reflect the managers' new role vis-à-vis the self-managed work teams they oversee.[22]

Group Leadership

All groups and teams need leadership. Indeed, as we discussed in detail in Chapter 9, effective leadership is a key ingredient for high-performing groups, teams, and organizations. Sometimes managers assume the leadership role, as is the case in many command groups and top-management teams. Or a manager may appoint a member of a group who is not a manager to be group leader or chairperson, as is the case in a task force or standing committee. In other cases, group or team members may choose their own leaders, or a leader may emerge naturally as group members work together to achieve group goals. When managers empower members of self-managed work teams, they often let group members choose their own leaders. Some self-managed work teams find it effective to rotate the leadership role among their members. Whether leaders of groups and teams are managers or not, and whether they are appointed by managers or emerge naturally in a group, they play an important role in ensuring that groups and teams perform up to their potential.

Group Development Over Time

Every group's development over time is somewhat unique. However, researchers have identified five stages of group development that many groups seem to pass through (see Figure 10.3):[23]

- *Forming.* Members try to get to know each other and reach a common understanding of what the group is trying to accomplish and how group members should behave. During this stage, managers should strive to make each member feel like a valued part of the group.

- *Storming.* Group members experience conflict and disagreements because some members do not wish to submit to the demands of other group members. Disputes may arise over who should lead the group. Self-managed work teams can be particularly vulnerable during the storming stage. Managers need to keep an eye on groups at this stage to make sure that conflict does not get out of hand.

- *Norming.* Close ties between group members develop, and feelings of friendship and camaraderie emerge. Group members arrive at a consensus about what goals they should be aiming to achieve and how group members should behave toward one another.

- *Performing.* The real work of the group gets accomplished during this stage. Depending on the type of group in question, managers need to take different steps at this stage to help ensure that groups are effective. Managers of command groups need to make sure that group members are motivated and that they are effectively leading group members. Managers overseeing self-managed work teams have to empower team members and make sure that teams are given enough responsibility and autonomy at the performing stage.

- *Adjourning.* This stage applies only to groups that eventually are disbanded, such as task forces. During adjourning, a group is dispersed. Sometimes, adjourning takes place when a group completes a finished product, such as when a task force evaluating the pros and cons of providing on-site child care produces a report supporting its recommendation.

Managers need a flexible approach to group development and need to keep attuned to the different needs and requirements of groups at the various stages.[24] Above all else, and regardless of the stage of development, managers need to think of themselves as *resources* for groups. Thus, managers always should be trying to find ways to help groups and teams function more effectively.

Group Norms

group norms

Shared guidelines or rules for behaviour that most group members follow.

All groups, whether top-management teams, self-managed work teams, or command groups, need to control their members' behaviour to ensure that the group performs well and meets its goals. Roles as well as group norms control behaviour in groups.[25] **Group norms** are shared guidelines or rules for behaviour that most group members follow. Groups develop norms for a wide variety of behaviours, including working hours, the sharing of information among group members, how

Figure 10.3 | **Five Stages of Group Development**

certain group tasks should be performed, and even how members of a group should dress.

Managers should encourage members of a group to develop norms that contribute to group performance and the attainment of group goals. These could include group norms that dictate that each member of a cross-functional team should always be available for the rest of the team when his or her input is needed, return phone calls as soon as possible, inform other team members of travel plans, and give team members a phone number at which he or she can be reached when travelling on business. Virtual teams such as those at Ryder System Inc. in Mississauga, Ontario establish such norms as how often to have conference calls and how often they should meet face to face in order to increase their ability to communicate effectively.

Conformity and Deviance

Group members conform to norms for three reasons:[26]

- They want to obtain rewards and avoid punishments.

- They want to imitate group members whom they like and admire.

- They have internalized the norm and believe it is the right and proper way to behave.

Failure to conform, or deviance, occurs when a member of a group violates a group norm. Deviance signals that a group is not controlling one of its members' behaviours. Groups generally respond to members who behave deviantly in one of three ways:[27]

- The group might try to get the member to change his or her deviant ways and conform to the norm. Group members might try to convince the member of the need to conform, or they might ignore or even punish the deviant.

- The group might expel the member.

- The group might change the norm to be consistent with the member's behaviour.

That last alternative suggests some deviant behaviour can be functional for groups. Deviance is functional for a group when it causes group members to stop and evaluate norms that may be dysfunctional but that are taken for granted by the group. Often, group members do not think about why they behave in a certain way or why they follow certain norms. Deviance can cause group members to reflect on their norms and change them when appropriate, such as when a new employee comes up with a new procedure, because she wasn't aware of "the right way" to do something, and everyone realizes it's a better way.

Encouraging a Balance of Conformity and Deviance

In order for groups and teams to be effective and help an organization gain a competitive advantage, they need to have the right balance of conformity and deviance (see Figure 10.4). A group needs a certain level of conformity to ensure that it can control members' behaviour and channel it in the direction of high performance and group goal accomplishment. A group also needs a certain level of deviance to ensure that dysfunctional norms are discarded and replaced with functional ones. Balancing conformity and deviance is a pressing concern for all groups, whether they are top-management teams, R&D teams, command groups, or self-managed work teams.

Managers can take several steps to ensure that there is enough tolerance of deviance in groups so that group members are willing to deviate from dysfunctional norms:

Figure 10.4 | Balancing Conformity and Deviance in Groups

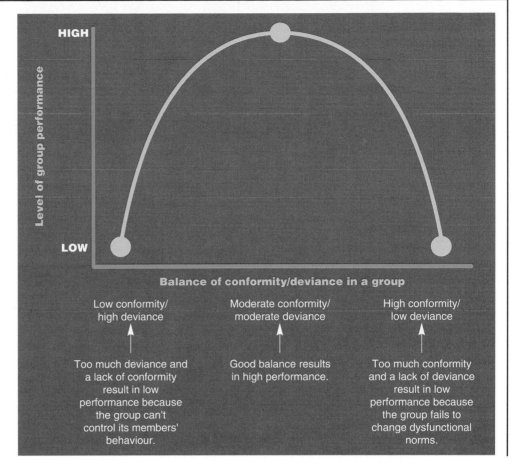

- Be role models by not rigidly insisting on existing norms and procedures.

- Encourage openness to new norms and procedures.

- Encourage the evaluation of existing norms.

Group Cohesiveness

group cohesiveness
The degree to which members are attracted or loyal to a group.

Another important element of group dynamics that affects group performance and effectiveness is **group cohesiveness**, the degree to which members are attracted or loyal to their group or team.[28] When group cohesiveness is high, individuals strongly value their group membership, find the group very appealing, and have strong desires to remain part of the group. When group cohesiveness is low, group members do not find their group particularly appealing and have little desire to retain their group membership. Research suggests that managers should aim to have a moderate level of cohesiveness in the groups and teams they manage because that is most likely to contribute to an organization's competitive advantage.

Consequences of Group Cohesiveness

There are three major consequences of group cohesiveness: level of participation within a group, level of conformity to group norms, and emphasis on group goal accomplishment (see Figure 10.5).[29]

Figure 10.5 | Sources and Consequences of Group Cohesiveness

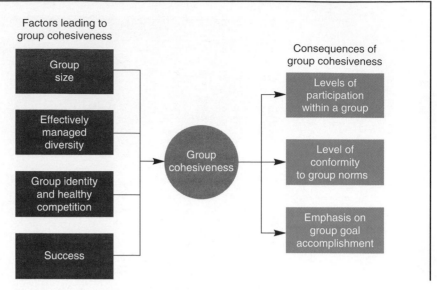

As group cohesiveness grows, the extent of group members' participation within the group increases. A moderate level of group cohesiveness helps to ensure that group members take an active part in the group and communicate effectively with each other. Increasing levels of group cohesiveness result in increasing levels of conformity to group norms. Groups need a balance of conformity and deviance, so a moderate level of cohesiveness often yields the best outcome. And finally, as group cohesiveness grows, emphasis on group goal accomplishment also increases within a group. A moderate level of cohesiveness motivates group members to accomplish both group and organizational goals.

MANAGING GROUPS AND TEAMS FOR HIGH PERFORMANCE

Think About It

Dofasco Uses Teams to Beat Other Steelmakers

Hamilton, Ontario-based Dofasco Inc., under the leadership of CEO John Mayberry, has posted impressive results in recent years.[30] It posted a profit in 2002, while famous steelmakers Bethlehem Steel and National Steel were looking at bankruptcy protection. (Bethlehem Steel has since been bought by International Steel Group Inc., and National Steel by United States Steel Corp.)

Before retiring in spring 2003, Mayberry relied on his employees to help with Dofasco's success, and he involved them in various team-building exercises, including taking them all to a ski resort for "experiential learning" exercises. Multidisciplinary teams have a lot of responsibility at Dofasco. They receive improvement goals from management, but are required to develop their own plans to reach the goals. When explaining how the teams work, Mayberry reported that "The supervisor became less of an a—-kicker and more of a resource person."

Question

1.   How can organizations create effective teams?

Dofasco Inc.
www.dofasco.ca

Now that you have a good understanding of the reasons why groups and teams are so important for organizations, the types of groups that managers create, and group dynamics, we consider additional steps that managers can take to make sure groups and teams perform highly and contribute to organizational effectiveness. Managers who want top-performing groups and teams need to (1) motivate group members to work toward the achievement of organizational goals, (2) prevent groupthink, (3) reduce social loafing, and (4) help groups to manage conflict effectively.

Motivating Group Members to Achieve Organizational Goals

Managers can motivate members of groups and teams to reach organizational goals and create a competitive advantage by making sure that the members themselves benefit when the group or team performs highly. If members of a self-managed work team know that they will receive a percentage of any cost savings that the team discovers and implements, they probably will try to cut costs. For example, Canadian Tire offers team incentives to employees of its gas bars. "Secret" retail shoppers visit the outlets on a regular basis, and score them on such factors as cleanliness, manner in which the transaction was processed, and the types of products offered, using a 100-point scoring system. Scores above a particular threshold provide extra compensation that is shared by the team. Xerox Canada, through its XTRA program, rewards districts for achieving profit and customer satisfaction targets. Everyone in the district shares equally in the bonuses.

Managers often rely on some combination of individual and group-based incentives to motivate members of groups and teams to work toward reaching organizational goals and a competitive advantage. When individual performance within a group can be assessed, pay is often determined by individual performance or by both individual and group performance. When individual performance within a group cannot be assessed accurately, then group performance should be the key determinant of pay levels.

Benefits that managers can make available to group members when a group performs highly could also include equipment and computer software, awards and other forms of recognition, and choice future work assignments. For example, members of self-managed work teams that develop new software at companies such as Microsoft often value working on interesting and important projects, and so members of teams that perform highly are rewarded with interesting and important new projects.

Preventing Groupthink

groupthink
A pattern of faulty and biased decision making that occurs in groups whose members strive for agreement among themselves at the expense of accurately assessing information relevant to a decision.

We have been focusing on the steps that managers can take to encourage high levels of performance in groups. Managers, however, need to be aware of an important downside to group and team work: the potentials for groupthink, social loafing, and conflict, all of which can reduce group performance. **Groupthink** occurs when group members become so focused on reaching agreement that they stop examining alternative courses of action and try to prevent the full expression of deviant, minority, or unpopular views within the group. The group pressure to conform causes a deterioration in an individual's mental efficiency, reality testing, and moral judgment.[31]

Groupthink does not affect all groups. It seems to occur most often where there is a clear group identity, where members hold a positive image of their group that they want to protect, and where the group perceives an outside threat to this positive image.[32] Groupthink is less about preventing dissent among group members and more about ways for a group to protect its positive image.

Groupthink can be minimized.[33] Group leaders need to play an impartial role, actively seek input from all members, and avoid expressing their own opinions early on in the discussion. One group member could be appointed to the role of devil's advocate, explicitly challenging the majority position and offering a different perspective. The group should also actively seek out discussion of diverse alternatives, and consider the negative sides of all alternatives. By doing so, the group is less likely to prevent dissenting views and more likely to gain an objective evaluation of each alternative.

Reducing Social Loafing in Groups

social loafing

The tendency of individuals to put forth less effort when they work in groups than when they work alone.

Social loafing is the tendency of individuals to put forth less effort when they work in groups than when they work alone.[34] Have you ever watched one or two group members who never seemed to be pulling their weight?

Social loafing can occur in all kinds of groups and teams and in all kinds of organizations. It can result in lower group performance and may even prevent a group from reaching its goals. Fortunately, managers can take steps to reduce social loafing, by making sure that individual contributions are recognizable, emphasizing the valuable contributions of each individual, and making sure that the group size is not too large (see Figure 10.6). Individuals who feel their contributions matter will be less likely to engage in social loafing.

Helping Groups to Manage Conflict Effectively

At some point or other, practically all groups experience conflict either within the group (intragroup conflict) or with other groups (intergroup conflict). In Chapter 12, we discuss conflict in depth and explore ways to manage it effectively. As you will learn there, managers can take several steps to help groups manage conflict and disagreements.

Tips for Managers

Group Dynamics and Managing Groups and Teams for High Performance

1. Make sure that members of groups and teams personally benefit when the group or team performs highly.

2. Form groups and teams with no more members than are necessary to achieve group and team goals.

3. Clearly communicate to members of groups and teams the expectations for their roles and how the different roles in the group fit together.

4. Encourage group and team members to periodically assess the appropriateness of existing norms.

Figure 10.6 | Three Ways to Reduce Social Loafing

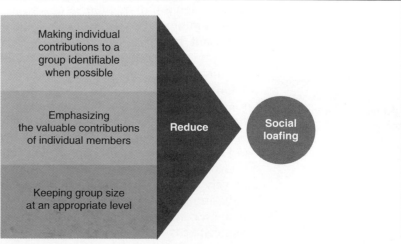

Chapter Summary

SUMMARY AND REVIEW

WHY THE POPULARITY OF GROUPS AND TEAMS IN THE WORKPLACE? A group is two or more people who interact with each other to reach certain goals or meet certain needs. A team is a group whose members work intensely with each other to achieve a specific common goal or objective. Groups and teams can contribute to organizational effectiveness by enhancing performance, increasing responsiveness to customers, increasing innovation, and being a source of motivation for their members.

TYPES OF GROUPS AND TEAMS Managers can establish a variety of groups and teams to reach organizational goals. These include cross-functional teams, top-management teams, research and development teams, command groups, task forces, self-managed work teams, and virtual teams. Teams may not always be the answer for reaching a goal, however.

GROUP DYNAMICS Key elements of group dynamics are group size and roles; group leadership; group development; group norms; and group cohesiveness. The advantages and disadvantages of large and small groups suggest that managers should form groups with no more members than are needed to provide the human resources the group needs to reach its goals and use a division of labour. A group role is a set of behaviours and tasks that a member of a group is expected to perform because of his or her position in the group. All groups and teams need leadership.

Five stages of development that many groups pass through are *forming, storming, norming, performing,* and *adjourning.*

Group norms are shared rules for behaviour that most group members follow. To be effective, groups need a balance of conformity and deviance. Conformity allows a group to control its members' behaviour in order to achieve group goals; deviance provides the impetus for needed change.

Group cohesiveness is the attractiveness of a group or team to its members. As group cohesiveness increases, so, too, do the level of participation and communication within a group, the level of conformity to group norms, and the emphasis on group goal accomplishment. Managers should strive to achieve a moderate level of group cohesiveness in the groups and teams they manage.

MANAGING GROUPS AND TEAMS FOR HIGH PERFORMANCE To make sure that groups and teams perform highly, managers need to motivate group members to work toward the achievement of organizational goals, prevent groupthink, reduce social loafing, and help groups to manage conflict effectively. Managers can motivate members of groups and teams to work toward the achievement of organizational goals by making sure that members personally benefit when their group or team performs highly.

Roles in Contrast: Considerations

MANAGERS	EMPLOYEES
Teams should be used when an individual cannot do the job alone, if a variety of skills or knowledge is needed, and if individuals need to rely on each other to get the work done.	Teams can be more effective than individuals in a variety of situations. Thus it is helpful to learn how to be an effective team member.
As a manager, it's important to consider group size, diversity of team members, and ways to encourage team identity as part of developing an effective team.	Groups that are cohesive are more effective, as long as they are not so cohesive that they don't question each other. You might want to encourage positive group inter-actions, and a spirit of challenging each other positively to allow alternative viewpoints to be expressed.
Team members should be encouraged to avoid conformity, and to explore diverse ideas and opinions to help them avoid groupthink.	Teams can go through stages, and storming (conflict) is one of those stages. If the conflict seems temporary, as team members try to sort out their roles, this may not really be a problem.

MANAGEMENT in Action

Topics for Discussion and Action

1. Why do all organizations need to rely on groups and teams to achieve their goals and gain a competitive advantage?
2. Interview one or more managers in an organization in your local community to identify the types of groups and teams that the organization uses to achieve its goals.
3. Think about a group of which you are a member, and describe your group's current stage of development. Does the development of this group seem to be following the forming-storming-norming-performing-adjourning stages described in the chapter?
4. Discuss the reasons why too much conformity can hurt groups and their organizations.
5. Why do some groups have very low levels of cohesiveness?
6. Imagine that you are the manager of a hotel. What steps will you take to reduce social loafing by members of the cleaning staff who are responsible for keeping all common areas and guest rooms spotless?

Building Management Skills

DIAGNOSING GROUP FAILURES

Think about the last dissatisfying or discouraging experience you had as a member of a group or team. Perhaps the group did not accomplish its goals, perhaps group members could agree about nothing, or perhaps there was too much social loafing. Now answer the following questions.

1. What type of group was this?
2. Were group members motivated to achieve group goals? Why or why not?
3. What were the group's norms? How much conformity and deviance existed in the group?
4. How cohesive was the group? Why do you think the group's cohesiveness was at this level? What consequences did this level of group cohesiveness have for the group and its members?
5. Was social loafing a problem in this group? Why or why not?
6. What could the group's leader or manager have done differently to increase group effectiveness?
7. What could group members have done differently to increase group effectiveness?

Management for You

One of your professors has just informed your class that you will be working on a new major assignment worth 30 percent of your course mark. The assignment is to be done in teams of 7. Realistically you will need to function as a virtual team, because it turns out that each of you has a different work and class schedule, so that there is almost no time when more than 3 people could meet face to face. As you know, virtual teams have benefits, but they can also face problems. How will you build group cohesiveness of this team? What norms might help the team function, and how should the norms be decided? What will you do to prevent social loafing?

Small Group Breakout Exercise

CREATING A CROSS-FUNCTIONAL TEAM

Form groups of 3 or 4 people, and appoint 1 member as the spokesperson who will communicate your findings to the whole class when called on by the instructor. Then discuss the following scenario.

You are a group of managers in charge of food services for a large university. Recently, a survey of students, faculty, and staff was conducted to evaluate customer satisfaction with the food services provided by the university's 8 cafeterias. The results were disappointing, to put it mildly. Complaints ranged from dissatisfaction with the type and range of meals and snacks provided, operating hours, and food temperature, to unresponsiveness to current concerns about the importance of low-carb/high-protein diets and the preferences of vegetarians. You have decided to form a cross-functional team to further evaluate reactions to the food services and to develop a proposal for changes that can be made to increase customer satisfaction.

1. Indicate who should be on this important cross-functional team and why.
2. Describe the goals the team should be trying to achieve.
3. Describe the different roles team members will need to perform.
4. Describe the steps you will take to help ensure that the team has a good balance between conformity and deviance and a moderate level of cohesiveness.

Managing Ethically

Strana Corporation uses self-managed teams to develop and produce new greeting cards. Some of the members of the team are engaged in social loafing, and other members of the team are reluctant to say anything. Team members are supposed to provide performance evaluations of each other at the end of each project, but some rate everyone equally, to avoid conflict. This practice has caused low morale on the team, because hard work results in the same pay as loafing. Some team members are complaining that it's unethical to rate everyone the same way when individual performance differs so much. One team member has come to you for advice, because you are an expert in team performance and ethics. What would you advise this team member to do? How could the team's performance be improved?

Exploring the World Wide Web

SPECIFIC ASSIGNMENT

Many companies are committed to the use of teams, including Sears Canada. Scan Sears' website to learn more about this company (www.sears.ca). Then click on "Corporate Information," "Careers at Sears," and "Mission, Vision & Values."

1. What principles or values underlie Sears' use of teams?
2. How does Sears use teams to build employee commitment?

GENERAL ASSIGNMENT

Find the website of a company that relies heavily on teams to accomplish its goals. What kinds of teams does this company use? What steps do managers take to ensure that team members are motivated to perform at a high level?

You're the Management Consultant

VIRTUAL TEAM MEMBERS AVOID COMMUNICATING

Jill St. Pierre was recently hired in a boundary-spanning role for the global unit of an educational and professional publishing company. The company is headquartered in Halifax (where St. Pierre works) and has divisions in other countries. Each division is responsible for translating, manufacturing, marketing, and selling a set of books in its country. St. Pierre's responsibilities include interfacing with managers in each of the divisions in her region (Central and South America), overseeing their budgeting and financial reporting to headquarters, and heading up a virtual team consisting of herself and the top managers in charge of each of the divisions in her region. The virtual team is to promote global learning, explore new potential opportunities and markets, and address ongoing problems. She communicates directly with division managers via telephone and email, as well as written reports, memos, and faxes. When virtual team meetings are convened, videoconferencing is often used.

After her first few virtual team meetings, St. Pierre noticed that the managers seemed reluctant to speak up. Interestingly enough, when each manager communicates with her individually, mainly in telephone conversations, they tend to be very talkative and frank and she feels she has a good rapport with each of them. However, getting them to communicate with each other as a virtual team has been a real challenge. At the last meeting, she tried to prompt some of the managers to raise issues relevant to the agenda that she knew were on their minds from her individual conversations with them. Surprisingly, the managers skillfully avoided informing their fellow teammates about the heart of the issues in question. St. Pierre is confused and troubled. While she feels her other responsibilities are going well, she knows that her virtual team is not operating like a team at all and no matter what she tries, discussions in virtual team meetings are forced and generally unproductive. As an expert on team functioning, she has come to you for advice. What do you think is the cause of the problem and how should St. Pierre address it?

MANAGEMENT CASE

Teams Manage AES (With the Help of a Few Managers)

In the late 1970s, Dennis W. Bakke and R.W. Sant founded AES Corporation, a power company that sells electricity to public utilities and steam to industrial corporations. Since the early days, AES's revenues have been increasing, on average, about 23 percent per year, annual profits have reached the $155 million mark, and the company has grown to 1500 employees. AES has only four levels in its corporate hierarchy: workers, plant managers, division managers, and corporate managers. There are no corporate departments or managers in charge of areas such as purchasing, finance, human resources, or operations. Who oversees such activities? They are all handled by volunteer teams formed by plant managers and composed of rank-and-file workers. In a nutshell, AES appears to be a well-managed company with a minimum of managers and many teams.[35]

Do workers in an electric power plant make million-dollar investment decisions or negotiate major contracts with suppliers? This is exactly what is done at AES. Jeff Hatch, an employee in the Montville, Connecticut plant who performs activities such as unloading coal from barges, and Joe Oddo, a maintenance technician at the plant, are both part of a voluntary team that manages the plant's $51-million investment fund. Other teams of technicians handle the purchasing of materials—ranging from mops to turbines—and teams of engineers arrange financing for new plants. Multimillion-dollar contracts normally negotiated by CEOs are handled by teams of engineers as well. New employees are hired by teams with diverse members ranging from pipefitters to accountants.

Why does AES manage with teams (and without many managers)? According to Bakke and

Sant, four core values underlie this unique approach to management: integrity, social responsibility, fairness, and fun. Observes Sant, "Fun is when you're intellectually excited and you are interacting with others. . . . It's the struggle, and even the failures that go with it, that makes work fun."[36]

AES has experienced its share of failures as well as successes.

In 1992, seven workers falsified emission-control reports at the Shady Point, Oklahoma plant. When managers discovered and reported this violation to the authorities, the result was a $194 000 fine. Why did the violation occur? Sometimes team members feel so responsible for what happens at AES that they are afraid to admit when they make a mistake. The Shady Point workers who falsified the reports had been afraid they would be fired when managers realized emissions were high.

When problems like this occur, managers interpret them as a signal that the AES values are not coming through. Bakke and Sant felt so personally responsible for not getting AES's values across to the plant's employees that they reduced their own bonuses by more than 50 percent in 1992. To avoid a recurrence of this kind of problem, they also made it clear that employees in the plant can trust managers to stand by them even when they make a mistake.

True to the spirit of social responsibility, a team of employees in the Montville, Connecticut plant determined how much carbon dioxide the plant would release into the environment in the foreseeable future. The team then had thousands of trees planted in Guatemala to offset the omissions, to the tune of $3.1 million.

Making high-powered decisions can be stressful for AES employees. Paul Burdick, for example, described how he felt when, after being on the job as a mechanical engineer at AES for only a few months, he had major responsibility in a team to complete a $1.55-billion purchase of coal: "I'd never negotiated anything before, save for a used car . . . I was afraid to make some of the decisions." He found the experience very motivating, challenging, and energizing, however, while also feeling intense pressure to do "right" by other AES employees. As Burdick suggests, such intellectual stimulation has "a flip side . . . You're given a lot of leeway and a lot of rope. You can use it to climb or you can hang yourself."[37]

It seems that most employees might actually enjoy the stimulation of making important decisions and being responsible for them (and do not find it overly stressful), because AES's turnover rate is less than 1 percent. Nevertheless, suppliers, financiers, and company presidents often balk at having to negotiate and deal with rank-and-file workers in order to do business with AES. As Sant puts it, "Outside parties clearly are frustrated at having to deal with people who have more authority than top management. So many people want to come to the CEO, but we generally back off and say, 'It's up to these guys. You've just got to work these relationships.'"

What does coal handler Jeff Hatch think about this innovative use of teams at AES? "Who would have thought I'd be reading the *Wall Street Journal* every day and second-guessing Alan Greenspan? . . . It definitely makes it a lot more fun to show up for work every day."[38]

Questions

1. What are the advantages of AES's innovative use of teams?
2. What are the potential disadvantages of having teams of workers rather than managers make most of the important decisions?
3. Do you think Sant and Bakke's approach to managing AES would work in other companies? Why or why not?

MANAGEMENT CASE

From the Pages of the *Ottawa Citizen* Team Building Adventures More Than Game

When 40 employees from Hewlett-Packard's technology-finance division gathered in late November for a retreat at Chateau Montebello, they spent four days engaged in a variety of activities—discussing corporate strategy, upgrading their customer-support skills and navigating their way across a river infested with piranhas.

Piranha-infested rivers?

OK, so the flesh-eating fish were fictitious and the river turned out to be a harmless sandpit. But organizers of the retreat are hopeful that this make-believe adventure, in which colleagues had to help each other across a fake river using barrels and planks of plywood, will play a crucial role in the company's efforts to encourage teamwork and improve communication among its employees.

"We learned, as individuals, the value of communication, and how important it is to acknowledge the strengths that everyone brings to the group," said participant Lilie Venditti, who, when not sidestepping around imaginary piranhas or defusing fake bombs, manages Hewlett-Packard's Canadian Business Centre.

"These exercises really brought us closer together," she said. "Once we got back . . . I noticed that people were more open with each other."

These mock adventure games, in which groups of employees are forced to rely on each other to overcome adverse challenges, might seem like an unorthodox way to train personnel, but the concept is catching on with an increasing number of Canadian companies, who, wanting to foster teamwork and trust among employees, are forsaking traditional classroom-style lectures in favour of hands-on learning.

"When you have a talking head, be it on video or in front of a class, there's a low level of retention," said John Cross, vice-president, human resources, for Hewlett-Packard Canada Ltd. "We find that experiential learning is a far, far better learning experience. People tend to remember things through stories and this is a story that they can recall."

Stuart Robertson, a physical-education professor at Champlain College and veteran outdoor educator, put it even more simply: "You can sit in a classroom and talk all you want about downhill skiing," he said. "But you can't teach someone to ski without taking them on to a mountain."

Mr. Robertson, who is also an adjunct professor at Concordia University's department of exercise science, recently signed on to develop and facilitate team-building adventure programs for Atmosp(here) Communications, a Montreal firm that has built a reputation as an event planner but is now focusing its attention on experiential learning, through a new division entitled Naviquest.

Atmosp(here) Communications founder Jason Katz, who organized the Hewlett-Packard program, is working feverishly to build up his company's client base, convinced that corporations are ready to offer their employees more hands-on training. The company's program has just been accredited by Emploi Quebec—making it eligible under the provincial law requiring corporations to spend one per cent of their total salary on training and development programs each year. And the company is expected to launch a flagship outdoor-adventure centre at Hotel l'Esterel in the Laurentians next spring.

Working with Mr. Robertson and fellow outdoor educator Keith Wilkinson, Mr. Katz's company has crafted a series of activities that draw on the skills that employees need to develop in order to become more productive in the workplace. Challenges might include working together to defuse an imaginary bomb or getting a whole team of employees through an electrified spider web.

"Our goal is to put employees into situations that they have to conquer together; they need to find the best path in order to complete the task or defuse the situation, and that often means finding better ways of communicating with each other," Mr. Katz said.

"The activities may last only 20 minutes, but they are metaphors for what happens in life," Mr. Robertson added.

"While the impact of such programs is often difficult to measure, a growing body of literature suggests that companies benefit greatly when putting their employees through experiential-type learning activities," said Dan Romano, who oversees corporate training programs for H2O Adventures. He cites one survey that indicates companies can expect a 30-percent increase in productivity and a significant drop in employee absenteeism in the six months following the program.

"The investment comes back to these companies," he said. "It's often a question of how companies cannot afford to do this."

Starting out as a kayak company offering white-water rafting adventures along the Rouge River in Western Quebec, H2O Adventures began courting corporate clients about three years ago. Today, that slice of their business is growing exponentially and now represents about two-thirds of the company's total revenue.

Mr. Romano said some corporate executives are skeptical about the idea, mistaking the programs as nothing more than fun and games. And participants often enter with reservations of their own. "When they hear that there is a learning component to it, they think they'll be forced to sit through a lecture, where they will be told how to perform," he said.

A typical program often lasts anywhere from three hours to a full day, but can be tailored to cover up to an entire week. The two companies' client lists include corporations like Pfizer Canada Inc., Bristol-Myers Squibb Co., Future Electronics, London Life Insurance Company and hi-tech startups Hyperchip Inc. and Zero-Knowledge Systems.

Mr. Romano said it is no coincidence that his company's list of clients includes a high proportion of firms in the technology and pharmaceutical industries—not only do company heads from those milieus tend to be more progressive in their thinking, and thus more apt to try unorthodox training methods, but Mr. Romano said those industries are also most vulnerable to losing employees through corporate raiding.

"In the high-tech industry, for example, where staff are continuously being headhunted, and where the knowledge and ability inside an employee's head is the most valuable asset they have, it behooves them to have a really good team-building program in place, in order to develop a really loyal staff," he said.

But Steven Appelbaum, a management professor at Concordia's John Molson School of Business, cautions companies not to rely too much on off-site team-building programs, saying the lessons learned through simulated games and activities rarely translate into better working habits at the office. "The problem is that (these activities) do not correlate back to the workplace."

Employees participate in these activities "because they know it's what their managers want, so they get along with each other and play the role that's expected of them," he said. "But then, when they get back to the office on Monday morning, they put their armour back on and go back to their old patterns."

Instead, Mr. Appelbaum suggests companies that want to keep their employees motivated need to concentrate on old-fashioned, textbook style management techniques, such as opening communication channels and involving personnel in decision-making processes.

"It's the structures and behaviour of the organization that are the critical factors that determine whether you can get people to play ball for you, not whether your employees can rely on each other in a game," he said. "If an organization creates an environment where people feel empowered, where they feel motivated and where they are involved in making decisions, then you don't have to do all of this extra stuff."

But those involved in organizing experiential-learning programs disagree, insisting that the lessons learned do in fact translate back to the workplace. Activities are followed by debriefing sessions, where participants have a chance to analyse the skills they relied upon to complete their tasks. And Atmosp(here) Communications runs followup sessions back at the client's office within a month of the program.

"If we just ran these scenarios and left it at that, it could be considered fun and games,"

Mr. Robertson said. "But we go back to these people and help them transfer what they learned to the workplace."

"A lot of the success ends up being anecdotal," Hewlett-Packard's Mr. Cross admitted. "But clearly, relationships among employees tend to be stronger and communication is better."

Source: D. Cassoff, "Team Building Adventures More Than Game: Experts Disagree on the Usefulness of Mock Adventures Used to Motivate Employees," *Ottawa Citizen*, December 26, 2000, p. F6. Used with permission of Derek Cassoff.

Questions

1. What strategies does IBM Canada use to help develop teamwork?
2. There is clearly a debate regarding the usefulness of off-site team-building exercises. To what extent do you think these kinds of programs might be useful for team building?

CHAPTER 11

MANAGING HUMAN RESOURCES

Learning Objectives

1. Explain why strategic human resource management can help an organization gain a competitive advantage.

2. Describe the steps managers take to recruit and select organizational members.

3. Discuss the training and development options that ensure organizational members can perform their jobs effectively.

4. Explain the issues managers face in determining levels of pay and benefits.

5. Explain why performance appraisal and feedback is such a crucial activity, and list the choices managers must make in designing effective performance appraisal and feedback procedures.

Roles in Contrast: Questions

MANAGERS	EMPLOYEES
Is it better to outsource jobs or perform them within the organization?	Why do companies do so much outsourcing these days?
Is it better to recruit internally or hire from the outside?	Why does my manager hire new people rather than recruiting from within the organization?
What can I learn by using 360-degree appraisals?	Why would my manager ask those above *and* below me to evaluate me?

A CASE IN CONTRAST

TRAINING AND DEVELOPMENT AT COMTEK AND TD CANADA TRUST

Burlington, Ontario-based Comtek Advanced Structures Ltd. (www.comtekadvanced.com) manufactures aircraft parts.[1] The company also repairs the parts it makes for airliners, and for this task it needs experienced repair people.

"It's fairly specialized work, and we can only grow the business as fast as we have people available," says Patrick Whyte, Comtek's president. Getting enough trained people has been so difficult that Whyte decided to take matters into his own hands. In 1995, he created a three-year part-time apprenticeship program for his employees. The program consists of 12 learning modules on the repair of different aircraft parts, and is taught in-house. New employees can apply for the program after they have been with the firm for six months. Ontario's provincial government recognizes the program, and even supplies a certificate of accomplishment to graduates. The company, not the employee, pays for the program, which costs $15 000 per employee.

Whyte sees his investment in training as a good expenditure: The program attracts new hires, and it reduces turnover substantially. Employees stay with the company because they feel a sense of accomplishment through the course. "The return for us is that they may decide to spend the rest of their career here," he says. "People these days get a lot of their job satisfaction from the training."

Whyte has also been able to use the training to grow his business. When he started the company as a first-time CEO in 1994, the economy was booming and it was easy for the company to expand. By 2001, Comtek had grown to more than 100 employees from a start of 6 in 1994. In 2000 alone, Comtek doubled the number of its employees. Revenue grew more than 1500 percent to slightly more than $7 million between 1995 and 2000.

Both Comtek Advanced Structures and TD Bank Financial Group invest heavily in employee training and development. Both companies see this as an investment in their employees.

When Comtek faced a downturn in the turbulent environment of 2001, Whyte was philosophical. "If the economy slows down, regional airlines don't take on new airplanes, but they still have to repair the ones they have," he said. "I don't think in our sector we'd have any layoffs, but it's a question of growing more slowly." Whyte's training program may well be the key that keeps his company going.

Comtek is a small company, especially compared to something like TD Bank Financial Group (www.tdcanadatrust.com). So how does training differ for a big corporation? Instead of an apprenticeship program, TD takes a classroom approach, using satellites to deliver programs to 300 sites.[2] Some of these sites are in training centres where 100 people can attend a course together, while other sites are the lunchrooms of remote branches. TD's approach, offering much greater face-to-face delivery of material, differs from that of the Bank of Montreal (BMO), which delivers almost 80 percent of its training through computer programs and similar activities. BMO finds that its method allows students to forge their own path of learning, at their own pace, while Jane Hutcheson, TD's vice-president of learning and development, suggests that the benefit of TD's approach is that "You can interact in real time."

To find out what kinds of courses they should take, TD's employees log on to PeopleDevelopment@TD, a program that catalogues their strengths and also lets them see the skills required for all positions in the bank, including that of CEO. Employees are encouraged to sketch out a program with their manager to develop added competencies.

Like Whyte, Hutcheson sees training as an investment in employees, not a cost. She points out that employee education provides a 15-percent return to the bank. Although their means are dramatically different, Comtek's training and TD's development programs are achieving similar goals: ensuring that the companies are building the human resources they need to be effective and gain a competitive advantage. Moreover, managers in both companies realize how valuable training and development are for employees at all hierarchical levels, from entry level to top management.

OVERVIEW

Managers are responsible for acquiring, developing, protecting, and using the resources that an organization needs to be efficient and effective. One of the most important resources in all organizations is human resources—the people involved in the production and distribution of goods and services. Human resources include all members of an organization, ranging from top managers to entry-level employees. Effective managers such as Patrick Whyte and Jane Hutcheson in the *Case in Contrast* realize how valuable human resources are and take active steps to make sure that their organizations build and make best use of their human resources to gain a competitive advantage.

This chapter examines how managers can tailor their human resource management system to their organization's strategy and structure. We discuss in particular the major components of human resource management: recruitment and selection, training and development, pay and benefits, performance appraisal, and labour relations. By the end of this chapter, you will understand the central role that human resource management plays in creating a high-performing organization.

STRATEGIC HUMAN RESOURCE MANAGEMENT

Think About It

At Greenarm Management, Family Comes First

Earl Brewer, chair of Greenarm Management Ltd., believes in hiring employees who put people first.[3] "We don't want people working excessively and neglecting their families," he says. Turnover is low at the Fredericton, New Brunswick-based developer and property management firm. Brewer says that is because the company hires the right people: "They have to have passion for the job."

When *Atlantic Progress* magazine surveyed the employees, it found that they raved about working for the company. The employees commented that senior management leads by example. Because senior managers find it important to balance work life and family life, employees feel comfortable doing the same. As one employee explains, "I tell people that my company expects hard, good quality work, but also expects me and others to have a family life and to be happy."

Greenarm, named a Best Company to Work For in Atlantic Canada in 2001, is also a successful company. It is New Brunswick's largest private sector property management company.

Question

1. How do a company's human resource policies contribute to its success?

---

human resource management (HRM)

Activities that managers engage in to attract and retain employees and to ensure that they perform at a high level and contribute to the accomplishment of organizational goals.

strategic human resource management

The process by which managers design the components of a human resource management system to be consistent with each other, with other elements of organizational architecture, and with the organization's strategy and goals.

Human resource management (**HRM**) includes all the activities that managers engage in to attract and retain employees and to ensure that they perform at a high level and contribute to the accomplishment of organizational goals. **Strategic human resource management** is the process by which managers design the components of an HRM system to be consistent with each other, with other elements of organizational architecture, and with the organization's strategy and goals.[4] The objective of strategic HRM is the development of an HRM system that enhances an organization's efficiency, quality, innovation, and responsiveness to customers—the four building blocks of competitive advantage, which we discussed in Chapter 1.

Overview of the Components of HRM

An organization's human resource management system has five major components: recruitment and selection, training and development, performance appraisal and feedback, pay and benefits, and labour relations (see Figure 11.1). Managers use *recruitment and selection*, the first component of an HRM system, to attract and hire new employees who have the abilities, skills, and experiences that will help an organization achieve its goals. For instance, managers at New Brunswick's Greenarm Management hire people who put people first and are family-focused, because they believe this brings the right type of person to the company.

After recruiting and selecting employees, managers use the second component, *training and development*, to ensure that organizational members develop skills and abilities that will enable them to perform their jobs effectively in the present and the future. Training and development is an ongoing process, because changes in technology and the environment, as well as in an organization's goals and strategies, often require organizational members to learn new techniques and ways of working. The *Case in Contrast* describes Comtek's heavy investment in the development of repair people to ensure that they acquire the technical skills needed to find new ways to increase Comtek's revenues and profits.

The third component, *performance appraisal and feedback*, serves two purposes in HRM. First, performance appraisal can provide managers with the information

Figure 11.1 | Components of a Human Resource Management System

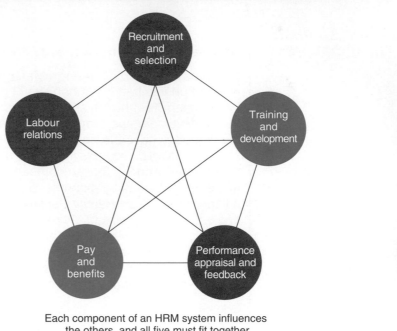

Each component of an HRM system influences
the others, and all five must fit together

they need to make good human resources decisions—decisions about how to train, motivate, and reward organizational members.[5] Thus, the performance appraisal and feedback component is a kind of control system that can be used with management by objectives (discussed in Chapter 7). Second, performance feedback from performance appraisal serves a developmental purpose for members of an organization. When managers regularly evaluate their subordinates' performance, they can provide subordinates with valuable information about their strengths and weaknesses and the areas in which they need to concentrate. On the basis of performance appraisals, managers distribute pay to employees.

In the fourth component of HRM, *pay and benefits,* managers distribute pay to employees, first by determining their starting salaries, and then later by determining whether raises or bonuses should be given. By rewarding high-performing organizational members with pay raises, bonuses, and the like, managers increase the likelihood that an organization's most valued human resources are motivated to continue their high levels of contribution to the organization. Moreover, when pay is linked to performance, high-performing employees are more likely to stay with the organization, and managers are more likely to be able to fill open positions with highly talented individuals. Benefits, such as health insurance, are important outcomes that employees receive by virtue of their membership in an organization.

Last but not least, *labour relations* includes the steps that managers take to develop and maintain good working relationships with the labour unions that may represent their employees' interests. For example, an organization's labour relations component can help managers establish safe working conditions and fair labour practices in their offices and plants.

Managers must ensure that all five of these components fit together and complement their companies' structure and control systems.[6] For example, if managers decide to decentralize authority and empower employees, they need to invest in training and development to ensure that lower-level employees have the knowledge and expertise they need to make the decisions that top managers would make in a more centralized structure.

Each of the five components of HRM influences the others (see Figure 11.1).[7] The kinds of people that the organization attracts and hires through recruitment and selection, for example, determine (1) the training and development that are necessary, (2) the appropriate levels of pay and benefits, and (3) the way performance is appraised.

RECRUITMENT AND SELECTION

Think About It

Amusement Parks Hire Seniors

Calgary's Calaway Park, Vancouver's Pacific National Exhibition (PNE), and Canada's Wonderland, in Vaughan, Ontario, used to hire only students to sell hot dogs, run the rides, and collect tickets each summer.[8] Now, they look to senior citizens for staffing needs as well.

Calaway Park's marketing director, Bob Williams, believes that senior citizens offer a good source of employees. "I think that the seniors market is more viable today than it was years ago. Seniors are hard workers. They're great workers." Lowell Schrieder, spokesperson for Canada's Wonderland, agrees: "We're trying to break the perception that we wouldn't hire beyond students. Seniors are just as good as the young ones. They're very congenial."

Question
1. Why would a company need to look for nontraditional employees when hiring?

recruitment
Activities that managers use to develop a pool of qualified candidates for open positions.

selection
The process that managers use to determine the relative qualifications of job applicants and the individuals' potential for performing well in a particular job.

human resource planning
Activities that managers use to forecast their current and future needs for human resources.

Recruitment includes all the activities that managers use to develop a pool of qualified candidates for open positions.[9] **Selection** is the process by which managers determine the relative qualifications of job applicants and their potential for performing well in a particular job. Before actually recruiting and selecting employees, managers need to make use of two important activities: human resource planning and job analysis (see Figure 11.2).

Human Resource Planning

Human resource planning includes all the activities that managers use to forecast their current and future needs for human resources. Current human resources are the employees an organization needs today to provide high quality goods and services to customers. Future human resources are the employees the organization will need at some later date to achieve its longer-term goals. As part of human resource planning, managers must make both demand forecasts and supply forecasts. *Demand forecasts* estimate the qualifications and numbers of employees an organization will need given its goals and strategies. *Supply forecasts* estimate the availability and qualifications of current employees now and in the future, and the

Figure 11.2 | The Recruitment and Selection System

supply of qualified workers in the external labour market. One of the factors facing some amusement parks was that not enough teenagers are available or willing to work at them. With low supply, they have had to look to senior citizens as an alternative supply of labour.

The assessment of both current and future human resource needs helps managers determine whom they should be trying to recruit and select to achieve organizational goals now and in the future. In recent years, Montreal-based BCE has created a new position, "chief talent officer," and appointed Léo Houle to the post. Houle reports directly to BCE's CEO, Michael Sabia. He is responsible for executive recruitment, compensation, and succession planning to make sure that BCE's companies have the right leadership and talent as BCE looks toward the future.[10]

As a result of their human resource planning, managers sometimes use **outsourcing** to fill some of their human resource needs. Instead of recruiting and selecting employees to produce goods and services, managers contract with people who are not members of their organization to produce goods and services. Outsourcing can be used for functional activities such as legal work, after-sales service on appliances and equipment, and the management of human resources or information systems. Outsourcing is increasingly being used on a global level. Managers in some Canadian computer software companies are outsourcing some of their programming work to programmers in India who are highly skilled but cost the companies substantially less than if the programming work were done in-house.

There are at least two reasons why human resource planning sometimes leads managers to outsource: flexibility and cost. First, outsourcing provides flexibility, especially if it is difficult to forecast human resource needs accurately or find skilled workers in a particular area, or if human resource needs fluctuate over time. Second, outsourcing can save money. When work is outsourced, the organization does not have to provide benefits to workers, managers are able to contract for work only when the work is needed, and managers do not have to invest in training.

Outsourcing does have disadvantages, however. When work is outsourced, managers may lose some control over the quality of goods and services. Also, individuals performing outsourced work may have less knowledge of organizational practices, procedures, and goals and less commitment to an organization than regular employees. In addition, unions resist outsourcing because it has the potential to eliminate the jobs of some of their members.

Job Analysis

Job analysis is a second important activity that managers need to undertake before recruitment and selection.[11] **Job analysis** is the process of identifying (1) the tasks, duties, and responsibilities that make up a job (the *job description*), and (2) the knowledge, skills, and abilities needed to perform the job (the job specifications).[12] For each job in an organization, a job analysis needs to be done.

A job analysis can be done in a number of ways, including by observing current employees as they perform the job or by interviewing them. Often, managers rely on questionnaires completed by job holders and their managers. The questionnaires ask about the skills and abilities needed to perform the job, job tasks and the amount of time spent on them, responsibilities, supervisory activities, equipment used, reports prepared, and decisions made.[13]

When managers complete human resource planning and job analyses for all jobs in an organization, they know their human resource needs and the jobs they need to fill. They also know what knowledge, skills, and abilities potential employees will need to perform those jobs. At this point, recruitment and selection can begin.

BCE Inc.
www.bce.ca

outsourcing
Using outside suppliers and manufacturers to produce goods and services.

job analysis
Identifying the tasks, duties, and responsibilities that make up a job and the knowledge, skills, and abilities needed to perform the job.

External and Internal Recruitment

As noted earlier, recruitment is what managers use to develop a pool of qualified candidates for open positions.[14] They generally use two types of recruiting: external and internal.

External Recruiting

When managers recruit externally to fill open positions, they look outside the organization for people who have not worked for the organization before. There are many ways in which managers can recruit externally—advertisements in newspapers and magazines, open houses for students, career counsellors at high schools and colleges, career fairs at colleges, recruitment meetings with groups in the local community, and notices on the web.

External recruitment can also take place through informal networks, such as when current employees inform friends about open positions in their companies or recommend people they know to fill vacant spots. Some organizations use employment agencies for external recruitment, and some external recruitment takes place simply through walk-ins, where job hunters come to an organization and inquire about employment possibilities.

External recruiting has both advantages and disadvantages for managers. Advantages include having access to a potentially large applicant pool; being able to hire people who have the skills, knowledge, and abilities the organization needs to achieve its goals; and being able to bring in newcomers who may have a fresh approach to problems and be up to date on the latest technology. These advantages have to be weighed against the disadvantages, however, including lower morale if current employees feel that there are individuals within the company who should be promoted. External recruitment also has high costs. Employees recruited externally lack knowledge about the inner workings of the organization and may need to receive more training than those recruited internally. InSystems uses its website to inform potential employees about its culture and strategic plans, as shown in *Exploring the World Wide Web*. Finally, when employees are recruited externally, there is always uncertainty about whether they actually will be good performers. Vancouver-based Angiotech Pharmaceuticals, Inc. solves this problem by working with potential employees years before they are ready to be hired. The company provides research money to graduate students at the University of British Columbia who are working on projects closely related to Angiotech's needs.

Angiotech
Pharmaceuticals, Inc.
www.angiotech.com

lateral move
A job change that entails no major changes in responsibility or authority levels.

Internal Recruiting

When recruiting is internal, managers turn to existing employees to fill open positions. Employees recruited internally want either **lateral moves** (job changes that entail no major changes in responsibility or authority levels) or promotions. Internal recruiting has several advantages. First, internal applicants are already familiar with the organization (including its goals, structure, culture, rules, and norms). Second, managers already know internal candidates; they have considerable information about their skills and abilities and actual behaviour on the job. Third, internal recruiting can help boost levels of employee motivation and morale, both for the employee who gets the job and for other workers. Those who are not seeking a promotion or who may not be ready for a promotion can see that it is a possibility for the future, or a lateral move can alleviate boredom once a job has been fully mastered and also provide a useful way to learn new skills. Finally, internal recruiting is normally less time-consuming and expensive.

Given the advantages of internal recruiting, why do managers rely on external recruiting as much as they do? The answer is that there are disadvantages to internal recruiting—among them, a limited pool of candidates and a tendency among those candidates to be "set" in the organization's ways. Often, the organization simply does not have suitable internal candidates. Sometimes, even when suitable internal applicants are available, managers may rely on external recruiting to find the very best candidate or to help bring new ideas and approaches into the organization. When organizations are in trouble and performing poorly, external recruiting is often relied on to bring in managerial talent with a fresh approach. Thus, when Nortel Networks announced in October 2001 that it would promote the company's chief financial officer, Frank Dunn, as the replacement for John Roth, some analysts expressed disappointment, because Dunn was a career number cruncher, not a dynamic strategist.

The Selection Process

Once managers develop a pool of applicants for open positions through the recruitment process, they need to find out whether each applicant is qualified for the position and whether he or she is likely to be a good performer. If more than one applicant meets these two conditions, managers must further determine which applicants are likely to be better performers than others. They have several selection tools to help them sort out the relative qualifications of job applicants and to appraise applicants' potential for being good performers in a particular job. Those tools include background information, interviews, tests, and references.[15]

Background Information

To aid in the selection process, managers obtain background information from job applications and from résumés. Such information might include highest levels of education obtained, university or college majors and minors, type of college or university attended, years and type of work experience, and mastery of foreign languages. Background information can be helpful both to screen out applicants who are lacking key qualifications (such as a post-secondary degree) and to determine which qualified applicants are more promising than others (e.g., applicants with a BSc may be acceptable, but those who also have an MBA are preferable).

Interviews

Virtually all organizations use interviews during the selection process. Two general types of interviews are structured and unstructured. In a structured interview, managers ask each applicant the same standard questions (such as "What are your unique qualifications for this position?" and "What characteristics of a job are most important for you?"). Particularly informative questions may be those where the actual answering allows an interviewee to demonstrate skills and abilities needed for the job. Sometimes called *situational interview questions*, these questions present interviewees with a scenario that they would likely encounter on the job and ask them to indicate how they would handle it.[16] For example, applicants for a sales job may be asked to indicate how they would respond to a customer who complains about waiting too long for service, a customer who is indecisive, and a customer whose order is lost.

An *unstructured interview* proceeds more like an ordinary conversation. The interviewer feels free to ask probing questions to discover what the applicant is like and does not ask a fixed set of questions prepared in advance. In general, structured interviews are superior to unstructured interviews because they are more likely to yield information that will help identify qualified candidates

Earl Brewer, president of Greenarm Management, wants employees who have a passion for the job and who understand balance. In job interviews, one consideration is whether "family is first," something Brewer thinks is important in the people he hires.

and they are less subjective. Also, evaluations based on structured interviews may be less likely to be influenced by the biases of the interviewer than evaluations based on unstructured interviews.

Even when structured interviews are used, however, there is always the potential for the biases of the interviewer to influence his or her judgment. Recall from Chapter 3 how the similar-to-me effect can cause people to perceive others who are similar to themselves more positively than they perceive those who are different and how stereotypes can result in inaccurate perceptions. It is important for interviewers to be trained to avoid these biases and sources of inaccurate perceptions as much as possible. Many of the approaches to increasing diversity awareness and diversity skills described in Chapter 3 can be used to train interviewers to avoid the effects of biases and stereotypes. In addition, using multiple interviewers can be advantageous, for their individual biases and idiosyncrasies may cancel one another out.[17]

When conducting interviews, managers have to be careful not to ask questions that are irrelevant to the job in question, or their organizations run the risk of costly lawsuits. It is inappropriate and illegal, for example, to inquire about an interviewee's spouse or to ask questions about whether an interviewee plans to have children. Questions such as these, which are irrelevant to job performance, may be viewed as discriminatory and as violating human rights legislation. Thus, interviewers also need to be instructed in what is required under the legislation and informed about questions that may be seen as violating those laws.

Testing

Potential employees may be asked to take ability tests, personality tests, physical ability tests, or performance tests. Ability tests assess the extent to which applicants possess skills necessary for job performance, such as verbal comprehension or numerical skills.

Personality tests measure personality traits and characteristics relevant to job performance. Some retail organizations, for example, give job applicants honesty tests to determine how trustworthy they are. The use of personality tests (including honesty tests) for hiring purposes is controversial. Some critics maintain that honesty tests do not really measure honesty (i.e., they are not valid) and can be subject to faking by job applicants. For jobs that require physical abilities—such as firefighting, garbage collecting, and package delivery—managers' selection tools include physical ability tests that measure physical strength and stamina.

Performance tests measure job applicants' performance on actual job tasks. Applicants for secretarial positions, for example, are typically required to complete a typing test that measures how quickly and accurately they are able to type. Applicants for middle- and top-management positions are sometimes given short-term projects to complete—projects that mirror the kinds of situations that arise in the job being filled—to assess their knowledge and problem-solving capabilities.[18]

Lisa Cedars grimaces as she hauls a 74-kilogram dummy to the finish line during a physical fitness test for firefighting applicants. The physical test is just one of many used to determine the top candidates.

References

Applicants for many jobs are required to provide references from former employers or other knowledgeable sources (such as a college instructor or adviser) who know the applicants' skills, abilities, and other personal characteristics. These individuals are asked to provide candid information about the applicants. References are often used at the end of the selection process to confirm a decision to hire. Yet the fact that many former employers are reluctant to provide negative information in references sometimes makes it difficult to interpret what a reference is really saying about an applicant.

In fact, several recent lawsuits filed by applicants who felt that they were unfairly denigrated or had their privacy invaded by unfavourable references from former employers have caused managers to be increasingly wary of providing any kind of negative information in a reference, even if it is accurate. For jobs in which the job holder is responsible for the safety and lives of other people, however, failing to provide accurate negative information in a reference does not just mean that the wrong person might get hired; it also may mean that other people's lives will be at stake.

Tips for Managers

Recruitment and Selection

1. Before recruiting and selecting new employees, use human resource planning and job analysis to determine your human resource needs now and in the future.

2. Provide job applicants with an honest assessment of the advantages and disadvantages of a job.

3. Use other selection tools in addition to interviews to decide which applicants to hire.

4. Make sure that the selection tools you use are reliable and valid.

TRAINING AND DEVELOPMENT

Think About It

At SaskPower, Leaders are Trained, Not Born

Regina-based SaskPower Corp. does not assume that leadership skills come naturally. Instead, the company searches among its employees for individuals with leadership potential, and then gives them the training they need to be leaders.[19] Individuals who want to be part of the leadership training program have to persuade management with examples of why they would make great managers.

The program has a definite advantage over the way managers were chosen previously at SaskPower. "It was unorganized, and the 'old boys network' was still at work," said Bill Hyde, vice-president of human resources. The program is similar to a mini-MBA, and introduces participants to leadership skills and other areas of business.

Question

1. What is the purpose of training and development in the workplace?

training

Teaching organizational members how to perform their current jobs and helping them acquire the knowledge and skills they need to be effective performers.

Training and development help to ensure that organizational members have the knowledge and skills they need to perform their jobs effectively, take on new responsibilities, and adapt to changing conditions. **Training** focuses mainly on teaching organizational members how to perform their current jobs and on helping them acquire the knowledge and skills they need to be effective performers.

Figure 11.3 | Training and Development

NEEDS ASSESSMENT

Training

Development

Classroom instruction

On-the-job training

Apprenticeships (can include classroom instruction and on-the-job training)

Classroom instruction

On-the-job training

Varied work experiences

Formal education

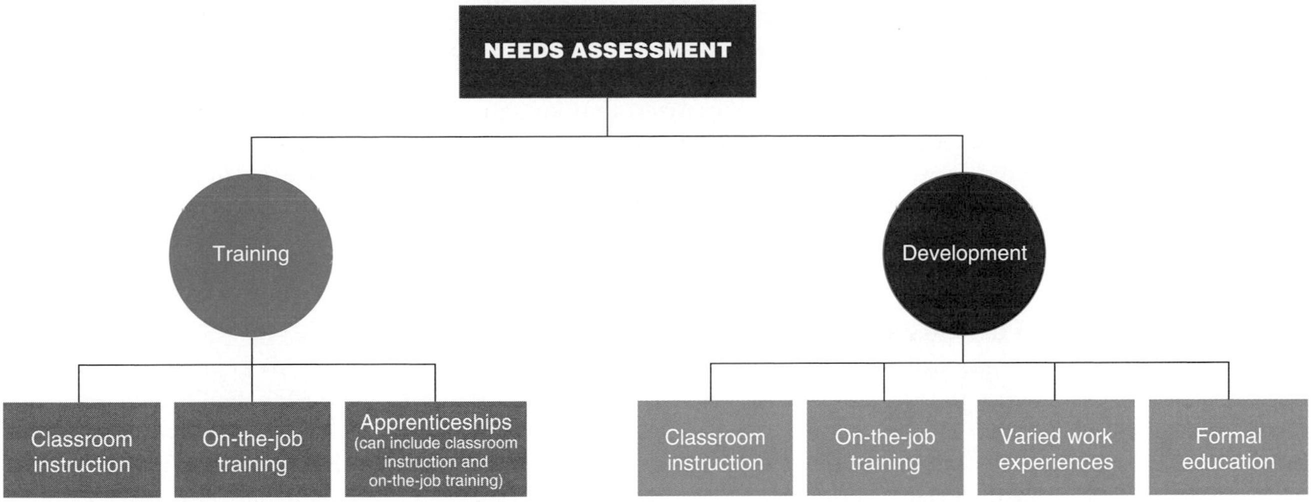

development

Building the knowledge and skills of organizational members so that they will be prepared to take on new responsibilities and challenges.

needs assessment

An assessment of which employees need training or development and what type of skills or knowledge they need to acquire.

Development focuses on building the knowledge and skills of organizational members so that they will be prepared to take on new responsibilities and challenges. Training tends to be used more often at lower levels of an organization; development tends to be used more often with professionals and managers. Comtek's apprenticeship program, described in the *Case in Contrast,* focuses in large part on ensuring that entry-level employees have the skills they need to perform their jobs effectively. The program aims to ensure that when employees start their first jobs at Comtek, they have the knowledge and skills needed for good performance.

Before creating training and development programs, managers should perform a **needs assessment** in which they determine which employees need training or development and what type of skills or knowledge they need to acquire (see Figure 11.3).[20]

Issues in Career Development

A career is "the evolving sequence of a person's work experiences over time."[21] As individuals progress through their lives, they may get promoted, or they may change employers, or even become self-employed. All of this constitutes one's career. There are benefits to effective career development: It improves satisfaction and self-esteem, reduces stress, and strengthens an individual's psychological and physical health.[22] It also helps the organization, because employees are better suited to meet organizational needs.

The issue of career development, and who is responsible for making sure it happens, has become a national issue. The federal government is predicting "a looming national employment crisis" because of an aging and shrinking labour force.[23] Within 10 to 15 years, there will not be enough young people to replace those who are retiring. There is also concern that employees need to develop more job-related skills due to the increase in technology and the demands of the information economy. There is no single answer as to who should take action to resolve the issue of skills training: the government, employers, or employees.

Human Resources Development Canada (HRDC) proposed in 2001 a plan to increase the skills of Canada's workforce. The plan's main proposals included encouraging individuals to retrain and pursue lifelong learning; giving incentives to private industry to make employee training a top priority; increasing the numbers of skilled immigrants and speeding up their accreditation; and bringing traditionally unemployed groups into the labour force. The HRDC proposal faced serious controversy and is only one way of trying to resolve the skills crisis in Canada.

Human Resources Development Canada www.hrdc-drhc.gc.ca

Organizations benefit when they offer career development programs:[24] They can make sure that the right people will be available for changing staffing needs, they can increase workforce diversity, and they can help employees get a better understanding of what is expected in various positions, that is, to have more realistic job expectations. At SaskPower, the leadership training program was started because management recognized that an aging workforce, and rapid turnover in the executive ranks, would otherwise lead to a lack of leadership experience in the company. The training program also helps individuals see whether they really want to move up the management ranks.

Below, we describe both the organization's and employee's responsibilities for career development today.

The Organization's Responsibilities

What, if any, responsibility does the organization have for career development? Organizations take a variety of positions on this question. At Montreal-based Alcan Inc., employees are assessed annually, and then the individual employee's manager provides feedback regarding the potential for advancement and career prospects.[25] At the same time, employees discuss their career aspirations with their manager. High-potential employees are brought to the attention of senior management so that divisions anywhere within Alcan have knowledge about employees and their skills. Alcan's managers also develop an annual five-year plan to examine their human resource needs so that appropriate individuals can be identified and given training. At Hewlett-Packard Canada, by contrast, employees are expected to develop their own career plans and seek out the development they need. This is done with encouragement by their managers.

Employers that have successful career development programs provide support for employees to continually add to their skills, abilities, and knowledge. This support includes:[26]

"1. *Clearly communicating the organization's goals and future strategies.* When people know where the organization is headed, they're better able to develop a personal plan to share in that future.

2. *Creating growth opportunities.* Employees should have the opportunity to get new, interesting, and professionally challenging work experiences.

3. *Offering financial assistance.* The organization should offer tuition reimbursement to help employees keep their skills and knowledge current.

4. *Providing the time for employees to learn.* Organizations should be generous in providing paid time off from work for off-the-job training. Additionally, workloads should not be so demanding that they preclude employees having the time to develop new skills, abilities, and knowledge."

The Employee's Responsibilities

While it is to an organization's advantage to develop its employees, Canada's employers do not have a good reputation for employee training. The country ranks 17th in terms of private sector employers placing a "high priority" on employee training—falling behind Sweden, Japan, Norway, Germany, Australia, and the United States.[27] Therefore, it is wise for individuals to take a more entrepreneurial approach to their careers. By maintaining flexibility and keeping skills and knowledge up to date, individuals will have more job opportunities available to them. Author and consultant Barbara Moses makes the following suggestions for how to be a career activist and take charge of your own career.[28]

1. *Ensure your employability.* Make sure you have alternatives, in case you lose your job. Gain new skills, and pursue opportunities that will stretch you.

2. *Have a fallback position.* Have multiple options for your career, and try to see yourself in multiple roles. This means you could be an employee, a contract worker, or a freelance consultant using a broader set of skills.

3. *Know your key skills.* Know how to package your existing skills and experience in new ways (e.g., an architect who has a hobby as a gardener may start a business designing and building greenhouses). Identify your key talents and skills, and don't limit yourself to a job title.

4. *Market! Market! Market!* Always keep your eyes open for new work assignments, and position yourself for these. Let key people know your skills, and how you can bring value to the organization. Be sure to network. Be sure to treat everyone you meet as a potential client.

5. *Act Type A, be Type B.* While it is important to have the drive and achievement orientation of a Type A personality, it is also important to have the more relaxed Type B attitude of feeling good about yourself, even if you are not producing at a mile a minute. Your sense of self should not be completely tied to your job and the workplace.

6. *Stay culturally current.* Make sure that you are aware of world and cultural events. Being in the know helps you establish relationships with other people, and can help you manage your career effectively.

7. *Be a compelling communicator.* Everyone is busy these days, so it's important to communicate effectively and efficiently. You may be communicating with people halfway around the globe, or individuals who know little about the technical details of what you do. So being clear is important.

8. *Manage your finances.* If you have your finances in order, this will give you greater opportunities to explore new options.

9. *Act like an insider, think like an outsider.* Work as a team player and be self-aware, and able to evaluate your performance with some objectivity. It is important to be able to think independently. Sometimes you will have to make decisions without the help of a group.

10. *Be capable of rewarding yourself.* With increased demands on everyone, you may not receive all of the external feedback you might like. Learn how to give yourself a pat on the back when you do things well. Celebrate your successes, and take time to nourish yourself.

PERFORMANCE APPRAISAL AND FEEDBACK

Think About It

How Much Appraisal, How Often?

Montreal-based Proximi-T Inc., a business application software consulting firm, reviews its employees' performance every three months.[29] Some may view the frequency as excessive, but Proximi-T also evaluates a broad set of skills and traits. Team leaders evaluate their team members on such points as whether individuals are transparent, proactive, and balanced in their lives, behaviours viewed as important to the company.

Proximi-T employees are also evaluated on 10 technical abilities, such as programming and change management, and personal qualities. For instance, employees are evaluated on how well they write and speak in English and French, how they deal with diversity, and what kind of leaders they are. One reason for this frequent and extensive evaluation is that the management at Proximi-T knows where it needs to invest in more training for the staff. This helps the company be at the leading edge in consulting.

Questions
1. Who should do performance appraisals?
2. What is the best way to give performance feedback?

performance appraisal
The evaluation of employees' job performance and contributions to their organization.

performance feedback
The process through which managers share performance appraisal information with subordinates, give subordinates an opportunity to reflect on their own performance, and develop, with subordinates, plans for the future.

The recruitment and selection and the training and development components of a human resource management system ensure that employees have the knowledge and skills they need to be effective now and in the future. Performance appraisal and feedback complement recruitment, selection, training, and development. **Performance appraisal** is the evaluation of employees' job performance and contributions to their organization. **Performance feedback** is the process through which managers share performance appraisal information with their subordinates, give subordinates an opportunity to reflect on their own performance, and develop, with subordinates, plans for the future. In order for there to be performance feedback, performance appraisal must take place. Performance appraisal could take place without providing performance feedback, but wise managers are careful to provide feedback because it can contribute to employee motivation and performance.

Performance appraisal and feedback contribute to the effective management of human resources in two ways. Performance appraisal gives managers important information on which to base human resource decisions.[30] Decisions about pay raises, bonuses, promotions, and job moves all hinge on the accurate appraisal of performance. Performance appraisal also can help managers determine which workers are candidates for training and development, and in what areas. Performance feedback encourages high levels of employee motivation and performance. It lets good performers know that their efforts are valued and appreciated and lets poor performers know that their lacklustre performance needs improvement. Performance feedback can provide both good and poor performers with insight into their strengths and weaknesses and ways in which they can improve their performance in the future.

Who Appraises Performance?

We have been assuming that managers or the supervisors of employees evaluate performance. This is a pretty fair assumption, for supervisors are the most common appraisers of performance. Performance appraisal is an important part of most managers' job duties. It is managers' responsibility to motivate their subordinates to perform at a high level, and managers make many of the decisions that hinge on performance appraisals, such as decisions about pay raises or promotions. Appraisals by managers can, however, be usefully supplemented by appraisals from other sources (see Figure 11.4).

Although appraisals from each of these sources can be useful, managers need to be aware of potential issues that may arise when they are used. Subordinates sometimes may be inclined to inflate self-appraisals, especially if organizations are downsizing and they are worried about their job security. Managers who are appraised by their subordinates may fail to take needed but unpopular actions for fear that their subordinates will appraise them negatively.

360-Degree Performance Appraisals

360-degree appraisal
A performance appraisal by peers, subordinates, superiors, and sometimes clients who are in a position to evaluate a manager's performance.

To improve motivation and performance, some organizations include **360-degree appraisals** and feedback in their performance appraisal systems, especially for managers. In a 360-degree appraisal, an individual's performance is appraised by a variety of people, such as one's self and one's peers or co-workers, subordinates, superiors, and sometimes even customers or clients. The individual receives feedback based on evaluations from these multiple sources.

The growing number of companies using 360-degree appraisals and feedback includes Toronto-based Celestica; Markham, Ontario-based InSystems; Burnaby, BC-based Dominion Information Services; and Toronto-based Hudson's Bay. A 360-degree appraisal and feedback is not always as clear-cut as it might seem. On

Figure 11.4 | Who Appraises Performance?

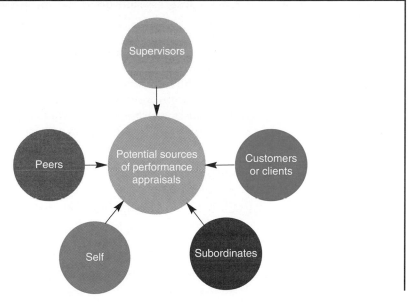

the one hand, some subordinates may try to get back at their managers by giving them negative evaluations, especially when evaluations are anonymous (to encourage honesty and openness). On the other hand, some managers may coach subordinates to give—or even threaten punishment if they fail to give—positive evaluations.

Peers often are very knowledgeable about performance but may be reluctant to provide an accurate and negative appraisal of someone they like or a positive appraisal of someone they dislike. In addition, whenever peers, subordinates, or anyone else evaluates an employee's performance, managers must be sure that the evaluators are actually knowledgeable about the performance dimensions being assessed. For example, subordinates should not evaluate their supervisor's decision making if they have little opportunity to observe this dimension of his or her performance.

These potential problems with 360-degree appraisals and feedback do not mean that they are not useful. Rather, they suggest that in order for 360-degree appraisals and feedback to be effective, trust is needed throughout the organization. More generally, trust is a critical ingredient in any performance appraisal and feedback procedure. Managers using 360-degree appraisals and feedback also have to consider carefully the pros and cons of using anonymous evaluations and of using the results of the appraisals for decision making about important issues such as pay raises.[31]

Effective Performance Feedback

formal appraisal

An appraisal conducted at a set time during the year and based on performance dimensions and measures that were specified in advance.

In order for the performance appraisal and feedback component of a human resource management system to encourage and motivate high performance, managers must provide their subordinates with performance feedback. To generate useful information to pass on to subordinates, managers can use both formal and informal appraisals. **Formal appraisals** are conducted at set times during the year and are based on performance dimensions and measures that have been specified in advance. A salesperson, for example, may be evaluated by his or her manager twice a year on the performance dimensions of sales and customer service, sales being measured from sales reports and customer service being measured by the

informal appraisal
An unscheduled appraisal of ongoing progress and areas for improvement.

number of complaints received. **Informal appraisals**—unscheduled appraisals of ongoing progress and areas for improvement—may occur at the request of the employee.

An integral part of a formal appraisal is a meeting between the manager and the subordinate in which the subordinate is given feedback on his or her performance. Performance feedback shows subordinates areas in which they are excelling and areas in which they are in need of improvement. It should also provide them with guidance for improving performance. Canadian workers report that the practice of performance appraisals is not carried out well in many workplaces. A survey of 2004 Canadian workers from a variety of industrial sectors by Watson Wyatt Worldwide, an international consulting firm, found the following:[32]

- Only 60 percent said they understood the measures used to evaluate their performance.

- Only 57 percent thought their performance was rated fairly.

- Only 47 percent said their managers clearly expressed goals and assignments.

- Only 42 percent reported regular, timely performance reviews.

- Only 39 percent reported that their performance review was helpful in improving their on-the-job performance.

- Only 19 percent reported a clear, direct, and compelling linkage between their performance and their pay.

Managers often dislike providing performance feedback, especially when the feedback is negative, but doing so is an important managerial activity. Here are some guidelines for effectively giving performance feedback that will contribute to employee motivation and performance:

- Be specific and focus on behaviours or outcomes that are correctable and within a worker's ability to improve. *Example:* Telling a salesperson that he or she is too shy when interacting with customers is likely to do nothing more than lower the person's self-confidence and prompt him or her to become defensive. A more effective approach is to give the salesperson feedback about specific behaviours to engage in—greeting customers as soon as they enter the department, asking customers whether they need help, and volunteering to help customers find items if they seem to be having trouble.

- Approach performance appraisal as an exercise in problem-solving and solution-finding, not criticizing. *Example:* Rather than criticizing a financial analyst for turning reports in late, the manager helps the analyst determine why the reports are late and identify ways to better manage time.

- Express confidence in a subordinate's ability to improve. *Example:* Instead of being skeptical, a first-level manager tells a subordinate of confidence that the subordinate can increase quality levels.

- Provide performance feedback both formally and informally. *Example:* The staff of a preschool receives feedback from formal performance appraisals twice a year. The director of the school also provides frequent informal feedback, such as complimenting staff members on creative ideas for special projects, noticing when they do a particularly good job of handling a difficult child, and pointing out when they provide inadequate supervision.

- Praise instances of high performance and areas of a job in which an employee excels. *Example:* Rather than focusing on just the negative, a manager discusses the areas the subordinate excels in as well as areas in need of improvement.

- Avoid personal criticisms, and treat subordinates with respect. *Example:* An engineering manager acknowledges subordinates' expertise and treats them as professionals. Even when the manager points out performance problems to subordinates, it is important to refrain from criticizing them personally.

- Agree to a timetable for performance improvements. *Example:* A first-level manager and subordinate decide to meet again in one month to determine whether quality has improved.

In following these guidelines, managers need to keep in mind why they are giving performance feedback: to encourage high levels of motivation and performance. Moreover, the information that managers gather through performance appraisal and feedback helps them determine how to distribute pay raises and bonuses.

Tips for Managers

Performance Appraisal

1. Supplement periodic formal performance appraisals with more frequent informal appraisals and give performance feedback often.

2. When high performance can be reached by different kinds of behaviours and the way that employees perform their jobs is not important, use results appraisals to evaluate performance and give feedback.

3. When providing performance feedback, focus on specific behaviours or outcomes, adopt a problem-solving mode, express confidence in employees, praise instances of high performance, and agree to a timetable for improvements.

4. Avoid personal criticisms and treat employees with respect when providing feedback.

5. Provide performance feedback from both formal and informal performance appraisals.

PAY AND BENEFITS

Think About It

How Do Wages Get Set?

Young Canadians wonder how much a job should pay, as they move back in with Mum and Dad to save money.[33] The average full-time employee earned more than $43 231 in 2002, a modest increase over 10 years.[34] However, this increase is not reflected in the earnings of young Canadians, who are making about the same as (or even less than) young people did 20 years ago.

Thomas Lemieux, an economics professor at the University of British Columbia, suggests young adults earn less because they are less likely to have jobs that are unionized or jobs in the public service.

Question
1. Why is there variation in pay levels across organizations?
2. How is pay determined?

In Chapter 8, we discussed the ways in which pay can be used to motivate organizational members to perform at a high level. Here we focus on how organizations determine their pay levels and pay structures.

Pay Level

Pay includes employees' base salaries, pay raises, and bonuses and is determined by a number of factors, including characteristics of the organization and of the job and levels of performance. **Pay level** is a broad comparative concept that refers to how an organization's pay incentives compare, in general, to those of other organizations in the same industry employing similar kinds of workers. Managers must decide whether they want to offer relatively high wages, average wages, or relatively low wages. High wages help ensure that an organization is going to be able to recruit, select, and retain high performers, but high wages also raise costs. Low wages give an organization a cost advantage but may undermine the organization's ability to select and recruit high performers and motivate current employees to perform at a high level. Either of these situations may lead to inferior quality or inferior customer service.

In determining pay levels, managers should take their organization's strategy into account. A high pay level may prohibit managers from effectively pursuing a low-cost strategy. But a high pay level may be well worth the added costs in an organization whose competitive advantage lies in superior quality and excellent customer service. As one might expect, hotel and motel chains with a low-cost strategy, such as Days Inn and Hampton Inns, have lower pay levels than chains striving to provide high quality rooms and services, such as Four Seasons and Hyatt Regency.

Pay Structure

After deciding on a pay level, managers have to establish a pay structure for the different jobs in the organization. A **pay structure** clusters jobs into categories that reflect their relative importance to the organization and its goals, levels of skill required, and other characteristics that managers consider to be important. Pay ranges are established for each job category. Individual job holders' pay within job categories is then determined by factors such as performance, seniority, and skill levels.

There is quite a difference between public and private sector pay structures. On average, governments at all three levels (federal, provincial, and local) pay a premium of about 9 percent to their employees, compared with private sector jobs. Public sector employees are also more likely to be covered by pension plans. Despite the seeming differences between public and private sector wages, it is generally women and less-skilled workers who get higher wages for working in the public sector. Managers, especially male managers, do not get paid much more for working in the public sector. Moreover, at the federal level, senior managers are paid less than they might earn in the private sector. There is also far more wage compression in the public sector. In the private sector, on average, individuals in managerial, administrative, or professional occupations are paid 41-percent more than those in service occupations. In the public sector, it is not uncommon for managers to be paid only 10-percent more than other employees.[35]

The Stride Rite Corporation, which makes children's shoes, has established an intergenerational daycare centre for its employees in which the families of employees are encouraged to take an active interest in the care of employees' children.

Benefits

Employee benefits are based on membership in an organization (and not necessarily on the particular job held) and include sick days, vacation days, and medical and life insurance. Organizations are legally required to provide certain benefits to their employees, including workers' compensation, social insurance, and employment insurance. Workers' compensation provides employees with financial assistance if they become unable to work because of a work-related injury or illness. Social insurance provides financial assistance to retirees and disabled former employees. Employment insurance provides financial assistance to employees who lose their jobs through no fault of their own.

Other benefits—such as extended health insurance, dental insurance, vacation time, pension plans, life insurance, flexible working hours, company-provided day-care, and employee assistance and wellness programs—are provided at the option of employers. Benefits mandated by public policy and benefits provided at the option of employers cost organizations a substantial amount of money.

In some organizations, top managers decide which benefits might best suit the organization and employees, and offer the same benefit package to all employees. Other organizations, realizing that employees' needs and desires for benefits might differ, offer **cafeteria-style benefit plans** that let employees themselves choose the benefits they want, from among such options as flextime, tuition credits, and extended medical and dental plans. Some organizations have success with cafeteria-style plans, while others find them difficult to manage.

cafeteria-style benefit plan
A plan from which employees can choose the benefits that they want.

Labour Relations

Think About It

Students Join Union in Montreal

Employees at a downtown Montreal branch of Indigo Books & Music became members of the Confédération des syndicate nationaux (CSN) in February 2003.[36] The employees are mostly students, and they faced electing an executive and then forming a negotiating committee to negotiate their first union contract. The employees joined the union to improve their working conditions at Indigo.

Questions
1. Why do people join labour unions?
2. What do labour unions do?

labour relations
The activities that managers engage in to ensure that they have effective working relationships with the labour unions that represent their employees' interests.

Labour relations are the activities that managers engage in to ensure that they have effective working relationships with the labour unions that represent their employees' interests. As a way to deal with the potential for unethical organizations and managers to treat workers unfairly, the federal and provincial governments created and enforce the Canada Labour Code, the Canadian Human Rights Act, and provincial Employment Standards laws. However, some employees believe that unions will be more effective than codes and laws in protecting their rights.

Labour Unions

Labour unions exist to represent workers' interests in organizations. Given that managers have more power than rank-and-file employees and that organizations have multiple stakeholders, there is always the potential that managers might take steps that will benefit one set of stakeholders (such as shareholders) while hurting another (such as employees). For example, managers might decide to speed up a production line to lower costs and increase production in the hope of increasing returns to shareholders. This action could, however, hurt employees who are forced to work at a rapid pace, who may have increased risk of injuries as a result of the line speedup, and who receive no additional pay for the extra work they are performing. Unions represent employees' interests in such scenarios. The students working at Montreal's downtown Indigo bookstore were unhappy with their working conditions, for instance, when they voted to join the CSN.

Employees might vote to have a union represent them for any number of reasons.[37] They may feel that their wages and working conditions are in need of improvement. They may feel that managers are not treating them with respect. They may think that their working hours are unfair or that they need more job security or a safer work environment. Or they may be dissatisfied with management and find it difficult to communicate their concerns to their managers. Regardless of the specific reason, one overriding reason is power: A united group inevitably wields more power than an individual, and this type of power may be especially helpful to employees in some organizations.

Although these would seem to be potent forces for unionization, some workers are reluctant to join unions. Sometimes this reluctance is due to the perception that union leaders are corrupt. Some workers may simply feel that belonging to a union might not do them much good or might actually cause more harm than good while costing them money in membership dues. Employees also might not want to be "forced" into doing something they do not want to do (such as striking) because the union thinks it is in their best interest. Moreover, although unions can be a positive force in organizations, they sometimes can be a negative force, impairing organizational effectiveness. For example, when union leaders resist needed changes in an organization or are corrupt, organizational performance can suffer.

About 31 percent of Canadian employees are represented by unions today.[38] Representation has remained fairly consistent for the past 20 years, although it is a decline from 30 years ago, when more than 40 percent of employees were unionized.[39] In the United States, where union representation peaked in the 1950s at about 35 percent, today it stands at about 13 percent.[40]

Union membership and leadership, traditionally dominated by white men, is also becoming increasingly diverse.

Chapter Summary

SUMMARY AND REVIEW

STRATEGIC HUMAN RESOURCE MANAGEMENT Human resource management (HRM) includes all the activities that managers use to ensure that their organizations are able to attract, retain, and utilize human resources effectively. *Strategic HRM* is the process by which managers design the components of a human resource management system to be consistent with each other, with other elements of organizational architecture, and with the organization's strategies and goals.

RECRUITMENT AND SELECTION Before recruiting and selecting employees, managers must engage in human resource planning and job analysis. *Human resource planning* includes all the activities managers engage in to forecast their current and future needs for human resources. *Job analysis* is the process of identifying (1) the tasks, duties, and responsibilities that make up a job and (2) the knowledge, skills, and abilities needed to perform the job. *Recruitment* includes all the activities that managers engage in to develop a pool of qualified applicants for open positions. *Selection* is the process by which managers determine the relative qualifications of job applicants and their potential for performing well in a particular job.

TRAINING AND DEVELOPMENT Training focuses on teaching organizational members how to perform effectively in their current jobs. Development focuses on broadening organizational members' knowledge and skills so that employees will be prepared to take on new responsibilities and challenges. As part of the training and development process, organizations and individuals need to consider career development of employees.

PERFORMANCE APPRAISAL AND FEEDBACK Performance appraisal is the evaluation of employees' job performance and contributions to their organization. *Performance feedback* is the process through which managers share performance appraisal information with their subordinates; give subordinates an opportunity to reflect on their own performance; and help subordinates develop plans for the future. Performance appraisal provides managers with useful information for decision making. Performance feedback can encourage high levels of motivation and performance.

PAY AND BENEFITS Pay level is the relative position of an organization's pay incentives in comparison with those of other organizations in the same industry employing similar kinds of employees. A *pay structure* clusters jobs into categories that reflect their relative importance to the organization and its goals, levels of skill required, and other characteristics. Pay ranges are established for each job category. Organizations are legally required to provide certain benefits to their employees; other benefits are provided at the discretion of employers.

LABOUR RELATIONS Labour relations are the activities that managers engage in to ensure that they have effective working relationships with the labour unions that may represent their employees' interests.

Roles in Contrast: Considerations

MANAGERS	EMPLOYEES
Outsourcing may have the advantages of flexibility and lower cost. However, managers lose some control over the quality of goods and services that are outsourced. It is important to weigh the costs and benefits.	Managers often feel that outsourcing increases flexibility and lowers cost. Employees might want to discuss with managers ways to avoid outsourcing while maintaining flexibility.
External recruitment increases the size of the labour pool, but it may reduce morale if individuals feel that there were suitable internal candidates. Thus, the effect on internal morale should be considered when making this decision.	External recruitment increases the size of the labour pool, and may bring a greater variety of skills, knowledge, and abilities to the organization. It may be helpful as an employee to be sure to keep developing your skills and abilities to increase the chances of being considered for other positions.
By allowing a variety of individuals to provide feedback about an employee, you get a clearer picture of whether the employee is performing well at all levels, or just performing for superiors while not being helpful with subordinates or co-workers.	Your manager might use 360-degree feedback to get a variety of perspectives on your performance, including those of superiors, subordinates, and clients. This gives a clearer perspective on how well you are performing, and encourages you to perform well, whether individuals are above or below you in rank.

MANAGEMENT
in Action

Topics for Discussion and Action

1. Discuss why it is important for the components of the human resource management system to be in sync with an organization's strategy and goals and with each other.
2. Interview a manager in a local organization to determine how that organization recruits and selects employees.
3. Discuss why training and development is an ongoing activity for all organizations.

4. Evaluate the pros and cons of 360-degree performance appraisals and feedback. Would you like your performance to be appraised in this manner? Why or why not?
5. Discuss why two restaurants in the same community might have different pay levels.
6. Explain why union membership is becoming more diverse.

Building Management Skills

ANALYZING HUMAN RESOURCE SYSTEMS

Think about your current job or a job that you had in the past. If you have never had a job, then interview a friend or family member who is currently working. Answer the following questions about the job you have chosen.

1. How are people recruited and selected for this job? Are the recruitment and selection procedures that the organization uses effective or ineffective? Why?
2. What training and development do people who hold this job receive? Is it appropriate? Why or why not?

3. How is performance of this job appraised? Does performance feedback contribute to motivation and high performance on this job?
4. What levels of pay and benefits are provided for this job? Are these levels of pay and benefits appropriate? Why or why not?

Management for You

Your instructor has asked class members to form teams to work on a major class project. You have worked on teams before, and have not always been pleased with the results. This time you are determined to have a good team experience. You have reason to believe that how people are recruited to and selected for teams might make a difference. You also know that evaluating performance and giving feedback are important. You have also heard that training can make a difference. With all of this in mind, write up a plan that indicates how you might recruit an excellent set of team members, and make sure that they perform well throughout.

Small Group Breakout Exercise

BUILDING A HUMAN RESOURCE MANAGEMENT SYSTEM

Form groups of 3 or 4 people, and appoint 1 group member as the spokesperson who will communicate your findings to the whole class when called on by the instructor. Then discuss the following scenario.

You and your 2 or 3 partners are engineers with a business minor who have decided to start a consulting business. Your goal is to provide manufacturing-process engineering and other engineering services to large and small organizations. You forecast that there will be an increased use of outsourcing for these activities. You discussed with managers in several large organizations the services you plan to offer, and they expressed considerable interest. You have secured funding to start the business and are now building the HRM system. Your human resource planning suggests that you need to hire between 5 and 8 experienced engineers with good communication skills, 2 clerical/secretarial workers, and 2 MBAs who between them will have financial, accounting, and human resource skills. You are striving to develop an approach to building your human resources that will enable your new business to prosper.

1. Describe the steps you will take to recruit and select (a) the engineers, (b) the clerical/secretarial workers, and (c) the MBAs.
2. Describe the training and development the engineers, the clerical/secretarial workers, and the MBAs will receive.
3. Describe how you will appraise the performance of each group of employees and how you will provide feedback.
4. Describe the pay level and pay structure of your consulting firm.

Managing Ethically

Nadia Burowsky has recently been promoted to a managerial position in a large downtown bank. Before her promotion, she was one of a group of bank tellers who got together weekly and complained about their jobs. Burowsky enjoyed these get-togethers, because she is recently divorced and they provided a bit of a social life for her. In Burowsky's new role, she will be conducting performance appraisals and making decisions about pay raises and promotions for these same tellers. Burowsky reports to you, and you are aware of her former weekly get-togethers with the tellers. Is it ethical for her to continue attending these social functions? How might she effectively manage having relationships with co-workers and evaluating them?

Exploring the World Wide Web

SPECIFIC ASSIGNMENT

Many companies take active steps to recruit and retain valuable employees. One such company is InSystems. Scan the InSystems Technologies, Inc. website (http://www.insystems.com) to learn more about this company, including clicking on "About Us." Then click on "Corporate Information" and, under that, "Corporate Profile," then "Careers," "Total Rewards," and "What Employees Say," to find out more about what it's like for employees to work at InSystems.

1. What steps is InSystems taking to recruit and retain employees?
2. Do you think that its approach is effective? Why or why not?

GENERAL ASSIGNMENT

Find websites of two companies that try to recruit new employees by means of the World Wide Web. Are their approaches to recruitment on the web similar or different? What are the potential advantages of the approaches of each? What are the potential disadvantages?

You're the Management Consultant

THE 360-DEGREE PERFORMANCE APPRAISAL SYSTEM IS JUST NOT WORKING

Walter Michaels has just received some disturbing feedback. Michaels is the director of human resources for Maxi Vision Inc., a medium-sized manufacturer of windows and glass doors. Michaels recently introduced a 360-degree performance appraisal system for all middle and upper managers at Maxi Vision, including himself but excluding the most senior executives and the top-management team.

Michaels was eagerly awaiting the feedback he would receive from the managers who report to him. He had recently made several important changes that affected them and their subordinates, including a complete overhaul of the organization's performance appraisal system. While the managers who reported to Michaels were now evaluated based on 360-degree appraisals, their own subordinates were evaluated using a new 20-question scale Michaels created that focuses on behaviours. Conducted annually, appraisals were an important input into pay raise and bonus decisions.

Michaels was so convinced that the new performance appraisal procedures were highly effective that he hoped his own subordinates would mention them in their feedback to him.

And boy, did they! Michaels was amazed to learn that the managers and their subordinates thought the new 20-question scale was unfair, inappropriate, and a waste of time. In fact, the managers' feedback to Michaels was that their own performance was suffering, based on the 360-degree appraisals they received, because their subordinates hated the new appraisal system and partly blamed their managers. Some managers even admitted giving all their subordinates around the same scores on the scale so their pay raises and bonuses would not be affected by their performance appraisals.

Michaels could not believe his eyes when he read these comments. He had spent so much time developing what he thought was the ideal rating scale for this group of workers. Evidently for some unknown reason, they were being very closed-minded and would not give it a chance. Michaels' own supervisor was aware of these complaints and said that it was a top priority for Michaels to fix "this mess" (with the implication that Michaels was responsible for creating it). Michaels has come to you, an expert in human resource management, for advice. What should he do?

MANAGEMENT CASE

From the Pages of *Business Week* Job Security, No. Tall Latte, Yes.

When dot-coms started building gourmet coffee bars modeled on Central Perk from the TV show *Friends*—complete with mood lighting, over-stuffed sofas, and 14 varieties of premium brews—some wondered if the New Economy frills were getting out of hand. It was one thing to hand out signing bonuses to janitors, and maids to summer interns. If a slowdown occurred, these perks could easily be whacked. But caffeine-addicted employees swarmed the espresso machines like druggies angling for a fix. Yanking this freebie could send them into convulsions of revolt.

Not to worry. The dot-com era may be dead, but, for the most part, connoisseur office coffee is here to stay. In fact, instead of worrying about being cut off from their caffeine supplies, employees can also look forward to mainlining free bottled water and subsidized snacks, both of which are in the offing at many companies—despite the slowdown-induced emphasis on cost-cutting.

Souped Up

What began as a dot-com dividend has "spilled over into a legacy," says Richard Wyckoff, president of corporate America's top coffee supplier, Aramark Refreshment Services, which reports that sales of souped-up coffee machines tripled in the past year. Many companies such as Philadelphia-based Omicrom say that no matter how bad things get, they wouldn't dare pull the perk. Even managers at MCI Worldcom Inc., who postmerger were told to can the coffee, have resumed re-ordering.

The any-kind-of-coffee-you-want largesse is not the only New Economy legacy. Far from being fads that will evaporate like so many market caps, many of the workplace revolutions developed to coddle employees and warehouse them in offices for as long as possible might very well strengthen during the next 15 years. Part of the reason is economic. Even with the slowdown, companies must still compete for valued knowledge workers. And as employees are forced to clock workaholic hours in the global, 24/7 economy, companies will have to make offices seem more and more like home.

Out Gen Y-ers

Attitudinal shifts about the workplace are also a key factor. Earlier in their lives, many of the boomers now running the show spat on bourgeois values, disdained all things corporate, and fancied themselves as bohemians. In fact, today's corporate chieftains make up the first generation that didn't serve in the armed forces and wasn't weaned on military models of organization. Thus, some have refashioned offices in the image of their freewheeling, anti-establishment values. They want to succeed, but they also want to be cool.

In Return of the Suit

Of course, not everything about the loosey-goosey New Economy workplace will stick. Skin-tight spandex and scruffy facial hair at the office are fading as fast as knee-length skirts on the runway. Underscored by a President who requires crisp, company-man dress, the suit is making a big comeback. Some firms such as recruiter Korn/Ferry have even reinstituted the button-down codes of yore—except in Silicon Valley. Already, retailer Men's Warehouses Inc. and fashion design Joseph Abboud are forming a marketing alliance aimed at the resurgence of professional dress.

Waning, too, is the reign of the unwrinkled. Seasoned, over-40 types bring a level of comfort to employers that post-pubescent wireheads never could. Another casualty: résumé puffery. Gone are the days when employers skipped the background and reference checks, allowing fakers to sail through. And the corporate carpetbaggers who bounced from job to job, collecting fatter paychecks and more options along the way, are no longer laughing at those "loyalist losers." They're asking them for jobs.

Bur for the most part, dot-com style perks will become permanent fixtures of the work landscape. Cultural changes wrought by the New Economy stem from when all those startups were siphoning off Old Economy workers amid the worst labor shortage in modern history. Rather than sit back and take it, Big Five accounting firms, Rust Belt stalwarts, investment banks, and law firms were forced to remake themselves in the image of their worker-snatching rivals. The strategy shifted the balance of power in employees' favor, and companies still haven't been able to completely regain their upper hand. That's why the recent pileup in layoffs isn't going to magically turn everyone back into a gold-watch seeker. Those days have been replaced by the free-agent mentality, in which the most talented workers can still afford to seek better deals within their companies and on the open market.

The smartest companies know this. Instead of ensnaring employees financially with more signing bonuses and huge salaries, they are trying to hook them emotionally with management retreats, specials awards, and assistance with elder and dependent care. And rather than resorting to their old strategy of assembling secret SWAT teams to psychologically pressure would-be defectors into staying, they are rechristening these leave-takers "alumni" and bidding them to boomerang back to the firm—if and when it's still hiring.

That's why Ernst & Young renamed its Office for Retention to the Center for the New Workforce. "People will have nine jobs by the time they are 30," says E&Y job czar Deborah K. Holmes. "We'd be delighted to be two or three of those jobs." And when skilled workers take those jobs, they'll do so with dot-com-style employment contracts in hand that protect them from mergers and downturns. After all, the Nasdaq may be in shreds, but if talented workers learned anything from the boom, it's that their careers—and offices—don't have to be.

Source: M. Conlin, "Job Security, No. Tall Latte, Yes," *Business Week*, April 2, 2001, pp. 62, 64.

Questions

1. Why does it appear that managers are preserving some traditions from the dot-com heyday and eliminating others?
2. How important are job benefits, perks, and work environment factors for organizational effectiveness?

MANAGEMENT CASE

IN THE NEWS

From the Pages of the *Ottawa Citizen* The Blessed: Under 30, They Are the Darlings of the Industry—But They Want More

In the last three years, something momentous has been happening at Nortel Networks Corp. While an army of startups—not to mention archrival Cisco Systems Inc.—has been siphoning workers from the telecom giant, Nortel has been forced to remake itself in the image of its talent-snatching competitors. Quite simply, Canada's oldest technology company could no longer afford to appear stodgy and out-of-date, especially if it wanted to appeal to a new generation of engineering and business talent.

The Brampton-based corporation—which employs some 15 000 workers in Ottawa—embarked on a systematic overhaul. It boosted salaries, moved to merit-based pay, and doled out signing bonuses. It offered stock options to half of its 85 000 employees worldwide—a five-fold increase from the 10 percent that used to qualify. Taking a page from the rec-room atmosphere at many startups, Nortel experimented with informal, café-and-lounge work spaces. And it devised some clever ways to show staff they're appreciated. One employee recognition plan, rolled out last year, awards "Pride Points" that can be converted into all kinds of prizes, whether they be camcorders, bikes, gift certificates, or cold, hard cash.

"That's something that does wonders for motivation," says Jacqui McGillivray, who studies what Nortel employees want. While such perks aren't aimed specifically at Nortel's under-30 population, [Linda] Duxbury's [a professor at the School of Business, University of Carleton] research shows this crowd is hungry for recognition from their bosses. They want to know that their contributions are valued, and they want regular feedback from their bosses. What these newbies think and want is very important to their employers.

While only one in four tech workers is under 30, they are the undisputed darlings of the industry: companies not only want to hire them, but they do everything they can to keep them. Employers associate youth with enthusiasm, new ideas, and an endless capacity for work.

For their part, those under 30 are intensely loyal to their own career goals, and they work hard to be noticed by their employers. In particular, they spend more effort developing office relationships, and they're eager to learn from older colleagues. They also like to take on big responsibilities. For those reasons, they're driven less by money than by challenging work.

At Nortel, recruiters count on the company's reputation for cutting-edge technology to attract and keep their best people. "That's the number one reason people stay here," says McGillivray.

To prove themselves, young workers take advantage of training programs, special projects, and strong mentors—all of which companies seem happy to provide. It should come as no surprise, then, that these workers are generally satisfied with their work environment. But that doesn't mean they feel any loyalty to the company. Despite their employer's efforts to keep them happy, an overwhelming 9 out of 10 workers in this age group think about leaving their jobs. The main reason for this paradox appears to be frustration with career advancement. Those who simply can't wait around for promotions inevitably find other opportunities—ones that promise greater job responsibility, better pay, and more cutting-edge work.

If there is one source of job stress for the under-30 crowd, it's the fast pace of the industry. Seven out of ten workers in this age group feel the pressure of rapid product cycles, which force punishing project deadlines on them. The speed of technology trends also leaves many young workers worried that their skills will quickly be out of date. Duxbury believes companies don't do enough to help their younger employees manage this change. Indeed, in an economic slowdown, it's the young ones that feel the greatest pressure. As companies start cutting their workforce, it's usually the under-30s who are asked to do more with less, Duxbury adds.

"Unlike their older colleagues, the young ones haven't yet learned the survival skills to cope with the pace, which is why many compensate by working long hours."

Source: Reprinted with permission. Pauline Tan, the *Ottawa Citizen.*

Questions

1. What is Nortel's approach to pay?
2. How might something like the technology downturn that occurred in 2001 affect how companies reward their younger employees?

CHAPTER 12

COMMUNICATION, CONFLICT, AND NEGOTIATION

Learning Objectives

1. Describe the communication process, and explain the role of perception in communication.

2. Define information richness, and describe the information richness of communication media available to managers.

3. Describe important communication skills that individuals need as senders and as receivers of messages.

4. Explain why conflict arises, and identify the difference between functional and dysfunctional conflict.

5. Describe conflict management strategies that individuals can use to resolve conflict effectively.

6. Describe how integrative bargaining can be used to resolve conflict.

Roles in Contrast: Questions

MANAGERS	EMPLOYEES
Can I just use email to communicate with my employees?	Can I just use email to communicate with my manager?
How can I be a better listener?	How can I be a better listener?
Should I do whatever possible to minimize conflict in my department?	Is it wrong to think that conflict is bad?

THE IMPORTANCE OF GOOD COMMUNICATION SKILLS

Managers and employees at Owen Sound, Ontario-based Transcontinental RBW Graphics (www.transcontinental-gtc.com) pride themselves on the family atmosphere of the company.[1] Brian Reid, general manager, speaks to every employee he encounters whenever he walks around the plant.

Good communication among management and employees is a hallmark of the company, and that attitude pays off. The company has consistently been on the leading edge of technology in the printing industry, as far back as 1927.

RBW empowers its staff to both make decisions and act on them. The average employee has worked there for 18 years. And though there have been several organizing attempts by unions (including a drive in 1999), there has never been a union at the plant.

"I believe our employees have more say with the current structure than they would with unions," says Reid. The company has never laid off a full-time employee. In agreeing with Reid, press technician Brad Fritzsch says, "I think the unions haven't been successful here because of the way we operate. Management does a pretty good job at trying to address all the people's concerns,

and there are a number of sub-committees that provide for good communication."

Committees at RBW include a joint health and safety committee, a shop committee, and a social committee. Employees volunteer to serve on the committees and they are responsible for exchanging information and investigating, recommending and implementing solutions, policies, and events to improve the working and personal lives of all the employees.

Because of good communication in the plant, the company has been able to achieve work structures that might have been difficult in other companies. For instance, in 1997 RBW switched to a 12-hour shift system, making the company a seven-day-a-week, 24-hour-a-day operation. The decision to do this was investigated and voted on by the staff. Thus, even though the impact was great, the transition was well received.

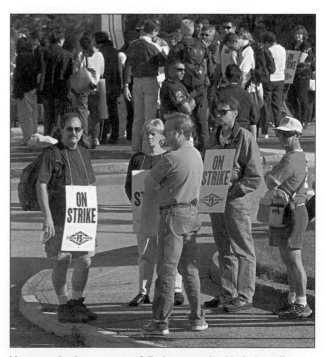

Vancouver's city managers failed to consult with their staff before abolishing the four-day workweek that had been in place for 22 years. Employees staged a seven-week strike because they could not reach agreement with the city.

At Transcontinental RBW Graphics, good communication empowers employees and creates a work environment that both employees and managers appreciate.

Bill Hiscox, a pressroom technician, says the atmosphere on the shop floor is "just like being in a small town." He adds, "It's a good family company and they really look after us well." The admiration is mutual, however. When Montreal-based Transcontinental Inc., RBW's parent corporation, won a coveted six-year contract to print the Canadian edition of *Time* magazine in 1999, Wayne Newson, Transcontinental's president at the time, noted that "the most gratifying thing to us is that we did not get this contract on price. We had to be competitive but it really came down to the capabilities of our plant in Owen Sound. We won the business based on our people and our competencies."

RBW exemplifies good communication among managers and employees, but not all employers treat their employees as well. When Canadian Union of Public Employees (CUPE; www.cupe.bc.ca) Local 15, which represents the City of Vancouver's inside workers, went on strike in early October 2000, the employees were responding to a long-simmering feud with the city's managers. In late April 1998, the city council had announced, without consulting its staff, that it would abolish its 22-year-old program of four-day workweeks, effective September 1, 1998. The program was very popular with the staff.

Within two weeks of the city's announcement, negative response from employees became widespread. Some resigned from the staff-appreciation committee, others withdrew voluntary services, and/or wrote anguished letters to councillors "about the emotional and financial impact it would have on them, city hall and the community if the city returned to more traditional work schedules." Ken Dobell, who was then city manager, showed no sympathy to the employees' complaints. He simply remarked that "the rest of the world is on a five-day workweek and the city is out of step." In other words, he refused to listen to his employees' concerns.

Two years later, city employees were still upset. Two dozen managers and professional staff had quit during that period, double the normal resignation rate for the city. In October 2000, the CUPE workers went on strike for seven weeks because they could not reach agreement with the city on the four-day workweek. At issue was the fact that the city would not communicate with its employees to resolve difficulties with the way the four-day workweek was implemented at City Hall. Early on in the debate the city claimed that there had been widespread complaints about disruptions caused by the four-day workweek, but during the strike city manager Judy Rogers said there was only "anecdotal evidence of dissatisfaction among business leaders with irregular city hours."

Employees were not offered the opportunity to address alleged concerns while preserving their flextime schedules. Dave Amy, an engineering technician, explained, "I worked with the developers who brought the complaints [about flextime] forward to council, and yes, they had some reasons to complain. But those were small issues that could very well have been worked out. It didn't need to come down to this."

Overview

As should be clear from the *Case in Contrast,* ineffective communication is detrimental for managers, employees, and organizations; it can lead to conflict, poor performance, strained interpersonal relations, poor service, and dissatisfied customers. Managers at all levels need to be good communicators in order for an organization to be effective and gain a competitive advantage.

In this chapter, we describe the nature of communication and the communication process and explain why it is so important for all managers and their subordinates to be effective communicators. We describe the communication media available to managers, and the factors that managers need to consider in selecting a communication medium for each message they send. We describe the communication skills that help individuals be effective senders and receivers of messages. We describe conflict, and the strategies that managers can use to resolve it effectively. We discuss one major conflict resolution technique—negotiation—in detail, outlining the steps managers can take to be good negotiators. By the end of this chapter, you will have a good appreciation of the nature of communication and the steps that all organizational members can take to ensure that they are effective communicators. You will also become aware of the skills necessary to manage organizational conflict.

COMMUNICATION IN ORGANIZATIONS

Think About It

FPI's Failed Communication Brings Restrictive Legislation

When St. John's, Newfoundland-based Fishery Products International (FPI) tried to restructure the company and merge with a rival in 2002, the plans created such a stir that the provincial government stepped in.[2] The plans called for modernizing the plant and laying off a number of employees. Former federal cabinet minister John Crosbie, a director of Fishery Products, acknowledges that the restructuring plans failed because the directors did not communicate them well to those affected.

"FPI should have consulted extensively with the union, employees, community leaders, elected members and both levels of government, developing . . . an adequate retirement plan for the displaced workers," he says. "Not doing so was a terrible mistake."

The result of this lack of communication was that the provincial government imposed restrictive legislation on the company. No investor can now own more than 15 percent of the company, and shareholders cannot sue the province for imposing tough new rules.

Question

1. Is good communication really that important?

communication

The sharing of information between two or more individuals or groups to reach a common understanding.

Communication is the sharing of information between two or more individuals or groups to reach a common understanding.[3] Some organizations are more effective at doing this than others. FPI did not spend enough time trying to make sure other groups understood the need for modernizing the fish plants in Newfoundland. From the *Case in Contrast,* it is clear that RBW Graphics encourages employees and managers to work together on solutions to problems. The City of Vancouver simply imposed a decision that would affect the personal lives of many of its employees.

Good communication is essential for organizations to function effectively. Managers spend about 85 percent of their time engaged in some form of communication, whether in meetings, in telephone conversations, through email, or in face-to-face interactions. Employees also need to be effective communicators.[4] When all members of an organization are able to communicate effectively with each other and with people outside the organization, the organization is much more likely to perform highly and gain a competitive advantage.

The Communication Process

The communication process consists of two phases. In the *transmission phase*, information is shared between two or more individuals or groups. In the *feedback phase,*

sender
The person or group wishing to share information.

message
The information that a sender wants to share.

encoding
Translating a message into understandable symbols or language.

noise
Anything that hampers any stage of the communication process.

receiver
The person or group for which a message is intended.

medium
The pathway through which an encoded message is transmitted to a receiver.

decoding
Interpreting and trying to make sense of a message.

verbal communication
The encoding of messages into words, either written or spoken.

nonverbal communication
The encoding of messages by means of facial expressions, body language, and styles of dress.

a common understanding is reached. In both phases, a number of distinct stages must occur for communication to take place (see Figure 12.1).[5]

The **sender** (the person or group wishing to share information with some other person or group) starts the transmission phase by deciding on the **message** (the information to communicate). Then the sender translates the message into symbols or language, a process called **encoding.** Often, messages are encoded into words but they could also be symbols, such as :-) or a stop sign. **Noise** is a general term that refers to anything that hampers any stage of the communication process. In the *Case in Contrast,* a source of noise was city manager Dobell's failure to pay attention and listen to employee concerns about how a change in the workweek would affect their lives.

Once encoded, a message is transmitted through a medium to the **receiver**, the person or group for which the message is intended. A **medium** is simply the pathway—such as a phone call, a letter, a memo, or face-to-face communication in a meeting—through which an encoded message is transmitted to a receiver. At the next stage, the receiver interprets and tries to make sense of the message, a process called **decoding**. This is a critical point in communication.

The feedback phase is begun by the receiver (who becomes a sender). The receiver decides what message to send to the original sender (who becomes a receiver), encodes it, and transmits it through a chosen medium (see Figure 12.1). The message might contain a confirmation that the original message was received and understood, a restatement of the original message to make sure that it was correctly interpreted, or a request for more information. The original sender decodes the message and makes sure that a common understanding has been reached. If the original sender determines that a common understanding has not been reached, the sender and receiver go through the whole process as many times as needed to reach a common understanding. As the *Case in Contrast* indicates, failure to listen to employees prevents many managers from receiving feedback and reaching a common understanding with their employees. Feedback eliminates misunderstandings, ensures that messages are correctly interpreted, and enables senders and receivers to reach a common understanding.

Nonverbal Communication

The encoding of messages into words, written or spoken, is **verbal communication**. We also encode messages without using written or spoken language. **Nonverbal communication** shares information by means of facial expressions (smiling, raising an eyebrow, frowning, dropping one's jaw), body language (posture, gestures, nods, shrugs), and even style of dress (casual, formal, conservative,

Figure 12.1 | The Communication Process

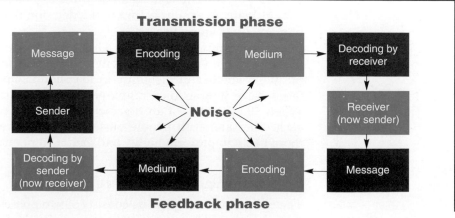

trendy). As we mentioned in Chapter 10, walk into Toronto-based Willow Manufacturing and you will find everyone who works there, even president Dennis Wild, wearing the same style of uniform.[6] That is one way the company conveys that everyone at Willow is part of the team, and equally important.

As Wild realizes, nonverbal communication can reinforce verbal communication. Just as a warm and genuine smile can back up words of appreciation for a job well done, a concerned facial expression can back up words of sympathy for a personal problem. In such cases, similarity between verbal and nonverbal communication helps to ensure that a common understanding is reached.

People tend to have less control over nonverbal communication, and often a verbal message that is withheld gets expressed through body language or facial expressions. For instance, studies show that maintaining eye contact while speaking is seen as being more credible and more competent than if eye contact wanders. A manager who agrees to a proposal that she or he actually is not in favour of may unintentionally communicate disfavour by grimacing.

It is important to be aware of nonverbal aspects of communication, as well as the literal meaning of the words. You should particularly be aware of contradictions between the messages. A manager may say it's a good time to discuss a raise, but then keep looking at the clock. This nonverbal signal may indicate that this is really *not* a good time to talk. Thus, actions can speak louder (and more accurately) than words. A variety of popular books help one interpret body language. However, do use some care. For instance, while it is often thought that crossing your arms in front of your chest is showing resistance to a message, you might also do this simply because you feel cold.

The Role of Perception in Communication

perception

The process through which people select, organize, and interpret sensory input to give meaning and order to the world around them.

Perception plays a central role in communication and affects both transmission and feedback. **Perception** is the process through which people select, organize, and interpret sensory input to give meaning and order to the world around them. But it is inherently subjective and influenced by people's personalities, values, attitudes, and moods, as well as by their experience and knowledge. Thus, when senders and receivers communicate with each other, they are doing so based on their own subjective perceptions. The encoding and decoding of messages and even the choice of a medium hinge on the perceptions of senders and receivers.

In addition, perceptual biases can hamper effective communication. Recall from Chapter 3 that *biases* are systematic tendencies to use information about others in ways that result in inaccurate perceptions. In Chapter 3, we described a number of biases that can result in diverse members of an organization being treated unfairly. These same biases also can lead to ineffective communication. For example, stereotypes—simplified and often inaccurate beliefs about the characteristics of particular groups of people—can interfere with the encoding and decoding of messages.

One of the issues that hurt the potential merger between Fishery Products International and Halifax-based Clearwater Fine Foods was a comment by Clearwater's John Risley (CEO at the time, and now chair). When Newfoundlanders protested the number of jobs that would be lost in the proposed merger, he declared: "This is a culture in which people think there's value in the number of jobs that become eligible for unemployment insurance."[7] He was stereotyping those in the fishery industry in Newfoundland. After he made this statement, any message he tried to encode to employees would be viewed with suspicion. Employees would effectively decode all of Risley's message as meaning he had no respect for them. As Allan Moulton, a union leader and worker at FPI's plant in Marystown, Newfoundland for 30 years, pointed out: "We're not the only seasonal workers in Canada and it's unfortunate Newfoundland really got pegged

Clearwater Fine Foods
www.clrwater.ca

Fishery Products
International Ltd.
www.fpil.com

with this." He added: "We worked long hours in this industry and every single worker worked hard to save Fishery Products International, and we were successful and we want to get back to doing that."[8] Instead of relying on stereotypes, effective communicators strive to perceive other people accurately by focusing on their actual behaviours, knowledge, skills, and abilities. Accurate perceptions, in turn, contribute to effective communication.

INFORMATION RICHNESS AND COMMUNICATION MEDIA

Think About It

Eavesdropping on Voice Mail and Email

National Post writer Jonathan Kay recently interviewed an employee who was fired for forwarding dirty jokes to clients via email.[9] The man did not want to be identified by his real name, so Kay referred to him as "Fred Jones." Jones sold network computers for a living, and during this employment had earned consistently good performance reviews and always received top bonuses. Jones believed he sent the jokes only to the clients he thought would like them, and assumed that a client would tell him if he or she did not. Unbeknownst to him, however, a client had complained to the company about the dirty jokes, and after the company investigated, it fired Jones. Jones still does not completely understand why he was fired. He feels his email was private, and no different from telling jokes at the water cooler.

Questions
1. When is email an appropriate way to communicate?
2. Should managers listen to their subordinates' voice mail messages or read their email?

To be effective communicators, individuals need to select an appropriate communication medium for *each* message they send. Should a change in procedures be communicated to subordinates in a memo or sent as email? Should a congratulatory message about a major accomplishment be communicated in a letter, in a phone call, or over lunch? Should a layoff announcement be made in a memo or at a plant meeting? Should the members of a purchasing team travel to Europe to finalize a major agreement with a new supplier, or should they do this through faxes?

There is no one best communication medium. In choosing a communication medium for any message, individuals need to consider three factors:

information richness

The amount of information that a communication medium can carry and the extent to which the medium enables sender and receiver to reach a common understanding.

- *The level of information richness that is needed.* **Information richness** is the amount of information a communication medium can carry and the extent to which the medium enables sender and receiver to reach a common understanding.[10] The communication media that managers use vary in their information richness (see Figure 12.2).[11] Media high in information richness are able to carry a lot of information and generally enable receivers and senders to come to a common understanding.

- *The time needed for communication.* Managers' and other organizational members' time is valuable, and this affects the way messages should be sent.

- *The need for a paper or electronic trail.* An individual may want written documentation that a message was sent and received.

In the remainder of this section, we examine four types of communication media that vary along these three dimensions: information richness, time, and need for a paper or electronic trail.[12]

Figure 12.2 | The Information Richness of Communication Media

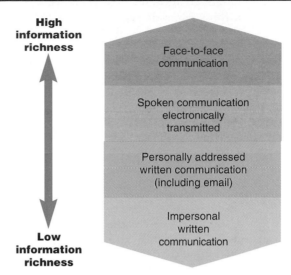

High
information
richness

Face-to-face
communication

Spoken communication
electronically
transmitted

Personally addressed
written communication
(including email)

Impersonal
written
communication

Low
information
richness

Face-to-Face Communication

Face-to-face communication has the highest information richness. When individuals communicate face to face, they not only can take advantage of verbal communication but also can interpret each other's nonverbal signals, such as facial expressions and body language. A look of concern or puzzlement can sometimes tell more than a thousand words, and individuals can respond to these nonverbal signals on the spot. Face-to-face communication also enables instant feedback. Points of confusion, ambiguity, or misunderstanding can be resolved, and individuals can cycle through the communication process as many times as they need to, to reach a common understanding.

Because face-to-face communication is highest in information richness, you might think that it should always be the medium of choice. This is not the case, however, because of the amount of time it takes and the lack of a paper or electronic trail resulting from it. For messages that are important, personal, or likely to be misunderstood, it is often well worth the time to use face-to-face communication and, if need be, supplement it with some form of written communication documenting the message.

Many organizations are using videoconferences to capture some of the advantages of face-to-face communication (such as access to facial expressions), while saving time and money because individuals in different locations do not have to travel to meet with one another. In addition to saving travel costs, videoconferences can speed up decisions, shorten new product development time, and lead to more efficient meetings. Some managers have found that meetings are 20- to 30-percent shorter when they use videoconferences instead of face-to-face meetings.[13]

Spoken Communication Electronically Transmitted

After face-to-face communication, spoken communication electronically transmitted over the phone is second-highest in information richness (see Figure 12.2).

Sally McNeil, a manager at HP Canada, knows that her telecommuting employees can feel disconnected from the workplace sometimes. She tries to call them once a week to offer support, and makes sure that they receive emails about office events and parties.

Although individuals communicating over the phone do not have access to body language and facial expressions, they do have access to the tone of voice in which a message is delivered, the parts of the message the sender emphasizes, and the general manner in which the message is spoken, in addition to the actual words themselves. Thus, phone conversations have the capacity to convey extensive amounts of information. Individuals also can ensure that mutual understanding is reached because they can get quick feedback over the phone and can answer questions.

Voice mail systems and answering machines also allow people to send and receive verbal electronic messages. Such systems are obviously a necessity when managers or employees are frequently out of the office, and those on the road are well advised to check their voice mail periodically.

Personally Addressed Written Communication

Lower than electronically transmitted verbal communication in information richness is personally addressed written communication (see Figure 12.2). One of the advantages of face-to-face communication and verbal communication electronically transmitted is that they both tend to demand attention, which helps ensure that receivers pay attention. Personally addressed written communication such as a memo or letter also has this advantage. Because it is addressed to a particular person, the chances are good that the person will actually pay attention to (and read) it. Moreover, the sender can write the message in a way that the receiver is most likely to understand. Like voice mail, written communication does not enable a receiver to have his or her questions answered immediately, but when messages are clearly written and feedback is provided, common understandings can still be reached. Even if managers use face-to-face communication, a follow-up in writing is often needed for messages that are important or complicated and need to be referred to later on.

Email

E-Mail Etiquette
www.emailreplies.com

Email also fits into this category of communication media because senders and receivers are communicating through personally addressed written words. The words are appearing on their personal computer screens, however, rather than on pieces of paper. Email is becoming so widespread in the business world that managers are even developing their own email etiquette. For instance, messages in capital letters are often perceived as being shouted or screamed. Here are some guidelines from polite emailers:

- Always punctuate messages.

- Do not ramble on or say more than you need to.

- Do not act as though you do not understand something when in fact you do understand it.

- Pay attention to spelling and format (put a memo in memo form).

While the growing use of email has enabled better communication within organizations, not all benefits have been positive. Many individuals complain of "email overload," and being unable to keep up with all the email that arrives, even personally addressed messages. In addition, some employees sexually harass co-workers through email, and employees often find their electronic mailboxes clogged with junk mail. In a recent survey, more than half of the organizations surveyed acknowledged some problems with their email systems.[14]

To avoid these and other costly forms of email abuse, managers need to develop a clear policy specifying what company email can and should be used for and what is out of bounds. Managers also should clearly communicate this policy to all members of an organization, as well as describe both the procedures that will be used when email abuse is suspected and the consequences that will result when email abuse is confirmed.

The increasing use of voice mail and email in companies large and small has led to some ethical concerns, as we noted at the beginning of this section. These forms of communication are not necessarily private. The federal Privacy and Access to Information Acts apply to all federal government departments, most federal agencies, and some federal Crown corporations, but many private sector employees are not covered by privacy legislation. Only Quebec's privacy act applies to the entire private sector.

The ethics of listening to other people's voice mail or reading their email are likely to be a growing concern for many managers. While no comparable Canadian data are available, a recent survey of more than 2000 large American firms found that 38 percent reported that they "store and review" employee email messages. This was up from 27 percent in 1999 and just 15 percent in 1997.[15] The Ontario, Manitoba, and BC governments have told their employees that email will be monitored if abuse is suspected. The governments' positions are that the internet and email should be used only for business purposes.

Impersonal Written Communication

Impersonal written communication is lowest in information richness and is well suited for messages that need to reach a large number of receivers. Because such messages are not addressed to particular receivers, feedback is unlikely, so managers must make sure that messages sent by this medium are written clearly in language that all receivers will understand.

Managers can use impersonal written communication, including company newsletters, for various types of messages, including rules, regulations, policies, newsworthy information, and announcements of changes in procedures or the arrival of new organizational members. Impersonal written communication also can be used to communicate instructions about how to use machinery or how to process work orders or customer requests. For these kinds of messages, the paper trail left by this communication medium can be invaluable for employees. Much of this information is also being posted to company intranets. The danger with impersonal communication, however, is that individuals will not read it, so it is important that employees are made aware of important messages.

Tips for Managers

Information Richness and Communication Media

1. For messages that are important, personal, or likely to be misunderstood, consider using face-to-face communication or videoconferences.

2. Consider using videoconferences instead of face-to-face meetings to save time and travel costs.

3. Frequently check voice mail when out of the office.

4. For messages that are complex and need to be referred to later on, use written communication either alone or in conjunction with face-to-face communication, verbal communication electronically transmitted, or videoconferences.

5. Develop a clear policy specifying what company email can and cannot be used for, and communicate this policy to all organizational members.

Developing Communication Skills

Think About It

Understanding Cultural Symbolisms

Communicating with someone of your own cultural background can sometimes cause confusion when you don't know them. Imagine communicating with someone from a different culture, where symbols have different meanings.[16] For instance, Tiffany boxes, much like Birks boxes, are blue, and often wrapped in white ribbons. But when gifts from the New York store were presented to officials of a Shanghai company, the ribbons had to be changed to red, because white stands for death in China. White ribbons would have made the gift recipients uncomfortable.

Business travellers to China have also had to learn how to use chopsticks appropriately. Stabbing them into a bowl of rice and leaving them there is viewed as an act of hostility, because it signifies death to the Chinese. Such faux pas are less likely to be the deal killers they once were, because globalization has helped individuals gain more understanding of each other, but they can lead to misunderstandings.

Question
1. What can you do to communicate more effectively with others?

There are various kinds of barriers to effective communication in organizations. Some barriers have their origins in senders. When messages are unclear, incomplete, or difficult to understand, when they are sent over an inappropriate medium, or when no provision for feedback is made, communication suffers. Other communication barriers have their origins in receivers. When receivers pay no attention to, or do not listen to messages, or when they make no effort to understand the meaning of a message, communication is likely to be ineffective.

To overcome these barriers and effectively communicate with others, managers (as well as other organizational members) must possess or develop certain communication skills. Some of these skills are particularly important when individuals send messages, and others are critical when individuals receive messages. These skills help ensure not only that individuals will be able to share information, but that they will have the information they need to make good decisions and take action, and also that they will be able to reach a common understanding with others.

Communication Skills for Senders

Individuals can make sure that they consider all of the steps of the communication process when they are engaging in communication. They can also develop their skills in giving feedback. We discuss each of these issues in turn.

Improving the Communication Process

Table 12.1 summarizes seven communication skills that help ensure that when individuals send messages, they are properly understood and the transmission phase of the communication process is effective. Let's see what each skill entails.

SEND CLEAR AND COMPLETE MESSAGES Individuals need to learn how to send a message that is clear and complete. A message is clear when it is easy for the receiver to understand and interpret, and it is complete when it contains all the information that the sender and receiver need to reach a common understanding. In trying to send messages that are both clear and complete, managers must learn

Table 12.1 | **Seven Communication Skills for Managers as Senders of Messages**

- Send messages that are clear and complete
- Encode messages in symbols that the receiver understands
- Select a medium that is appropriate for the message
- Select a medium that the receiver monitors
- Avoid filtering and information distortion
- Ensure that a feedback mechanism is built into messages
- Provide accurate information to ensure that misleading rumours are not spread

to anticipate how receivers will interpret messages, and adjust messages to eliminate sources of misunderstanding or confusion.

ENCODE MESSAGES IN SYMBOLS THE RECEIVER UNDERSTANDS

Individuals need to appreciate that when they encode messages, they should use symbols or language that the receiver understands. When sending messages in English to receivers whose native language is not English, for example, it is important to use commonplace vocabulary and to avoid clichés that, when translated, may make little sense and in some cases are unintentionally comical or insulting.

jargon

Specialized language that members of an occupation, group, or organization develop to facilitate communication among themselves.

Jargon, specialized language that members of an occupation, group, or organization develop to facilitate communication among themselves, should never be used to communicate with people outside the occupation, group, or organization. For example, truck drivers refer to compact cars as "roller skates," highway dividing lines as "paints," and orange barrels around road construction areas as "Schneider eggs." Using this jargon among themselves results in effective communication because they know precisely what is being referred to. But if a truck driver used this language to send a message (such as "That roller skate can't stay off the paint") to a receiver who did not drive trucks, the receiver would not know what the message meant.[17]

SELECT A MEDIUM APPROPRIATE FOR THE MESSAGE

When choosing among communication media, individuals need to take into account the level of information richness required, time constraints, and the need for a paper or electronic trail. A primary concern in choosing an appropriate medium is the nature of the message. Is it personal, important, nonroutine, and likely to be misunderstood and in need of further clarification? If it is, face-to-face communication is likely to be in order.

SELECT A MEDIUM THAT THE RECEIVER MONITORS

Another factor that individuals need to take into account when selecting a communication medium is whether it is one that the receiver uses. Not everyone checks voice mail and email routinely. Many people simply select the medium that they themselves use the most and are most comfortable with, but doing this can often lead to ineffective communication. No matter how much an individual likes email, sending an email message to someone else who never checks his or her email is useless. Learning which individuals like things in writing and which prefer face-to-face interactions and then using the appropriate medium enhances the chance that receivers will actually receive and pay attention to messages.

A related consideration is whether receivers have disabilities that limit their ability to decode certain kinds of messages. A blind receiver, for example, cannot read a written message. Managers should ensure that their employees with disabilities have resources available to communicate effectively with others.

filtering
Withholding part of a message out of the mistaken belief that the receiver does not need or will not want the information.

AVOID FILTERING AND INFORMATION DISTORTION Filtering occurs when senders withhold part of a message because they (mistakenly) think that the receiver does not need the information or will not want to receive it. Filtering can occur at all levels in an organization and in both vertical and horizontal communication. Rank-and-file employees may filter messages they send to first-line managers, first-line managers may filter messages to middle managers, and middle managers may filter messages to top managers. Such filtering is most likely to take place when messages contain bad news or problems that subordinates are afraid they will be blamed for.

information distortion
Changes in the meaning of a message as the message passes through a series of senders and receivers.

Information distortion occurs when the meaning of a message changes as the message passes through a series of senders and receivers. Some information distortion is accidental—due to faulty encoding and decoding or to a lack of feedback. Other information distortion is deliberate. Senders may alter a message to make themselves or their groups look good and to receive special treatment.

Managers themselves should avoid filtering and distorting information. But how can they eliminate these barriers to effective communication throughout their organization? They need to establish trust throughout the organization. Subordinates who trust their managers believe that they will not be blamed for things beyond their control and will be treated fairly. Managers who trust their subordinates provide them with clear and complete information and do not hold things back.

INCLUDE A FEEDBACK MECHANISM IN MESSAGES Because feedback is essential for effective communication, individuals should build a feedback mechanism into the messages they send. They either should include a request for feedback or indicate when and how they will follow up on the message to make sure that it was received and understood. When writing letters and memos or sending faxes, one can request that the receiver respond with comments and suggestions in a letter, memo, or fax; schedule a meeting to discuss the issue; or follow up with a phone call. Building feedback mechanisms such as these into messages ensures that messages are received and understood.

rumours
Unofficial pieces of information of interest to organizational members but with no identifiable source.

PROVIDE ACCURATE INFORMATION Rumours are unofficial pieces of information of interest to organizational members but with no identifiable source. Rumours spread quickly once they are started, and usually they concern topics that organizational members think are important, interesting, or amusing. Rumours, however, can be misleading and can cause harm to individual employees and to an organization when they are false, malicious, or unfounded. Managers can halt the spread of misleading rumours by providing organizational members with accurate information on matters that concern them.

Giving Feedback

We have discussed the importance of feedback in making sure that communication is understood. We can also talk about providing feedback more generally, because communicating feedback is an important task for managers. While positive feedback is easier to give, many individuals do not provide such feedback. Most people find giving negative feedback more difficult. Individuals can learn from feedback, whether it is positive or negative, so providing it in a timely fashion is important. The following suggestions can lead to more effective feedback:

- *Focus on specific behaviours.* Individuals should be told what it was that they did well or poorly, rather than simply being told that they did a good job. They can learn more from comments such as "You were very organized in your presentation," or "You managed your time effectively on this project," than when told simply, "Great job."

- *Keep feedback impersonal.* When giving feedback, you should describe the behaviour, rather than judge or evaluate the person.[18] Particularly when giving negative feedback, it is easy to focus on personal characteristics (rudeness, laziness, incompetence, etc.), but this rarely helps the person learn from mistakes. It is better to explain that the report was late, it contained a number of errors, and was missing an important section.

- *Keep feedback goal-oriented.* Feedback should not be given just because it will make you feel better. Rather, it should have a goal, such as improving performance for next time.

- *Make feedback well timed.* Feedback should be given shortly after the behaviour occurs. This ensures that the individual remembers the event, and also is more likely to result in change if change is needed. Giving feedback to someone six months later, during a performance review, is usually not helpful. If a situation has provoked an emotional response in you, however, delaying feedback until you have had time to lessen the emotional impact is wise.

- *Direct negative feedback toward behaviour that the receiver can control.* When giving negative feedback, consider which things the individual can fix, and which are out of his or her control. Criticizing someone's writing skills and then suggesting that the person take a writing course focuses on behaviour that can be controlled. Criticizing someone for not sending an important email when the company's network was down is not likely a situation the individual can fix or control.

Communication Skills for Receivers

Senders also receive messages, and thus they must possess or develop communication skills that allow them to be effective receivers of messages. Table 12.2 summarizes three of these important skills, which we examine in greater detail.

Pay Attention

When individuals are overloaded and forced to think about several things at once, they sometimes do not pay sufficient attention to the messages they receive. To be effective, however, individuals should always pay attention to messages they receive, no matter how busy they are. For example, when discussing a project with a subordinate, an effective manager focuses on the project and not on an upcoming meeting with his or her own boss. Similarly, when individuals are reading written forms of communication, they should focus their attention on understanding what they are reading and not be sidetracked into thinking about other issues.

Be a Good Listener

Part of being a good communicator is being a good listener. This is an essential communication skill for all organizational members. Being a good listener is surprisingly more difficult than you might realize, however. The average person speaks at a rate of 125 to 200 words per minute, but the average listener can effectively process up to 400 words per minute. Therefore listeners are often thinking about other things at the same time that a person is speaking.

Table 12.2 | **Three Communication Skills for Managers as Receivers of Messages**

- Pay attention
- Be a good listener
- Be empathetic

It is important to engage in active listening, which requires paying attention, interpreting, and remembering what was said. Active listening requires making a conscious effort to hear what a person is saying, and interpreting it to see that it makes sense. Being a good listener is an essential communication skill in many different kinds of organizations, from small businesses to large corporations.

Organizational members can practise the following behaviours to become active listeners:[19]

1. *Make eye contact.* Eye contact lets the speaker know that you are paying attention, and it also lets you pick up nonverbal cues.
2. *Exhibit affirmative head nods and appropriate facial expressions.* By nodding your head and making appropriate facial expressions, you further show the speaker that you are listening.
3. *Avoid distracting actions or gestures.* Do not look at your watch, shuffle papers, play with your pencil, or engage in similar distractions when you are listening to someone talk. These actions suggest to the speaker that you are bored or uninterested. The actions also mean that you probably are not paying full attention to what is being said.
4. *Ask questions.* The critical listener analyzes what he or she hears, and asks questions. Asking questions provides clarification, and reduces ambiguity, leading to greater understanding. It also assures the speaker that you are listening.
5. *Paraphrase.* Paraphrasing means restating in your own words what the speaker has said. The effective listener uses such phrases as "What I hear you saying is . . ." or "Do you mean . . . ?" Paraphrasing is a check on whether you are listening carefully and accurately.
6. *Avoid interrupting the speaker.* Interruptions can cause the speaker to lose his or her train of thought and cause the listener to jump to wrong conclusions based on incomplete information.
7. *Don't overtalk.* Most of us prefer talking to listening. However, a good listener knows the importance of taking turns in a conversation.
8. *Make smooth transitions between the roles of speaker and listener.* The effective listener knows how to make the transition from listener to speaker roles, and then back to being a listener. It's important to listen rather than plan what you are going to say next.

Be Empathetic

Receivers are empathetic when they try to understand how the sender feels and try to interpret a message from the sender's perspective, rather than viewing a message from only their own point of view.

Understanding Linguistic Styles

Deborah Tannen, who has written a number of books on communication, describes **linguistic style** as a person's characteristic way of speaking. Elements of linguistic style include tone of voice, speed, volume, use of pauses, directness or indirectness, choice of words, credit-taking, and use of questions, jokes, and other manners of speech.[20] When people's linguistic styles differ and these differences are not understood, ineffective communication is likely. Differences in linguistic style can cause problems because linguistic style is often taken for granted. People rarely think about their own linguistic styles and often are unaware of how linguistic styles can differ. Communication between men and women can be affected by differences in linguistic style, as can communication cross-culturally.

Gender Differences

Research conducted by Tannen and other linguists indicates that the linguistic styles of men and women differ in practically every culture and language.[21] Men

linguistic style
A person's characteristic way of speaking.

Deborah Tannen
www.georgetown.edu/
faculty/tannend/

and women take their own linguistic styles for granted and thus do not realize when they are talking with someone of the opposite sex that gender differences in style may lead to ineffective communication.

In Canada and the United States, women tend to downplay differences between people, are not overly concerned about receiving credit for their own accomplishments, and want to make everyone feel more or less on an equal footing so that even poor performers or low-status individuals feel valued. They are less likely to criticize poor performance, as a result. Men, in contrast, tend to emphasize their own superiority and are not reluctant to acknowledge differences in status or differences in performance.[22]

Do some women try to prove that they are better than everyone else, and are some men unconcerned about taking credit for ideas and accomplishments? Of course. The gender differences in linguistic style that Tannen and other linguists have uncovered are general tendencies evident in many women and men but not in all women and men.

Where do gender differences in linguistic style come from? Tannen suggests that they develop from early childhood on. Girls and boys tend to play with children of their own gender, and the ways in which girls and boys play are quite different. Girls play in small groups, engage in a lot of close conversation, emphasize how similar they are to each other, and view boastfulness negatively. Boys play in large groups, emphasize status differences, expect leaders to emerge who boss others around, and give each other challenges to try to meet. These differences in styles of play and interaction result in differences in linguistic styles when boys and girls grow up and communicate as adults. The ways in which men communicate emphasize status differences and play up relative strengths, while the ways in which women communicate emphasize similarities and downplay individual strengths.[23]

Cross-Cultural Differences

Managers from Japan tend to be more formal in their conversations and more deferential toward upper-level managers and people with high status than are managers from Canada. Japanese managers do not mind extensive pauses in conversations when they are thinking things through or when they think that further conversation might be detrimental. Canadian managers, in contrast, find very lengthy pauses disconcerting and feel obligated to talk to fill the silence.[24]

Another cross-cultural difference in linguistic style concerns the appropriate physical distance separating speakers and listeners in business-oriented conversations.[25] The distance between speakers and listeners is greater in Canada, for example, than it is in Brazil or Saudi Arabia. Citizens of different countries also

Differences in linguistic style may come from early childhood, when girls and boys are inclined to play with members of their own sex. Girls tend to play in small groups, noting how they are similar to each other. Boys tend to emphasize status differences, challenging each other and relying on a leader to emerge.

vary in how direct or indirect they are in conversations and in the extent to which they take individual credit for accomplishments. Japanese culture, with its collectivist or group orientation, tends to encourage linguistic styles in which group rather than individual accomplishments are emphasized. The opposite tends to be true in the United States, where Americans proudly reel off their accomplishments.

These and other cross-cultural differences in linguistic style can and often do lead to misunderstandings. Communication misunderstandings and problems can be overcome if managers make themselves familiar with cross-cultural differences in linguistic styles. Before managers communicate with people from abroad, they should try to find out as much as they can about the aspects of linguistic style that are specific to the country or culture in question. Expatriate managers who have lived in the country in question for an extended period of time can be good sources of information about linguistic styles because they are likely to have experienced first-hand some of the differences that citizens of a country are not aware of. Finding out as much as possible about cultural differences also can help managers learn about differences in linguistic styles, for the two are often closely linked.

Managing Differences in Linguistic Styles

Managers should not expect to change people's linguistic styles and should not try to. Instead, to be effective, managers need to understand differences in linguistic styles. Knowing that some individuals are slower to speak up, or that they wait for cues to jump into a conversation, managers can be more proactive about inviting quiet members to speak up. As Tannen points out, "Talk is the lifeblood of managerial work, and understanding that different people have different ways of saying what they mean will make it possible to take advantage of the talents of people with a broad range of linguistic styles."[26]

Tips for Managers

Sending and Receiving Messages

1. Make sure that the messages you send are clear, complete, encoded in symbols the receiver will understand, and sent over a medium the receiver monitors.

2. Establish a sense of trust in your organization to discourage filtering and information distortion.

3. Send your messages in a way that will ensure that you receive feedback.

4. Pay attention to the messages you receive, be a good listener, and try to understand the sender's perspective.

5. Be attuned to differences in linguistic style and try to understand the ways they affect communication in your organization.

ORGANIZATIONAL CONFLICT

Think About It

Cayoosh Resort

Olympic gold medallist Nancy Greene-Raine's hopes of building a ski resort in Melvin Creek, near Lillooet, BC, have not gone as smoothly as her athletic competitions once did.[27] Green-Raine's business, NGR Resort Consultants Inc., which she runs with her developer husband, Al Raine, has spent years trying to gain permission to build Cayoosh Resort, a $500-million investment that would create 1000 jobs. Vancouver-based environmental groups say that the resort would destroy the grizzly bear habitat and threaten a pristine valley. The St'at'imc Nation, which includes 11 bands, has also objected to the development proposal, and has threatened road blockades if it proceeds.

"The only thing that would get talks going," Chief Gary John said, "would be if cabinet ministers from Ottawa and Victoria came to discuss 'the big picture,' which involves BC Rail, BC Hydro, and the sharing of resource revenues. Canada and British Columbia are very wealthy. They should be sharing some of that wealth, instead of leaving us in this welfare state."

Question

1. How do we effectively manage conflict?

organizational conflict

The discord that arises when the goals, interest, or values of different individuals or groups are incompatible and those individuals or groups block or thwart each other's attempts to achieve their objectives.

Organizational conflict often arises as the result of communication breakdowns among individuals or units. **Organizational conflict** is the discord that arises when the goals, interests, or values of different individuals or groups are incompatible and those individuals or groups block or thwart each other's attempts to achieve their objectives.[28] Conflict is an inevitable part of organizational life because the goals of different stakeholders such as managers and workers are often incompatible. Organizational conflict also can exist between departments and divisions that compete for resources or even between managers who may be competing for promotion to the next level in the organizational hierarchy.

Though many people dislike conflict, it is not always dysfunctional. Too little conflict can be as bad as too much conflict, but a medium level of conflict can encourage a variety of perspectives that improve organizational functioning and effectiveness and help decision making. Conflict is a force that needs to be managed rather than eliminated.[29] Managers should never try to eliminate all conflict but rather should try to keep conflict at a moderate and functional level to promote change efforts that benefit the organization. To manage conflict, one should understand the types and sources of conflict and to be familiar with certain strategies that can be effective in dealing with it.

Conflict Management Strategies

Organizational conflict can happen between individuals, within a group or department, between groups or departments, or even across organizations. Conflict can arise for a variety of reasons. Within organizations conflict occurs for such reasons as incompatible goals and time horizons, overlapping authority, task interdependencies, incompatible evaluation or reward systems, scarce resources, and status inconsistencies (see Figure 12.3).[30] Regardless of the source of the conflict, knowing how to handle conflict is an important skill.

The behaviours for handling conflict fall along two dimensions: *cooperativeness* (the degree to which one party tries to satisfy the other party's concerns) and *assertiveness* (the degree to which one party tries to satisfy his or her own concerns).[31] This can be seen in Figure 12.4. From these two dimensions emerge five conflict-handling behaviours:

- *Avoiding.* Withdrawing from conflict.

- *Competing.* One person tries to satisfy his or her own interests, without regard to the interests of the other party.

- *Compromising.* Each party is concerned about its own goal accomplishment and the goal accomplishment of the other party and is willing to engage in a give-and-take exchange and to make concessions until a reasonable resolution of the conflict is reached.

- *Accommodating.* One person tries to please the other person by putting the other's interests ahead of his or her own.

Figure 12.3 | Sources of Conflict in Organizations

• *Collaborating.* The parties to a conflict try to satisfy their goals without making any concessions and instead come up with a way to resolve their differences that leaves them both better off.

When the parties to a conflict are willing to cooperate with each other and devise a solution that each finds acceptable (through compromise or collaboration), an organization is more likely to achieve its goals. The difficulties faced by Nancy Greene-Raine in building a ski resort in British Columbia are considerable.

Figure 12.4 | Dimensions of Conflict-Handling Behaviours

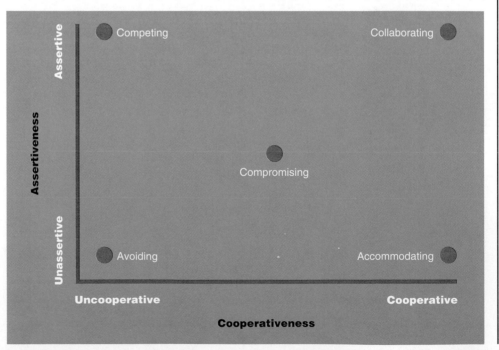

Source: K.W. Thomas, "Conflict and Negotiation in Organizations," in M.D. Dunnette and L.M. Hough (eds.), *Handbook of Industrial Psychology*, 2nd ed., vol. 3 (Palo Alto, CA: Consulting Psychologists Press, 1992), p. 668. Copyright 2001 by Acad. of Mgmt. Reproduced with permission of Acad. of Mgmt. in the format Textbook via Copyright Clearance Center.

Though the resort would bring a great number of jobs, as well as money to the area, Chief Gary John of the St'at'imc Nation sees these as short-term solutions to problems that have plagued the bands for years. He has taken a competing position, whereas the developers have tried to find some compromises.

Conflict management strategies that ensure conflicts are resolved in a functional manner focus on individuals and on the organization as a whole. Below, we describe four strategies that focus on individuals: increasing awareness of the sources of conflict, increasing diversity awareness and skills, practising job rotation or temporary assignments, and using permanent transfers or dismissals when necessary. We also describe two strategies that focus on the organization as a whole: changing an organization's structure or culture, and directly altering the source of conflict.

Strategies Focused on Individuals

INCREASING AWARENESS OF THE SOURCES OF CONFLICT Much conflict arises because individuals are not aware of how differences in linguistic styles, personality, background, and job requirements affect interactions. For example, differences in linguistic styles may lead some men in work teams to talk more, and take more credit for ideas, than women in those teams. These communication differences can result in conflict when the men incorrectly assume that the women are uninterested or less capable because they participate less, and the women incorrectly assume that the men are being bossy and are not interested in their ideas because they seem to do all the talking. Conflict can also arise when co-workers are unaware of the demands of each other's jobs, and place unrealistic expectations on someone to complete a project. When individuals are aware of the source of conflict, they can take steps to interact with each other more effectively. Awareness can be increased through diversity training, open communication, and job rotation or temporary assignments that increase understanding of the work activities and demands that others in an organization face.

USING PERMANENT TRANSFERS OR DISMISSALS Sometimes when other conflict resolution strategies do not work, managers may need to take more drastic steps, including permanent transfers or dismissals.

Suppose two first-line managers who work in the same department are always at each other's throats; frequent bitter conflicts arise between them even though they both seem to get along well with the other people they work with. No matter what their supervisor does to increase their understanding of each other, these conflicts keep occurring. In this case, the supervisor may want to transfer one or both managers so that they do not have to interact as frequently.

When dysfunctionally high levels of conflict occur among top managers who cannot resolve their differences and understand each other, it may be necessary for one of them to leave the company.

One of the issues in the dispute between the nurses in British Columbia and the Health Employers Association of BC is whether nurses are paid enough. Another one that British Columbia Nurses' Union president Debra McPherson raises is the chronic understaffing that hospitals seems unwilling to address.

Strategies Focused on the Organization

CHANGING STRUCTURE OR CULTURE Conflict can signal the need for changes in an organization's structure or culture. Sometimes, managers can effectively resolve conflict by changing the organizational structure they use to group people and tasks.[32] As an organization grows, for example, the *functional structure* that was effective when the organization was small may no longer be effective, and a shift to a product structure might effectively resolve conflicts (see Chapter 6).

Managers also can effectively resolve conflicts by increasing levels of integration in an organization. When individuals from different departments are assigned to the same team, they can directly resolve issues on the spot, rather than going through departments.

Sometimes managers may need to take steps to change an organization's culture to resolve conflict (see Chapter 7). Norms and values in an organizational culture might inadvertently promote dysfunctionally high levels of conflict that are difficult to resolve. For instance, norms that stress respect for formal authority may create conflict that is difficult to resolve when an organization creates self-managed work teams. Values stressing individual competition may make it difficult to resolve conflicts when organizational members need to put others' interests ahead of their own. In circumstances such as these, taking steps to change norms and values can be an effective conflict resolution strategy.

ALTERING THE SOURCE OF CONFLICT When conflict is due to overlapping authority, status inconsistencies, and incompatible evaluation or reward systems, managers can sometimes effectively resolve the conflict by directly altering the source of conflict–the overlapping authority, the status inconsistency, or the evaluation or reward system. For example, managers can clarify the chain of command and reassign tasks and responsibilities to resolve conflicts due to overlapping authority.

Tips for Managers

Handling Conflict

1. Try to handle conflicts by compromise or collaboration.
2. Analyze how differences among parties to a conflict (such as in linguistic styles, personality, age, or gender) may be contributing to misunderstandings and conflict.
3. Consider using job rotation or temporary assignments to help your subordinates understand the work activities and demands of other organizational members.
4. Analyze the extent to which conflict in your organization is due to a faulty organizational structure or a dysfunctional culture.

NEGOTIATION STRATEGIES

Think About It

Debra McPherson and the BC Nurses' Union

Debra McPherson, president of the British Columbia Nurses' Union (BCNU), is seen as an uncompromising person, one who stands her ground.[33] As head of the 25 000-member union, she points out that she needs to be firm, otherwise nurses would be treated even more poorly than they already are. In leading a recent job action against hospitals in British Columbia, she told administrators and the public alike that nurses should have a say in how health care is delivered, and that wages need to be a lot better than what has been offered. "Why should I be paid less than a freaking plumber?" she asks.

McPherson feels that the union is the only hope that nurses have to get better working conditions and pay. She sees hospital management "as oppressors and as barriers to good health management practices."

Questions
1. How does one engage in bargaining effectively?
2. What is a win-win solution?

A particularly important conflict resolution technique for managers and other organizational members to use in situations in which the parties to a conflict have approximately equal levels of power is negotiation. During **negotiation**, the parties to a conflict try to come up with a solution acceptable to themselves by considering various alternative ways to allocate resources to each other.[34]

There are two major types of negotiation—distributive negotiation and integrative bargaining.[35] In **distributive negotiation**, the parties perceive that they have a "fixed pie" of resources that they need to divide up.[36] They take a competitive, adversarial stance. Each party realizes that he or she must concede something but is out to get the lion's share of resources.[37] The parties see no need to interact with each other in the future and do not care if their interpersonal relationship is damaged or destroyed by their competitive negotiations.[38] To some extent, this is the stance that the BC Nurses' Union and hospital administrators have taken with each other.

In **integrative bargaining**, the parties perceive that they might be able to increase the resource pie by trying to come up with a creative solution to the conflict. They do not view the conflict competitively, as a win-or-lose situation; instead, they view it cooperatively, as a win-win situation in which all parties can gain. Integrative bargaining is characterized by trust, information sharing, and the desire of all parties to achieve a good resolution of the conflict.[39] For the BC Nurses' Union and the hospital administrators to show a commitment to integrative bargaining, each side would need to figure out ways to address some of the needs of the other, rather than simply taking an adversarial position.

There are five strategies that individuals can rely on to increase the odds of a win-win solution:[40]

- *Emphasize the big-picture goals.* This reminds individuals that they are working together for a larger purpose or goal despite their disagreements.

- *Focus on the problem, not the people.* All parties to a conflict need to keep focused on the source of the conflict and avoid the temptation to discredit each other by personalizing the conflict.

- *Focus on interests, not demands.* Demands are what a person wants, and interests are why the person wants them. When two people are in conflict, it is unlikely that the demands of both can be met. Their underlying interests often can be met, creating a win-win solution.

- *Create new options for joint gain.* Rather than having a fixed set of alternatives from which to choose, the parties can come up with new alternatives that might even expand the resource pie.

- *Focus on what is fair.* Emphasizing fairness will help the parties come to a mutual agreement about what is the best solution to the problem.

Any and all of these strategies would help the BC Nurses' Union and the hospital administrators negotiate with each other more effectively. When managers pursue these five strategies and encourage other organizational members to do so, they are more likely to resolve their conflicts effectively, through integrative bargaining. In addition, throughout the negotiation process, managers and other organizational members need to be aware of, and on their guard against, the biases that can lead to faulty decision making (see Chapter 4).[41]

Collective Bargaining

Collective bargaining is negotiation between labour unions and managers to resolve conflicts and disputes about important issues such as working hours, wages, benefits, working conditions, and job security. Before sitting down with

---

negotiation

A method of conflict resolution in which the parties in conflict consider various alternative ways to allocate resources to each other in order to come up with a solution acceptable to them all.

distributive negotiation

Adversarial negotiation in which the parties in conflict compete to win the most resources while conceding as little as possible.

integrative bargaining

Cooperative negotiation in which the parties in conflict work together to achieve a resolution that is good for them all.

British Columbia Nurses' Union (BCNU) www.bcnu.org

collective bargaining

Negotiation between labour unions and managers to resolve conflicts and disputes about issues such as working hours, wages, benefits, working conditions, and job security.

management to negotiate, union members sometimes go on strike to drive home their concerns to managers. Once an agreement that union members support has been reached (sometimes with the help of a neutral third party called a *mediator),* union leaders and managers sign a contract spelling out the terms of the collective bargaining agreement.

Collective bargaining is an ongoing consideration in labour relations. The signing of a contract, for example, does not bring collective bargaining to a halt. Disagreement and conflicts can arise over the interpretation of the contract. In these cases, a neutral third party known as an *arbitrator* is usually called in to resolve the conflict. An important component of a collective bargaining agreement is a *grievance procedure* through which workers who feel they are not being fairly treated are allowed to voice their concerns and have their interests represented by the union. Employees who feel they were unjustly fired in violation of a union contract, for example, may file a grievance, have the union represent them, and get their jobs back if an arbitrator agrees with them.

Tips for Managers

Negotiation

1. Whenever feasible, use integrative bargaining rather than distributive negotiation.
2. To help ensure that conflicts are effectively resolved through integrative bargaining, emphasize big-picture goals, focus on the problem not the people, focus on interests not demands, create new options for joint gain, and focus on what is fair.

SUMMARY AND REVIEW

Chapter Summary

COMMUNICATION IN ORGANIZATIONS

- The Communication Process
- The Role of Perception in Communication

INFORMATION RICHNESS AND COMMUNICATION MEDIA

- Face-to-Face Communication
- Spoken Communication Electronically Transmitted
- Personally Addressed Written Communication
- Impersonal Written Communication

COMMUNICATION IN ORGANIZATIONS Communication is the sharing of information between two or more individuals or groups to reach a common understanding. Good communication is necessary for an organization to gain a competitive advantage. Communication takes place in a cyclical process that has two phases: *transmission* and *feedback.*

INFORMATION RICHNESS AND COMMUNICATION MEDIA Information richness is the amount of information a communication medium can carry and the extent to which the medium enables the sender and receiver to reach a common understanding. Four categories of communication media in descending order of information richness are *face-to-face communication* (includes videoconferences), *spoken communication electronically transmitted* (includes voice mail), *personally addressed written communication* (includes email), and *impersonal written communication.*

DEVELOPING COMMUNICATION SKILLS There are various barriers to effective communication in organizations. To overcome these barriers and effectively communicate with others, individuals must possess or develop certain communication skills. As senders of messages, individuals should send messages that are clear and complete, encode messages in symbols the receiver understands, choose a medium that is appropriate for the message and monitored by the receiver, avoid filtering and information distortion, include a feedback mechanism in the message, and provide accurate information to ensure that misleading rumours are not spread. Communication skills for individuals as receivers of messages include paying *attention,* being a *good listener,* and being *empathetic.* Understanding linguistic styles is also an essential communication skill. Linguistic styles can vary by geographic region, gender, and country or culture. When these differences are not understood, ineffective communication can occur.

ORGANIZATIONAL CONFLICT Organizational conflict is the discord that arises when the goals, interests, or values of different individuals or groups clash, and those individuals or groups block or thwart each other's attempts to achieve their objectives. Conflict management strategies focused on individuals include increasing awareness of the sources of conflict, increasing diversity awareness and skills, practising job rotation or temporary assignments, and using permanent transfers or dismissals when necessary. Strategies focused on the whole organization include changing an organization's structure or culture and altering the source of conflict.

NEGOTIATION STRATEGIES Negotiation is a conflict resolution technique used when parties to a conflict have approximately equal levels of power and try to come up with an acceptable way to allocate resources to each other. In *distributive negotiation,* the parties perceive that there is a fixed level of resources for them to allocate, and each competes to receive as much as possible at the expense of the others, not caring about their relationship in the future. In *integrative bargaining,* the parties perceive that they may be able to increase the resource pie by coming up with a creative solution to the conflict, trusting each other, and cooperating with each other to achieve a win-win resolution. Five strategies that managers can use to facilitate integrative bargaining are to emphasize big-picture goals; focus on the problem, not the people; focus on interests, not demands; create new options for joint gain; and focus on what is fair. *Collective bargaining* is the process through which labour unions and managers resolve conflicts and disputes and negotiate agreements.

Roles in Contrast: Considerations

MANAGERS	EMPLOYEES
For routine information, email can be an appropriate mechanism of communication. Email is not a particularly good way to communicate important information such as performance appraisals, however.	Before communicating an important message, I should determine what forms of communication my manager prefers, and also consider that email overload could result in a message being overlooked.
To be a better listener, I should engage in active listening. This includes making eye contact, asking questions, and paraphrasing to make sure you understand what is being communicated.	To be a better listener, I should engage in active listening. This includes making eye contact, asking questions, and paraphrasing to make sure you understand what is being communicated.
While conflict can be dysfunctional if individuals refuse to work with each other, I should understand that some conflict is needed for effective decision making and high performance.	It is not necessary for me to be afraid of conflict. While it can be dysfunctional in some situations, some conflict is needed for effective decision making and high performance.

MANAGEMENT in Action

Topics for Discussion and Action

1. Interview a manager in an organization in your community to determine with whom he or she communicates on a typical day and what communication media he or she use.

2. Which medium (or media) do you think would be appropriate for each of the following kinds of messages that a subordinate could receive from his or her manager: messages about (a) a raise, (b) not receiving a promotion, (c) an error in a report prepared by the subordinate, (d) additional job responsibilities, and (e) the schedule for company holidays for the upcoming year? Explain your choices.

3. Why do some managers find it difficult to be good listeners?

4. Explain why subordinates might filter and distort information about problems and performance shortfalls when communicating with their managers.

5. Explain why differences in linguistic style, when not understood by senders and receivers of messages, can lead to ineffective communication.

6. Discuss why too little conflict in an organization can be just as detrimental as too much conflict.

7. Interview a manager in a local organization to determine the kinds of conflicts that occur in that manager's organization and the strategies that are used to manage them.

8. Why is integrative bargaining a more effective way of resolving conflicts than distributive negotiation?

Building Management Skills

DIAGNOSING INEFFECTIVE COMMUNICATION

Think about the last time you experienced very ineffective communication with another person—someone you work with, a classmate, a friend, or a member of your family. Describe the incident. Then answer the following questions.

1. Why was your communication ineffective in this incident?

2. What stages of the communication process were particularly problematic and why?

3. Describe any filtering or information distortion that occurred.

4. Do you think differences in linguistic styles adversely affected the communication that took place? Why or why not?

5. How could you have handled this situation differently so that communication would have been effective?

6. Are there conflict management strategies or bargaining strategies you could have used to improve the communication?

Management for You

Consider a person with whom you have had difficulty communicating. Using the communication skills for senders as a start, analyze what has gone wrong with the communication process with that person. What can be done to improve communication? To what extent did sender and receiver problems contribute to the communication breakdown?

Small Group Breakout Exercise

NEGOTIATING A SOLUTION

Form groups of 3 or 4 people. One member of your group will play the role of Jane Rister, 1 member will play the role of Michael Schwartz, and 1 or 2 members will be observer(s) and spokesperson(s) for your group.

Jane Rister and Michael Schwartz are assistant managers in a large department store. They report directly to the store manager. Today they are meeting to discuss important problems that they need to solve but on which they disagree.

The first problem hinges on the fact that either Rister or Schwartz needs to be on duty whenever the store is open. For the last six months, Rister has taken most of the least desirable hours (nights and weekends). They are planning their schedules for the next six months. Rister hoped Schwartz would take more of the undesirable times, but Schwartz has informed Rister that his wife has just started a nursing job that requires her to work weekends, so he needs to stay home on weekends to take care of their infant daughter.

The second problem concerns a department manager who has had a hard time retaining salespeople in his department. The turnover rate in his department is twice that of the other departments in the store. Rister thinks the manager is ineffective and wants to fire him. Schwartz thinks the high turnover is a fluke and the manager is effective.

The last problem concerns Rister's and Schwartz's vacation schedules. Both managers want to take off the week of July 1, but one of them needs to be in the store whenever it is open.

1. The group members playing Rister and Schwartz assume their roles and negotiate a solution to these 3 problems.
2. Observers take notes on how Rister and Schwartz negotiate solutions to their problems.
3. Observers determine the extent to which Rister and Schwartz use distributive negotiation or integrative bargaining to resolve their conflicts.
4. When called on by the instructor, observers communicate to the rest of the class how Rister and Schwartz resolved their conflicts, whether they used distributive negotiation or integrative bargaining, and their actual solutions.

Managing Ethically

About 75 percent of medium and large companies that were surveyed engaged in some kind of monitoring of employees' email and internet activities. Critics say this is an invasion of privacy. Proponents say that web surfing costs millions of dollars in lost productivity. What is your opinion of web surfing? To what extent should it be allowed? When does internet use at work become unethical? To what extent should it be monitored? When does monitoring become unethical?

Exploring the World Wide Web

SPECIFIC ASSIGNMENT

Many companies use the World Wide Web to communicate with prospective employees, including Ford Motor Company of Canada, Ltd. Scan the Ford website (www.ford.ca) to learn more about this company and the kinds of information it communicates to prospective employees through its website. Then click on "About Ford" and "Career Centre." Click on the various selections in this location of the website, such as "Ford in Canada," "Career Starting Points," "Empowerment, Diversity, Teamwork," and "Sharing in the Rewards."

1. What kinds of information does Ford communicate to prospective employees through its website?
2. How might providing this information on the web help Ford Canada attract new employees?

GENERAL ASSIGNMENT

Find the website of a company that you know very little about. Scan the website of this company. Do you think it effectively communicates important information about the company? Why or why not? Can you think of anything that customers or prospective employees might want to see on the website that is not currently there? Is there anything on the website that you think should not be there?

You're the Management Consultant

COMMUNICATION PROBLEMS AT AN INTERNET MERCHANDISER

Mark Chen supervises support staff for an internet merchandising organization that sells furniture over the internet. Chen has always thought that he needed to expand his staff, but just when he was about to approach his boss with such a request, the economy slowed down and other areas of the company have experienced layoffs. Thus, Chen's plans for trying to add to his staff are on indefinite hold.

However, he has noticed a troubling pattern of communication with his staff. Usually, when he wants one of his staff members to work on a task, he emails the individual with the necessary information. For the past few months, his email requests have been ignored and his subordinates have done what he asked only after he has visited them in person and given them specific deadlines. Each time, they apologized for not getting to it sooner but said that they were so overloaded with requests that they sometimes even stop answering their phones. Unless someone asks for something more than once, they feel that it is not that urgent and can be put on hold. Chen thinks this state of affairs is deplorable. Also, he realizes that his subordinates have no way of prioritizing tasks—thus, some very important projects he asked them to complete were put on hold until he followed up. Knowing he cannot add to his staff in the short term, Chen has come to you for advice. In particular, he wants to develop a system whereby his staff will provide some kind of response to requests within 24 hours; will be able to prioritize tasks, identifying their relative importance; and will not feel so overloaded that they ignore their manager's requests and do not answer their phones. As an expert in communication, advise Chen.

MANAGEMENT CASE IN THE NEWS

From the Pages of *The Globe and Mail* Stinging Office E-Mail Lights 'Firestorm'

The only things missing from the office memo were expletives. It had everything else. There were lines berating employees for not caring about the company. There were words in all capital letters like "SICK" and "NO LONGER." There were threats of layoffs and hiring freezes and a shutdown of the employee gym.

The memo was sent by e-mail on March 13 [2001] by the chief executive officer of Cerner Corp., which develops software for the health care industry and is based in Kansas City, Mo., with 3100 employees around the world.

Originally intended only for 400 or so company managers, it quickly took on a life of its own.

The e-mail message was leaked and posted on Yahoo. Its belligerent tone surprised thousands of readers, including analysts and investors. In the stock market, the valuation of the company, which was $1.5-billion (US) on March 20, plummeted 22 per cent in three days.

Now Neal Patterson, the 51-year-old CEO, variously described by people who know him as "arrogant," "candid" and "passionate," says he wishes he had never hit the send button.

"I was trying to start a fire," he said. "I lit a match, and I started a firestorm."

That's not hard to do in the internet age, when all kinds of messages in cyberspace are capable of stirring reactions and moving markets.

But in this case, Mr. Patterson was certainly not trying to manipulate the market; he was simply looking to crack the whip on his troops. That sometimes requires sharp language, he said, and his employees know how to take it with a grain of salt.

Business professors and market analysts apparently need more convincing. They are criticizing not only Mr. Patterson's angry tone, but also his mode of communication.

Mr. Patterson ran afoul of two cardinal rules for modern managers, they say. Never try to hold large-scale discussions over e-mail. And never, ever, use the company e-mail system to convey sensitive information or controversial ideas to more than a handful of trusted lieutenants. Not unless you want the whole world looking over your shoulder, that is.

In Mr. Patterson's case, this is what the world saw:

"We are getting less than 40 hours of work from a large number of our K.C.-based EMPLOYEES. The parking lot is sparsely used at 8 a.m.; likewise at 5 p.m. As managers—you either do not know what your EMPLOYEES are doing; or you do not CARE. You have created expectations on the work effort which allowed this to happen inside Cerner, creating a very unhealthy environment. In either case, you have a problem and you will fix it or I will replace you.

"NEVER in my career have I allowed a team which worked for me to think they had a 40-hour job. I have allowed YOU to create a culture which is permitting this.

NO LONGER."

Mr. Patterson went on to list six potential punishments, including laying off 5 per cent of the staff in Kansas City. "Hell will freeze over," he vowed, before he would dole out more employee benefits. The parking lot would be his yardstick of success, he said; it should be "substantially full" at 7:30 a.m. and 6:30 p.m. on weekdays and half full on Saturdays. "You have two weeks," he said. "Tick, tock."

That message, management experts say, created an atmosphere of fear without specifying what, if anything, was actually going wrong at the company. Moreover, it established a simplistic gauge of success—measuring worker productivity by the number of cars in a parking lot is like judging a book by its word count.

"It puts you at war with your employees and with your basic tendencies in human nature," said Jeffrey Pfeffer, a professor at the Stanford University Graduate School of Business. "It's the corporate equivalent of whips and ropes and chains."

But the more costly error was releasing such an inflammatory memo to a wide audience. Whenever a company does that these days, it is practically inviting a recipient to relay it to friends or even corporate rivals. At that point, a message of even the mildest interest to others will start churning through the farthest corners of the internet.

"I would not advocate the use of e-mail for a problem-solving discussion," said Ralph Biggadike, a professor at the Columbia University Graduate School of Business.

"E-mail does not really promote dialogue."

For Cerner, it apparently promoted a market upheaval. On March 22, the day after the memo was posted on the Cerner message board on Yahoo, trading in Cerner's shares, which typically runs at about 650 000 a day, shot up to 1.2 million shares. The following day, volume surged to four million. In three days, the stock price fell to US$34 from US$44.

Stephen Savas, an analyst with Goldman Sachs, said the memo got overblown. "But it did raise two real questions for investors. One: Has anything potentially changed at Cerner to cause such a seemingly violent reaction? And two: Is this a CEO that investors are comfortable with?"

Questions

1. How might Neal Patterson have more effectively communicated his message to his managers?
2. What were the particular problems associated with sending this kind of message via email?

MANAGEMENT CASE

From the Pages of *Canadian Press Newswire* Unions Find Fertile Ground at Newspapers

The war between Canada's newspaper fiefdoms has many of the front-line troops diving for the cover of organized labour.

Unions have been organizing newsrooms, capitalizing on the uncertainty of a shifting industry where the likes of Conrad Black have built up empires.

Reporters and editors at Southam Inc.'s *Calgary Herald* said Yes last week to union representation after a drive that caught many in the traditionally anti-union city off guard.

Several other newsrooms—including the independent *Halifax Chronicle-Herald* and *Mail-Star* and Southam's *Regina Leader-Post*—have also organized.

The *Thunder Bay Chronicle-Journal*, owned by Thomson Newspapers Co. Ltd., recently negotiated its first contract, as did the *St. Catharines Standard*, another of Black's Southam properties.

Bob Hackett of Simon Fraser University's School of Communications says Black, who controls 58 Canadian dailies through the Southam and Hollinger chains, is cutting back at papers like the *Leader-Post* to finance his bigger properties.

"In smaller and medium markets they have no competition and they don't have to worry about producing exceptional journalism," Hackett says. "All they have to be is acceptable to keep the optimum number of readers and advertisers."

He says employees fear for their jobs, especially when they've seen 25 per cent of the workforce lopped off, as was the case in Regina two years ago.

"But in Calgary, and it's a very encouraging development to me, journalists are worried about questions of editorial integrity."

Certification at the *Herald* leaves the *Edmonton Journal*, *Saskatoon StarPhoenix* and new *National Post* as the only major Black-controlled papers without a union in the newsroom.

Orland French, a former reporter with the *Globe and Mail* and now visiting professor at the University of Regina journalism program, says Black's purchase of Southam and its marriage with Hollinger has stirred the business like never before.

"On many of those papers they've gone through a lot of turmoil in the past year or two with Hollinger taking over, and this is the survivors trying to maintain some kind of security," French says of the unionizing.

The Toronto Star recently made a hostile takeover bid for Sun Media, which owns 15 dailies. That merger would further concentrate ownership.

"It really frightens people," says Arnold Amber, Canadian director of The Newspaper Guild Canada. "Uncertainty leads people to seek co-operative protection, and in a work setting that's a union."

The ownership trend is putting new demands on unions to become defenders of newsroom independence, says Simon Fraser's Hackett.

"Now with the *National Post* out, how long can we sustain competition between two national papers? What if the *Globe and Mail* goes under or if there's a merger?

"Some people are talking about journalistic chill. If you work in Canada and you run afoul of Conrad Black, you've hardly got anywhere else to go."

The Guild's Amber says fears about concentrated ownership have been a common theme in recent union drives.

Don Babick, president and chief operating officer of Southam, dismisses the suggestion that journalistic integrity is being threatened, calling it "a nice ploy for the organizing drive."

"If someone is preaching the bogeyman of interference from the top, then that's totally unfounded," Babick says. "There is no evidence of that happening at our newspapers."

Whether there's a union or not, local editorial managers will still decide what appears in their newspapers, he says.

Babick sees the organizing drives more as a function of two aggressive unions, the Guild and the Communications, Energy and Paperworkers Union of Canada, looking to expand.

Calgary Herald publisher Ken King says a communication breakdown between senior management and staff during an era of rapid change was one factor that led to the organizing drive by the Communications union.

"It's one thing to have problems; it's another thing to be seen to seemingly ignore them," says King.

"I indicated to staff that I was very regretful and accepted the responsibility that was associated with that and acknowledged to them that their concerns had been validated in large part."

King says the *Herald* is overhauling its structure with a major emphasis on opening new channels of communication.

A union news release identified the key issues at the *Herald* as "unfair and arbitrary treatment by management as well as concerns about editorial integrity." The *Herald* responded by suing the union for defamation.

Union vice-president Gail Lem says wage inequalities were also an issue in Calgary—senior reporters earn about $65 000 a year but many in the newsroom make considerably less.

She says many employees believe they were left no choice but to organize because of the overwhelming size of their employer.

"It's not the old *Calgary Herald* any more," she says. "It's part of a big chain where unfortunately quality journalism sometimes takes a back seat to the bottom line."

Source: R. Curren, "Unions Find Fertile Ground at Newspapers," *Canadian Press Newswire*, November 8, 1998.

Questions

1. What are the sources of conflict at the various newspapers between publishers and the editors and reporters?
2. What strategies could be used to reduce the conflict?
3. What negotiation strategies could be used to reach agreement between the unions and the publishers?

CHAPTER 13
ORGANIZATIONAL CONTROL

Learning Objectives

1. Define organizational control, and describe the four steps of the control process.

2. Identify the main output controls, and discuss their advantages and disadvantages as means of coordinating and motivating employees.

3. Identify the main behaviour controls, and discuss their advantages and disadvantages as means of coordinating and motivating employees.

4. Explain why clan control is most effective for control in innovative organizations.

5. Explain how culture can control managerial behaviour.

Roles in Contrast: Questions

MANAGERS	EMPLOYEES
What are the goals that were set for my unit during this time frame?	What aspects of my performance are being measured?
What standards of performance will be used to determine whether the goals are being met?	Do the rewards match what I'm being told is being measured?
Have I conveyed the standards of performance to employees, and have I made sure that what gets measured also gets rewarded?	What do I need to understand in order to improve my performance?

A CASE IN CONTRAST

DIFFERENT APPROACHES TO OUTPUT CONTROL CREATE DIFFERENT MANAGERIAL RESPONSES

Giddings and Lewis (www.giddings.com)—the well-known manufacturer of automated factory equipment for companies such as General Motors (www.gm.com), Boeing (www.boeing.com), and Ford (www.ford.com)—was in trouble when CEO William J. Fife took control of the company. Fife had been given the responsibility to turn the company's performance around; it had been suffering because of rising costs and falling sales. Fife began the turn-around by embarking on a program to develop new products to widen the company's product range. Moreover, he coupled innovation with a focus on responsiveness to customers, even flying all over the United States to talk to customers to make sure that the products being developed would suit their needs.[1]

To motivate Giddings and Lewis's managers to raise the company's performance, Fife established exacting performance targets and goals. For example, managers were told to achieve goals such as "a 20-percent increase in sales" or "a 20-percent reduction in costs," and their bonuses were closely tied to their ability to reach their goals. Periodically, Fife met with his managers and reviewed their progress toward

meeting the goals. Measured by his managers' success in achieving their goals, Fife's turn-around program was successful. In five years, Giddings and Lewis was the most profitable firm in its industry.

In 2001, Gateway, Inc. (www.gateway.com), the personal computer maker, saw its customer satisfaction rating drop from third to fifth in consumer satisfaction with personal computer makers. This drop caused Gateway's managers considerable anxiety because they use this measure of customer satisfaction as an important indicator of their company's ongoing performance. They had already seen sales drop 11 percent over the past year.

After an investigation, management discovered that the source of customer dissatisfaction was 15 new rules the company had instituted for its customer-service reps to follow to reduce costs. Mike Ritter, director of Gateway consumer marketing, reported to Gateway CEO Ted Waitt that 2 rules in particular were the source of customer dissatisfaction. The first rule concerned the issue of customer-installed software. Gateway had told its service reps to inform customers that if they

Differing performance goals, and delivery of those performance goals, can often have positive effects on the outcomes, but different effects on managers and workers within the organizations. Both William J. Fife and Ted Waitt were successful in using goals to solve problems, but Fife destroyed the work values, norms, and culture of Giddings and Lewis in the process.

installed any other software on their machines this would invalidate Gateway's warranty. This angered customers. The second rule was one that rewarded customer-support reps on the basis of how quickly they handled customer calls, meaning that the more calls they handled in an hour or day, the higher their bonuses.

Because of these rules, customer reps were motivated to minimize the length of a service call, and in particular were unwilling to help solve customer problems that resulted from installation of "outlawed software," since this took a lot of time. Once Gateway's managers realized the source of the problem, they abolished the 15 rules immediately. Within one month in 2001, the 30-day survey saw customer satisfaction jump by more than 10 percent. Gateway was again struggling to contain costs in 2003, but its problems were related more to the high competition from Dell and Hewlett-Packard, rather than customer dissatisfaction.

CEOs Fife and Waitt both seem to have had considerable success in using performance goals to solve problems and control their managers, but the ways in which each CEO reacted to difficulties with these goals had very different effects on managers and employees within the organizations. At Gateway, Waitt listened to a critique of the rules, and then abolished them. Waitt's managers felt they had been heard, and that the company would indeed return to its culture of providing excellent customer service.

Fife's use of goals at Giddings and Lewis resulted in a very different response. Fife alone dictated the goals that his managers were expected to achieve. When the results did not please him (i.e., when a manager did not meet his or her goals), Fife verbally abused the offending manager in front of other managers, who were forced to sit through the attacks in embarrassed silence. Managers began to claim that Fife's use of goals to control behaviour was creating a competitive rather than a cooperative environment and was destroying Giddings and Lewis's culture. Giddings and Lewis's board of directors took the managers' side and asked Fife to resign.

 OVERVIEW

As the *Case in Contrast* suggests, the different ways in which Fife and Waitt decided to control the behaviour of their managers had very different effects on the way those managers behaved. Waitt was open to feedback on the goals, particularly when customer satisfaction dropped. Fife alone established the performance standards that managers at Giddings and Lewis were expected to achieve, and he closely monitored their progress. As a result of their different ways of controlling their employees, Fife and Waitt created very different cultures in their organizations. When managers make choices about how to influence and regulate their subordinates' behaviour and performance, they are choosing among different styles of control.

As discussed in Chapter 6, one major task facing managers is organizing—that is, establishing the structure of task and reporting relationships that allows organizational members to use resources most efficiently and effectively. Structure alone, however, does not provide the incentive or motivation for people to behave in ways that help achieve organizational goals. The purpose of organizational control is to provide managers with a means of motivating subordinates to work toward achieving organizational goals, and to provide managers with specific feedback on how well an organization and its members are performing. Organizational structure provides an organization with a skeleton, for which organizational control and culture provide the muscles, sinews, nerves, and sensations that allow managers to regulate and govern the organization's activities. The managerial functions of organizing and controlling are inseparable, and effective managers must learn to make them work together harmoniously.

In this chapter, we look in detail at the nature of organizational control and describe the steps in the control process. We discuss three types of control available to managers for controlling and influencing organizational members: *output control, behaviour control,* and *clan control* (which operates through the values and norms of an organization's culture).[2] By the end of this chapter, you will appreciate the rich variety of control systems available to managers and understand why developing an appropriate control system is vital to increasing the performance of an organization and its members.

WHAT IS ORGANIZATIONAL CONTROL?

Think About It

Nacan Products Promotes Safety

Collingwood, Ontario-based Nacan Products Ltd., a starch manufacturer, reached one million hours without a lost-time claim at the beginning of 2001.[3] The company is understandably pleased with its safety record. The potential safety hazards in the company include high-speed machinery, forklifts, and accidental slips, trips, and falls. Safety is an important concern at Nacan.

Corporate manager Terry Gates says that "All management personnel have safety [activities] in their development goals that [are] reviewed and used in their performance assessment to a weighted level of 25 percent of their overall salary increase." Employees who show a strong commitment to safety also get salary increases.

Nacan benchmarks itself against DuPont Canada, "which is hands down the top safety organization," says Gates. DuPont Canada has had more than 24 million hours without a lost-time injury. Gates thinks Nacan can duplicate DuPont's record because of the company's incentive programs. "Safety initiatives at our company don't just mean we walk the walk or talk the talk," says Gates. "It's also attached to our pay cheques."

Questions
1. How does planning relate to control?
2. What can organizations do to make sure they reach the standards they set for themselves?

Nacan Products Ltd.
www.nacan.com

DuPont Canada Inc.
www.dupont.ca

As noted in Chapter 1, *controlling* is the process that managers use to monitor and regulate how efficiently and effectively an organization and its members are performing the activities necessary to achieve organizational goals. As discussed in previous chapters, in *planning* and *organizing,* managers develop the organizational strategy and then create the structure that they hope will allow the organization to use resources most effectively to create value for customers. In *controlling,* managers monitor and evaluate whether their organization's strategy and structure support the plans they have created. Based on this evaluation they determine what could be improved or changed. In the case of Nacan Products, their plan is to benchmark the company against DuPont Canada. Having decided on that "plan," the managers then determine the controls they will put in place to achieve such a

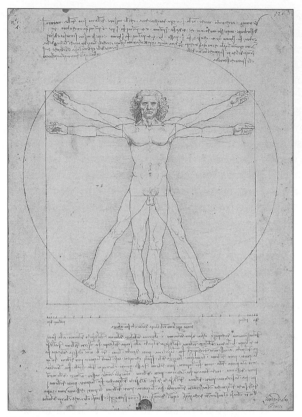

This famous Leonardo da Vinci drawing illustrates the artist's concern for understanding how the human body controls its own movements and how the different parts of the body work together to maintain the body's integrity. The interconnection of the body is similar to the way in which various departments operate in an organization.

safety record. We consider some of Nacan's control policies later in the chapter.

The Importance of Organizational Control

Control systems are intended to make organizations more successful. As we see in Figure 13.1, they help managers do the following:[4]

1. *Adapt to change and uncertainty.* We described in Chapter 2 how managers face uncertain task and external environments. New suppliers and customers can appear, as well as new technologies and regulations. Control systems help managers to anticipate these changes and be prepared for them.
2. *Discover irregularities and errors.* There may be problems with quality control, customer service, or even human resource management. Control systems help managers uncover these problems before they become too serious to overcome.
3. *Reduce costs, increase productivity, or add value.* Control systems can be used to reduce labour or production costs, to improve productivity, or to add value to a product, making it more attractive to a customer.
4. *Detect opportunities.* Control systems can help managers identify new markets, demographic changes, new suppliers, and other opportunities.
5. *Deal with complexity.* When organizations become large, it sometimes becomes impossible to know what the different units are doing. This is particularly the case when two companies merge. There may be redundancies in product lines or employees. Control systems help managers deal with these complexities.
6. *Decentralize decision making and facilitate teamwork.* When control systems are in place, managers can allow employees to make more decisions, and work in teams.

Figure 13.1 | How Does Control Help Managers?

Figure 13.2 | Steps in Organizational Control

| Establish standards against which performance is evaluated | Measure actual performance | Compare actual performance against chosen standards | Evaluate results and take corrective action when the standard is not being achieved |

Operating costs?

Time?

Quality?

Output?

Behaviour standards?

Monitoring Output
• Financial performance
• Organizational goals
• Operating budgets

Monitoring Behaviour
• Direct supervision
• Management by objectives
• Bureaucratic control

Is performance higher than expected?

Is performance as expected?

Is performance lower than expected?

Were standards too low? Should they be raised?

Confirm that standards are appropriate. Give appropriate rewards

Were standards unrealistic? Were the resources appropriate for the task?

Steps in the Control Process

The control process can be broken down into four steps: establishing standards of performance, then measuring, comparing, and evaluating actual performance (see Figure 13.2).[5]

Step 1: *Establish the standards of performance*

At Step 1 in the control process, managers decide on the standards of performance, goals, or targets that they will use to evaluate the performance of either the entire organization or some part of it, such as a division, a function, or an individual. The standards of performance that managers select measure efficiency, quality, responsiveness to customers, and innovation.[6] If managers decide to pursue a low-cost strategy, for example, they need to measure efficiency at all levels in the organization.

At the corporate level, a standard of performance that measures efficiency is *operating costs*—the actual costs associated with producing goods and services, including all employee-related costs. Top managers might set a corporate goal of "reducing operating costs by 10 percent for the next three years" to increase efficiency. Corporate managers might then evaluate divisional managers for their ability to reduce operating costs within their respective divisions, and divisional managers might set cost-savings targets for functional managers. Thus, performance standards selected at one level affect those at the other levels, and ultimately individual managers are evaluated for their ability to reduce costs. For example, S.I. Newhouse, the owner of Condé Nast Publications Inc., which produces magazines such as *GQ, Vanity Fair, Vogue,* and *Wired,* started an across-the-board attempt to reduce costs so he could reverse the company's losses, and instructed all divisional managers to begin a cost-cutting program. When Newhouse decided to retire he chose Steven T. Florio to replace him. Florio had been the division head

Condé Nast Publications Inc.
condenast.com

who had been most successful in reducing costs and increasing efficiency at *The New Yorker* magazine.

Managers can set a variety of standards, including time, output, quality, and behaviour standards. *Time standards* refer to how long it is supposed to take to complete a task. Some companies, for instance, instruct staff that all emails must be answered within 24 hours. *Output standards* refer to the quantity of the service or product the employee is to produce. *Quality standards* refer to the level of quality expected in the delivery of goods or services. For instance, a company might set what it considers an acceptable level of defects. Or a retail store might set a standard of one complaint per thousand customers served. Finally, a company might set *behaviour standards,* which can govern factors such as hours worked, dress code, or how one interacts with others.

Managers must be careful to choose standards of performance that are not harmful in unintended ways. If managers focus on just one issue (such as efficiency) and ignore others (such as determining what customers really want and innovating a new line of products to satisfy them), managers may end up hurting their organization's performance. This is what happened to Gateway. Its managers tried to increase efficiency and reduce costs by using policies that led customer-service representatives to cut short customer calls. Although this might have reduced costs, it resulted in a large decrease in customer satisfaction which hurt Gateway's effectiveness.

Step 2: *Measure actual performance*

Once managers have decided which standards or targets they will use to evaluate performance, the next step in the control process is to measure actual performance. In practice, managers can measure or evaluate two things: (1) the actual *outputs* that result from the behaviour of their members and (2) the *behaviours* themselves (hence the terms *output* control and *behaviour control).*[7]

Sometimes both outputs and behaviours can be easily measured. Measuring outputs and evaluating behaviour are relatively easy in a fast-food restaurant, for example, because employees are performing routine tasks. Managers of a fast-food restaurant can measure outputs quite easily by counting how many customers their employees serve and how much money customers spend. Managers can easily observe each employee's behaviour and quickly take action to solve any problems that may arise.

When an organization and its members perform complex, nonroutine activities that are difficult to measure, it is much more difficult for managers to measure outputs or behaviour.[8] It is very difficult, for example, for managers in charge of R&D departments at Merck or Microsoft to measure performance or to evaluate the performance of individual members because it can take 5 or 10 years to determine whether the new products that scientists are developing are going to be profitable. Moreover, it is impossible for a manager to measure how creative a research scientist is by watching his or her actions.

In general, the more nonroutine or complex organizational activities are, the harder it is for managers to measure outputs or behaviours.[9] Outputs, however, are usually easier to measure than behaviours because they are more tangible and objective. Therefore, the first kind of performance measures that managers tend to use are those that measure outputs. Then managers develop performance measures or standards that allow them to evaluate behaviours in order to determine whether employees at all levels are working toward organizational goals. Some simple behaviour measures are: Do employees come to work on time? Do employees consistently follow the established rules for greeting and serving customers? Each type of output and behaviour control and the way it is used at the different organizational levels—corporate, divisional, functional, and individual—is discussed in detail later in the chapter.

Step 3: *Compare actual performance against chosen standards of performance*

During Step 3, managers evaluate whether—and to what extent—performance deviates from the standards of performance chosen in Step 1. If performance is higher than expected, managers might decide that performance standards are too low and may raise them for the next time period to challenge subordinates.[10] Managers at Japanese companies are well known for the way they try to raise performance in manufacturing settings by constantly raising performance standards to motivate managers and employees to find new ways to reduce costs or increase quality.

However, if performance is too low and standards were not reached, or if standards were set so high that employees could not achieve them, managers must decide whether to take corrective action.[11] If managers are to take any form of corrective action, Step 4 is necessary.

Step 4: *Evaluate the result and initiate corrective action if necessary*

The final step in the control process is to evaluate the results. Whether performance standards have been met or not, managers can learn a great deal during this step. If managers decide that the level of performance is unacceptable, they must try to solve the problem. Sometimes, performance problems occur because the standard was too high—for example, a sales target was too optimistic and impossible to achieve. In this case, adopting more realistic standards can reduce the gap between actual performance and desired performance. However, if managers determine that something in the situation is causing the problem, then to raise performance they will need to change the way in which resources are being used.[12] Perhaps the latest technology is not being used, perhaps workers lack the advanced training they need to perform at a higher level, perhaps the organization needs to buy its inputs or assemble its products abroad to compete against low-cost rivals, or perhaps it needs to restructure itself or re-engineer its work processes to increase efficiency. If managers decide that the level has been achieved or exceeded, they can consider whether the standard set was too low. However, they might also consider rewarding employees for a job well done.

Establishing targets and designing measurement systems can be difficult for managers. Because of the high level of uncertainty in the organizational environment, managers rarely know what might happen. Thus, it is vital for managers to design control systems to alert them to problems so that these can be dealt with before they become threatening. Another issue is that managers are not just concerned with bringing the organization's performance up to some predetermined standard; they want to push that standard forward, to encourage employees at all levels to find new ways to raise performance.

Control Systems

control systems
Formal target-setting, monitoring, evaluation, and feedback systems that provide managers with information about how well the organization's strategy and structure are working.

As we see from the control process described above, managers need effective control systems to help them evaluate whether they are staying on target with their planned performance. **Control systems** are formal target-setting, monitoring, evaluation, and feedback systems that provide managers with information about whether the organization's strategy and structure are working efficiently and effectively.[13] Effective control systems alert managers when something is going wrong and give them time to respond to opportunities and threats. An effective control system has three characteristics:

- It is flexible enough to allow managers to respond as necessary to unexpected events.

- It provides accurate information and gives managers a true picture of organizational performance.

- It provides managers with the information in a timely manner because making decisions on the basis of outdated information is a recipe for failure.

New forms of information technology have revolutionized control systems because they ease the flow of accurate and timely information up and down the organizational hierarchy and between functions and divisions. Today, employees at all levels of the organization routinely feed information into a company's information system or network and start the chain of events that affect decision making at some other part of the organization. This could be the department-store clerk whose scanning of purchased clothing tells merchandise managers what kinds of clothing need to be reordered; or the salesperson in the field who uses a wireless laptop to send information about customers' changing needs or problems.

Control and information systems are developed to measure performance at each stage in the work process, from gathering inputs to delivering finished goods and services (see Figure 13.3).

Feedforward Control

feedforward control
Control that allows managers to anticipate and deal with potential problems.

Before the work begins, managers use **feedforward control** to anticipate possible problems that they can then avoid once the work is underway.[14] For example, by giving stringent product specifications to suppliers in advance (a form of performance target), an organization can control the quality of the inputs it receives from its suppliers and thus avoid potential problems at the conversion stage (see Figure 13.3). Similarly, by screening job applicants and using several interviews to select the most highly skilled people, managers can lessen the chance that they will hire people who lack the skills or experience needed to perform effectively. Another form of feedforward control is the development of management information systems that provide managers with timely information about changes in the task and general environments that may impact their organization later on. Effective managers always monitor trends and changes in the external environment to try to anticipate problems.

Concurrent Control

concurrent control
Control that gives managers immediate feedback on how efficiently inputs are being transformed into outputs so that managers can correct problems as they arise.

During the actual production phase, **concurrent control** gives managers immediate feedback on how efficiently inputs are being transformed into outputs so that managers can correct problems as they arise. Concurrent control alerts managers to the need for quick reaction to the source of the problem, be it a defective batch of inputs, a machine that is out of alignment, or an employee who lacks the skills necessary to perform a task efficiently. Concurrent control is at the heart of total

Figure 13.3 | Three Types of Control

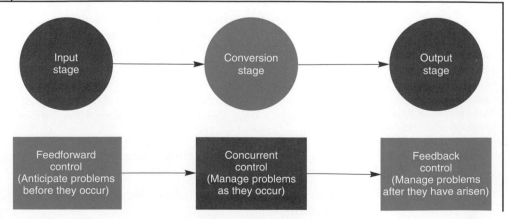

Figure 13.4 | Three Organizational Control Systems

Type of control	Mechanisms of control
Output control	Financial measures of performance Organizational goals Operating budgets
Behaviour control	Direct supervision Management by objectives Rules and standard operating procedures
Clan control	Values Norms Socialization

quality management programs, in which employees are expected to constantly monitor the quality of the goods or services they provide at every step of the production process and inform managers as soon as they discover problems. One of the strengths of Toyota's production system, for example, is that individual employees are given the authority to push a button to stop the assembly line whenever they discover a quality problem. When all problems have been corrected, the result is a finished product that is much more reliable.

Feedback control

feedback control

Control that gives managers information about customers' reactions to goods and services so that corrective action can be taken if necessary.

Once the work is completed, managers use **feedback control** to provide information about customers' reactions to goods and services so that corrective action can be taken if necessary. For example, a feedback control system that monitors the number of customer returns alerts managers when defective products are being produced, and a system that measures increases or decreases in product sales alerts managers to changes in customer tastes so they can increase or reduce the production of specific products.

Styles of Control

Managers need to determine internal control systems that will motivate employees and ensure that they perform effectively. In the following sections, we consider the three most important styles of control that managers use to coordinate and motivate employees: *output control, behaviour control,* and *clan control* (see Figure 13.4). Managers use all three to govern and regulate organizational activities, no matter what specific organizational structure is in place.

OUTPUT CONTROL

Think About It

ScotiaMcLeod Looks to Become a Conservative Blue-Chip Safe House

For decades, retail brokerage ScotiaMcLeod rewarded brokers by giving them a commission for every trade they made.[15] This type of reward ensured that brokers would actively trade in client accounts, thus increasing their commissions. Managing director James Werry, who runs Toronto-based Scotia-McLeod, wants brokers to be more accountable for the performance of the portfolios they manage. Under the commission system, it was the number of trades that generated income for the brokers, not how well the portfolio did. Now he wants brokers to generate fee-based accounts instead, where investors pay a quarterly or annual fee based on the size of their accounts. Accounts that are managed well by brokers will grow larger, so both the investor and the broker gain.

Questions
1. How do different mechanisms for control affect behaviour?
2. Why might ScotiaMcLeod want to change from a commission system to fee-based accounts?
3. How are organizational goals linked to control?

All managers, like William Fife and Ted Waitt (profiled in the *Case in Contrast)*, develop a system of output control for their organizations. First, they choose the goals or output performance standards or targets that they think will best measure factors such as efficiency, quality, innovation, and responsiveness to customers. Then they measure to see whether the performance goals and standards are being achieved at the corporate, divisional or functional, and individual levels of the organization. If the goals are being met, usually organizations give rewards to employees and managers. If goals are not being met, senior management needs to evaluate the reasons why performance standards are missed. Scotia McLeod had been measuring the number of trades that brokers made, and commissions were used as rewards for all trades. The company became concerned, however, that brokers were carrying out too many trades.

Financial Measures of Performance

Top managers are most concerned with overall organizational performance and use various financial measures to evaluate performance. The most common are *profit ratios, liquidity ratios, leverage ratios,* and *activity ratios.* They are discussed below and summarized in Table 13.1.[16]

Profit Ratios

Profit ratios measure how efficiently managers are using the organization's resources to generate profits. *Return on investment (ROI),* an organization's net income before taxes divided by its total assets, is the most commonly used financial performance measure because it allows managers of one organization to compare performance with that of other organizations. ROI allows managers to assess an organization's competitive advantage. *Gross profit margin* is the difference between the amount of revenue generated by a product and the resources used to produce the product. This measure provides managers with information about how efficiently an organization is using its resources and about how attractive customers find the product. It also provides managers with a way to assess how well an organization is building a competitive advantage.

Liquidity Ratios

Liquidity ratios measure how well managers have protected organizational resources so as to be able to meet short-term obligations. The *current ratio* (current assets divided by current liabilities) tells managers whether they have the resources available to meet the claims of short-term creditors. The *quick ratio* tells whether they can pay these claims without selling inventory.

Leverage Ratios

Leverage ratios such as the *debt-to-assets ratio* and the *times-covered ratio* measure the degree to which managers use debt (borrow money) or equity (issue new shares) to

Table 13.1 | Four Measures of Financial Performance

Profit Ratios			
Return on investment	$=$	$\dfrac{\text{Net profit before taxes}}{\text{Total assets}}$	Measures how well managers are using the organization's resources to generate profits.
Gross profit margin	$=$	$\dfrac{\text{Sales revenue—cost of goods sold}}{\text{Sales revenue}}$	The difference between the amount of revenue generated from the product and the resources used to produce the product.
Liquidity Ratios			
Current ratio	$=$	$\dfrac{\text{Current assets}}{\text{Current liabilities}}$	Do managers have resources available to meet claims of short-term creditors?
Quick ratio	$=$	$\dfrac{\text{Current assets—inventory}}{\text{Current liabilities}}$	Can managers pay off claims of short-term creditors without selling inventory?
Leverage Ratios			
Debt-to-assets ratio	$=$	$\dfrac{\text{Total debt}}{\text{Total assets}}$	To what extent have managers used borrowed funds to finance investments?
Times-covered ratio	$=$	$\dfrac{\text{Profit before interest and taxes}}{\text{Total interest charges}}$	Measures how far profits can decline before managers cannot meet interest charges. If ratio declines to less than 1, the organization is technically insolvent.
Activity Ratios			
Inventory turnover	$=$	$\dfrac{\text{Cost of goods sold}}{\text{Inventory}}$	Measures how efficiently managers are turning inventory over so excess inventory is not carried.
Days sales outstanding	$=$	$\dfrac{\text{Accounts receivable}}{\dfrac{\text{Total Sales}}{360}}$	Measures how efficiently managers are collecting revenues from customers to pay expenses.

finance ongoing operations. An organization is highly leveraged if it uses more debt than equity. Debt can be very risky when profits fail to cover the interest on the debt.

Activity Ratios

Activity ratios provide measures of how well managers are creating value from organizational assets. *Inventory turnover* measures how efficiently managers are turning inventory over so that excess inventory is not carried. *Days sales outstanding* provides information on how efficiently managers are collecting revenue from customers to pay expenses.

The objectivity of financial measures of performance is the reason why so many managers use them to assess the efficiency and effectiveness of their organizations. When an organization fails to meet performance standards such as ROI, revenue, or stock price targets, managers know that they must take corrective action. Thus, financial controls tell managers when a corporate reorganization might be necessary, when they should sell off divisions and exit from businesses, or when they should rethink their corporate-level strategies.[17] For example, Nortel Networks, JDS Uniphase Corp., and Lucent Technologies had to rethink corporate strategies in the spring and summer of 2001 after their stock prices plummeted.

While financial information is an important output control, on its own it does not provide managers with all the information they need about whether the plans they have made are being met. Financial results inform managers about the results of decisions they have already made; they do not tell managers how to find new opportunities to build competitive advantage in the future. To encourage a future-oriented approach, top managers, in their planning function, establish organizational goals that provide direction to middle and first-line managers. As part of the control function, managers evaluate whether those goals are being met.

Organizational Goals

Once top managers, in consultation with lower-level managers, have set the organization's overall goals, they then establish performance standards for the divisions and functions. These standards specify for divisional and functional managers the level at which their units must perform if the organization is to reach its overall goals.[18] For instance, if the goals for the year include improved sales, quality, and innovation, sales managers might be evaluated for their ability to increase sales, materials management managers for their ability to increase the quality of inputs or lower their costs, and R&D managers for the number of products they innovate or the number of patents they receive. By evaluating how well performance matches up to the goals set, managers at all levels can determine whether the plans they had made are being met, or whether adjustments need to be made in either the plans or the behaviours of managers and employees. Thus goals can be a form of control by providing the framework for what is evaluated and assessed.

Operating Budgets

operating budget
A budget that states how managers intend to use organizational resources to achieve organizational goals.

Once managers at each level have been given a goal or target to achieve, the next step in developing an output control system is to establish operating budgets that regulate how managers and employees reach those goals. An **operating budget** is a blueprint that states how managers intend to use organizational resources to achieve organizational goals efficiently. Typically, managers at one level allocate to subordinate managers a specific amount of resources to use to produce goods and services. Once they have been given a budget, these lower-level managers must decide how to allocate resources for different organizational activities. They are then evaluated for their ability to stay within the budget and to make the best use of available resources. The failure of many dot-com companies illustrates what happens when organizations do not emphasize control. It would appear that many dot-com companies focused more on spending whatever money came in (i.e., had a high "burn rate") without consideration of developing and then staying within a budget. This practice proved to be disastrous when investors decided to stop pouring money into these companies after they had little in the way of performance that they could show investors.

Large organizations often treat each division as a singular or stand-alone responsibility centre. Corporate managers then evaluate each division's contribution to corporate performance. Managers of a division may be given a fixed budget for resources and evaluated for the amount of goods or services they can produce using those resources (this is a *cost* or *expense* budget approach). Or managers may be asked to maximize the revenues from the sales of goods and services produced (a *revenue* budget approach). Or managers may be evaluated on the difference between the revenues generated by the sales of goods and services and the budgeted cost of making those goods and services (a *profit* budget approach). Japanese companies' use of operating budgets and challenging goals to increase efficiency is instructive in this context.

In summary, three components—objective financial measures, performance standards derived from goals, and appropriate operating budgets—are the essence of effective output control. Most organizations develop sophisticated output control systems to allow managers at all levels to maintain an accurate picture of the organization so that they can move quickly to take corrective action as needed.[19] Output control is an essential part of management.

Problems with Output Control

When designing an output control system, managers must be careful to avoid some pitfalls, as shown in Figure 13.5. First, they must be sure that their output standards motivate managers at all levels and do not cause managers to behave in inappropriate ways to achieve organizational goals. ScotiaMcLeod's system of rewarding for each individual trade ended up creating "churning." Brokers advised clients to trade too much, and this led to investigations by regulatory bodies, as well as fines and discipline against the brokerages and individual brokers.

Problems can also occur if the standards that are set turn out to be unrealistic. Suppose that top managers give divisional managers the goal of doubling profits over a three-year period. This goal seems challenging and reachable when it is jointly agreed upon, and in the first two years profits go up by 70 percent. In the third year, however, an economic recession hits and sales plummet. Divisional managers think it is increasingly unlikely that they will meet their profit goal. Failure will mean losing the substantial monetary bonus tied to achieving the goal. How might managers behave to try to preserve their bonus?

One course of action they might take is to find ways to reduce costs, since profit can be increased either by raising revenues or by reducing costs. Thus, divisional managers might cut back on expensive research and development activities, delay maintenance on machinery, reduce marketing expenditures, and lay off middle managers and employees to reduce costs so that at the end of the year they will make their target of doubling profits and will receive their bonus. This tactic might help them achieve a short-run goal—doubling profits—but such actions could hurt long-term profitability or ROI (because a cutback in R&D can reduce the rate of product innovation, a cutback in marketing will lead to the loss of customers, and so on).

The long term is what corporate managers should be most concerned about. Thus, top managers must consider carefully how flexible they should be when using output control. If conditions change (as they will because of uncertainty in the task and general environments), it is probably better for top managers to communicate to managers lower in the hierarchy that they are aware of the changes taking place and are willing to revise and lower goals and standards. Indeed, most organizations schedule yearly revisions of their five-year plan and goals.

Second, the inappropriate use of output control systems can lead lower-level managers and employees to behave unethically. If goals are too challenging, employees may be motivated to behave unethically toward customers, as sometimes happens in brokerage firms. ScotiaMcLeod has moved to a fee-based system to change the way in which its brokers are rewarded in order to reduce potential ethical conflicts.

Figure 13.5 | Pitfalls of Output Control

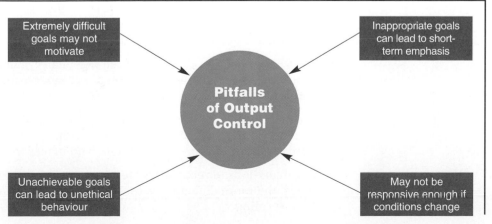

The message is clear: Although output control is a useful tool for keeping managers and employees at all levels motivated and the organization on track, it is only a guide to appropriate action. Output controls need to be flexible enough to accommodate changes in the organization's environment. Therefore, managers must be sensitive to how they use output control and constantly monitor its effects at all levels in the organization.

BEHAVIOUR CONTROL

Think About It

Nacan Products Revisited

Earlier in the chapter we discussed Nacan Products' safety record. The company has a series of controls in place to make sure that safety gets carried out. Each month, a new safety topic is discussed on the shop floor. There is a full-time safety coordinator who assists with safety initiatives. The company conducts safety audits to ensure compliance with all safety, environmental, and procedural regulations. Supervisors and staff conduct training programs.

Question
1. How are policies and procedures part of the control system?

Organizational structure is often viewed as a way of achieving control by designating who reports to whom, and what the responsibilities of each individual are. However, structure by itself does not provide any mechanism that motivates managers and nonmanagerial employees to behave in ways that make the structure work or even improve the way it works—hence the need for control. Output control is one way to motivate employees; behaviour control is another. In this section, we examine three mechanisms of behaviour control that managers can use to keep subordinates on track and make organizational structures work as they are designed to work: *direct supervision, management by objectives,* and *rules and standard operating procedures* (see Figure 13.4).

Direct Supervision

The most immediate and potent form of behaviour control is direct supervision by managers who actively monitor and observe the behaviour of their subordinates, teach subordinates the behaviours that are appropriate and inappropriate, and intervene to take corrective action as needed. When managers personally supervise subordinates, they lead by example and in this way can help subordinates develop and increase their own skill levels (leadership is the subject of Chapter 9). Thus, control through personal supervision can be a very effective way of motivating employees and promoting behaviours that increase efficiency and effectiveness.[20]
Nevertheless, certain problems are associated with direct supervision.

- It is very expensive. A manager can personally manage only a small number of subordinates effectively. Therefore, direct supervision requires a lot of managers and this will raise costs.

- It can demotivate subordinates if they feel that they are not free to make their own decisions. Subordinates may avoid responsibility if they feel that their manager is waiting to reprimand anyone who makes the slightest error.

- For many jobs, direct supervision is simply not feasible. The more complex a job is, the more difficult it is for a manager to evaluate how well a subordinate is performing.

For all of these reasons, output control is usually preferred to behaviour control. Indeed, output control tends to be the first type of control that managers at all levels use to evaluate performance.

Management by Objectives

To provide a framework within which to evaluate subordinates' behaviour and, in particular, to allow managers to monitor progress toward achieving goals, many organizations implement some version of management by objectives (MBO), which we described in Chapter 5.

From a control perspective, the important element of MBO is that managers and their subordinates need to periodically review the subordinates' progress toward meeting goals. Normally, salary raises and promotions are linked to the goal-setting process, and managers who achieve their goals receive greater rewards than those who fall short. (The issue of how to design reward systems to motivate managers and other organizational employees is discussed in Chapter 8.)

In companies that decentralize responsibility for the production of goods and services to empowered teams and cross-functional teams, management would review the accomplishments of the team, and then the rewards would be linked to team performance, not to the performance of any one team member. For either the individual or team situation, MBO creates the conditions for providing standards that are evaluated.

Bureaucratic Control

bureaucratic control

Control of behaviour by means of a comprehensive system of rules and standard operating procedures.

When direct supervision is too expensive and management by objectives is inappropriate, managers might turn to another mechanism to shape and motivate employee behaviour: bureaucratic control. **Bureaucratic control** is control by means of a comprehensive system of rules and standard operating procedures (SOPs) that shape and regulate the behaviour of divisions, functions, and individuals. In the appendix to Chapter 1, we discussed Max Weber's theory of bureaucracy and noted that all organizations use bureaucratic rules and procedures but some use them more than others.[21]

Rules and SOPs guide behaviour and specify what employees are to do when they confront a problem that needs a solution. It is the responsibility of a manager to develop rules that allow employees to perform their activities efficiently and effectively. When employees follow the rules that managers have developed, their behaviour is *standardized*—actions are performed in the same way time and time again—and the outcomes of their work are predictable. In addition, to the degree that managers can make employees' behaviour predictable, there is no need to monitor the outputs of behaviour because standardized behaviour leads to standardized outputs.

Suppose a worker at Toyota comes up with a way to attach exhaust pipes that reduces the number of steps in the assembly process and increases efficiency. Always on the lookout for ways to standardize procedures, managers make this idea the basis of a new rule: "From now on, the procedure for attaching the exhaust pipe to the car is as follows . . ." If all workers followed the rule to the letter, every car would come off the assembly line with its exhaust pipe attached in the new way, and there would be no need to check exhaust pipes at the end of the line. In practice, mistakes and lapses of attention do happen, so output control is used at the end of the line, and each car's exhaust system is given a routine inspection. However, the number of quality problems with the exhaust system is minimized because the rule (bureaucratic control) is being followed.

Service organizations such as retail stores and fast-food restaurants try to standardize the behaviour of employees by instructing them on the correct way to greet customers or the appropriate way to serve and bag food. Employees are trained to follow the rules that have proven to be most effective in a particular situation. The better trained the employees are, the more standardized is their behaviour, and the more trust managers can have that outputs (such as food quality) will be consistent.

Problems with Bureaucratic Control

All organizations make extensive use of bureaucratic control because rules and SOPs effectively control routine organizational activities. With a bureaucratic control system in place, managers can manage by exception and intervene and take corrective action only when necessary. However, managers need to be aware of a number of problems associated with bureaucratic control, because they can reduce organizational effectiveness.[22]

First, establishing rules is always easier than discarding them. Organizations tend to become overly bureaucratic over time if managers do everything according to the rule book. When the amount of "red tape" becomes too great, decision making slows and managers react slowly to changing conditions. This slowness can harm an organization's survival if quicker new competitors emerge.

Second, because rules constrain and standardize behaviour and lead people to behave in predictable ways, people may become so used to automatically following rules that they stop thinking for themselves. By definition, new ideas do not come from blindly following standardized procedures. Similarly, the pursuit of innovation implies a commitment by managers to discover new ways of doing things; innovation, however, is incompatible with the use of extensive bureaucratic control.

Managers must therefore be sensitive about the way they use bureaucratic control. It is most useful when organizational activities are routine and well understood and employees are making programmed decisions such as in mass-production settings or in a routine service setting, for example such restaurants and stores as Tim Horton's, Canadian Tire, and Midas Muffler. Bureaucratic control is not nearly as useful in situations where nonprogrammed decisions have to be made and managers have to react quickly to changes in the organizational environment.

To use output control and behaviour control, managers must be able to identify the outcomes they want to achieve and the behaviours they want employees to perform to achieve these outcomes.

Tips for Managers

Control

1. Identify the source(s) of an organization's competitive advantage (efficiency, quality, innovation, and customer responsiveness). Then design control systems that allow managers to evaluate how well they are building competitive advantage.

2. Involve employees in the goal-setting process and make MBO an organization-wide activity.

3. Choose the right balance of direct supervision and bureaucratic controls to allow managers to monitor progress toward goals and to take corrective action as needed.

4. Periodically evaluate the output and behaviour control system to keep it aligned with your current strategy and structure.

CLAN CONTROL

Think About It

WestJet's Employees Control Costs

WestJet's strategy is to keep costs low, and Clive Beddoe, WestJet's CEO and chair, says it's really his employees who contribute the most to cost-cutting.[23] The airline's profit margins are considerably higher than those of rival airlines, especially Air Canada. Beddoe wanted to make sure that employees felt responsible for WestJet's profitability, so he introduced a generous profit-sharing plan. The company's accountants say that the profit-sharing plan turns each employee into a 'cost cop' who is always looking for waste and savings. "We are one of the few companies that has to justify [to employees] its Christmas party every year," Derek Payne, treasury director, boasted and lamented.

WestJet encourages teamwork among its employees. There are no rigid job descriptions for positions, so employees have a lot of freedom to determine and carry out their day-to-day duties. However, all employees are required to help with all tasks. Sometimes even pilots load baggage. When a plane lands, all employees on the flight, even those flying on their own time, are expected to prepare the plane for its next takeoff. This saves the company $2.5 million annually in cleaning costs. It also means that planes usually have a half-hour turnaround, although turnarounds have been achieved in as little as six minutes.

Questions
1. What happens if you can neither measure output effectively nor use standard operating procedures?
2. How do you motivate employees to act as owners, and go above and beyond the call of duty for the organization?

For many of the most important organizational activities, output control and behaviour control are inappropriate for several reasons:

- Not all employees can be observed on a day-to-day basis.

- Rules and SOPs are of little use in either crisis situations or situations requiring innovation.

- Output controls can be a very crude measure of the quality of performance, and could in fact harm performance, in some instances.

Professionals such as scientists, engineers, doctors, and professors often have jobs that are relatively ambiguous in terms of standard operating procedures, and which may require individualized response based on the situation.

How can managers try to control and regulate the behaviour of their subordinates when personal supervision is of little use, when rules cannot be developed to tell employees what to do, and when outputs and goals cannot be measured at all or can be measured usefully only over long periods? One source of control increasingly being used by organizations is clan control, which relies on a strong organizational culture. This form of control is also increasingly being used in organizations that value innovation, and want to empower their employees.

How Clan Control Works

William Ouchi used the term **clan control** to describe the control exerted on individuals and groups in an organization by shared values, norms, standards of

clan control

Control exerted on individuals and groups in an organization by shared values, norms, standards of behaviour, and expectations.

behaviour, and expectations. The control arising from clan control is not an externally imposed system of constraints, such as direct supervision or rules and procedures, but constraints that come from organizational culture (discussed in Chapter 7).

Clan control is an important source of control for two reasons. First, it makes control possible in situations where managers cannot use output or behaviour control. Second and more important, when a strong and cohesive set of organizational values and norms is in place, employees focus on thinking about what is best for the organization in the long run—all their decisions and actions become oriented toward helping the organization perform well. For example, a teacher spends personal time after school coaching and counselling students; an R&D scientist works 80 hours a week, evenings and weekends, to help speed up a late project; a sales clerk at a department store runs after a customer who left a credit card at the cash register. Many researchers and managers believe that employees of some organizations go out of their way to help their organization because the organization has a strong and cohesive organizational culture—a culture that controls employee attitudes and behaviours. Strong bureaucratic control is less likely to foster positive attitudes and behaviours that encourage employees to go above and beyond. WestJet is an example of how effective clan culture can be in encouraging effective behaviour from all employees. CEO Clive Beddoe comments that he has "1400 sets of sharp eyes belonging to employees watching costs."[24]

WestJet Airlines Ltd.
www.westjet.com

How Culture Controls Managerial Action

The way in which organizational culture shapes and controls behaviour is evident in the way managers perform their four main functions—planning, organizing, leading, and controlling—when they work in different types of organizations (see Table 13.2). As we consider these functions, we continue to distinguish between two kinds of top managers: those who create organizational values and norms that encourage creative, *innovative* behaviour, and those who encourage a *conservative*, cautious approach by their subordinates. We noted earlier that both kinds of values and norms may be appropriate in different situations.

Planning

Top managers in an organization with an *innovative* culture are likely to encourage lower-level managers to take part in the planning process and develop a flexible approach to planning. They are likely to be willing to listen to new ideas and to take risks involving the development of new products.

In contrast, top managers in an organization with *conservative* values are likely to emphasize formal top-down planning. Suggestions from lower-level managers are

Table 13.2 | How Culture Controls Action

Managerial Function	Type of Organization	
	Conservative	**Innovative**
Planning	Formal, top-down planning	All managers encouraged to participate in decision making
Organizing	Well-defined hierarchy of authority and clear reporting relationships	Organic, flexible structure
Leading	Rigid MBO and constant monitoring	Managers lead by example, encourage risk-taking
Controlling	Bureaucratic control	Clan control

likely to be subjected to a formal review, which can significantly slow decision making. Although this deliberate approach may improve the quality of decision making in a nuclear power plant, it also can have unintended consequences. At conservative IBM, for example, before its more recent turnaround, the planning process became so formalized that managers spent most of their time assembling complex slide shows and overheads to defend their current positions rather than thinking about what they should be doing to keep IBM abreast of the changes taking place in the computer industry.

Organizing

Valuing creativity, managers in an *innovative* culture are likely to try to create an organic structure, one that is flat, with few levels in the hierarchy, and in which authority is decentralized so that employees are encouraged to work together to find solutions to ongoing problems. A product team structure may be very suitable for an organization with an innovative culture.

In contrast, managers in a *conservative* culture are likely to create a well-defined hierarchy of authority and establish clear reporting relationships so that employees know exactly to whom to report, and how to react to any problems that arise.

Leading

In an *innovative* culture, managers are likely to lead by example, encouraging employees to take risks and experiment. They are supportive regardless of whether employees succeed or fail.

In contrast, managers in a conservative culture are likely to develop a rigid management by objectives system and to constantly monitor subordinates' progress toward goals, overseeing their every move.

Controlling

As this chapter makes clear, there are many control systems that managers can adopt to shape and influence employee behaviour. The control systems managers choose reflect a choice about how they want to motivate organizational members and keep them focused on organizational goals. Managers who want to encourage the development of *innovative* values and norms that encourage risk-taking choose output and behaviour controls that match this objective. They are likely to choose output controls that measure performance over the long run and develop a flexible MBO system suited to the long and uncertain process of innovation.

In contrast, managers who want to encourage the development of conservative values choose the opposite combination of output and behaviour controls. They develop specific, difficult goals for subordinates, frequently monitor progress toward these goals, and develop a clear set of rules that subordinates are expected to adhere to. Sometimes managers who are hired by a company do not fit into the existing culture. Calgary-based WestJet fired CEO Steve Smith, who was far more controlling than the rest of the company's culture. WestJet's founders sent a strong message to the employees by firing Smith in a year when the company had done very well financially.

The values and norms of an organization's culture strongly affect the way managers perform their management functions. The extent to which managers buy into the values and norms of their organization shapes their view of the world and their actions and decisions in particular circumstances.[25] In turn, the actions that managers take can have an impact on the performance of the organization. Thus, organizational culture, managerial action, and organizational performance are linked together. Geoffrey Relph, interviewed as IBM's director of services marketing, notes that his previous company (GE Appliances in Louisville, Kentucky) had a

GE Appliances Company
www.geappliances.com

very different set of expectations than IBM Canada. "The priorities in GE are: 'Make the financial commitments. Make the financial commitments. Make the financial commitments.' At IBM, the company's attention is divided among customer satisfaction, employee morale, and positive financial results."[26] GE Appliances' focus on financial commitments may deter employees from also looking at customer satisfaction. Relph's experience at GE Appliances may also suggest that managers need to be concerned with employee morale.

Although organizational culture can give rise to managerial actions that ultimately benefit the organization, this is not always the case. Sometimes culture can become so much a part of the organization that it becomes difficult to improve performance.[27] For example, Wayne Sales, the new president and CEO of Canadian Tire, is trying desperately to revitalize customer service in the company's stores. Canadians have become so used to poor service that employees don't necessarily see the need to change. However, with alternatives such as Home Hardware, Revy Home Centres, and Home Depot Canada, lack of customer service is likely to become an increasing issue as Sales sets out to "drive away the chain's 'crappy tire' image."[28] He will need to change the control system to encourage employees to be more customer-focused.

Chapter Summary

WHAT IS ORGANIZATIONAL CONTROL?

- The Importance of Organizational Control
- Steps in the Control Process
- Control Systems
- Styles of Control

OUTPUT CONTROL

- Financial Measures of Performance
- Organizational Goals
- Operating Budgets
- Problems with Output Control

BEHAVIOUR CONTROL

- Direct Supervision
- Management by Objectives
- Bureaucratic Control
- Problems with Bureaucratic Control

CLAN CONTROL

- How Clan Control Works
- How Culture Controls Managerial Action

SUMMARY AND REVIEW

WHAT IS ORGANIZATIONAL CONTROL? Controlling is the process that managers use to monitor and regulate how efficiently and effectively an organization and its members are performing the activities necessary to reach organizational goals. Controlling is a four-step process: (1) establishing performance standards, (2) measuring actual performance, (3) comparing actual performance against performance standards, and (4) evaluating the results and taking corrective action if needed.

OUTPUT CONTROL To monitor output or performance, managers choose goals or performance standards that they think will best measure efficiency, quality, innovation, and responsiveness to customers at the corporate, divisional, departmental or functional, and individual levels. The main mechanisms that managers use to monitor output are financial measures of performance, organizational goals, and operating budgets.

BEHAVIOUR CONTROL In an attempt to shape behaviour and induce employees to work toward achieving organizational goals, managers use direct supervision, management by objectives, and bureaucratic control by means of rules and standard operating procedures.

CLAN CONTROL *Clan control* operates on individuals and groups through shared values, norms, standards of behaviour, and expectations. The way managers perform their management functions influences the kind of culture that develops in an organization.

Roles in Contrast: Considerations

MANAGERS	EMPLOYEES
It is important to understand the goals of the organization, and of my unit, to make sure that I put appropriate controls in place.	If I don't understand how I'm being evaluated for performance, I should ask my manager for that information.
Developing appropriate controls (output, behavioural, and clan) will help my unit achieve the required standards of performance.	I need to consider what behaviours get rewarded by my manager, and then make sure that I engage in those behaviours.
If I don't measure what I say is important for performance, or I don't reward what gets measured, then employees will engage in the behaviours that bring them rewards, even if these behaviours are not part of the intended goals.	If my rewards are not what I expect, I should consider whether my behaviours are meeting the goals of the organization and the unit, and adjust my behaviour accordingly.

MANAGEMENT
in Action

Topics for Discussion and Action

1. What is the relationship between organizing and controlling?
2. How do output control and behaviour control differ?
3. Ask a manager to list the main performance measures that he or she uses to evaluate how well the organization is achieving its goals.
4. Ask the same or a different manager to list the main forms of output control and behav-

iour control that he or she uses to monitor and evaluate employee behaviour.
5. Why is it important for managers to involve subordinates in the control process?
6. What is clan control, and how does it affect the way employees behave?
7. What kind of controls would you expect to find most used in (a) a hospital, (b) the Armed Forces, (c) a city police force. Why?

Building Management Skills

UNDERSTANDING CONTROLLING

For this exercise, you will analyze the control systems used by a real organization such as a department store, restaurant, hospital, police department, or small business. It can be the organization that you investigated for previous *Building Management Skills* exercises or a different one. Your objective is to uncover all the different ways in which managers monitor and evaluate the performance of the organization and employees.

1. At what levels does control take place in this organization?
2. Which output performance standards (such as financial measures and organizational goals) do managers use most often to evaluate performance at each level?
3. Does the organization have a management by objectives system in place? If it does, describe it. If it does not, speculate about why not.
4. How important is behaviour control in this organization? For example, how much of

managers' time is spent directly supervising employees? How formal is the organization? Do employees receive a book of rules to instruct them about how to perform their jobs?
5. To what extent does clan control have an impact on the organization? What is its relative importance compared with output and behaviour control?
6. Based on this analysis, do you think there is a fit between the organization's control systems and its culture? What is the nature of this fit? How could it be improved?

Management for You

Your parents have let you know that they are expecting a big party for their 25th wedding anniversary, and that you are in charge of planning it. Develop a timeline for carrying out the project, and then identify ways to monitor

progress toward getting the party planned. How will you know that your plans have been successful? At what critical points do you need to examine your plans to make sure that everything is on track?

Small Group Breakout Exercise

HOW BEST TO CONTROL THE SALES FORCE?

Form groups of 3 or 4 people, and appoint 1 member as the spokesperson who will communicate your findings to the whole class when called on by the instructor. Then discuss the following scenario.

You are the regional sales managers of an organization that supplies high quality windows and doors to building supply centres nationwide. Over the last three years, the rate of sales growth has slackened. There is increasing evidence that, to make their jobs easier, salespeople are primarily servicing large customer accounts and ignoring small accounts. In addition, the salespeople are not dealing promptly with customer questions and complaints, and this inattention has resulted in a drop in after-sales service. You have talked about these problems, and you are meeting to design a control system to increase both the amount of sales and the quality of customer service.

1. Design the control system that you think will best motivate salespeople to achieve these goals.

2. What relative importance do you put on (a) output control, (b) behaviour control, and (c) organizational culture in this design?

Managing Ethically

You are a manager of a group of 10 employees in their 20s. They are very innovative and are not accustomed to tight rules and regulations. Managers at the company want order and control on every front. Your team is fighting the rules and regulations, which is creating an ethical dilemma. They are being very productive and innovative but clearly not in the way the top management wants things run. You have been asked to bring more order to your team. You really like your team and think they are effective and will leave if they are forced to conform. And the company needs their expertise and energy to remain competitive in the high-tech world. What would you do?

Exploring the World Wide Web

SPECIFIC ASSIGNMENT

Enter Creo's website (www.creo.com). Under "Company" click on "About Creo" and then read the "Company Overview," "Awards and Recognition (where you will find a number of articles describing Creo's culture)," and "Philosophy." Also explore "Careers."

1. What evidence did you find that Creo engages in clan control?
2. How does Creo's organizational culture help the company to achieve its strategies?
3. How easy would it be to copy what Creo does in other companies?

GENERAL ASSIGNMENT

Search for the website of a company that actively uses organizational culture (or one of the other types of control) to build competitive advantage. What kind of values and norms is the culture based on? How does it affect employee behaviour?

You're the Management Consultant

DESIGNING CONTROL SYSTEMS FOR EFFECTIVE TEAM PERFORMANCE

You have been called in to advise the managers in charge of teams of web-design and web-hosting specialists and programmers. Each team is working on a different aspect of website production. While each team is responsible for the quality of its own performance, individual team performance also depends on how well the other teams perform. You are meeting to design a control system that will be used to motivate and reward all the teams. Your objective is to create a control system that will help to increase the performance of each team separately and facilitate cooperation between the teams, something that is necessary because the various projects are interlinked and affect one another—just as the different parts of the car must fit together. Since competition in the website production market is intense, the website has to be up and running as quickly as possible and must incorporate all the latest advances in website software technology.

Questions

1. What kind of outputs controls will best facilitate positive interactions both within the teams and between the teams?
2. What kind of behaviour controls will best facilitate positive interactions both within the teams and between the teams?
3. How would you use clan controls to promote high team performance?

MANAGEMENT CASE

Mutual Life Goes Public, and Changes Its Name

In June 1999, Waterloo, Ontario-based Mutual Life of Canada's policy holders voted to accept a plan to go public, which was presented by the company's management team.[29]

The company started issuing shares, and took on a new identity, as Clarica Life Insurance Co., to begin its life as a shareholder-owned company.

Bob Astley, Mutual's and then Clarica's president and CEO, told policy holders that the change to the company's operating procedures would be dramatic, and would include "Tough competition, new rules and a lot more people-watching."

Four of Canada's life insurers had gone public in recent years: Clarica, Sun Life Assurance Co., Manulife Financial Corp., and Canada Life Assurance Co. Doing so allowed the insurers to have opportunities similar to the banks, such as raising capital in the equity and debt markets. However, it also forced them to focus more on efficiency and profitability.

The trend to go public is the opposite of what some Canadian life insurers did in the 1950s and '60s. Back then the trend was to go from publicly traded companies to mutuals in order to be protected from possible foreign takeovers. Today, demutualization (i.e., becoming publicly traded) is a response to globalization and the need to raise capital for domestic or foreign expansion.

The shift from a mutual company to a publicly held company has had an impact on both Astley's way of managing and on his employees. The company used to make annual plans regarding strategy and performance. Within a short time, Astley said, the pace had increased considerably, and staff were "on 90-day business planning and individuals have 90-day personal plans."

Working for a publicly traded company is a new experience for many of the company's employees. The pace is different, and there is more stress involved in meeting performance standards. As Astley explains, "The single-minded focus on profitability in each of the business segments has been sharpened as a result of the public disclosure, the need to report earnings on a quarterly basis and the need to satisfy investors."

Astley spends his day a lot differently as well. Being a CEO for a publicly listed company caused him "to be much more focused on results and probably more demanding of the people around me. I spend more of my time thinking about and meeting with investors and analysts, explaining the company. I delegate more and I pick my spots. I don't get involved in activities inside the company that I can't afford the time for."

Eighteen months after Mutual became Clarica, Astley expressed annoyance at the constant jokes that "Clarica sounds like a brand of toilet bowl cleanser." He acknowledged that the company still had a ways to go to become a household name. "The name Clarica had no meaning in itself. Our task was to infuse it with meaning. We're working at that. It takes many, many months, indeed years, to build up name awareness to the highest level that we'd all want to have. We're still on that path."

Clarica's legal environment changed after the company first became a publicly listed company. New financial services legislation was expected to mean that Clarica, the smallest of the four life insurance companies that went public in 1999 and 2000, would face "a strategic alliance, merger with another insurance company or outright acquisition by a bank."

Astley set about getting his company ready for sale. "My goal in running the company is going to be to make us the most effective company we can, to have the highest share price we can, to be innovative and to continue to grow." The plan worked. On December 31, 2002, Clarica amalgamated with Sun Life Assurance, becoming a subsidiary of Sun Life Financial Services of Canada Inc., of which Astley is now president.

Questions

1. How have controls changed over time at the company that used to be known as Mutual Life?

2. Why might you expect changes in control systems for the company to become publicly traded?

Source: R. McQueen, "Polishing up Clarica Life: Sale Possible. Federal Legislation Would Make Insurer a Likely Target," *Financial Post (National Post),* December 4, 2000, p. C6; S. Gordon, "En Garde! Insurance Companies are Taking on the Banks More Directly, in the Marketplace and in the Regulatory Arena," *Canadian Banker,* March 2000, pp. 20–24; M. Strathdee, "Mutual Group to Meet June 10 on Issuing Shares," *Canadian Press Newswire,* March 25, 1999.

MANAGEMENT CASE ——————————————— IN THE NEWS

From the Pages of *The Vancouver Sun* Fast Ferry Directors Resign

VICTORIA—The cost of the troubled fast-ferry project is now expected to reach about $450 million, according to a scathing financial and management audit released Wednesday.

And senior BC Ferries managers misled both their board of directors and the minister responsible for the troubled fast ferries project, the audit finds.

The board of directors of BC Ferries Corp. and Catamaran Ferries International, the subsidiary building the ships, resigned following the release of the report on Wednesday.

Accountant Hugh Gordon said the plan to build three high-speed aluminum catamarans was doomed from the start by unrealistic budgets and construction timetables and later hampered by efforts to pretend the ships were on schedule.

Gordon found that there never was a final business plan for the project and that construction started without either complete designs or a final contract with one of the primary builders.

It also started before the training of the shipyard workers was complete.

Once under way, pressure to show progress added to the costs, Gordon found.

In 1997, sections of the hull of the first ferry were assembled prematurely to impress visiting APEC leaders.

In June of the following year, the first ship was launched long before it was ready by Premier Glen Clark and his wife Dale, who broke a bottle of champagne over the bow of what has now been revealed to have been little more than a brightly painted hull.

Gordon also confirmed that the original board of directors at Catamaran Ferries International, the wholly owned subsidiary of BC Ferries set up to build and market the new ships, had serious questions about the viability of the project.

Those questions were never answered. Instead, the original board, which had considerable business expertise, was replaced by members of the BC Ferries board.

The new board was headed by former union leader and long-time NDP supporter Jack Munro.

"Thereafter, board minutes are briefer and generally do not deal as fully with substantive management or financial issues," Gordon said.

When the fast ferry project was launched in 1994 under Clark, who was then the minister responsible for BC Ferries, it was estimated to cost $210 million "right down to the toilet paper."

The original estimate came from Tom Ward, Gordon said. Ward was then working for Vancouver Shipyards, one of the primary contractors on the fast ferry contract. He subsequently went to work for CFI and when Frank Rhodes stepped down in 1997, he became the head of both BC Ferries Corp and CFI.

In January Dan Miller, then the minister responsible for BC Ferries, accepted Ward's resignation when he learned that the projected cost of the first ship has risen to $113 million.

Gordon found that the cost of that ship is now more than $116 million. The second and third ships are expected to cost more than $100 million each.

Add to that about $90 million in financing costs, costs related to the building of the shed for construction of the ships, money spent developing B.C.'s ship-building industry and the expense of modifying some BC Ferries docks, among other things.

As recently as last September, the CFI board was told the projected cost of the first ship was $86 million, while accountants within CFI were forecasting a cost of $107 million.

Contacted by *The Vancouver Sun* Wednesday, Ward denied misleading anyone and said the cost projections in the Gordon report have been padded.

"It looks like everyone is trying to give themselves a hedge . . . I think at least $22 million has been added," Ward said.

He also denied that the schedule was unrealistic.

"They are saying the schedule was overly aggressive, but this project will have taken longer than it took to fight World War Two."

Rhodes, who was president of BC Ferries from the start of the project, could not be reached for comment.

After meeting with the board of CFI on Wednesday, Gordon Wilson, the new minister responsible for the ferry service, said the report detailed "a serious lack of governance over a huge project. We're now faced with a huge fiscal problem which we're going to have to deal with in this fiscal year."

Wilson refused to say who was responsible for the fiasco.

"I think it's safe to say I'm wanting a new direction and that's going to require a new board."

Bob Lingwood, who was appointed president of BC Ferries just three weeks ago, will serve as the interim chairman of the BC Ferries board until new members can be appointed.

Liberal ferry critic Doug Symons also blamed the premier and the minister responsible for BC Ferries. "Obviously there's been a cover-up," he said, repeating his call for a full public inquiry.

The Gordon report found that the cost overruns ran throughout the project.

Some costs were anticipated but underestimated. Labour on the first ship was more than double the budgeted cost.

Others, including the $102,000 cost of the mountain-lion decal on the side of the ship, were not anticipated.

The Soaring Cost of Fast Ferries:

June 1994—[Premier Glen] Clark announces cost as $210 million for three ferries, first one due in early 1996.

June 1995—Clark insists $210-million cost is all inclusive, "right down to the toilet paper."

July 1997—Cost now estimated at $74 million each, $222 million for all three.

March 1998—First vessel now to cost $86 million, total cost projected to be $260 million.

Jan. 17, 1999—Cost of first vessel now projected to be $113 million, cost of total program could be $300 million, minister admits.

Jan. 21, 1999—Philip Halkett, then president of BC Ferries, releases figures showing that total cost could reach $400 million, with $267 million already spent and none of the ships ready for service.

Feb. 24, 1999—An audit finds that the total cost of the fast-ferry project is now about $450 million, with the first ship costing $116 million.

Source: C. McInnes, J. Beatty and J. Hunte, "Fast Ferry Directors Resign as Projected Cost Hits $450 Million: A Scathing Audit Finds Senior BC Ferries Managers Misled Their Board and the Minister Responsible for the Project," *The Vancouver Sun,* February 25, 1999, p. A1.

Questions

1. Describe how control failed with the fast ferries project.
2. How would you design control systems to prevent what happened with the fast ferries project?

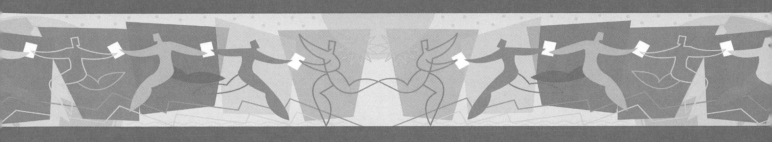

Integrated
Cases

IntegratedCase

From the Pages of the *National Post*
Canadian Tire at
Crossroads, Once Again

For Wayne Sales, the past is always present. As chief executive of Canadian Tire Corp. since last summer, he can't just denounce everything that happened before he took over because he was among the architects of the retailer's plan to renovate old stores and build new ones.

But in two years that strategy, the legacy of Mr. Sales' predecessor, Steve Bachand, will have run its course. There will be 480 Canadian Tire stores in Canada and no room for any more. That could be a problem because any retailer that doesn't keep growing can wither and die.

The United States beckons, but Canadian Tire tried southern exposure twice in the last 20 years and lost a total of $350-million. As soon as talk turns to such a plan, anyone with institutional memory around head office in Toronto wags a finger and gives a warning.

But why not try again? After all, this is a different Canadian Tire since all those U.S. banners began arriving after the Canada-U.S. Free Trade Agreement was signed. "We withstood everything that North America could throw at us," said Mr. Sales. "Not only have we been survivors, we've grown market share. You have to play your game. It's a horrible mistake when you see some of our competitors try to out-Depot Home Depot, out-Wal-Mart Wal-Mart. This is the thing I love about Canadian Tire. We're so unique in the marketplace. Canadians understand our format."

And yet after successfully defending itself, Canadian Tire began slipping last year. Mr. Bachand announced his retirement in January and the following month the company took a surprise $58.5-million writedown. "Canadian Tire was put in the penalty box," said Mr. Sales. "The stock was trading at the $29 range and then the day we announced the writedown went to $19. [Analysts] were blindsided and it became a surprise. I don't think it was a reaction to Steve retiring. CEOs retire all the time. For me, it was timing. There's a difference between information versus surprise."

For the next six months, the company conducted a global search before picking Mr. Sales, 50. The Virginia-born Mr. Sales is the third American to head Canadian Tire since Dean Muncaster was fired in 1985. Among those Mr. Sales beat out for the job was Andy Giancamilli, who has since resigned as president and chief operating officer of Kmart Corp., of Troy, Mich. "I came in a very difficult time, trying to refocus earnings momentum and giving it a strategy," said Mr. Sales.

Meanwhile, competition in Canada intensified. In the last five years, 120 big box stores have been built in Canada by Home Depot, Wal-Mart, Revy Home Centres and the rest. Canada has seen proportionately as much big-box growth in those five years as the United States did in 15.

Under Mr. Sales, some aspects of the past are being de-emphasized. Mr. Sales has put on hold Mr. Bachand's four-year plan to have two hundred PartSource stores. He still likes the stand-alone PartSource outlets because they can capture heavy do-it-yourself auto parts users where Canadian Tire only has 11% of market share and commercially installed parts where Tire has no market share. PartSource also has a defensive advantage in keeping out U.S. retailers such as Auto Zone. "I don't want to send any signal that it is a bad business model," Mr. Sales said. "It is a very profitable business model."

But the capital outlay required is substantial and 50 new PartSource stores would increase annual revenue, now $5.2-billion, by only $100-million. For the time being, Mr. Sales has decided to invest instead in new distribution centres in Montreal and Calgary. (PartSource outlets are unlike Canadian Tire outlets that are owned by independent dealers. Local Canadian Tire dealers own three, the other 25 are franchise operations.) Substantially increased revenue from other sources seems unlikely. E-commerce was begun in 2000, but sales from the 12,000 items available online is difficult to predict.

So, if there are no new stores, where will future revenue growth

come from? Mr. Sales has been meeting with Canadian Tire's controlling shareholder Martha Billes and the other members of the board of directors, aiming to produce a new strategy by Labour Day. He downplays expectations. "I don't think you're looking at a revolutionary strategic plan. To some, it'll be a yawner."

Canadian Tire went through a similar thought process in the past. In the late 1970s, the company believed it had run out of room east of the Rockies. In 1980, Canadian Tire expanded to British Columbia and lost money for years. In 1982, Canadian Tire bought a bankrupt chain in Texas and lost $250-million before the company bailed out in 1985. In the 1990s, a second, much smaller foray into the Northern Tier states caused a further loss of $100-million.

One thing is certain, Canadian Tire is unlikely to stray from its core business. Before joining Canadian Tire in 1992, Mr. Sales worked at Kmart in the United States for 25 years and has been distressed by Kmart's recent problems after it acquired too many unrelated companies.

Since taking over as chief executive Mr. Sales has replaced two officers, Ralph Trott, senior vice-president, business development, and John Rankin, senior vice-president, dealer relations, both of whom were part of the Bachand regime

He also reorganized the corporate structure into three divisions reporting to him: retail, credit cards and new business.

Mr. Sales is a more political and less prickly chief executive than Mr. Bachand. He will finish what they began together in terms of the building program but whatever the outcome of the strategic planning, three elements are already clear. First, he wants to improve in-store product availability, particularly on advertised specials. More inventory is not the answer; a just-in-time approach is. "There's this misconception that the higher the inventory the lower the out-of-stock position is. There's no correlation. When you have too much inventory you lose some degree of control. If I had one general complaint, on average, inventory is too heavy."

Second, he intends to take Canadian Tire in a new direction, one that permits less individuality among the dealers. To make his point, Mr. Sales cited his own travels in China where he soon grew tired of local food and yearned for the familiarity of a Big Mac. That has become his template for Canadian Tire; he wants every outlet to be as predictable as a McDonald's.

Some dealers are reluctant to cede autonomy. "They're beginning to use the 'm' word, mandatory. We're trying to seek the right balance. They do have a tendency to slow down the process, but in the

end, they help you get it right, they help prevent costly mistakes. Customers will choose to shop where they feel they have personal relationships."

As part of the plan, Mr. Sales has targeted the 40 worst dealers. "If you can't make the trip you have to exit the organization," Mr. Sales has told them. "I have a stewardship of this triangle that I take very seriously and how Canadians think about Canadian Tire. The strength of this is limited to the weakest link that we have in the organization."

The third part of the strategy is improved customer service. Surveys found 75% of customers think Canadian Tire is as good as or better than its competitors, but only 19% say Canadian Tire is the best. In response, Mr. Sales has increased in-store staff training and product knowledge. Fifty 30-minute self-teaching courses were already available via the Internet to employees; within 18 months, there will be 250 such programs. "Consumers were confused about what Canadian Tire represented. We must deliver a constant shopping experience in format, pricing and product. We have to become absolutely the best at what customers tell us today we're pretty good at."

Source: R. McQueen, "Canadian Tire at Crossroads, Once Again: Retailer Haunted by Past Attempts at Strategic Growth," *Financial Post (National Post)*, May 7, 2001, p. C7.

IntegratedCase

From the Pages of the *National Post*
Firm Encounters China
Syndrome

When Ray Perez was at business school in Canada in the late 1980s, he dreamed of opening up new consumer markets.

After graduating in 1989, Mr Perez, 33, joined Kooshies Baby Products, the family concern. The Toronto-based enterprise had just launched a range of non-disposable nappies and Mr Perez was soon appointed to run the factory. Convinced of the products' international sales potential, he helped to open up markets in more than 40 countries.

In 1996, with help from the Canadian International Development Agency, Kooshies entered into a joint venture with Diqiu, a Changzhou state-owned enterprise that was famous across China for its dyeing and flannel cotton products. Kooshies had a 51 per cent stake in Changzhou Kooshies Garments. Mr Perez himself took on the task of establishing a factory in China and opening up the Chinese market.

Kooshies' first factory was located in the suburbs of Changzhou, which is in Jiangsu province, around 100 miles inland from Shanghai. It took several months longer than expected to get the plant up and running. "Production has been the least of my problems," says Mr Perez.

Instead, his headaches were caused by the failure of the joint venture set-up, the management team he inherited and the difficulty of selling products to the local market. Neither Mr Perez nor the Shanghai-based consultancy that had recommended Diqiu realised it was on the verge of bankruptcy. Having contributed the plant and supplies of textiles, Diqiu failed to provide the agreed financial investment so Mr Perez was forced to run the business with 40 per cent less operating capital than planned.

The joint venture struggled on for a year before Kooshies bought out Diqiu's stake. For the next year, Mr Perez ran the business as a wholly foreign-owned concern. Unable to access credit locally or from the Canadian operation, he kept Kooshies afloat by stipulating that all distributors had to pay up front in cash.

In retrospect, Mr Perez believes his biggest mistake was taking on a management team from Diqiu. "The state-owned enterprise gave me all the riff-raff, people who had just slept for 10 years," he recalls. When he arrived in Changzhou Mr Perez drew up a list of raw materials to be sourced locally. Diqiu's procurement managers assured him that many of the products were unavailable in China. At first he deferred to their experience but then, on regular trips to Shanghai, began to source the materials himself.

He started to fire the local managers and within two years they had all been replaced, mostly by people under 25. For Mr Perez, they were "people with fresh minds, uncorrupted and much easier to train." It was not easy finding suitable management staff. Few Changzhou residents can speak English, and negotiating through interpreters took longer than Mr Perez had imagined. Finding people with creative talent, such as designers, has also been difficult. It has been harder still to find staff he can trust; information that was supposed to remain secret, such as salesmen's commissions, has often become common knowledge across the business.

Building up domestic sales to just under half of total turnover has been an uphill struggle, says Mr Perez. Around 20m Chinese babies are born each year, but Mr Perez observes that "the figures are a lot more beautiful in theory than in reality."

With severely scaled-back resources, the marketing budget was minimal and Kooshies' promotion relied mainly on Mr Perez and one local assistant. Travelling around China, they managed to place Kooshies products in 200 department stores in 14 provinces within 18 months.

Initially, the company relied on local distributors in each province. Now it also sells direct to some 20 local department stores. This needs a team of sales staff and stores only pay when they have sold the products.

Operating as a wholly foreign-owned concern gave Mr Perez full

control, but he had no support. In August 1999, however, he teamed up with Chen Qiao Yu, the boss of a local private company that makes beach chairs for US retailers such as Wal-Mart. Mr Chen bought a 49 per cent stake in Changzhou Kooshies. Work began immediately on a new factory at Wujing, a small town near Changzhou.

In western markets, Kooshies promotes its products as environmentally friendly. Just 20 of Kooshies non-disposable nappies can replace up to 7,000 disposable nappies. However, the company has had to adapt its marketing strategy in China, a country without an independent green lobby. Environmental benefits are placed behind health and cost.

Kooshies Ultra, which Mr Perez describes as a "revolutionary diaper" made from cotton flannel, has been a poor seller in China. Flannel is Kooshies' main product in 45 countries around the world, including Hong Kong, but in China, "the flannel capital of the world", it is considered an inferior product and the preference is for brushed cotton.

In the venture's early days, business was hindered because Diqiu's contribution had included 100,000 metres of flannel, making it hard to change the product line.

Although hindered by a lack of resources, Kooshies has begun to customise products for the Chinese market. For example, while Canadian customers prefer nappies with a white waistband, Chinese pattern-makers warned Mr Perez that local consumers would associate white with funerals.

Even within China, product markets differ from one province to the next. For instance, popular western designs featuring big animal prints do not sell in most parts of China; people prefer softer traditional baby colours. Guangzhou and Shanghai, though, are more open to western designs.

Source: J. Gamble, "Firm Encounters China Syndrome," *Financial Post (National Post)*, May 31, 2001, p. C2.

Glossary

A

ACCOMMODATIVE APPROACH
Moderate commitment to social
responsibility; willingness to do more
than the law requires if asked.

ADMINISTRATIVE MANAGEMENT
The study of how to create an organizational structure that leads to high
efficiency and effectiveness.

ADMINISTRATIVE MODEL An
approach to decision making that
explains why decision making is basically uncertain and risky and why
managers usually make satisficing
rather than optimum decisions.

AMBIGUOUS INFORMATION
Information that can be interpreted in
multiple and often conflicting ways.

ARTIFACTS Aspects of an organization's culture that one sees, hears, and
feels.

ASSUMPTIONS The taken-for-
granted notions of how something
should be in an organization.

AUTHORITY The power to hold
people accountable for their actions
and to make decisions concerning the
use of organizational resources.

B

BARRIERS TO ENTRY Factors that
make it difficult and costly for an
organization to enter a particular task
environment or industry.

BEHAVIOURAL MANAGEMENT
The study of how managers should
behave in order to motivate employees and encourage them to perform at
high levels and be committed to
achieving organizational goals.

BELIEFS The understandings of how
objects and ideas relate to each other.

BENCHMARKING Comparing performance on specific dimensions with
the performance of high-performing
organizations.

BIAS The systematic tendency to use
information about others in ways that
result in inaccurate perceptions.

BOTTOM-UP CHANGE Change that
is introduced gradually and involves
managers and employees at all levels
of an organization.

BOUNDARYLESS ORGANIZATION
An organization whose members are
linked by computers, faxes, computer-
aided design systems, and video teleconferencing, and who rarely, if ever,
see one another face to face.

BOUNDED RATIONALITY
Cognitive limitations that constrain
one's ability to interpret, process, and
act on information.

BRAINSTORMING A group problem-solving technique in which individuals meet face to face to generate
and debate a wide variety of alternatives from which to make a decision.

BRAND LOYALTY Customers' preference for the products of organizations that currently exist in the task
environment.

BUREAUCRACY A formal system of
organization and administration
designed to ensure efficiency and
effectiveness.

BUREAUCRATIC CONTROL
Control of behaviour by means of a
comprehensive system of rules and
standard operating procedures.

BUSINESS-LEVEL PLAN
Divisional managers' decisions relating to divisions' long-term goals, overall strategy, and structure.

BUSINESS-LEVEL STRATEGY A
plan that indicates how a division
intends to compete against its rivals in
an industry.

**BUSINESS-TO-BUSINESS (B2B)
NETWORKS** A group of organizations that join together and use software to link themselves to potential
global suppliers to increase efficiency
and effectiveness.

C

**CAFETERIA-STYLE BENEFIT
PLAN** A plan from which employees
can choose the benefits that they want.

CHARISMATIC LEADER An enthusiastic, self-confident leader able to
communicate clearly his or her vision
of how good things could be.

CLAN CONTROL Control exerted
on individuals and groups in an
organization by shared values, norms,
standards of behaviour, and expectations.

CLOSED SYSTEM A system that is
self-contained and thus not affected
by changes that occur in its external
environment.

CODES OF ETHICS Formal standards and rules, based on beliefs about right or wrong, that managers can use to help themselves make appropriate decisions with regard to the interests of their stakeholders.

COERCIVE POWER The ability of a manager to punish others.

COLLECTIVE BARGAINING Negotiation between labour unions and managers to resolve conflicts and disputes about issues such as working hours, wages, benefits, working conditions, and job security.

COMMAND ECONOMY An economic system in which the government owns all businesses and specifies which and how many goods and services are produced and the prices at which they are sold.

COMMAND GROUP A group composed of subordinates who report to the same supervisor; also called a department or unit.

COMMUNICATION The sharing of information between two or more individuals or groups to reach a common understanding.

COMPETITIVE ADVANTAGE The ability of one organization to outperform other organizations because it produces desired goods or services more efficiently and effectively than competitors do.

COMPETITORS Organizations that produce goods and services that are similar to a particular organization's goods and services.

CONCEPTUAL SKILLS The ability to analyze and diagnose a situation and to distinguish between cause and effect.

CONCURRENT CONTROL Control that gives managers immediate feedback on how efficiently inputs are being transformed into outputs so that managers can correct problems as they arise.

CONTINGENCY THEORY The idea that managers' choice of organizational structures and control systems depends on—is contingent on—characteristics of the external environment in which the organization operates.

CONTROL SYSTEMS Formal target-setting, monitoring, evaluation, and feedback systems that provide managers with information about how well the organization's strategy and structure are working.

CONTROLLING Evaluating how well an organization is achieving its goals and taking action to maintain or improve performance; one of the four principal functions of management.

CORPORATE-LEVEL PLAN Top management's decisions relating to the organization's mission, overall strategy, and structure.

CORPORATE-LEVEL STRATEGY A plan that indicates the industries and national markets in which an organization intends to compete.

COST-LEADERSHIP STRATEGY Driving the organization's costs down below the costs of its rivals.

CREATIVITY A decision maker's ability to discover original and novel ideas that lead to feasible alternative courses of action.

CROSS-FUNCTIONAL TEAM A group of individuals from different departments brought together to perform organizational tasks.

CUSTOMERS Individuals and groups that buy the goods and services that an organization produces.

D

DATA Raw, unsummarized, and unanalyzed facts.

DECISION MAKING The process by which managers analyze the options facing them and make decisions about specific organizational goals and courses of action.

DECODING Interpreting and trying to make sense of a message.

DEFENSIVE APPROACH Minimal commitment to social responsibility; willingness to do what the law requires and no more.

DELPHI TECHNIQUE A decision-making technique in which group members do not meet face to face but respond in writing to questions posed by the group leader.

DEMOGRAPHIC FORCES Outcomes of changes in, or changing attitudes toward, the characteristics of a population, such as age, gender, ethnic origin, race, sexual orientation, and social class.

DEPARTMENT A group of people who work together and possess similar skills or use the same knowledge, tools, or techniques to perform their jobs.

DEVELOPMENT Building the knowledge and skills of organizational members so that they will be prepared to take on new responsibilities and challenges.

DEVELOPMENTAL CONSIDERATION Behaviour a leader engages in to support and encourage followers and help them develop and grow on the job.

DEVIL'S ADVOCACY Critical analysis of a preferred alternative, made by a group member who plays the role of devil's advocate to defend unpopular or opposing alternatives for the sake of argument.

DIFFERENTIATION STRATEGY Distinguishing an organization's products from the products of competitors in dimensions such as product design, quality, or after-sales service.

DISTRIBUTIVE JUSTICE A moral principle calling for the distribution of pay raises, promotions, and other organizational resources to be based on meaningful contributions that individuals have made and not on personal characteristics over which they have no control.

DISTRIBUTIVE NEGOTIATION Adversarial negotiation in which the parties in conflict compete to win the most resources while conceding as little as possible.

DISTRIBUTORS Organizations that help other organizations sell their goods or services to customers.

DIVERSIFICATION Expanding operations into a new business or industry and producing new goods or services.

DIVERSITY Differences among people in age, gender, race, ethnicity, religion, sexual orientation, socioeconomic background, and capabilities or disabilities.

DIVISION A business unit that has its own set of managers and functions or departments and competes in a distinct industry.

DIVISION OF LABOUR Splitting the work to be performed into particular tasks and assigning tasks to individual workers.

DIVISIONAL MANAGERS Managers who control the various divisions of an organization.

DIVISIONAL STRUCTURE An organizational structure composed of separate business units within which are the functions that work together to produce a specific product for a specific customer.

DRIVING FORCES Forces that direct behaviour away from the status quo.

E

ECONOMIC FORCES Interest rates, inflation, unemployment, economic growth, and other factors that affect the general health and well-being of a nation or the regional economy of an organization.

ECONOMIES OF SCALE Cost advantages associated with large operations.

EFFECTIVENESS A measure of the appropriateness of the goals an organization is pursuing and of the degree to which the organization achieves those goals.

EFFICIENCY A measure of how well or productively resources are used to achieve a goal.

EMOTIONAL INTELLIGENCE The ability to understand and manage one's own moods and emotions and the moods and emotions of other people.

EMPLOYEE-CENTRED BEHAVIOUR Behaviour indicating that a manager trusts, respects, and cares about subordinates.

EMPOWERMENT The process of giving employees the authority to make decisions and be responsible for their outcome.

ENCODING Translating a message into understandable symbols or language.

ENTROPY The tendency of a system to dissolve and disintegrate because it loses the ability to control itself.

ENVIRONMENTAL CHANGE The degree to which forces in the task and general environments change and evolve over time.

EQUITY The justice, impartiality, and fairness to which all organizational members are entitled.

EQUITY THEORY A theory of motivation that focuses on people's perceptions of the fairness of their work outcomes relative to their work inputs.

ESCALATING COMMITMENT A source of cognitive bias resulting from the tendency to commit additional resources to a project even if evidence shows that the project is failing.

ETHICAL DECISION A decision that reasonable or typical stakeholders would find acceptable because it aids stakeholders, the organization, or society.

ETHICS Moral principles or beliefs about what is right or wrong.

ETHICS OMBUDSMAN An ethics officer who monitors an organization's practices and procedures to be sure they are ethical.

EXPECTANCY In expectancy theory, a perception about the extent to which effort will result in a certain level of performance.

EXPECTANCY THEORY The theory that motivation will be high when employees believe that high levels of effort will lead to high performance, and high performance will lead to the attainment of desired outcomes.

EXPERT POWER Power that is based in the special knowledge, skills, and expertise that a leader possesses.

EXTERNAL ENVIRONMENT The forces operating outside an organization that affect how the organization functions.

EXTINCTION Stopping the performance of dysfunctional behaviours by eliminating whatever is reinforcing them.

EXTRINSICALLY MOTIVATED BEHAVIOUR Behaviour that is performed to acquire material or social rewards or to avoid punishment.

F

FEEDBACK CONTROL Control that gives managers information about customers' reactions to goods and services so that corrective action can be taken if necessary.

FEEDFORWARD CONTROL Control that allows managers to anticipate and deal with potential problems.

FILTERING Withholding part of a message out of the mistaken belief that the receiver does not need or will not want the information.

FIRST-LINE MANAGERS Managers who are responsible for the daily supervision and coordination of non-managerial employees.

FOCUSED DIFFERENTIATION STRATEGY Serving only one segment of the overall market and trying to be the most differentiated organization serving that segment.

FOCUSED LOW-COST STRATEGY Serving only one segment of the overall market and being the lowest-cost organization serving that segment.

FORMAL APPRAISAL An appraisal conducted at a set time during the year and based on performance dimensions and measures that were specified in advance.

FREE-MARKET ECONOMY An economic system in which private enterprise controls production, and the interaction of supply and demand determines which and how many goods and services are produced and how much consumers pay for them.

FUNCTION A unit or department in which people have the same skills or use the same resources to perform their jobs.

FUNCTIONAL MANAGERS Managers who supervise the various functions–such as manufacturing, accounting, and sales–within a division.

FUNCTIONAL STRUCTURE An organizational structure composed of all the departments that an organization requires to produce its goods or services.

FUNCTIONAL-LEVEL PLAN Functional managers' decisions relating to the goals that functional managers propose to pursue to help the division reach its business-level goals.

FUNCTIONAL-LEVEL STRATEGY A plan that indicates how a function intends to achieve its goals.

G

GENERAL ENVIRONMENT The economic, technological, socio-cultural, demographic, political and legal, and global forces that affect an organization and its task environment.

GEOGRAPHIC STRUCTURE An organizational structure in which each region of a country or area of the world is served by a self-contained division.

GLOBAL FORCES Outcomes of changes in international relationships; changes in nations' economic, political, and legal systems; and changes in technology–such as falling trade barriers, the growth of representative democracies, and reliable and instantaneous communication.

GLOBAL ORGANIZATIONS Organizations that operate and compete in more than one country.

GLOBAL STRATEGY Selling the same standardized product and using the same basic marketing approach in each national market.

GOAL A desired future outcome that an organization strives to achieve.

GOAL-SETTING THEORY A theory that focuses on identifying the types of goals that are most effective in producing high levels of motivation and performance and explaining why goals have these effects.

GROUP Two or more people who interact with each other to reach certain goals or meet certain needs.

GROUP COHESIVENESS The degree to which members are attracted or loyal to a group.

GROUP NORMS Shared guidelines or rules for behaviour that most group members follow.

GROUP ROLE A set of behaviours and tasks that a member of a group is expected to perform because of his or her position in the group.

GROUPTHINK A pattern of faulty and biased decision making that occurs in groups whose members strive for agreement among themselves at the expense of accurately assessing information relevant to a decision.

H

HERZBERG'S MOTIVATOR-HYGIENE THEORY A needs theory that distinguishes between motivator needs (related to the nature of the work itself) and hygiene needs (related to the physical and psychological context in which the work is performed). Herzberg proposed that motivator needs must be met in order for motivation and job satisfaction to be high.

HEURISTICS Rules of thumb that simplify decision making.

HIERARCHY OF AUTHORITY An organization's chain of command, specifying the relative authority of each manager.

HOSTILE WORK ENVIRONMENT SEXUAL HARASSMENT Telling lewd jokes, displaying pornography, making sexually oriented remarks about someone's personal appearance, and other sex-related actions that make the work environment unpleasant.

HUMAN RESOURCE MANAGEMENT (HRM) Activities that managers engage in to attract and retain employees and to ensure that they perform at a high level and contribute to the accomplishment of organizational goals.

HUMAN RESOURCE PLANNING Activities that managers use to forecast their current and future needs for human resources.

HUMAN SKILLS The ability to understand, alter, lead, and control the behaviour of other individuals and groups.

I

ILLUSION OF CONTROL A source of cognitive bias resulting from the tendency to overestimate one's own ability to control activities and events.

INDIVIDUAL ETHICS Personal standards that govern how individuals interact with other people.

INEQUITY Lack of fairness.

INFORMAL APPRAISAL An unscheduled appraisal of on-going progress and areas for improvement.

INFORMAL ORGANIZATION The system of behavioural rules and norms that emerge in a group.

INFORMATION Data that are organized in a meaningful fashion.

INFORMATION DISTORTION Changes in the meaning of a message as the message passes through a series of senders and receivers.

INFORMATION RICHNESS The amount of information that a communication medium can carry and the extent to which the medium enables sender and receiver to reach a common understanding.

INFORMATION TECHNOLOGY
The means by which information is acquired, organized, stored, manipulated, and transmitted.

INNOVATION The process of creating new goods and services or developing better ways to produce or provide goods and services.

INSTRUMENTALITY In expectancy theory, a perception about the extent to which performance will result in the attainment of outcomes.

INTEGRATIVE BARGAINING
Cooperative negotiation in which the parties in conflict work together to achieve a resolution that is good for them all.

INTELLECTUAL STIMULATION
Behaviour a leader engages in to make followers aware of problems and view these problems in new ways, consistent with the leader's vision.

INTERNAL ENVIRONMENT The forces operating within an organization and stemming from the organization's structure and culture.

INTRINSICALLY MOTIVATED BEHAVIOUR Behaviour that is performed for its own sake.

INTUITION Ability to make sound decisions based on past experience and immediate feelings about the information at hand.

J

JARGON Specialized language that members of an occupation, group, or organization develop to facilitate communication among themselves.

JOB ANALYSIS Identifying the tasks, duties, and responsibilities that make up a job and the knowledge, skills, and abilities needed to perform the job.

JOB DESIGN The process by which managers decide how to divide tasks into specific jobs.

JOB ENLARGEMENT Increasing the number of different tasks in a given job by changing the division of labour.

JOB ENRICHMENT Increasing the degree of responsibility a worker has over his or her job.

JOB SIMPLIFICATION Reducing the number of tasks that each worker performs.

JOB SPECIALIZATION The process by which a division of labour occurs as different employees specialize in different tasks over time.

JOB-ORIENTED BEHAVIOURS
Behaviours that managers engage in to ensure that work gets done, subordinates perform their jobs acceptably, and the organization is efficient and effective.

JOINT VENTURE A strategic alliance among two or more companies that agree to establish jointly and share the ownership of a new business.

JUDGMENT Ability to develop a sound opinion based on one's evaluation of the importance of the information at hand.

L

LABOUR RELATIONS The activities that managers engage in to ensure that they have effective working relationships with the labour unions that represent their employees' interests.

LATERAL MOVE A job change that entails no major changes in responsibility or authority levels.

LEADER An individual who is able to exert influence over other people to help achieve group or organizational goals.

LEADER SUBSTITUTE
Characteristics of subordinates or characteristics of a situation or context that act in place of the influence of a leader and make leadership unnecessary.

LEADERSHIP The process by which an individual exerts influence over other people and inspires, motivates,

and directs their activities to help achieve group or organizational goals.

LEADING Articulating a clear vision and energizing and empowering organizational members so that everyone understands their individual roles in achieving organizational goals; one of the four principal functions of management.

LEARNING ORGANIZATION An organization in which managers try to maximize the ability of individuals and groups to think and behave creatively and thus maximize the potential for organizational learning to take place.

LEGITIMATE POWER The authority that a manager has by virtue of his or her position in an organization's hierarchy.

LINGUISTIC STYLE A person's characteristic way of speaking.

M

MAINTENANCE ROLES Roles performed by group members to make sure there are good relations among group members.

MANAGEMENT The planning, organizing, leading, and controlling of resources to achieve organizational goals effectively and efficiently.

MANAGEMENT BY OBJECTIVES
A system of evaluating subordinates for their ability to achieve specific organizational goals or performance standards.

MANAGEMENT SCIENCE THEORY
An approach to management that uses rigorous quantitative techniques to help managers make full use of organizational resources.

MANAGER A person who is responsible for supervising the use of an organization's resources to achieve its goals.

MARKET STRUCTURE An organizational structure in which each kind of customer is served by a self-contained division; also called *customer structure*.

MASLOW'S HIERARCHY OF NEEDS An arrangement of five basic needs that, according to Maslow, motivate behaviour. Maslow proposed that the lowest level of unmet needs is the prime motivator and that only one level of needs is motivational at a time.

MATRIX STRUCTURE An organizational structure that simultaneously groups people and resources by function and by product.

MECHANISTIC STRUCTURE An organizational structure in which authority is centralized at the top of the hierarchy, tasks and roles are clearly specified, and employees are closely supervised.

MEDIUM The pathway through which an encoded message is transmitted to a receiver.

MESSAGE The information that a sender wants to share.

MIDDLE MANAGERS Managers who supervise first-line managers and are responsible for finding the best way to use resources to achieve organizational goals.

MISSION STATEMENT A broad declaration of an organization's purpose that identifies the organization's products and customers, and distinguishes the organization from its competitors.

MIXED ECONOMY An economic system in which some sectors of the economy are left to private ownership and free-market mechanisms and others are owned by the govern-ment and subject to government planning.

MOTIVATION Psychological forces that determine the direction of a person's behaviour in an organization, a person's level of effort, and a person's level of persistence.

MULTIDOMESTIC STRATEGY Customizing products and marketing strategies to specific national conditions.

N

NEED A requirement or necessity for survival and well-being.

NEEDS ASSESSMENT An assessment of which employees need training or development and what type of skills or knowledge they need to acquire.

NEEDS THEORIES Theories of motivation that focus on what needs people are trying to satisfy at work and what outcomes will satisfy those needs.

NEGATIVE REINFORCEMENT Eliminating or removing undesired outcomes once people have performed organizationally functional behaviours.

NEGOTIATION A method of conflict resolution in which the parties in conflict consider various alternative ways to allocate resources to each other in order to come up with a solution acceptable to them all.

NETWORK STRUCTURE A series of strategic alliances that an organization creates with suppliers, manufacturers, and distributors to produce and market a product.

NOISE Anything that hampers any stage of the communication process.

NOMINAL GROUP TECHNIQUE A decision-making technique in which group members write down ideas and solutions, read their suggestions to the whole group, and discuss and then rank the alternatives.

NONPROGRAMMED DECISION MAKING Nonroutine decision making that occurs in response to unusual, unpredictable opportunities and threats.

NONVERBAL COMMUNICATION The encoding of messages by means of facial expressions, body language, and styles of dress.

NORMS Unwritten rules and informal codes of conduct that prescribe how people should act in particular situations.

O

OBSTRUCTIONIST APPROACH Disregard for social responsibility; willingness to engage in and cover up unethical and illegal behaviour.

OPEN SYSTEM A system that takes in resources from its external environment and converts them into goods and services that are then sent back to that environment for purchase by customers.

OPERATING BUDGET A budget that states how managers intend to use organizational resources to achieve organizational goals.

OPTIMUM DECISION The best decision in light of what managers believe to be the most desirable future consequences for their organization.

ORGANIC STRUCTURE An organizational structure in which authority is decentralized to middle and first-line managers and tasks and roles are left ambiguous to encourage employees to cooperate and respond quickly to the unexpected.

ORGANIZATIONAL BEHAVIOUR The study of the factors that have an impact on how individuals and groups respond to and act in organizations.

ORGANIZATIONAL BEHAVIOUR MODIFICATION (OB MOD) The systematic application of operant conditioning techniques to promote the performance of organizationally functional behaviours and discourage the performance of dysfunctional behaviours.

ORGANIZATIONAL CONFLICT The discord that arises when the goals, interest, or values of different individuals or groups are incompatible and those individuals or groups block or thwart each other's attempts to achieve their objectives.

ORGANIZATIONAL CULTURE A system of shared meaning, held by organization members, that distinguishes the organization from other organizations.

ORGANIZATIONAL DESIGN The process by which managers make specific organizing choices that result in a particular kind of organizational structure.

ORGANIZATIONAL ENVIRON-MENT The set of forces and conditions that operate beyond an organization's boundaries but affect a manager's ability to acquire and use resources.

ORGANIZATIONAL LEARNING The process through which managers seek to improve employees' desire and ability to understand and manage the organization and its task environment.

ORGANIZATIONAL PERFOR-MANCE A measure of how efficiently and effectively a manager uses resources to satisfy customers and achieve organizational goals.

ORGANIZATIONAL SOCIALIZA-TION The process by which newcomers learn an organization's values and norms and acquire the work behaviours necessary to perform jobs effectively.

ORGANIZATIONAL STAKEHOLD-ERS Shareholders, employees, customers, suppliers, and others who have an interest, claim, or stake in an organization and in what it does.

ORGANIZATIONAL STRUCTURE A formal system of both task and reporting relationships that coordinates and motivates organizational members so that they work together to reach organizational goals.

ORGANIZATIONS Collections of people who work together and co-ordinate their actions to achieve goals.

ORGANIZING Structuring workplace relationships in a way that allows members of an organization to work together to achieve organizational goals; one of the four principal functions of management.

OUTSOURCING Using outside suppliers and manufacturers to produce goods and services.

OVERPAYMENT INEQUITY Inequity that exists when a person perceives that his or her own outcome/input ratio is greater than the ratio of a referent.

OVERT DISCRIMINATION Knowingly and willingly denying diverse individuals access to opportunities and outcomes in an organization.

P

PATH-GOAL THEORY A contingency model of leadership proposing that leaders can motivate subordinates by identifying their desired outcomes, rewarding them for high performance and the attainment of work goals with these desired outcomes, and clarifying for them the paths leading to the attainment of work goals.

PAY LEVEL The relative position of an organization's pay incentives in comparison with those of other organizations in the same industry employing similar kinds of workers.

PAY STRUCTURE The arrangement of jobs into categories that reflect their relative importance to the organization and its goals, levels of skill required, and other characteristics.

PERCEPTION The process through which people select, organize, and interpret sensory input to give meaning and order to the world around them.

PERFORMANCE APPRAISAL The evaluation of employees' job performance and contributions to their organization.

PERFORMANCE FEEDBACK The process through which managers share performance appraisal information with subordinates, give subordinates an opportunity to reflect on their own performance, and develop, with subordinates, plans for the future.

PLANNING Identifying and selecting appropriate goals and courses of action; one of the four principal functions of management.

POLICY A general guide to action.

POLITICAL AND LEGAL FORCES Outcomes of changes in laws and regulations, such as the deregulation of industries, the privatization of organizations, and increased emphasis on environmental protection.

POSITION POWER The amount of legitimate, reward, and coercive power that a leader has by virtue of his or her position in an organization; a determinant of how favourable a situation is for leading.

POSITIVE REINFORCEMENT Giving people outcomes they desire when they perform organizationally functional behaviours well.

PRIOR HYPOTHESIS BIAS cognitive bias resulting from the tendency to base decisions on strong prior beliefs even if evidence shows that those beliefs are wrong.

PRIVATELY HELD ORGANIZA-TIONS Companies whose shares are not available on the stock exchange but are privately held.

PROACTIVE APPROACH Strong commitment to social responsibility; eagerness to do more than the law requires and to use organizational resources to promote the interests of all organizational stakeholders.

PROCEDURAL JUSTICE A moral principle calling for the use of fair procedures to determine how to distribute outcomes to organizational members.

PROCESS THEORIES Theories of motivation that explore how one actually motivates someone.

PRODUCT STRUCTURE An organizational structure in which each product line or business is handled by a self-contained division.

PRODUCT TEAM STRUCTURE An organizational structure in which employees are permanently assigned to a cross-functional team and report only to the product team manager or to one of his or her direct subordinates.

PRODUCTION BLOCKING A loss of productivity in brainstorming sessions due to the unstructured nature of brainstorming.

PROFESSIONAL ETHICS Standards that govern how members of a profession are to make decisions when the way they should behave is not clear-cut.

PROGRAMMED DECISION MAKING Routine, virtually automatic decision making that follows established rules or guidelines.

PUBLICLY HELD ORGANIZATIONS Companies whose shares are available on the stock exchange for public trading by brokers or dealers.

PUNISHMENT Administering an undesired or negative consequence when dysfunctional behaviour occurs.

Q

QUID PRO QUO SEXUAL HARASSMENT Asking or forcing an employee to perform sexual favours in exchange for some reward or to avoid negative consequences.

R

RATIONAL DECISION-MAKING MODEL A prescriptive approach to decision making based on the idea that the decision maker can identify and evaluate all possible alternatives and their consequences and rationally choose the most suitable course of action.

REAL-TIME INFORMATION Frequently updated information that reflects current conditions.

RECEIVER The person or group for which a message is intended.

RECRUITMENT Activities that managers use to develop a pool of qualified candidates for open positions.

REFERENT POWER Power that comes from subordinates' and co-workers' respect, admiration, and loyalty.

REINFORCEMENT Anything that causes a given behaviour to be repeated or stopped.

REINFORCEMENT THEORY A motivation theory based on the relationship between a given behaviour and its consequence.

RELATED DIVERSIFICATION Entering a new business or industry to create a competitive advantage in one or more of an organization's existing divisions or businesses.

REPRESENTATIVE DEMOCRACY A political system in which representatives elected by citizens and legally accountable to the electorate form a government whose function is to make decisions on behalf of the electorate.

REPRESENTATIVENESS BIAS A cognitive bias resulting from the tendency to generalize inappropriately from a small sample or from a single vivid case or episode.

REPUTATION The esteem or high repute that individuals or organizations gain when they behave ethically.

RESEARCH AND DEVELOPMENT TEAM A team whose members have the expertise and experience needed to develop new products.

RESOURCES Assets such as people, machinery, raw materials, information, skills, and financial capital.

RESTRAINING FORCES Forces that prevent movement away from the status quo.

RESTRUCTURING Downsizing an organization by eliminating the jobs of large numbers of top, middle, and first-line managers and nonmanagerial employees.

REWARD POWER The ability of a manager to give or withhold tangible and intangible rewards.

ROLE The specific tasks that a person is expected to perform because of the position he or she holds in an organization.

ROLE MAKING Taking the initiative to modify an assigned role by taking on extra responsibilities.

RULES Formal written instructions that specify actions to be taken under different circumstances to achieve specific goals.

RUMOURS Unofficial pieces of information of interest to organizational members but with no identifiable source.

S

SATISFICING Searching for and choosing acceptable, or satisfactory, ways to respond to problems and opportunities, rather than trying to make the best decision.

SCENARIO PLANNING The generation of multiple forecasts of future conditions followed by an analysis of how to respond effectively to each of those conditions; also called *contingency planning*.

SCIENTIFIC MANAGEMENT The systematic study of relationships between people and tasks for the purpose of redesigning the work process to increase efficiency.

SELECTION The process that managers use to determine the relative qualifications of job applicants and the individuals' potential for performing well in a particular job.

SELF-MANAGED (OR SELF-DIRECTED) WORK TEAMS Groups of employees who supervise their own activities and monitor the quality of the goods and services they provide.

SELF-MANAGED TEAMS Groups of employees who supervise their own activities and monitor the quality of the goods and services they provide.

SENDER The person or group wishing to share information.

SEXUAL HARASSMENT Unwelcome behaviour of a sexual nature in the workplace that negatively affects the work environment or leads to adverse job-related consequences for the employee.

SITUATIONAL LEADERSHIP THEORY (SLT) A contingency model of leadership that focuses on the followers' readiness.

SOCIAL AUDIT A tool that allows managers to analyze the profitability and social returns of socially responsible actions.

SOCIAL LOAFING The tendency of individuals to put forth less effort when they work in groups than when they work alone.

SOCIAL RESPONSIBILITY A manager's duty or obligation to make decisions that promote the well-being of stakeholders and society as a whole.

SOCIETAL ETHICS Standards that govern how members of a society are to deal with each other on issues such as fairness, justice, poverty, and the rights of the individual.

SPAN OF CONTROL The number of subordinates who report directly to a manager.

STANDARD OPERATING PROCEDURES (SOPs) Specific sets of written instructions about how to perform a certain aspect of a task.

STEREOTYPE Simplistic and often inaccurate beliefs about the typical characteristics of particular groups of people.

STRATEGIC ALLIANCE An agreement in which managers pool or share their organization's resources and know-how with a foreign company, and the two organizations share the rewards and risks of starting a new venture.

STRATEGIC HUMAN RESOURCE MANAGEMENT The process by which managers design the components of a human resource management system to be consistent with each other, with other elements of organizational architecture, and with the organization's strategy and goals.

STRATEGY A cluster of decisions about what goals to pursue, what actions to take, and how to use resources to achieve goals.

STRATEGY FORMULATION Analysis of an organization's current situation followed by the development of strategies to accomplish the organization's mission and achieve its goals.

SUPPLIERS Individuals and organizations that provide an organization with the input resources that it needs to produce goods and services.

SWOT ANALYSIS A planning exercise in which managers identify organizational strengths (S) and weaknesses (W), and environmental opportunities (O) and threats (T).

SYNERGY Performance gains that result when individuals and departments coordinate their actions.

SYSTEMATIC ERRORS Errors that people make over and over again and that result in poor decision making.

T

TASK ENVIRONMENT The set of forces and conditions that start with suppliers, distributors, customers, and competitors and affect an organization's ability to obtain inputs and dispose of its outputs, because they influence managers on a daily basis.

TASK FORCE A committee of managers or nonmanagerial employees from various departments or divisions who meet to solve a specific, mutual problem; also called an ad hoc committee.

TASK STRUCTURE The extent to which the work to be performed is clear-cut so that a leader's subordinates know what needs to be accomplished and how to go about doing it; a determinant of how favourable a situation is for leading.

TASK-ORIENTED ROLES Roles performed by group members to make sure the task gets done.

TEAM A group whose members work intensely with each other to achieve a specific common goal or objective.

TECHNICAL SKILLS Job-specific knowledge and techniques that are required to perform an organizational role.

TECHNOLOGICAL FORCES Outcomes of changes in the technology that managers use to design, produce, or distribute goods and services.

TECHNOLOGY The combination of skills and equipment that managers use in the design, production, and distribution of goods and services.

THEORY X Negative assumptions about employees that lead to the conclusion that a manager's task is to supervise them closely and control their behaviour.

THEORY Y Positive assumptions about employees that lead to the conclusion that a manager's task is to create a work setting that encourages commitment to organizational goals and provides opportunities for employees to be imaginative and to exercise initiative and self-direction.

360-DEGREE APPRAISAL A performance appraisal by peers, subordinates, superiors, and sometimes clients who are in a position to evaluate a manager's performance.

TIME HORIZON The intended duration of a plan.

TOP MANAGERS Managers who establish organizational goals, decide how departments should interact, and monitor the performance of middle managers.

TOP-DOWN CHANGE Change that is introduced quickly throughout an organization by upper-level managers.

TOP-MANAGEMENT TEAM A group composed of the CEO, the president, and the heads of the most important departments.

TOTALITARIAN REGIME A political system in which a single party, individual, or group holds all political power and neither recognizes nor permits opposition.

TRAINING Teaching organizational members how to perform their current jobs and helping them acquire the knowledge and skills they need to be effective performers.

TRANSACTIONAL LEADERSHIP Leaders who guide their subordinates toward expected goals with no expectation of exceeding expected behaviour.

TRANSFORMATIONAL LEADER-SHIP Leadership that makes subordinates aware of the importance of their jobs and performance to the organization and aware of their own needs for personal growth, and that motivates subordinates to work for the good of the organization.

U

UNCERTAINTY Unpredictability.

UNDERPAYMENT INEQUITY Inequity that exists when a person perceives that his or her own outcome/input ratio is less than the ratio of a referent.

UNETHICAL DECISION A decision that a manager would prefer to disguise or hide from other people because it enables a company or a particular individual to gain at the expense of society or other stakeholders.

UNRELATED DIVERSIFICATION Entering a new industry or buying a company in a new industry that is not related in any way to an organization's current businesses or industries.

V

VALENCE In expectancy theory, how desirable each of the outcomes available from a job or organization is to a person.

VALUES The stable, long-lasting beliefs about what is important.

VERBAL COMMUNICATION The encoding of messages into words, either written or spoken.

VERTICAL INTEGRATION A strategy that allows an organization to create value by producing its own inputs or distributing and selling its own outputs.

VIRTUAL TEAM A team whose members rarely or never meet face to face and interact by using various forms of information technology such as email, computer networks, telephones, faxes, and videoconferences.

VISION STATEMENT A broad declaration of the big picture of the organization and/or a statement of its dreams for the future.

Endnotes

Chapter 1

1. *Case in Contrast* based on C. Cattaneo, "WestJet CEO Fired to Head off Revolt: WestJet Founder Feared Defections by Key Executives," *Financial Post (National Post)*, September 26, 2000, pp. C1, C2; P. Fitzpatrick, "Morale Uplifted as CEO Departs: WestJet Demands Resignation of Stephen Smith," *Financial Post (National Post)*, September 12, 2000, pp. C1, C11; and P. Verburg, "Prepare for Takeoff," *Canadian Business*, December 25, 2000, pp. 94–96.

2. G.R. Jones, *Organizational Theory* (Reading, MA: Addison-Wesley, 1995).

3. J.P. Campbell, "On the Nature of Organizational Effectiveness," in P.S. Goodman, J.M. Pennings, and Associates, *New Perspectives on Organizational Effectiveness* (San Francisco: Jossey-Bass, 1977).

4. P. Drucker, *Management: Tasks, Responsibilities, Practices* (New York: Harper and Row, 1974).

5. *Think About It* based on P. Willcocks, "Yours and Mine? Can the New Owner of the Once-Troubled Myra Falls Copper and Zinc Mine Near Campbell River Forge a New Relationship With Workers and Their Union to Create a True Partnership?" *BCBusiness Magazine*, September 2000, pp. 114–120.

6. H. Fayol, *General and Industrial Management* (New York: IEEE Press, 1984). Fayol's work was first published in 1916. Fayol actually identified five different managerial functions but most scholars today believe these four capture the essence of Fayol's ideas.

7. P.F. Drucker, *Management Tasks, Responsibilities, and Practices* (New York: Harper and Row, 1974).

8. G. Dixon, "Clock Ticking for New CEOs," *The Globe and Mail*, May 8, 2001.

9. *Think About It* based on G. Mallet, "Spotlight on Success: The Canadian Woman Entrepreneur of the Year Awards," *Financial Post Magazine*, December 1997, pp. 82–91; "Innovators Alliance: Ontario's Leading Growth Firms," *Profit: The Magazine for Canadian Entrepreneurs*, June 1999, pp. Insert 1–8; D. Peters, H. Davidson, J. McCann, and D. Luciani, "Working at Balance: Canada's Top Women Entrepreneurs Have to Balance a Lot More Than Their Books. It's All About Growing a Company While Growing as a Person," *Chatelaine*, November 2002; and http://www.southmedic.com.

10. J. Kotter, *The General Managers* (New York: Free Press, 1992).

11. C.P. Hales, "What Do Managers Do? A Critical Review of the Evidence," *Journal of Management Studies*, January 1986, pp. 88–115; A.I. Kraul, P.R. Pedigo, D.D. McKenna, and M.D. Dunnette, "The Role of the Manager: What's Really Important in Different Management Jobs," *Academy of Management Executive*, November 1989, pp. 286–293.

12. A.K. Gupta, "Contingency Perspectives on Strategic Leadership," in D.C. Hambrick (ed.), *The Executive Effect: Concepts and Methods for Studying Top Managers* (Greenwich, CT: JAI Press, 1988), pp.147–178.

13. D.G. Ancona, "Top Management Teams: Preparing for the Revolution," in J.S. Carroll (ed.), *Applied Social Psychology and Organizational Settings* (Hillsdale, NJ: Erlbaum, 1990); D.C. Hambrick and P.A. Mason, "Upper Echelons: The Organization as a Reflection of Its Top

Managers," *Academy of Management Journal*, 9, 1984, pp. 193–206.

14. T.A. Mahony, T.H. Jerdee, and S.J. Carroll, "The Jobs of Management," *Industrial Relations*, 4, 1965, pp. 97–110; L. Gomez-Mejia, J. McCann, and R.C. Page, "The Structure of Managerial Behaviours and Rewards," *Industrial Relations*, 24, 1985, pp. 147–154.

15. *Think About It* based on P. Verburg, "Prepare for Takeoff," *Canadian Business*, December 25, 2000, pp. 94–96+.

16. K. Labich, "Making Over Middle Managers," *Fortune*, May 8, 1989, pp. 58–64.

17. "'Haves & Have-Nots': Canadians Look for Corporate Conscience," *Maclean's*, December 30, 1996/January 6, 1997, pp. 26, 37.

18. "'Haves & Have-Nots': Canadians Look for Corporate Conscience," *Maclean's*, December 30, 1996/January 6, 1997, pp. 26, 37.

19. "'Haves & Have-Nots': Canadians Look for Corporate Conscience," *Maclean's*, December 30, 1996/January 6, 1997, pp. 26, 37.

20. W.F. Cascio, "Downsizing: What Do We Know? What Have We Learned?" *Academy of Management Executive*, 7, 1993, p. 100.

21. T.H. Wagar, "Exploring the Consequences of Workforce Reduction," *Canadian Journal of Administrative Sciences*, December 1998, pp. 300–309.

22. S.R. Parker, T.D. Wall, and P.R. Jackson, "That's Not My Job: Developing Flexible Work Orientations," *Academy of Management Journal*, 40, 1997, pp. 899–929.

23. B. Dumaine, "The New Non-Manager," *Fortune*, February 22, 1993, pp. 80–84.

24. N. Kelleher, "Short-Term Rentals Is All Booked Up," *Boston Herald*, January 17, 1995, p. 26.

25. R.H. Guest, "Of Time and the Foreman," *Personnel*, 32, 1955, pp. 478–486.

26. C.W.L. Hill, *Becoming a Manager: Mastery of a New Identity* (Boston: Harvard Business School Press, 1992).

27. H. Mintzberg, "The Manager's Job: Folklore and Fact," *Harvard Business Review*, July–August 1975, pp. 56–62.

28. H. Mintzberg, *The Nature of Managerial Work* (New York: Harper and Row, 1973).

29. H. Mintzberg, *The Nature of Managerial Work* (New York: Harper and Row, 1973).

30. R.L. Katz, "Skills of an Effective Administrator," *Harvard Business Review*, September–October 1974, pp. 90–102.

31. R.L. Katz, "Skills of an Effective Administrator," *Harvard Business Review*, September–October 1974, pp. 90–102.

32. *Think About It* based on "Army Lags Behind Navy, Air Force in Attitudes Toward Women, Minorities: Report," *Canadian Press Newswire*, April 7, 2000.

33. Data on manufacturing, public sector, and service sector employment for July 2003. Statistics Canada, "Latest Release From the Labour Force Survey," August 8, 2003, http://www.statcan.ca/english/Subjects/Labour/LFS/lfs-en.htm.

34. Statistics Canada, "Establishments by Industry," http://www.statcan.ca/english/Pgdb/econ18.htm.

35. C. Harris, "Prime Numbers: A Statistical Look at the Trends and Issues That Will Dominate Our Future," *The Financial Post*, November 15/17, 1997, p. P13.

36. Statistics Canada, "Latest Release From the Labour Force Survey," August 8, 2003, http://www.statcan.ca/english/Subjects/Labour/LFS/lfs-en.htm.

37. J.A. Brander, *Government Policy Toward Business*, 3rd ed. (Toronto: John Wiley and Sons, 2000), p. 380.

38. D. Jamieson and J. O'Mara, *Managing Workforce 2000: Gaining a Diversity Advantage* (San Francisco: Jossey-Bass, 1991).

39. T.H. Cox and S. Blake, "Managing Cultural Diversity: Implications for Organizational Competitiveness," *Academy of Management Executive*, August 1991, pp. 49–52.

40. *Think About It* based on "Mountain Equipment Co-Op Grapples with Human Rights," *The Vancouver Sun*, February 24, 2001, pp. F1, F12, and information at the company's website (www.mec.ca).

41. A. Shama, "Management Under Fire: The Transformation of Management in the Soviet Union and Eastern Europe," *Academy of Management Executive*, 1993, pp. 22–35.

42. "Radio Canada and Montreal *La Presse* Sign Partnership Agreement," *Canadian Press Newswire*, January 20, 2001.

43. K. Seiders and L.L. Berry, "Service Fairness: What It Is and Why It Matters," *Academy of Management Executive*, 12, 1998, pp. 8–20.

44. C. Anderson, "Values-Based Management," *Academy of Management Executive*, 11, 1997, pp. 25–46.

45. W.H. Shaw and V. Barry, *Moral Issues in Business*, 6th ed. (Belmont, CA: Wadsworth, 1995); and T. Donaldson, *Corporations and Morality* (Englewood Cliffs, NJ: Prentice-Hall, 1982).

46. T. Tedesci, "Nesbitt Burns Procedures Investigated," *The Vancouver Sun*, April 7, 2001, pp. A1, A4; and D. DeCloet, "Industry Owes a Duty of Care," *The Vancouver Sun*, April 7, 2001, pp. D1, D6.

47. D.R. Tobin, *The Knowledge Enabled Organization* (New York: AMACOM, 1998).

48. "Canadian Productivity Rising Because of High Tech Investment, Says Conference Board," *Canadian Press Newswire*, November 30, 2000.

49. C. Cobb, "Mistrust Reigns at CBC: Survey," *National Post,* May 22, 2001, pp. A1, A8; M. Fraser, "This Dish May Be Too Hot to Handle: CBC's Bold Plan to Sell off Infrastructure Faces Stiff Opposition," *Financial Post (National Post),* February 5, 2001, p. C2; A. Clark, "Remaking the CBC: The Public Broadcaster Faces More Job Losses," *Maclean's,* February 14, 2000, p. 57; and A. Wilson-Smith, "The CBC's New Boss: Bob Rabinovitch Says Canada's Beleaguered Public Broadcaster Must Build on Its Strengths, and Not Try to Be All Things to All People," *Maclean's,* November 1, 1999, p. 30.

Appendix to Chapter 1

1. A. Smith, *The Wealth of Nations* (London: Penguin, 1982).

2. A. Smith, *The Wealth of Nations* (London: Penguin, 1982), p. 110.

3. J.G. March and H.A. Simon, *Organizations* (New York: Wiley, 1958).

4. F.W. Taylor, *Shop Management* (New York: Harper, 1903); F.W. Taylor, *The Principles of Scientific Management* (New York: Harper, 1911).

5. J.A. Litterer, *The Emergence of Systematic Management as Shown by the Literature from 1870–1900* (New York: Garland, 1986).

6. H.R. Pollard, *Developments in Management Thought* (New York: Crane, 1974).

7. F.B. Gilbreth, *Primer of Scientific Management* (New York: Van Nostrand Reinhold, 1912).

8. D. Roy, "Efficiency and the Fix: Informal Intergroup Relations in a Piece Work Setting," *American Journal of Sociology*, 60, 1954, pp. 255–266.

9. M. Weber, in H.H. Gerth and C.W. Mills (eds.), *From Max Weber: Essays in Sociology* (New York: Oxford University Press, 1946); M. Weber, in G. Roth and C. Wittich (eds.), *Economy and Society* (Berkeley: University of California Press, 1978).

10. C. Perrow, *Complex Organizations*, 2nd ed. (Glenview IL: Scott, Foresman, 1979).

11. M. Weber in H.H. Gerth and C.W. Mills (eds.), *From Max Weber: Essays in Sociology* (New York: Oxford University Press, 1946), p. 331.

12. See C. Perrow, *Complex Organizations*, 2nd ed. (Glenview IL: Scott, Foresman, 1979), Ch. 1, for a detailed discussion of these issues.

13. H. Fayol, *General and Industrial Management* (New York: IEEE Press, 1984).

14. L.D. Parker, "Control in Organizational Life: The Contribution of Mary Parker Follett," *Academy of Management Review*, 9, 1984, pp. 736–745.

15. E. Mayo, *The Human Problems of Industrial Civilization* (New York: Macmillan, 1933); F.J. Roethlisberger and W.J. Dickson, *Management and the Worker* (Cambridge, MA: Harvard University Press, 1947).

16. D. Roy, "Banana Time: Job Satisfaction and Informal Interaction," *Human Organization*, 18, 1960, pp. 158–161.

17. For an analysis of the problems in determining cause from effect in the Hawthorne studies and in social settings in general, see A. Carey, "The Hawthorne Studies: A Radical Criticism," *American Sociological Review*, 33, 1967, pp. 403–416.

18. D. McGregor, *The Human Side of Enterprise* (New York: McGraw-Hill, 1960).

19. W.E. Deming, *Out of the Crisis* (Cambridge, MA: MIT Press, 1986).

20. D. Katz and R.L. Kahn, *The Social Psychology of Organizations* (New York: Wiley, 1966); J.D. Thompson, *Organizations in Action* (New York: McGraw-Hill, 1967).

21. T. Burns and G.M. Stalker, *The Management of Innovation* (London: Tavistock, 1961); P.R. Lawrence and J.R. Lorsch, *Organization and Environment* (Boston: Graduate School of Business Administration, Harvard University, 1967).

Chapter 2

1. C. Cattaneo, "PetroCan Profit Rises Fourfold to $893M: Cash Flow Doubles. Cost Cutting and Strong Crude, Gas Prices Credited," *Financial Post (National Post)*, January 24, 2001, pp. C1, C9.

2. "Market Welcomes Petro-Can," *The Financial Post*, December 23/25, 1995, p. 23.

3. C. Cattaneo, "Petrocan Rids Itself of Pariah Legacy: Once Viewed as a Federal Government Invader, the Firm Is Now Accepted in Its Home Town," *Financial Post (National Post)*, November 17, 1999, p. C8.

4. P. Foster, "Hopper's Last Stand, Excerpt From *Self-Serve: How Petro-Canada Pumped Canadians Dry* [Toronto: Macfarlane Walter and Ross, 1992]," *Canadian Business*, September 1993, pp. 56–65.

5. "Petrocan's New Boss Angles for a Sell-Off: Company CEO James Stanford Says State Ownership Scares off Investors," *Western Report*, October 4, 1993, p. 30.

6. "Petrocan's New Boss Angles for a Sell-Off: Company CEO James Stanford Says State Ownership Scares off Investors," *Western Report*, October 4, 1993, p. 30.

7. C. Cattaneo, "Petrocan Rids Itself of Pariah Legacy: Once Viewed as a Federal Government Invader, the Firm Is Now Accepted in Its Home Town," *Financial Post (National Post)*, November 17, 1999, p. C8.

8. C. Howes, "Exxon Veteran Takes Petro-Can Helm: Stanford Retiring. No Idea When Ottawa Will Sell Its $1B Stake," *Financial Post (National Post)*, December 18, 1999, pp. D1, D9.

9. C. Cattaneo, "Petrocan Rids Itself of Pariah Legacy: Once Viewed as a Federal Government Invader, the Firm Is Now Accepted in Its Home Town," *Financial Post (National Post)*, November 17, 1999, p. C8.

10. C. Cattaneo, "Petrocan Rids Itself of Pariah Legacy: Once Viewed as a Federal Government Invader, the Firm Is Now Accepted in Its Home Town," *Financial Post (National Post)*, November 17, 1999, p. C8.

11. G. Livingston, "PetroCan Sees 55% Output Rise: Looks to Expand Further," *Financial Post (National Post)*, February 20, 2003, p. FP9.

12. L.J. Bourgeois, "Strategy and Environment: A Conceptual Integration," *Academy of Management Review*, 5, 1985, pp. 25–39.

13. *Think About It* based on N. Boomer, "Playing to Win," *Canadian Printer*, November 1998, pp. 26–31.

14. M.E. Porter, *Competitive Strategy* (New York: Free Press, 1980).

15. M.E. Porter, *Competitive Advantage* (New York: Free Press, 1985).

16. For views on barriers to entry from an economics perspective, see M.E. Porter, *Competitive Strategy* (New York: Free Press, 1980). For the sociological perspective, see J. Pfeffer and G.R. Salancik, *The External Control of Organization: A Resource Dependence Perspective* (New York: Harper and Row, 1978).

17. M.E. Porter, *Competitive Strategy* (New York: Free Press, 1980); J.E. Bain, *Barriers to New Competition* (Cambridge, MA: Harvard University Press, 1956); R.J. Gilbert, "Mobility Barriers and the Value of Incumbency," in R. Schmalensee and R.D. Willig (eds.), *Handbook of Industrial Organization*, vol. 1 (Amsterdam: North Holland, 1989).

18. C.W.L. Hill, "The Computer Industry: The New Industry of Industries," in C.W.L. Hill and G.R. Jones, *Strategic Management: An Integrated Approach*, 3rd ed. (Boston: Houghton Mifflin, 1995).

19. *Think About It* based on "NB Outlines Plans for Energy Competition but Says It's Not Deregulation," *Canadian Press Newswire*, January 30, 2001.

20. J. Schumpeter, *Capitalism, Socialism and Democracy* (London: Macmillan, 1950), p. 68. Also see R.R. Winter and S.G. Winter, *An Evolutionary Theory of Economic Change* (Cambridge, MA: Harvard University Press, 1982).

21. Rates reported for women aged 25–54. I. Ip, S. King, and G. Verdier, "Structural Influences on Participation Rates: A Canada–US Comparison," *Canadian Business Economics*, May 1999, pp. 25–41; and Organisation for Economic Co-operation and Development, *Labour Force Statistics 1978–1999* (Paris, 2000).

22. For a detailed discussion of the importance of the structure of law as a factor explaining economic change and growth, see D.C. North, *Institutions, Institutional Change and Economic Performance* (Cambridge: Cambridge University Press, 1990).

23. R.B. Reich, *The Work of Nations* (New York: Knopf, 1991).

24. Jagdish Bhagwati, *Protectionism* (Cambridge, MA: MIT Press, 1988).

25. P.M. Sweezy and H. Magdoff, *The Dynamics of US Capitalism* (New York: Monthly Review Press, 1972).

26. The ideology is that of individualism, which dates back to Adam Smith, John Stuart Mill, and the like. See H.W. Spiegel, *The Growth of Economic Thought* (Durham, NC: Duke University Press, 1991).

27. M. Magnier, "Chiquita Bets Czechoslovakia Can Produce Banana Bonanza," *Journal of Commerce*, August 29, 1991, pp. 1, 3.

28. Based on S. Erlanger, "An American Coffeehouse (or 4) in Vienna," June 1, 2002, *NYTimes.com*.

29. R.B. Duncan, "Characteristics of Organization Environment and Perceived Environment," *Administrative Science Quarterly*, 17, 1972, pp. 313–327.

30. Not everyone agrees with this assessment. Some argue that organizations and individual managers have little impact on

the environment. See M.T. Hannan and J. Freeman, "Structural Inertia and Organizational Change," *American Sociological Review*, 49, 1984, pp. 149–164.

31. D. Olive, "In Beermaking, Two's a Crowd," *Financial Post (National Post)*, January 10, 2001, p. C2.

32. "Sleeman Poised for US Moves After Building Beer Company with Crafty Deals," *Canadian Press Newswire*, December 28, 2000.

33. "Sleeman Poised for US Moves After Building Beer Company with Crafty Deals," *Canadian Press Newswire*, December 28, 2000.

34. "Sleeman Poised for US Moves After Building Beer Company with Crafty Deals," *Canadian Press Newswire*, December 28, 2000.

35. "Smaller Brewers Want to Face Smaller Excise Tax Than Labatt and Molson," *Canadian Press Newswire*, September 19, 2000.

36. "Smaller Brewers Want to Face Smaller Excise Tax Than Labatt and Molson," *Canadian Press Newswire*, September 19, 2000.

37. "Smaller Brewers Want to Face Smaller Excise Tax Than Labatt and Molson," *Canadian Press Newswire*, September 19, 2000.

Chapter 3

1. N. Ramage, "Honesty Wins the Day: A Case Study in Effective Media Relations," *Marketing*, September 25, 2000, p. 7.

2. E. Gibbs, "Bridgestone Vows to Restore Battered Firestone Brand: President Apologizes. Plans to Overhaul US Subsidiary by End of the Year," *Financial Post (National Post)*, September 12, 2000, p. C13.

3. C.W. Wolf, "Bridgestone Has No Plans to Expand Tire Recall: Blames Ford for Crashes. Says Deficiencies in Explorer Caused Many Fatalities," *Financial Post (National Post)*, September 13, 2000, p. C11.

4. "Massive Tire Recall Sends Bridgestone Profits Skidding: Down 80%," *Financial Post (National Post)*, February 23, 2001, p. C10.

5. A. Harney, "Bridgestone Boss to Quit: Denies Move Related to Firestone Tire Recall in the US," *Financial Post (National Post)*, January 12, 2001, p. C10.

6. M. Ellis, "North American Slump Leads to Ford Earnings Slide: 33% Drop in Fourth Quarter. Sales Revenue for Canadian Operations Declines 5.7%," *Financial Post (National Post)*, January 19, 2001, p. C13.

7. "Ford Canada Posts Higher Sales Despite Bridgestone/Firestone Tire Scandal," *Canadian Press Newswire*, October 3, 2000.

8. C. Cattaneo, "Lingering Sudan Effect Likely to Tarnish Talisman," *Financial Post (National Post)*, February 24, 2000, pp. D1, D3.

9. "Talisman Shares Jump in Wake of Sudan Report," *Financial Post (National Post)*, February 16, 2000, p. C3.

10. C. Harrington, "Talisman Says Peacemaking Is the Business of Governments, Not Business," *Canadian Press Newswire*, February 17, 2000.

11. C. Harrington, "Talisman Says Peacemaking Is the Business of Governments, Not Business," *Canadian Press Newswire*, February 17, 2000.

12. T.L. Beauchamp and N.E. Bowie (eds.), *Ethical Theory and Business* (Englewood Cliffs, NJ: Prentice-Hall, 1979); and A. Macintyre, *After Virtue* (South Bend, IN: University of Notre Dame Press, 1981).

13. R.E. Goodin, "How to Determine Who Should Get What," *Ethics*, July 1975, pp. 310–321.

14. T.M. Jones, "Ethical Decision Making by Individuals in Organizations: An Issue Contingent Model," *Academy of Management Journal*, 16, 1991, pp. 366–395; and G.F. Cavanaugh, D.J. Moberg, and M. Velasquez, "The Ethics of Organizational Politics," *Academy of Management Review*, 6, 1981, pp. 363–374.

15. L.K. Trevino, "Ethical Decision Making in Organizations: A Person–Situation Interactionist Model," *Academy of Management Review*, 11, 1986, pp. 601–617; and W.H. Shaw and V. Barry, *Moral Issues in Business*, 6th ed. (Belmont, CA: Wadsworth, 1995).

16. A.S. Waterman, "On the Uses of Psychological Theory and Research in the Process of Ethical Inquiry," *Psychological Bulletin*, 103, no. 3, 1988, pp. 283–298.

17. www.shell.ca/code/values/ethics/ethics.html.

18. J.A. Pearce, "The Company Mission as a Strategic Tool," *Sloan Management Review*, Spring 1982, pp. 15–24.

19. C.I. Barnard, *The Functions of the Executive* (Cambridge, MA: Harvard University Press, 1948).

20. R.E. Freeman, *Strategic Management: A Stakeholder Approach* (Marshfield, MA: Pitman, 1984).

21. M. McClearn, "African Adventure," *Canadian Business*, September 1, 2003.

22. "Corruption Still Tainting Asian Financial Picture, Study Says," *The Vancouver Sun*, March 20, 2001, p. D18.

23. "Canadian Firms Ink New Ethics Code [for International Operations]," *Plant*, October 6, 1997, p. 4.

24. B. Victor and J.B. Cullen, "The Organizational Bases of Ethical Work Climates," *Administrative Science Quarterly*, 33, 1988, pp. 101–125.

25. H. Demsetz, "Towards a Theory of Property Rights," *American Economic Review*, 57, 1967, pp. 347–359.

26. K.M. Grace, "The Last Chapter Isn't Written: Misfortunes of Book Discounters Give Hope to Canada's Battered Independents," *Report Newsmagazine*, November 20, 2000, pp. 32–33.

27. L. McKnight, "Will the Sky Fall? Publishers Worry About Chapters' Survival," *Maclean's*, August 14, 2000, p. 33.

28. D. Hasselback, "BC Hydro Overcharging California Utilities, Report Says," *Financial Post (National Post)*, April 12, 2001, p. C4.

29. D. Baines, "BC Hydro Unit Cited for Blame in California's Electricity Crisis," *The Vancouver Sun*, April 12, 2001, pp. F1, F5.

30. C. Howes, "Ethics as More Than Just a Course: More Companies Are Promoting Ethical Practices in Work," *National Post*, October 28, 2000, p. D4.

31. C. Howes, "Ethics as More Than Just a Course: More Companies Are Promoting Ethical Practices in Work," *National Post*, October 28, 2000, p. D4.

32. C. Howes, "Ethics as More Than Just a Course: More Companies Are Promoting Ethical Practices in Work," *National Post*, October 28, 2000, p. D4.

33. P.E. Murphy, "Creating Ethical Corporate Structure," *Sloan Management Review*, Winter 1989, pp. 81–87.

34. G.R. Jones, *Organizational Theory: Text and Cases* (Reading, MA: Addison-Wesley, 1997).

35. "When It Comes to Ethics, Canadian Companies Are All Talk and Little Action, a Survey Shows," *Canadian Press Newswire,* February 17, 2000.

36. Based on L. Kallenbach, "The Web of Change," *Yoga Journal,* October 2002; and J. Jedras, "Social Workers," *Silicon Valley NORTH,* July 30, 2001, p. 1.

37. E. Gatewood and A.B. Carroll, "The Anatomy of Corporate Social Response," *Business Horizons,* September–October 1981, pp. 9–16.

38. M. Friedman, "A Friedman Doctrine: The Social Responsibility of Business Is to Increase Its Profits," *New York Times Magazine,* September 13, 1970, p. 33.

39. "Wal-Mart Canada Says Imports From Myanmar Ended in Spring," *Canadian Press Newswire,* July 18, 2000.

40. W.G. Ouchi, *Theory Z: How American Business Can Meet the Japanese Challenge* (Reading, MA: Addison-Wesley, 1981).

41. J.B. McGuire, A. Sundgren, and T. Schneewis, "Corporate Social Responsibility and Firm Financial Performance," *Academy of Management Review,* 31, 1988, pp. 854–872.

42. J. Jedras, "Social Workers," *Silicon Valley NORTH,* July 30, 2001, p. 1.

43. M. Friedman, "A Friedman Doctrine: The Social Responsibility of Business Is to Increase Its Profits," *New York Times Magazine,* September 13, 1970, pp. 32, 33, 122, 124, 126.

44. E.D. Bowman, "Corporate Social Responsibility and the Investor," *Journal of Contemporary Business,* Winter 1973, pp. 49–58.

45. *Think About It* based on M. O'Brien, "Heritage Room for Native Cadets," *The Leader-Post* (Regina), December 5, 2000, p. A3.

46. Information for this paragraph was based on *Canada's Ethnocultural Portrait: The Changing Mosaic,* January 2003, http://www12.statcan.ca/english/census01/products/analytic/companion/etoimm/provs.cfm (accessed May 16, 2003).

47. M. O'Brien, "Heritage Room for Native Cadets," *The Leader-Post* (Regina), December 5, 2000, p. A3.

48. R. Folger and M.A. Konovsky, "Effects of Procedural and Distributive Justice on Reactions to Pay Raise Decisions," *Academy of Management Journal,* 32, 1989, pp. 115–130; and J. Greenberg, "Organizational Justice: Yesterday, Today, and Tomorrow," *Journal of Management,* 16, 1990, pp. 399–402.

49. G. Glynn, "Bank of Montreal Invests in Its Workers," *Workforce,* December 1997, pp. 30–38.

50. D. Calleja, "Equity or Else: Employment Equity Has Been Around for a Long Time With No One to Enforce it," *Canadian Business,* March 19, 2001, pp. 29–30+.

51. J. Greenberg, "Organizational Justice: Yesterday, Today, and Tomorrow," *Journal of Management,* 16, 1990, pp. 399–402.

52. D. Calleja, "Equity or Else," *Canadian Business,* March 19, 2001, p. 31.

53. G. Robinson and K. Dechant, "Building a Case for Business Diversity," *Academy of Management Executive,* 1997, pp. 3, 32–47.

54. K. Kalawsky, "US Group Wants Royal's Centura Buy Delayed: Alleges Takeover Target Discriminates Against Minorities," *Financial Post (National Post),* April 10, 2001, p. C4.

55. H. Branswell, "When Nestlé Canada Said Last Month It Would No Longer Be Making Chocolate Bars in a Nut-Free Facility, Thousands Wrote in to Protest," *Canadian Press Newswire,* May 14, 2001.

56. H. Branswell, "When Nestlé Canada Said Last Month It Would No Longer Be Making Chocolate Bars in a Nut-Free Facility, Thousands Wrote in to Protest," *Canadian Press Newswire,* May 14, 2001.

57. A.P. Carnevale and S.C. Stone, "Diversity: Beyond the Golden Rule," *Training & Development,* October 1994, pp. 22–39.

58. "Selling Equity," *Financial Post Magazine,* September 1994, pp. 20–25.

59. "Study Shows Women Who Are Unhappy with Corporate Life Plan to Start Own Businesses," *Women in Management,* December–January 1999, pp. 1–3.

60. Based on "Sask. NDP Deflect Sex Harassment Barbs With Opposition Leader's Duck Joke," *Canadian Press Newswire,* April 3, 2003; and "Sask. Deputy Minister Takes Severance Package

Over Ruling in Harassment Case," *Canadian Press Newswire,* April 23, 2003.

61. J. Goddu, "Sexual Harassment Complaints Rise Dramatically," *Canadian Press Newswire,* March 6, 1998.

62. B. Carton, "Muscled Out? At Jenny Craig, Men Are Ones Who Claim Sex Discrimination," *The Wall Street Journal,* November 29, 1994, pp. A1, A7.

63. R.L. Paetzold and A.M. O'Leary-Kelly, "Organizational Communication and the Legal Dimensions of Hostile Work Environment Sexual Harassment," in G.L. Kreps (ed.), *Sexual Harassment: Communication Implications* (Cresskill, NJ: Hampton Press, 1993).

64. M. Galen, J. Weber, and A.Z. Cuneo, "Sexual Harassment: Out of the Shadows," *Fortune,* October 28, 1991, pp. 30–31.

65. "Employers Underestimate Extent of Sexual Harassment, Report Says," *The Vancouver Sun,* March 8, 2001, p. D6.

66. A.M. O'Leary-Kelly, R.L. Paetzold, and R.W. Griffin, "Sexual Harassment as Aggressive Action: A Framework for Understanding Sexual Harassment," paper presented at the annual meeting of the Academy of Management, Vancouver, August 1995.

67. "Employers Underestimate Extent of Sexual Harassment, Report Says," *The Vancouver Sun,* March 8, 2001, p. D6.

68. Information in this paragraph based on Ian Jack, "Magna Suit Spotlights Auto Industry Practices," *The Financial Post Daily,* September 10, 1997, p. 1.

69. I. Jack, "Magna Suit Spotlights Auto Industry Practices," *The Financial Post Daily,* September 10, 1997, p. 1.

70. S.J. Bresler and R. Thacker, "Four-Point Plan Helps Solve Harassment Problems," *HR Magazine,* May 1993, pp. 117–124.

Chapter 4

1. The CSI story is based on a real incident experienced by a consulting client of one of the authors of this text. The dates and the names of the company and individuals involved have been changed.

2. Based on Mary Lamey, "A Monument to the Environment: Focus on Recycling. Mountain Equipment Is Building First 'Green' Retail Outlet in Quebec," *montrealgazette.com,* November 22, 2002, http://www.Canada.com/montreal.

3. H.A. Simon, *The New Science of Management* (Englewood Cliffs, NJ: Prentice-Hall, 1977).

4. *Think About It* based on S. Reinhardt, "Company Stays Local After Bosses Inspired by Employee," *Asheville Citizen-Times,* April 15, 2003, http://cgi.citizen-times.com/cgi-bin/story/news/32955 (accessed April 20, 2003).

5. H.A. Simon, *Administrative Behavior* (New York: Macmillan, 1947), p. 79.

6. H.A. Simon, *Models of Man* (New York: Wiley, 1957).

7. K.J. Arrow, *Aspects of the Theory of Risk Bearing* (Helsinki: Yrjo Johnssonis Saatio, 1965).

8. R.L. Daft and R.H. Lengel, "Organizational Information Requirements, Media Richness and Structural Design," *Management Science,* 32, 1986, pp. 554–571.

9. R. Cyert and J. March, *Behavioral Theory of the Firm* (Englewood Cliffs, NJ: Prentice-Hall, 1963).

10. J.G. March and H.A. Simon, *Organizations* (New York: Wiley, 1958).

11. H.A. Simon, "Making Management Decisions: The Role of Intuition and Emotion," *Academy of Management Executive,* 1, 1987, pp. 57–64.

12. M.H. Bazerman, *Judgment in Managerial Decision Making* (New York: Wiley, 1986); G.P. Huber, *Managerial Decision Making* (Glenview, IL: Scott, Foresman, 1993); and J.E. Russo and P.J. Schoemaker, *Decision Traps* (New York: Simon and Schuster, 1989).

13. M.D. Cohen, J.G. March, and J.P. Olsen, "A Garbage Can Model of Organizational Choice," *Administrative Science Quarterly,* 17, 1972, pp. 1–25.

14. P.C. Nutt, *Why Decisions Fail: Avoiding the Blunders and Traps That Lead to Debacles* (San Francisco: Berrett-Koehler Publishers, 2002); and M.H. Bazerman, *Judgment in Managerial Decision Making* (New York: Wiley, 1986).

15. J.E. Russo and P.J. Schoemaker, *Decision Traps* (New York: Simon and Schuster, 1989).

16. M.H. Bazerman, *Judgment in Managerial Decision Making* (New York: Wiley, 1986).

17. P.C. Nutt, *Why Decisions Fail: Avoiding the Blunders and Traps That Lead to Debacles* (San Francisco: Berrett-Koehler Publishers, 2002).

18. P.C. Nutt, *Why Decisions Fail: Avoiding the Blunders and Traps That Lead to Debacles* (San Francisco: Berrett-Koehler Publishers, 2002).

19. J.E. Russo and P.J. Schoemaker, *Decision Traps* (New York: Simon and Schuster, 1989).

20. *Think About It* based on G. Hamilton, "Log Home Builders Turn Pestilence into Profit," *The Vancouver Sun,* April 10, 2001, pp. D1, D8.

21. D. Kahneman and A. Tversky, "Judgment Under Uncertainty: Heuristics and Biases," *Science,* 185, 1974, pp. 1124–1131.

22. C.R. Schwenk, "Cognitive Simplification Processes in Strategic Decision Making," *Strategic Management Journal,* 5, 1984, pp. 111–128.

23. An interesting example of the illusion of control is Richard Roll's hubris hypothesis of takeovers. See R. Roll, "The Hubris Hypothesis of Corporate Takeovers," *Journal of Business,* 59, 1986, pp. 197–216.

24. B.M. Staw, "The Escalation of Commitment to a Course of Action," *Academy of Management Review,* 6, 1981, pp. 577–587.

25. J.E. Russo and P.J. Schoemaker, *Decision Traps* (New York: Simon and Schuster, 1989).

26. J.E. Russo and P.J. Schoemaker, *Decision Traps* (New York: Simon and Schuster, 1989).

27. *Think About It* based on A. Muoio, "Brainstorming at Switzerland's BrainStore: Building an Assembly Line for Ideas," *Financial Post (National Post),* April 12, 2000, p. C15.

28. I.L. Janis, *Groupthink: Psychological Studies of Policy Decisions and Fiascoes,* 2nd ed. (Boston: Houghton Mifflin, 1982).

29. I.L. Janis, *Groupthink* (Boston: Houghton Mifflin, 1982).

30. J.N. Choi and M.U. Kim, "The Organizational Application of Groupthink and Its Limitations in Organizations," *Journal of Applied Psychology,* 84, 1999, pp. 297–306.

31. C. McCauley, "The Nature of Social Influence in Groupthink: Compliance and Internalization," *Journal of Personality and Social Psychology,* 57, 1989, pp. 250–260; P.E. Tetlock, R.S. Peterson, C. McGuire, S. Chang, and P. Feld, "Assessing Political Group Dynamics: A Test of the Groupthink Model," *Journal of Personality and Social Psychology,* 63, 1992, pp. 781–796; S. Graham, "A Review of Attribution Theory in Achievement Contexts," *Educational Psychology Review,* 3, 1991, pp. 5–39; and G. Moorhead and J.R. Montanari, "An Empirical Investigation of the Groupthink Phenomenon," *Human Relations,* 39, 1986, pp. 399–410.

32. J. Longley and D.G. Pruitt, "Groupthink: A Critique of Janis' Theory," in L. Wheeler (ed.), *Review of Personality and Social Psychology* (Newbury Park, CA: Sage, 1980), pp. 507–513; and J.A. Sniezek, "Groups Under Uncertainty: An Examination of Confidence in Group Decision Making," *Organizational Behavior and Human Decision Processes,* 52, 1992, pp. 124–155.

33. J.N. Choi and M.U. Kim, "The Organizational Application of Groupthink and Its Limitations in Organizations," *Journal of Applied Psychology,* 84, 1999, pp. 297–306.

34. See N.R.F. Maier, *Principles of Human Relations* (New York: Wiley, 1952); I.L. Janis, *Groupthink: Psychological Studies of Policy Decisions and Fiascoes,* 2nd ed. (Boston: Houghton Mifflin, 1982); and C.R. Leana, "A Partial Test of Janis' Groupthink Model: Effects of Group Cohesiveness and Leader Behavior on Defective Decision Making," *Journal of Management,* Spring 1985, pp. 5–17.

35. See R.O. Mason, "A Dialectic Approach to Strategic Planning," *Management Science,* 13, 1969, pp. 403–414; R.A. Cosier and J.C. Aplin, "A Critical View of Dialectic Inquiry in Strategic Planning," *Strategic Management Journal,* 1, 1980, pp. 343–356; I.I. Mitroff and R.O. Mason, "Structuring III–Structured Policy Issues: Further Explorations in a Methodology for Messy Problems," *Strategic Management Journal,* 1, 1980, pp. 331–342.

36. Mary C. Gentile, *Differences That Work: Organizational Excellence Through Diversity* (Boston: Harvard Business School Press, 1994).

37. *Think About It* based on J. Mackintosh, "How BMW Put the Mini Back on Track," *Financial Times,* March 18, 2003, http://www.ft.com (accessed March 19, 2003).

38. B. Hedberg, "How Organizations Learn and Unlearn," in W.H. Starbuck and P.C. Nystrom (eds.), *Handbook of*

Organizational Design, vol. 1 (New York: Oxford University Press, 1981), pp. 1–27.

39. See P. Senge, *The Fifth Discipline: The Art and Practice of the Learning Organization* (New York: Doubleday, 1990).

40. T.A. Stewart, "3M Fights Back," *Fortune*, February 5, 1996, pp. 94-99; and T.D. Schellhardt, "David in Goliath," *The Wall Street Journal*, May 23, 1996, p. R14.

41. R.W. Woodman, J.E. Sawyer, and R.W. Griffin, "Towards a Theory of Organizational Creativity," *Academy of Management Review*, 18, 1993, pp. 293–321.

42. M. Ullmann, "Creativity Cubed: Burntsand Has Found a Novel Program to Motivate Its Most Creative Employees. Can It Work for You?" *SVN Canada*, February 2001, pp. B22–B23+.

43. T.J. Bouchard Jr., J. Barsaloux, and G. Drauden, "Brainstorming Procedure, Group Size, and Sex as Determinants of Problem Solving Effectiveness of Individuals and Groups," *Journal of Applied Psychology*, 59, 1974, pp. 135–138.

44. L. Thompson and L.F. Brajkovich, "Improving the Creativity of Organizational Work Groups," *Academy of Management Executive*, 17, no. 1, 2003, pp. 96–111, B. Mullen, C. Johnson, and E. Salas, "Productivity Loss in Brainstorming Groups: A Meta-Analytic Integration," *Basic and Applied Social Psychology*, 12, no. 1, 1991, pp. 3–23; and M. Diehl and W. Stroebe, "Productivity Loss in Brainstorming Groups: Towards the Solution of a Riddle," *Journal of Personality and Social Psychology*, 53, 1987, pp. 497–509.

45. D.H. Gustafson, R.K. Shulka, A. Delbecq, and W.G. Walster, "A Comparative Study of Differences in Subjective Likelihood Estimates Made by Individuals, Interacting Groups, Delphi Groups, and Nominal Groups," *Organizational Behavior and Human Performance*, 9, 1973, pp. 280–291.

46. N. Dalkey, *The Delphi Method: An Experimental Study of Group Decision Making* (Santa Monica, CA: Rand Corp., 1989).

47. P. Fitzpatrick, "Wacky WestJet's Winning Ways: Passengers Respond to Stunts That Include Races to Determine Who Leaves the Airplane First," *Financial Post (National Post)*, October 16, 2000, p. C1.

48. N.B. Macintosh, *The Social Software of Accounting Information Systems* (New York: Wiley, 1995).

49. R.I. Benjamin and J. Blunt, "Critical IT Issues: The Next Ten Years," *Sloan Management Review*, Summer 1992, pp. 7–19; W.H. Davidow and M.S. Malone, *The Virtual Corporation* (New York: Harper Business, 1992).

50. C.A. O'Reilly, "Variations in Decision Makers' Use of Information: The Impact of Quality and Accessibility," *Academy of Management Journal*, 25, 1982, pp. 756–771.

51. G. Stalk and T.H. Hout, *Competing Against Time* (New York: Free Press, 1990).

52. R. Cyert and J. March, *Behavioral Theory of the Firm* (Englewood Cliffs, NJ: Prentice-Hall, 1963).

Chapter 5

1. B. Simon, "Upstart Cott Shakes Cola Kings," *Financial Times*, June 14, 1994, p. 18; "Coca-Cola Versus Pepsi-Cola and the Soft Drink Industry," *Harvard Business School Case* #9-391-179.

2. A. Levy, "Pepsi Ceding Cola War Victory to Rival Coke: Fails to Take Advantage of Leader's Stumbles," *Financial Post (National Post)*, January 19, 2000. p. C12; and "Coke Rides Vanilla, Diet Flavours Over Rival Pepsi," *Calgary Herald*, February 25, 2003, p. C4.

3. "Cott Pays $72M US for Concord Beverage, Posts Profitable Quarter," *Canadian Press Newswire*, October 18, 2000.

4. Based on A. Lam, "The Entrepreneurial Bug Hits Business Students Before Graduation," *Business Sense*, 2000, p. 33; http://www.grocery gopher.ca/aboutus.php; L. Kukurudza, "Make-up Master Teaches Craft," *The StarPhoenix* (Saskatoon), September 14, 2000, p. C1; and "Women of Distinction," *The StarPhoenix* (Saskatoon), March 20, 2000; p. D1.

5. A. Chandler, *Strategy and Structure: Chapters in the History of the American Enterprise* (Cambridge, MA: MIT Press, 1962).

6. M. Ingram, "Our Job Is to Be Better," *The Globe and Mail*, May 12, 2001, p. F3.

7. A. Chandler, *Strategy and Structure: Chapters in the History of the American Enterprise* (Cambridge, MA: MIT Press, 1962).

8. V. Pilieci, "The Lost Generation of Business Talent," *The Vancouver Sun*, May 2, 2001, pp. D1, D9.

9. F.J. Aguilar, "General Electric: Reg Jones and Jack Welch," in *General Managers in Action* (Oxford: Oxford University Press, 1992).

10. F.J. Aguilar, "General Electric: Reg Jones and Jack Welch," in *General Managers in Action* (Oxford: Oxford University Press, 1992).

11. F.J. Aguilar, "General Electric: Reg Jones and Jack Welch," in *General Managers in Action* (Oxford: Oxford University Press, 1992).

12. www.ge.com, 2001.

13. C.W. Hofer and D. Schendel, *Strategy Formulation: Analytical Concepts* (St. Paul, MN: West, 1978).

14. H. Fayol, *General and Industrial Management* (New York: IEEE Press, 1984). Fayol's work was first published in 1916.

15. H. Fayol, *General and Industrial Management* (1916; New York: IEEE Press, 1984), p. 18.

16. R. Phelps, C. Chan, S.C. Kapsalis, "Does Scenario Planning Affect Firm Performance?" *Journal of Business Research*, March 2001, pp. 223–232.

17. Laura Ramsay, "Lessons Learned From SARS Crisis," *The Globe and Mail*, May 22, 2003, p. B16.

18. *Think About It* based on S. Bartlett, "Healing Centre Opens at General Hospital," *Windspeaker*, February 2000, p. 22; the Regina Health District's web page, http://www.reginahealth.sk.ca; and "Native Healing Centre Officially Opens," *Regina Health District's News Release*, December 10, 1999.

19. J.A. Pearce, "The Company Mission as a Strategic Tool," *Sloan Management Review*, Spring 1992, pp. 15–24.

20. P.C. Nutt and R.W. Backoff, "Crafting Vision," *Journal of Management Inquiry*, December 1997, p. 309.

21. D.F. Abell, *Defining the Business: The Starting Point of Strategic Planning* (Englewood Cliffs, NJ: Prentice-Hall, 1980).

22. www.worksafebc.com/corporate/about/goals/default.asp.

23. G. Hamel and C.K. Prahalad, "Strategic Intent," *Harvard Business Review*, May–June 1989, pp. 63–73.

24. E.A. Locke, G.P. Latham, and M. Erez, "The Determinants of Goal

Commitment," *Academy of Management Review*, 13, 1988, pp. 23–39.

25. P.F. Drucker, *The Practice of Management* (New York: Harper and Row, 1954).

26. S.J. Carroll and H.L. Tosi, *Management by Objectives: Applications and Research* (New York: Macmillan, 1973).

27. R. Rodgers and J.E. Hunter, "Impact of Management by Objectives on Organizational Productivity," *Journal of Applied Psychology*, 76, 1991, pp. 322–326.

28. M.B. Gavin, S.G. Green, and G.T. Fairhurst, "Managerial Control Strategies for Poor Performance Over Time and the Impact on Subordinate Reactions," *Organizational Behaviour and Human Decision Processes*, 63, 1995, pp. 207–221.

29. K.R. Andrews, *The Concept of Corporate Strategy* (Homewood, IL: Irwin, 1971).

30. Based on G. Pitts, "Tide Turns for P&G Canada President," *The Globe and Mail*, October 14, 2002, p. B3.

31. *Think About It* based on O. Bertin, "E.D. Smith Caught in a Bit of a Jam," *The Globe and Mail*, April 23, 2001, p. B5; R. McQueen, "Llewellyn Smith Is Planting His Legacy: ED Smith and Sons' Owner Puts Best Face on Sale of Company," *Financial Post (National Post)*, April 30, 2001, p. C6; and "Jam Today: Imperial Capital Merchant Bank Takes Over E.D. Smith," *Canadian Press Newswire*, January 28, 2002.

32. M. McNeill, "Peak of the Market Buys Competitor," *Winnipeg Free Press*, June 2001, pp. B1, B3.

33. E. Penrose, *The Theory of the Growth of the Firm* (Oxford: Oxford University Press, 1959).

34. M.E. Porter, "From Competitive Advantage to Corporate Strategy," *Harvard Business Review*, 65, 1987, pp. 43–59.

35. "Jam Today: Imperial Capital Merchant Bank Takes Over E.D. Smith," *Canadian Press Newswire*, January 28, 2002.

36. G. Pitts, "Small Is Beautiful, Conglomerates Signal," *The Globe and Mail*, April 1, 2002, pp. B1, B4.

37. For a review of the evidence, see C.W.L. Hill and G.R. Jones, *Strategic Management: An Integrated Approach,* 3rd ed. (Boston: Houghton Mifflin, 2000), Ch. 10.

38. V. Ramanujam and P. Varadarajan, "Research on Corporate Diversification: A

Synthesis," *Strategic Management Journal*, 10, 1989, pp. 523–551. Also see A. Shleifer and R.W. Vishny, "Takeovers in the 1960s and 1980s: Evidence and Implications," in R.P. Rumelt, D.E. Schendel, and D.J. Teece, *Fundamental Issues in Strategy* (Boston: Harvard Business School Press, 1994).

39. J.R. Williams, B.L. Paez, and L. Sanders, "Conglomerates Revisited," *Strategic Management Journal*, 9, 1988, pp. 403–414.

40. H. Shaw, "Fish, Dairy Units Sacrificed to Help Raise Cash for Baked Goods: Bestfoods Deal," *Financial Post (National Post)*, February 20, 2001, pp. C1, C6.

41. C.A. Bartlett and S. Ghoshal, *Managing Across Borders* (Boston: Harvard Business School Press, 1989).

42. C.K. Prahalad and Y.L. Doz, *The Multinational Mission* (New York: Free Press, 1987).

43. M.K. Perry, "Vertical Integration: Determinants and Effects," in R. Schmalensee and R.D. Willig, *Handbook of Industrial Organization*, vol. 1 (New York: Elsevier Science Publishing, 1989).

44. T. Muris, D. Scheffman, and P. Spiller, "Strategy and Transaction Costs: The Organization of Distribution in the Carbonated Soft Drink Industry," *Journal of Economics and Management Strategy*, 1, 1992, pp. 77–97.

45. "Matsushita Electric Industrial (MEI) in 1987," *Harvard Business School Case* #388-144.

46. P. Ghemawat, *Commitment: The Dynamic of Strategy* (New York: Free Press, 1991).

47. D. McMurdy, "The Human Cost of Mergers," *Maclean's*, November 20, 2000, p. 128.

48. M.E. Porter, *Competitive Strategy* (New York: Free Press, 1980).

49. Gordon Pitts, "Ganong Boss Aims for Sweet Spot," *The Globe and Mail*, March 3, 2003, p. B4.

50. C.W.L. Hill, "Differentiation Versus Low Cost or Differentiation and Low Cost: A Contingency Framework," *Academy of Management Review*, 13, 1988, pp. 401–412.

51. For details see J.P. Womack, D.T. Jones, and D. Roos, *The Machine That Changed the World* (New York: Rawson Associates, 1990).

52. M.E. Porter, *Competitive Strategy* (New York: Free Press, 1980).

53. C.W.L. Hill and G.R. Jones, *Strategic Management: An Integrated Approach,* 3rd ed. (Boston: Houghton Mifflin, 2000).

54. See D. Garvin, "What Does Product Quality Really Mean?" *Sloan Management Review*, 26, Fall 1984, pp. 25–44; P.B. Crosby, *Quality Is Free* (New York: Mentor Books, 1980); and A. Gabor, *The Man Who Discovered Quality* (New York: Times Books, 1990).

Chapter 6

1. G. Cheesbrough, "Guidelines for Corporate Transformation," *Canadian Speeches*, 13, no. 1, 1999, pp. 56–60.

2. G. Cheesbrough, "Guidelines for Corporate Transformation," *Canadian Speeches*, 13, no. 1, 1999, pp. 56–60.

3. G. Cheesbrough, "Guidelines for Corporate Transformation," *Canadian Speeches*, 13, no. 1, 1999, pp. 56–60.

4. G. Cheesbrough, "Guidelines for Corporate Transformation," *Canadian Speeches*, 13, no. 1, 1999, pp. 56–60.

5. G. Cheesbrough, "Guidelines for Corporate Transformation," *Canadian Speeches*, 13, no. 1, 1999, pp. 56–60.

6. S. Heinrich, "Steering Altamira in a New Direction: Gordon Cheesbrough has Set out to Improve the Performance of the Mutual Fund Company and Win Back Lost Investors by Shifting the Focus From Single Star Managers to the Team Approach and by Introducing a Broader Range of Products, Such as Competitors' Funds," *Financial Post (National Post)*, November 28, 1998, p. D9.

7. D. Yedlin, "Buyer Saw Value in Out-of-Favour Altamira: The National Bank Still Finds Potential in a Company Whose Success Depended on Booming Equity Markets," *Ottawa Citizen*, July 28, 2002, p. D2.

8. *Think About It* based on L. Millan, "Who's Scoffing Now? The Lemaire Brothers Started out Using Recycled Fibre in One Small Paper Mill in Rural Quebec," *Canadian Business*, March 27, 1998, pp. 74–77; and *cascades.com*, http://www.cascades.com/cas/en/ 0_0/0_0.jsp (accessed September 15, 2003).

9. G.R. Jones, *Organizational Theory: Text and Cases* (Reading, MA: Addison-Wesley, 1995).

10. J. Child, *Organization: A Guide for Managers and Administrators* (New York: Harper and Row, 1977).

11. S. Erwin, "Chrysler, CAW Far Apart, Union Says," *The Canadian Press*, October 11, 2002; and P. Brent, "'Sadie Hawkins' Day Survives Torrid Talks: Workers May Pick Jobs," *Financial Post (National Post)*, October 17, 2002, pp. FP1, FP9.

12. F.W. Taylor, *The Principles of Scientific Management* (New York: Harper, 1911).

13. R.W. Griffin, *Task Design: An Integrative Approach* (Glenview, IL: Scott, Foresman, 1982).

14. R.W. Griffin, *Task Design: An Integrative Approach* (Glenview, IL: Scott, Foresman, 1982).

15. *Think About It* based on B. Critchley, "Royal Bank/DS Now Restructured," *Financial Post (National Post)*, February 10, 2000, p. D2.

16. J.R. Galbraith and R.K. Kazanjian, *Strategy Implementation: Structure, System, and Process*, 2nd ed. (St. Paul, MN: West, 1986).

17. P.R. Lawrence and J.W. Lorsch, *Organization and Environment* (Boston: Graduate School of Business Administration, Harvard University, 1967).

18. G.R. Jones, *Organizational Theory: Text and Cases* (Reading, MA: Addison-Wesley, 1995).

19. P.R. Lawrence and J.W. Lorsch, *Organization and Environment* (Boston: Graduate School of Business Administration, Harvard University, 1967).

20. R.H. Hall, *Organizations: Structure and Process* (Englewood Cliffs, NJ: Prentice-Hall, 1972); and R. Miles, *Macro Organizational Behaviour* (Santa Monica, CA: Goodyear, 1980).

21. A.D. Chandler, *Strategy and Structure* (Cambridge, MA: MIT Press, 1962).

22. G.R. Jones and C.W.L. Hill, "Transaction Cost Analysis of Strategy–Structure Choice," *Strategic Management Journal*, 9, 1988, pp. 159–172.

23. S.M. Davis and P.R. Lawrence, *Matrix* (Reading, MA: Addison-Wesley, 1977); and J.R. Galbraith, "Matrix Organization Designs: How to Combine Functional and Project Forms," *Business Horizons*, 14, 1971, pp. 29–40.

24. L.R. Burns, "Matrix Management in Hospitals: Testing Theories of Matrix Structure and Development," *Administrative Science Quarterly*, 34, 1989, pp. 349–368.

25. C.W.L. Hill, *International Business* (Homewood, IL: Irwin, 1997).

26. C.A. Bartlett and S. Ghoshal, *Transnational Management* (Homewood, IL: Irwin, 1992).

27. G.R. Jones, *Organizational Theory: Text and Cases* (Reading, MA: Addison-Wesley, 1995).

28. "P&G Divides to Rule," *Marketing*, March 23, 1995, p. 15.

29. P. Blau, "A Formal Theory of Differentiation in Organizations," *American Sociological Review*, 35, 1970, pp. 684–695.

30. J. Child, *Organization: A Guide for Managers and Administrators* (New York: Harper and Row, 1977).

31. Information about Ducks Unlimited from "Salute! Celebrating the Progressive Employer," advertising supplement, *Benefits Canada*, March 1999, p. Insert 1–23; and http://www.ducksunlimited.ca.

32. P.M. Blau and R.A. Schoenherr, *The Structure of Organizations* (New York: Basic Books, 1971).

33. G.R. Jones, *Organizational Theory: Text and Cases* (Reading, MA: Addison-Wesley, 1995).

34. T. Burns and G.M. Stalker, *The Management of Innovation* (London: Tavistock, 1961).

35. L.A. Perlow, G.A. Okhuysen, and N.P. Repenning, "The Speed Trap: Exploring the Relationship Between Decision Making and Temporal Context," *Academy of Management Journal*, 45, 2002, pp. 931–955.

36. P.R. Lawrence and J.W. Lorsch, *Organization and Environment* (Boston: Graduate School of Business Administration, Harvard University, 1967).

37. R. Duncan, "What Is the Right Organizational Design?" *Organizational Dynamics*, Winter 1979, pp. 59–80.

38. T. Burns and G.R. Stalker, *The Management of Innovation* (London: Tavistock, 1966).

39. D. Miller, "Strategy Making and Structure: Analysis and Implications for Performance," *Academy of Management Journal*, 30, 1987, pp. 7–32.

40. A.D. Chandler, *Strategy and Structure* (Cambridge, MA: MIT Press, 1962).

41. J. Stopford and L. Wells, *Managing the Multinational Enterprise* (London: Longman, 1972).

42. J. Woodward, *Management and Technology* (London: Her Majesty's Stationery Office, 1958).

43. *Think About It* based on K. Cox, "Joint Ventures Key to Success for Cape Breton Reserve," *The Globe and Mail*, May 9, 2001, p. B12.

44. B. Kogut, "Joint Ventures: Theoretical and Empirical Perspectives," *Strategic Management Journal*, 9, 1988, pp. 319–332.

45. See, for example, B. Hedberg, G. Dahlgren, J. Hansson, and N.-G. Olve, *Virtual Organizations and Beyond: Discovering Imaginary Systems* (New York: Wiley, 2001); N.A. Wishart, J.J. Elam, and D. Robey, "Redrawing the Portrait of a Learning Organization Inside Knight-Ridder, Inc.," *Academy of Management Executive*, 10, no. 1 (1996), pp. 7–20; G.G. Dess, A.M.A. Rasheeed, K.J. McLaughlin, and R.L. Priem, "The New Corporate Architecture," *Academy of Management Executive*, 9, no. 3 (1995), p. 720; and R. Keidel, "Rethinking Organizational Design," *Academy of Management Executive*, November 1994, pp. 12–27.

46. B. Hedberg, G. Dahlgren, J. Hansson, and N.-G. Olve, *Virtual Organizations and Beyond: Discovering Imaginary Systems* (New York: Wiley, 2001).

47. "Outsourcing," advertising supplement in *PurchasingB2B*, October 2000, pp. Insert 1–12.

48. J. Barthelemy and D. Adsit, "The Seven Deadly Sins of Outsourcing." *Academy of Management Executive*, 17, no. 2, 2003, pp. 87–100.

49. © 1996, Gareth R. Jones.

50. M. Meyer, "Culture Club," *Newsweek*, July 11, 1994, pp. 38–42.

Chapter 7

1. Information about NASA based on M.L. Wald and J. Schwartz, "Shuttle Inquiry Uncovers Flaws in Communication," *NYTimes.com*, August 4, 2003; Associated Press, "NASA 'Culture' Resists Change, Says Investigator," *The Baltimore Sun*, August 3, 2003, http://www.sunspot.net/bal-te.nasa02aug03,0,7833936.story (accessed

August 3, 2003); Associated Press, "NASA Official Defends Handling of Columbia Safety," *The Baltimore Sun,* July 22, 2003, http://www.sunspot.net/news/nation-world/bal-nasa0722,0,6092519.story?coll=bal-nationworld-headlines (accessed August 3, 2002); and http://www.caib.us.

2. Information about Creo based on P. Withers, "Culturally Creative [Best Companies to Work for in BC, #2]," *BCBusiness Magazine,* January 2002, p. 27; and C. Taylor, "Best Companies to Work for in BC," *BCBusiness Magazine,* November 1999, pp. 31–51.

3. *Think About It* based on http://www.nokia.com, 2001; and P. de Bendern, "Quirky Culture Paves Nokia's Road to Fortune," http://www.yahoo.com, 2000.

4. See, for example, H.S. Becker, "Culture: A Sociological View," *Yale Review,* Summer 1982, pp. 513–527; and E.H. Schein, *Organizational Culture and Leadership* (San Francisco: Jossey-Bass, 1985), p. 168.

5. T.E. Deal and A.A. Kennedy, "Culture: A New Look Through Old Lenses," *Journal of Applied Behavioral Science,* November 1983, p. 501.

6. M. Rokeach, *The Nature of Human Values* (New York: Free Press, 1973).

7. D. Yedlin, "Entwistle Faces Potholes at Telus," *The Globe and Mail,* March 17, 2003, p. B2.

8. E.H. Schein, "Leadership and Organizational Culture," in F. Hesselbein, M. Goldsmith, and R. Beckhard (eds.), *The Leader of the Future* (San Francisco: Jossey-Bass, 1996), pp. 61–62.

9. J.B. Sorensen, "The Strength of Corporate Culture and the Reliability of Firm Performance," *Administrative Science Quarterly,* 47, no. 1, 2002, pp. 70–91.

10. D.C. Feldman, "The Development and Enforcement of Group Norms," *Academy of Management Review,* 9, 1984, pp. 47–53.

11. M.L. Wald and J. Schwartz, "Shuttle Inquiry Uncovers Flaws in Communication," *NYTimes.com,* August 4, 2003.

12. D. Yedlin, "Merging Corporate Cultures Not Always Easy," *Calgary Herald,* June 2, 2001, p. E1.

13. G.R. Jones, *Organizational Theory: Text and Cases* (Reading, MA: Addison-Wesley, 1995).

14. H. Schein, "The Role of the Founder in Creating Organizational Culture," *Organizational Dynamics,* 12, 1983, pp. 13–28.

15. J.M. George, "Personality, Affect, and Behaviour in Groups," *Journal of Applied Psychology,* 75, 1990, pp. 107–116.

16. J. Van Maanen, "Police Socialization: A Longitudinal Examination of Job Attitudes in an Urban Police Department," *Administrative Science Quarterly,* 20, 1975, pp. 207–228.

17. P.L. Berger and T. Luckman, *The Social Construction of Reality* (Garden City, NY: Anchor Books, 1967).

18. H.M. Trice and J.M. Beyer, "Studying Organizational Culture Through Rites and Ceremonials," *Academy of Management Review,* 9, 1984, pp. 653–669.

19. "Bonding and Brutality: Hazing Survives as a Way of Forging Loyalty to Groups," *Maclean's,* January 30, 1995, p. 18.

20. B. Ortega, "Wal-Mart's Meeting Is a Reason to Party," *The Wall Street Journal,* June 3, 1994, p. A1.

21. C. Stephenson, "Corporate Values Drive Global Success at Lucent Technologies," *Canadian Speeches,* November/December 1999, pp. 23–27.

22. A. Rafaeli and M.G. Pratt, "Tailored Meanings: On the Meaning and Impact of Organizational Dress," *Academy of Management Review,* January 1993, pp. 32–55.

23. J. Greenwood, "Job One: When Bobbie Gaunt Became Ford of Canada President Earlier This Year, the Appointment Put a Spotlight on the New Rules of the Auto Industry: It's Less About Manufacturing These Days Than About Marketing and Sales," *Financial Post Magazine,* June 1997, pp. 18–22.

24. D. Akin, "Big Blue Chills Out: A Canadian Executive Leads the Campaign to Turn IBM into Cool Blue," *Financial Post (National Post),* October 11, 1999, pp. C1, C6.

25. *Think About It* based on J.W. Schulz, L.C. Hauck, R.M. Hauck, "Using the Power of Corporate Culture to Achieve Results: A Case Study of Sunflower Electric Power Corporation," *Management Quarterly,* 2, 2001, pp. 2–19.

26. J. Lee, "Canadian Businesses Not Good at Adjusting, Survey Says," *The Vancouver Sun,* December 14, 1998, pp. C1–2.

27. E. Schein, *Organizational Culture and Leadership* (San Francisco, Jossey-Bass, 1985).

28. *Think About It* based on D. Steinhart, "US Headquarters to Bear the Brunt of Moore's Axe: Cutting 1,400 Jobs," *Financial Post (National Post),* January 5, 2001, p. C5; "Business Form Company Moore Selling Carbonless Copy Paper Operation to Mead," *Canadian Press Newswire,* November 13, 2000; P. Kuitenbrouwer, "Angry Investors Slam Moore Boss: Blue Chip No More. Company Admits Strategic Options in Short Supply," *Financial Post (National Post),* April 29, 2000, p. D4; and M.C. Goldman, "Paper Lives, Moore Corp. Learned the Hard Way," *torontostar.com,* May 5, 2003 (accessed May 5, 2003).

29. L. Brown, "Research Action: Organizational Feedback, Understanding and Change," *Journal of Applied Behavioral Research,* 8, 1972, pp. 697–711; P.A. Clark, *Action Research and Organizational Change* (New York: Harper and Row, 1972); and N. Margulies and A.P. Raia (eds.), *Conceptual Foundations of Organizational Development* (New York: McGraw-Hill, 1978).

30. W.L. French and C.H. Bell, *Organizational Development* (Englewood Cliffs, NJ: Prentice-Hall, 1990).

31. K. Lewin, *Field Theory in Social Science* (New York: Harper and Row, 1951).

32. W.L. French, "A Checklist for Organizing and Implementing an OD Effort," in W.L. French, C.H. Bell, and R.A. Zawacki (eds.), *Organizational Development and Transformation* (Homewood, IL: Irwin, 1994), 484–495.

33. *Think About It* based on "Back on the Rails: Years of Cutting Have Produced a Leaner and Meaner CN," *Maclean's,* January 13, 1997, pp. 36–38.

34. J.R. Stepp and T.J. Schneider, "Fostering Change in a Unionized Environment," *Canadian Business Review,* Summer 1995, pp. 13–16.

35. J.R. Stepp and T.J. Schneider, "Fostering Change in a Unionized Environment," *Canadian Business Review,* Summer 1995, pp. 13–16.

Chapter 8

1. W. Bounds, "Kodak's CEO Got $1.7 Million Bonus in 1994 Despite Below-Target Profit," *The Wall Street Journal*, March 13, 1995, p. B9; C.J. Cantoni, "Manager's Journal: A Waste of Human Resources," *The Wall Street Journal*, May 15, 1995, p. A22; D. Defotis, "Kodak's Moment May Be Near," *Financial Post (National Post)*, August 12, 2000, p. C8; M. Maremont, "Kodak's New Focus," *Business Week*, January 30, 1995, pp. 62–68; and P. Nulty, "Kodak Grabs for Growth Again," *Fortune*, May 16, 1994, pp. 76–78; B. Saporito, "The Eclipse of Mars," *Fortune*, November 28, 1994, p. 82.

2. B. Saporito, "The Eclipse of Mars," *Fortune*, November 28, 1994, p. 82.

3. *Think About It* based on Marina Strauss, "Pay of Store Workers Fails to Entice," *The Globe and Mail*, June 4, 2003, p. B4.

4. R. Kanfer, "Motivation Theory and Industrial and Organizational Psychology," in M.D. Dunnette and L.M. Hough (eds.), *Handbook of Industrial and Organizational Psychology*, 2nd ed., vol. 1 (Palo Alto, CA: Consulting Psychologists Press, 1990), pp. 75–170.

5. *Think About It* based on G. Bellett, "Firm's Secret to Success Lies in Treating Workers Right," *The Vancouver Sun*, March 21, 2001, pp. D7, D11.

6. A.H. Maslow, *Motivation and Personality* (New York: Harper and Row, 1954); and J.P. Campbell and R.D. Pritchard, "Motivation Theory in Industrial and Organizational Psychology," in M.D. Dunnette (ed.), *Handbook of Industrial and Organizational Psychology* (Chicago: Rand McNally, 1976), pp. 63–130.

7. R. Kanfer, "Motivation Theory and Industrial and Organizational Psychology," in M.D. Dunnette and L.M. Hough (eds.), *Handbook of Industrial and Organizational Psychology*, 2nd ed., vol. 1 (Palo Alto, CA: Consulting Psychologists Press, 1990), pp. 75–170.

8. S. Ronen, "An Underlying Structure of Motivational Need Taxonomies: A Cross-Cultural Confirmation," in H.C. Triandis, M.D. Dunnette, and L.M. Hough (eds.), *Handbook of Industrial and Organizational Psychology*, vol. 4 (Palo Alto, CA: Consulting Psychologists Press, 1994), pp. 241–269.

9. N.J. Adler, *International Dimensions of Organizational Behavior*, 2nd ed. (Boston: P.W.S.-Kent, 1991); G. Hofstede, "Motivation, Leadership and Organization: Do American Theories Apply Abroad?" *Organizational Dynamics*, Summer 1980, pp. 42–63.

10. F. Herzberg, *Work and the Nature of Man* (Cleveland: World, 1966).

11. N. King, "Clarification and Evaluation of the Two-Factor Theory of Job Satisfaction," *Psychological Bulletin*, 74, 1970, pp. 18–31; and E.A. Locke, "The Nature and Causes of Job Satisfaction," in M.D. Dunnette (ed.), *Handbook of Industrial and Organizational Psychology* (Chicago: Rand McNally, 1976), pp. 1297–1349.

12. R.A. Clay, "Green Is Good for You," *Monitor on Psychology*, April 2001, pp. 40–42.

13. "Motorola Inc.: Company Is Chosen to Build Cellular System in Calcutta," *The Wall Street Journal*, January 5, 1995, p. B4; and "Motorola Inc. Plans to Increase Business With Chinese Ventures," *The Wall Street Journal*, February 13, 1995, p. B11.

14. T.R. Mitchell, "Expectancy-Value Models in Organizational Psychology," in N.T. Feather (ed.), *Expectations and Actions: Expectancy-Value Models in Psychology* (Hillsdale, NJ: Erlbaum, 1982), pp. 293–312; V.H. Vroom, *Work and Motivation* (New York: Wiley, 1964).

15. P. Engardio and G. DeGeorge, "Importing Enthusiasm," *Business Week/21st Century Capitalism*, 1994, pp. 122–123.

16. E.A. Locke and G.P. Latham, *A Theory of Goal Setting and Task Performance* (Englewood Cliffs, NJ: Prentice-Hall, 1990).

17. E.A. Locke and G.P. Latham, *A Theory of Goal Setting and Task Performance* (Englewood Cliffs, NJ: Prentice-Hall, 1990); J.J. Donovan and D.J. Radosevich, "The Moderating Role of Goal Commitment on the Goal Difficulty–Performance Relationship: A Meta-Analytic Review and Critical Analysis," *Journal of Applied Psychology*, 83, 1998, pp. 308–315; and M.E. Tubbs, "Goal Setting: A Meta-Analytic Examination of the Empirical Evidence," *Journal of Applied Psychology*, 71, 1986, pp. 474–483.

18. *Think About It* based on L. Perreaux, "When 'The Job Sucks,' Maple Leaf Raffles Trucks: Company Incentives at Slaughterhouse in Manitoba," *National Post*, May 19, 2001, p. A3.

19. F. Luthans and R. Kreitner, *Organizational Behavior Modification and Beyond* (Glenview, IL: Scott, Foresman, 1985); A.D. Stajkovic and F. Luthans, "A Meta-Analysis of the Effects of Organizational Behavior Modification on Task Performance, 1975–95," *Academy of Management Journal*, 40, 1997, pp. 1122–1149.

20. J.S. Adams, "Toward an Understanding of Inequity," *Journal of Abnormal and Social Psychology*, 67, 1963, pp. 422–436; J. Greenberg, "Approaching Equity and Avoiding Inequity in Groups and Organizations," in J. Greenberg and R.L. Cohen (eds.), *Equity and Justice in Social Behavior* (New York: Academic Press, 1982), pp. 389–435; J. Greenberg, "Equity and Workplace Status: A Field Experiment," *Journal of Applied Psychology*, 73, 1988, pp. 606–613; and R.T. Mowday, "Equity Theory Predictions of Behavior in Organizations," in R.M. Steers and L.W. Porter, (eds.), *Motivation and Work Behavior* (New York: McGraw-Hill, 1987), pp. 89–110.

21. *Think About It* based on "Paying Workers Well Is Not Enough, Surveys Finds," *Financial Post (National Post)*, May 16, 2001, p. C10.

22. E.E. Lawler III, *Pay and Organization Development* (Reading, MA: Addison-Wesley, 1981).

23. Based on S.E. Gross and J.P. Bacher, "The New Variable Pay Programs: How Some Succeed, Why Some Don't," *Compensation & Benefits Review*, January–February 1993, p. 51; and J.R. Schuster and P.K. Zingheim, "The New Variable Pay: Key Design Issues," *Compensation & Benefits Review*, March–April 1993, p. 28.

24. *Peter Brieger*, "Variable Pay Packages Gain Favour: Signing Bonuses, Profit Sharing Taking Place of Salary Hikes," *Financial Post (National Post)*, September 13, 2002, p. FP5.

25. E. Beauchesne, "Pay Bonuses Improve Productivity, Study Shows," *The Vancouver Sun*, September 13, 2002, p. D5.

26. "Hope for Higher Pay: The Squeeze on Incomes Is Gradually Easing Up," *Maclean's*, November 25, 1996, pp. 100–101.

27. R. Jacob, "Corporate Reputations," *Fortune*, March 6, 1995, pp. 54–64; J.R. Norman, "Choose Your Partners," *Forbes*,

November 21, 1994, pp. 88–89; S. Tully, "Why to Go for Stretch Targets," *Fortune*, November 14, 1994, pp. 145–158.

28. S. Tully, "Why to Go for Stretch Targets," *Fortune*, November 14, 1994, pp. 145–158.

29. S. Tully, "Why to Go for Stretch Targets," *Fortune*, November 14, 1994, pp. 145–158.

Chapter 9

1. *Case in Contrast* based on K. Barker, "Dr Boss: Julie Levy Tells Kate Barker About Her Reluctant Transition From Scientist to CEO," *National Post Business*, July 2000, p. 33; D. Calleja, "Now We're in Business," *Canadian Business*, December, 25, 2000, pp. 119–120+; D. Hasselback, "QLT Soars as Sales Outlook Brightens: Shares Gain 35%. Potential Market Grows but Revenue Forecast Still Falls," *Financial Post (National Post)*, February 9, 2001, pp. D1, D2; I. MacNeill, "Entrepreneurs of the Year 2000," *BCBusiness Magazine*, September 2000, pp. 45, 47+; I. MacNeill, "Pacific Canada Entrepreneur of the Year," *BCBusiness Magazine*, October 2000, pp. 36–39; L. Pratt, "Stressful Times: Managers Ignore the Impact of Severe Stress at Their Peril. *Financial Post (National Post)*, March 31, 2003, pp. BE1, BE6; S. Silcoff, "Irwin Toy in Discussions With Potential Private Buyer: Negotiating Cash Offer," *Financial Post (National Post)*, February 28, 2001, pp. C1, C6; S. Silcoff, "There Is No Joy in Irwin Toy Land: Feud Involving Family Members Ended in Departure of Chief Executive," *Financial Post (National Post)*, December 11, 2000, pp. C1, C6; S. Silcoff, "Irwin Toy Bows Out as Publicly Traded Company," *Financial Post (National Post)*, May 24, 2001, p. C11; P. Verburg, "The Light Stuff: Julia Levy and QLT Phototherapeutics Inc Have Spent 20 Years Perfecting a Light-Activated Cure for Elderly Blindness. It Could Mean Blockbuster Revenues, If They Can Master the Switch From Discovery to Manufacturing," *Canadian Business*, February 7, 2000, pp. 66–70; and P. Withers, "M(i)s-Matched? Why So Few Women Seem to be Taking Advantage of the High-Tech Bonanza," *BCBusiness Magazine*, October 2000, pp. 102–111.

2. J. Fierman, "Winning Ideas From Maverick Managers," *Fortune*, February 6, 1995, pp. 66–80.

3. J. Fierman, "Winning Ideas From Maverick Managers," *Fortune*, February 6, 1995, p. 70.

4. J. Fierman, "Winning Ideas From Maverick Managers," *Fortune*, February 6, 1995, pp. 66–80.

5. G. Yukl, *Leadership in Organizations*, 2nd ed. (New York: Academic Press, 1989); and R.M. Stogdill, *Handbook of Leadership: A Survey of the Literature* (New York: Free Press, 1974).

6. J. Fierman, "Winning Ideas From Maverick Managers," *Fortune*, February 6, 1995, p. 70.

7. H. Mintzberg, *Power in and Around Organizations* (Englewood Cliffs, NJ: Prentice-Hall, 1983); and J. Pfeffer, *Power in Organizations* (Marshfield, MA: Pitman, 1981).

8. R.P. French Jr. and B. Raven, "The Bases of Social Power," in D. Cartwright and A.F. Zander (eds.), *Group Dynamics* (Evanston, IL: Row, Peterson, 1960), pp. 607–623.

9. J.A. Lopez, "A Better Way? Setting Your Own Pay–and Other Unusual Compensation Plans," *The Wall Street Journal*, April 13, 1994, p. R6; "Maverick: The Success Story Behind the World's Most Unusual Workplace," *HRMagazine*, April 1994, pp. 88–89; J. Pottinger, "Brazilian Maverick Reveals His Radical Recipe for Success," *Personnel Management*, September 1994, p. 71.

10. T.M. Burton, "Visionary's Reward: Combine 'Simple Ideas' and Some Failures; Result: Sweet Revenge," *The Wall Street Journal*, February 3, 1995, pp. A1, A5.

11. L. Nakarmi, "A Flying Leap Toward the 21st Century? Pressure From Competitors and Seoul May Transform the Chaebol," *Business Week*, March 20, 1995, pp. 78–80.

12. J. Schaubroeck, J.R. Jones, and J.L. Xie, "Individual Differences in Utilizing Control to Cope With Job Demands: Effects on Susceptibility to Infectious Disease," *Journal of Applied Psychology*, 86, no. 2, 2001, pp. 265–278; and A.M. Owens, "Empowerment Can Make You Ill, Study Says," *National Post*, April 30, 2001, pp. A1, A8.

13. "Delta Promotes Empowerment," *The Globe and Mail*, May 31, 1999, advertising supplement, p. C5.

14. J.P. Kotter, "What Leaders Really Do," *Harvard Business Review*, May–June 1990, pp. 103–111.

15. R.N. Kanungo, "Leadership in Organizations: Looking Ahead to the 21st Century," *Canadian Psychology*, 39, no. 1–2, 1998, p. 77. For more evidence of this consensus, see N. Adler, *International Dimensions of Organizational Behavior*, 3rd ed., (Cincinnati, OH: South Western College Publishing), 1997; R.J. House, "Leadership in the Twenty-First Century," in A. Howard (ed.), *The Changing Nature of Work* (San Francisco: Jossey-Bass), 1995, pp. 411–450; R.N. Kanungo and M. Mendonca, *Ethical Dimensions of Leadership* (Thousand Oaks, CA: Sage Publications, 1996); and A. Zaleznik, "The Leadership Gap," *Academy of Management Executive*, 4, no. 1, 1990, pp. 7–22.

16. U. Gupta, "Starting Out; How Much? Figuring the Correct Amount of Capital for Starting a Business Can Be a Tough Balancing Act," *The Wall Street Journal*, May 22, 1995, p. R7; R. Jacob, "How One Red Hot Retailer Wins Customer Loyalty," *Fortune*, July 10, 1995, pp. 72–79; and "Staples Taps Hanaka from Lechmere Inc. to Become Its CEO," *The Wall Street Journal*, July 29, 1994, p. B2.

17. B.M. Bass, *Bass and Stogdill's Handbook of Leadership: Theory, Research, and Managerial Applications*, 3rd ed. (New York: Free Press, 1990); R.J. House and M.L. Baetz, "Leadership: Some Empirical Generalizations and New Research Directions," in B.M. Staw and L.L. Cummings (eds.), *Research in Organizational Behavior*, vol. 1 (Greenwich, CT: JAI Press, 1979), pp. 341–423; S.A. Kirpatrick and E.A. Locke, "Leadership: Do Traits Matter?" *Academy of Management Executive*, 5, no. 2, 1991, pp. 48–60; and G. Yukl, *Leadership in Organizations*, 2nd ed. (New York: Academic Press, 1989); and G. Yukl and D.D. Van Fleet, "Theory and Research on Leadership in Organizations," in M.D. Dunnette and L.M. Hough (eds.), *Handbook of Industrial and Organizational Psychology*, 2nd ed., vol. 3 (Palo Alto, CA: Consulting Psychologists Press, 1992), pp. 147–197.

18. E.A. Fleishman, "Performance Assessment Based on an Empirically Derived Task Taxonomy," *Human Factors*, 9, 1967, pp. 349–366; E.A. Fleishman, "The Description of Supervisory Behavior," *Personnel Psychology*, 37, 1953, pp. 1–6; A.W. Halpin and B.J. Winer, "A

Factorial Study of the Leader Behavior Descriptions," in R.M. Stogdill and A.I. Coons (eds.), *Leader Behavior: Its Description and Measurement* (Columbus Bureau of Business Research, Ohio State University, 1957); and D. Tscheulin, "Leader Behavior Measurement in German Industry," *Journal of Applied Psychology*, 56, 1971, pp. 28–31.

19. R. Likert, *New Patterns of Management* (New York: McGraw-Hill, 1961); and N.C. Morse and E. Reimer, "The Experimental Change of a Major Organizational Variable," *Journal of Abnormal and Social Psychology*, 52, 1956, pp. 120–129.

20. R.R. Blake and J.S. Mouton, *The New Managerial Grid* (Houston: Gulf, 1978).

21. U. Gupta, "Starting Out; How Much? Figuring the Correct Amount of Capital for Starting a Business Can Be a Tough Balancing Act," *The Wall Street Journal*, May 22, 1995, p. R7; R. Jacob, "How One Red Hot Retailer Wins Customer Loyalty," *Fortune*, July 10, 1995, pp. 72–79; and "Staples Taps Hanaka from Lechmere Inc. to Become Its CEO," *The Wall Street Journal*, July 29, 1994, p. B2.

22. E.A. Fleishman and E.F. Harris, "Patterns of Leadership Behavior Related to Employee Grievances and Turnover," *Personnel Psychology*, 15, 1962, pp. 43–56.

23. F.E. Fiedler, *A Theory of Leadership Effectiveness* (New York: McGraw-Hill, 1967); and F.E. Fiedler, "The Contingency Model and the Dynamics of the Leadership Process," in L. Berkowitz (ed.), *Advances in Experimental Social Psychology* (New York: Academic Press, 1978).

24. R.J. House and M.L. Baetz, "Leadership: Some Empirical Generalizations and New Research Directions," in B.M. Staw and L.L. Cummings (eds.), *Research in Organizational Behavior*, vol. 1 (Greenwich, CT: JAI Press, 1979), pp. 341–423; L.H. Peters, D.D. Hartke, and J.T. Pohlmann, "Fiedler's Contingency Theory of Leadership: An Application of the Meta-Analysis Procedures of Schmidt and Hunter," *Psychological Bulletin*, 97, 1985, pp. 274–285; and C.A. Schriesheim, B.J. Tepper, and L.A. Tetrault, "Least Preferred Co-Worker Score, Situational Control, and Leadership Effectiveness: A Meta-Analysis of Contingency Model Performance Predictions," *Journal of Applied Psychology*, 79, 1994, pp. 561–573.

25. P. Hersey and K.H. Blanchard, "So You Want to Know Your Leadership Style?" *Training and Development Journal*, February 1974, pp. 1–15; and P. Hersey and K.H. Blanchard, *Management of Organizational Behavior: Utilizing Human Resources*, 6th ed. (Englewood Cliffs, NJ: Prentice-Hall, 1993).

26. Cited in C.F. Fernandez and R.P. Vecchio, "Situational Leadership Theory Revisited: A Test of an Across-Jobs Perspective," *Leadership Quarterly*, 8, no. 1, 1997, p. 67.

27. M.G. Evans, "The Effects of Supervisory Behavior on the Path–Goal Relationship," *Organizational Behavior and Human Performance*," 5, 1970, pp. 277–298; M.G. Evans, "Leadership and Motivation: A Core Concept," *Academy of Management Journal*, 13, 1970, pp. 91–102; R.J. House, "A Path–Goal Theory of Leader Effectiveness," *Administrative Science Quarterly*, September 1971, pp. 321–338; R.J. House and T.R. Mitchell, "Path–Goal Theory of Leadership," *Journal of Contemporary Business*, Autumn 1974, p. 86; M.G. Evans, "Leadership," in S. Kerr (ed.), *Organizational Behavior* (Columbus, OH: Grid Publishing, 1979); R.J. House, "Retrospective Comment," in L.E. Boone and D.D. Bowen (eds.), *The Great Writings in Management and Organizational Behavior*, 2nd ed. (New York: Random House, 1987), pp. 354–364; M.G. Evans, "Fuhrungstheorien, Weg-ziel-theorie" (trans. G. Reber), in A. Kieser, G. Reber, and R. Wunderer (eds). *Handworterbuch Der Fuhrung*, 2nd ed. (Stuttgart, Germany: Schaffer Poeschal Verlag, 1995), pp. 1075–1091; and J.C. Wofford and L.Z. Liska, "Path–Goal Theories of Leadership: A Meta-Analysis," *Journal of Management*, 19, 1993, pp. 857–876.

28. R. McQueen, "The Long Shadow of Tom Stephens: He Branded MacBlo's Crew as Losers, Then Made Them into Winners," *Financial Post (National Post)*, June 22, 1999, pp. C1, C5.

29. S. Kerr and J.M. Jermier, "Substitutes for Leadership: Their Meaning and Measurement," *Organizational Behavior and Human Performance*, 22, 1978, pp. 375–403; P.M. Podsakoff, B.P. Niehoff, S.B. MacKenzie, and M.L. Williams, "Do Substitutes for Leadership Really Substitute for Leadership? An Empirical Examination of Kerr and Jermier's Situational Leadership Model,"

Organizational Behavior and Human Decision Processes, 54, 1993, pp. 1–44.

30. S. Kerr and J.M. Jermier, "Substitutes for Leadership: Their Meaning and Measurement," *Organizational Behavior and Human Performance*, 22, 1978, pp. 375–403; and P.M. Podsakoff, B.P. Niehoff, S.B. MacKenzie, and M.L. Williams, "Do Substitutes for Leadership Really Substitute for Leadership? An Empirical Examination of Kerr and Jermier's Situational Leadership Model," *Organizational Behavior and Human Decision Processes*, 54, 1993, pp. 1–44.

31. "Combo Push From Goldstar, Zenith," *Dealerscope*, February 1995, p. 38; "L.G. Electronics Co.: South Korean Firm Raises 1995 Sales Target by 22.6%," *The Wall Street Journal*, January 5, 1995, p. 10; and L. Nakarmi, "Goldstar Is Burning Bright," *Business Week*, September 26, 1994, pp. 129–130.

32. "Combo Push From Goldstar, Zenith," *Dealerscope*, February 1995, p. 38; "L.G. Electronics Co.: South Korean Firm Raises 1995 Sales Target by 22.6%," *The Wall Street Journal*, January 5, 1995, p. 10; and L. Nakarmi, "Goldstar Is Burning Bright," *Business Week*, September 26, 1994, pp. 129–130.

33. J.M. Howell and B.J. Avolio, "The Leverage of Leadership," in *Leadership: Achieving Exceptional Performance*, supplement prepared by the Richard Ivey School of Business, *The Globe and Mail*, May 15, 1998, pp. C1, C2.

34. J.M. Howell and B.J. Avolio, "The Leverage of Leadership," in *Leadership: Achieving Exceptional Performance*, supplement prepared by the Richard Ivey School of Business, *The Globe and Mail*, May 15, 1998, pp. C1, C2.

35. V. Smith, "Leading Us On," *Report on Business Magazine*, April 1999, pp. 91–96.

36. A. Bryman, "Leadership in Organizations," in S.R. Clegg, C. Hardy, and W.R. Nord (eds.), *Handbook of Organization Studies* (London: Sage Publications, 1996), pp. 276–292.

37. B.M. Bass, *Leadership and Performance Beyond Expectations* (New York: Free Press, 1985); B.M. Bass, *Bass and Stogdill's Handbook of Leadership: Theory, Research, and Managerial Applications*, 3rd ed. (New York: Free Press, 1990); and G. Yukl and D.D. Van Fleet, "Theory and Research on Leadership in Organizations," in M.D.

Dunnette and L.M. Hough (eds.), *Handbook of Industrial and Organizational Psychology*, 2nd ed., vol. 3 (Palo Alto, CA: Consulting Psychologists Press, 1992), pp. 147–97.

38. L. Nakarmi, "Goldstar is Burning Bright," *Business Week*, September 26, 1994, p. 129.

39. J.A. Conger and R.N. Kanungo, "Behavioral Dimensions of Charismatic Leadership," in J.A. Conger, R.N. Kanungo, and Associates, *Charismatic Leadership* (San Francisco: Jossey-Bass, 1988).

40. J.A. Conger and R.N. Kanungo, *Charismatic Leadership in Organizations* (Thousand Oaks, CA: Sage, 1998).

41. "Building a Better Boss," *Maclean's*, September 30, 1996, p. 41.

42. T. Dvir, D. Eden, B.J. Avolio, and B. Shamir, "Impact of Transformational Leadership on Follower Development and Performance: A Field Experiment," *Academy of Management Journal*, 45, no. 4, 2002, pp. 735–744; R.J. House, J. Woycke, and E.M. Fodor, "Charismatic and Noncharismatic Leaders: Differences in Behavior and Effectiveness," in J.A. Conger and R.N. Kanungo, *Charismatic Leadership in Organizations,* (Thousand Oaks, CA: Sage, 1998), pp. 103–104; D.A. Waldman, B.M. Bass, and F.J. Yammarino, "Adding to Contingent-Reward Behavior: The Augmenting Effect of Charismatic Leadership," *Group & Organization Studies,* December 1990, pp. 381–394; S.A. Kirkpatrick and E.A. Locke, "Direct and Indirect Effects of Three Core Charismatic Leadership Components on Performance and Attitudes," *Journal of Applied Psychology,* February 1996, pp. 36–51; and J.A. Conger, R.N. Kanungo, and S.T. Menon, "Charismatic Leadership and Follower Outcome Effects," paper presented at the 58th Annual Academy of Management Meetings, San Diego, CA, August 1998.

43. J.M. Howell and P.J. Frost, "A Laboratory Study of Charismatic Leadership," *Organizational Behavior & Human Decision Processes*, 43, no. 2, April 1989, pp. 243–269.

44. "Building a Better Boss," *Maclean's*, September 30, 1996, p. 41.

45. A. Elsner, "The Era of CEO as Superhero Ends Amid Corporate Scandals," *globeandmail.com*, July 10, 2002.

46. B.M. Bass, *Leadership and Performance Beyond Expectations* (New York: Free Press, 1985); B.M. Bass, *Bass and Stogdill's Handbook of Leadership: Theory, Research, and Managerial Applications*, 3rd ed. (New York: Free Press, 1990); and G. Yukl and D.D. Van Fleet, "Theory and Research on Leadership in Organizations," in M.D. Dunnette and L.M. Hough (eds.), *Handbook of Industrial and Organizational Psychology*, 2nd ed., vol. 3 (Palo Alto, CA: Consulting Psychologists Press, 1992), pp. 147–197.

47. B.M. Bass, *Leadership and Performance Beyond Expectations* (New York: Free Press, 1985); B.M. Bass, *Bass and Stogdill's Handbook of Leadership: Theory, Research, and Managerial Applications*, 3rd ed. (New York: Free Press, 1990); G. Yukl and D.D. Van Fleet, "Theory and Research on Leadership in Organizations," in M.D. Dunnette and L.M. Hough (eds.), *Handbook of Industrial and Organizational Psychology*, 2nd ed., vol. 3 (Palo Alto, CA: Consulting Psychologists Press, 1992), pp. 147–197.

48. Cited in B.M. Bass and B.J. Avolio, "Developing Transformational Leadership: 1992 and Beyond," *Journal of European Industrial Training,* January 1990, p. 23.

49. J.M. Howell and B.J. Avolio, "The Leverage of Leadership," in *Leadership: Achieving Exceptional Performance*, supplement prepared by the Richard Ivey School of Business, *The Globe and Mail,* May 15, 1998, p. C2.

50. B.M. Bass, *Bass and Stogdill's Handbook of Leadership;* B.M. Bass and B.J. Avolio, "Transformational Leadership: A Response to Critiques," in M.M. Chemers and R. Ayman (eds.), *Leadership Theory and Research: Perspectives and Directions* (San Diego: Academic Press, 1993), pp. 49–80; B.M. Bass, B.J. Avolio, and L. Goodheim, "Biography and the Assessment of Transformational Leadership at the World Class Level," *Journal of Management,* 13, 1987, pp. 7–20; J.J. Hater and B.M. Bass, "Supervisors' Evaluations and Subordinates' Perceptions of Transformational and Transactional Leadership," *Journal of Applied Psychology,* 73, 1988, pp. 695–702; R. Pillai, "Crisis and Emergence of Charismatic Leadership in Groups: An Experimental Investigation," *Journal of Applied Psychology,* 26, 1996, pp. 543–562; J. Seltzer and B.M.

Bass, "Transformational Leadership: Beyond Initiation and Consideration," *Journal of Management*, 16, 1990, pp. 693–703; and D.A. Waldman, B.M. Bass, and W.O. Einstein, "Effort, Performance, Transformational Leadership in Industrial and Military Service," *Journal of Occupation Psychology,* 60, 1987, pp. 1–10.

51. R. Pillai, C.A. Schriesheim, and E.S. Williams, "Fairness Perceptions and Trust as Mediators of Transformational and Transactional Leadership: A Two-Sample Study," *Journal of Management,* 25, 1999, pp. 897–933.

52. *Think About It* based on R. McQueen, "Meet Canada's Top Business Women [The Power 50]," *Financial Post (National Post)*, March 31, 2001, pp. F1, F2; and A. Kingston, "The Carmaker's Daughter," *National Post Business*, September 2002, pp. 42–55;

53. R. McQueen, "Frank's Daughter Doesn't Ride Any Coattails: Belinda Stronach: 'I'm Responsible for This Ship,'" *Financial Post (National Post)*, March 31, 2001, p. F3.

54. R. McQueen, "Glitter Girls No More," *National Post Business*, March 2001, p. 68; and J. McFarland, "Women Still Find Slow Rise to Power Positions," *The Globe and Mail*, March 13, 2003, pp. B1, B7.

55. L. Ramsay, "A League of Their Own," *The Globe and Mail*, November 23, 2002, p. B11.

56. A.H. Eagly and B.T. Johnson, "Gender and Leadership Style: A Meta-Analysis," *Psychological Bulletin*, 108, 1990, pp. 233–256.

57. A.H. Eagly and B.T. Johnson, "Gender and Leadership Style: A Meta-Analysis," *Psychological Bulletin*, 108, 1990, pp. 233–256.

58. A.H. Eagly and B.T. Johnson, "Gender and Leadership Style: A Meta-Analysis," *Psychological Bulletin*, 108, 1990, pp. 233–256.

59. A.H. Eagly and B.T. Johnson, "Gender and Leadership Style: A Meta-Analysis," *Psychological Bulletin*, 108, 1990, pp. 233–256.

60. A.H. Eagly and B.T. Johnson, "Gender and Leadership Style: A Meta-Analysis," *Psychological Bulletin*, 108, 1990, pp. 233–256.

61. A.H. Eagly, S.J. Karau, and M.G. Makhijani, "Gender and the Effectiveness of Leaders: A Meta-Analysis," *Psychological Bulletin*, 117, 1995, pp. 125–145.

62. A.H. Eagly, S.J. Karau, and M.G. Makhijani, "Gender and the Effectiveness of Leaders: A Meta-Analysis," *Psychological Bulletin*, 117, 1995, pp. 125–145.

63. R. Calori and B. Dufour, "Management European Style," *Academy of Management Executive*, 9, no. 3, 1995, pp. 61–70.

64. R. Calori and B. Dufour, "Management European Style," *Academy of Management Executive*, 9, no. 3, 1995, pp. 61–70.

65. J.M. George and K. Bettenhausen, "Understanding Prosocial Behavior, Sales Performance, and Turnover: A Group-Level Analysis in a Service Context," *Journal of Applied Psychology*, 75, 1990, pp. 698–709.

66. N.M. Ashkanasy and C.S. Daus, "Emotion in the Workplace: The New Challenge for Managers," *Academy of Management Executive*, 16, no. 1, 2002, pp. 76–86; and J.M. George, "Emotions and Leadership: The Role of Emotional Intelligence," *Human Relations*, 53, 2002, pp. 1027–1055.

67. J.M. George, "Emotions and Leadership: The Role of Emotional Intelligence," *Human Relations*, 53, 2000, pp. 1027–1055.

68. *Management Case* based on I. Austen, "Problem Child [Can Cynthia Trudell Save Saturn?]," *Canadian Business*, March 26, 1999, pp. 22–31; M. Ellis, "Trudell Jumps Saturn Ship to Steer Sea Ray Boats: Highest-Ranking Woman Auto Exec Moves to Brunswick," *Financial Post (National Post)*, March 30, 2001, p. C10; R. McQueen, "Saturn Boss Aims to Make Difference: Trudell's Mantra: 'I Lived, I Laughed, I Learned and I Loved,'" *Financial Post (National Post)*, April 1, 2000, pp. D1, D2; and "Saturn Corporation's Trudell to Lead Sea Ray," Brunswick Corporation *Press Release*, March 29, 2001.

Chapter 10

1. *Case in Contrast* based on C. McLean, "Reinventing a Clean, Lean Manufacturing Machine: Willow Pulls Together as a Team to Survive in the Competitive Metal Working Industry,"
Plant, September 27, 1999, p. 13; B. Wheatley, "Innovation in ISO Registration," *CMA Management Accounting Magazine*, June 1998, p. 23; L. Wichmann, "Taking the Fight out of Your Workplace Environment: Aggressive Behavior Costs Manufacturers Time and Money," *Plant*, May 8, 2000, p. 13.

2. W.R. Coradetti, "Teamwork Takes Time and a Lot of Energy," *HR Magazine*, June 1994, pp. 74–77; and D. Fenn, "Service Teams That Work," *Inc.*, August 1995, p. 99; "Team Selling Catches on, but Is Sales Really a Team Sport?" *The Wall Street Journal*, March 29, 1994, p. A1.

3. *Think About It* based on K. Rude, "Retrofitting a Community of Spaces: When Steelcase Canada Moved Its Toronto-Area Operations Under One Roof, Quadrangle Architects Provided a Renovated Facility in Markham That Showcases the Latest Workplace Strategies," *Canadian Interiors*, January–February 2001, pp. 42–45.

4. P. Booth, *Challenge and Change: Embracing the Team Concept*, Report 123-94, Conference Board of Canada, 1994.

5. Cited in C. Joinson, "Teams at Work," *HRMagazine*, May 1999, p. 30; and P. Strozniak, "Teams at Work," *Industry Week*, September 18, 2000, p. 47.

6. *Think About It* based on L Berglund, "So, You Think You're a Good Manager . . . Find out for Sure With a Reverse Appraisal of Your Staff," *Modern Purchasing*, May 1998, p. 32.

7. T.M. Mills, *The Sociology of Small Groups* (Englewood Cliffs, NJ: Prentice Hall, 1967); M.E. Shaw, *Group Dynamics* (New York: McGraw-Hill, 1981).

8. P. Willcocks, "Yours and Mine? Can the New Owner of the Once-Troubled Myra Falls Copper and Zinc Mine Near Campbell River Forge a New Relationship With Workers and Their Union to Create a True Partnership?" *BCBusiness Magazine*, September 2000, pp. 114–120.

9. J.A. Pearce II and E.C. Ravlin, "The Design and Activation of Self-Regulating Work Groups," *Human Relations*, 11, 1987, pp. 751–782.

10. P. Booth, *Challenge and Change: Embracing the Team Concept*, Report 123-94, Conference Board of Canada, 1994.

11. B. Dumaine, "Who Needs a Boss?" *Fortune*, May 7, 1990, pp. 52–60; and J.A.
Pearce II and E.C. Ravlin, "The Design and Activation of Self-Regulating Work Groups," *Human Relations*, 11, 1987, pp. 751–782.

12. B. Dumaine, "Who Needs a Boss?" *Fortune*, May 7, 1990, pp. 52–60; and A.R. Montebello and V.R. Buzzotta, "Work Teams That Work," *Training & Development*, March 1993, pp. 59–64.

13. T.D. Wall, N.J. Kemp, P.R. Jackson, and C.W. Clegg, "Outcomes of Autonomous Work Groups: A Long-Term Field Experiment," *Academy of Management Journal*, 29, 1986, pp. 280–304.

14. W.R. Pape, "Group Insurance," *Inc. (Inc. Technology Supplement)*, June 17, 1997, pp. 29–31; A.M. Townsend, S.M. DeMarie, and A.R. Hendrickson, "Are You Ready for Virtual Teams?" *HRMagazine*, September 1996, pp. 122–126; and A.M. Townsend, S.M. DeMarie, and A.M. Hendrickson, "Virtual Teams: Technology and the Workplace of the Future," *Academy of Management Executive*, 12, no. 3, 1998, pp. 17–29.

15. A.M. Townsend, S.M. DeMarie, and A.R. Hendrickson, "Are You Ready for Virtual Teams?" *HRMagazine*, September 1996, pp. 122–126.

16. W.R. Pape, "Group Insurance," *Inc. (Inc. Technology Supplement)*, June 17, 1997, pp. 29–31; and A.M. Townsend, S.M. DeMarie, and A.R. Hendrickson, "Are You Ready for Virtual Teams?" *HRMagazine*, September 1996, pp. 122–126.

17. A.B. Drexler and R. Forrester, "Teamwork–Not Necessarily the Answer," *HRMagazine*, January 1998, pp. 55–58.

18. R. Forrester and A.B. Drexler, "A Model for Team-Based Organization Performance," *Academy of Management Executive*, August 1999, p. 47. See also S.A. Mohrman, with S.G. Cohen and A.M. Mohrman Jr., *Designing Team-Based Organizations* (San Francisco: Jossey-Bass, 1995); and J.H. Shonk, *Team-Based Organizations* (Homewood, IL: Business One Irwin, 1992).

19. *Think About It* based on G. Crone, "Welcome to the Other Web: Loose Clusters, Not Rigid Contracts, Are the Future in Business," *The Financial Post Daily*, January 22, 1998, p. 11.

20. A. Deutschman, "The Managing Wisdom of High-Tech Superstars," *Fortune*, October 17, 1994, pp. 197–206.

21. A. Deutschman, "The Managing Wisdom of High-Tech Superstars," *Fortune*, October 17, 1994, pp. 197–206.

22. J.S. Lublin, "My Colleague, My Boss," *The Wall Street Journal*, April 12, 1995, pp. R4, R12.

23. B.W. Tuckman, "Developmental Sequences in Small Groups," *Psychological Bulletin*, 63, 1965, pp. 384–399; and B.W. Tuckman and M.C. Jensen, "Stages of Small Group Development," *Group and Organizational Studies*, 2, 1977, pp. 419–427.

24. C.J.G. Gersick, "Time and Transition in Work Teams: Toward a New Model of Group Development," *Academy of Management Journal*, 31, March 1988, pp. 9–41; C.J.G. Gersick, "Marking Time: Predictable Transitions in Task Groups," *Academy of Management Journal*, 32, June 1989, pp. 274–309.

25. J.R. Hackman, "Group Influences on Individuals in Organizations," in M.D. Dunnette and L.M. Hough (eds.), *Handbook of Industrial and Organizational Psychology*, 2nd ed., vol. 3 (Palo Alto, CA: Consulting Psychologists Press, 1992), pp. 199–267.

26. J.R. Hackman, "Group Influences on Individuals in Organizations," in M.D. Dunnette and L.M. Hough (eds.), *Handbook of Industrial and Organizational Psychology*, 2nd ed., vol. 3 (Palo Alto, CA: Consulting Psychologists Press, 1992), pp. 199–267.

27. J.R. Hackman, "Group Influences on Individuals in Organizations," in M.D. Dunnette and L.M. Hough (eds.), *Handbook of Industrial and Organizational Psychology*, 2nd ed., vol. 3 (Palo Alto, CA: Consulting Psychologists Press, 1992), 199–267.

28. L. Festinger, "Informal Social Communication," *Psychological Review*, 57, 1950, pp. 271–282; and M.E. Shaw, *Group Dynamics* (New York: McGraw-Hill, 1981).

29. J.R. Hackman, "Group Influences on Individuals in Organizations," in M.D. Dunnette and L.M. Hough (eds.), *Handbook of Industrial and Organizational Psychology*, 2nd ed., vol. 3 (Palo Alto, CA: Consulting Psychologists Press, 1992), pp. 199–267; and M.E. Shaw, *Group Dynamics* (New York: McGraw-Hill, 1981).

30. G. Keenan, "Steely John: Dofasco Lifer John Mayberry Is Not Your Typical Steel CEO. He's Making Money," *Report on Business Magazine,* September 2002, pp. 12–15.

31. I.L. Janis, *Groupthink* (Boston: Houghton Mifflin, 1982); W. Park, "A Review of Research on Groupthink," *Journal of Behavioral Decision Making,* July 1990, pp. 229–245; C.P. Neck and G. Moorhead, "Groupthink Remodeled: The Importance of Leadership, Time Pressure, and Methodical Decision Making Procedures," *Human Relations,* May 1995, pp. 537–558; and J.N. Choi and M.U. Kim, "The Organizational Application of Groupthink and Its Limits in Organizations," *Journal of Applied Psychology,* April 1999, pp. 297–306.

32. M.E. Turner and A.R. Pratkanis, "Mitigating Groupthink by Stimulating Constructive Conflict," in C. De Dreu and E. Van de Vliert (eds.), *Using Conflict in Organizations* (London: Sage, 1997), pp. 53–71.

33. See N.R.F. Maier, *Principles of Human Relations* (New York: Wiley, 1952); I.L. Janis, *Groupthink: Psychological Studies of Policy Decisions and Fiascoes,* 2nd ed. (Boston: Houghton Mifflin, 1982); and C.R. Leana, "A Partial Test of Janis' Groupthink Model: Effects of Group Cohesiveness and Leader Behavior on Defective Decision Making," *Journal of Management,* Spring 1985, pp. 5–17.

34. P.C. Earley, "Social Loafing and Collectivism: A Comparison of the United States and the People's Republic of China," *Administrative Science Quarterly*, 34, 1989, pp. 565–581; J.M. George, "Extrinsic and Intrinsic Origins of Perceived Social Loafing in Organizations," *Academy of Management Journal*, 35, 1992, pp. 191–202; S.G. Harkins, B. Latane, and K. Williams, "Social Loafing: Allocating Effort or Taking it Easy," *Journal of Experimental Social Psychology*, 16, 1980, pp. 457–465; B. Latane, K.D. Williams, and S. Harkins, "Many Hands Make Light the Work: The Causes and Consequences of Social Loafing," *Journal of Personality and Social Psychology*, 37, 1979, pp. 822–832; and J.A. Shepperd, "Productivity Loss in Performance Groups: A Motivation Analysis," *Psychological Bulletin*, 113, 1993, pp. 67–81.

35. B. Birchard, "Power to the People," *CFO*, March 1995, pp. 38–43.

36. A. Markels, "A Power Producer Is Intent on Giving Power to Its People," *The Wall Street Journal,* July 3, 1995, pp. A1, A12.

37. A. Markels, "A Power Producer Is Intent on Giving Power to Its People," *The Wall Street Journal,* July 3, 1995, pp. A1, A12.

38. A. Markels, "A Power Producer Is Intent on Giving Power to Its People," *The Wall Street Journal,* July 3, 1995, pp. A1, A12.

Chapter 11

1. Information on Comtek based on R. Wright, "21 Ways to Build Great People," *Profit: The Magazine for Canadian Entrepreneurs,* June 2000, pp. 122–132; and "Businesses Founded in Flush Times Deal with Looming Slowdown," *Canadian Press Newswire,* January 2, 2001.

2. Information on TD Bank based on H. Schachter, "Leading-Edge Learning: Banks Look for Results From Their Investments in Employee Education," *Canadian Banker,* 107, no. 2, pp. 16–20+.

3. K. Harley, "Zero Churn," *Atlantic Progress,* May 2001, pp. 30–33.

4. J.E. Butler, G.R. Ferris, and N.K. Napier, *Strategy and Human Resource Management* (Cincinnati, OH: South Western, 1991); P.M. Wright and G.C. McMahan, "Theoretical Perspectives for Strategic Human Resource Management," *Journal of Management*, 18, 1992, pp. 295–320.

5. C.D. Fisher, L.F. Schoenfeldt, and J.B. Shaw, *Human Resource Management* (Boston: Houghton Mifflin, 1990).

6. P.M. Wright and G.C. McMahan, "Theoretical Perspectives for Strategic Human Resource Management," *Journal of Management*, 18, 1992, pp. 295–320.

7. L. Baird and I. Meshoulam, "Managing Two Fits for Strategic Human Resource Management," *Academy of Management Review*, 14, 1989, pp. 116–128; J. Milliman, M. Von Glinow, and M. Nathan, "Organizational Life Cycles and Strategic International Human Resource Management in Multinational Companies: Implications for Congruence Theory," *Academy of Management Review*, 16, 1991, pp. 318–339; R.S. Schuler and S.E. Jackson, "Linking Competitive Strategies With Human Resource Management Practices," *Academy of Management Executive*, 1, 1987, pp. 207–219; P.M. Wright and S.A. Snell, "Toward an

Integrative View of Strategic Human Resource Management," *Human Resource Management Review*, 1, 1991, pp. 203–225.

8. *Think About It* based on C. Alphonso, "It's Not Just Students in the Hot Dog Suits: Theme Parks Are Now Recruiting Seniors and Parents," *The Globe and Mail*, Monday, April 23, 2001, p. B8.

9. S.L. Rynes, "Recruitment, Job Choice, and Post-Hire Consequences: A Call for New Research Directions," in M.D. Dunnette and L.M. Hough (eds.), *Handbook of Industrial and Organizational Psychology*, vol. 2 (Palo Alto, CA: Consulting Psychologists Press, 1991), pp. 399–444.

10. M. Lewis, "BCE Appoints Alcan Recruit 'Chief Talent Officer,'" *Financial Post (National Post)*, May 24, 2001, p. C11.

11. R.J. Harvey, "Job Analysis," in M.D. Dunnette and L.M. Hough (eds.), *Handbook of Industrial and Organizational Psychology*, vol. 2 (Palo Alto, CA: Consulting Psychologists Press, 1991), pp. 71–163.

12. E.L. Levine, *Everything You Always Wanted to Know About Job Analysis: A Job Analysis Primer* (Tampa, FL: Mariner, 1983).

13. R.L. Mathis and J.H. Jackson, *Human Resource Management*, 7th ed. (St. Paul, MN: West, 1994).

14. S.L. Rynes, "Recruitment, Job Choice, and Post-Hire Consequences: A Call for New Research Directions," in M.D. Dunnette and L.M. Hough (eds.), *Handbook of Industrial and Organizational Psychology*, vol. 2 (Palo Alto, CA: Consulting Psychologists Press, 1991), pp. 399–444.

15. R.M. Guion, "Personnel Assessment, Selection, and Placement," in M.D. Dunnette and L.M. Hough (eds.), *Handbook of Industrial and Organizational Psychology*, vol. 2 (Palo Alto, CA: Consulting Psychologists Press, 1991), pp. 327–397.

16. R.A. Noe, J.R. Hollenbeck, B. Gerhart, and P.M. Wright, *Human Resource Management: Gaining a Competitive Advantage* (Burr Ridge, IL: Irwin, 1994); J.A. Wheeler and J.A. Gier, "Reliability and Validity of the Situational Interview for a Sales Position," *Journal of Applied Psychology*, 2, 1987, pp. 484–487.

17. R.A. Noe, J.R. Hollenbeck, B. Gerhart, and P.M. Wright, *Human*

Resource Management: Gaining a Competitive Advantage (Burr Ridge, IL: Irwin, 1994).

18. "Wanted: Middle Managers, Audition Required," *The Wall Street Journal*, December 28, 1995, p. A1.

19. *Think About It* based on K. Harding, "Once and Future Kings," *The Globe and Mail*, April 9, 2003, pp. C1, C6.

20. I.L. Goldstein, "Training in Work Organizations," in M.D. Dunnette and L.M. Hough (eds.), *Handbook of Industrial and Organizational Psychology*, vol. 2 (Palo Alto, CA: Consulting Psychologists Press, 1991), pp. 507–619.

21. M.B. Arthur, D.T. Hall, and B.S. Lawrence (eds.), *Handbook of Career Theory* (Cambridge: Cambridge University Press, 1989), p. 8.

22. S.L. McShane, *Canadian Organizational Behaviour*, 4th ed. (Whitby, ON: McGraw-Hill Ryerson, 2001), p. 548.

23. L. Chwialkowska, "Ottawa Plan Targets Jobs Crisis," *National Post*, June 18, 2001, p. A1.

24. See, for example, P.O. Benham Jr., "Developing Organizational Talent: The Key to Performance and Productivity," *SAM Advanced Management Journal*, January 1993, pp. 34–39.

25. Information about Alcan and Hewlett-Packard based on L. Duxbury, L. Dyke, and N. Lam, "Career Development in the Federal Public Service: Building a World-Class Workforce," *Treasury Board of Canada*, January 1999.

26. S.P. Robbins and N. Langton, *Organizational Behaviour: Concepts, Controversies, Applications*, 3rd Canadian ed. (Toronto: Pearson Education Canada, 2003), pp. 512–513.

27. L. Chwialkowska, "Ottawa Plan Targets Jobs Crisis," *National Post*, June 18, 2001, p. A1.

28. For further elaboration of these points see B. Moses, *Career Intelligence: Mastering the New Work and Personal Realities*, (Toronto: Stoddart, 1997).

29. *Think About It* based on R. Wright, "21 Ways to Build Great People," *Profit: The Magazine for Canadian Entrepreneurs*, June 2000, pp. 122–132.

30. C.D. Fisher, L.F. Schoenfeldt, and J.B. Shaw, *Human Resource Management* (Boston: Houghton Mifflin, 1990).

31. M.A. Peiperl, "Getting 360° Feedback Right," *Harvard Business Review*, January 2001, pp. 142–147.

32. T. Davis and M.J. Landa, "A Contrary Look at Employee Performance Appraisal," *Canadian Manager*, Fall 1999, pp. 18–19+.

33. E. Anderssen, "Paycheques Show Generational Split," *The Globe and Mail*, March 12, 2003, p. A6.

34. http://www12.statcan.ca/english/census01/Products/Analytic/companion/earn/canada.cfm#8

35. L. Duxbury, L. Dyke, and N. Lam, "Career Development in the Federal Public Service: Building a World-Class Workforce," *Treasury Board of Canada*, January 1999.

36. *Think About It* based on M. King, "Union at Indigo," *The Gazette* (Montreal), February 11, 2003, p. B3.

37. S. Premack and J.E. Hunter, "Individual Unionization Decisions," *Psychological Bulletin*, 103, 1988, pp. 223–234.

38. *The Daily* (Statistics Canada), "Fact-Sheet on Unionization in Canada," August 28, 2003.

39. F. Milhar, "Leaders out of Step With Members," *Financial Post (National Post)*, September 2, 2003, pp. FP1, FP4.

40. S. Greenhouse, "Unions to Push to Make Organizing Easier," *NYTimes.com*, August 31, 2003, http://www.nytimes.com/2003/08/31/national/31SWEE.html.

Chapter 12

1. *Case in Contrast* based on V. Hempsall, "Family Matters: Strong Employee Relations Help RBW Graphics Manage Change," *Canadian Printer*, June 1999, pp. 24–26; "Transcontinental Wins *Time Canada* Contract, Buys Plesman," *Canadian Printer*, October 1999, p. 14; F. Bula, "City Staff Face Losing Four-Day Work Week," *The Vancouver Sun*, April 28, 1998, pp. B2, B3; F. Bula, "City's Plan to End 4-Day Week Sparks Backlash," *The Vancouver Sun*, May 15, 1998, pp. B1, B3; F. Bula, "Bid to Alter Work Week in City Shop for Repairs," *The Vancouver Sun*, May 26, 1998, pp. B1, B3; and P. Brooke, "Civic Strike More About Time Than Money," *The Vancouver Sun*, November 1, 2000, p. A6.

2. R. Foot, "FPI Goofed Restructuring, Crosbie says," *Financial Post (National Post)*, April 6, 2002, p. FP7.

3. C.A. O'Reilly and L.R. Pondy, "Organizational Communication," in S. Kerr (ed.), *Organizational Behavior* (Columbus, OH: Grid, 1979).

4. D.A. Adams, P.A. Todd, and R.R. Nelson, "A Comparative Evaluation of the Impact of Electronic and Voice Mail on Organizational Communication," *Information & Management*, 24, 1993, pp. 9–21.

5. E.M. Rogers and R. Agarwala-Rogers, *Communication in Organizations* (New York: Free Press, 1976).

6. B. Wheatley, "Innovation in ISO Registration," *CMA Management Accounting Magazine*, June 1998, p. 23; C. McLean, "Reinventing a Clean, Lean Manufacturing Machine: Willow Pulls Together as a Team to Survive in the Competitive Metal Working Industry," *Plant*, September 27, 1999, p. 13.

7. K. Cox, "Risley's Wagging Tongue Doomed FPI Deal," *The Globe and Mail*, February 19, 2002, p. B14.

8. K. Cox, "Risley's Wagging Tongue Doomed FPI Deal," *The Globe and Mail*, February 19, 2002, p. B14.

9. J. Kay, "Someone Will Watch Over Me: Think Your Office E-Mails are Private? Think Again," *National Post Business*, January 2001, pp. 59–64.

10. R.L. Daft, R.H. Lengel, and L.K. Trevino, "Message Equivocality, Media Selection, and Manager Performance: Implications for Information Systems," *MIS Quarterly*, 11, 1987, pp. 355–366; R.L. Daft and R.H. Lengel, "Information Richness: A New Approach to Managerial Behavior and Organization Design," in B.M. Staw and L.L. Cummings (eds.), *Research in Organizational Behavior* (Greenwich, CT: JAI Press, 1984).

11. R.L. Daft, *Organization Theory and Design* (St. Paul, MN: West, 1992).

12. R.L. Daft, *Organization Theory and Design* (St. Paul, MN: West, 1992).

13. "Lights, Camera, Meeting: Teleconferencing Becomes a Time-Saving Tool," *The Wall Street Journal*, February 21, 1995, p. A1.

14. "E-Mail Abuse: Workers Discover High-Tech Ways to Cause Trouble in the Office," *The Wall Street Journal*, November

22, 1994, p. A1; and "E-Mail Alert: Companies Lag in Devising Policies on How It Should Be Used," *The Wall Street Journal*, December 29, 1994, p. A1.

15. J. Kay, "Someone Will Watch Over Me: Think Your Office E-Mails are Private? Think Again," *National Post Business*, January 2001, pp. 59–64.

16. Examples based on C.S. Smith, "Beware of Cross-Cultural Faux Pas in China," *NYTimes.com*, April 30, 2002.

17. "On the Road," *Newsweek*, June 6, 1994, p. 8.

18. C.R. Mill, "Feedback: The Art of Giving and Receiving Help," in L. Porter and C.R. Mill (eds), *The Reading Book for Human Relations Training* (Bethel, ME: NTL Institute of Applied Behavioral Science, 1976), pp. 18–19.

19. Based on S.P. Robbins and P.L. Hunsaker, *Training in Interpersonal Skills: TIPS for Managing People at Work*, 2nd ed. (Upper Saddle River, NJ: Prentice-Hall, 1996), Ch 3.

20. D. Tannen, "The Power of Talk," *Harvard Business Review*, September–October 1995, pp. 138–148; D. Tannen, *Talking from 9 to 5* (New York: Avon Books, 1995).

21. D. Tannen, "The Power of Talk," *Harvard Business Review*, September–October 1995, pp. 138–148.

22. D. Tannen, *Talking from 9 to 5* (New York: Avon Books, 1995).

23. D. Tannen, *Talking from 9 to 5* (New York: Avon Books, 1995).

24. D. Tannen, "The Power of Talk," *Harvard Business Review*, September–October 1995, pp. 138–148; and D. Tannen, *Talking from 9 to 5* (New York: Avon Books, 1995).

25. D. Tannen, "The Power of Talk," *Harvard Business Review*, September–October 1995, pp. 138–148; and D. Tannen, *Talking from 9 to 5* (New York: Avon Books, 1995).

26. D. Tannen, "The Power of Talk," *Harvard Business Review*, September–October 1995, pp. 138–148; and D. Tannen, *Talking from 9 to 5* (New York: Avon Books, 1995).

27. *Think About It* based on M. Hume, "Trouble on Perfect Mountain," *National Post*, April 30, 2001, p. A17.

28. J.A. Litterer, "Conflict in Organizations: A Reexamination,"

Academy of Management Journal, 9, 1966, pp. 178–186; S.M. Schmidt and T.A. Kochan, "Conflict: Towards Conceptual Clarity," *Administrative Science Quarterly*, 13, 1972, pp. 359–370; and R.H. Miles, *Macro Organizational Behavior* (Santa Monica, CA: Goodyear, 1980).

29. S.P. Robbins, *Managing Organizational Conflict: A Nontraditional Approach* (Englewood Cliffs, NJ: Prentice-Hall, 1974); and L. Coser, *The Functions of Social Conflict* (New York: Free Press, 1956).

30. L.R. Pondy, "Organizational Conflict: Concepts and Models," *Administrative Science Quarterly*, 2, 1967, pp. 296–320; and R.E. Walton and J.M. Dutton, "The Management of Interdepartmental Conflict: A Model and Review," *Administrative Science Quarterly*, 14, 1969, pp. 62–73.

31. K.W. Thomas, "Conflict and Negotiation Processes in Organizations," in M.D. Dunnette and L.M. Hough (eds.), *Handbook of Industrial and Organizational Psychology,* 2nd ed., vol. 3 (Palo Alto, CA: Consulting Psychologists Press, 1992), pp. 651–717.

32. P.R. Lawrence, L.B. Barnes, and J.W. Lorsch, *Organizational Behavior and Administration* (Homewood, IL: Irwin, 1976).

33. *Think About It* based on J. Lee, "Leader Takes a Hard Line," *The Vancouver Sun*, May 15, 2001, p. A10.

34. R.J. Lewicki and J.R. Litterer, *Negotiation* (Homewood, IL: Irwin, 1985); G.B. Northcraft and M.A. Neale, *Organizational Behavior* (Fort Worth, TX: Dryden, 1994); J.Z. Rubin and B.R. Brown, *The Social Psychology of Bargaining and Negotiation* (New York: Academic Press, 1975).

35. L. Thompson and R. Hastie, "Social Perception in Negotiation," *Organizational Behavior and Human Decision Processes*, 47, 1990, pp. 98–123.

36. K.W. Thomas, "Conflict and Negotiation Processes in Organizations," in M.D. Dunnette and L.M. Hough (eds.), *Handbook of Industrial and Organizational Psychology*, 2nd ed., vol. 3 (Palo Alto, CA: Consulting Psychologists Press, 1992), pp. 651–717.

37. R.J. Lewicki, S.E. Weiss, and D. Lewin, "Models of Conflict, Negotiation and Third Party Intervention: A Review

and Synthesis," *Journal of Organizational Behavior*, 13, 1992, pp. 209–252.

38. G.B. Northcraft and M.A. Neale, *Organizational Behavior* (Fort Worth, TX: Dryden, 1994).

39. R.J. Lewicki, S.E. Weiss, and D. Lewin, "Models of Conflict, Negotiation and Third Party Intervention"; G.B. Northcraft and M.A. Neale, *Organizational Behavior* (Fort Worth, TX: Dryden, 1994); and D.G. Pruitt, "Integrative Agreements: Nature and Consequences," in M.H. Bazerman and R.J. Lewicki (eds.), *Negotiating in Organizations* (Beverly Hills, CA: Sage, 1983).

40. R. Fischer and W. Ury, *Getting to Yes* (Boston: Houghton Mifflin, 1981); and G.B. Northcraft and M.A. Neale, *Organizational Behavior* (Fort Worth, TX: Dryden, 1994).

41. P.J. Carnevale and D.G. Pruitt, "Negotiation and Mediation," *Annual Review of Psychology,* 43, 1992, pp. 531–582.

Chapter 13

1. R.L. Rose, "After Turning Around Giddings and Lewis, Fife Is Turned out Himself," *The Wall Street Journal*, June 22, 1995, p. A1.

2. W.G. Ouchi, "Markets, Bureaucracies, and Clans," *Administrative Science Quarterly*, 25, 1980, pp. 129–141.

3. *Think About It* based on C. McLean, "Incorporating Safety into the Corporate Culture: Nacan Closes in on One Million Hours, No Lost-Time Claims," *Plant*, November 27, 2000, p. 17.

4. A. Kinicki and B.K. Williams, *Management: A Practical Introduction"* (Boston: McGraw-Hill Irwin, 2003).

5. E.E. Lawler III and J.G. Rhode, *Information and Control in Organizations* (Pacific Palisades, CA: Goodyear, 1976).

6. C.W.L. Hill and G.R. Jones, *Strategic Management: An Integrated Approach*, 4th ed. (Boston: Houghton Mifflin, 1997).

7. W.G. Ouchi, "The Transmission of Control Through Organizational Hierarchy," *Academy of Management Journal*, 21, 1978, pp. 173–192.

8. W.G. Ouchi, "The Relationship Between Organizational Structure and Organizational Control," *Administrative Science Quarterly*, 22, 1977, pp. 95–113.

9. W.G. Ouchi, "Markets, Bureaucracies, and Clans," *Administrative Science Quarterly*, 25, 1980, pp. 129–141.

10. W.H. Newman, *Constructive Control* (Englewood Cliffs, NJ: Prentice-Hall, 1975).

11. J.D. Thompson, *Organizations in Action* (New York: McGraw-Hill, 1967).

12. R.N. Anthony, *The Management Control Function* (Boston: Harvard Business School Press, 1988).

13. P. Lorange, M. Morton, and S. Ghoshal, *Strategic Control* (St. Paul, MN: West, 1986).

14. H. Koontz and R.W. Bradspies, "Managing Through Feedforward Control," *Business Horizons*, June 1972, pp. 25–36.

15. *Think About It* based on D. DeCloet, "Scotia Bid to Jump off Percentage Treadmill," *Financial Post (National Post)*, May 16, 2001, p. C3.

16. W.G. Ouchi, "Markets, Bureaucracies, and Clans," *Administrative Science Quarterly*, 25, 1980, pp. 129–141.

17. C.W.L. Hill and G.R. Jones, *Strategic Management: An Integrated Approach*, 4th ed. (Boston: Houghton Mifflin, 1997).

18. R. Simons, "Strategic Orientation and Top Management Attention to Control Systems," *Strategic Management Journal*, 12, 1991, pp. 49–62.

19. J.A. Alexander, "Adaptive Changes in Corporate Control Practices," *Academy of Management Journal*, 34, 1991, pp. 162–193.

20. G.H.B. Ross, "Revolution in Management Control," *Management Accounting*, 72, 1992, pp. 23–27.

21. D.S. Pugh, D.J. Hickson, C.R. Hinings, and C. Turner, "Dimensions of

Organizational Structure," *Administrative Science Quarterly*, 13, 1968, pp. 65–91.

22. P.M. Blau, *The Dynamics of Bureaucracy* (Chicago: University of Chicago Press, 1955).

23. *Think About It* based on P. Fitzpatrick, "Wacky WestJet's Winning Ways: Passengers Respond to Stunts That Include Races to Determine Who Leaves the Airplane First," *Financial Post (National Post)*, October 16, 2000, p. C1.

24. P. Fitzpatrick, "Wacky WestJet's Winning Ways: Passengers Respond to Stunts That Include Races to Determine Who Leaves the Airplane First," *Financial Post (National Post)*, October 16, 2000, p. C1.

25. S. Mcgee, "Garish Jackets Add to Clamor of Chicago Pits," *The Wall Street Journal*, July 31, 1995, p. C1.

26. T. Cole, "How to Stay Hired," *Report on Business Magazine*, March 1995, pp. 46–48.

27. K.E. Weick, *The Social Psychology of Organization* (Reading, MA: Addison-Wesley, 1979).

28. J. McCann, "Cutting the Crap," *National Post Business*, March 2001, pp. 47–57.

29. Based on R. McQueen, "Polishing up Clarica Life: Sale Possible. Federal Legislation Would Make Insurer a Likely Target," *Financial Post (National Post)*, December 4, 2000, p. C6; S. Gordon, "En Garde! Insurance Companies Are Taking on the Banks More Directly, in the Marketplace and in the Regulatory Arena," *Canadian Banker*, March 2000, pp. 20–24; M. Strathdee, "Mutual Group to Meet June 10 on Issuing Shares," *Canadian Press Newswire*, March 25, 1999; and "Sun Life Financial and Clarica Life Insurance Company Confirm Amalgamation," *Canada NewsWire*, http://www.newswire.ca/releases/December 2002/30/c6810.html (accessed September 6, 2003).

Photo Credits

Chapter 1
Page 3, Courtesy of Ernst & Young; Page 3, CP/Jeff McIntosh; Page 12, Jim Cooper/AP/Wide World Photos; Page 24, Michael Rosenfeld/Tony Stone Images.

Chapter 2
Page 41, *The National Post*; Page 24, CP/Jeff McIntosh; Page 47, CP/AP/ Cliff Schiappa; Page 50, CP/Frank Gunn.

Chapter 3
Page 65, CP/Cam Mcalpine; Page 65, CP/AP/Luis Alvarez; Page 71, CP/ Maclean's/Peter Bregg; Page 76, Courtesy McDonald's Corporation; Page 80, Patti Gower/*The Globe and Mail*. Reprinted with permission from *The Globe and Mail*, Woman in Hajib, G&M, 18 Dec. 2002, A10. Accompanying photo of Safia Shire in headscarf credited to Patti Gower/ *The Globe and Mail*; Page 82, Don Healy/ *The Leader-Post*.

Chapter 4
Page 93, Charly Franklin/FPG; Page 93, Telegraph Colour Library/FPG; Page 96, *The National Post*; Page 101, CP/AP/Chris Meara.

Chapter 5
Page 121, Sharon Hoogstraten; Page 121, Courtesy of CLEO Photography, Whitby Ontario; Page 124, Gary Beechey, BDS Studios; Page 139, Peter Blakely/SABA; Page 142, Courtesy of Sleeman Brewery.

Chapter 6
Page 155, CP/*Toronto Star*/John Mahler; Page 155, CP/Macleans/Phill Snel; Page 159, Bernard Boutrit/Woodfin Camp & Associates, Inc.; Page 169, Tony Bock/ *Toronto Star*; Page 176, © *Winnipeg Free Press*, May 7, 2001.

Chapter 7
Page 185, AP/NASA/Bill Ingalls; Page 185, Courtesy of Creo Inc.; Page 191, Courtesy of Southwest Airlines; Page 195, CP/*Toronto Star*/Andrew Stawicki.

Chapter 8
Page 209, James Leynse/SABA; Page 209, Sharon Hoogstraten; Page 213, Pazmac Enterprises, *Vancouver Sun*/Bill Keay; Page 218, John Abbot; Page 225, James Schnepf/Liaison Agency, Inc.

Chapter 9
Page 235, Courtesy of QLT; Page 235, CP/*Toronto Star*/Ron Bull; Page 254, *National Post*; Page 255, Mark Segal/ Index Stock.

Chapter 10
Page 265, Courtesy of Willow MFG. Ltd. Established in 1954. www.willowcnc.com; Page 267, Courtesy of Burnaby, BC-based Dominion Information Services Inc ™.

Chapter 11
Page 291, Courtesy of Comtek Advanced Structures Ltd.; Page 291, Courtesy of CLEO Photography, Whitby Ontario; Page 298, Sandor Fizli photographer. Atlantic Progress; Page 299, AP/Stephen Reed; Page 308, Richard Howard/Black Star;

Chapter 12
Page 319, Courtesy of RBW Graphics/ Transcontinental; Page 319, *Vancouver Sun*/Ward Perrin; Page 325, Reprinted with permission from *The Globe and Mail*; Page 333, Ellen Senisi/The Image Works; Page 333, © Tony Freeman/Photo Edit; Page 337, *Vancouver Sun*/Stuart Davis.

Chapter 13
Page 349, Christopher Bissel/Tony Stone Images; Page 349, Loren Santow/Tony Stone Images; Page 352, Scala/Art Resource, NY.

Index
Name/Company/URL

Subject

A

ability tests, 299
access to information legislation, 327
accommodation, 335
accommodative approach, 75
accurate information, 330
achievement-oriented behaviours, 248
active listening, 331–332
activity ratios, 359–360
adjourning, 275
administrative management
bureaucracy, 35–36
defined, 34
Fayol's principles of management, 36
administrative model of decision making
bounded rationality, 98
defined, 98
and incomplete information, 98
satisficing, 98–99
age
aging of population, 50
discrimination, 90–91
agents of change, 54–55
ambiguous information, 98
artifacts, 188
assertiveness, 335–337
assumptions, 188
authority
allocation of, 167
centralization, 169–170
decentralization, 169–170
defined, 35, 167
hierarchy of, 167
avoidance, 335

B

barriers to entry, 46–48
behaviour control
bureaucratic control, 363–364
direct supervision, 362–363
management by objectives, 363
behaviour standards, 354
behavioural management
defined, 37
Follett's work, 37
Hawthorne Studies, 37
Theory X, 37–38
Theory Y, 38
behavioural models of leadership, 243–244
beliefs, 188
benchmarking, 198, 351
bias
decision making biases, 103–104
defined, 82
perceptual, 323
prior hypothesis bias, 103
representativeness bias, 103–104
Blake and Mouton's Managerial Grid, 243
bottom-up change, 196
boundaryless organization, 175–176
bounded rationality, 98

brainstorming, 108–109
brand loyalty, 47
bureaucracy
defined, 35
principles of, 35–36
bureaucratic control, 363–364
business-level plan, 127
business-level strategy
cost-leadership strategy, 141–142
defined, 127
differentiation strategy, 142
focused differentiation strategy, 143
focused low-cost strategy, 143
"stuck in the middle," 142–143
business-to-business (B2B) networks, 176

C

cafeteria-style benefit plan, 309
Canada
business regulations in, 21
diversity in, 77–78
global challenge, 22–23
management challenges, 19–22
Canada Labour Code, 309
Canadian Human Rights Act, 80, 309
career development issues
described, 301–302
employee's responsibilities, 302–303
organization's responsibilities, 302
centralization of authority, 169–170
change. See organizational change
charismatic leaders, 251–252
clan control
defined, 365–366
as important source of control, 366
managerial action, control of, 366–368
classical model, 97
closed system, 39
codes of ethics, 69
coercive power, 240
collaboration, 336
collective agreements, negotiation of, 199
collective bargaining, 339–340
command economy, 51
command group, 269
communication
decoding, 322
defined, 321
medium, 322
nonverbal, 322–323
perception, role of, 323–324
process, 321–322
verbal, 322
communication media
email, 326–327
face-to-face communication, 325
impersonal written communication, 327
and information richness, 324
monitored by receiver, 329
paper or electronic trail, need for, 324
personally addressed written communication, 326–327

selection of appropriate medium, 329
spoken communication electronically
transmitted, 325–326
and time, 324
communication process
encoding, 322
feedback phase, 321–322
message, 322
noise, 322
receiver, 322
sender, 322
transmission phase, 321
communication skills
accurate information, 330
appropriate medium, selection of, 329
clear and complete messages, 328–329
effective listening, 331–332
empathy, 332
feedback, 330–331
feedback mechanism, inclusion of, 330
filtering, avoidance of, 330
information distortion, avoidance of, 330
linguistic styles, understanding, 332–334
paying attention, 331
for receivers, 331
for senders, 328–331
understandable encoding, 329
compensation, and motivation, 224–226
competition
and barriers to entry, 47
as conflict-handling behaviour, 335
Competition Act, 50
competitive advantage
and efficiency, 23–24
global competition, 23–24
and quality, 24
self-managed work teams, 270
teams and, 267
and total quality management, 24
competitors, 46
compromise, 335
concentration on single business, 136–137
conceptual skills, 18
concurrent control, 356–357
conflict-handling behaviours, 335–336
conflict management
collective bargaining, 339–340
conflict-handling behaviours, 335–336
distributive negotiation, 339–340
in groups, 280
integrative bargaining, 339–340
negotiation, 339–340
strategies. See conflict management strategies
conflict management strategies
alteration of source of conflict, 338
assertiveness, 335–337
awareness of sources of conflict, 337
cooperativeness, 335–337
individuals, focus on, 337
organizational culture, change in, 337–338
organizational structure, change in, 337–338
organizations, focus on, 337–338
permanent transfers or dismissals, use of, 337
contingency models of leadership